Lecture Notes in Compute

Commenced Publication in 1973
Founding and Former Series Editors:
Gerhard Goos, Juris Hartmanis, and Jan van

T0092507

Xavier Masip-Bruin   Dominique Verchere
Vassilis Tsaoussidis   Marcelo Yannuzzi (Eds.)

Wired/Wireless Internet Communications

9th IFIP TC 6 International Conference, WWIC 2011
Vilanova i la Geltrú, Spain, June 15-17, 2011
Proceedings

 Springer

Volume Editors

Xavier Masip-Bruin
Marcelo Yannuzzi
Universitat Politècnica de Catalunya (UPC)
Advanced Network Architectures Lab (CRAAX)
Rambla Exposició, 61-69, 08800 Vilanova i la Geltrú, Spain
E-mail: {xmasip,yannuzzi}@ac.upc.edu

Dominique Verchere
Alcatel-Lucent Bell Labs France
Route de Villejuste, 91620 Nozay, France
E-mail: dominique.verchere@alcatel-lucent.com

Vassilis Tsaoussidis
Democritus University of Thrace
Dept. of Electrical and Computer Engineering
Panepistimioiupoli Xanthis, Kimmeria, 67100, Xanthi, Greece
E-mail: vtsaousi@ee.duth.gr

ISSN 0302-9743   e-ISSN 1611-3349
ISBN 978-3-642-21559-9   e-ISBN 978-3-642-21560-5
DOI 10.1007/978-3-642-21560-5
Springer Heidelberg Dordrecht London New York

Library of Congress Control Number: 2011929031

CR Subject Classification (1998): C.2, H.4, D.4.4, H.3.5, I.2, D.2, H.5, K.6.4

LNCS Sublibrary: SL 5 – Computer Communication Networks and Telecommunications

Typesetting: Camera-ready by author, data conversion by Scientific Publishing Services, Chennai, India

Printed on acid-free paper

Springer is part of Springer Science+Business Media (www.springer.com)

Preface

The IFIP International Conference on Wired/Wireless Internet Communications (WWIC) was organized and hosted by the Advanced Network Architectures Lab (CRAAX) at the Technical University of Catalonia (UPC), in Vilanova i la Geltrú, Spain, during June 15–17, 2011. In this edition, the conference was for the first time technically sponsored by IFIP TC6. In particular, WWIC 2011 got the endorsement of WG 6.2 (Network and Internetwork Architectures) and WG 6.8 (Mobile and Wireless Communications).

The conference attracted 50 submissions from 21 different countries in Asia, Europe, North America and Africa. All submitted papers went through a meticulous review by the Technical Program Committee members as well as other additional reviewers. After this strict review process, 22 high-quality papers were selected for publication in the conference proceedings as part of the IFIP *Lecture Notes in Computer Science* series. The Technical Program Committee also selected five additional papers that although were considered somewhat less mature technically, satisfied the criteria of novelty, presentation, relevance and in addition demonstrated clear potential for significant impact. All accepted papers were thematically distributed into six technical sessions making up the conference program, which covered highly relevant topics in the conference area grouped in major themes: quality through routing, naming and control, performance and simulation analysis, energy efficiency and cooperation in wireless networks, transmission and management, mobility and LTE networks.

The WWIC 2011 conference started with an outstanding keynote from Telefónica I+D, that gave way to the technical program. The technical program included five keynotes, two invited talks, two invited papers and one interesting panel on "Delay Tolerant Networking." The conference was completed by two invited sessions, one on "Adaptive Approaches to Guarantee E2E Network Services" (organized by AbdelhamidMellouk from the University of Paris-Est Creteil and Eva Marín from Universitat Politècnica de Catalunya), and the other on "Wireless Multi-hop Communications Challenges in the Future Internet" (organized by Marilia Curado from the University of Coimbra and EnzoMingozzi from the University of Pisa). Keeping the tradition of previous WWIC editions, WWIC 2011 was pleased to host the 5th ERCIM Workshop on eMobility which took place on June 14, 2011, and was organized by Torsten Braun from the University of Bern and Geert Heijenk from the University of Twente.

This year's edition the WWIC conference was preceded by the Cost IC0806 Workshop, that was hosted by UPC during June 13–14.

The conference organization team would like to express its gratitude to the WWIC Steering Committee, which decided on the WWIC 2011 location. It has been a pleasure for the CRAAX team at UPC to organize and host WWIC 2011.

Finally, we would also like to record our appreciation of the efforts of many people in bringing about the WWIC2011 conference: all authors that submitted papers to the conference; the Technical Program Committee and the additional reviewers devoting time on creating these proceedings; the financial institutions (CISCO, SPICE, Spanish Ministry of Science and Education, UPC and i2cat); the technically sponsoring institution IFIP; and the sponsors, since all of them made this challenge feasible. In particular we appreciate the commitment of the CRAAX Lab staff for their dedication and the support received from the UPC Campus in Vilanova and the City Council.

April 2011   Xavi Masip
                                                     Dominique Verchere
                                                    Vassilis Tsaoussidis
                                                     Marcelo Yannuzzi

Organization

WWIC was organized by the Advanced Network Architectures Lab (CRAAX) located on the campus of the Universitat Politècnica de Catalunya (UPC) in the nice city of Vilanova i la Geltrú in June 2011.

General Co-chairs

Xavier Masip-Bruin	Universitat Politècnica de Catalunya, UPC, Spain
Dominique Verchere	Alcatel-Lucent Bell Labs, France

Steering Committee

Torsten Braun	University of Bern, Switzerland
Georg Carle	TU München, Germany
Geert Heijenk	University of Twente, The Netherlands
Yevgeni Koucheryavy	Tampere University of Technology, Finland
Peter Langendörfer	IHP Microelectronics, Germany
Ibrahim Matta	Boston University, USA
Vassilis Tsaoussidis	Democritus University of Thrace, Greece

Technical Program Co-chairs

Vassilis Tsaoussidis	Democritus University of Thrace, Greece
Marcelo Yannuzzi	Universitat Politècnica de Catalunya, UPC, Spain

Technical Program Committee

Ozgur B. Akan	Middle East Technical University, Turkey
Khalid Al-Begain	University of Glamorgan, UK
Onur Altintas	Toyota InfoTechnology Center, Japan
Brice Augustin	University Paris Est Creteil (UPEC), France
Lenoardo Badia	IMT Lucca Institute for Advanced Studies, Italy
Mortaza Bargh	Novay, The Netherlands
Jalel Ben-Othman	University of Versailles, France
Fernando Boavida	University of Coimbra, Portugal
Thomas Michael Bohnert	SAP Research, Switzerland
Richard Boucherie	Universiteit Twente, The Netherlands

Vassilis Tsaoussidis	Demokritos University, Greece
Hans van den Berg	TNO ICT / University of Twente, The Netherlands
Rob van der Mei	Centre for Mathematics and Computer Science, The Netherlands
Miki Yamamoto	Kansai University, Japan
Marcelo Yannuzzi	Universitat Politècnica de Catalunya, Spain
Chi Zhang	Juniper Networks, USA

Publicity Chairs

Eduardo Cerqueira	UFPA, Brazil
Alex Sprintson	Texas A&M, USA

Publication Chair

Eva Marín Tordera	Universitat Politècnica de Catalunya, UPC, Spain

Local Organization Chair

René Serral Gracià	Universitat Politècnica de Catalunya, UPC, Spain

Workshop Chairs (5th ERCIM eMobility Workshop)

Torsten Braun	University of Bern, Switzerland
Geert Heijenk	University of Twente, The Netherlands

Reviewers

Belal Abuhaija	Thomas Michael Bohnert
Khalid Al-Begain	Richard Boucherie
Onur Altintas	Torsten Braun
Carlos Anastasiades	Wojciech Burakowski
Brice Augustin	Scott Burleigh
Leonardo Badia	Maria Calderon
Mortaza Bargh	Eduardo Cerqueira
Abdussalam Baryun	Bong Dae Choi
Jalel Ben-othman	Mieso Denko
Vitor Bernardo	Sotiris Diamantopoulos
Nikolaos Bezirgiannidis	Michel Diaz
A. Ozan Bicen	Stylianos Dimitriou
Fernando Boavida	Ozgur Ergul

Sergi Figuerola
Erik Fledderus
Simon Gansel
Victor Govindaswamy
Mohsen Guizani
Jarmo Harju
Adriana Hava
Sonia Heemstra de Groot
Geert Heijenk
Michael Howarth
Byung-Guk Kim
Murat Kocaoglu
Yevgeni Koucheryavy
Christos Koulamas
Giada Landi
Peter Langendoerfer
Remco Litjens
Pascal Lorenz
Lefteris Mamatas
Eva Marín Tordera
Patrick McDonagh
Abdelhamid Mellouk
Enzo Mingozzi
Dmitri Moltchanov
Edmundo Monteiro

Marc Necker
Ioanis Nikolaidis
Guevara Noubir
Cristian Olariu
Evgeny Osipov
Joerg Ott
Philippe Owezarski
Giorgos Papastergiou
George Pavlou
Aikaterini Petraki
Ioannis Psaras
Jukka Rinne
KeithScott
Patrick Senac
Dimitrios Serpanos
René Serral-Gracià
Vasilios Siris
Dirk Staehle
Thomas Staub
Vassilis Tsaoussidis
Hans van den Berg
Robvan der Mei
Marcelo Yannuzzi
Chi Zhang
Zhongliang Zhao

Sponsoring Institutions

Table of Contents

Mobility and LTE Networks

Performance and Simulation Analysis

Adaptive Approaches to Guarantee E2E Network Services

Energy Efficiency and Cooperation in Wireless Networks

Transmission and Management

Quality through Routing, Naming and Control

Wireless Multi-hop Communications Challenges in the Future Internet

Emerging Contributions

TRAWL – A Traffic Route Adapted Weighted Learning Algorithm

Enda Fallon[1,2], Liam Murphy[1], John Murphy[1], and Chi Ma[2]

[1] School of Computer Science and Informatics. University College Dublin, Ireland
[2] Software Research Institute, Athlone Institute of Technology, Athlone, Ireland
efallon@ait.ie, {Liam.Murphy,j.murphy}@ucd.ie,
cma@research.ait.ie

Abstract. Media Independent Handover (MIH) is an emerging standard which supports the communication of network-critical events to upper layer mobility protocols. One of the key features of MIH is the event service, which supports predictive network degradation events that are triggered based on link layer metrics. For set route vehicles, the constrained nature of movement enables a degree of network performance prediction. We propose to capture this performance predictability through a Traffic Route Adapted Weighted Learning (TRAWL) algorithm. TRAWL is a feed forward neural network whose output layer is configurable for both homogeneous and heterogeneous networks. TRAWL uses an unsupervised back propagation learning mechanism, which captures predictable network behavior while also considering dynamic performance characteristics. We evaluate the performance of TRAWL using a commercial metropolitan heterogeneous network. We show that TRAWL has significant performance improvements over existing MIH link triggering mechanisms.

Keywords: MIH, vehicular systems, handover, neural networks.

1 Introduction

The IEEE 802.21 working group propose the MIH standard [1] to support the communication of network critical events to upper layer mobility protocols. While the MIH standard defines the interface for communication of link layer metrics to upper layer mobility protocols it does not provide specifics on the mechanisms which should be employed to trigger such events. Many existing algorithms [2][3][4] define static thresholds for performance metrics such as RSS. When these thresholds are exceeded events such as Link_Going_Down (LGD) and Link_Down (LD) are triggered. For set route vehicle systems such approaches are limited as they do not consider how the predictable nature of movement enables historic performance metrics to influence predictive link triggering.

In this paper we focus on the optimisation of network handover for set route vehicles such as public transport busses and trains. Such vehicles typically operate in preconfigured routes which are repeated at routine intervals sometimes many times a

X. Masip-Bruin et al. (Eds.): WWIC 2011, LNCS 6649, pp. 1–14, 2011.

day. We propose TRAWL, an unsupervised feed forward neural network, which captures repetitive network behaviour while also considering the dynamic performance characteristics of heterogeneous networks.

TRAWL consists of 2 major components; Route Identification and Management (RIM) and an Unsupervised Vehicle Learning Algorithm (UVLA). RIM is responsible for the configuration and removal of routes in the system. RIM also maintains the relationship between Access Points (APs) and vehicle routes. UVLA consists of a feed forward neural network which implements the decision logic for TRAWL. UVLA input consists of a selection of normalised performance metrics. The number of neurons in the output layer is dependent on the network configuration; 1 for homogeneous networks, 2 or more for heterogeneous networks. When the stimulation of a neuron exceeds a user defined activation threshold, the neuron "fires" producing a binary positive output. Positive binary output triggers path switchover to the path specified by the inputs. UVLA aims to maximise throughput per route cycle. In order to determine the learning rate we calculate the rate of change of a linear regression line through historic cycle throughput. A large rate of change results in a large alteration of weights. A small rate of change results in a small alteration of weights.

We evaluate our approach against the standard MIH approach used in [2] using performance metrics from a commercial heterogeneous network installation. The standard MIH approach is limited as uses a static RSS threshold of typically -80dBm to -85dBm to determine when connection termination should occur. For a commercial heterogeneous network implementation where APs are positioned for hot spot coverage, RSS ranging for -80dBm to -90dBm is common. By exploiting historic performance trends TRAWL determines that significant throughput can still be achieved at this RSS level, particularly for uncongested heterogeneous networks. Results illustrate that TRAWL has up to a 400% performance improvement over [2].

This paper is organised as follows; related work is described in section 2. An introduction to neural networks is provided in section 3. In section 4 TRAWL is described. In section 5 and 6 experimental and simulated results are presented. Conclusions and future work is presented in section 7.

2   Related Work

Many existing MIH implementations utilize a performance threshold P_{thres} to generate the MIH LGD event. In such scenarios the relationship between the time that P_{thres} (actual or projected) is exceeded, T_{deg}, and the time at which path handover is initiated, $T_{h\text{-}init}$, can be expressed as follows:

$$T_{h-init} = \alpha_{\lg d}(T_{deg})$$

α_{lgd} is an anticipation factor applied to T_{deg} to adjust the aggressiveness of LGD event triggering. Many implementations are based on pre-defined P_{thres}, mostly associated with RSS. If the current RSS crosses P_{thres} the LGD event is generated [2]. The NIST MIH implementation in NS2 [2] utilizes the power level of packets RXThresh (P_{thres}) and Pr_limit (α_{lgd}) to control event triggering. A number of studies utilize a predictive indication of RSS in this manner [3][4].In [5] the MN velocity and handover duration are used in conjunction with the predicted RSS level to improve LGD event triggering. While [6][7] use a predictive model which uses the neighbor information to generate timely link triggers so that handover procedures can finish before the link goes down. While these mechanisms utilise metrics which provide a static representation and dynamic view of performance they do not provide a mechanism by which the handover algorithm can tune performance thresholds for changing network conditions.

There are a significant number of recent studies in the area of network handover for vehicle based systems. These studies can be generally categorized in the area of Vehicle Ad-hoc NETworks (VANET) or infrastructure mode network access. Our investigation relates to the latter. In [9], SWiFT focuses on handover optimisation for vehicles travelling greater than 200kmph. SWiFT uses the speed of MN movement and RSS as the basis for link event triggering. It does not consider the condition of the link in the handover decision. [10] proposes a MIP handover mechanism for VANET which maintains the original Care of Address (CoA) configured at the original AP. [11] uses Proxy Mobile IPv6 (PMIP) and Host Identity Protocol (HIP) to reduce handover latency for urban vehicular systems. In [12] we propose multi-homing rather than MIP to pre-configure alternate paths prior to network handover. [13] proposes a collaborative approach in which APs use MN position prediction to limit the potential for retransmission. Such an approach has significant network infrastructure requirements. [14] proposes an architecture for network selection in vehicular systems based on network metrics, user requirements and application QoS. We propose that the predictable nature of public transport vehicles enables performance predictability which is not exploited by any of these approaches. Other studies have investigated how network performance can be optimised by predicting network holes [15][16]. These studies are ad hoc network based and assume an autonomic approach which allows the sensor nodes to self learn/configure. As an end point oriented solution our approach has no ability to change network configuration.

There are a number of ongoing studies which evaluate how artificial intelligence techniques can be used in the optimisation of network handover. [17] [18] propose a mutually connected neural network in order to optimise load balancing and QoS for the entire network. Our work focuses on the optimisation of throughput for client devices. [19] proposes a Hopfield neural network which considers multiple input parameters in the selection of networks. However that study does not consider how the predictable nature of routes used by public vehicles can be used in the optimisation of weights.

3 Artificial Neural Networks

ANN are data processing models which are based on the operation of the brain. The first work on ANN was presented by Mc Cullock and Pitts in 1943 [20]. The work proposed a Threshold Logic Unit (TLU) which used weighted binary inputs. If the weighted sum of inputs exceeded a threshold value, the neuron fired. Many enhancements to the original model have been introduced. The first unsupervised learning approach, Hebbian Learning, was proposed by [21] in 1949. Classification of inputs was introduced by the perceptron model in [22]. The introduction of back propagation enabled the training of synaptic weights based on a desired output. This paper proposes TRAWL, an ANN used to capture historic performance trends for predictable route vehicle systems. These trends are weighted against dynamic metrics.

Fig. 1 illustrates a supervised learning ANN. Values x_0, x_1, x_2,.... x_n are provided as input to the neuron. The neuron has 2 modes of operation; training or trained. In trained mode, the neuron applies synaptic weights w_{k0}, w_{k1},..... w_{kn} which enhance or degrade the input values. These weighted values are summed and an activation function $\varphi(.)$ is applied. $\varphi(.)$ determines whether the neuron should "fire", producing an output y_k which classifies the input pattern.

Training mode can be implemented through supervised or unsupervised learning. In supervised learning the ANN will have an offline training phase in which neural outputs are compared against a training set. Alterations are made to the synaptic weights to limit the error in classification between the output y_k and the training set d_k. When the ANN correctly classifies the input pattern, the ANN operates in trained mode. Unsupervised learning has no external training patterns. In this mode the ANN self organizes data presented to the network and detects recurrent properties.

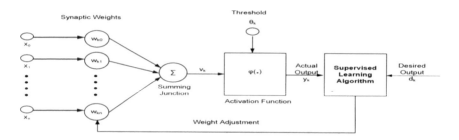

Fig. 1. A Supervised Learning Neural Network

4   TRAWL – A Traffic Route Adapted Weighted Learning Algorithm

Our TRAWL algorithm consists of 2 components:

Route Identification and Management (RIM) – is responsible for the identification and management of vehicle routes. Using the geographical position of the vehicle RIM distinguishes existing, altered or new routes.

Unsupervised Vehicle Learning Algorithm (UVLA) – implements the path selection intelligence within TRAWL. UVLA is a feed forward neural network which operates with a single output neuron for homogeneous networks or 2 output neurons for heterogeneous networks. Back propagation and weight adjustment are implemented each time the vehicle completes a cycle of a route.

The fig 2 illustrates the pseudo code for the TRAWL algorithm. TRAWL dynamically configures and maintains traffic routes using GPS coordinates. Having read the GPS coordinates, TRAWL determines if the current position uniquely identifies a route. If the position is not previously configured, a new route is created and training is initiated. If the position uniquely identifies a previously defined route, the TRAWL algorithm determines if ANN training is required for that route.

```
Struct Route
  param trainingmode = false //training or trained
  param GPS_Cord startOfRoute
  param GPS_Cord[] existingRoute // cc-ords for existing route
  param float[] weights  // synaptic weights
  param float activationThreshold //if summation > then fire
  param float[] historicThroughput  //previous cycle throughput
  param float learningRate // rate of altering of synaptic weights
  param  float  accuracyThreashold  //  if  throughput  <  reinitiate
training
Routine::TRAWL()
  GPS_Cord CurrentPosition = get GPS_Position()
  foreach(Route)   // RIM route management
    if(CurrentPosition    contained    in    Route.StartOfRoute)//cycle
complete
      historicThroughput[] += throughputforcurrentcycle
      UVLAcheckAccuracy(historicThroughput)
      if(trainingmode==true)
        UVLATraining()
      else
      UVLAcalculatehandover()
    else if(CurrentPosition contained in Route.ExistingRoute)
      UVLAcalculatehandover()
    else // coords will form a new route
      if(start of new route)
        create Route newRoute
        newRoute.StartofRoute = CurrentPosition
      newRoute.ExistingRoute[] += CurrentPosition
      if(trainingmode==false)
        trainingmode = true
        UVLAcalculatehandover()
      else if(trainingmode==true)
        UVLAcalculatehandover()
Routine::UVLAcalculatehandover()
  foreach(AP)
    param float[] normalisedmetric
    foreach(performancemetric)
      normalisedmetric[] = NormaliseMetric(GetPerformanceMetric())
    param activationValue = (weights[0]*normalisedmetric[0])+......
    if(activationValue>threshold)
      implementhandover(AP)   // neuron fires
Routine:: UVLATraining ()
  param slope = slopeofLinearRegression(HistoricThroughput)
  param errorCorrection = slope*learningRate
  foreach(weight)
    weight+=errorCorrection // alter weights
Routine:: UVLAcheckAccuracy()
  Param slope = slopeofLinearRegression(HistoricThroughput)
  if(abs(slope)>accuracyThreashold)
    trainingmode = true   //reinitiate training
```

Fig. 2. Pseudo code for the TRAWL algorithm

TRAWL operates in either training or trained mode. As an unsupervised algorithm TRAWL does not have an offline training phase. TRAWL uses initial end user synaptic weights to determine if hndover is required. Following each route cycle the throughput is calculated and synaptic weights are adjusted. TRAWL is trained when (a) the training process does not update synaptic weights (b) synaptic weight updates have no effect on throughput. TRAWL ensures that synaptic weights remain relevant to changing network conditions by applying an `accuracyThreshold`. Throughput is measured for every route cycle and if the `accuracyThreshold` is exceeded training is reinitiated.

The ULVA model consists of X_0, X_1,... X_n neuron inputs corresponding to the selected performance metrics. Each neuron is a linear threshold gate producing a binary output for path switchover. O_y is defined as follows:

$$V_y = \sum_{i=0}^{N} X_i W_i \qquad (1) \qquad O_y = \begin{cases} 1 \ if \ V_y \geq \theta \\ 0 \ if \ V_y < \theta \end{cases} \qquad (2)$$

Fig 3 illustrates a UVLA configuration with 2 output neurons for a heterogeneous network with wireless and mobile components.

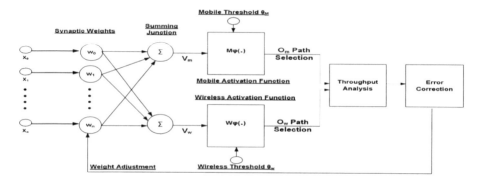

Fig. 3. UVLA Neural Network with 2 Output Neurons

W_i are synaptic weights for each performance metric. V_y is the sum of weighted inputs. θ_y is a user configured activation threshold. If the stimulation of the neuron V_y meets the activation threshold θ_y, the neuron "fires" producing a binary positive output. A positive output indicates that path switchover should occur. The aim is to maximise throughput per route cycle, therefore we calculate the rate of change, c, of a linear regression line for historic throughput as follows:

$$c = \frac{\sum (x - x')(y - y')}{\sum (x - x')^2} \qquad (3)$$

Using c we can determine the rate by which alterations to synaptic weights affect throughput. A positive c indicates that synaptic weight alterations have a beneficial effect on throughput. A negative c indicates that synaptic weight alterations have a detrimental effect on throughput.

these values exceeds the activation threshold switchover occurs. On the first cycle of the route this approach resulted in a throughput of 66.82Mbytes. A slope of a line from the origin to the point (1,66.82) is calculated resulting in a slope of 66.82. This slope is then multiplied by the learning rate, .002, resulting in a weight adjustment of 0.13364. On the second cycle the synaptic weights w_1=.484, w_2=.3, w_3=.4, w_4=.25 result in a throughput of 164.9Mbytes. We calculate the slope of a linear regression line through the points (0,0), (1,66.82), (2,82.45) as 82.45. Multiplying the learning rate .002 by 82.45 results in a synaptic weight adjustment following the second cycle of .1649. Weights are adjusted in this manner following every cycle until the slope of the linear regression line is 0 or until adjustments in the synaptic weights have no effect on throughput.

Local maxima can have a negative effect on ANN performance as learning is centred on a local maximum value. Table 1 illustrates the TRAWL parameters for learning cycles 5-10 for the non congested heterogeneous network. After 9 cycles the slope of the throughput linear regression is 0 indicating that no error correction is required. The synaptic weight configuration w_1=.575, w_{12}=.518, w_3=.590, w_1=.516 has been optimised around a local maximal value. In order to avoid local maxima we introduce a positive or negative random weight adjustment in the range 0-0.2 every 5 learning cycles. In cycle 10 the random weight adjustments w_1=.-.112, w_{12}=-.181, w_3=.-.069, w_1=.-.145 are applied avoiding the local maxima and resulting in the final trained throughput of 74.4Mbytes.

Table 1. Local Maxima in a non congested heterogeneous network configuration

Cycle	w1 (Loss)	w2 (RTT)	w3 (RSS)	w4 (Bw)	Thres	Throughput	Slope	Error Correction	Learning Rate
5	0582	0.525	0.597	0.523	1	49.15	5.141	0.010	0.002
6	0.592	0.535	0.607	0.533	1	49.15	-3.939	-0.008	0.002
7	0.585	0.528	0.600	0.526	1	49.15	-3.89	-0.008	0.002
8	0.577	0.520	0.592	0.518	1	49.15	-0.928	-0.002	0.002
9	0.575	0.518	0.590	0.516	1	49.15	0	0.000	0.002
10	0.463	0.337	0.521	0.371	1	59.38	2.046	0.004	0.002

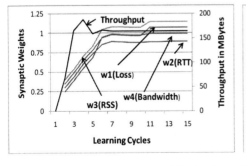

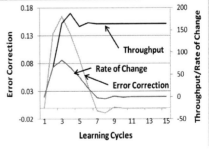

Fig. 7. Throughput and Synaptic Weights for a Non Congested Homogenous Configuration

Fig. 8. Throughput and Error Correction for a Non Congested Homogenous Configuration

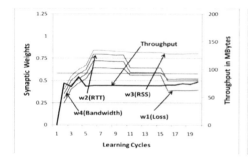

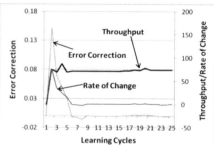

Fig. 9. Throughput and Synaptic Weights for a Non Congested Heterogeneous Configuration

Fig. 10. Throughput and Error Correction for a Non Congested Heterogeneous Configuration

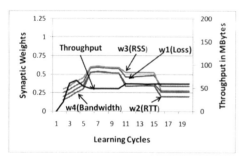

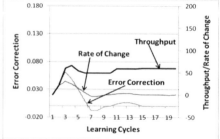

Fig. 11. Throughput and Synaptic Weights for a Congested Heterogeneous Configuration

Fig. 12. Throughput and Error Correction for a Congested Heterogeneous Configuration

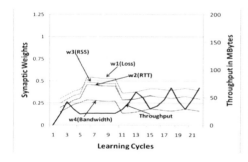

Fig. 13. Throughput and Synaptic Weights for a Congested Homogeneous Configuration

Fig. 14. Throughput and Error Correction for a Congested Homogenous Configuration

TRAWL uses an unsupervised back propagation learning mechanism which captures predictable network behaviour while also considering dynamic performance characteristics. We evaluate TRAWL using performance metrics from a commercial heterogeneous network. Results presented illustrate up to a 400% performance improvement over traditional MIH link triggering approaches for this network installation. For an unsupervised ANN such as TRAWL the optimisation of synaptic weights is a trade off between learning time and throughput. While a number of cycles are required to fully train TRAWL, we illustrate that early in the training cycle throughput is close to its final trained value. Future work will extend the TRAWL algorithm to consider metrics applicable to media streaming applications.

References

[1] Institute of Electrical and Electronics Engineers, IEEE Standard for Local and metropolitan area networks – Part 21: Media Independent Handover Services, January 21 (2009)
[2] NIST, The Network Simulator NS-2 NIST Add-on – Neighbor Discovery (January 2007)
[3] Mhatre, V., Papagiannaki, K.: Using Smart Triggers for Improved User Performance in 802.11 Wireless 24 Networks. In: ACM Mobisys 2006, pp. 246–259 (2006)
[4] Woon, S., Golmie, N., Sekercioglu, Y.A.: Effective Link Triggers to Improve Handover Performance. In: IEEE PIMRC 2006, pp. 1–5 (2006)
[5] Zhang, R., Hong Wang, Y., Zhi Huang, K., Quan Wei, H.: Link Quality Oriented Proactive Vertical Handover in Heterogeneous Wireless Networks. In: CNMT 2009, pp. 1–4 (January 2009)
[6] Yoo, S., Cypher, D., Golmie, N.: Predictive Handover Mechanism based on Required Time Estimation in Heterogeneous Wireless Networks. In: MILCOM 2008, pp. 1–7. IEEE, Los Alamitos (2008)
[7] Yoo, S., Cypher, D., Golmie, N.: Timely Effective Handover Mechanism in Heterogeneous Wireless Networks. Journal, Wireless Personal Communications (2008)
[8] UC Berkeley, LBL, UCS/ISI, Xerox Parc (2005). NS-2 Documentation and Software, Version 2.29
[9] Kumar, K.R., Angolkar, P., Das, D.: SWiFT: A Novel Architecture for Seamless Wireless Internet for Fast Trains. In: Ramalingam, R. (ed.) VTC Spring 2008, pp. 3011–3015. IEEE, Los Alamitos (2008)
[10] Hayoung, O., Chong-kwon, K.: A Robust handover under analysis of unexpected vehicle behaviors in Vehicular Ad-hoc Network. In: Vehicular Technology Conference, VTC 2010-Spring, pp. 1–7 (2010)
[11] Céspedes U, S., (Sherman) Shen, X.: An Efficient Hybrid HIP-PMIPv6 Scheme for Seamless Internet Access in Urban Vehicular Scenarios. In: IEEE GLOBECOM 2010, Miami, USA (2010)
[12] Fallon, E., Qiao, Y., Murphy, L., Muntean, G.: SOLTA: a service oriented link triggering algorithm for MIH implementations. In: IWCMC, Caen, France, pp. 1146–1150 (2010)
[13] Ryo, A., et al.: Control of transmission timing using information on predicted movement in opportunistic roadside-to-vehicle communication. In: Proceedings of ICUFN, pp. 262–267 (2010)
[14] Chantaksinopas, I., Oothongsap, P., Prayote, A.: Framework for network selection transparency on vehicular networks. In: Proceedings of ECTI-CON, pp. 593–597 (2010)

[15] Ahmed, N., Kanhere, S., Jha, S.: The Holes Problem in Wireless Sensor Networks. ACM SIGMOBILE Mobile Computing and Communications Review 9(2) (April 2005)

[16] Ghosh, A.: Estimating Coverage Holes and Enhancing Coverage in Mixed Sensor Networks. In: IEEE International Conference on Local Computer Networks (2004)

[17] Hasegawa, M., Ishizu, K., Murakami, H., Harada, H.: Experimental evaluation of distributed radio resource optimization algorithm based on the neural networks for Cognitive Wireless Cloud. In: Proceedings of IEEE PIMRC Workshops, pp. 32–37 (2010)

[18] Hasegawa, M., et al.: Design and Implementation of A Distributed Radio Resource Usage Optimization Algorithm for Heterogeneous Wireless Networks. In: Proceedings of VTC Fall, pp. 1–7 (2009)

[19] Rakovic, V., Gavrilovska, L.: Novel RAT selection mechanism based on Hopfield neural networks. In: Proceedings of ICUMT (2010)

[20] McCulloch, W., Pitts, W.: A logical calculus of the ideas immanent in nervous activity

[21] Hebb, D.: The Organization of Behavior. Wiley, Chichester

[22] Rosenblatt, F.: A comparison of several perceptron models

[23] Framework and overall objectives of the future development of IMT-2000 and systems beyond IMT-2000. Recommendation M.1645 (2000)

[24] Heikkilä, S.: Business Models of Mobile Operators for WLAN: Case Examples, http://www.netlab.tkk.fi/opetus/s383042/2006/papers_pdf/G2.pdf

[25] Netstumbler Network Analysis Software, http://www.netstumbler.com/

[26] Palazzi, C., Chin, B., Ray, P., Pau, G., Gerla, M., Roccetti, M.: High Mobility in a Realistic Wireless Environment: a Mobile IP Handoff Model for NS-2. In: Proceedings of TridentCom 2007 (2007)

Adaptive Packet Scheduling for the Support of QoS over DVB-S2 Satellite Systems

Elizabeth Rendon-Morales, Jorge Mata-Díaz, Juanjo Alins,
José Luis Muñoz, and Oscar Esparza

Departamento de Ingeniería Telemática
Universidad Politécnica de Cataluña
C. Jordi Girona, 31. 08034 Barcelona. Spain
elizabeth.rendon@entel.upc.edu

Abstract. This paper presents an adaptive algorithm for managing the weights of a weighted round robin (WRR) scheduler. The weights calculation depends on the capacity variations present in a Digital Video Broadcasting-Second Generation (DVB-S2) satellite link. The algorithm optimizes the bandwidth utilization while satisfying the QoS requirements for different traffic classes. The operation of the proposed algorithm is demonstrated by using the NS-2 simulator environment. The results show that the proposed adaptive WRR algorithm optimizes the bandwidth utilization while enforcing the priority level of each service class even in an extreme reduction of bandwidth caused by rain events.

Keywords: QoS, DiffServ DVB-S2, BSM and WRR.

1 Introduction

Nowadays, the support of IP-based applications over Internet has experienced a fast and continuous growth together with the expansion of the World Wide Web. As a consequence, new IP applications such as Voice over IP (VoIP) and multimedia services require considering different levels of individual packet treatment through the network. This differentiation must include not only the Quality of Service (QoS) parameters to specify packet transmission priorities across the network nodes but also, the required amount of bandwidth assignment to guarantee its transport.

To provide this type of IP services, the geostationary (GEO) satellite infrastructure plays a crucial role. Specially, because the satellite systems can provide ubiquity and broadband access, being feasible to reach large and disperse populations around the world.

However, to provide a variety of services over satellite systems with QoS, it is important to consider the intrinsic characteristics present in GEO satellite systems that affect the QoS provisioning. Such characteristics are: delay, losses and link bandwidth variations. The presence of these link bandwidth variations need to be seriously considered, as it is necessary to preserve the QoS levels when rain events in the atmosphere are experienced, which can also reduce the available capacity in the

X. Masip-Bruin et al. (Eds.): WWIC 2011, LNCS 6649, pp. 15–26, 2011.

Digital Video Broadcasting-Second Generation (DVB-S2) [1] forward channel. To address this, the DVB-S2 specification implements the Adaptive Code and Modulation (ACM) techniques to achieve quasi-error free channel conditions for each individual user, by providing them with the most suitable modulation and code (*ModCod*) value according to the measured signal-to-noise-plus-interference ratio (SNIR). In addition, the Broadband Satellite Multimedia (BSM) working group has defined a QoS functional architecture (ETSI-BSM-QoS) standardized in [2]. This framework establishes the required QoS mechanisms (supported in the Hub) to define the priorities among users and applications based on the Differentiated Services (DiffServ) architecture [3].

Nevertheless, most of the predefined QoS mechanisms usually have static input parameters resulting in an inefficient resource allocation. Therefore, a solution is to use an adaptive approach that manages the bandwidth distribution (among service classes) considering the fact that the available capacity present in a satellite system is constantly changing. This adaptive approach enables sharing bandwidth resources in a more suitable way, ensuring that the required QoS levels are maintained while the satellite link capacity is optimized.

In this paper, we propose a resource sharing model that manages the QoS requirements and at the same time optimizes the utilization of the DVB-S2 satellite link capacity. The aim of this model is to share the available bandwidth between various service classes having a certain QoS level. The proposed adaptive scheme calculates the optimal weight values considering two factors used to determine the minimum required amount of resources, these are: the QoS requirements of each traffic class and the link bandwidth availability present on the satellite system.

The proposed adaptive IP packet scheduling mechanism is based on the Weighted Round Robin (WRR) scheme which is evaluated using the NS-2 simulation tool. In the simulation environment we consider both the adoption of a DiffServ model to provide QoS guarantees and the most representative characteristics affecting the DVB-S2 forward channel (i.e. delay, losses and mainly the presence of link bandwidth variations). The presented simulation results demonstrate that when our adaptive WRR mechanism is implemented, an enhanced satellite performance is achieved while maintaining the QoS levels even though a severe reduction of bandwidth is experienced.

The presented work is organized in 5 sections: in section 2 a characterization of the bandwidth link variation is presented together with a description of the adaptive Hub and the adaptive WRR algorithm. In section 3, the proposed adaptive model is evaluated using the NS-2 simulation tool and the performance evaluation results are presented. In section 4 the related studies are presented and conclusions are formulated in section 5.

2   Adaptive WRR Model

In this section we present a characterization of the bandwidth link variations present in GEO satellite systems, a description of the adaptive Hub and the proposed adaptive WRR algorithm.

2.1 Characterization of the Bandwidth Link Variation

In practice, transmission rate variations in the satellite link are mainly caused by atmospheric conditions such as rain events. In order to define an adaptive WRR model that considers these link bandwidth variations, we have analyzed a rain event affecting the bandwidth availability in the DVB-S2 forward channel.

Particularly, we have considered the study presented in [4] that provides an estimation of the physical layer performance over the DVB-S2 forward link under a heavy rain event. By considering this approach, the physical layer behavior is adapted taking into account the effects of the satellite delay and the implementation of the ACM techniques. Using such techniques, it is possible to achieve an optimal operation point by selecting the most suitable *ModCod* depending on the satellite terminal propagation conditions. To simplify and use these results in our proposed adaptive model we approximated the physical layer estimation reported in [4] by a sinusoidal wave (see Fig. 1-dotted line) to represent a rain event in the satellite DVB-S2 link.

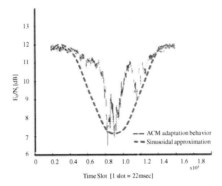

Fig. 1. ACM adaptation behavior during a heavy rain event in the forward link [4]

In this way, satellite terminals allocated under clear sky conditions are characterized for having high link bandwidth availability (see Fig. 1 at the peak of the sinusoidal link wave). Therefore, those terminals will be provided with an efficient *ModCod* according to the satellite propagation conditions. In contrast, terminals allocated under a heavy rain event are characterized for having reduced link bandwidth availability (see Fig. 1 at the valley of the sinusoidal link wave). Therefore those terminals will be provided with a *ModCod* including a robust channel protection mechanism and a specific modulation scheme. As a result, the bandwidth capacity will fluctuate between the minimum (valley) and maximum (peak) values, since the ACM mechanism will be continuously working to mitigate the atmospheric impairments. This bandwidth characterization will be the input parameter of our proposed IP adaptive scheduler.

2.2 Architecture of the Adaptive Hub

The proposed DiffServ model implemented over the adaptive DVB-S2 Hub fulfills the ETSI QoS Broadband Satellite Multimedia Services and Architectures standard [2].

The QoS policy implemented in the DiffServ model allows the EF traffic class to have the highest priority, while the AF traffic class has more priority than the BE traffic class. As a results, the BE traffic class, which is based on a best effort scheme, uses the remaining link capacity, being able to use the bandwidth that any other class does not use.

The architecture of the adaptive Hub that supports the DiffServ model and exploits our adaptive packet scheduler based on the WRR mechanism is shown in Fig. 2. The DiffServ model includes a traffic classifier that decides if a packet needs to be reassigned with a different QoS level by remarking its DSCP. Notice that the proposed scheme allows multiple flows to be aggregated and treated as a single flow per traffic class. The enqueuing system supported at the Hub has three traffic classes allowing each of them to have its own physical queue and implementing a drop tail mechanism.

Every traffic class implements a token bucket (TB) as a rate limiter to guarantee the transmission rate according to the bandwidth assignment established in the Service Level Agreement (SLA). Each TB limiting rate is set to μ_{EF}, μ_{AF} and μ_{BE} for the EF, AF and BE traffic classes respectively. Here, it is worth mentioning that our proposal considers the buffer length of each traffic class as a function of the Bandwidth Delay Product (BDP). This BDP value is set considering the minimum Round Trip Time (RTT_{MIN}) present in the satellite system and the associated TB limiting rate.

All packets coming from each traffic class are sent directly to the IP scheduler. The IP scheduler is based on the Weighted Round Robin (WRR) mechanism [5] that controls the order in which packets are extracted out from its queues. Along with the WRR scheduler, there is a new module which is responsible for calculating the parameters of the WRR scheduler. This component is referred as the *Weights calculator* that takes into account the adaptive WRR model (further defined in subsection 2.3) to compute the suitable weight values. The *Weights calculator's* input parameter is the bandwidth availability considering the sinusoidal wave variation defined in subsection 2.1. Such value is sent from the physical layer to the network layer by means of a cross-layer mechanism.

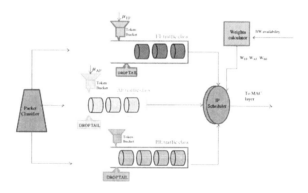

Fig. 2. Structure of the adaptive DVB-S2 Hub

The corresponding weight values (W_{EF}, W_{AF} and W_{BE}) are set within the IP scheduler to prioritize the resources for each traffic class. As it is observed, in Fig. 2 the *Weights calculator* module is decoupled from the IP scheduler. Therefore, the scheduler complexity is not increased and both modules can work independently based on their own settings.

2.3 The Adaptive WRR Algorithm

In order to calculate the weight values, different criteria can be used (e.g. the mean packet size [6], queue sizes [7], revenue-based [8]). In this paper, we propose to use the current capacity of the DVB-S2 satellite link (C_{OUT}) as the main criteria for the allocation of network resources. To the best of our knowledge, this is the first time that such scenario has been analyzed over a DVB-S2 satellite system.

The adaptive IP scheduler design proposed in this paper actively adjusts the weight of each traffic class to enforce its QoS level. This adaptive design is linked to the ACM mechanism specification. In this way, considering the three traffic classes defined in the DiffServ architecture (EF, AF and BE), the adaptive model will therefore prioritize the EF traffic class over the AF and BE traffic classes when the satellite system experiences a capacity reduction in the presence of a heavy rain event. This prioritization is done by assigning high weight values to the EF traffic class while the AF and BE traffic classes will have the lowest weight values. Similarly, when the intensity of the rain event has diminished and the link capacity increases, the adaptive model will keep the priority levels of the EF and AF traffic classes over the BE traffic by assigning high weight values to the EF and AF traffic classes while the BE traffic class will have the lowest weight value. Finally when the rain event has ended and the bandwidth availability is enough to guarantee the high priority traffic (EF and AF), the assigned bandwidth for the BE traffic class will be reestablished and the weight values will be assigned according to the rate of the high priority classes.

To adaptively distribute the available capacity among each traffic class, two thresholds are defined: the LowerCap$_{THR}$ and the UpperCap$_{THR}$. The LowerCap$_{THR}$ is set to the EF limiting rate (μ_{EF}) specifying when the system capacity (C_{OUT}) is scarce but is still enough to guarantee the EF traffic class. The upper threshold UpperCap$_{THR}$ is set to the sum of the EF and AF limiting rates ($\mu_{EF}+\mu_{AF}$) specifying when the system capacity is enough to guarantee the rate of both priority classes. If the bandwidth capacity is kept beyond the UpperCap$_{THR}$, it is considered that the available bandwidth in the system is broad enough to transport all the traffic classes.

In order to specify such functionality on an adaptive WRR scheduler, Fig. 3 shows the weight values at each interval as a function of the DVB-S2 system capacity (C_{OUT}).

Here, the sum of the weights is set to K, where K is considered as a constant value that must be significantly high to avoid weight rounding errors:

$$W_{EF} + W_{AF} + W_{BE} = K \qquad (1)$$

Given that the BE traffic class has the lowest priority level, our adaptive model allocates the excess of resources in this class. Therefore, in all cases W_{BE} is set to W^R representing a residual and constant weight value.

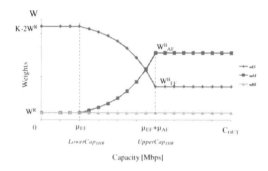

Fig. 3. The weight values as a function of the DVB-S2 system capacity (C_{OUT})

$$W_{BE} = W^R \tag{2}$$

As it is shown in Fig. 3 when the system capacity is broad enough, $C_{OUT} >$ UpperCap$_{THR}$, our adaptive model assigns constant weight values to guarantee high priority classes (EF and AF). We assume that the weight values of each traffic class are set to W^B_{EF} and W^B_{AF} for the high priority classes and W^R for the BE class. Following this assumption the next relationship is obtained:

$$W^B_{AF} + W^B_{EF} = K - W^R \tag{3}$$

To proportionally distribute the system resources [9], the ratio of W^B_{EF} over W^B_{AF} is set equal to the ratio of the associated TB limiting rates, thus:

$$\frac{W^B_{EF}}{W^B_{AF}} = \frac{\mu_{EF}}{\mu_{AF}} \tag{4}$$

As a result, the W^B_{EF} and W^B_{AF} values can be expressed as a function of the TB limiting rates (μ_{EF} and μ_{AF}) as:

$$W^B_{AF} = \frac{K - W^R}{(\mu_{EF} + \mu_{AF})} \mu_{AF} \tag{5}$$

$$W^B_{EF} = \frac{K - W^R}{(\mu_{EF} + \mu_{AF})} \mu_{EF} \tag{6}$$

In a similar way, when the system capacity is scarce, $C_{OUT} <$ LowerCap$_{THR}$, our adaptive model assigns constant weight values to guarantee the EF priority class over the AF and BE traffic classes. Therefore, W_{EF}, W_{AF} and W_{BE} are set as:

$$W_{AF} = W_{BE} = W^R \tag{7}$$

$$W_{EF} = K - 2W^R \tag{8}$$

Finally, to guarantee the EF traffic class over the AF traffic class, when the system capacity is constrained, $LowerCap_{THR} < C_{OUT} < UpperCap_{THR}$, our adaptive model allocates most of the resources to the EF traffic class. At this interval, we can apply either a linear or an exponential relationship between the weights of the higher priority classes (W_{EF} and W_{AF}) and the satellite link capacity (C_{OUT}).

We have performed a practical analysis between the high priority weights and the available bandwidth at the constrained interval. Such analysis has enabled us to conclude that the weight variations must change in a progressive way following an exponential function. However, we have also analyzed the case when a linear weight function is used, resulting in a faster variation where it is not possible to guarantee the EF priority traffic class when the available capacity is close to the $UpperCap_{THR}$. Therefore, in order to build a continuous weight function for each traffic class, we define W_{AF} as follows:

$$W_{AF} = W^R \left[\frac{W^B_{AF}}{W^R} \right]^{\frac{C_{out} - \mu_{EF}}{\mu_{AF}}} \qquad (9)$$

Similarly, the W_{EF} is obtained as follows:

$$W_{EF} = K - W^R - W_{AF} \qquad (10)$$

3   Performance Evaluation

In this section the satellite network settings and performance metrics are presented. Then, the proposed adaptive WRR model is simulated over a DVB-S2 satellite network and compared with the Round Robin (RR) and the ordinary WRR scheduler.

3.1   Satellite Network Settings

The simulation is carried out employing the NS-2 simulator tool version 2.29. For QoS purposes the DiffServ module was developed using the library described in [10] where our adaptive WRR model has been added. The network topology used for the simulation is shown in Fig. 4. Here, three sources send data to a remote destination. Each source node supports different services, having a predefined PHB. The EF class is represented by a real-time Voice over IP (VoIP) application employing the User Data Protocol (UDP). The AF class represents Hypertext Transfer Protocol (HTTP) traffic. The BE class represents bulk data transfer generated by a persistent File Transfer Protocol (FTP) transaction server. The transport protocol used to transport the AF and BE traffic classes is the Sack [11] variant of the Transmission Control Protocol (TCP). We used the TCP Linux version [12], which includes this TCP variant. The details of each service class are presented on Table I.

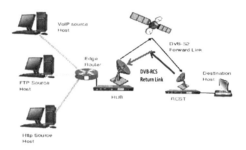

Fig. 4. DiffServ-satellite network topology

All the traffic entering the edge router is directly sent to the adaptive Hub that supports the DiffServ architecture to guarantee the predefined QoS level for each traffic type. The Hub, which is the main element in the satellite system, is responsible for applying the adaptive WRR model and sending the data to the destination host via the DVB-S2 forward channel. The return channel is used to transport signaling data, based on the DVB-RCS specification [13]. The DVB-S2 satellite network settings used throughout the simulation are configured as follows:

The satellite channel capacity considered as the bottleneck link is set considering the terminals in clear sky conditions will have 3.4 Mbps of bandwidth while terminals under a rain event will have a reduced capacity set to 0.4 Mbps. Therefore, the sinusoidal link variation will fluctuate between 0.4 to 3.4 Mbps. The minimum Round Trip Time (RTT_{MIN}) experienced by the satellite system is set to 560 msec. The buffer length of each traffic class is set to the BDP value. Particularly, the buffer length of the BE traffic class is set to 90 packets. The Packet Error Rate (PER) is set to 1×10^{-7}.

The transfer speed for each traffic class considered for the simulation is: 400 Kbps for the EF traffic class and 800 Kbps for the AF traffic class, while the BE traffic class will use the remaining bandwidth. The $LowerCap_{THR}$ and the $UpperCap_{THR}$ values are set to 0.4 Mbps and 1.2 Mbps respectively.

Table 1. Parameters of each service class

Traffic Class	Max Flows	Rate per-class [Kbps]	Packet Size [bytes]	C_{OUT} [Mbps]
EF	10	400	1500	0.4-3.4
AF	10	800	1500	0.4-3.4
BE	10	3400	1500	0.4-3.4

3.2 Performance Metrics

The proposed analysis is carried out at the bottleneck-satellite link, therefore, the relevant TCP information such as: the transmitted/acknowledged packets, the congestion window and the RTT are collected at the sender's side. Additionally, in order to asses the system performance with the proposed adaptive WRR scheduler, two metrics are considered: the goodput and the buffer occupancy.

The goodput is defined as the average amount of correctly received data (excluding retransmissions) measured over a certain period of time. The goodput per-class is calculated by dividing the amount of transmitted data by the number of active data flows (10 flows) within a service class in a given interval.

The buffer occupancy represents the fullness of the DiffServ queue during the simulation time. In our case, the simulation results consider the buffer occupancy for the IP queues allocated at the Hub.

3.3 Simulation Results

In order to evaluate the performance of the proposed adaptive scheduler, three simulation tests are considered: the first test is performed to assess the DVB-S2 system response when the Round Robin (RR) mechanism is employed. The second test considers the Weighted Round Robin mechanism with static weight values set to 6, 8 and 1 ($K = 15$) for W_{EF}, W_{AF} and W_{BE} respectively. These values are set considering the proportional distribution of resources, where the EF traffic class has higher weight value than its corresponding proportional value. Finally, a third simulation test is performed considering our proposed adaptive WRR scheduler to adjust the weight values taking into account the capacity variations. Here, we have calculated the weight values at the constrained interval considering both functions: the linear weight function and the exponential weight function. The results of plotting the dynamics of weights as a function of the sinusoidal link variation are shown in Fig. 5.

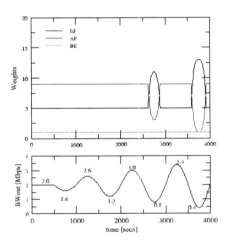

Fig. 5. Dynamics of Weights

In this case, the link bandwidth variation (C_{OUT}) oscillates between 0.4 and 3.4 Mbps. These results consider the exponential adaptive WRR algorithm (using the analysis presented in section 2.3) and the bandwidth rate previously set for each traffic class. The K value is set to 15 and W^R is set to 1.

Fig. 6a illustrates the simulation results of goodput and queue occupancy considering the RR algorithm. Using this algorithm it is observable that the EF and AF traffic classes are not guaranteed when a reduction of bandwidth (due to a rain event) is experienced. Moreover, the queue occupancy is overloaded in most of the cases leading to an increase of the system latency.

In a similar way, by using the WRR mechanism (see Fig. 6b) with static weight values, the EF traffic class is able to reach its 400 Kbps. However, its goodput is affected in specific time points when the capacity is reduced (see the valleys of the sine wave).

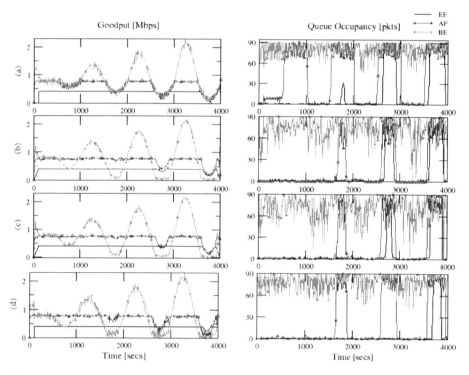

Fig. 6. Goodput performance results and queue occupancy with different scheduler types: (a) Round Robin mechanism, (b) Weighted Round Robin, (c) Linear Adaptive WRR and (d) Exponential Adaptive WRR

Likewise, the AF traffic class tries to keep its 800 Kbps of goodput, while the BE traffic class uses the remaining bandwidth. The buffer occupancy (considering the three traffic classes) is overloaded, allowing an increase of the system latency which is reduced compared to the latency experienced in the RR scenario. It is also observable that when an extreme reduction of bandwidth is experienced (see the interval between 3500-4000 sec) the priority levels of each traffic class are lost, being unable to guarantee the EF traffic class over the AF and BE traffic classes.

Similarly, by using the linear adaptive WRR mechanism (Fig. 6c), it is observable that the EF buffer occupancy is reduced compared to the previous case. However, given that a linear function generates a faster weight variation, it is not possible to guarantee the EF priority traffic class when the available capacity is reduced (see the interval between 3500-4000 sec).

Finally, considering our proposed exponential adaptive WRR mechanism (Fig. 6d) it is observable that the buffer occupancy for the EF traffic class is kept at lower levels and that the rate for the EF traffic class is totally guaranteed (400 Kbps) even though an extreme reduction of bandwidth is experienced. In addition, the transmission rate for the AF traffic class reaches its 800 Kbps of goodput and the BE traffic class uses the remaining bandwidth, being able to follow the sine wave when an increase of bandwidth is experienced by the system. It is also observable that when an extreme reduction of bandwidth is experienced (see the interval between 3500-4000 sec) the priority levels of each traffic class are kept, guaranteeing the EF traffic class over the AF and BE traffic classes.

4 Related Works

In order to calculate the optimal weight values based on the QoS requirements, different criteria have been researched in the literature e.g. the mean packet size, queue sizes, revenue-based etc.

In [6], a Variable WRR (VWRR) scheduler is proposed. This model uses the average packet length to adapt its weights. A weight value is calculated considering two parameters: the bandwidth requirements and the average length of packets. The problem of adjusting weights for the WRR scheduler guaranteeing the premium service has been analyzed in [7]. This work proposes a resource allocation model considering the average queue size, which is calculated using a low-pass filter. In [8], an adaptive scheduling scheme using the revenue-based WRR is presented. This proposal has been considered for guaranteeing the maximum service provider revenue. The proposed scheme, adjusts its weights using the revenue criteria to control the resource allocation. In [14], a modified Fair WRR (FWRR) scheduler has been proposed to protect the best effort traffic from the assured forwarding out-of- profile packets in the core routers based on the DiffServ architecture. This policy dynamically adjusts the weights and the buffer allocation using congestion hints to avoid unfair bandwidth sharing.

5 Conclusions

We have presented an adaptive resource management algorithm based on a WRR scheduler. This proposed algorithm uses the link bandwidth variations present in the DVB-S2 forward link to determine the minimum amount of resources for each traffic class considering the DiffServ architecture. To calculate the optimal weight values, we have applied two functions to associate the weights of the higher priority classes and the satellite link capacity: a linear and an exponential weight function. By employing the NS-2 simulator tool we have demonstrated that using our adaptive WRR algorithm it is possible to ensure the QoS requirements for each traffic class and to optimize the bandwidth utilization when bandwidth fluctuations caused by rain events are faced. The simulation results have shown that our exponential adaptive WRR model enforces the priority levels and guarantees the QoS parameters established in the SLA, while maintaining the queue occupancy at lower levels (compared to the RR and WRR mechanism), leading to a reduction of the system latency.

References

1. ETSI ES 302 307, ETSI Standard for Digital Video Broadcasting (DVB); Second generation framing structure, channel coding and modulation systems for Broadcasting, Interactive Services, News Gathering and other broadband satellite applications (DVB-S2) (2004)
2. ETSI TS 102 462, ETSI Standard for Satellite Earth Stations and Systems (SES); Broadband Satellite Multimedia (BSM); QoS Functional Architecture (2006)
3. IETF RFC 2475, Standard for an Architecture for Differentiated Services (December 1998)
4. Cioni, S., Gaudency, R., Rinaldo, R.: Channel estimation a physical layer adaptation techniques for satellite networks exploiting adaptive coding and modulation. International Journal of Satellite Communication and Networking 26(2), 157–188 (2008)
5. Shimonishi, H., Suzuki, H.: Performance Analysis of Weighted Round Robin Cell Scheduling and Its Improvement in Atm Networks. IEICE Transactions on Communications E81B(5), 910–918 (1998)
6. Ito, Y., Tasaka, S., Ishibashi, Y.: Variably weighted round robin for core IP networks. In: Performance, Computing and Communication Conference, pp. 159–166 (2002)
7. Wang, H., Shen, C., S.K.G.: Adaptive-weighted packet scheduling for premium service. In: IEEE International Conference on Communications, vol. 6, pp. 1846–1850 (2001)
8. Sayenko, A., Hamalainen, T., Raatikainen, P.: Adaptive scheduling using the revenue-based weighted round robin. In: IEEE International Conference on Networks, pp. 743–749 (2004)
9. Dovrolis, C., Ramanathan, P.: A case for relative Differentiated Services and Proportional Differentiation Model. IEEE Network Magazine, 26–34 (1999)
10. Pieda, P., Ethridge, J., Bainess, M., Shallwani, F.: A Network Simulator Differentiated Services Implementation. Open IP Nortel Networks (2000)
11. IETF RFC 3517. IETF Standard for a Conservative Selective Acknowledgment (SACK)-based. Loss Recovery Algorithm for TCP (2003)
12. Wei, D., Cao, P.: A Linux TCP implementation for NS2, available at the Internet (2006)
13. ETSI EN 301 790, ETSI Standard for Digital Video Broadcasting (DVB); Interaction Channel for Satellite Distribution Systems; (DVB-RCS) (2005)
14. Yi, S., Deng, X., Kesidis, G., Das, C.R.: Providing fairness in DiffServ architecture. IEEE Global Telecommunications Conference 2, 1435–1439 (2002)

Presence-Based Architecture for Wireless Sensor Networks Using Publish/Subscribe Paradigm

Ernesto García Davis[1] and Anna Calveras Augé[1,2]

[1] Department of Telematic Engineering, Universitat Politècnica de Catalunya
C/Jordi Girona 1-3, Mòdul C3, 08034 Barcelona, Spain
{ernesto.garcia,anna.calveras}@entel.upc.edu
[2] i2CAT Foundation, Barcelona, Spain

Abstract. Ubiquitous communication is a key component of Ambient Intelligence, enabling objects to communicate with each-other by means of a wireless ad-hoc network. A presence service allows knowing the availability or responsiveness status of elements in a communication (entities). Traditionally, only human use this service, however all smart devices or objects (with embedded wireless sensor nodes) could interact with each other thus a presence service could also enhance communication among them. To achieve this objective we look into existing protocols to propose the requirements needed to provide presence service on Wireless Sensor Networks (WSN). The main contribution of this paper is the discussion of requirements for presence services on WSN and the new proposed architecture to cope with presence services in WSN.

Keywords: Distributed Architecture, Wireless Sensor Networks, Presence Service, Embedded Devices.

1 Introduction

Wireless Sensor Networks (WSN) consist of small distributed sensor nodes capable of communicate in a wireless network. WSN are providing tremendous benefits for a number of industries. In recent years, uses of WSN are moving from the mere monitoring of certain environmental variables towards its adoption for context aware systems. In this sense, WSN are able to capture a rich set of contextual information (e.g. spatial, physiological and environmental data) and to respond regarding to a situation without user interaction. In addition, context information could also contain another type of information called presence information. This information is related to user and communication conditions, capacity and preferences. Traditionally, presence information has been used by personal applications such as Instant Messaging (IM) in which human user can know the willingness or responsiveness of other human users to engage a communication. In a similar manner, presence information can also be used by other type of users such smart objects or devices in order to discover the status, conditions and capacity with the purpose of interacting with each other. In this paper, a "smart object or device" refers to anything that has specific functionality and that is able to compute and communicate on its own. For instance, an energy meter can be programmed in a specific way. When consumption reaches a threshold it

X. Masip-Bruin et al. (Eds.): WWIC 2011, LNCS 6649, pp. 27–38, 2011.

should send a command to turn off all devices with less priority, so we can save energy. Without presence information (such as on/off/standby/consumption level, user preferences, etc) the energy meter would try to send this command to all devices complying this condition. However, the energy meter would not know which of them are turned off. Therefore, unnecessary packets will be transmitted into the network resulting in waste of resources (energy, processing and bandwidth) at each node along the path to reach the destination device.

Some use cases to apply presence services on WSN are related to smart grid or Internet of Things. Firstly, Home Area Network (HAN) devices are capable of receiving messages from the Utility (service provider) and adjusting its operational mode based on Consumer preferences (e.g., energy saving mode, delayed turn on/off, etc). In these scenarios, a presence service could enhance decisions interacting between HAN devices and Utility equipment. Each HAN device will publish its presence information to the Utility equipment. The Utility will check the state of HAN devices presence before transmitting a command. In this manner, only HAN devices with availability status will receive a command, thus the Utility only will transmit necessary messages to the network. Secondly, the Internet of Things will be an open network in which auto-organized or intelligent entities will be interoperable and able to act independently pursuing their own objectives or shared ones, depending on the context, circumstances or environments. In the cases aforementioned, each object or device could incorporate an embedded sensor able to capture, to process and to communicate presence information through wireless media to enhance system performance.

Our motivation for this research is based on the fact that an efficient communication among users is possible if we know its presence information. Nevertheless, the presence service as we know it in Internet cannot be directly applied to the devices based on WSN. That is because these types of networks have constrained resources on processing, energy and bandwidth. The requirements in its architecture must be defined in an efficient manner.

Presence services, in general, are based on Publish/Subscribe communication model [1] [2]. Also, this model has been integrated in several protocols specifically designed for WSN (e.g., service discovery protocols and middleware technologies). However, as far as we know there is not a protocol or mechanism which considers the whole requirements to provide presence services in WSNs.

In this paper, we present the requirements to provide a presence service on WSN and then we propose a presence-based architecture using the Publish/Subscribe communication model. The remainder of this paper is organized as follows. In section 2, we provide background information about Presence Service. Followed, section 3 presents related work for Publish/Subscribe Protocols on WSN. In Section 4 we discuss the requirements to provide presence service on WSN and a new presence-based architecture for WSN. Finally, conclusions and future work are discussed in section 5.

2 Presence Service

Presence information is a subset of context information. It expresses the determining factors around communication between users or devices (such as their availability, willingness, environment, preferences, etc). The presence service architecture [3] fits into publish/subscribe communication model. This architecture works as follows (Fig. 1): the presence entities, called presentities (devices or objects), provide their presence information to the presence service. The presence service accepts, stores, and distributes the presence information to everyone subscribed to get the notification about presence changes. The entities (devices or objects) receiving notification about presence information are called watchers.

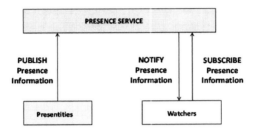

Fig. 1. General Presence Service Architecture

The presence information will improve the whole communication because watchers only will transmit messages to presentities taking into account their presence information. Therefore, we achieve an efficient communication on WSNs taking into account the constrained resources on this type of networks. Presentities and watchers communicate by exchanging presence events. Presentities are publishers in Publish/Subscribe Communication Model and watchers are subscribers that are interested in a presence event.

In the next section, we briefly present publish/subscribe protocols already known in the area of sensor networks. We focus on the issues they are addressing in their design.

3 Related Work of Publish/Subscribe on WSN

Several authors [11] [12] have proposed protocols making use of publish/subscribe communication model. In this section, we summarize these protocols focusing on relevant aspects for presence services on WSN.

3.1 Message Queuing Telemetry Transport for Sensor Networks

Message Queuing Telemetry Transport for Sensor Networks (MQTT-S) is an extension of Message Queuing Telemetry Transport (MQTT) [13] originally developed for telemetry applications using constrained devices. It is based on a centralized architecture where a broker node is placed in the backbone network to provide publish/subscribe service to the nodes in this part of the network and in the WSN. MQTT-S allows subscribing to one topic and receiving information of several nodes by using the "wildcard" concept. Therefore we can reduce the number of transmitted messages to only one SUBSCRIBE message instead of sending one for each device. That results in energy saving for the subscriber nodes which is very relevant in large WSN. MQTT-S defines three QoS levels. Level 0 offers a best effort delivery service and no retransmission or acknowledgment is defined. Level 1 allows the retransmission of messages until they are acknowledged by the receivers. However, certain messages may arrive multiple times at the destination because of the retransmissions (duplicated). Finally, level 2 ensures not only the reception of the messages, but also that they are delivered only once to the destination. In addition, this protocol considers the message size to be no longer than 64 bytes of the payload of an 802.15.4 packet (127 bytes). That is because the remaining 64 bytes should be used by the overhead information required to support functions such as MAC layer, networking, security, etc.

3.2 Tiny Session Initiation Protocol

Tiny Session Initiation Protocol (TinySIP) is based on Session Initiation Protocol (SIP) protocol. It incorporates a messaging mechanism for accessing sensor-based services. It provides a communication abstraction which allows session signaling, publish/subscribe services and instant messaging features. Basically, this protocol is based on centralized architecture. A SIP-TinySIP Gateway(s) situated on the edge of WSN. All communication between clients on outsider networks and WSN nodes is through the SIP-TinySIP Gateway(s). In addition, TinySIP uses a more compact message size than MQTT-S. A TinySIP message can be transmitted within a small payload, such as the 29-byte of a regular TinyOS payload message.

4 Proposed Architecture

In this section, we firstly present the requirements for presence service. Next, we propose a new architecture based on publish/subscribe to cope with presence service on WSN.

4.1 Requirements for Presence Service on WSN

In general, presence services on Internet have certain limitations to be used on WSN. The most relevant are:

— Limited vocabulary to express presence information: In the case of human users, the presence information was contained in PIDF [4] format. It includes a simple status of presence information (e.g.: offline, busy, away), and this is not enough to convey a user's real situation and to decide how to establish a communication with an entity. Some authors have identified this insufficiency of basic information and responded with several extensions of presence information [5] [6] [7] that are RPID, CPID and GEOPRIV respectively. However, to enable the integration with objects or devices, we need to define others extensions. Therefore, we can accommodate additional type of information provided by sensor nodes embedded on devices or objects. A first approach to extend the vocabulary is presented in [8] where authors propose the addition of two new attributes to the GEOPRIV. Nowadays, there is not yet consensus in the used data model to describe the presence information of objects or devices.

— The presence status is generally updated manually by the user: There is not a way to deduce automatically presence status of a user. Some presence technologies can change presence information status to "away" assuming that there is not activity from the user in the device during some period of time. In the case of objects or devices acting as presentities, it should be necessary that they change their status without user interaction. That can be made by means of context information acquired by sensor nodes.

Moreover, there are other requirements we have to consider based on the specific characteristics of WSN such as:

— Reduced size of MTU: the size of presence information messages used by traditional presence services is incompatible to fit into the data packets used in embedded devices with constrained resources, such as sensor nodes. It is needed an encoding/compressing mechanism to convey presence information on WSN.
— Limited resources in terms of energy, computing and storage: The availability of these resources depends on the number of transmissions and the length of transmitted packets. Authors in [11] [12] do not provide a mechanism to manage resources in an efficient manner. In this case, we could apply data aggregation techniques [9] that allow, for example, concatenating individual data items into larger packets thus reducing network traffic load and saving energy.
— Wireless communication: WSN are susceptible to loss packets due to transmission errors. If presence information cannot be delivered to watcher nodes, the communication among entities could be affected. Therefore, it is necessary to implement a reliable data delivery. In this case we could consider using Transmission Control Protocol (TCP). However, the header overhead, connection management, end-to-end flow and congestion control lead to TCP poor performance on wireless environment and resource constrained nodes, such as WSN [10]. This issue is still opened and some authors [11] suggest assign this functionality to the application layer.

4.2 General Description of the Proposed Architecture

Taking into account the relevant features of current publish/subscribe protocols and the requirements above mentioned, we propose a new approach for a presence-based architecture. There are three entities that interact in our architecture. The first is a publisher entity that is used to produce presence information and publish it when it is requested. Second, there is a subscriber which is the entity that makes a subscription in order to receive presence information for its interest. Finally, there is a broker entity responsible for distributing the published information from publishers to subscribers. Our architecture, contrary to centralized architecture such [11], is based on distributed architecture.

In centralized architecture there is only one broker node located between WSN and the external network. So, the broker node makes the sink node functionality. Therefore, when many nodes are forwarding messages to the sink node at high rates, it could become a bottleneck leading to low network performance. In addition, this architecture is unsuitable for providing a presence service on WSN because these protocols consider the communication will only occur between sensor nodes and external users or vice versa. Thus, all the information is sent to the broker node (sink) located between WSN and external network. However, a presence service on WSN and new trends such as "Internet of Things" consider that objects can interact among them. Thus, publish/subscribe protocols should consider publisher nodes not always will send information to the sink node as the only destination. We propose a distributed architecture, where there are other broker nodes inside WSN aside from the broker node acting as sink node. We can see this distributed architecture in Fig. 2 where there are, as example, two broker nodes inside WSN, and another broker node at the edge of the network. This one is also acting as gateway to communicate with the external network. Thus, it allows distributing the load in the network by grouping publisher and subscriber nodes in different broker nodes.

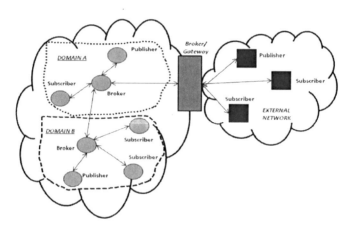

Fig. 2. Proposed Presence Service Architecture for WSN

We call *broker domain* to the group of subscribers and publishers nodes managed by a broker node. The broker nodes will be the only responsible to exchange message between broker domains, as we can see in Fig. 3. When a potential publisher or subscriber node enters into the network, it sends a broadcast message to discovery a broker node in its domain. Once the publisher or subscriber node receives a reply, it will establish a connection with the broker node.

Also, a broker node might play a publisher or subscriber role on behalf of its domain. Fig. 3 shows this situation. "Subscriber 1" and "Publisher 1" are placed in different broker domains. "Subscriber 1" on broker domain A wants to receive presence information from "Publisher 1" on broker domain B. So, "Subscriber 1" makes a subscription (1) in its respective broker node ("Broker A"). This one makes a subscription (2) in the broker node responsible for broker domain B ("Broker B"). When "Publisher 1" sends presence information (3) to its broker node, this one will forward it (4) to broker node of Broker Domain A, and this one; will transmit it (5) to the "Subscriber 1". In this way, nodes located in different Broker's domains will exchange messages through corresponding broker nodes. It should be noticed that a broker node learns the identities of brokers in other domains. That is because it receives a broadcast message of available topics to subscribe in each broker. Then, it will store this information to be available when a potential subscriber node wants to subscribe to a topic. On the other hand, publisher and subscriber nodes located in the same broker domain, will exchange messages through the broker node responsible for this domain. Thus, exchanged traffic is kept inside the broker domain. This situation is also depicted on Fig. 3, where "Subscriber 2" makes a subscription (6) through "Broker B" to receive presence information from "publisher 2" on the same broker domain B. When "Publisher 2" publishes presence information (7) to its broker node, "Broker B" will forward it (8) to "Subscriber 2". In conclusion, the proposed architecture contributes to isolate the exchanged traffic in broker domains, and will exchange traffic between broker domains through corresponding broker nodes only when it is needed.

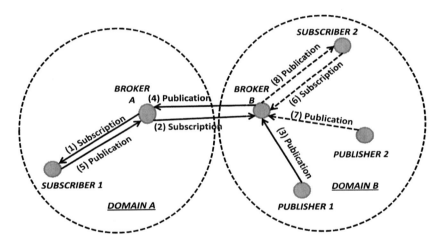

Fig. 3. Broker roles and broker domain

The proposed architecture not only improves scalability but also provides mechanisms for an efficient energy management. Moreover, it reduces the subscriber nodes spent time to receive the first publication. These mechanisms are explained in following sections.

4.2.1 Publication on Demand of Presence Information

Generally, publish/subscribe protocols allow a publisher to publish data regardless of the presence of a subscriber. This would result in extra power consumption at publisher node. Moreover, unnecessary network traffic increases the risk of network congestion. To overcome this situation, in our architecture, publisher nodes only send publications when there is a subscriber. So, the broker sends a notification message to the publisher the first time it receives a subscription. That is shown in Fig. 4.

Also, similar notification message is sent to publisher when the last subscriber decides unsubscribe to presence information event (un-subscription). In this case, the publisher node stops events of presence information publication. This mechanism is referred as publication on demand of presence information. It should be noted that previously publishers communicate to the broker the events they are able to publish. This way, a broker knows about the publishers to send them the notification of subscription.

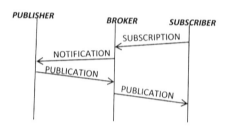

Fig. 4. Publication on demand

4.2.2 Data Aggregation

As we mentioned previously, data aggregation is a well known and essential technique to achieve energy efficiency when propagating data from WSN nodes. In our architecture, we make use of wildcards in similar way as MQTT-S [11] does it. This allows that we can transmit only one SUBSCRIBE message to subscribe us to a topic related to several publishers. In addition, we propose two ways to perform data aggregation with the purpose to decrease the number of messages into the network. Data aggregation will be performed either in the publisher or in the broker node.

— *Data aggregation in publisher node*: we propose the publisher nodes can aggregate packets in a "lossless way". That means that publisher will not transmit publications to the broker node until a timer expires. They will aggregate in a single message all publication events produced during the timer period. Then, they will create only one packet to transmit to the broker node. This technique results in reducing the number of transmissions and thus energy saving of network nodes. However, there is a trade-off between the number of transmissions and the delivery delay. The more the number of gathered data; the less is the number of transmissions. Nevertheless, waiting for more data increases the delivery delay. This issue is addressed by the new proposed architecture. Therefore, we recommend this technique only be applied in situations where network congestion is detected or an application parameter has been defined. We can see the algorithm in Fig. 5 where a publisher node detects a congestion indication (i.e. received from the broker or from MAC layer) or there is an application parameter defined. Then, the publisher node will activate a timer, we call "aggregation timer". During this period, publication events produced locally will be buffered and marked for "lossless" aggregation.
The number of packets to be buffered will depend on memory resources. Also, the number of data that one packet can carry will depend on the packet size

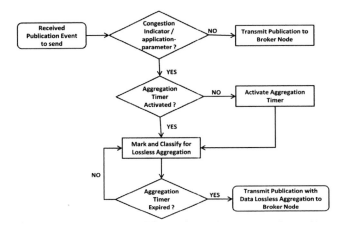

Fig. 5. Lossless Aggregation Algorithm

limit. For example, 127 bytes is the maximum size of PHY service data unit defined in IEEE 802.15.4 standard. When the "aggregation timer" expires, the publisher node performs the lossless aggregation, and transmits the packet to the broker node. In case of congestion network, this mechanism prevents the publisher nodes continue transmitting packets. Thus, it avoids the increment of network congestion. Furthermore, it contributes to save energy. That is because of, during congestion, the transmission of packet would result in packet loss, thus extra packet retransmission.

— *Data aggregation in broker node*: The broker node aggregates publication of concerning publishers (i.e. by configurable function: average, min, max, status, etc). Then, it transmits only one packet to the subscriber nodes.

4.2.3 Advertisement of Presence Information to Subscribers

Another important issue in presence services over WSN is that subscriber nodes receive presence information as soon as this has been published. The proposed architecture allows publisher nodes to include presence information (initial value) when they register the topics at the broker node as is showed in Fig. 6(a). This presence information will be stored in the broker node and will be available immediately in the subscriber.

Let suppose node 1 is the first subscriber for the registered topic A. Now, let consider T_w as the waiting time experimented by subscriber node 1 to receive the first publication. T_{pb} is the time used by the broker node to process the subscription of topic A and transmit the publication message to subscriber node 1. Then,

$$T_w = T_{pb} \tag{1}$$

Otherwise, if publisher node does not register topic with initial value as it is showed in Fig. 6(b), T_w would be calculated by,

$$T_w = T_{np} + T_{ep} + T_{pp} + T_{pb} \tag{2}$$

Where T_{np} is the time used by the broker node to send a notification message indication to publisher to initiate the publication for topic A; T_{ep} is the time until the next event for topic A is produced; and T_{pp} is the time used by publisher node to generate publication message and transmit it to the broker node.

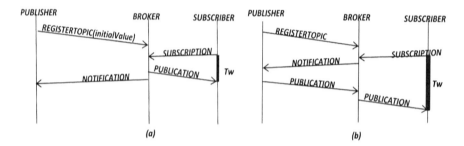

Fig. 6. Spent Time in the first publication

4.3 Evaluation

A first glance to the mechanisms provided by the proposed architecture can indicate several valuable advantages. It reduces the traffic in the whole network by isolating it inside broker domains. That is an important issue in large WSN. Moreover, it addresses the energy efficiency applying data aggregation techniques. Also, the architecture contributes to reduce the spent time of subscriber nodes to receive publications. Simulations were carried out to make a preliminary evaluation of the proposed architecture. We use OMNet++ [14] simulation environment to perform several experiments. The network topology consisted of one broker node, one subscriber node and up to 32 publisher nodes depending on test scenarios. Each node is provided by an 802.15.4 network interface working in 2.4 GHz frequency. We have analysed two main aspects. Firstly, we measured the spent time of subscriber nodes to receive publications. In this case, Fig. 7 shows that the mechanism described in section 4.2.3, where publisher node is able to include initial value when it registers a topic reduces the waiting time around 38% comparing if we don't use this. Secondly, we evaluated the relation between the impact of the amount of publication messages without subscription in the network traffic when we increase the number of publisher nodes and the energy consumption when we increase the publication rate.

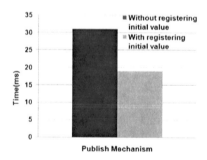

Fig. 7. Spent Time until reception of the first publication by subscriber node

From Fig. 8 we can note a proportional direct relation between the number of publish messages transmitted without subscription and the number of publisher nodes.

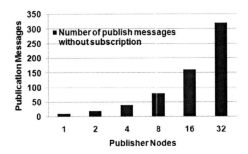

Fig. 8. Publish messages transmitted without subscription

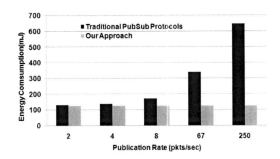

Fig. 9. Energy Consumption of Publications on Demand

In the simulations, each publisher node has a publish rate equal to 10 messages per second with a regular inter-packet interval. As we mentioned previously, this way to work has a high impact on energy resource of nodes and also generates unnecessary traffic on the network. Therefore, the advertisement of presence information to subscribers has a great benefit. Fig. 9 shows that our approach described in section 4.2.1 results in an energy saving between 3.6% for the lower publication rate and 80% for the higher one. There is an important benefit of using publication on demand mechanism.

5   Conclusions

In this paper, we analyse the implementation of presence service in WSN. We discuss its requirements and present a new architecture to provide presence services in WSN. The mechanisms provided by our architecture bring significant advantages with respect to other publish/subscribe protocols in WSN. The publication on demand mechanism prevents to transmit publication messages without related subscriber nodes. In addition, this architecture provides a mechanism to avoid that subscriber node waits for the next presence information produced by publisher node. It reduces waiting time of subscriber nodes. Preliminary results presented in this paper show that the proposed architecture is suitable for WSN. The implemented "lossless" data aggregation algorithm would result in energy saving for publisher nodes. Moreover, it would reduce the traffic load in situations of network congestion. At the present time, more results are being obtained by simulation to quantify how much energy can be saved if we apply "lossless" data aggregation. Also we intend to concentrate our efforts in building and testing a hardware/software prototype.

Acknowledgments. This research has been funded by The Professional Excellence Program IFARHU-SENACYT-Panama and Spanish Government CICYT-TEC2009-11453.

References

1. Eugster, P.T.: The many faces of publish/subscribe. ACM Computing Surveys (June 2003)
2. Tran, D.A., et al.: Publish/Subscribe Techniques for Sensor Networks (May 2009)
3. Day, M., et al.: Presence and Instant Messaging Model (RFC 2778) (February 2000)
4. Sugano, H., et al.: Presence Information Data Format. PIDF (RFC 3863) (August 2004)
5. Schulzrinne, H., et al.: Rich Presence Extensions to the PIDF (RFC 4480) (July 2006)
6. Schulzrinne, H., et al.: Contact Information for the PIDF (RFC 4482) (July 2006)
7. Peterson, J.: GEOPRIV Location Object Format (RFC 4119) (December 2005)
8. El Barachi, M., et al.: A Presence-Based Architecture for the Integration of the Sensing Capabilities of WSN in IM Subsystem. In: IEEE WCNC 2008, pp. 1525–3511 (2008)
9. Abdelzaher, T., et al.: Feedback Control of Data Aggregation in Sensor. In: 43rd IEEE Conference on Decision and Control, pp. 191–2216 (2004)
10. Kuorilehto, M., et al.: Experimenting TCP/IP For Low-Power Wireless Sensor Networks. In: IEEE PIMRC 2006, pp. 1–6 (September 2006)
11. Hunkeler, U., et al.: MQTT-S. A publish/subscribe protocol for Wireless Sensor Networks. In: COMSWARE 2008, pp. 791–798 (2008)
12. Krishnamurthy, S.: TinySIP: Providing Seamless Access to Sensor-based Services. In: 3rd International Conference on Mobile and Ubiquitous Systems (July 2006)
13. MQTT, http://mqtt.org
14. OMNet++ Simulator, http://www.omnetpp.org

Dynamic Spectrum Trade and Game-Theory Based Network Selection in LTE Virtualization Using Uniform Auctioning

Manzoor Ahmed Khan[1] and Yasir Zaki[2]

[1] DAI-Labor/Technical University, Berlin, Germany
manzoor-ahmed.khan@dai-labor.de
[2] ComNets, University of Bremen, Germany

Abstract. It is expected that in future user-centric wireless network scenario the concept of dynamic spectrum trade will provide operators with opportunities to utilize the spectrum more efficiently. Wireless market players (both incumbent and new entrants) trade the spectrum chunks on the *provide, when needed* basis with the spectrum broker. In this paper, we model the interaction between different stake-holders such as users, operators and spectrum brokers at different hierarchical level and investigate the equilibria. We also model the utility functions of all the stake-holders. We propose and implement the realization framework for the proposed dynamic spectrum allocation approach using Long Term Evolution (LTE) virtualization.

Keywords: LTE, Wireless virtualization, Spectrum sharing, Uniform auctioning format.

1 Introduction

The evolution of wireless communication technologies places the scarce radio spectrum as the main pillar of future wireless communication, which in turn dictates that spectrum should be efficiently managed. The current practices for spectrum management in any country is regulated by the governmental body (e.g., FCC in USA or ECC in Europe) and the current trend of spectrum allocation is driven by the rigid frequency distribution through auctioning. Such spectrum allocation approaches are static and specific to the usage parameters (i.e., power, geographical scope etc.) and usage purposes (i.e., cellular communication, TV broadcasting, radio broadcasting etc.). Although spectrum auctions have been a success in this regard by putting essential spectrum in the hands of those who best value it. However, such spectrum management may not cope with the growing and dynamic needs of spectrum, particularly in environments, where the network selection decision is delegated to users (user-centric paradigm) and /or where market is shared by the small scaled new entrants such as Mobile Virtual Network Operators (MVNO) etc. We now make an attempt to define the spectrum inefficiency by discussing a prevalent bidding procedures. In the current fixed spectrum allocation scenario, the telecommunication operators bid for the amount of frequencies they are interested in, when declared winner, the bidding operators are

X. Masip-Bruin et al. (Eds.): WWIC 2011, LNCS 6649, pp. 39–55, 2011.
© IFIP International Federation for Information Processing 2011

allocated with some amount of frequencies for periods spanning over years. This dictates that the operators frequency demands are the results of their peak traffic planning i.e., busy hour, which represents the peak network usage time. It should be noted
that bandwidth demands are exposed to
variation not only with respect time, but
also depends on location (spatial variation). This, in a way addresses the issue
of satisfying the operators' demands and
reducing the call blocking at the operator
end, but at the same time it causes temporal under-utilization in less busy periods.
Hence the static spectrum allocation often leads to low spectrum utilization and
results in fragmentation of the spectrum
creating *white space* that can not be used
for either licensed or unlicensed. Thus
the potential candidate solution that one
could think of is the *Dynamic Spectrum
Allocation* (DSA) approach.

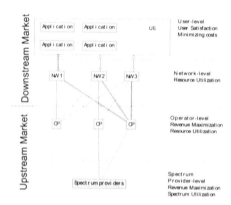

Fig. 1. Hierarchical position of telecommunication stake-holders and their objectives

DSA can significantly improve the spectrum utilization and provide a more flexible spectrum management method and promises much higher spectrum utilization efficiency. DSA concept brings a good news for the wireless service providers, as the
flexible spectrum acquisition gives a particular provider the chance to easily adapt its
system capacity to fit the end users demands. One could wish for situations, where
solutions are not accompanied by the issues. The DSA solution is also brings few challenges e.g., frequency interference problem and DSA implementation in user-centric
wireless communication paradigm etc. In this paper, we confine our discussion more on
dynamic spectrum allocation in user-centric paradigm, the interaction of stake-holders
in the mentioned paradigm, and the related issues. Obviously the DSA problems turns
out to be more complicated, when it comes to user-centric network selection scenarios,
where the operators' associated size of user pool is dynamic, in this case the operators
are faced with two obvious competitions. We term these competitions with respect to
their positions in the telecommunication hierarchical figure i.e., Fig 1. The competition
or the interaction that takes place vertically between spectrum provider and operators is
termed as *upstream competition* and the competition vertically between users and operators is termed as *downstream competition*. Our focus in this paper is to capture the
interaction among spectrum broker, wireless service providers and end users. Intuitively
all the stake-holders in this scenario aim at maximizing their own profits (the objectives
of each stake-holders are mentioned on the respective level in the Fig 1).

2   Related Work

The concept of DSA first came up in the DARPA XG program [1], the project aims to
develop, integrate, and evaluate the technology. The emphasis is on enabling the user
equipment that automatically selects spectrum and operating modes to both minimize

disruption of existing users, and to ensure operation of U.S. systems. In [2], the authors propose a spectrum broker model that controls and provides operators the time bound access to a spectrum band. The authors investigated spectrum allocation algorithms for spectrum allocation in homogeneous CDMA networks and executed spectrum measurements in order to study the realizable spectrum gain that can be achieved using DSA. Authors in [3] propose a scheme, where the spectrum manager periodically allocates short-term spectrum licenses. The spectrum rights are traded amongst the operators for a fixed amount of time, the license for the allocated spectrum automatically expires after the predefined time period. However, [4] assumes that the operators follow the multi-unit auction format for the spectrum trade, where the sealed bids are submitted for the spectrum resources and the winner operator pays the second highest price (the price of resource is assumed to be charged on per unit basis). Buddhikot and Ryans [5] in their seminal work discuss the DSA management, where the authors focus on spectrum allocation and pricing. The paper introduces the concept of coordinated DSA and the spectrum broker, the paper illustrates over various allocation algorithm types e.g., online vs. batched, in addition it also highlights the notion of interference conflict graph, and the cascading effects among brokers on blocked list. Linear programming formulation is used to solve the problem of the spectrum allocation with feasibility constraints i.e., maximal service vs. minimal interference, maximal broker revenue vs. max-min fairness. A deviation from the use of distributed approaches is observed in the centralized auction based approach [6], where authors assume pairwise interference conflict graph, piece-wise linear bidding functions, and homogeneous non-overlapping channels. The efficiency of spectrum utilization is also addressed in European Union projects such as Dynamic Radio for IP Services in Vehicular Environments (DRiVE) [7] and overDRiVE [8], that investigates co-existence, sharing rules with broadcast and military systems and scenarios for a dynamic regional/temporal spectrum allocation.

2.1   Motivation

The hierarchical business model presented in Fig 1 dictates interdependency of the stake-holders i.e., the stake-holders at the operators' level depend on the service demands pattern from underlying common user-pool for formulating their (operators') spectrum demand at different times and for different geographical locations. The service demands do not only influence the operators spectrum demands but also the operators valuation for the spectrum. On the similar lines, the offered service prices and service quality by the operator drive the user demands, which in turn has impact on the spectrum demands and consequently on the profit of spectrum broker and the operators. As can be seen in the Fig 1, the consequence of such interdependency is the integration of two markets (upstream and downstream). Thus investigating the efficiency (e.g., resource utilization at operator level, user satisfaction maximization at user-level etc.) at one of the hierarchical level and not considering their dependency at different levels may not lead to realistic efficient solution. Considering the future user-centric wireless network paradigm, the characteristics of attractive LTE like technologies, and the interaction among all the stake-holders, one can think of a more realistic spectrum distribution. We are also convinced that the interaction model is different for different geographical regions, hence there is a need for a generic model that captures the interaction for the regions and define all the markets on granule level. In the current literature, these aspects are widely oversimplified and many frameworks have been presented lacking to fulfill the basic requirements of general distribution systems, where limited resource is to be divided among the participants. Although the existing literature that discusses the possible spectrum allocation models and related issues is vast, our work focuses on modeling the interaction at different levels, we also take an opportunity here to justify the technical feasibility of dynamic spectrum allocation concept i.e., investigating the support of flexible transmission frequencies in new generation technologies e.g., LTE promises the flexible operational frequencies. Future wireless network communication is boosted by the concept of technology virtualization. When it comes to technical realization of the dynamic spectrum allocation concept, one of the attractive solutions is *virtualization*. The choice of *Virtualization* as a technical solution is driven by the widespread and yet growing presence of this concept in the research literature e.g., many research projects including PlanetLab and GENI [9] [10] in the United States, AKARI [11] in Asia and 4WARD [12] in Europe. The basic definition of virtualization comes from the environment, where the technical setup with under-utilized resources can share its unused resources with other entities and processes (which require resources), this argument forms the basis for the growing importance and existence of virtualization in the time to come. There is a number of research activities in virtualization as well as a number of commercial solutions using virtualization: e.g., Server Virtualization, Router Virtualization, XEN, Cloud Computing etc.

Wireless virtualization is yet another very important aspect specially for the future. The best candidate for applying virtualization in the wireless domain is mobile networks. In [13] it was shown that virtualization in mobile networks (represented by the LTE) has a number of advantages. Multiplexing gain as well as better overall resource utilization were the key gains achieved. In [14], a more practical framework was investigated for LTE virtualization and spectrum sharing among multiple virtual network operators. The framework focused on a contract based algorithm to share the spectrum between the operators.

3   Downstream Market

In this market, we model the interaction between operators and users. We propose the user and operator utilities, focus on the learning aspects of the proposed utilities, and study the interactive trial and error learning for finding equilibria. Extending the concept of service priorities i.e., *Guaranteed Bit Rate (GBR* and *Non-Guaranteed Bit Rate (Non-GBR)* in LTE, we assume that there are three different types of users namely; i) Excellent, ii) Good, and iii) Fair. These users are characterized by the their preference profiles e.g., an excellent user prefers the service quality, whereas a fair user is interested in the service costs. We further assume that users broadcast the application requests in an abstract area a for three different types of applications namely; i) Voice over IP (VoIP), ii) File Transfer Protocol (FTP), and iii) Video streaming. The modeling in this market is decomposed as following:

- Operator level: Each operator uses a network pricing scheme and allocates the resource to the users under the associated quality of service constraints (which is translated in to users QoE). Operators with lowest cost but with good QoS will be more and more congested. This will lead to saturation and bad QoS. When, increasing the prices, the users will switch to another class or operator in order to get better utility. This means that strategy of the operators are interdependent (the pricing of operator influence the others via the network repartition of users for each user type and service class).

- User level: At this level, each user seeks to maximize his utility with as low cost as possible.
- Interdependency between the levels: The prices fixed by the operators influence the user decisions: network selection based the set of operators that are the QoS requirement with lowest costs. In parallel, the decision of the users leads to a sub-network for each operator. When maximizing his revenue, the operator needs to readapt its price in function of the user choice and the other operators. This leads to a interdependent multi-level system.

3.1 Network Operator Resource Allocation Problem

Each operator seeks to optimize its total revenue $R_o := \sum_{k,c} \pi(o, k, c) n_{o,k}^c$ subject to the QoS constraints. For the accepted users, a bandwidth allocation between the users is established. Then, each operator o designs the function π for each type k and each service class c.

3.2 User Centric Network Selection Problem

At user level, the user problem is to select the suitable network operator. In this connection we need to model the user preferences and performance metrics. This will be captured by the utility function. Let K be the set of three different types of users, and U_i represents the utility of user i, $\forall i \in K$. The expression of $U_i(.)$ is given as follows:

$$U_{i,k,c}(o,n) := u_{i,o}\left(\frac{b_{o,k}^c}{n_{o,k}}\right) \prod_{l \in L} (\nu_{il,o}(k,c,n))^{w_{il}} . \pi(o,k,c)$$
$$+ \sum_{j \in J} \omega_j v_{ij,o}(k,c,n,\psi), \qquad (1)$$

The user utility function (equation-1) has four components:

- The term $u_{i,o}\left(\frac{b_{o,k}^c}{n_{o,k}}\right)$ is the function of network state $n = (n_{o,k}^c)_{o,k,c}$ and the offered bandwidth $b_{o,k}^c$ by the operator $\dot{o}$. The collection n is the vector that represent the total number of users those request the service of specific class.
- $\prod_{l \in L}(\nu_{il,o}(k,c,n))^{w_{il}}$ is the weighted multiplicative approach for *dependent* associated QoE attributes.
- $\sum_{j \in J} \omega_j v_{ij,o}(k,c,n,\psi)$ is the weighted sum of different *independent* QoE attributes.
- $\pi(o,k,c)$ is the price of operator o to the user type k for service class c.

The first two multiplicative terms take into account both the congestion level of the operator and expected QoE, which is translated from the Operators QoS indices. The weight values w are dictated by the sensitivity of user type, service class to the attribute j. Here $k \in \Theta$, where Θ is the finite set of user types. Each operator o chooses its price vector π_o in a competitive way.

In order to formulate a utility function that respect the preference of the users and the performance metric of the network we use an experimental approach. *The expression of utility functions are given by experimental observations*. The objective measurement validation of the proposed utility function can be seen in [15]

Bandwidth dependent utility. Availability of bandwidth / transmission data rate plays the key role in evaluating the user QoE, therefore most of the literature work focus on the impact of varying data rate/bandwidth over QoE. However the user satisfaction should be analyzed with respect to different technical and non-technical attributes, and QoE evaluation metric vary with respect to application used by the user. We capture the bandwidth dependent user satisfaction with the following utility function:

$$
t_{i,k,c}(o,n) := \begin{cases}
0 & \text{if } \frac{b_{o,k}^c}{n_{o,k}} \leq \underline{b}_{o,k}^c \\
\alpha_k(n_{o,k}) \frac{1-e^{\beta(b_{o,k}^c - \underline{b}_{o,k}^c)}}{1-e^{\beta(\overline{b}_{o,k}^c - \underline{b}_{o,k}^c)}} & \text{if } \underline{b}_{o,k}^c \leq b_{o,k}^c \leq \overline{b}_{o,k}^c \\
\alpha_k(n_{o,k}) \frac{1-e^{\beta(b_{o,k}^c - \overline{b}_{o,k}^c)}}{1-e^{\beta(\tilde{b}_{o,k}^c - \overline{b}_{o,k}^c)}} & \text{if } \overline{b}_{o,k}^c \leq b_{o,k}^c \leq \tilde{b}_{o,k}^c \\
\alpha_k(n_{o,k}) \frac{1-e^{\beta(b_{o,k}^c - \tilde{b}_{o,k}^c)}}{1-e^{\beta(\hat{b}_{o,k}^c - \tilde{b}_{o,k}^c)}} & \text{if } \tilde{b}_{o,k}^c \leq b_{o,k}^c \leq \hat{b}_{o,k}^c \\
\alpha_k(n_{o,k}) & \text{if } b_{o,k}^c \geq \hat{b}_{o,k}^c
\end{cases}
\tag{2}
$$

where $\alpha_k(n_{0,k})$, represent the maximum utility of user types k and $n_{o,k} = \sum_c n_{o,k}^c$ is the number of users of type k for application quality of service class c from the operator o. In order to capture the congestion level, we choose the function α as strictly decreasing function in the number of users that request services at the same operator. The number $b_{o,k}^c$ represents the offered bandwidth to user type k for application quality of service class c, similarly $\underline{b}_{o,k}^c$, $\overline{b}_{o,k}^c$ etc represents the minimum and maximum required bandwidth by the application quality of service class c and user type k.

Now, we examine the outcome of the network selection in a competitive manner at the user level with the utility $t_i(.)$. At this level, each type of user seeks to maximize its utility $t_{i,k}(o,n)$. In this setting a well-studied solution concept is the called Cournot-Nash equilibrium. It is network configuration n^* such that for any i, k, the utility $t_{i,k,c}(o,n)$ is maximized by fixing the choice of the other users.

Next, we show that the user-centric game (the game at the user-level when the pricing functions chosen the operators are fixed) is in the class of congestion game [16]. A finite game in strategic form is a potential game [17] if the incentive of all players to change their strategy can be expressed in one global function called the potential function.

Proposition 1. *The user-centric game is a finite potential game.*

Proof. Let π the pricing function chosen the operators. Since the utility $t_{i,k,c}$ contains only a congestion part via the total number of users $n_{o,k}$ for each range of bandwidth, one gets a standard congestion game which is known to be isomorphic to a *potential game*. The exact expression of the potential function can be obtained from [16,17].

Corollary 1. *The user-centric game has at least one pure Nash equilibrium.*

This result follows from the fact that the existence of pure Cournot-Nash equilibria holds in finite potential game [17]. Here we apply it for each range of bandwidth.

The second issue that we address is the computation and the learning aspect of such equilibrium configurations. Different learning techniques have been developed for this specific class of games: finite improvement path, fictitious play, best response dynamics, stochastic fictitious play etc. Most of these learning schemes require at least the information of the network states at the previous step which seems to be very strong assumption in our context.

Because the number of users in the hull network can be arbitrary large, observing and responding to the individual choice of all users on a frame of time units would be a formidable task for any individual user. Therefore, the standard fictitious play and the iterative best reply are not directly applicable. Note that in the finite improvement path procedure (FIP) only one user moves at a given time slot (simultaneous moves are not allowed). For this reason, the FIP is not adapted when the network does not follows a prescribed rule evolution.

One of the well-known learning scheme for simultaneous-move games is the trial and error learning. Interactive trial and error learning is a recent version of standard trial and error learning studied in [18] that takes into account the interactive and dynamic nature of the learning environment. In ordinary trial and error learning, users occasionally try out new operators and classes and accept them if and only if they lead to higher performance. In an interactive situation, however, "errors" can arise in two different ways:

- the active errors, those done by trying some new operator that turns out to be not better (in terms of QoS, price and performance) than what one was chosen, or
- the passive errors, those done by continuing to keep the old strategy that turns out to be worse than it was before (due to congestion, new traffic conditions etc) .

In [18], it is shown that the interactive trial and error learning, implements Nash equilibrium behavior in any game with generic utilities and which has at least one pure Nash equilibrium. The interactive trial and error learning is a fully distributed learning rule such that, when used by all users in a game, period-by-period play comes close to pure Nash equilibrium play a high proportion of the time, provided that the game has such an equilibrium and the payoffs satisfy an interdependency condition. Since our finite utility given by the $t_i(.)$ has at least one equilibrium, the learning procedure implements one of the equilibrium with proportion of the time.

We assume that each user makes selection and service request decisions in random frames to optimize its own objectives in response to their own observations and local clocks and is able to measure a numerical value of its benefit and pay a cost for the service that he/she consumed. He is able to evaluate $t_{i,k,o}$ if the tried operator is o. Based on this measurement the user update his/her strategy when he/she will be active: keep the strategy with probability $(1 - \epsilon)$ if the performance is greater or try another strategy with probability ϵ. All this is done for a well-chosen $\epsilon \in (0, 1)$.

Proposition 2. *The interactive trial and error learning algorithm implements a pure Nash equilibrium of the user-centric game with high proportion of times.*

Proof. We verify that the conditions in [18] are satisfied. First, the user-centric game is a finite game for any fixed pricing function π. Second, the game is not degenerated because the utility functions are strongly interdependent via the network state. Third, we know that the game has at least one equilibrium from the corollary 1. Combining together all the conditions in [18] are satisfied. The result follows.

Learning in dynamic environment. Since the network is dynamic the associated game model should capture the variabilities, network traffic and the randomness in the environment. To this end, we extend the learning framework to dynamic game. For more details, we refer to [19] in which the number of active users may be random, new users come in, and exit etc. Without knowledge of the network state, without knowledge of the distribution of users, each active user tries to find out his/her utility function and associated payoff in the long-term [19].

Price of Anarchy and Suboptimality. Note that, even if this learning algorithm implements Nash equilibria of the game, the convergence time to be close to an equilibrium can be arbitrary high. Moreover, it is known that the equilibrium can be inefficient in term social welfare. The performance gap between the total equilibria utilities and global optimum is sometimes referred to *price of anarchy.*

In order to reduce this gap, the operators can design new game via their pricing functions. Under appropriate pricing functions π, one can design a game such that the equilibrium configuration of the new game (the utility is the difference between profit and cost) is near-optimal. This leads to the utility U_i (instead of t_i). Important components of U_i are the attributes dependent utilities v_{ij} and the cost functions π. For more details on the associated dependent and independent utilities refer to [15].

4   Upstream Market

In this market, we model the interaction between operators and the spectrum broker using the uniform price auctioning theory. The motivation for choosing the mentioned auction format is it common use in financial and other markets, which is evident by a large economic literature devoted to its study (e.g., Ofcom, Award of available spectrum: 1781.7-1785 MHz paired with 1876.7-1880 MHz: A Consultation, 16 September 2005.). It is also argued that to a large extent, the FCC spectrum auctions can be viewed as a uniform-price auction [20]. In a uniform-price auction, small bidders can simply bid their valuations and be assured of paying only the market-clearing price [21]. The fact highlighted in [22] that in uniform price auctions the downstream playing field is level, in the sense that each licensee begins with the same foundational asset at the same price is also one of the motivating force to user the uniform price auctioning for spectrum trade. More on auction clearing algorithms can be found in [23].

In our formulation, the spectrum broker (virtualized LTE framework) is analogous to *auctioneer*, network operators are analogous to *bidders*, and the resource to be auctioned is analogous to *auctioned-item*. We assume that the *auctioned-items* are *homogeneous* and *perfectly divisible*. This assumption is strengthen by the fact that current trend of introducing flexibility in frequencies licensing i.e., providing operators with the technology neutral spectrum allocation. Let the distribution of auctioned item size has support in the range $[X_{min}, X_{max}]$, which defines the resource limits, where X_{min} is a single PRB (Physical Resource Block) size and X_{max} is the total capacity of the spectrum resource, hereafter we use $\tilde{C}$ to represent the total resource capacity of the infrastructure provider. Let there are $\mathcal{N}$ symmetric risk-neutral bidders (operators), who compete by simultaneously submitting their non-increasing demand functions $x_{i,k}$. These bidders have independent private valuation function of the auctioned item, which is driven by the bidders' demand and the service types. Although the resource is homogeneous, the bidders have different valuations for different amounts of the resource. Such valuation is strictly influenced and is the consequence of service types for which the resource is required. We assume that the market comprises of demands of two service types namely *Guaranteed service* and *Non-guaranteed*, intuitively the former has more strict resource requirements when compared with the later. Let the $\tilde{\nu}_i$ be the bidder private valuation of the auctioned item. Influenced by the comment given in the preceding sentence, the bidder valuation varies for demands of different service types, this is captured by the index k, thus the bidder valuation now can be represented by $\tilde{\nu}_{i,k}$ such that $\tilde{\nu}_{i,k} \neq \tilde{\nu}_{i,\tilde{k}} \forall k \neq \tilde{k}$. To illustrate this one has to consider the service demand patterns of the operators or putting it the other way operators spectrum valuation is driven by the operators' target market segment e.g., an operator targeting the fair users values the amount of spectrum demands for fair users more than the amount of spectrum for other user (service) types, the similar argument holds for the converse situation. Thus the strategy for bidder $i \in \mathcal{N}$ is non-increasing function $X_i : [0, \infty) \to [0, X_{max}]$, and the his private valuation $\tilde{\nu}_{i,k}$, which is the evaluated spectrum price by the operator, the details of computing such valuation is given later in this section. Thus the operator bid is given by $\{x_{i,k}, \tilde{\nu}_{i,k}\}$. It should be noted that the valuation is computed as price per unit of the spectrum.

We assume that the market behavior is represented by Equation 3, and we term this market as *spectrum trade market* hereafter. As can be see that the demand curve is linear that expresses the demand as a linear function of the unit price. The choice of this market behavior is influence by its simplicity and wide presence in the literature.

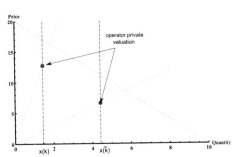

Fig. 2. figure representing the valuation of the operators for different services

$$\tilde{\pi}(x) := -\zeta x + \varsigma, \qquad (3)$$

where ζ and ς are positives, the negative gradient represents the sensitivity of market towards the price, and ς represents the bound on price. We know that the gradient introduces the elasticity in the curve. However, the proposed problem formulation dictates an inelastic spectrum demand behavior i.e., irrespective of how price may change the demand remains the same. This is represented by a perpendicular to the quantity axis in Fig 2. Given such inelastic scenario, what about the operators' valuation computation? So far the valuation is the price value at the intersection of the demand perpendicular and normal negatively sloped (going down from left to right) linear demand curve. However, this does not capture the operator preference for different services. To address this issue, we introduce the operator valuation function. Thus now the operator valuation corresponds to the intersection of operator valuation function slope and the demand perpendicular. As depicted in Fig 2, we map the operator demands over the spectrum trade market. The operator's the *valuation function*, given by Equation 4.

$$\tilde{\pi}_{i,k}(x) = \frac{x_{i,k}}{\gamma_k} \qquad (4)$$

where γ_k tunes the operators' valuation for the given demand and the service type such that; if the service type is of higher importance to the operator γ_k takes comparatively lower value than that of lower importance service. γ_k further can be translated as the function of number of operators in the spectrum competition and demands of service type i.e., real time service has higher value than that of background or non-real-time values i.e., $\gamma(k, \mathcal{N} - 1)$. Although one may come up with any suitable $\gamma(.)$ function, in this work, we simply represent it by a real-value exposed to simple constraint of $\gamma_{k,i} \neq \gamma_{\bar{k},i} \forall k \neq \bar{k}$ and $\gamma_{k,i} \neq \gamma_{k,\bar{i}} \forall i \neq \bar{i}$. Furthermore, it should be noted from the Fig 2 that the price given by the intersection of the demand perpendicular and the negative slope of market curve is the upper bound on the prices set by the regulatory body.

Remark 1. *We observe that downstream market demands (user service demands) influences the operator demands (operator resource demands). Although the optimal estimation of the service demands by users can be computed analytically, in this paper, we adopt the methodology for estimating the downstream demands based on the carried out simulation runs for all the virtual operators. In this connection we use the* Exponential Moving Average (EMA) *function to compute the estimated demands based on 20 seconds time intervals. Given the downstream demand, the upstream demand function can be computed.*

Definition 1. *The operator valuation $\gamma_{i,k}$ is directly translated in to $\tilde{\pi}_{i,k}$ i.e., based on service types and downstream market demands the operator reflects its valuation as $\tilde{\pi}_{i,k}$ such that $\gamma_{k,u} = \tilde{\pi}_{i,k}$. Intuitively the false valuation $\tilde{\pi}_{i,k}$ is given by $\gamma_{k,u} \neq \tilde{\pi}_{i,k}$.*

Let f be the mapping function that maps the downstream demands Y over the upstream demand function X, such that $f(Y) \mapsto X$. For simplicity we assume that the mapping is *bijective*. Given the upstream demand function an operator computes its valuation of resource using Equation 4. Realizing the upstream demand and by *Definition 1* the operator formulates its bid for the resource, which is given by $d_i(X, \pi)$.

Allocation Rule. Given the uniform price auctioning format, let $\bar{d}$ represents the highest bid, and p represents the stop out price;

$$a_i(X_i, d_i) := \begin{cases} X_i & \text{if} \quad d_{i,k} = \bar{d} \wedge X_i \leq \tilde{C} \wedge d_{i,k} > p \\ min\{X_i, \tilde{C} - \displaystyle\sum_{\bar{d}_i \in B, \bar{d}_i \setminus d_i} X_{\bar{d}_i}\} & \text{otherwise} \end{cases} \qquad (5)$$

As can be seen from Equation 5 the operator which is declared as the highest bidder gets the resources equivalent to its demands. In case the operator does not occupy the highest bidder position and resides in the winner list then it is allocated the residual resources not necessarily equivalent to its demands. The operator gets the residual demand when the infrastructure resource capacity is less than the operator demands(lower part of Equation 5). The resource allocated to each operator is independent of the auctioning format, however the payments do depend on the auction format.

Operator utility function. As we know that operators have different valuation of different amounts (i.e., spectrum for k and $\tilde{k}$ type services) of spectrum. However, the allocation rule dictates that operators are allocated according to their aggregated demand request. Thus the operator profit function involves both spectrum amounts of different operator valuation values. We define the operator utility function for resource allocation a_i to operator $i \in \mathcal{N}$ and the stop-out price be p as:

$$u_i(a, p) := (\gamma_k - p)x_k + (\gamma_{\tilde{k}} - p)x_{\tilde{k}} \tag{6}$$

As can be seen that operator utility increases in its valuation and demands and decreases in stop-out price.

Auctioneer utility function. The profit function or utility function of auctioneer (LTE virtualition framework) is the function of bidder demands and stop-out price and is given by:

$$u(\sum_{i \in \mathcal{N}} X_i, p) := \sum_{\tilde{d} \in B} a_{\tilde{d}} \times (p - \frac{\sqrt{x}}{\lambda}) \tag{7}$$

where $\frac{\sqrt{x}}{\lambda}$ represents the incurring cost of auctioneer, λ is the controller that enables the auctioneer to scale the cost that follows the operator specific deployment pattern (i.e., co-location, site rentals, tower rental etc.), the detail modeling of cost function (modeling operational and maintenance, deployment costs etc.) is out of the scope of this paper. However the choice of square-root function to capture the operator cost function is influenced by the continuous nature of the function for all non-negative numbers and differentiable for all positive numbers, the function also capture the realistic nature of the operator cost i.e., the operator initially incur more cost on improving service and such cost decreases with increase in demands. Spectrum broker maximizes its utility i.e., $max_p u_j(\sum_{i \in \mathcal{N}} X_i, p)$, which increases in p and allocated resources and constrained by the operators' capacities. Thus the problem that the auctioneer solves is to decide the auction clearing or stop-out price and resource allocation (for allocation rule see Equation 5) i.e., $p = sup \left\{ p | \sum_{i \in \mathcal{N}} X_i \geq K \right\}$. We also present the algorithm that is implemented by the auctioneer to take the decision over resource allocation and stop-out price as follows:

4.1 Equilibrium Analysis - A Two States Tale

We characterize the Nash equilibria in the mentioned model in weakly dominant strategies.

Algorithm 1. Calculate p and a_i

Given the available spectrum $\tilde{C}$, clock index $t = 0$, the auctioneer (LTE virtualization framework) sets the reservation price R. Set t = 0 // Bids submissions start
Ensure: $d_i \geq$ R // Ensure that bids are equal or above the *Reserve price (R)*
  while $t \neq t_{max}$ **do**
    B ← $d_i \forall i \in \mathcal{N}$ // Update the bid vector B for every income bid d_i
  end while
  Determine the set of winning bids $LIST\overline{B}$ ← d_i // The set of highest bids of B that do not
  violate the capacity constraint $\sum_{i \in \mathcal{N}} a_i \leq \tilde{C}$
  SORT $LIST\overline{B}$ in ascending order.
  p← $LIST\overline{B}.d_i(\tilde{\pi})$ // select the price of lowest winning bidder as stop-out price.
  while $\tilde{C} \neq 0$ && $LIST\overline{B} \neq$ empty **do**
Ensure: $d_i \in \overline{B}$
    if $\tilde{C} > d_i(X)$ **then**
      $\overline{B}.B_i(a) = X_i$
    else
      $\overline{B}.B_i(a) = \tilde{C}_r$ // $\tilde{C}_r$ is the residual capacity
    end if
  end while

Lemma 1. *In an homogeneous item uniform price auctions, the operators with multiple
bids have a unique dominant strategy for each bid in different instances i.e.,*

$$d_{i,t_1} := \gamma_{i,t_1,k} \tag{8}$$

and $d_{i,t_2} := min\{R, \gamma_{i,t_2,\tilde{k}}\}$.

Proof. Proof omitted due to space restrictions.

4.2 Sequence of Actions

1. Each bidder observes the demands (based on EMA, mentioned earlier).
2. Infrastructure provider announces the start of auction time t_{init} and duration of bid
   submission i.e., $t_{init} - t_{max}$.
3. Bidders submit their demands to the auctioneer at each per-unit price, which is the
   valuation of the bidder and attained from the Equation-4.
4. After the elapse of the submission time, the infrastructure provider observes the
   aggregated demand and sets the stop out price, which is equal or greater than the
   incurring cost over the unit resource. The auctioneer also decides each bidder's
   allocation.
5. The allocation is executed through the hypervisor
6. The process iterates over $1 - 4$, after the inter-auction time δt expires.

5 Dynamic Spectrum Trade Realization Framework

In this section, we present the LTE virtualization framework that we implement extensively to realize the proposed dynamic spectrum allocation concept. We virtualize the

LTE network infrastructure (i.e., eNodeB, routers, ethernet links, and aGW etc.) so that multiple mobile network operators can create their own virtual network (depending on their requirements) on a common infrastructure. In the proposed virtualized network, we mainly foresee two different aspects; i) Physical infrastructure virtualization: virtualizing the LTE nodes and links and ii) Air interface virtualization: being able to virtualize the LTE spectrum. However, we in this paper focus on the later aspect, since virtualizing the air interface of the LTE system is a completely new concept and also the earlier aspect is extensively investigated in the research literature.

5.1   Air Interface Virtualization

The eNodeB is the entity responsible for accessing the radio channel and scheduling the air interface resources between the users. The eNodeB has to be virtualized so as to virtualize the LTE air interface. Virtualizing the eNodeB is similar to node virtualization. The physical resource of the node (e.g., CPU, memory, I/O devices ... etc.) are shared between multiple virtual instances. XEN [24] is a well known PC virtualization solution that insert a layer called "Hypervisor" on top of the physical hardware to schedule the resources. From that, our LTE virtualization framework follows the same principle. A hypervisor is added on top of the PHY layer of the eNodeB, it is responsible for virtualizing the eNodeB node as well as the spectrum. The proposed framework can be seen in Figure 3b.

The architecture shows the physical eNodeB virtualized into a number of virtual eNodeBs. This is achieved by the hypervisor that sits on top of the physical resources of the eNodeB. In addition, the hypervisor is responsible for scheduling the spectrum, i.e., scheduling the air interface resources (OFDMA sub-carriers) between the virtual eNodeBs running on top. In the framework architecture two new entities should be highlighted: the "*Spectrum configuration and Bandwidth estimation*" which is responsible for setting the spectrum the virtual eNodeB is supposed to operate in as well as estimating the required bandwidth of the operator. And the "*Spectrum allocation unit*" which is responsible for scheduling the spectrum among the different virtual eNodeBs. LTE uses OFDMA in the downlink, which means that the frequency band is divided into a number of sub-bands that are called Physical Resource Blocks (PRBs). A PRB is the smallest unit the LTE MAC scheduler can assign to a user. The Hypervisor schedule the PRBs between the different virtual operators, this process could be done by different mechanisms. In this paper, an auction based mechanism is used in the "*Spectrum allocation unit*" to auction the PRBs to the different virtual operators that bid for them.

6   Simulation Model and Results Analysis

The LTE virtualization simulation model is developed using OPNET [25] based on the 3GPP specifications. As explained earlier, the focus of the model is on the air interface virtualization and spectrum sharing between multiple virtual operators (all sharing the same eNodeB). An example scenario of the simulation model can be seen in Figure-3a. Two scenarios are investigated based on the Auctioneer's (Infrastructure Provider) reserved price "R". The reserved price is the minimum price the Auctioneer is willing

Table 1. Simulation configurations

Parameter	Assumption
Number of virtual operators	4 virtual operators with circular cells of 375 meters radius
Total Number of PRBs (Spectrum)	75 PRBs, i.e., about 15 MHz
Mobility model	Random Way Point (RWP) with vehicular speed (120 Km/h)
Number of active users per virtual operator	VO1: 16 GBR (video users) and 4 non-GBR (FTP users)
	VO2: 10 GBR (video users) and 10 non-GBR (FTP users)
	VO3: 4 GBR (video users) and 16 non-GBR (FTP users)
VO1 price valuation	$\gamma1=2$ and $\gamma2=(2, 4, 6, 8, 10$ and $20)$
VO2 price valuation	$\gamma1=2$ and $\gamma2=4$
VO3 price valuation	$\gamma1=2$ and $\gamma2=2$
Video traffic model	24 frames per second with frame size = 1562 Bytes
	Video call duration = Exponential with 60 seconds mean
	Inter video call time = Poison with 30 seconds mean
FTP traffic model	FTP file size = 8M bytes
	Inter request time = uniform between 50 and 75 seconds
Auctioning parameters	Auction done every 20 seconds with $\gamma = 0.25$
Simulation runtime	1000 seconds

to sell the resources with, and any bid with a price lower than the reserved one will be rejected. The first scenario is configured no reserved price (i.e., R = 0). The second scenario is configured with a dynamic reserved price that is a function of the total resources demand, this is calculated as follows:

$$R = \gamma \cdot \sqrt[3]{\sum_i \sum_k x_{i,k}} \qquad (9)$$

The rest of the configurations can be seen in Table 1.

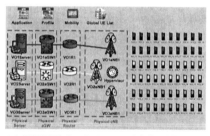

(a) OPNET simulation model for LTE virtualization

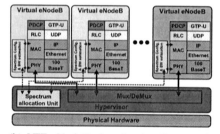

(b) LTE eNodeB virtualization framework architecture

Fig. 3. Figure representing the OPNET based LTE eNodeB virtualization framework

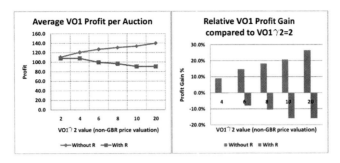

Fig. 4. Virtual Operator 1 profit and relative profit gain

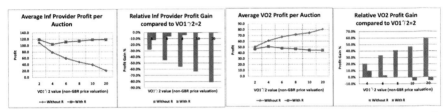

(a) Infrastructure provider (Auctioneer) profit (b) Virtual Operator 2 profit and relative profit
and relative profit gain   gain

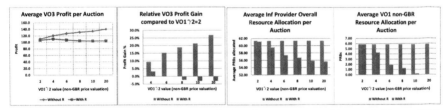

(c) Virtual Operator 3 profit and relative profit (d) Infrastructure provider and VO1 non-GBR
gain   overall resource utilization

Fig. 5. Figure presenting the profit and relative profit results and virtual operator resources

6.1 Results and Analysis

The idea behind the simulations is to show how the uniform auctioning framework performs in a practical scenario, highlight some of the foreseen problems and how it can be
solved. First, what happens if the infrastructure provider does not set any reserved price.
Since the resources are homogeneous (in the perspective of the infrastructure provider)
and they are soled by a uniform price determined by the lowest winner price, there is a
possibility that the virtual operators try to exploit this by reducing their bidding prices
in order to maximize their profit. This could be seen in Figure 4, where virtual operator 1 manipulates the price and maximizes his profit (blue curve of the figure). Since
the spectrum broker (or infrastructure provider) has no reserved price set in that scenario, the virtual operator succeeds in reducing the resource price and thus increasing
his profit. On the other hand, in the 2nd scenario (red curve of the figure) even though

the virtual operator tries to manipulate his bidding price he is unable to increase his profit. This is because the spectrum broker sets a reserved price that the operator can not bid below. Figure 5a shows the spectrum broker (or infrastructure provider) profit. The profit decreases in the case with no reserved price due to the virtual operator's price manipulation, but when the spectrum broker (infrastructure provider) sets a reserved price he can stop the operator manipulation. Figure 5b and 5c show the average profit of virtual operator 2 and 3 respectively. The results are similar to virtual operator 1 results. The average number of PRBs (spectrum utilization) for both the spectrum broker (infrastructure provider) as well as virtual operator 1 can be seen in Figure 5d. Similar trend as before can be observed, in the scenario with no reserved price the amount of resources is the same in all cases because the virtual operator gets all of his demand but with different prices. In the scenario with a reserved price it can be seen that the overall resources granted to the virtual operator starts decreasing, this is because when the virtual operator starts manipulating the bidding price he will not be granted his demand if the price is lower than the reserved one.

7 Conclusion

In this paper, we discussed different market dynamics, the strategies of involved stakeholders at different hierarchical levels of telecommunication landscape, and investigated the equilibria in the upstream and downstream market. We also discussed the infrastructure resource auctioning in future wireless paradigm by focusing on both technical and theoretical aspects. We provide the technical realization of the proposed future market behavior with the state-of-the-art technical solution on the granule level. We have investigated how the uniform auctioning format performs when used to trade the spectrum between different virtual operators in a virtualized LTE system environment.

References

1. DARPA Next Generation Communication Program, http://www.sharedspectrum.com/resources/darpa-next-generation-communications-program/
2. Buddhikot, M.M., Kolodzy, P., Miller, S., Ryan, K., Evans, J.: Dimsumnet: New directions in wireless networking using coordinated dynamic spectrum access. In: IEEE WoWMoM 2005, pp. 78–85 (2005)
3. Rodriguez, V., Moessner, K., Tafazolli, R.: Market-driven dynamic spectrum allocation: Optimal end-user pricing and admission control for cdma. In: The Proceedings of IST Mobile and Wireless Communication Summit (2005)
4. Rodriguez, V., Moessner, K., Tafazolli, R.: Auction driven dynamic spectrum allocation: optimal bidding, pricing and service priorities for multi-rate, multi-class cdma. In: The Proceedings of 16th Internation Symposium on Personal, Indoor and Mobile Radio Communications (PIMRC), pp. 1850–1854 (2005)
5. Ryan, K., Aravantinos, E., Buddhikot, M.M.: A new pricing model for next generation spectrum access. In: Proceedings of the First International Workshop on Technology and Policy for Accessing Spectrum, TAPAS 2006. ACM, New York (2006)
6. Sorabh, G., Buragohain, C., Cao, L., Zheng, H., Suri, S.: A general framework for wireless spectrum

7. IST-DRIVE PRoject, http://www.ist-drive.org
8. http://smartradioview.blogspot.com/2007/07/
   overdrive-projecthomepage.html (Link last accessed on Febraury 24, 2011)
9. Bavier, A., Bowman, M., Culler, D., Chun, B., Karlin, S., Muir, S., Peterson, L., Roscoe, T., Spalink, T., Wawrzoniak, M.: Operating system support for planetary-scale network services (March 2004)
10. Paul, S., Seshan, S.: Geni technical document on wireless virtualization (September 2006)
11. AKARI architecture conceptual design for new generation network
12. Bauck, S., Görg, C.: Virtualisation as a co-existence tool in a future internet. In: ICT Mobile Summit - 4WARD Workshop, Stockholm, Sweden (June 2008)
13. Zaki, Y., Zhao, L., Timm-Giel, A., Görg, C.: A Novel LTE Wireless Virtualization Framework. In: Second International ICST Conference on Mobile Networks And Management (Monami), pp. 1–13. CD publication, Santander (2010)
14. Zaki, Y., Zhao, L., Timm-Giel, A., Görg, C.: LTE Wireless Virtualization and Spectrum Management. In: Third Joint IFIP Wireless and Mobile Networking Conference (WMNC), Budapest, Hungary (October 2010)
15. Khan, M.A., Toseef, U.: User utility function as quality of experience (qoe). In: Proceedings of the ICN 2011, pp. 99–104 (2011)
16. Rosenthal, R.W.: A class of games possessing pure-strategy nash equilibria. International Journal of Game Theory 2, 65–67 (1973), doi:10.1007/BF01737559
17. Monderer, D., Shapley, L.S.: Games and economic behavior 14, 124–143 (1996)
18. Young, H.P.: Learning by trial and error. Games and Economic Behavior 65, 626–643 (2009)
19. Tembine, H.: Distributed learning in dynamic robust games: dynamics, algorithms and network applications. Lecture Notes (2010)
20. Cramton, P.: The efficiency of the fcc spectrum auctions. Journal of Law and Economics 41 (October 1998)
21. Spectrum auctions. Auction design issues for spectrum awards market analysis ltd
22. French, R.: Spectrum auctions 101. The Journal of Public Sector Management (2008)
23. Sandholm, T., Suri, S.: Market clearability. In: Proceedings of the Seventeenth International Joint Conference on Artificial Intelligence, pp. 1145–1151 (2001)
24. Williams, D.E., Garcia, J.: Virtualization with Xen^{TM}: Including XenEnterprise^{TM}, XenServer^{TM}, and XenExpress^{TM}. SYNGRESS (2007)
25. OPNET website, http://www.opnet.com

Combining MBSFN and PTM Transmission Schemes for Resource Efficiency in LTE Networks

Antonios Alexiou[2], Konstantinos Asimakis[1,2], Christos Bouras[1,2],
Vasileios Kokkinos[1,2], and Andreas Papazois[1,2]

[1] Research Academic Computer Technology Institute, Patras, Greece
[2] Computer Engineering and Informatics Dept., Univ. of Patras, Greece
{Alexiua,asimakis,papazois}@ceid.upatras.gr,
{bouras,Kokkinos}@cti.gr

Abstract. Long Term Evolution (LTE) systems allow the transmission of rich multimedia services by utilizing the Multimedia Broadcast/Multicast Service (MBMS) over a Single Frequency Network (MBSFN). During MBSFN transmission a time-synchronized common waveform is transmitted from multiple cells. The 3rd Generation Partnership Project (3GPP) has specified that Point-to-Multipoint (PTM) transmission can be used in combination with MBSFN to provide MBMS-based services. In this paper we evaluate the combined transmission scheme in terms of Resource Efficiency (RE). The evaluation is performed through simulation experiments for various user distributions and LTE network configurations. The experiments are conducted with the aid of a proposed algorithm, which estimates the Spectral Efficiency (SE) of each cell and the RE of the network, and is also able to formulate the optimal network deployment that maximizes the network's RE. For each of the examined scenarios, we present the most efficient solution (in terms of RE) selected by our algorithm and we compare it with other transmission schemes.

Keywords: long term evolution; multimedia broadcast and multicast; single frequency network; point-to-multipoint; resource efficiency.

1   Introduction

The 3rd Generation Partnership Project (3GPP) has introduced the Multimedia Broadcast/Multicast Service (MBMS) as a means to broadcast and multicast information to mobile users, with mobile TV being the main service offered. The Long Term Evolution (LTE) infrastructure offers to MBMS an option to use an uplink channel for interaction between the service and the user, which is not a straightforward issue in common broadcast networks [1], [2].

In the context of LTE systems, the MBMS will evolve into e-MBMS ("e-" stands for evolved). This will be achieved through increased performance of the air interface that will include a new transmission scheme called MBMS over a Single Frequency Network (MBSFN). In MBSFN operation, MBMS data are transmitted simultaneously over the air from multiple tightly time-synchronized cells. A group of those cells, which are targeted to receive these data, is called MBSFN area [2]. Since the MBSFN

X. Masip-Bruin et al. (Eds.): WWIC 2011, LNCS 6649, pp. 56–67, 2011.
© IFIP International Federation for Information Processing 2011

transmission greatly enhances the Signal to Interference plus Noise Ratio (SINR), the MBSFN transmission mode leads to significant improvements in Spectral Efficiency (SE) in comparison to multicasting over Universal Mobile Telecommunications System (UMTS) [3], [4]. The higher the SE is, the faster the transmissions get per Hz of bandwidth that is devoted to the transmission.

3GPP has also proposed Point-to-Multipoint (PTM) transmissions for individual cells. The main disadvantage of PTM when compared to MBSFN is that it has a much lower SE because nearby transmitting cells cause destructive interference. On the other hand, in PTM transmissions there is no need for complex synchronization with adjacent cells as in the MBSFN case. This means that the cost of synchronization in PTM case is lower than that of MBSFN.

Different aspects of MBSFN have been studied in previous research works. For example, in [5] and [6], the authors evaluated the SE of four different approaches when selecting the Modulation and Coding Scheme (MCS) to be utilized for MBSFN data transmission under various scenarios. The authors in [7] evaluated the SE and the Resource Efficiency (RE) under varying numbers of MBSFN assisting rings. The RE takes into account the SE of all cells and shows how well are the system resources (essentially the active cells and bandwidth) used for the transmissions. Furthermore, the authors of [8] proposed analytical approaches for the evaluation and validation of MBSFN enabled networks. Finally, there have been several studies for PTM over UMTS networks [9], [10].

To the best of our knowledge there is little to no research regarding the combination of MBSFN and PTM as a way to increase the RE of a system. In this paper, we investigate the provision of MBMS service through a new scheme that combines MBSFN and PTM transmissions. The evaluation of RE is performed through simulation experiments for various user distributions and LTE network configurations. The experiments are conducted with the aid of a proposed algorithm, which estimates the SE of each cell, the RE of the network and gradually formulates the optimal network deployment that maximizes the network's RE. The tool implementing this algorithm is available at [11]. In the first experiment, we compare different network deployments for a simple user distribution scenario, where a single interested UE drop cell is located at different distances from an extensive UE drop area. In this experiment we present how the RE changes as the distance between the two areas changes for different network deployments. In the second experiment, we re-evaluate the resulting RE of hexagonal interested UE drop areas when MBSFN is used along with a varying number of assisting rings. This experiment is similar to the one performed in [7] but in this case we use a method that provides more precise approximations of the SE of individual cells compared to the one used in [7]. In the third experiment, we try to optimize the network deployment in order to achieve the highest possible RE for different interested UE drop deployment scenarios.

The remainder of the paper is structured as follows: Section 2 presents an overview of the MBSFN area configuration. In Section 3, we describe our simulation tools and in Section 4 the experiments that we have conducted. Finally, the conclusions and the planned next steps are described in Section 5.

2 MBSFN Area Configuration

We define the MBSFN area as the group of cells that contain UEs, which requests media (the interested UE drop location cells) plus any number of assisting cells. A cell is assumed to be assisting when it broadcasts MBSFN data while it does not actually contain any users that request any media service. Although their SE is not useful (i.e. they do not contribute to the RE of the system), assisting cells may increase the SE of nearby MBSFN cells by constructive combination of their transmissions. This is the main difference between MBSFN and PTM, MBSFN transmissions are synchronized so their combination can be constructive while PTM transmissions cause interference to any other nearby transmission.

If an area is completely surrounded by assisting neighboring cells then we say that it is surrounded by an assisting ring.

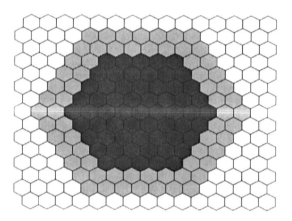

Fig. 1. Example topology with 2 assisting rings

Fig. 1 illustrates a network topology. The dark blue cells are interested UE drop location cells that contain users requiring the MBSFN data, while the light blue cells are assisting cells, which form two assisting rings. In the remainder of the paper, we call this kind of network deployment as AAI (using the terminology from [7], meaning that two rings around the interested UE drop area are Assisting and the third one is Interfering). In the same manner we define all cases from III (three interfering rings) to AAA (three assisting rings).

3 Simulation Scheme

3.1 Spectral Efficiency in MBSFN

We define a simulation scheme that, among other parameters, uses the coordinates of interested UE drop locations and an initial MBSFN topology. After the network has been populated, the mechanism evaluates the RE and, if desired, starts optimizing the current MBSFN deployment in order to increase the RE.

In general, RE is a measure for monitoring how efficiently the resources of a system are utilized. It is tightly associated with the SE, but also considers the amount of resources that are utilized to achieve a certain SE. To calculate the RE of the system, the SE of each cell must be known. Therefore, the first step is to approximate the SE of each cell. We suppose an inter site distance of 500m and therefore we use the SE values given in [7]. The remainder of the simulation parameters are given in Table 1.

Table 1. Simulation settings

Parameter	Units	Value
Cellular layout		Hexagonal grid, 19 cell sites
Inter Site Distance (ISD)	m	500
Carrier frequency	MHz	2000
System bandwidth	MHz	1.4
Channel model		3GPP Typical Urban
Path loss	dB	Okumura-Hata
BS transmit power	dBm	46
BS # antennas		1
UE # Rx antennas		2
UE speed	Km/h	3

If no users requesting media are resided in the cell then there is no need to calculate the SE as it does not affect the RE of the system. As suggested in [7], a cell transmitting with PTM has a spectral efficiency of 0.4bps/Hz. If the cell is transmitting with MBSFN we use the values shown in Table 2.

Table 2. SE with different number of assisting rings [7]

1st ring	2nd ring	3rd ring	Central cell SE (bps/Hz)
Assisting	Assisting	Assisting	2.4
Assisting	Assisting	Interfering	2.2
Assisting	Interfering	Interfering	1.3
Interfering	Interfering	Interfering	0.4

The performance of the MBSFN increases rapidly when rings of neighboring cells outside the interested UE drop area assist the MBSFN service and transmit the same MBSFN data. More specifically according to [7] and [12] even the presence of one assisting ring can significantly increase the overall spectral efficiency. Moreover, we assume that a maximum of 3 neighboring rings outside the interested UE drop area can transmit in the same frequency and broadcast the same MBSFN data (assisting rings), since additional rings do not offer any significant additional gain in the MBSFN transmission [7], [12]. In our case by adding one assisting ring the SE goes from 0.4bps/Hz to 1.3bps/Hz, which constitutes a difference of 0.9bps/Hz. By adding one more assisting ring, it goes up to 2.2bps/Hz and by adding the third one we can gain only 0.2bps/Hz.

For cases not matching any of the calculated data of the work presented in [7], we use the following approach for estimating the SE. We suppose that the change of the SE when transiting between different numbers of assisting rings is approximately linear. Our method can be summarized in the following table.

Table 3. The linear approximation used for calculating the spectral efficiency (X is the percentage of the ring that is assisting)

1st ring	2nd ring	3rd ring	SE of cell
X%	Any	Any	X% * 0.9 + 0.4
100%	X%	Any	X% * 0.9 + 1.3
100%	100%	X%	X% * 0.2 + 2.2

As an example, let us consider the leftmost cell in Fig. 2. It is transmitting using MBSFN. It has 6 adjacent cells and 3 of them are transmitting with MBSFN, while the transmissions of the other 3 are interfering. Therefore 50% of the cells in the 1st ring are Assisting while the other 50% are Interfering and the SE of this cell is 0.4+50%*0.9=0.85bps/Hz.

3.2 Configuration Optimization Algorithm

The RE of the system for a given service is calculated by dividing the sum of all useful SE with the number of cells transmitting data for that service via PTM or MBSFN. We consider the SE of a cell useful if there is at least one user in that cell that are interested in receiving the PTM or MBSFN transmission. For example, if there are 3 interested UE drop cells with SE 0.4, 1.4 and 1.2 respectively but only the first two cells actually contain users interested into the service then the resulting RE is (0.4 + 1.4) / 3 = 0.6bps/Hz.

The algorithm is summarized using pseudo-code in the table that follows. In brief, the algorithm starts with an arbitrary distribution of MBSFN cells (for a given interested UE drop area) and then makes random changes to it. For every change it calculates the RE of the system, if it has decreased, it rolls back to the best-known configuration. In many cases though, the changes happen to be beneficial for the RE and thus they are accepted. Gradually, this procedure leads to better configurations. The computational overhead of the algorithm is reasonably low. For example, for medium size interested UE drop areas (consisting of approximately 20 cells) the algorithm requires less than 5 seconds to find the configuration that leads to the maximum value for RE. It is theoretically impossible for the algorithm to get trapped forever in local optima because the mutation function (the one that produces the changes) has a small chance to produce so radical changes that it will overcome such problems, given adequate time. Although the algorithm cannot and does not provide any information on whether it has reached the globally optimal configuration, it is fairly obvious when the search can be safely stopped. For example the algorithm might make rapid changes for a few seconds and then stabilize for more than a minute, which almost surely indicates that this is the optimal configuration. Additionally one can perform the experiments with different starting configurations to be further reassured that the optimum found is the global one.

```
% MBSFN area optimization algorithm

Grid = create_grid()
create_rings(grid,number_of_assisting_rings)
RE = evaluate(grid)
best = RE
print("Initial SE: ",best)
While not user_requested_break
        mutations = mutate(grid)
        For each cell in grid do
                If cell.MBSFN and cell.UE_drop then
                        % MBSFN cell
                        cell.SE=calculate_MBSFN_SE(cell)
                Elseif cell.MBSFN then
                        % Assisting cell.
                        % SE=0 because it is useless
                        cell.SE=0
                Elseif cell.UE_drop then
                        % PTM cell.
                        SE=0.4
                Else
                        % Cell off
                        SE=0
                Endif
        Next
        % The SE have been calculated. We can calculate the RE.
        RE = evaluate_RE(grid)
        If RE > best then
                best = RE
                print("Current SE: ",best)
                export_grid_to_file(grid)
        Elseif RE==best then
                best = RE
        Else
                demutate(grid,mutations)
        Endif
Endwhile
```

The evaluate subroutine calculates the SE for each cell and then the RE of the system which is also returned. The mutate subroutine randomly enables and disables MBSFN cells and returns the changes that have been made so that the demutate subroutine can undo those changes later if the evaluation of the grid shows a decrease in the RE of the system because of them.

4 Experimental Evaluation

In this section, we present the experiments we have conducted along with their results. The experiments are grouped in the three following subsections.

4.1 Deployments for Moving Adjacent Cell

The first part of our simulation experiments attempts to estimate how the optimal MBSFN deployment varies as the multicast user distribution changes. Although the current 3GPP specification does not allow on-the-fly changes to the MBSFN deployment, our algorithm is fast and efficient enough to propose on-the-fly changes, if they get ever allowed by the standard. The optimal RE is estimated and compared with the RE estimated for other typical configurations. For this purpose we consider a set of adjacent cells where the multicast users are located in a way that a primary area with multicast users is formed (Fig. 2). The next step is to define a cell where multicast user(s) exist and to see how the optimal MBSFN deployment varies as the position of this cell recedes from the primary area.

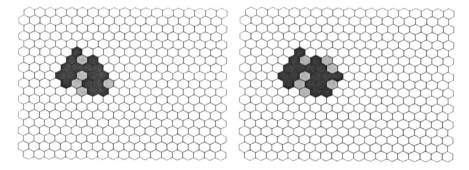

Fig. 2. The primary interested UE drop area is the one covered by dark blue cell cells

Fig. 3. A new single-cell interested UE drop location at distance 1 from the initial area

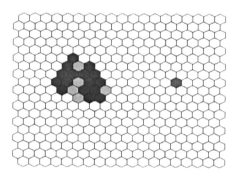

Fig. 4. The last step evaluated. The single-cell interested UE drop location at a distance equal to 7.

In this experiment, we use a randomly shaped area of 16 cells as primary area and a single cell at different distances from the primary area are used as a base for this scenario. For example, in Fig. 2, the primary interested UE drop area is visible with dark blue color. In the same picture, the optimal coverage proposed by our algorithm is also shown. All interested UE drop location cells are covered with MBSFN transmissions along with some assisting cells (light blue).

Fig. 3 presents the second step of our experiment, where users appear in a new cell at a distance of 1 from the initial area. Our optimization algorithm proposes that the new cell should be covered with MBSFN while its addition triggers the activation of two more assisting cells.

We continue moving the new users' location to the right until distance 7 (a further increase in the distance would not change the RE of any of the transmission schemes). That last step of our experiment can be seen in Fig. 4 along with the proposed coverage configuration. What is worth mentioning is that our algorithm selects the combination of MBSFN and PTM transmissions (blue and red colored cells respectively) as the optimal network configuration.

In order to give an overview of the improved performance of our algorithm we compare the optimal RE with the RE estimated for the five typical configurations 2-6 listed below. It should be noted that the configurations 3-6 are proposed in work [7].

1. **MBSFN+PTM**: This is the configuration using MBSFN and/or PTM as proposed by our optimization algorithm. Assisting rings or MBSFN area are not predefined.
2. **III (MBSFN only)**
3. **AII (MBSFN only)**
4. **AAI (MBSFN only)**
5. **AAA (MBSFN only)**
6. **PTM**: All interested UE drop cells are covered by PTM. MBSFN is not used at all and therefore no assisting rings exist either.

The results of the aforementioned experiments are presented in Fig. 5.

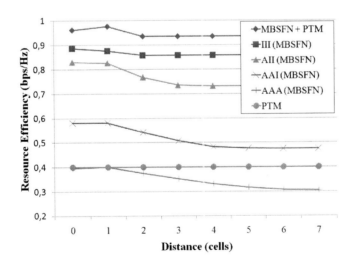

Fig. 5. The RE for different distances and coverage schemes

From the results we can conclude that the best would be to use a few assisting cells (as shown in the previous figures). If this is not possible the second best solution is to use pure MBSFN without any assisting rings. Adding assisting rings only dropped the RE of the system in our scenarios to the point that, with three assisting rings, it was lower than that of pure PTM.

4.2 Optimal Configuration for Hexagonal Areas

In this paragraph we re-evaluate some of the experiments conducted in [7]. We aim to provide more accurate results using the linear approximation of SE presented in Section 3. The central area in all cases is one cell plus a number of rings around it. Around that area we apply 0 to 3 assisting rings (deployments III to AAA). As an example, in Fig. 1 we can see an area with 4 inner rings and 2 assisting ones.

We found results that differ considerably from those presented in [7] which are listed in Table 4. The underlined values of RE correspond to the highest value and therefore to the optimal MBSFN deployment. In contrast to [7], our approximation algorithm supposes that cells are also assisted by other MBSFN cells that contain users and not just by cells in assisting rings. For example in the case of 15 inner rings, we suppose that the inner 12 rings form an area already surrounded by 3 "assisting" rings, therefore their SE is already maximal and adding additional rings will not improve the RE as much as the authors of [7] suggest. Therefore out of a total of 721 interested UE drop location cells, 469 have a SE of 2.4bps/Hz (that of a fully assisted cell). Moreover, if our linear approximation is accurate enough, then using assisting rings around hexagonal areas is only lowering the RE of the system. Indeed, the assisting rings just increase the SE of the outmost rings of the interested UE drop area while the majority of cells already have a high SE because they assist each other. Our results are presented in Table 5.

Table 4. RE (in bps/Hz) for hexagonal areas of different sizes and different numbers of assisting rings, as presented in [7]

Assisting rings	0 inner rings	1 inner rings	2 inner rings	3 inner rings	4 inner rings	5 inner rings	15 inner rings	Infinite inner rings
AAA	0.06	0.28	0.50	0.70	0.87	1.01	1.68	2.4
AAI	0.12	0.42	0.69	0.89	1.11	1.18	1.73	2.2
AII	0.19	0.48	0.67	0.79	0.87	0.93	1.15	1.3
III	0.4	0.4	0.4	0.4	0.4	0.4	0.4	0.4

Table 5. RE (in bps/Hz) for hexagonal areas of different sizes and different numbers of assisting rings

Assisting rings	0 inner rings	1 inner rings	2 inner rings	3 inner rings	4 inner rings	5 inner rings	15 inner rings	Infinite inner rings
AAA	0.06	0.28	0.5	0.7	0.87	1.01	1.68	2.4
AAI	0.12	0.44	0.74	0.96	1.14	1.28	1.88	2.4
AII	0.19	0.69	1.06	1.3	1.48	1.6	2.07	2.4
III	0.4	0.91	1.28	1.52	1.68	1.8	2.17	2.4

From Table 5, it is clear that the addition of assisting rings does not improve the overall performance in terms of RE. Irrespectively of the number of inner rings, the RE when adding assisting rings decreases. However, this difference decreases with the number of inner rings and for an infinite area the RE for all deployments equals to 2.4bps/Hz.

4.3 Examination of Typical Cases

The third part of our simulation experiments determines the optimal network configuration and the corresponding RE for some indicative typical examples of user distribution. As in the previous figures, we use dark and light blue colors to indicate the area where MBMS is provided with MBSFN transmission scheme. Dark blue color is used for MBSFN transmissions in interested UE drop locations while light blue is used to indicate the assisting cells that are added to the MBSFN area and transmit the same MBSFN data as in interested UE drop locations. Finally, red color is used for the cells where for PTM transmission scheme is used.

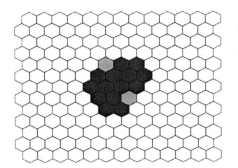
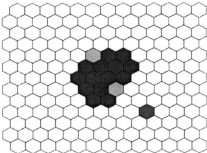

Fig. 6. A random interested UE drop area and the optimal coverage

Fig. 7. A random interested UE drop area with one distant cell and the optimal coverage

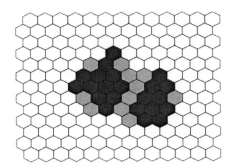
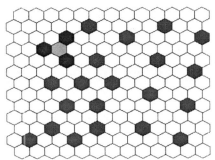

Fig. 8. Two random nearby interested UE drop areas and the optimal coverage

Fig. 9. Scattered interested UE drop cells and the optimal coverage

The first case is the randomly shaped interested UE drop area shown in Fig. 6 with blue cells. The algorithm stabilizes at the proposed coverage, which covers all interested UE drop locations with MBSFN transmissions. Also two cells (light blue) transmit with MBSFN in order to increase the SE of the interested UE drop cells (these are the assisting cells). Both assisting cells fill alcoves in the initial area and therefore adding them to the MBSFN area makes it more rounded. The proposed coverage results in a RE of 1.0766bps/Hz while if we did cover that area with PTM the RE would be 0.4bps/Hz (which is the case for any PTM only coverage).

The second case considers that the majority of the multicast users are located in a set of adjacent cells formulating a primary area, while a small minority roams to a single-cell area. The optimal network configuration is depicted in Fig. 7. The optimization algorithm selects the combination of MBSFN and PTM, which provides a RE of 1.0368bps/Hz.

In third case there are two nearby, randomly shaped, interested UE drop areas. The optimization algorithm selects the network configuration shown in Fig. 8. All interested UE drop locations are covered with MBSFN transmissions and there are a lot of assisting cells especially between the two interested UE drop areas. It is clear that the algorithm tries to make the MBSFN area more rounded and achieves a RE of 0.9999bps/Hz.

In the last case, which is depicted in Fig. 9, we consider the case where the multicast user population is sparsely distributed. In more detail, 23 cells are randomly scattered throughout the LTE network topology. The algorithm selects PTM for the majority of the interested UE drop cells while only the three interested UE drop cells (and the one assisting) at the top left of the grid are covered with MBFSN because of their proximity. The selected configuration achieves a RE slightly above 0.4bps/Hz (specifically 0.4021bps/Hz).

5   Conclusions and Future Work

From our results we concluded that using a combination of MBSFN and PTM yields much higher RE than using any of the other coverage schemes described in this paper. We also concluded that on the contrary of the claims in [7] using even one assisting ring usually lowers the RE of the system. Instead in our experiments, while covering all interested UE drop locations with MBSFN and nothing more than them, yields a RE higher than not using MBSFN at all, adding a few more strategically placed assisting cells can increase the RE even more. In most cases those assisting cells tend to make the MBSFN area more round. In the current release of 3GPP LTE the definition of the MBSFN area is static and operator dependent. Therefore the results of this work can be used by LTE network operators for the definition of the MBSFN area in an optimal way. At a later stage, these results could constitute a basis for dynamic MBSFN area configuration.

In the future the current algorithm could be extended to support more metrics (for example air interface costs), with minimal changes. During our experimentation we found a minor flaw in RE as a metric. Specifically, one would expect that if the optimal coverage scheme for two different interested UE drop areas is known, putting those two areas along with their coverage scheme on the same grid at a big distance (so that there is no interference between the two) would also be optimal. This is not always the case. We observed two cases where the optimal coverage scheme of an area changed when we added another area at a great distance from the first.

The algorithm could also be extended to support more transmission schemes in addition to MBSFN and PTM. Finally replacing the optimization part of the algorithm with a genetic algorithm might be more efficient when optimizing huge network topologies as well as less prone to local optima in the network topology space (the search space).

References

1. Holma, H., Toskala, A.: LTE for UMTS – OFDMA and SC-FDMA based radio access. John Wiley & Sons, Chichester (2009)
2. 3GPP TS 36.300, V9.3.0, Technical specification group radio access network; Evolved universal terrestrial radio access (E-UTRA) and evolved universal terrestrial radio access network (E-UTRAN); Overall description; Stage 2 (Release 9) (2010)
3. 3GPP TS 36.201, V9.0.0, Technical Specification Group Radio Access Network; Evolved Universal Terrestrial Radio Access (E-UTRA); LTE Physical Layer - General Description (Release 9) (2009)
4. 3GPP TS 36.213, V9.1.0, Technical specification group radio access network; Evolved Universal Terrestrial Radio Access; Physical Layer Procedures (Release 9) (2010)
5. Alexiou, A., Bouras, C., Kokkinos, V., Papazois, A., Tsichrintzis, G.: Efficient MCS selection for MBSFN transmissions over LTE networks. In: Proc. IFIP Wireless Days Conference 2010 (WD 2010) (October 2010)
6. Alexiou, A., Bouras, C., Kokkinos, V., Papazois, A., Tsichrintzis, G.: Spectral Efficiency Performance of MBSFN-enabled LTE Networks. In: Proc. of the 6th IEEE International Conference on Wireless and Mobile Computing, Networking and Communications (WiMob 2010), Niagara Falls, Canada, October 11-13 (2010)
7. 3GPP TSG RAN WG1#47-bis R1-070051, Performance of MBMS transmission configurations (2007)
8. Alexiou, A., Bouras, C., Kokkinos, V., Tsichrintzis, G.: Communication Cost Analysis of MBSFN in LTE. In: Proc. of the 21st Annual IEEE International Symposium on Personal, Indoor and Mobile Radio Communications (PIMRC 2010), Istanbul, Turkey (2010)
9. Rummler, R., Chung, Y., Aghvami, H.: Modeling and Analysis of an Efficient Multicast Mechanism for UMTS. IEEE Transactions on Vehicular Technology 54(1), 350–365 (2005)
10. Alexiou, A., Bouras, C.: Multicast in UMTS: Evaluation and Recommendations. International Journal of Wireless Communications and Mobile Computing 8(4), 463–481 (2008)
11. MBSFN / PTM Resource Efficiency Estimation Tool,
    http://ru6.cti.gr/ru6/MBSFN_exe.zip
12. Rong, L., Ben Haddada, O., Elayoubi, S.: Analytical Analysis of the Coverage of a MBSFN OFDMA Network. In: Proc. of IEEE Global Communications Conference (IEEE GLOBECOM 2008), New Orleans, LA, USA, November 30-December 4 (2008)

A Comparative Study of Network Mobility Paradigms

Pedro Vale Pinheiro[1,2], Shivam Jain[3], and Fernando Boavida[2]

[1] Centro de Informática, Universidade de Coimbra, Portugal
[2] Faculdade de Ciências e Tecnologia da Universidade de Coimbra, Portugal
[3] Indian Institute of Technology Roorkee, India
`{Vapi,boavida}@uc.pt, shivam.jain.iitr@gmail.com`

Abstract. Effective solutions for the mobility of whole networks are essential for ubiquitous Internet access. Different network mobility paradigms have different consequences in terms of signalling load, performance and scalability. In this paper, a comparison of three network mobility paradigms is presented, namely the legacy-compatible, the infrastructure-centric and the end-node-centric network mobility paradigms. The study is unprecedented not only because the three paradigms encompass most of the existing network mobility solutions, but also because it involves scenarios with up to 22,800 routers, 11,250 networks, more than 27,000 nodes (fixed and mobile) and up to 16 levels of network mobility nesting. The obtained results point to the very good potential of the end-node-centric network mobility paradigm.

Keywords: network mobility; route optimisation.

1 Introduction

Moving entire networks raises problems that are not trivial, due to the potentially large number of flows involved in such movement. The problem can be considerably more complex in nested scenarios, where mobile networks exist inside other mobile networks.

Several solutions for network mobility have been proposed in the recent past. Despite their differences in detail, they fall into one of three paradigm classes: i) legacy class (LC), with no impact on end-nodes in order to maximize compatibility with legacy networks and nodes; ii) infrastructure-centric class (IC), in which mobile routers take up the management of most of the mobility-related tasks on behalf of the end-nodes, and iii) end-node-centric class (EC), in which end-nodes are aware of their mobility condition and perform most of the mobility functions, making mobility as transparent as possible to the networks.

The NEMO Basic Support Protocol, specified in RFC 3963 [1], belongs to the first paradigm class. NEMO has been developed in order to provide a basic solution for network mobility, having as main requirement complete mobility transparency, that is, requiring no need for any modifications to the nodes.

The well-known limitations of NEMO – of which lack of route optimization is the main one – have led to a whole class of more elaborate network mobility proposals, with the common characteristic that they rely on additional functionality on the part of

X. Masip-Bruin et al. (Eds.): WWIC 2011, LNCS 6649, pp. 68–79, 2011.
© IFIP International Federation for Information Processing 2011

the networking infrastructure (e.g., mobile routers, routers, agents, etc.) which, for instance, take up the burden of performing route optimization on behalf of the mobile nodes they give access to. These proposals – which we collectively designate as infrastructure-centric paradigm – aim at minimal impact on the end-nodes, as opposed to the network.

The third network mobility paradigm is based on mobility awareness on the part of end nodes. In this case, nodes have enough 'intelligence' to know if they are mobile or not and to react accordingly.

Naturally, each of the above-mentioned paradigms has different consequences on the performance, scalability and signalling load of each particular mobility solution. These translate into different behaviour in terms of round trip time, route optimisation time and signalling overhead. In order to clearly identify and assess these consequences, a large-scale comparative study has been performed and the results are presented in this paper.

A clear option to compare paradigms instead of comparing particular network mobility solutions has been made for several reasons. First, it is not practical to compare the large number of specific solutions that exist. Second, the differences between solutions belonging to the same paradigm class are minor and can only have very limited impact on the results. Last, but not least, comparing paradigms provides a more independent and general view on the consequences of architectural choices, as opposed to detailed and often irrelevant views of very particular proposals and/or implementations.

Another important aspect of the presented study is the fact that it has an unprecedented scale. Typically, proposals are accompanied by some form of assessment involving tens of nodes and few networks. In contrast, in the present case we are interested in analyzing the consequences of the mobility paradigms at a very large scale, in generalised mobility environments, such as the one foreseen for the future Internet, in which it is anticipated that a very large percentage of nodes and networks will be mobile.

Before presenting the simulation study, a brief description of the various network mobility paradigms and a comparative analysis are made in section 2. In section 3 the simulation scenarios are detailed, followed by a presentation and discussion of extensive simulation results in section 4. The objective of this discussion is to clearly identify the advantages and drawbacks of each paradigm under study. Section 5 summarises the key findings and identifies guidelines for further work.

2 Network Mobility Paradigms

Network mobility can be achieved by implementations obeying to different architectural approaches or paradigms. The chosen paradigm will impact the effectiveness and efficiency of the actual solution and, thus, it is important to carefully analyse the existing paradigms before generalised, large-scale deployment takes place.

This section provides an overview of existing network mobility paradigms. It also places existing proposals for network mobility in the presented paradigm landscape, thus providing a clear high-level view of relevant work. As the purpose of the paper is to assess and compare paradigms, we will not go into the detail of each particular proposal, as this detail can easily be found in the literature.

2.1 Legacy Paradigm

The idea behind the Legacy-compatible (LC) network mobility paradigm is to readily allow network mobility without the need to change mobile network nodes (MNN) and correspondent nodes (CN). The NEMO Basic Support Protocol [1] is the reference solution for this paradigm.

Whenever a packet destined to the mobile network prefix (MNP) arrives at the home network, a home agent (HA) encapsulates the packet and sends it to the care-of-address (CoA) of the mobile router (MR) over a tunnel (the MRHA tunnel). The MR will then decapsulate the packet and deliver it to the MNN. Conversely, packets from an MNN to a CN are encapsulated, sent from the MR to the HA over the MRHA tunnel, decapsulated at the HA and routed to the CN.

Although extremely simple and fully compatible with legacy devices, the NEMO Basic Support solution suffers from several important problems, such as triangular routing, potential bottleneck in the home network and amplified sub-optimality in nested mobile networks, as thoroughly discussed in [2], [3] and [4]. Virtually all problems affecting the LC paradigm have to do with lack of route optimization.

2.2 Infrastructure-Centric Paradigm

In the case of the infrastructure-centric (IC) network mobility paradigm, most of the tasks inherent to network mobility – with emphasis on route optimisation – are carried out by infrastructure elements, such as mobile routers, home agents and correspondent entities. The main idea behind this paradigm is that end nodes are as unaffected as possible by mobility, at the cost of higher infrastructure complexity. Nevertheless, in contrast with the LC paradigm, changes to correspondent nodes are allowed, in order to support route optimisation.

Route optimisation mechanisms differ, depending on the type of mobile network node. Typically, in the case of local fixed nodes (LFN) and local mobile nodes (LMN), all traffic to/from these nodes must be optimized by some network element, such as a mobile router, a transit router, or a special purpose agent, which, in this context, we will designate MR for simplicity. This means that MRs must keep track of all LFN-CN optimisations and must perform route optimisation, using the return routability mechanism, whenever the mobile network moves. For visiting mobile nodes (VMN), the MR must somehow provide a temporary address to the node and enable that address to be routable inside the moving network. Also, typically, nested networks are treated by MRs as VMNs.

Several network mobility proposals fall into the infrastructure-centric paradigm class. Examples are Optimised Route Cache (ORC) [5] [6], Path Control Header (PCH) [7] [8], Global HA to HA [9] and Mobile IPv6 Router Optimisation for Network Mobility (MIRON) [10] [11] [12].

2.3 End-Node-Centric Paradigm

In the case of the end-node-centric (EC) network mobility paradigm, nodes are aware of their mobility condition. This means that end nodes play an active part in mobility management tasks, such as route optimisation, relieving mobile routers from them.

For this to be possible, when a mobile router acquires a new care-of-address (CoA) it informs its inside network, so that all the mobile network nodes may then use the MR's CoA as their own CoA. From this point onward, mobile nodes decide when to optimise routes and perform optimisation by themselves. On the other hand, mobile routers largely limit their role to plain routing.

Up to the present, only one network mobility proposal uses the EC paradigm. Optimised Mobility for Enhanced Networking (OMEN) was proposed by the authors and first presented in [13]. In addition to detailed description of OMEN, reference [13] also provides preliminary validation and assessment of the proposal, in a limited way and for small-scale scenarios.

Although it is based on an innovative paradigm, OMEN exclusively relies on existing protocols. Instead of creating a new protocol for informing MNNs of their MR's CoA, OMEN uses Neighbor Discovery (RFC4861) [14]. Thus, either as response to a router solicitation message or by its own initiative, an MR can send router advertisement messages that will be used by MNNs to learn their CoA. The CoA will be carried in a new option. As the definition of new options is already accounted for in RFC4861, there is no need to change the protocol. On the other hand, route optimisation uses standard MIPv6 mechanisms.

2.4 Preliminary Analysis

The end-node-centric paradigm eliminates several problems inherent to the legacy and infrastructure-centric paradigms.

One of the issues with the IC paradigm is to decide if and when to perform route optimisation, as it is recognized that not all traffic needs it. In fact, in some cases route optimisation may not be advisable, as the process takes longer than the traffic flow itself, as is the case of DNS traffic.

Another issue is that the load put on mobile routers may be excessive, as all the route optimisation work for all MNNs must be performed by their MR. For small mobile networks this may be acceptable, but in large ones the burden may be too high for mobile routers. Of course, the processing power of router devices has been increasing over the time, but the lighter the mobile router the smaller and the more energy-efficient it can be, and these are important factors when mobility is concerned.

The advantage of the EC paradigm mobility-awareness is that the nodes themselves can take decisions on whether to perform route optimization or not, depending on their needs, and will not be subject to a global, general-purpose, undifferentiated 'route optimisation'. Whenever a node is informed that it is under a mobile network, it can be given all the needed information for it to perform route optimisation, using the existing mechanisms of MIPv6. This, of course, does not preclude legacy nodes from using plain, sub-optimal NEMO Basic Support mechanisms or any other solution that they implement and understand.

The advantage of passing the responsibility of route optimisation to the mobile nodes is that it allows MRs to be extremely light, taking care of network access tasks and MRHA tunnel handling, thus leading to lower complexity and lower processing needs. The price to pay for this approach is very low. LMNs need to be updated, in order for them to take advantage of mobility. VMNs and MRs will also have to perform very few EC-specific tasks. On the other hand, there is no need to change any of the protocols in order to adapt hem to the EC paradigm, as it either uses existing capabilities of existing protocols, or it resorts to local processing in MRs and MNs.

Of course, the potential advantages of the end-node-centric network mobility paradigm may only be apparent and significant in generalised mobility scenarios, such as the one anticipated for the future Internet, where a vast amount of networks and nodes will be mobile. Thus, it is essential to study and compare the behaviour of the three network mobility paradigms in large-scale scenarios, which, naturally, can only be done by simulation due to the necessarily high number of involved networks and nodes. The simulations set up and the results of such study are presented in the following sections.

3   Simulations Setup

The comparison of the LC, IC and EC paradigms in a large-scale scenario was only possible because three critical requirements were met: large processing power, a realistic and flexible network mobility emulation tool capable of running in a parallel processing environment and, last but not least, a set of scenarios suitable for drawing conclusions on the behaviour of the various paradigms under study in terms of round trip time, route optimisation time and signalling overhead. In the next sub-sections we will briefly present the mobility emulator and describe the simulation scenarios. The simulation results are presented and discussed in section 4.

3.1   The Mobsim Network Mobility Emulator

A network mobility emulator tool – named mobSim [15] – was especially built for this study due to the following reasons: 1) the large-scale of the study required the use of a cluster and the tool should be built and optimised for parallel execution; 2) the simulation detail should be as high as possible, ranging from protocol fields implementation to high-level mobility mechanisms and allowing for a configuration granularity ranging from individual hosts to routers, networks and global scenarios; 3) total flexibility to define the simulation scenarios, from the global dynamic behaviour to topologies, with any mix of mobile and fixed networks and nodes, any number of networks and any number of levels of nested mobility; 4) ability to perform any simulation using the exact same parameters, conditions and settings for the three paradigms under study.

Table 1 presents the standard functionality implemented by mobSim. This functionality is used to construct generic implementations of the paradigms under study. It should be noted that mobSim actually implements the specified mechanisms down to packet field level, and that all messages are actually generated and sent between emulated devices, thus maximising the fidelity of the tool. Configurable delays include the time for data link layer handoff, the time needed for acquiring a new IP address (through DHCP), the binding update procedure time, the binding acknowledgement procedure time, line speed, HoTi time, CoTi time, HoT time, CoT time, encapsulation and decapsulation times.

Table 1. mobSim standard functionality

IPv6 basic support (RFC 2460	MIPv6 (RFC 3775)
Hop limit	Binding update
Next Next header implementations	Binding acknowledgement (binding accept,
ICMPv6 (RFC4443)	reject)
ICMP echo, reply, unreachable,	Return routablity procedure
time exceeded	Home test init (HoTi)
IPv6 encapsulation (RFC2473)	Care-of test init (CoTi)
Mobility Header (RFC3775)	Home test (HoT)
Type 2 routing header	Care-of test (CoT)
Home address option (specific for T2RH)	Nonce utilisation (RFC3775 section 5.2.2)
	Binding refresh

Neighbor Discovery (RFC 4861)	NEMO basic support (RFC 3963)
Router advertisement	Bidireccional tunnel (MRHA tunnel)
Router solicitation	Binding update
	Binding acknowledgement
	Home agent implementation
	Mobile router implementation

The LC paradigm implementation closely follows the NEMO basic support specification (RFC 3963). In the case of the IC paradigm implementation, mobility functions – including route optimisation – are performed by mobile routers, on behalf of mobile nodes. The actual approach is a mix of the most important features of the proposals in [5] and [12]. In the case of the EC paradigm implementation, mobility functions are carried out by end-nodes, closely following the specification presented in [13].

3.2 Simulation Scenarios

Fig. 1 presents the base topology of the overall network used in all simulation scenarios. This base topology is made up of fixed and mobile networks, and can change in the course of a simulation, as mobile networks change their point of attachment, in non-nested and/or nested configurations. For simplicity, networks are represented by their border router only. Moreover, end-nodes are not depicted.

The overall network consists of a tree-like structure with seven levels. This organisation was chosen due to its natural ability to model network mobility nesting in the mobile part of the network, as well as different path lengths in the fixed part of the network. Level 1 of the hierarchy comprises 50 routers. Every level 1 router is directly connected to the other 49 level 1 routers. Each of these routers is connected to 5 level 2 routers. In turn, each level 2 router is connected to 3 level 3 routers, and so on, according to the diagram shown in Fig. 1. With this configuration, there are 456 routers under each level 1 router. In addition, the number of end-nodes under each level 1 router was configured to be between 225 and nearly 54,000. In total, the simulated network had 22,800 routers, 11,250 networks, and more than 27,000 end nodes (fixed and mobile).

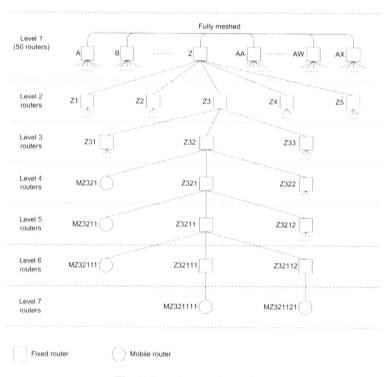

Fig. 1. Overall network topology

Seventeen simulation scenarios were used. For scenario 1, no mobile nesting was used, i.e., all mobile networks were directly connected to fixed networks. For scenarios 2 to 17, one to sixteen levels of nesting (i.e., mobile networks inside mobile networks) were used, respectively. In all scenarios, up to 1,000 mobile nodes could be transmitting and/or receiving packets at the same time, although, in the course of the simulation runs, all mobile nodes were active at some point in time. Each mobile node transmitted a total of around 140 packets. The exact same conditions and settings were used for each of the paradigms under study.

In addition to the above, several delay parameters were used for all simulations, aiming to represent the time taken to perform the various actions associated with mobility procedures (e.g., table look up and update, security verifications, etc.). The chosen values are an approximation of actual values measured in a lab implementation, and were the following: DHCP delay – 300 ms; Return Routability delay – 200 ms; HoTi, CoTi, HoT or CoT messages processing delay – 100 ms; MAC-layer handoff delay – 500 ms; MR-HA tunnel setup delay – 10 ms; BU or BA messages processing delay – 10 ms.

Another important aspect of the simulations was that, for the EC paradigm, different ratios of number of nodes not performing route optimisation and number of nodes performing it were used. For instance, a ratio of 1:2 means that for each node not performing route optimisation two other nodes perform it. On the other hand, by design, in the case of the IC paradigm, route optimisation is performed for all nodes, whether their traffic requires it or not. This, of course, has influence in the performance of the mobile routers and on the amount of necessary signalling.

Finally, it is important to note that the objective of all simulations was to obtain results that could clearly show the impact of each paradigm on networks and routers. This impact can only be measured if no other factors distort the results. This is why all scenarios assumed unloaded networks. Naturally, if a given paradigm has poorer performance than another in an unloaded network, its behaviour will be even worse in networks with background traffic for which, possibly, some links will have little available capacity and some network elements will be overloaded. Moreover, there was no intention to perform stress tests to the various paradigms under study, in order to identify their limits and, thus, the number of packets transmitted per node was relatively low. Stress tests will be performed in future work.

4   Simulation Results

Several simulation sets were run, each with a particular feature in mind, namely the effect of each paradigm on the average round-trip time (RTT), average route optimisation time and signalling overhead. The following sub-sections present and discuss the results of each set in detail

4.1   Average Round-Trip Time

This set comprised a considerable number of simulations, each for each of the paradigms under study and for each scenario (1 to 17). In addition, each simulation was run for the following ratios of nodes not performing route optimisation and nodes performing route optimisation: 1:1, 1:2, 1:10, 1:100 and 1:1000. Fig. 2 presents the results for the 1:10 ratio.

It is possible to see that, as expected, the average round-trip time increases with the level of nesting for the case of the LC paradigm – as opposed to the case of the IC and EC paradigms – as in the LC paradigm there is no route optimization: as the level of nesting increases so increases the number of tunnels inside tunnels and, consequently, the number of networks that have to be traversed by the packets in order to reach the destination. Note that, for visibility purposes, the maximum value in Fig. 2 is cut at 2 seconds, although the LC RTT values go up to 23.4 seconds.

Fig. 3 presents the evolution of the average RTT, for three levels of nested mobile networks, as the number of nodes performing route optimization increases, according to the ratios 1:1, 1:2, 1:10, 1:100 and 1:1000.

As the number of nodes requiring optimization increases, the EC paradigm gets better than the IC paradigm in terms of RTT. The reason is that the impact on MRs gets lower and lower in the case of the EC paradigm as MRs simply become routing devices, as opposed to the case of the IC paradigm, for which MRs have to perform all routing optimization operations for all nodes. This extra load on mobile routers leads to poorer IC RTT in all cases, except in the 1:1 case, for which the EC RTT is worse due to the fact that half of the packets do not follow an optimal path, as opposed to the IC case where all packets follow optimal paths.

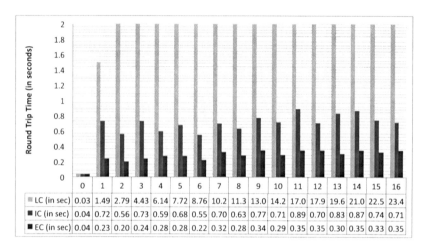

	0	1	2	3	4	5	6	7	8	9	10	11	12	13	14	15	16
LC (in sec)	0.03	1.49	2.79	4.43	6.14	7.72	8.76	10.2	11.3	13.0	14.2	17.0	17.9	19.6	21.0	22.5	23.4
IC (in sec)	0.04	0.72	0.56	0.73	0.59	0.68	0.55	0.70	0.63	0.77	0.71	0.89	0.70	0.83	0.87	0.74	0.71
EC (in sec)	0.04	0.23	0.20	0.24	0.28	0.28	0.22	0.32	0.28	0.34	0.29	0.35	0.35	0.30	0.35	0.33	0.35

Fig. 2. Average RTT, for the three paradigms, all scenarios and optimization ratio of 1:10

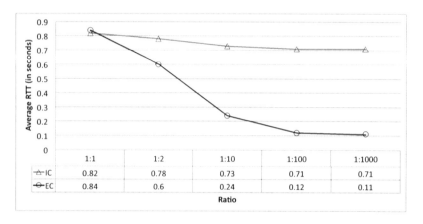

	1:1	1:2	1:10	1:100	1:1000
IC	0.82	0.78	0.73	0.71	0.71
EC	0.84	0.6	0.24	0.12	0.11

Fig. 3. Average RTT for three levels of nested mobile networks and different route optimization ratios

4.2 Average Route Optimisation Time

The second batch of simulations aimed at determining the average route optimisation time as a function of the number of nodes requiring it. Fig. 4 presents this evolution, for up to 51 nodes.

It is apparent that, as more nodes requiring route optimisation are present, the average route optimisation time increases steadily in the case of the IC paradigm and remains more or less constant in the case of the EC paradigm. This is due to the fact that in the case of the IC paradigm the mobile routers' processing load is higher, as all the tasks concerning route optimisation are performed by these network elements, as opposed to the EC paradigm, for which route optimisation tasks are performed by the end-nodes themselves.

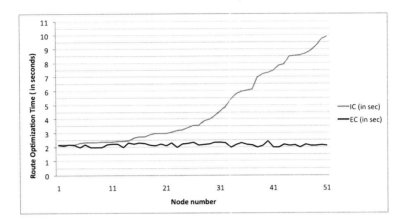

Fig. 4. Average time for route optimization, as a function of the number of nodes requiring it

4.3 Signalling Overhead

The final set of simulations addressed the issue of signalling overhead, resulting from the transmission of HoTi, CoTi, HoT, CoT, BU and BA messages, according to RFC 3775, during route optimisation processes. Signalling overhead increases with the number of moves of mobile routers and with the number of route optimisation operations.

Fig. 5 presents the signalling overhead for a scenario in which the point of attachment of a mobile router was changed 5 times, for different optimisation ratios. As can be seen, the simulation results clearly confirm that the signalling overhead of the EC paradigm is always lower than the one for the IC paradigm, due to the fact that IC performs route optimisation for all nodes, regardless their need for route optimisation. As the percentage of nodes requiring route optimisation increases, the signalling overhead of the EC paradigm approaches that of the IC paradigm.

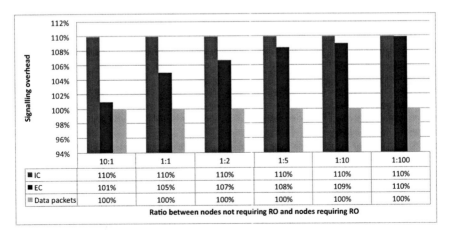

Fig. 5. Signalling overhead for 5 moves and for different optimization ratios

5   Conclusion

We have presented a comparison of three network mobility paradigms – the legacy-compatible paradigm, the infrastructure-centric paradigm, and the end-node-centric paradigm – that span the existing solutions for network mobility. The comparison targeted a very large scenario, having in mind generalised mobility environments anticipated for the future Internet.

The obtained simulation results clearly point to several conclusions. The first conclusion is that the legacy paradigm has several performance limitations and, consequently, will hardly scale. Clearly, this paradigm was developed for allowing network mobility despite the presence of legacy nodes.

The simulation results concerning the infrastructure-centric paradigm clearly show that the concentration of functionality in network elements affects the overall performance of these elements and, consequently, the quality characteristics of end-to-end communication.

On the other hand, the performed simulations have clearly shown that the end-node-centric paradigm has very good potential and should be explored in the future. By relieving mobile routers and other infrastructure elements from several mobility tasks, significant benefit can be achieved in terms of round trip time, route optimisation time and signalling overhead. All simulation results confirmed this.

The presented comparative study opens up a large field for further research. Naturally, stress tests to the paradigms can be performed. The study of their behaviour under different network loads will surely be carried out in the near future. Last but not least, the implementation and detailed study of an end-node-centric network mobility solution – as a follow up of the preliminary solution proposed in [13] – is a natural step.

Acknowledgments. This work was partially financed by project PTDC/EIA-EIA/116173/2009 (CoFiMoM) of the Portuguese Foundation for Science and Technology (FCT) and the Centre for Informatics and Systems of the University of Coimbra (CISUC). The authors would also like to thank Pedro Vieira Alberto, Luis Pinto and Pedro Almeida, from the Laboratory of Advanced Computing (LCA) of the University of Coimbra, for providing access the Milipeia cluster, without which this work would not have been possible.

References

1. Devarapalli, V., et al.: Network Mobility (NEMO) Basic Support Protocol. RFC 3963, Internet Engineering Task Force (January 2005)
2. Ng, C.-W., et al.: Network Mobility Route Optimization Problem Statement, draft-ietf-nemo-ro-problem-statement-03, Internet Engineering Task Force (September 2006)
3. Ng, C.-W., et al.: Network Mobility Route Optimization Solution Space Analysis, draft-ietf-nemo-ro-space-analysis-03, Internet Engineering Task Force (September 2006)
4. Bernardos, C.J., et al.: NEMO: Network Mobility in IPv6. Upgrade IV(2) (April 2005)
5. Wakikawa, R., et al.: Optimized Route Cache Protocol (ORC), draft-wakikawa-nemo-orc-01, work in progress, Internet Engineering Task Force (November 2004)

6. Wakikawa, R., et al.: ORC: Optimized Route Cache Management Protocol for Network Mobility. In: 10th International Conference on Telecommunications, vol. 2, pp. 1194–1200 (February 2003)
7. Na, J., et al.: Route Optimization Scheme based on Path Control Header, draft-na-nemo-path-control-header-00, work in progress, Internet Engineering Task Force (April 2004)
8. Jonkeun Na, Seoul National University, Supporting Route Optimization in Network MObility (NEMO) (September 2004)
9. Thubert, P., et al.: Global HA to HA protocol., draft-thubert-nemo-global-haha-01.txt, work in progress, Internet Engineering Task Force (October 2005)
10. Bernardos, C., et al.: MIRON: MIPv6 Route Optimization for NEMO. In: 4th Workshop on Applications and Services in Wireless Network (August 2004)
11. Bernardos, C., et al.: Mobile IPv6 Route Optimisation for Network Mobility (MIRON), draft-bernardos-nemo-miron-00, work in progress, Internet Engineering Task Force (July 2005)
12. Bernardos, C.: Route Optimisation for Mobile Networks in IPv6 Heterogeneous Environments. PhD thesis, Universidad Carlos III de Madrid, Spain (September 2006)
13. Pinheiro, P.V., Boavida, F.: OMEN – A New Paradigm for Optimal Network Mobility. In: Harju, J., Heijenk, G., Langendörfer, P., Siris, V.A. (eds.) WWIC 2008. LNCS, vol. 5031, pp. 115–126. Springer, Heidelberg (2008)
14. Narten, T., et al.: Neighbor Discovery for IP version 6 (IPv6). RFC 4861, Internet Engineering Task Force (September 2007)
15. Pinheiro, P.V., Boavida, F.: mobSim – A Network Mobility Simulation Tool for Very Large-Scale Scenarios. In: Proceedings of NTMS 2011 - 4th IFIP International Conference on New Technologies, Mobility and Security, Paris, France, February 7-10 (2011)

Comparison of Wireless Network Simulators with Multihop Wireless Network Testbed in Corridor Environment

Rabiullah Khattak, Anna Chaltseva, Laurynas Riliskis, Ulf Bodin, and Evgeny Osipov

Department of Computer Science Electrical and Space Engineering
Luleå University of Technology,
971 87 Luleå, Sweden
Rabiullah.Khattak@ltu.se

Abstract. This paper presents a comparative study between results of a single channel multihop wireless network testbed and the network simulators ns-2 and ns-3. We explore how well these simulators reflect reality with their standard empirical radio modeling capabilities. The environment studied is a corridor causing wave-guiding propagation phenomena of radio waves, which challenges the radio models used in the simulators. We find that simulations are roughly matching with testbed results for single flows, but clearly deviate from testbed results for concurrent flows. The mismatch between simulations and testbed results is due to imperfect wireless propagation channel modeling. This paper reveals the importance of validating simulation results when studying single channel multihop wireless network performance. It further emphasizes the need for validation when using empirical radio modeling for more complex environments such as corridors.

1 Introduction

Nowadays most of the research in the field of wireless networking is based on network simulators. Simulators are attractive for researching network protocols and mechanisms since they allow creating controlled and reproducible environments. Creating such an environments in real test beds is both expensive and time consuming. Real production networks at the same time often do not allow to obtain repeatable data sets needed for research analysis. Various network settings and large parameter ranges can be tested through simulations at low effort since creation and modification of network scenarios as well as data gathering are easy.

In this paper we study how well simulations reflect the reality with commonly used empirical models of wireless propagation channel that requires little configuration and are memory and computationally sparse. In particular, we explore disparities between simulations in ns2[1] and ns3[2] and testbed results for a multihop wireless network located in a corridor. This environment challenges the wireless propagation channel model present in the network simulators.

---

[1] ns-2 NetworkSimulator. Online. Available: http://www.isi.edu/nsnam/ns/
[2] ns-3 Network Simulator. Online. Available: http://www.nsnam.org

X. Masip-Bruin et al. (Eds.): WWIC 2011, LNCS 6649, pp. 80–91, 2011.

The performance of network protocols in a testbed is affected by wireless channel properties that depend on the physical environment, location and mobility of the nodes, and the external interference. Accurate wireless channel modeling for simulations is known to be difficult. The commonly used wireless propagation channel for path loss in simulators is empirically modeled, and path loss is computed depending on distance between transmitter and receiver. Consequently, accumulative interference caused by hidden terminals' concurrent transmissions, and spatial reuse ratios of testbed network may not be correctly represented by the simulators. Due to these reasons simulation results often do not match perfectly with the testbed results [2, 5].

The modeling of wave-guiding propagation phenomena of radio waves in corridors as well as modeling of the losses caused by reflections, diffraction and scattering of radio waves are more accurately captured by deterministic channel modeling methods [7]. The deterministic wireless channel modeling, e.g based on ray tracing techniques require the exact knowledge of location, shape, dielectric and conductive properties of all objects in the environments and it also requires extensive computational efforts for accuracy. Thus such models are site specific. In addition these models also considerably increase simulations' run time [12].

The aim of our paper is to make the wireless network researchers aware of the differences of the simulations from real wireless testbed. The differences are mainly caused by empirically modeled wireless propagation channel of the simulators. Empirical wireless propagation channel models of the simulators are simple from implementation perspective but they do not cover all the properties of the wireless propagation channel such as losses due to reflections, diffraction, scattering and penetration of the radio waves. We demonstrate the differences between simulations and testbed for two specific scenarios composed of single and concurrent flows transmissions over a single multihop path.

We find that for single flow transmissions over multiple radio links, ns2 and ns3 simulations roughly match the testbed results. Deviations between simulations and the testbed results are explained by the wireless propagation channel models used in the simulations are not accurately reflecting the accumulative interference caused by hidden terminals' concurrent transmissions and the spatial reuse ratio[3] of the testbed network. This shortcoming of the wireless propagation channel model becomes more evident for simultaneous flows transmissions, which have higher strength of accumulative interference than single flow. Simulations indicate considerably worse matching of the throughput fairness of simultaneous flows with testbed results, which reveals that the wireless propagation channel models of the simulators are not correctly representing the wireless channel properties in the corridors.

The article is organized as follows. Section II presents a brief overview of the background and related works. Section III presents the details and specifications of the testbed network and experiments. Section IV gives the details of the simulation setup and also provides an overview of path loss and multipath fading models. Section V presents the comparison of the experimental results with simulations. Section VI concludes this comparative study.

---

[3] Spatial reuse ratio is the total number of concurrent transmissions accommodated in network.

2   Background and Related Work

Network simulators ns-2 and ns-3 are de-facto standard simulation tools in the academic networking research community. Simulations in ns-2 are constructed with C++ code and OTcl scripts; the former provides modeling of applications, simulation nodes, communication channels and other mechanisms involved in networking, while the latter is used to control simulations and define additional features, for example the network topology.

Simulations in ns-3 are fully based on C++, but can also be created with Python. The ns-3 simulator was developed from scratch and cannot directly use the code developed for ns2. Many objects are ported from ns-2 to ns-3 but not all, and hence ns-2 incorporate capabilities not present in ns-3. However, ns-3 has capabilities not implemented in ns-2 such as support for multiple interfaces on nodes, use of IP addressing and closer resemblance with the TCP/IP model, and more detailed 802.11a/b/s models.

The accuracy of wireless channel models for simulations naturally determines the quality of the outcome. It could be expected that the more detailed modeling of the IEEE 802.11 MAC protocol in ns-3 would result in more accurate results for certain network scenarios. Obviously it is expected that the simulations results may deviate from the reality. It is therefore important to understand the degree of reality reflection by the simulators.

Other studies presenting comparisons between simulations of IEEE 802.11 based networks and testbeds include [9], which presents a comparative study between an IEEE 802.11a based testbed and three network simulators (ns-2, QualNet and OPNET). It aims to assess the relevance of these simulators in indoor and outdoor environments. The simulation results match to some extent with the testbed. The authors highlight that tuning of physical layer parameters and selected propagation models have great impact on the results. This study is conducted for a single hop network and no comparison with ns-3 simulations is presented.

In [1] the authors present a validation study of the IEEE 802.11b MAC model in ns-3 by comparing simulations with testbed results. The study shows that ns-3 simulations nearly match with reality after proper tuning of the devices in the testbed. It is also shown that for mismatching between the simulation and testbed results, simulator is not always wrong but specific selection and configuration of the devices in the testbed can be culprit. However, in the testbed wireless channel propagation effects on measurements are ignored because the communication between the devices is via coaxial cables.

The authors in [14] point out the disparities between a wireless network tesbed and ns-2 and Qualnet. The disparities are explored based on antenna diversity, path loss, multihop, transmission rate, interference and routing stability. However, ns-3 simulations have not been taken into account and intra-path interference[4] is discussed only for a single flow traffic over a linear multihop network.

3   Testbed and Experiments Description

We built an IEEE802.11b based multihop wireless testbed in an indoor corridor environment. The network consists of eight nodes placed as illustrated in Fig. 1. The logical

---

[4] Interference between the packets of the same end-to-end flow due to hidden terminals.

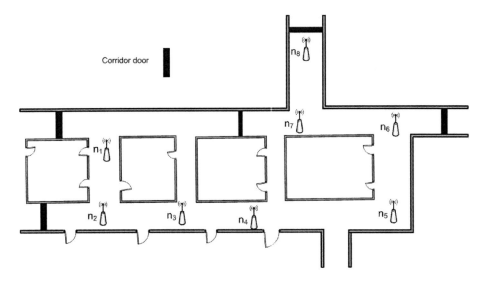

Fig. 1. Testbed: Layout of nodes in corridors

topology is a chain, the placement of nodes ensures the line-of-sight communications with the immediate neighbors. All nodes are Intel Pentium 4 based desktop PCs with 2.40 GHz processor, cache size 512 KB, RAM memory 256 MB and six USB 1.0 ports supporting the data transfer rate of 12 Mb/s.

For wireless connectivity each node is equipped with D-Link DWL-G122 wireless USB adapter[5] with an omni-directional antenna. The operating system is Linux (kernel 2.6.29) and the WLAN driver is p54[6]. At the MAC layer we switched off the options for frame fragmentation, dynamic rate adaption and disabled the RTS/CTS exchange. The transceivers operate on channel 3, the transmit power at each node was set to 18dBm, the physical channel data rate is set to 11Mb/s.

We experimented with TCP traffic generated by Iperf (version 2.0.8) traffic generator. We used TCP-Cubic configured with the default settings. The routes were configured statically in order to eliminate the effect of routing protocols on network performance [8].

In the testbed we conducted two types of experiments. The first experiment (further on referred to as *experiment-1*) was performed with a single flow running over a different number of hops. The second experiment (further on referred to as *experiment-2*) was conducted with multiple TCP flows running concurrently over different number of hops. To obtain the results from both experiments, we used tcpdump (version 3.9.8) to capture all the traffic generated in the network and measure the per-flow throughput.

The setup for experiment-1 is shown in Fig. 2(a). The experiment consists of seven scenarios with different number of wireless hops for the monitored flow. In order to

---

[5] DWL-G122 High Speed 2.4GHz (802.11g) Wireless USB Adapter. Online. Available: http://www.dlink.com/products/?pid=334

[6] Online. Available: http://linuxwireless.org/en/users/Drivers/p54

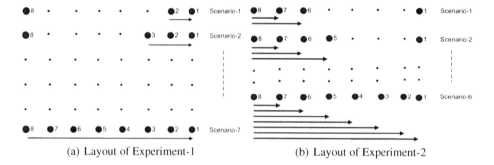

Fig. 2. Setup of experiments in the testbed

capture the effects of multipath fading and the accumulative interference on the network performance each scenario was repeated six times by changing the position of the
source and destination node along the multihop chain for a given number of hops. The
duration of each trial is three minutes.

In experiment-2 (see Fig. 2(b)) the layout of the nodes and the network specification
had been kept the same as in experiment-1. The experiment consists of six scenarios.
In all scenarios the traffic is alway generated from node 8. We start experimenting with
two flows of one and two hops running in parallel. In each subsequent scenario we add
flows as shown in the figure. As a result in the sixth scenario we experiment with seven
concurrent TCP flows. We perform two trials for each scenario and record an average
value of the per-flow throughput. The duration of each experiment is two minutes. The
throughput values are used to compute a fairness index as explained below.

4   Simulation Setup

We replicate the testbed experiments in ns-2 and ns-3 simulators. Firstly, we configure the parameters of the simulators with the corresponding values in the testbed. In
particular, the transmission power, characteristics of the antenna and the corresponding
transmission ranges are set according to the specification of the D-Link DWL-G122
wireless USB adapter. According to the device's data sheet the transmission range is set
to 100 m. According to [11] the carrier sensing range in commercial wireless cards is
twice or more than the transmission range.

On the transport layer we used TCP-Cubic as in the testbed experiments. Note that
while the implementation of TCP-Cubic in ns-2 is a simulator-specific, ns3- links the
real implementation from Linux via the Network Simulator Cradle (NCS).

Special attention was paid to the proper configuration of the path loss and multipath
fading models in order to reflect the radio environment of the testbed. In the indoor environment, the propagation of radio waves is mainly affected by two types of losses: the
path loss and the loss due to small and large scale fading. The small scale fading arises

due to the multipath propagation effect and the large scale fading is due to the shadow-ing effect. The model which closely reflects the path loss in the indoor environment is the log-distance path loss model [10]:

$$L_p = L_0 + 10n \log_{10} \frac{d}{d_0} + X_\theta. \tag{1}$$

In (1) n is the path loss distance exponent, d_0 is the reference distance (1 m), d is the distance in meters between the transmitting and the receiving nodes, L_0 is the reference path loss at the reference distance (dB), L_p is the path loss (dB) and X_θ is a log-normally distributed random variable (dB) with standard deviation σ and zero mean describing the attenuation caused by the obstacles due to shadowing effect.

Note that the value of n depends on the operating frequency and the characteristics of the propagation environment. In the case of the indoor environment, the type of the construction material and the position of the nodes within the building. In corridors due to wave-guiding propagation phenomena of radio waves, n takes values in the range $[1.3, 1.9]$ at 2.4 GHz [3, 6]. From Friis propagation loss model $L_0 = 20 \log_{10} \frac{4\pi d_0}{\lambda}$ where λ is the wave length in meters.

Note that in our testbed there is no large scale fading due to line-of-sight communi-cation between the adjacent nodes, therefore, $X_\theta = 0$ and (1) reduces to

$$L_p = L_0 + 10n \log_{10} \frac{d}{d_0}. \tag{2}$$

However, the small scale fading exists in the corridors due to multipath propagation. In corridors the small scale fading is described by Nakagami distribution [15, 13]. The probability density function for the Nakagami m-distribution is

$$pdf_r = \frac{2}{\Gamma(m)} \left(\frac{m}{\omega}\right)^m r^{2m-1} \exp\left(-\frac{m}{\omega} r^2\right) \qquad . \tag{3}$$

In (3) $r \geq 0$ is the amplitude of the received signal, $\Gamma(m)$ is the Euler's Gamma function, $\omega = \bar{r}^2$ is the mean square received power and $m = \frac{\omega^2}{(r^2 - \omega)^2}$ is the fading depth, where $m \geq 1/2$. For $m = 1$, the Nakagami m-distribution becomes Rayleigh distribution.

In ns-3 the log-distance path loss and Nakagami fading models are implemented sep-arately. Both models can be used and configured individually. In ns-2 the log-distance path loss model is not yet implemented, however, the Nakagami fading model is imple-mented together with three-log-distance path loss model. The three-log-distance path loss model of ns-2 is different from the log-distance path loss model with three distance fields namely near, middle and far. Each field has different path loss exponent. For the three-log-distance model a fourth distance field is also defined from 0 to near distance, however, the loss over this field is zero. The limits of four distance fields along with their corresponding path loss exponents are explained as

$$\underbrace{0 \cdots\cdots d_0}_{0} \underbrace{\cdots\cdots d_1}_{n_0} \underbrace{\cdots\cdots d_2}_{n_1} \underbrace{\cdots\cdots \infty}_{n_2}$$

So each field starts at the end of the preceding one and hence the resultant three-log-distance path loss model is a continuous function of the distance:

$$
L_p = \begin{cases}
0 & d \leq d_0 \\
L_0 + 10n_0 \log_{10} \frac{d}{d_0} & d_0 \leq d < d_1 \\
L_0 + 10n_0 \log_{10} \frac{d_1}{d_0} + 10n_1 \log_{10} \frac{d}{d_1} & d_1 \leq d < d_2 \\
L_0 + 10n_0 \log_{10} \frac{d_1}{d_0} + 10n_1 \log_{10} \frac{d_2}{d_1} + 10n_2 \log_{10} \frac{d}{d_2} & d_2 \leq d.
\end{cases}
\tag{4}
$$

In (4) n_0, n_1, n_2 are the path loss distance exponents and d_0, d_1, d_2 are three distance fields(meter). The Nakagami fading model in ns-2 defines three parameters m for three distance fields as

$$
\underbrace{0 \cdots\cdots}_{m_0} \underbrace{d_1 \cdots\cdots}_{m_1} \underbrace{d_2 \cdots\cdots}_{m_2} \infty
$$

The defaults values of distances and fading parameters m in ns-2 are $d_1 = 80$ meter, $d_2 = 200$ meter, $m_0 = 1.5$ and $m_1 = m_2 = 0.75$. In the testbed the maximum distance between the adjacent nodes per hop is less than 80 meter, so ns-2 is using log-distance path loss model part of (4).

In order to find a better match of the path loss and multipath fading with the real testbed the simulations are conducted for five combinations of the path loss exponent $n = 1.9$ and five Nakagami fading parameters m i.e. 1.5, 1.75, 2.0, 2.25 and 2.50. Note that doing simulations with higher values of the fading parameter m is not realistic because the higher m means stronger LOS component of the propagation model. This is not the case with the D-Link devices used in the testbed, which are equipped with omni-directional antennas. The next section report the results of the analysis.

5   Comparative Analysis

5.1   Experiment-1: Testbed vs. Simulations

Fig. 3(a) and Fig. 3(b) show ns-3 and ns-2 simulations of experiment-1 along with corresponding testbed results of experiment-1. As expected the TCP throughput decreases with increasing number of hops. This is because of the increase in accumulative interference due to hidden terminal problem and the decrease in spatial reuse ratio of the network due to the exposed terminal problem.

In case of testbed results, the most severe effect of accumulative interference and lower spatial reuse ratio on the throughput is observed in the five hops scenario. This severe effect is due to the specific positions of the hidden and exposed terminals in the connected corridors. It is, however, observed that the throughput of the six hops is higher than that of the five hops due to its higher spatial reuse ratio and hence lower effect of the accumulative interference. Similarly the seven hops has higher throughput as compared to both six and five hops because of its further higher spatial reuse ratio. The higher spatial reuse ratios in the six and seven hops scenarios are attained due to the specific positions of the nodes in the corridors.

Fig. 3(a) shows that ns-3 simulated results are matching with the results from the testbed in the single hop scenario for fading parameter $m = 2.0$ while diverging in

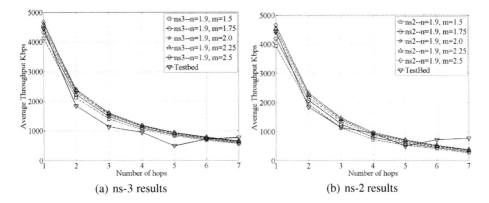

Fig. 3. TCP throughput in experiment-1 versus ns-3 and ns-2 results for path loss exponent $n = 1.9$ and different Nakagami parameters m

all other scenarios except for the six hops scenario. There the simulation results of all fading parameters m are almost identical with the testbed results. Fig. 3(b) shows that for the single hop scenario the ns-2 simulation results are almost identical with that of the testbed for fading parameter $m = 2.0$. The figure shows that ns-2 simulated results in three and four hops scenarios are matching with the testbed for various fading parameters m. Notably, simulations of ns-2 and ns-3 fail to reflect the higher spatial reuse ratio behavior of the six and seven hops than five hops like the testbed.

The simulation results from both ns-2 and ns-3 show that none of the fading parameters m has a persistent match with the testbed results in all multihop scenarios. We also observe that in contrast to ns-3, the ns-2 simulations have a closer match with the testbed results except for six and seven hops cases, where ns-2 results are diverging from the testbed larger than ns-3. It is observed as well that the throughput of a single hop TCP flow is higher in the testbed than the simulated results for certain values of fading parameter m. This is due to wave-guiding signal propagation phenomena not correctly captured by the propagation models in the simulators. It is, therefore, hard to conclude which of the two simulators closer reflect the reality except for stating that both simulators give a rough match of the testbed results.

5.2 Experiment-2: Testbed vs. Simulations

In experiment-2, from the simulations of each simulator, we are getting five plots for the average throughputs (over all scenarios) for five Nakagami parameters. So for sake of simplicity of explanation and limitation of pages of the article, we present comparison of the results with a concise performance metric call throughput fairness index. We find that fairness index behaviours of both the simulators are quite different from the testbed, which implies that average throughputs behaviours of simultaneous flows of simulations are also different from those of experiment-2 of the testbed. The details of the throughput fairness index are given as follows.

In experiment-2 we compared the performance of the simulators with the testbed using Jain fairness index f_s (5). The index takes values between 0 and 1. In (5) $X_i^{(s)}$ is the network's throughput share obtained by i^{th} flow and s is the number of simultaneous flows.

$$f_s = \frac{\left(\sum_{i=1}^{s} X_i^{(s)}\right)^2}{s \sum_{i=1}^{s} (X_i^{(s)})^2}. \tag{5}$$

In order to use the index in the case of flows with unequal characteristics we have to relate the actual measured throughput with a throughput share of the flow under ideal sharing condition [4]. Therefore, $X_i^{(s)}$ is computed as in (6). There $a_i^{(s)}$ is the actual throughput of the ith flow measured in simulations and in the testbed and $d_k^{(s)} = \frac{T_k}{s}$ is the throughput share under ideal sharing conditions over k hops. It is computed by dividing the throughput T_k of a single flow over k hops measured in experiment-1 by s.

$$X_i^{(s)} = \begin{cases} \frac{a_i^{(s)}}{d_k^{(s)}} & \text{if } a_i^{(s)} < d_k^{(s)} \\ 1 & \text{otherwise} \end{cases} \tag{6}$$

As we observe from Fig. 4(a) and Fig. 4(b) the fairness indices obtained from the ns-2 and ns-3 simulators have opposite trends for different values of simultaneous flows and the number of hops. It is observed from ns-3 simulations in the Fig. 4(a) that the fairness index is decreasing in scenarios one to four. The lowest fairness indices are observed in scenarios five, six and seven for certain values of fading parameters m. Like in the testbed, ns3 simulations of scenarios five and greater show an increasing trends in the fairness indices for different fading parameters. Clearly the fairness index obtained from ns3 simulations is lower than the one in the testbed for all values of the fading parameters. It is however worth pointing out that the overall behavior of the index for Nakagami parameters $m = 1.5$ and $m = 1.75$ matches the index's behavior in the testbed in scenarios three to seven.

Looking at the results from ns-2 simulations in Fig. 4(b) we observe that the fairness indices increase with increasing number of simultaneous flows and hops. In scenario three the fairness index in simulations matches exactly the values in the testbed. Although the absolute values of the index obtained from ns-2 do not significantly deviate from the measured in the testbed, however the overall development of the index is different from testbed.

It is to be noted that wave-guiding propagation phenomena of radio waves in the testbed are present in both single and simultaneous flow scenarios. However, in the simultaneous flow scenarios the probability of concurrent transmissions along the multihop path is higher than single flow scenarios. This results in higher value of the accumulative interference in experiment-2. We know that wave-guiding propagation phenomena of radio waves reduce the signal strength loss as compared to common radio waves propagation in space. So due to wave-guiding propagation, the accumulative interference has higher range to affect the desired reception of the signal along the multihop path. Hence the deviations of the simulations of simultaneous flow scenarios from testbed are larger than single flow scenarios.

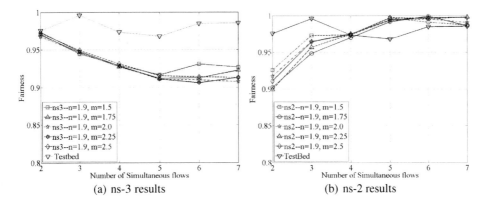

Fig. 4. Jain fairness index in experiment-2 versus ns-3 and ns-2 results for path loss exponent $n = 1.9$ and different Nakagami parameters m

Overall, as in the case with experiment-1 none of the simulators was able to exactly reproduce the performance of the testbed. Partially it depends on simulator specific implementation of protocols on MAC and (or) Transport layers. ns-2, for example, uses own implementation of TCP-Cubic congestion control. We however observe a better match of the network behavior produced by ns-3 simulator which uses native Linux implementation of TCP. The major problem in our opinion comes however from inability of the simulator's propagation models to capture all signal impairments mechanisms in the particular communication environment. The corridor environment of the tesbed exposes strong wave-guiding propagation phenomena, which places a great impact on the accumulative interference and the spatial reuse ratio.

6   Conclusion

This paper presents a comparative study between testbed and simulations of the network simulators ns-2 and ns-3. The testbed is multihop wireless network deployed in corridors in a non-linear chain topology, which challenges the commonly used empirical models of wireless propagation channel that are currently available in these simulators. The experiments done for this study include single and concurrent flows transmissions over a single multihop path. The goal is to explore how well these simulators reflect the reality represented by this testbed carrying those flows.

Our simulations roughly match with testbed results for single flow transmissions, which cause only limited accumulated interference and allow for good spatial reuse ratio of the network. Simulations deviate however more clearly from testbed results for simultaneous flows transmissions. These transmissions increase the accumulative interference compared to single flow transmissions and thereby decreases the spatial reuse ratio of the network. In particular, for simultaneous flows transmissions simulations indicate considerably worse fairness between flows compared to testbed results.

This reveals that the wireless propagation channel models of the simulators are not correctly representing the wireless channel properties in the corridors, especially in scenarios involving accumulated interference in difficult environments such as corridors.

Deterministic wireless channel modeling for example based on ray tracing techniques can better capture reality into simulators, but require exact knowledge of location, shape, dielectric and conductive properties of all objects in the environments and it also requires extensive computational efforts for accuracy. This complexity motivates the use of empirical radio modeling although its shortcomings in correctly modeling complex environments. Our paper emphasizes the need for validation when using such modeling to study single channel multihop wireless network performance for more complex environments.

Future work include to extend this study by exploring how results match between simulations and real multihop wireless networks with linear chain topology for other indoor environments as well as outdoor environments. Thereby we can further characterize possible discrepancies important to be aware of when using simulations to predict performance in real networks.

References

1. Baldo, N., Requena-Esteso, M., Nú nez-Martínez, J., Portolès-Comeras, M., Nin-Guerrero, J., Dini, P., Mangues-Bafalluy, J.: Validation of the ieee 802.11 mac model in the ns3 simulator using the extreme testbed. In: SIMUTools 2010: Proceedings of the 3rd International ICST Conference on Simulation Tools and Techniques, pp. 1–9. ICST (Institute for Computer Sciences, Social-Informatics and Telecommunications Engineering), ICST, Brussels, Belgium (2010)
2. Cavin, D., Sasson, Y., Schiper, A.: On the accuracy of manet simulators. In: POMC 2002: Proceedings of the Second ACM International Workshop on Principles of Mobile Computing, pp. 38–43. ACM, New York (2002)
3. Giannopoulou, K., Katsareli, A., Dres, D., Vouyioukas, D., Constantinou, P.: Measurements for 2.4 GHz spread spectrum system in modern office buildings, p. 21 (2000)
4. Jain, R., Chiu, D., Hawe, W.: A quantitative measure of fairness and discrimination for resource allocation in shared systems. dec research report TR-301 (1984)
5. Kotz, D., Newport, C., Gray, R.S., Liu, J., Yuan, Y., Elliott, C.: Experimental evaluation of wireless simulation assumptions. In: MSWiM 2004: Proceedings of the 7th ACM International Symposium on Modeling, Analysis and Simulation of Wireless and Mobile Systems, pp. 78–82. ACM, New York (2004)
6. Lu, D., Rutledge, D.: Investigation of indoor radio channels from 2.4 GHz to 24 GHz, vol. 2, pp. 134–137 (June 2003)
7. Molisch, A.: Wireless Communications. John Wiley & Sons, Chichester (2005)
8. Osipov, E., Tschudin, C.: Evaluating the effect of ad hoc routing on tcp performance in ieee 802.11 based manets. In: Koucheryavy, Y., Harju, J., Iversen, V.B. (eds.) NEW2AN 2006. LNCS, vol. 4003, pp. 298–312. Springer, Heidelberg (2006)
9. Rachedi, A., Lohier, S., Cherrier, S., Salhi, I.: Wireless network simulators relevance compared to a real testbed in outdoor and indoor environments. In: IWCMC 2010: Proceedings of the 6th International Wireless Communications and Mobile Computing Conference, pp. 346–350. ACM, New York (2010)
10. Rappaport, T.S.: Wireless Communications Principles and Practice. Prentice-Hall, Upper Saddle River (2002)

11. Razak, S., Kolar, V., Abu-Ghazaleh, N.B., Harras, K.A.: How do wireless chains behave?: the impact of mac interactions. In: MSWiM 2009: Proceedings of the 12th ACM International Conference on Modeling, Analysis and Simulation of Wireless and Mobile Systems, pp. 212–220. ACM, New York (2009)
12. Schmitz, A., Wenig, M.: The effect of the radio wave propagation model in mobile ad hoc networks. In: MSWiM 2006: Proceedings of the 9th ACM International Symposium on Modeling Analysis and Simulation of Wireless and Mobile Systems, pp. 61–67. ACM Press, New York (2006)
13. Sheikh, A., Abdi, M., Handforth, M.: Indoor mobile radio channel at 946 mhz: Measurements and modeling, pp. 73–76 (May 1993)
14. Tan, K., Wu, D. (Jack) Chan, A., Mohapatra, P.: Comparing simulation tools and experimental testbeds for wireless mesh networks, pp. 1–9 (June 2010)
15. Tarng, J., Liu, W.S., Huang, Y.F., Huang, J.M.: A novel and efficient hybrid model of radio multipath-fading channels in indoor environments. IEEE Transactions on Antennas and Propagation 51(3), 585–594 (2003)

UEF: Ubiquity Evaluation Framework

Bruno Sousa[1], Kostas Pentikousis[2], and Marilia Curado[1]

[1] CISUC, University of Coimbra
Polo II, Pinhal de Marrocos 3030-290, Coimbra, Portugal
{bmsousa,marilia}@dei.uc.pt
[2] Huawei Technologies European Research Center
Carnotstrasse 4, 10587 Berlin, Germany
k.pentikousis@huawei.com

Abstract. Ubiquitous computing (UbiComp) systems rely on hetero-geneous technologies to enable the anytime-anywhere communication paradigm. Despite the momentum that UbiComp systems have, most new proposals are typically evaluated through varying sets of criteria, making direct comparisons that are far from straightforward. In this paper, we introduce the Ubiquity Evaluation Framework (UEF) aim-ing to overcome the limitations of hitherto evaluation mechanisms. UEF is unique, as particular protocols of a UbiComp system can be evalu-ated without requiring a functional system or involving questionnaries to a group of experts in the field. UEF enables the comparison of pro-tocols intended for the same task in the design phase, by employing objective metrics. The generic applicability of UEF is demonstrated in this paper through a case study comparing UbiComp support in two well-established mobility management protocols, namely Mobile IPv6 (MIPv6) and Host Identity Protocol (HIP).

Keywords: Ubiquitous computing, Multihoming, MIPv6, HIP, model-ing and performance evaluation.

1 Introduction

Ubiquitous computing (UbiComp) is a model where computers live in the world of people, aware of their location, but in a transparent form to the user [1]. Modern devices and networks to some degree implement this vision for ubiq-uitous computing as they enable users to access online services 24-hours a day at "any time" and from "any place". In principle, the choice of technologies, system architecture and protocols must be considered in the design phase of UbiComp systems. However, the evaluation approaches taken for UbiComp Sys-tems so far [2, 3] typically consider user-perspective ratings only, or assess a limited set of functionalities. For example, some assessments follow a prototype-based approach and thus have high development costs while not always fully representative of the final system. Others rely on user surveys requiring at least a partially complete and functional system. Moreover, when multiple choices for the software components are available, said approaches do not provide insights for the selection of the best ones during the design phase.

X. Masip-Bruin et al. (Eds.): WWIC 2011, LNCS 6649, pp. 92–103, 2011.

This paper introduces the Ubiquity Evaluation Framework (UEF), which assess the ubiquity support of a protocol by considering its technical features (i.e., those related with the capabilities of UbiComp systems, including security and extensibility), as well as protocol extensions, i.e. features that improve the capabilities of UbiComp systems, but are not mandatory. Both technical features and extensions of UbiComp systems are considered regarding the functionalities of the assessed protocol. To showcase the use of UEF we consider in this paper two mobility management protocols, namely MIPv6 [4] and HIP [5], and study their respective ubiquity support. In doing so, we demonstrate the accuracy and general applicability of UEF.

The contributions of UEF in the evaluation of UbiComp systems are three-fold. First, evaluations do not require prototypes or working systems or even experts in the UbiComp area, as UEF does not rely on user interviews. Second, performance can be assessed at any phase of system development, ranging from the design phase to deployment. Third, UEF establishes objective metrics that allow the comparison of protocols intended for the same task in an objective manner. The remainder of this paper starts with Section 2, which reviews related work. Then, Section 3 introduces UEF and Section 4 assesses ubiquity support in MIPv6 and HIP based on our framework. Finally, Section 5 concludes the paper.

2   Related Work

UbiComp systems include different components, namely the computing platform, such as the hardware technologies supported, the software platform, and the users interacting with the system [6]. In this section, we overview the approaches so far taken when evaluating, on the one hand UbiComp systems, and on the other mobility management protocols.

UbiComp systems can be evaluated in terms of quality, which assesses the level of capabilities (i.e., technical characteristics) and the level of extensions [7, 8]. The assignment for each capability/item usually relies on interviews with experts in the field (e.g., with ubiquitous computing experience), giving a classification in the range $\{1, 2, ..., 7\}$. These solutions require the involvement of experts, limiting a general applicability of this type of methodology.

UCAN is a ubiquitous computing application development and evaluation process model [2] that allows the evaluation of ubiquitous applications, such as radio frequency identification (RFID) applications. The evaluation includes different stages and methods, for instance, the original idea can be evaluated using interviews, while the prototype (pilot) is assessed through user acceptance methods. Whilst UCAN requires prototypes and is tailored for applications relying on user satisfaction metrics, in [7] the overall system is evaluated.

Ontonym [3] is a framework that allows the evaluation of pervasive systems. The framework models context based on ontologies. For instance, people are modeled by using classes with different attributes such as Name and Religious-Name. The evaluation considers three aspects: design principles, (e.g., extensibility and documentation); content (e.g., clarity and consistency); and purpose (in which domain the evaluation is performed). Despite using established standards, Ontonym focuses on the context representation problem, and therefore does not provide objective and comparable metrics to evaluate UbiComp systems.

The performance of IP mobility management protocols has been a popular research topic. Due to space considerations, we only review the most salient work in this area in terms of performance metrics support. Usually, metrics include packet delivery cost, handover delay, location update cost, signaling cost, multiple interfaces and simultaneous mobility support. The packet delivery cost metric, for instance, determines the cost (e.g., processing or transmission) of the different packet delivery mechanisms (e.g., tunnel, direct) [9]. The handover delay metric includes movement detection, address configuration, security operations and location registration [10, 11]. The signaling cost is a compound metric that combines the packet delivery cost and the handover cost, commonly designated by location update cost [9]. The location update cost is determined according to the network model (e.g., number of hops, number of domains, wired and wireless links), message rate and respective message length. The difference between the different proposals resides on the fact that some of them include the functions of each involved entity (e.g., home agent, correspondent node), while others only include the mobile node or only the cost of specific operations (e.g., tunneling) [12]. The support of simultaneous mobility metrics is often neglected in evaluations, assuming fixed correspondent nodes [9, 12], although some consider the probability of simultaneous movement as in [13]. Paging efficiency is another metric to consider when evaluating mobility management protocols in a ubiquitous environment, specially due to energy efficiency. Paging support evaluations assess the power consumption cost, the paging delay cost but in a technology-dependent or application-dependent way [14–16].

Based on this survey of previous work in these two areas, we conclude that none of the existing approaches can assess protocol performance regarding its functionality and taking into consideration technical features and extensions of UbiComp systems. As will see later, UEF addresses these limitations, providing a consistent benchmark toolset for a variety of protocols.

3   UEF - Ubiquity Evaluation Framework

UEF defines the ubiquity metric - U_{MH} (see Def. 1) that combines aspects of UbiComp systems with the functionalities of a protocol. Metrics and methods to assess technical features and extensions of UbiComp systems are presented first. The degree of mobility support assesses IP mobility management performance, which is then combined with features of UbiComp systems, expressing the Ubiquity metric.

Definition 1 - *Ubiquity is the ability to support secure and optimized mobility to enable access to services anywhere and anytime, with acceptable quality levels.*

Table 1. Technical Capabilities of UbiComp systems in UEF for (S) - Software, (U) - User and (H) - Hardware components (with a total of 39)

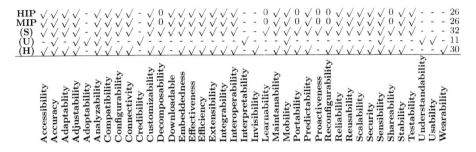

Table 2. Extensions of UbiComp systems in UEF for (S) - Software, (U) - User and (H) - Hardware components (total of 22)

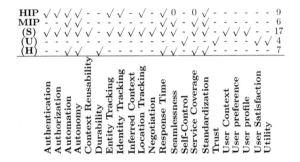

3.1 Formulation

The first contribution of UEF is the ubiquity metric that combines technical capabilities, lC, and extensions, lU, of UbiComp systems, according to the degree of mobility, Ψ, supported by a protocol. Eq.1 formulates Ubiquity - U_{MH}, where W_{lC} and W_{lU} are the weights for technical characteristics and extensions aspects, respectively. Weights are assigned as follows: $W_{lC} + W_{lU} \leq 1$. A simple rule to assign weights relates the number of technical or extensions items and the overall number of items (technical + extensions), having $W_{lC} = nLC/(nLC + nLU) = 0.65$ and $W_{lU} = nLU/(nLC + nLU) = 0.35$.

$$U_{MH} = (W_{lC} * lC + W_{lU} * lU) \cdot \Psi \tag{1}$$

Technical capabilities and extensions are determined for each component of a UbiComp system, namely user (U), software (S) and hardware or computing platform (H), as shown in Table 1 and Table 2. MIPv6 and HIP fall in the software component category (S). Thus, capabilities and extensions of the protocols are evaluated by considering only the capabilities and extensions of the

software component. A "$\sqrt{}$" in the Table entries means that the respective capability is supported; "0" means that it is not supported; and "$-$" means that
the capability is not applicable.

UEF should be usable without full expertise in UbiComp systems and at any
stage of system development (from design to deployment phases). As such, capabilities and extensions are evaluated using a Boolean scale (0-not supported
and 1-fully/partially supported). Moreover, to avoid ambiguity in the evaluation,
UEF employs the meaning of each capability/extension according to standard
dictionaries [17]. Finally, UEF considers non-overlapping capabilities and extensions as opposed to [7, 8] that evaluates an item twice, namely as a capability
and as extension. Each capability/extension is determined according to Eq. 2
specified in [7], where n is the number of supported capacities/extensions, C_i is
the value of the capacity (0 or 1) with $MaxScale = 1$, and n_ξ is the number of
capacities/extensions that apply to the component.

$$C_\xi = \frac{\sum_{i=1}^{n} C_i}{n_\xi \cdot MaxScale}, with \; \xi \in \{u, s, h\} \tag{2}$$

UEF assesses mobility support through the degree of mobility Ψ, which is a
compound metric of performance and cost aspects of the mobility management
process, as per Eq. 3. Common approaches, such as [9, 12] consider cost aspects
only. Performance aspects include the level of energy efficiency Ef and handover procedure preparation rate λ_{prep}. Cost aspects include handover Hc and
signaling Sc costs as well as the handover procedure finalization rate λ_{fina}. The
term $N \cdot maxS$ corresponds to the number of cost aspects and the maximum
cost value, respectively, with $maxS = 1$, and $N = 3$. The weight W_m is used to
distinguish performance and cost aspects.

$$\Psi = N \cdot maxS + W_m(Ef + \lambda_{prep}) - (1 - W_m) \cdot (Hc + Sc + \lambda_{fina}) \tag{3}$$

In IP mobility management evaluation, UEF includes metrics for energy efficiency and the procedure preparation rate, a significant improvement over previous work that only evaluates mobility management performance by assessing
costs [9, 12, 13]. UEF explores the end-host mobility approach, when all procedures are triggered by the mobile node, and includes support for simultaneous
mobility events. In the latter case, the correspondent node plays a dual role as
it is also a mobile node. The procedure rates include the procedure preparation
rate before the handover, λ_{prep}, and the procedure finalization rate, λ_{fina}, after
the handover. Considering a total of n_{proc} procedures and $n_{proc} = n_{prep} + n_{fina}$,
the rates are $\lambda_{prep} = n_{prep}/n_{proc}$ and $\lambda_{fina} = n_{fina}/n_{proc}$.

The handover cost, Hc, quantifies cost in terms of handover delay, d, measuring the sum of procedure delays in the n_e entities. Handover delay, d, is
determined as follows: $d = \sum_{e=1}^{n_e} \sum_{j=0}^{n_{je}} \Delta t_{proc_{j,e}}$, with n_{je} procedures executed
at entity e with Δt_{proc} processing time. The handover cost, Eq. 4, includes the
cost of procedures invoked after handover only. A sigmoid function normalizes
delay values that have increased granularity by a factor of d_g (=1000 by default).

Handover cost could consider other metrics, such as handover delay at Layer 2 [11], but this would tie UEF to a specific radio access technology and prevent us from apportioning the performance of the assessed protocol.

$$Hc = 1/(1 + e^{-\frac{\sqrt{d+1}}{d_g}})$$ (4)

The signaling cost, Sc, Eq.5, determines the procedure overhead (Gp set) of the protocol, as in [9].

$$Sc = \left[1 + e^{-\sqrt{\sum C_p/max(C_p)}} \right]^{-1} \forall_p \in Gp$$ (5)

The relation between the sum of all procedures $\sum C_p$ and the maximum cost $max(C_p)$ of all the procedures is the base for the signaling cost formulation. In UEF, the cost of a procedure C_p is formulated according to the message size, the message transmission frequency or the number of transmissions, and the processing cost Φ of each entity. Common approaches rely mainly on the message size only [9]. Eq. 6 determines the cost of a procedure invoked nI times, with message size L_i and transmitted nTx times or at a frequency Q_i.

$$C_p = \sum_{n=0}^{nI} \left[\sum_{t=1}^{nTx} \sum_{i=1}^{nM} \left(L_{n,t,i} \cdot Q_{n,t,i} \cdot \sum_{e \in \{...\}} \Phi_{n,t,i,e} \right) \right]$$ (6)

For the number nTx and frequency Q_i of transmissions we make the following assumptions:

- $Q_i = 1$, if $nTx > 1$, i.e. when there are retransmissions;
- $nTx = 1$, if $Q_i > 1$, for instance, messages that do not require any reliability but are sent frequently (e.g., router advertisements).

The processing cost, Pc, of an entity Φ_e is the relation between the processing cost of a procedure and the number of interfaces of entity e, $\Phi_e = Nif_e \cdot Pc_e$. UEF considers multihomed nodes and does not rely on upper-layer parameters (e.g., session rate) to determine the processing cost. Instead, Pc corresponds to the relation between the processing delay $pDelay$ and the operation complexity, as given in Eq. 7. Complexity is modeled by the number of operations $nOper$, and the size of data structures $sizeData$. Whilst the size of the data structures can be dynamic, UEF only considers the size of a single record, for simplicity. When procedures do not involve data structures, $sizeData = 0$. $sizeData$ differs from message length, since it accounts for the size of structures necessary to perform the operations in procedures (e.g., record in a routing table).

$$Pc = [nOper \cdot (1 + sizeData)] \cdot pDelay$$ (7)

Energy efficiency, Ef, considers the rates of reducing the active area $\lambda_{rdActArea}$ and the paging cost λ_{rdPagC}, as per Eq. 8. N is the number of cost aspects and $maxS$ the maximum value of these costs, with $N = 1$ and $maxS = 1$. Power saving mechanisms at the physical layer are not included in order to meet the technology independence requirement.

$$Ef = N \cdot maxS + W_e \cdot \lambda_{rdPagC} - (1 - W_e) \cdot \lambda_{rdActArea}$$ (8)

The rate of active area reduction, $\lambda_{rdActArea}$, is the relation between the domain $dArea$ and the paging area $pArea$: $\lambda_{rdActArea} = \frac{dArea - pArea}{dArea}$. The paging area is determined by considering the node that initiates paging till the endpoint (e.g., mobile node). Additionally, the area can consider the radius coverage (in meters), or simply the number of hops between the paging initiator and the endpoint as discussed in [14]. The domain area is limited by the prefix management entity, for instance an IPv6 router, and the endpoints. Values close to 1 indicate that the paging area is too small, with reduced costs, but with few optimizations. The paging cost, $PagC$ is given in Eq. 9, where L represents the message size, transmitted nTx times. Each entity e participating in the paging group Ga has Nif interfaces in idle state during Δt interval, and for each paging message the processing cost is Pc. The paging group Ga includes all entities involved in paging signaling.

$$PagC = \sum_{t=1}^{nTx} L_t \cdot \sum_{\forall_e \in Ga} \left(Nif_{e,t} \cdot Pc_{e,t} \cdot \Delta t_{e,t} \right) \tag{9}$$

The processing cost, Pc, is determined according to Eq. 7 with $sizeData = 0$. The ratio of paging cost reduction, λ_{rdPagC}, is the relation between paging cost at effective idle intervals, Δt_idle, and theoretical intervals, Δt_Tidle, during which the MN could remain in idle state (e.g., no data transfer and no mobility management signaling exchanges), $\lambda_{rdPagC} = \frac{PagC_{\Delta t\_idle}}{PagC_{\Delta t\_Tidle}}$.

4 UEF Use Case: Ubiquity in MIPv6 and HIP

After detailing the UEF specification, we now proceed with the evaluation of MIPv6 [4] and HIP [5] with respect to the effectiveness of their ubiquity support.

4.1 Ubiquity Derivation for MIPv6 and HIP

HIP supports mobility management with the RendezVous extension. The ubiquitous support is determined according to its technical capabilities and extensions. Using Tables 1 and 2 we see that MIPv6 and HIP have similar technical capabilities, that is, $lC_{MIP} = lC_{HIP} = 26/32 = 0.81$. MIPv6 does not gain any from its extensions support, $lU_{MIP} = 6/17 = 0.35$, but HIP does, $lU_{HIP} = 9/17 = 0.53$.

The formulation of the degree of mobility for the registration (RG), security (AA), address configuration (AD) and movement detection (MD) procedures are based on Eq. 2. Mobility management in MIPv6 includes Mobile Node (MN), Home Agent (HA) and Correspondent Node (CN) entities. In HIP, the HIP Initiator (HI), the RendezVous Server (RVS) and the HIP Responder (HR) manage mobility. As some procedures rely on IPv6 mechanisms, we employ $E1$ as MN or HI, $E2$ as HA or RVS and $E3$ as CN or HR.

MIPv6 registration is based on binding messages. MN sends Binding Update (BU) to the HA and CN when new addresses are available. BUs are retransmitted till the reception of a Binding Acknowledgment (BA). Moreover, binding can be refreshed using Binding Refresh Request (BRR), or the CN can inform the MN about errors using Binding Error (BE) message. The cost is determined similarly to HIP.

HIP registration is performed in three steps (*s1, s2, s3*) according to the handover phase. In *s1*, HI and HR register with RVS using *I1, R1, I2* and *R2* messages. The cost of this step is determined by Eq. 10. The base exchange (step *s2*) corresponds to a four-way handshake between HI and HR and only involves the RVS to forward I1 messages.

$$
C_{RG-HIP_{s1,s2}} = \sum_{t=1}^{nTx} L_{I1,t} \cdot \sum_{e \in \{HI,RVS,HR\}} (Nif_{e,t} \cdot Pc_{e,t}) + L_{R1} \cdot \sum_{e \in \{HI,RVS,HR\}} (Nif_e \cdot Pc_e)
$$
$$
+ L_{I2} \cdot \sum_{e \in \{HI,RVS,HR\}} (Nif_e \cdot Pc_e) + L_{R2} \cdot \sum_{e \in \{HI,RVS,HR\}} (Nif_e \cdot Pc_e) \tag{10}
$$

After the handover (step *s3*), HI needs to update the locator information on *dest* nodes, which include RVS and HR. For such purpose, it employs the update message with locator information, and issues an *echo_request*, which status of update is reported in the *echo_response* message. The registration cost of the update is determined according to Eq. 11.

$$
C_{RG-HIP_{s3}} = \sum_{t=1}^{nTx} L_{UPD(locator),t} \cdot \sum_{e \in \{HI,dest\}} (Nif_{e,t} \cdot Pc_{e,t}) \tag{11}
$$
$$
+ L_{UPD(echo\_req)} \cdot \sum_{e \in \{dest,HI\}} (Nif_e \cdot Pc_e) + L_{UPD(echo\_resp)} \cdot \sum_{e \in \{HI,dest\}} (Nif_e \cdot Pc_e)
$$

MIPv6 can rely on external mechanisms, such as IPsec, to enable security. Nevertheless, our study focuses on the return routability, since it is an internal procedure of MIPv6 that allows the verification of addresses when the MN is at foreign networks. Eq. 12 formulates the cost of this procedure relying on the Home Test init (HoTI), Care-of Test init (CoTI) and respective reply messages. Integrity protection and encryption is performed in HIP by employing the Encapsulating Security Payload (ESP). The registration cost already includes the security cost C_{AA-HIP}, as ESP security association is part of the base exchange.

$$
C_{AA-MIP} = \sum_{t=1}^{nTx} L_{HoTi,t} \cdot \sum_{e \in \{MN,HA,CN\}} (Nif_{e,t} \cdot Pc_{e,t}) \tag{12}
$$
$$
+ \sum_{t=1}^{nTx} L_{CoTi,t} \cdot (Nif_{MN,t} Pc_{MN,t} + Nif_{CN,t} Pc_{CN,t})
$$
$$
+ L_{HoT} \cdot \sum_{e \in \{MN,HA,CN\}} (Nif_e \cdot Pc_e) + L_{CoT} \cdot (Nif_{MN} \cdot Pc_{MN} + Nif_{CN} \cdot Pc_{CN})
$$

Address configuration in MIPv6 and HIP nodes relies on IPv6 schemes that include Router Solicitation (RS), Router Advertisements (RA) and the messages in the Duplicate Address Detection (DAD) mechanism. Neighbor Solicitation (NS) messages are sent to multicast addresses with the reply of Neighbor Acknowledgement (NA) messages. In addition, IPv6 routers (at home and foreign networks, Rtr_h and Rtr_f, respectively) advertise prefixes via Router Advertisements (RA) frequently, while Router Solicitation messages are retransmitted on error events. Eq. 13 defines the cost of address configuration.

$$C_{AD} = \sum_{t=1}^{nTx} L_{NS,t} \cdot \sum_{e \in \{E1,E2,E3\}} (Nif_{e,t} \cdot Pc_{e,t}) + L_{NA} \cdot \sum_{e \in \{E1,E2,E3\}} (Nif_e \cdot Pc_e)$$

$$+ \sum_{t=1}^{nTx} L_{RS,t} \cdot \sum_{e \in \{E1,E2,E3\}} (Nif_{e,t} \cdot Pc_{e,t}) + Q_{RA_{home}} \cdot L_{RA_{home}} \cdot \sum_{e \in \{E1,Rtr_h,E2,E3\}} (Nif_e \cdot Pc_e)$$

$$+ Q_{RA_{foreign}} \cdot L_{RA_{foreign}} \cdot \sum_{e \in \{E1,Rtr_f,E2,E3\}} (Nif_e \cdot Pc_e) \tag{13}$$

Movement detection also relies in IPv6 schemes, namely the Neighbor Unreachability Detection (NUD) mechanism. NUD uses solicited NS and NA messages and the respective cost is formulated according to Eq. 14.

$$C_{MD} = \sum_{t=1}^{nTx} L_{NS,t} \cdot \sum_{e \in \{E1,E2,E3\}} (Nif_{e,t} \cdot Pc_{e,t}) + L_{NA} \cdot \sum_{e \in \{E1,E2,E3\}} (Nif_e \cdot Pc_e) \tag{14}$$

Finally, MIPv6 includes the tunnel cost, since packets can be forwarded to MNs at foreign networks via tunnels. The cost of tunnel establishment is determined in an application independent fashion, as tunneling relies on IPv6 encapsulation mechanisms. The tunnel establishment cost, as per Eq. 15, considers only the size of message headers and respective processing cost in MN, HA and CN.

$$C_{TU} = \sum_{t=1}^{nTx} HdrT_{MN,t} \cdot (Nif_{MN,t} \cdot Pc_{MN,t}) \tag{15}$$

$$+ \sum_{t=1}^{nTx} HdrT_{HA,t} \cdot (Nif_{HA,t} \cdot Pc_{HA,t}) + \sum_{t=1}^{nTx} HdrT_{CN,t} \cdot (Nif_{CN,t} \cdot Pc_{CN,t})$$

4.2   Evaluation Methodology

In this UEF study case we consider the problem of choosing a protocol for a UbiComp system at the design phase. Hence, the evaluation does not target a particular scenario with specific technologies, but examines ubiquity support in generic UbiComp systems. Thus, MIPv6 and HIP protocols are assumed to be operating with the maximum message length (e.g., with all options filled). In addition, only the mandatory messages are considered; optional messages, such as *HIP - NOTIFY*, are not included.

The nodes (e.g., MN, HI, CN, HR) are configured with three interfaces, $nif = \{1, 2, 3\}$, a common configuration in mobile terminals. Moreover, MN/HI can communicate simultaneously with several correspondent nodes, $ncns = \{1, 5, 10\}$, within which different types of applications can be used. In addition,

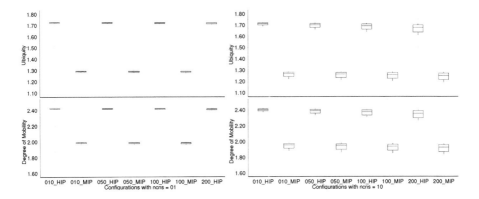

Fig. 1. Single (left) and 10 nodes (right) Ubiquity and degree of Mobility boxplots using UEF

nodes move with different speeds, thus having to handle a number of handovers $nho = \{10, 50, 100, 200\}$. All sessions last 300s. Assuming we are in the design phase of a UbiComp system, values of processing delay cannot be measured (as no prototype is available). Thus for this study case, we take all processing times to follow normal and exponential distributions, with different means $\{1s, 10s\}$. Different distributions are used to accommodate different modeling mechanisms for processing times. The analytical evaluation has been performed using the R framework [18] and considering that both MIPv6 and HIP do not include energy efficiency mechanisms $Ef = 0$, as no paging schemes are incorporated.

We use ubiquity weights $W_{lC} = 0.65$ and $W_{lU} = 0.35$ according to number of items in technical and extensions categories. The degree of mobility weight is equal to $W_m = 0.5$, as no energy efficiency mechanisms are considered and thus the degree of mobility relies mainly on the cost. Values higher then 0.5 tend to neglect the impact of cost in mobility support.

4.3   Results

Figs. 1 and 2 present our evaluation results ordered by the number of handovers and type of protocol under study. For instance, 200_HIP is an HIP study case with 200 handovers. Statistical significance is based on 100 runs for each case.

UEF can assess ubiquity taking into consideration protocol functionalities in different conditions that UbiComp systems can face. Under mobile scenarios, the number of handovers impacts the performance of mobile management protocols. All procedures required to handle mobility are triggered often, introducing degradation in the performance, (Fig. 1), as signaling overhead increases, (Fig. 2). The number of handovers also impacts handover performance; observe the difference between single and 10 simultaneous nodes on left and right sides of Fig. 1, respectively. Location updates, due to mobile events, need to be forwarded to more nodes.

Results also put in evidence the particularity of UEF that considers protocol functionalities in the assessment of ubiquity and degree of mobility. In the UEF

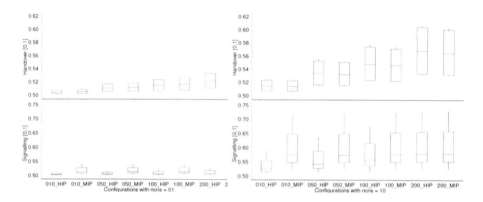

Fig. 2. Single (left) and 10 nodes (right) Handover and signalling costs boxplots using UEF

study case, HIP supports mobility better ($\sim$ 2.4) than MIP ($\sim$ 1.9 for 10 handovers with 10 simultaneous nodes) since some procedures are triggered before handover, as opposed to MIP, where procedures run after the handover.

5   Conclusion

We introduced UEF, a framework that assesses the ubiquity support of a protocol in an objective manner by considering multiple aspects of UbiComp systems regarding protocol functionalities. Evaluations carried out with UEF do not require any working system or prototype, as UEF metrics can be used at any phase in the development of a UbiComp System, ranging from system design to deployment. In addition, surveys involving users or field experts are not necessary. We used UEF in a study case to objectively evaluate MIPv6 and HIP concerning mobility management support. The study case showed that HIP supports ubiquity more efficiently than MIPv6, and for that reason HIP is a potential candidate to be deployed on UbiComp systems where mobility management and security are a concern.

To sum up, UbiComp systems integrate network protocols for diverse tasks. As multiple protocols can seemingly perform the same task, the choice of the most suitable and best-performing protocol is not always straightforward. UEF enables researchers and practitioners alike to objectively quantify the value of different technical features and extensions for mobility management in UbiComp systems.

Acknowledgment

The first author acknowledges the support of the PhD grant SFRH/BD/61256/ 2009 from Ministério da Ciência, Tecnologia e Ensino Superior, FCT, Portugal. This work is supported by CoFIMOM project PTDC/EIA-EIA/116173/2009.

References

1. Symonds, J.: Ubiquitous and Pervasive Computing: Concepts, Methodologies, Tools, and Applications. Information Science Reference I (2009)
2. Resatsch, F.: Ubiquitous Computing Developing and Evaluating Near Field Communication Applications. Gabler (2010)
3. Stevenson, G., Knox, S., Dobson, S., Nixon, P.: Ontonym: A Collection of Upper Ontologies for Developing Pervasive Systems. In: Proceedings of the 1st Workshop on Context, Information and Ontologies, pp. 1–8. ACM, New York (2009)
4. Johnson, D., Perkins, C., Arkko, J.: Mobility Support in IPv6. Internet Draft: draft-ietf-mext-rfc3775bis (March 2011)
5. Gurtov, A.: Host Identity Protocol (HIP): Towards the Secure Mobile Internet. Wiley Series (2008)
6. Niemel, E., Latvakoski, J.: Survey of Requirements and Solutions for Ubiquitous Software. In: Proceedings of the 3rd International Conference on Mobile and Ubiquitous Multimedia, ser. MUM 2004, pp. 71–78. ACM, New York (2004)
7. Kwon, O., Kim, J.: A Multi-layered Assessment Model for Evaluating the Level of Ubiquitous Computing Services. In: Ma, J., Jin, H., Yang, L.T., Tsai, J.J.-P. (eds.) UIC 2006. LNCS, vol. 4159, pp. 1059–1068. Springer, Heidelberg (2006)
8. Scholtz, J., Consolvo, S.: Toward a Framework for Evaluating Ubiquitous Computing Applications. IEEE Pervasive Comput. 3, 82–88 (2004)
9. Wang, Q., Abu-Rgheff, M.A.: Signalling Analysis of Cost-Efficient Mobility Support by Integrating Mobile IP and SIP in All IP Wireless Networks. International Journal of Communication Systems 19, 225–247 (2006)
10. Kong, K.-S., Lee, W., Han, Y.-H., Shin, M.-K., You, H.: Mobility Management for All-IP Mobile Networks: Mobile IPv6 vs. Proxy Mobile IPv6. IEEE Wireless Commun. 15(2), 36–45 (2008)
11. Liu, Y., Li, M., Yang, B., Qian, D., Wu, W.: Handover for Seamless Stream Media in Mobile IPv6 Network. In: Boavida, F., Monteiro, E., Mascolo, S., Koucheryavy, Y. (eds.) WWIC 2007. LNCS, vol. 4517, pp. 55–66. Springer, Heidelberg (2007)
12. Makaya, C., Pierre, S.: An Analytical Framework for Performance Evaluation of IPv6-Based Mobility Management Protocols. IEEE Trans. Wireless Commun. 7(3), 972–983 (2008)
13. Wong, K.D., Dutta, A., Schulzrinne, H., Young, K.: Simultaneous Mobility: Analytical Framework, Theorems and Solutions. Wireless Communications and Mobile Computing 7(5), 623–642 (2007)
14. Lee, J.-H., Chung, T.-M., Pack, S., Gundavelli, S.: Shall We Apply Paging Technologies to Proxy Mobile IPv6? In: Proceedings of MobiArch, pp. 37–42. ACM, New York (2008)
15. Do, H.T., Onozato, Y.: A Comparison of Different Paging Mechanisms for Mobile IP. Wirel. Netw. 13(3), 379–395 (2007)
16. Tang, H., Poyhonen, P., Strandberg, O., Pentikousis, K., Sachs, J., Meago, F., Tuononen, J., Aguero, R.: Paging issues and methods for multiaccess. In: CHINACOM 2007, pp. 769–776 (August 2007)
17. IEEE, IEEE Standard Computer Dictionary: A Compilation of IEEE Standard Computer Glossaries 610 (1990)
18. R Development Core Team, R: A Language and Environment for Statistical Computing, R Foundation for Statistical Computing (2010)

Traffic Engineering Approaches Using Multicriteria Optimization Techniques

Pedro Sousa[1], Paulo Cortez[3], Miguel Rio[2], and Miguel Rocha[1]

[1] Dept. of Informatics, University of Minho, Portugal
{pns,mrocha}@di.uminho.pt
[2] Dep. of Electronic and Electrical Engineering, UCL, UK
m.rio@ee.ucl.ac.uk
[3] Dep. of Information Systems, University of Minho, Portugal
pcortez@dsi.uminho.pt

Abstract. Nowadays, network planning and management tasks can be of high complexity, given the numerous inputs that should be considered to effectively achieve an adequate configuration of the underlying network. This paper presents an optimization framework that helps network administrators in setting the optimal routing weights of link state protocols according to the required traffic demands, contributing in this way to improve the service levels quality provided by the network infrastructure. Since the envisaged task is a NP-hard problem, the framework resorts to Evolutionary Computation as the optimization engine. The focus is given to the use of multi-objective optimization approaches given the flexibility they provide to network administrators in selecting the adequate solutions in a given context. Resorting to the proposed optimization framework the administrator is able to automatically obtain highly optimized routing configurations adequate to support the requirements imposed by their customers. In this way, this novel approach effectively contributes to enhance and automate crucial network planning and management tasks.

Keywords: Traffic engineering; Network design and network planning.

1 Introduction

Recently, several types of applications have been integrated over IP converged networks, increasing the requirements on the ability to provide adequate service levels. In order to achieve a generalized capable QoS infra-structure, many different Quality of Service (QoS) solutions and associated traffic control mechanisms were proposed, such as the examples of traffic prioritization and selective resource reservation solutions [1]. However, the fast growth of Internet users and events such as the proliferation of multimedia contents and the increasing use of P2P applications are being responsible for the change of traffic profiles in the Internet. Moreover, the heterogeneity of current Internet access networks including wireless technologies such as Wi-Fi, WiMAX, among others, along with the

X. Masip-Bruin et al. (Eds.): WWIC 2011, LNCS 6649, pp. 104–115, 2011.

mobility patterns of some users also pose new challenges to the wired supporting infrastructures, as regards to their correct planning and configuration.

In this context, it is crucial that network administrators carefully consider the traffic demands required to be supported by the network infra-structure during a given period of time, such as specific days of a week, particular periods during the year, seasonal intervals, etc. This information can be provided using distinct techniques, such as forecasting methods based on historical data, traffic accounting based mechanisms, demand matrix estimation techniques [6] [7] [8], among many others. Such inputs are of extreme importance to be used to enhance the provision of adequate QoS levels by the network. However, in general, achieving reasonable service quality requires several components of the network infrastructure working in a coordinated way. Moreover, and irrespective of the QoS mechanisms in place, there are other factors which also play a crucial role on the networking performance, such as the routing configuration of the network.

The optimization framework proposed in this work focuses on the Open Shortest Path First (OSPF) intra-domain routing protocol, an extremely popular and ease of implementation protocol [10]. In this protocol, the administrator sets weights to every link in the network, which then are used to compute the best paths from each source to destination pair, resulting on the nodes' routing tables [3]. This process has a major impact on the network performance. However, in practice, simple methods and heuristics are commonly used, but often leading to sub-optimal network resource utilization. To address these issues, innovative approaches were taken, many of them inspired by the work of Fortz et al. [2], where the OSPF weight setting process is implemented using Traffic Engineering (TE) techniques. Here, the routing configuration task is formulated as an optimization problem, by defining a cost function that measures the network congestion, assuming that the administrator has access to a matrix representing traffic demands between each pair of source and destination nodes of the network.

In previous work, the authors have enhanced such optimization efforts, proposing a new approach [4] [5] that also accommodates delay constraints, also crucial to implement QoS aware networking services. In such works, optimization algorithms were used to calculate link-state routing weights that optimize traffic congestion, while simultaneously complying with specific delay requirements. However, the objective of developing network management tools that could effectively help network administrators requires that more powerful, efficient and versatile optimization paradigms be used to underpin this complex optimization problem. Within this perspective, this work fosters the research efforts and the application of TE methods resorting to the use of Multiobjective Evolutionary Algorithms (MOEAs) as a means to provide near-optimal routing configurations able to be easily analyzed by the administrator and, if required, applied to the network environment. The devised optimization framework takes advantages of the nature of the MOEAs solutions, assuming the form of Pareto fronts which are, both from the administrator and the optimization engine perspectives, very appropriate to deal with this NP-hard multi-constrained problem.

The paper proceeds with Section 2 giving the description of the problem and explaining the devised optimization model; Section 3 describes the experimental platform and the corresponding illustrative results; Section 4 discusses computational issues and software availability; Section 5 presents the conclusions.

2   Optimizing OSPF Routing Configurations

2.1   Problem Definition

The optimization framework proposed in this work aims to provide network administrators with efficient OSPF link weights, taking into account the users demands, the network topology and other features of the network domain. In OSPF, all links are associated with an integer weight. Every node uses these weights as an input to the Dijkstra algorithm [3] to calculate the shortest paths to all other nodes. All the traffic from a given source to a destination travels along the shortest path, except when two or more paths have the same length, in that case, traffic is divided among the arcs in these paths (load balancing) [12]. The framework assumes that client demands are mapped into a matrix[1] summarizing, for each source/destination edge router pair, a given required bandwidth and, if also defined, a target edge-to-edge delay to be supported by the network domain.

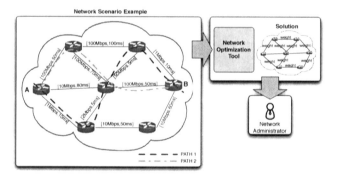

Fig. 1. Example of a network scenario

As an illustrative example, consider the network scenario included in Figure 1, involving only a single demand between the network $node_A$ and $node_B$. If such demand reflects only a delay target, the administrator should be able to use OSPF weights that result in a data path with the minimum delay between such nodes, i.e $path_1$. In a different perspective, if no delay requirements are assumed, and the unique constraint between such nodes is a given bandwidth target, the administrator would try to minimize the network congestion and assign OSPF weights to force a data path inducing the lowest level of losses in the traffic ($path_2$). These two distinct optimization aims would result in two

---

[1] There are several techniques to obtain traffic demand matrices which provide estimations regarding the overall requirements within a given domain (e.g. [6] [7]).

distinct sets of OSPF weights. Additionally, also considering that a given demand may have simultaneously bandwidth and delay constraints, then it is expected that the OSPF weight optimization process try to find a data path representing a trade-off between such requirements. The example of Figure 1 is, intentionally, extremely simple and only one demand was considered in the network domain. Assuming now that each router pair of a given Internet Service Provider (ISP) may have specific multi-constrained QoS requirements (i.e. traffic demands vs. delay restrictions), it is easy to understand how complex the problem can get, with the need of obtaining OSPF settings able to optimize multiple parameters.

The formulation model sustaining the proposed optimization framework follows the traditional mathematical networking model, representing routers and transmission links by a set of nodes (N) and arcs (A), respectively, in a directed graph $G = (N, A)$ [9], with each arc having a specific bandwidth capacity and a propagation delay, both intrinsic in the network topology[2]. Additionally, a demand matrix is available (D), where each element represents the traffic demand between a pair of nodes, allowing to calculate the total load on each arc. This value is used to define a congestion measure for each link, that can be used to compute a penalty function that exponentially penalizes high values of congestion (e.g. a function such the one used in [2]). The framework was also enriched with the possibility of including delay requirements for each pair of routers in the network. These are modeled as a matrix (DR) that, for each pair of nodes, gives the delay target for traffic between the origin and destination. In a similar way, a cost function was defined to evaluate the delay compliance for each scenario. This, in turn, allowed the definition of a delay minimization cost function. One illustrative example of the type of optimization problems addressed in our framework is to find the set of OSPF weights that simultaneously minimizes the cost functions associated with network congestion and with the edge-to-edge delay penalties of the network domain, making the problem addressed in this work clearly multi-objective. In the proposed model, given a specific network topology, a traffic demand matrix (D) and a delay requirements matrix (DR), the objective is to achieve a set of OSPF weights (w) that simultaneously minimize the functions $\Phi^*(w)$ and $\gamma^*(w)$, which are the penalty functions for congestion and edge-to-edge delays, respectively[3]. In this context, the cost of associated with a given weight solution w is evaluated using functions $\Phi^*(w)$ for congestion and $\gamma^*(w)$ for delays, with both functions normalized in the same range. The theoretical minimum value for the functions is 1; acceptable values for such network functions are in the range $[1, 10]$ meaning that the traffic demands and delays restrictions $(D, DR$ matrices$)$ are accomplished by the routing configuration.

2.2   Multi-Objective Evolutionary Algorithms

This section explains how multi-objective Evolutionary Algorithms (MOEAs) are adapted to be used in this work. The multi-objective nature of this problem

---

[2] It was considered that the delay in each path is dominated by propagation delays. However, if required, queuing delays are also easily incorporated in the framework.

[3] Details of these cost functions can be found in similar model formulations (e.g. [4]).

suggests MOEAs are good candidates for algorithms in the multi-objective optimization area, i.e. that return a set of solutions with distinct trade-offs between the two objectives, allowing the network administrator decide which solution to implement. Since the mid-1980's, MOEAs are being used to solve all kinds of multiple-criterion problems in distinct scenarios, being undoubtedly one of the most competitive approaches in this field [16]. The MOEAs chosen for this task are two of the most popular algorithms, namely the SPEA2 and the NSGA-II, widely accepted as two of the algorithms with the best overall performance.

In the proposed MOEAs based approach, each individual encodes a solution in the form of a vector of integer values. Here, each value (gene) corresponds to the weight of a link in the topology. Therefore, the size of the individual equals the number of links in the network. The individuals in the initial population are randomly generated, with link weights taken from an uniform distribution. To create new solutions, several reproduction operators were used, e.g. *crossover* and *mutation*. The *random mutation* replaces a given gene by a new value, randomly generated within the allowed range. The *incremental/decremental mutation* replaces a specific gene by the following or by the previous value (with same probabilities) constrained to the range of allowed values. The *uniform crossover* and *two-point crossover* are two standard crossover operators also applied to generate new solutions [11]. The fitness of an individual is derived from the analysis of functions $\Phi^*(w)$, for congestion, and $\gamma^*(w)$, for delays. On each algorithm iteration a sub-set of the best individuals proceeds to the next round, while a new subset of individuals is generated using the above mentioned reproduction operators. The process follows until the last iteration resulting in a set of solutions for the considered multi-objective problem. This process can be repeated several times (distinct runs) in order to obtain additional solutions.

The MOEAs return a Pareto front, i.e. a set of non-dominated solutions, for a given problem. When a solution is dominated by another one, it means that it is worse than the second in at least one of the objectives and it is not better in none. Given this, the Pareto front should be as near as possible to the optimal set of non-dominated solutions. In addition, it should also be as distributed as possible, i.e. it should cover the whole set of possible trade-offs between the optimization aims of the addressed problem. This specific characteristic of the Pareto front is adequate to be used in the context of optimization problems such the ones envisaged in this work. In this specific problem, the aim is to find routing configuration solutions where both objectives (congestion, delays) are within the range $[1, 10]$, as previously stated. The network administrator can then check the solutions within the returned Pareto front and select which is the trade-off that is more reasonable in a given context. Therefore, with a single run of the algorithm a set of alternatives are provided, which brings important advantages both in the administrator results perception and computational efforts perspectives.

2.3   Comparative Heuristics

In addition to the above mentioned optimization techniques, a number of traditional heuristic methods were also implemented, namely: *InvCap* - sets each

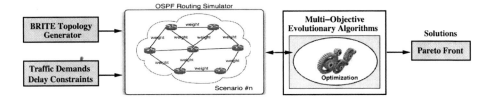

Fig. 2. Testbed for performance evaluation of the proposed framework

link weight to a value inversely proportional to its capacity; *L2* - sets each link weight to a value proportional to its Euclidean distance; *Random* - a number of randomly generated solutions are analyzed and the best is selected; and *Unit* - sets every link weight to one. These heuristic are used for comparative terms, i.e. to assess the order of magnitude of the improvements obtained by the MOEAs.

3   Performance Analysis

Figure 2 shows the experimental testbed used to assess the performance of the devised link weight setting optimization solution. The BRITE [13] topology generator was used to create distinct synthetic networks. The optimization results presented in this section were taken from two networks with $N \in \{30, 50\}$ nodes, with a node average degree of $m = 4$, resulting in topologies with 110 and 190 links, respectively. The capacity of the links varies in the interval $[1, 10]$ Gbits and the topology generation follows the Barabasi-Albert model[4].

In order to generate the traffic demands and delay constraints matrices two parameters (each one with three distinct values) were used, $D_p \in \{0.1, 0.2, 0.3\}$ and $DR_p \in \{3, 4, 5\}$, allowing to tune the difficulty levels of traffic demands and delay requirements, respectively. The precise values of D_p and DR_p parameters were selected in accordance with the overall congestion and delay constraints levels which are intended to be imposed to each network instance, given their particular characteristics. In the devised test methodology, scenarios assuming higher values for the D_p parameter and, simultaneously, lower values of the DR_p parameter are the ones harder to comply[5]. Based on the network topology, the demand matrices and on an initial weight assignment to the network links, a proprietary OSPF simulator will distribute the traffic along the paths, turning possible the computation of the $\Phi^*(w)$ and $\gamma^*(w)$ values. The optimization module of Figure 2 will then resort to the MOEA optimization approach explained before to find the solution for the optimization problem. In the following sections the results were obtained with the optimization module operating with the NSGA-II algorithm.

---

[4] A heavy-tail distribution was used along with an incremental grow type (the parameters HS and LS have values of 1000 and 100, respectively).

[5] Higher values of D_p mean that higher traffic demands are being considered, being harder to comply. In counterpoint, higher values for the DR_p mean that higher values for edge-to-edge delays requirements are being considered, being easier to comply.

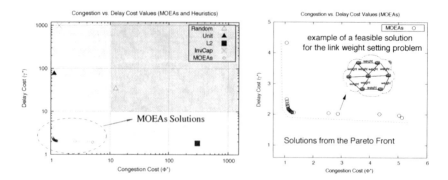

Fig. 3. a) Comparative perspective of the MOEAs and heuristics results (logarithmic scale); b) MOEAs results (i.e. only the white area from Fig. 3 a))

3.1 Illustrative Analysis of MOEAs Performance

As an initial illustrative example of the MOEAs optimization capabilities we select one particular instance of a network with 30 nodes and 110 links, with $D_p = 0.1$ and $DR_p = 3$. In this context, a brief analysis of the Pareto front returned by the MOEA is presented, along with comparative analysis of the performance obtained from the use of commonly used heuristics. This example will be complemented, in the next section, with additional optimization results for other network instances. However, in general terms, the conclusions drawn for this particular instance are representative of the overall performance capabilities of the proposed optimization framework. Figure 3 a) shows a particular subset of the solutions obtained by the MOEAs in the selected scenario and, for comparative terms, the ones obtained by common heuristics described before. Figure 3 a) has two distinct areas, the first one corresponds to solutions assuming routing configurations able to obey the considered traffic and delay demands (i.e. the white area, where cost function values are lower than 10), and a second area were the routing solutions lead to quality degradation of the network, with overloaded links or with the target delays requests not being assured by the network (gray filled area)[6].

As observed in Figure 3 a) the MOEA available in the proposed solution is able to provide the network administrator with a set of near-optimal routing configuration solutions for the network domain. In opposition, it is also noticeable that all the results of the heuristics for this instance lie outside the admissible range (i.e. outside the white area), and some of them with penalties which are one or two orders of magnitude higher than the ones obtained by MOEAs. This means that none of the heuristics is able to provide acceptable routing configurations[7].

---

[6] Note that in the dark gray filled area none of the requests are accomplished.

[7] Note that in Fig. 3 a) a logarithmic scale is used, meaning that points outside the white area represent, in fact, extremely poor quality routing solutions.

Figure 3 b) magnifies the white area of Figure 3 a) and now only the MOEAs solutions are plotted. As observed, the administrator achieves a set of near-optimal configuration solutions resulting from the Pareto front of the optimization process, all lying inside of the white area. Each one of such points (solutions) is associated with a routing weights table able to be used by the administrator according with the desired trade-off between the optimization objectives.

3.2   Optimization Results

This section analyzes the MOEAs optimization results for ten distinct network scenarios. The examples where taken from two networks with $N \in \{30, 50\}$ nodes and using five distinct combination of (D_p, DR_p) parameters, in this case the set $\{(0.1, 3), (0.1, 5), (0.2, 4), (0.3, 3), (0.3, 5)\}$. In the considered scenarios, the behavior of the heuristics is similar to the describe before, i.e. they are not capable of achieving acceptable performance, meaning that these solutions are completely outside of the white area of the graphs. For that reason, such results are not included in the following analysis.

Figure 4 shows the Pareto fronts obtained for each of the considered scenarios. It is important to note that results were obtained in the first runs of the MOEA optimization procedures, i.e. only a single run of the optimization algorithm has been performed for each of the network instances. As observed in Figure 4, for most of the scenarios the first run of the MOEA was sufficient to find acceptable results i.e. Pareto fronts with solutions (i.e. weight settings) in the white area of the figures. The administrator is then able to select these solutions in order to reach near-optimal routing configurations obeying to the imposed constraints.

As expected, the harder optimization scenarios are the ones imposing higher requirements regarding both the traffic demands and delay restrictions (e.g. $D_p = 0.3$, $DR_p = 3$). In such scenarios, the Pareto front patterns returned by the MOEAs are not so close to the graph origin as in other network configurations. As observed in Figure 4, the first run of the MOEA was not sufficient to find near-optimal configurations for the last two scenarios with $N = 50$ and (D_p, DR_p) values of $(0.3, 3)$ and $(0.3, 5)$. To improve such preliminary results additional runs of the MOEAs could be used to generate other weight setting configurations overcoming the performance obtained in previous runs.

In order to illustrate the previous reasoning, Figures 5 a), b) and c) plot additional optimization results obtained in other runs of the MOEAs for three specific scenarios (including the instances with lower quality results in the first run). The new Pareto fronts depicted in Figures 5 a), b) and c) are compared with the values obtained in the first runs (observed before in Figure 4). The analysis clearly shows an improvement of the Pareto front patterns for each scenario, containing now several points in the white regions of the figures. This behavior is visible in Figures 5 a), b) and c) and corresponds to a generalized displacement of the Pareto fronts to the feasible configuration area.

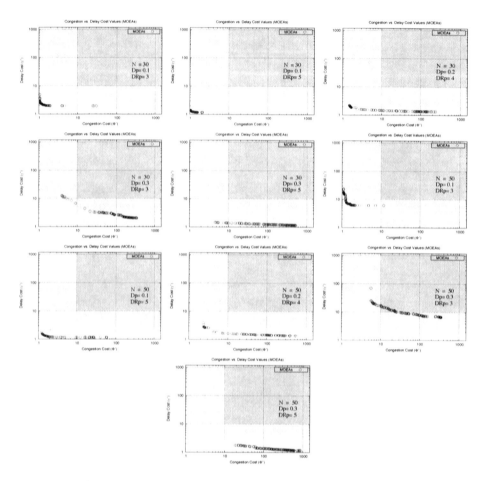

Fig. 4. MOEA optimization results - Pareto fronts - for two synthetic networks ($N =$ 30, 50) with distinct combinations of D_p and DR_p parameters (first runs)

3.3 Single-Objective vs. Multi-Objective Evolutionary Algorithms

This section compares the proposed framework approach with other approaches in the area which assume this problem under a single objective optimization perspective. In such works, a linear weighting scheme could be used to denote the overall cost of the solution, as expressed in Equation 1.

$$f(w) = \alpha \Phi^*(w) + (1 - \alpha)\gamma^*(w), \alpha \in [0, 1] \qquad (1)$$

When using a single objective evolutionary algorithm, the user specifies the parameter (α) defined above, that determines the importance that is given to each objective (congestion and delays). Examples of performance analysis of this approach can be found in [4], for a large set of distinct QoS constrained scenarios. Although this strategy has obtained acceptable results, it suffers from one

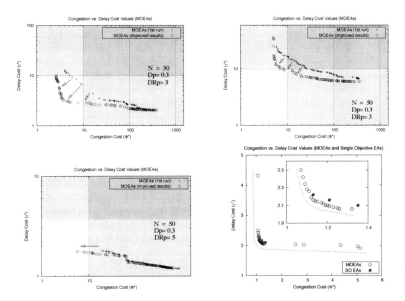

Fig. 5. a) b) c) Improved results for three particular network instances of Figure 4 (in runs 2, 23 and 16, respectively); d) MOEAs and single objective algorithm results

main drawback, since it assumes that there is one single trade-off that is optimum. Therefore, the algorithms typically return one single solution that has to be implemented by the administrator. To be able to analyze several distinct trade-offs between the two objectives, the user needs to execute different runs of the algorithm using different values of the parameter α. Moreover, for specific network configurations several tradeoffs between the congestion and delays requirements are not possible to be achieved, and the administrator will have the doubt about which values are admissible to tune the α parameter.

For comparative analysis, in addition to the MOEA used in the example of Figure 3 also a single objective evolutionary algorithm was run using the objective function of Equation 1. The single-objective algorithm was run with three distinct values of the parameter α (0.25, 0.5 and 0.75). Figure 5 d) shows the results obtained, showing a set of selected solutions obtained by the MOEA and also the best solution obtained by each of the single-objective evolutionary algorithms. It is important to note that all the solutions shown for the multi-objective optimization are obtained in a single run, while the solutions for the single objective need three distinct runs. Looking at the Figure 5 d), and although a direct comparison of the results obtained by the alternative approaches is not trivial, it is clear that running the MOEA the network administrator is provided with a set of alternatives, from where he can choose the best option, reflecting the ideal trade-off between the two objectives. The single objective evolutionary algorithm is normally restricted to a certain area of the working region of the network, making difficult the tuning process of the importance of each objective. Thus, the MOEA approach of the proposed framework presents advantages not only regarding the computational efforts perspective, but also improves the quality and the diversity of the results provided to the administrator.

4 Computational Efforts, Applicability and Availability

Even taking into account the complexity of the NP-hard problems here discussed, acceptable computational times were obtained when assessing the MOEA optimization process. As illustrative examples, on a current end-user computational platform (e.g. with a Core i7 processor) a single MOEAs run for the considered network examples required a computational time in the order of some minutes. As obvious, this value varies according with the network topology size and, when considering even harder optimization problems, the need of using several MOEAs runs may considerable increase the required computational times. In this perspective, if required, the use of computational clusters environments might be also an alternative to foster the process of obtaining high quality solutions.

It is important to note that, as known, frequent changes to the network routing configurations may lead to network instability. In this context, short-time updates to the routing configurations of a domain are not the scenarios envisioned by this work. Instead, the devised optimization framework was conceived with the aim of being an useful tool to assist network operators in the process of adjusting routing configurations for specific, stable and well known time periods, in conformity with previous studies expressing the demands required to be accomplished. This will allow that, in a first network configuration phase, a more efficient distribution of the traffic in the domain could be achieved. As obvious, other QoS oriented mechanisms are then expected to be applied, in a complementary way, in order to provide a finer-grain control of the service levels supported by the infra-structure. Another related area that could take advantage of the proposed solution, although not explored in this work, is the field of autonomic/self-management networks, as the devised optimization framework might also be useful to be integrated in such automated environments.

A preliminary version of the software implementing the proposed optimization framework was included in a traffic engineering platform which is made available in the home page accessible at `http://darwin.di.uminho.pt/netopt`.

5 Conclusions

This paper describes an evolutionary computation based traffic engineering framework, allowing the network administrator to improve the QoS levels on IP networks by obtaining near-optimal OSPF routing configurations. As an important contribution for the traffic engineering research efforts, the proposed framework integrates efficient multi-objective optimization algorithms from the evolutionary computation area. The presented results corroborate the idea that this optimization solution brings important advantages and enlarges the set of available options to network administrators, in shorter computation times, increasing the capacity of making informed decisions regarding the trade-offs between the different factors at stake. The supporting framework is currently under rapid development and additional functionalities may be also target of the MOEA optimization perspective. The class-based [15] and multicast [14] optimization mechanisms are two examples of developments which are suitable to be improved taking advantage of the presented MOEA based optimization approach.

References

1. Wang, Z.: Internet QoS: Architectures and Mechanisms for Quality of Service. Morgan Kaufmann Publishers, San Francisco (2001)
2. Fortz, B., Thorup, M.: Internet Traffic Engineering by Optimizing OSPF Weights. In: Proceedings of IEEE INFOCOM, pp. 519–528 (2000)
3. Dijkstra, E.W.: A note on Two Problems in Connexion with Graphs. Numerische Mathematik 1(269-271) (1959)
4. Sousa, P., Rocha, M., Rio, M., Cortez, P.C.: Efficient OSPF Weight Allocation for Intra-domain QoS Optimization. In: Parr, G., Malone, D., Ó Foghlú, M. (eds.) IPOM 2006. LNCS, vol. 4268, pp. 37–48. Springer, Heidelberg (2006)
5. Rocha, M., Sousa, P., Cortez, P., Rio, M.: Quality of Service Constrained Routing Optimization using Evolutionary Computation. Applied Soft Computing 11(1), 356–364 (2011)
6. Medina, A., et al.: Traffic matrix estimation: Existing techniques and new directions. Computer Communication Review 32(4), 161–176 (2002)
7. Davy, A., Botvich, D., Jennings, B.: An Efficient Process for Estimation of Network Demand for QoS-Aware IP Network Planning. In: Parr, G., Malone, D., Ó Foghlú, M. (eds.) IPOM 2006. LNCS, vol. 4268, pp. 120–131. Springer, Heidelberg (2006)
8. Gunnar, A., Johansson, M., Telkamp, T.: Traffic matrix estimation on a large IP backbone: a comparison on real data. In: IMC 2004: Proceedings of the 4th ACM SIGCOMM Conference on Internet Measurement, pp. 149–160 (2004)
9. Ahuja, R., Magnanti, T., Orlin, J.: Network Flows. Prentice Hall, Englewood Cliffs (1993)
10. Moy, J.: RFC 2328: OSPF version 2 (April 1998)
11. Michalewicz, Z.: Genetic Algorithms + Data Structures = Evolution Programs, 3rd edn. Springer, USA (1998)
12. Moy, J.: OSPF, Anatomy of an Internet Routing Protocol. Addison Wesley, Reading (1998)
13. Medina, A.L.A., Matta, I., Byers, J.: BRITE: Universal Topology Generation from a Users Perspective, Tech. Rep. 2001-003 (January 2001)
14. Sousa, P., Rocha, M., Cortez, P., Rio, M.: Multiconstrained Optimization of Networks with Multicast and Unicast Traffic. In: Pavlou, G., Ahmed, T., Dagiuklas, T. (eds.) MMNS 2008. LNCS, vol. 5274, pp. 139–150. Springer, Heidelberg (2008)
15. Sousa, P., Rocha, M., Rio, M., Cortez, P.: Class-Based OSPF Traffic Engineering Inspired on Evolutionary Computation. In: Boavida, F., Monteiro, E., Mascolo, S., Koucheryavy, Y. (eds.) WWIC 2007. LNCS, vol. 4517, pp. 141–152. Springer, Heidelberg (2007)
16. Coello, C.: A Comprehensive Survey of Evolutionary-Based Multiobjective Optimization Techniques. Knowledge and Information Systems 1(3), 129–156 (1999)

Storage-Enabled Access Points for Improved Mobile Performance: An Evaluation Study*

Efthymios Koutsogiannis[1], Lefteris Mamatas[1], and Ioannis Psaras[2]

[1] Democritus University of Thrace,
Dept. of Electrical and Computer Engineering/Space Internetworking Center,
12 Vas. Sofias Str., 67100 Xanthi, Greece
{ekoutsog,emamatas}@ee.duth.gr
[2] University College London,
Dept. of Electronic and Electrical Engineering,
WC1E 7JE, Torrington Place, London, UK
i.psaras@ee.ucl.ac.uk

Abstract. Due to existing networking paradigms and people communication habits, Internet is characterized by: (i) information that associates more and more with network edges, while corresponding traffic doesn't, (ii) a considerable amount of unexplored network resources that resides near mobile users, while their connectivity is usually poor and expensive in terms of financial cost and resource consumption.

To address the above challenges, we introduce a cooperative networking scheme where *Home Access Points* are equipped with storage capabilities and offer connectivity to mobile users. Whenever connectivity sharing is unavailable, the access points store the pending data and transmit it once connectivity becomes available. We explore how storage-enabled opportunistic routing algorithms can handle periods of intermittent connectivity. We experiment with realistic scenarios based on real network configurations and mobility maps. Our results demonstrate the potential of the proposed paradigm as well as guide us to define its follow-up evolution steps.

Keywords: user-centric networking, delay-tolerant networking, opportunistic routing.

1 Introduction

Research on *Opportunistic Mobile Networks* and DTNs has been mainly concerned with *storage and energy* constraints for mobile devices and optimization of *connectivity* opportunities between encounters. The more the encounters and data-exchanges between the mobile nodes, the more the energy and storage needed. The Delay-Tolerant and Opportunistic Networking research has

---

* The research leading to these results has received funding from the European Community's Seventh Framework Programme (FP7/2007-2013_FP7-REGPOT-2010-1, SP4 Capacities, Coordination and Support Actions) under grant agreement n° 264226 (project title: Space Internetworking Center-SPICE).

X. Masip-Bruin et al. (Eds.): WWIC 2011, LNCS 6649, pp. 116–127, 2011.

focused mainly on *mobile-only* devices. That is, researchers have been investigating ways to optimize communication opportunities between *the mobile devices themselves*[1]. This is indeed the case in rural areas, for instance, where connectivity points to the network are rare, or in case of applications that do not require Internet connectivity (e.g., distributed online social networks [1]).

In this study, we focus on metropolitan environments, where there are plenty of connectivity points to the Internet. We extend the operational spectrum of Opportunistic Networks and DTNs and consider Home Access Points (APs or HAPs) as integral part of these networks. We consider storage a cheap resource that can easily be integrated in future APs and evaluate the performance of existing DTN protocols in this setting. In particular, given that connectivity opportunities to APs/HAPs and therefore the Internet now increase, we investigate whether and to which extend the storage and energy constraints can now be somewhat relaxed.

We motivate our study based on the following facts:

- New applications and people communication habits call for approaches that go beyond the traditional client-server model. Users are increasingly active in uploading content to social networking sites, for instance, or hosting data, e.g., in P2P file-sharing platforms. Moreover, it is shown that Internet traffic is growing faster at the network edge than at the core [2]. In other words, future networks call for *user-centricity*, where applications demand that *content is closer to the user*.
- Internet traffic forecasts show that mobile users are expected to double-up every year through 2014[2]. Similar studies show that the amount of user-generated content is going to increase massively[3] and furthermore, that most of it will be generated by mobile devices, e.g., smart-phones *et simila*. This urges the need for easy access to the Internet for mobile users, since content has to be readily available.
- Statistics show that the vast majority of households (e.g., 70% in UK) own a broadband connection[4], which remains unexploited most of the day. It is obvious that an area of dense connectivity can be formed if the HAPs' network and storage resources are being shared between home- and mobile-users.
- User-Provided Networks and connectivity sharing schemes have already been investigated and implemented (e.g., FON [3]). In our previous studies [4], [5] we have presented algorithms for connectivity sharing among home- and guest-users and proved that careful design can guarantee seamless connectivity sharing for the home-user.

---

[1] Vehicular DTNs [6] and Infostations [7] can be considered as exceptions here, since these deployments are not constrained by energy and/or storage depletion in most cases.

[2] http://www.cisco.com/en/US/netsol/ns827/
networking_solutions_sub_solution.html

[3] http://newsroom.cisco.com/dlls/2009/prod_102109.html

[4] http://www.statistics.gov.uk/cci/nugget.asp?ID=8

In this study, we explore the performance benefits of extending the users' connectivity graph to include neighbor HAPs, exploiting this way local unused resources. *An occupied HAP that temporarily cannot forward packets from guest-users to the Internet may store the packets until a connection opportunity is available. The stored packets can be forwarded to another HAP in range, or relayed to a mobile node that may find another connectivity point.*

We focus on the evaluation of DTN routing protocols, when the opportunistic network infrastructure is extended to also include HAPs, whenever and wherever these are available. We have built a realistic scenario, where mobile users walk around the center of London. We assume that existing FON subscribers (i.e., we used the database from maps.btfon.com) employ the proposed paradigm. We apply different usage scenarios to the home-users (e.g., periodic use, away for the day, away for work) in order to emulate their on-off behavior in terms of connectivity offering. We assume that whenever the home-user is transmitting/receiving data the HAP is not available to the guest user. Therefore, the connection is available for guests whenever the home connection is idle. At this stage, we explore how existing opportunistic routing algorithms behave in this particular context; we evaluate the following well-known algorithms: *Epidemic* [8], *First contact* [9], *Spray and Focus* [10], *Spray and Wait* [11] and *MaxProp* [12]. We elaborate on these results in order to draw design guidelines for new algorithms, especially designed and optimized for the proposed paradigm. Our target is to identify the necessary properties that need to be integrated into opportunistic routing protocols in order to operate as efficiently as possible under this new setting, i.e., when storage resources are part of the HAP and are offered to mobile users. We leave these designs as our immediate future work task.

Our findings indicate that: (i) integrating storage capabilities to HAPs substantially increases connectivity opportunities for mobile nodes, (ii) service quality for mobile users increases with the number of available HAPs and their respective storage resources, (iii) there is a lot of space for improvement for opportunistic routing protocols, performance-wise, (iv) among the evaluated algorithms *Spray and Focus* is the most efficient, since it balances better between performance and overhead, and (v) an efficient routing algorithm for this new networking paradigm could offload routing sophistication or routing state info from mobile devices to HAPs, in order to reduce energy consumption at mobile users, without compromising performance.

In Section 2, we discuss the related work in terms of other broadband access sharing schemes and opportunistic routing algorithms. In Section 3, we describe our experimental setup and the associated methodology and in Section 4 we present our experimental results. We conclude the paper in Section 5, where we also discuss our future work.

2   Related Work

Broadly speaking, our study balances between *User-Provided Networks* and Opportunistic or Delay-Tolerant-Networks. Below, we briefly provide background, state of the art information on these areas and highlight how the present study advances research beyond the state of the art.

2.1 State of the Art

User-Provided Networks. UPNs have been recently proposed [13] as an umbrella framework for Broadband Access Sharing. Citywide Ubiquitous Wi-Fi Access sharing issues have been investigated in the past [14] and have shown that commercial deployment of such initiatives is indeed possible.

Famous commercial deployments include the FON Community, the OpenSpark Community and the Wifi.com[5]. Each of these deployments has a different starting point, incentive-wise, and therefore, comprises different scalability and efficiency properties. For instance, Wifi.com is based on a social networking approach, while FON is based on a business model that explicitly allocates resources to home- and guest-users. Recent studies have also investigated the wireless interface's capabilities to share resources [15].

The success of the above initiatives clearly shows that users are keen on giving away a portion of their bandwidth in order to have access when out of home or office. In our opinion, whatever the Broadband Access Sharing scheme, it has to balance between two fragile service-points: (i) the guarantee to the home-user for seamless sharing, performance-wise and (ii) the mobile-users' quality of experience. The former point has been our focus in previous studies [4], [5]. The latter constitutes our target in the present study, where we elaborate on the functionality of an efficient routing mechanism in order to achieve lower latency and reduced transmission redundancy. Hence, our target is increased responsiveness, efficient storage management and longer battery life for mobile devices.

Opportunistic Networks and DTNs. A lot of research has taken place recently to deal with routing issues in intermittently connected networks. Here, we briefly present the most prevalent DTN routing algorithms.

In *Epidemic routing* algorithm [8], a node copies a message to every other node it encounters. Variations of this algorithm include *Randomized flooding* and *Utility-based flooding*. *Randomized flooding* or *Gossiping (random-flood)* is quite similar to *Epidemic* although each message is copied with probability $p < 1$. In the *Utility-based flooding*, a message is copied only if the node encountered has a utility value higher than the current by some threshold U_{th}.

MaxProp [12] is another flooding-based mechanism which removes the messages once a copy is delivered. Moreover, *MaxProp* prioritizes both messages to be transmitted and dropped based on previous encounters.

Resource Allocation Protocol for Intentional DTN (*RAPID*) [16] treats DTN routing as a resource allocation problem. It uses a utility function that: (i) assigns a value based on the metric being optimized to every packet and (ii) first replicates packets that increase the utility function.

---

[5] URLs: http://www.btfon.com, http://open.spark.fi, http://www.wifi.com

Other approaches use a controlled replication or *spraying*. In *Spray and Wait* [11], a small fixed number of copies are distributed (sprayed) to different relays (i.e., the first few encountered). Each relay waits until it encounters the destination itself. A more sophisticated variation is *Spray and Focus* [10] which operates like *Spray and Wait* during *spraying*. Each relay, instead of waiting, can forward its copy to a potentially more appropriate relay, using a utility-based scheme.

For a complete survey on DTN routing protocols, we refer the reader to [17] and [18]. In addition, related work on exploiting WLAN hotspots in order to enhance opportunistic web access and offload cellular traffic can be found in [19] and [20], respectively.

2.2   Progress beyond the State of the Art

To release the boundaries that keep these two research fields separated and unleash the communication opportunities of the corresponding framework, we highlight the following:

– *UPNs exploit connectivity sharing opportunities only.* Broadband access is only one of the available resources that can be shared between home and mobile users. In this study, we explore the potential of sharing storage resources as well, given that storage is available at the HAPs. That is, we extend the sharing capabilities of UPNs to include storage resources as well.
– *DTN routing research has been mainly concerned with encounters between mobile nodes only.* Although in case of DTN nodes, both connectivity and storage resources are shared between the nodes, they do not consider collaborating with fixed points of the infrastructure. Here, we extend this trend to a boundless framework, where mobile nodes can also take advantage of both connectivity and storage resources of HAPs.

3   Experimental Setup and Methodology

We simulate a realistic mobility setup. We have chosen a geographical area in the center of London sized 2160m x 1600m, see Fig. 1. This area covers 349 different streets and 1876 landmarks. We have gathered detailed information from [3] regarding the exact position and the number of BTFON users in this particular area (i.e., 118 users). We parsed all this information into the ONE simulator [21].

We extended the ONE simulator with better support for wired networks and two new types of nodes: (i) the home-user that owns a HAP, and (ii) a server node, which hosts data for the mobile users (e.g., social profile photos). We assume that all home-users are permanently connected to a server node (e.g., a server farm) situated in Gower Street (see Fig. 1).

Mobile nodes are moving in the area and transmit periodically data (every 60 to 80 seconds, according to a uniform distribution) to the server node. Message sizes follow the uniform distribution [100kB, 200kB] (e.g., a typical social profile photo). Their movement is restricted to the streets in the map, according to the map route movement model and the shortest path algorithm in ONE simulator.

All nodes (mobile and static) have storage capabilities, but static nodes, i.e., HAPs, comprise extensive storage resources. In our setup, mobile nodes and HAPs have 30MB of storage available. These are only indicative figures and serve as pointers for future settings. As already mentioned, the HAP is only available to mobile users, whenever the home-user is idle. This practically means that when the home-user is using his Internet connection, only storage capabilities are offered to the mobile nodes within range. We assume three representative home-user profiles: (i) users that are idle for 8 hours per day only (e.g., during working hours), (ii) users that are permanently idle (e.g., they are absent), and (iii) users that are only periodically using their connection throughout the day (i.e., according to a normal probability distribution: 1-3 hours at home and 1-2 hours away). Nodes periodically transmit beacons to recognize each other's presence. Fig. 1, shows our experimental setup. The server is referenced as s-node, mobile-guests as g-nodes and home-users as h-nodes.

At this stage of investigation, we evaluate how existing opportunistic routing algorithms behave in this particular scenario, where HAPs offer storage resources apart from only connectivity. We selected five representative storage-enabled algorithms, namely: *Epidemic* [8], *First contact* [9], *Spray and Wait* [11], *Spray and Focus* [10] and *MaxProp* [12]. Our target is to *identify key requirements and design guidelines for a customized algorithm that exploits efficiently not only connection opportunities, but storage resources as well.*

Since a crucial aspect is to maximize energy efficiency of the mobile nodes, a maximum data delivery ratio should be combined with minimum communication / storage overhead and latency. In this context, we measure the following:

- $OverheadRatio = \frac{Packets\,Relayed - Packets\,Received}{Packets\,Received}$, which captures packet delivery ratio with respect to the number of packets relayed.
- *AverageLatency*, which captures the average packet latency that increases with the number of hops the packet crosses.
- *AverageBufferTime*, which reflects the average time the packets are buffered, in order to evaluate protocol storage efficiency.

4   Experimental Results

The experimental scenarios presented in the next section were designed in order to allow for:

- Studying the impact of the proposed extended networking scheme on the performance of a representative opportunistic routing algorithm. In this context, the *Epidemic*[6] protocol was evaluated in various deployment levels by increasing the number of HAPs in Scenario 1. In Scenario 2, evaluation is based on different usage profiles that home-users adopt.

---

[6] *Epidemic* protocol was selected for these scenarios and more specifically *EpidemicOracle* version, which upon message delivery removes that message from all nodes.

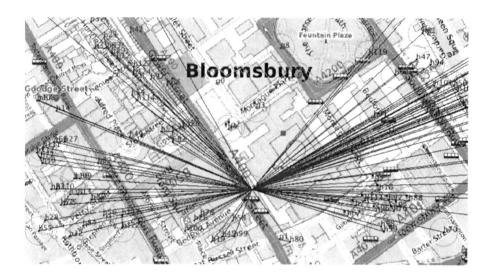

Fig. 1. Experimental Scenario

– Evaluating well-known DTN routing protocols' functionality used for communication between mobile nodes and static infrastructure. More specifically, we study their performance while scaling the proposed scheme with respect to mobile nodes' number, in Scenario 3. In scenario 4, we focus on the efficiency of the protocols with regards to guest-users' speed.

4.1   Scenario 1: Impact of Home-Users' Number

The purpose is to show the advantages of the proposed framework, i.e., the extension of mobile network's boundaries to also include storage-equipped HAPs. In this first scenario, we explore the performance of a representative opportunistic routing protocol and more specifically *Epidemic* with 100 mobile-users, where the availability of HAPs is gradually increased (0-100). Home-users can be perceived as points of guaranteed message delivery to the destination server.

We observe in Fig. 2(a), that as the number of home-users increases, the average Latency declines, since less time is needed to reach a connectivity point to the Internet. Consequently, the average buffering time declines as well, as is shown in Fig. 2(b), owing to timely message delivery. The peak in measurements (i.e., Figures 2(a), 2(b)) for 5 home-users can be justified as follows: most of the first five HAPs in our database are situated in peripheral streets. Hence, they have low interaction probability with mobile nodes and consequently they do not get involved in the replication process. Therefore, average buffering time increases (Fig. 2(b)), since mobile nodes need to carry data for more time. Clearly, there are still more delivery probabilities than in the case of zero home-users (Fig. 2(a)), where the server is the only data delivery point. In conclusion, increasing the availability of storage-equipped HAPs enhances network's connectivity, thus average Latency and Buffering time decrease.

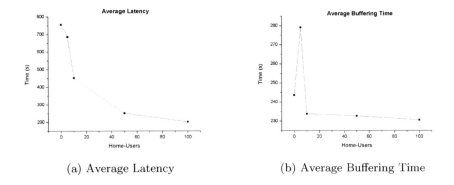

(a) Average Latency   (b) Average Buffering Time

Fig. 2. Scenario 1: Impact of Home-Users' Number

4.2 Scenario 2: Impact of Home-Users' Usage-Profiles

Here, each home-user adopts one of the three usage-profiles described in Section 3.1. This scenario intends to study the behavior of a representative opportunistic routing protocol in a topology consisting of 118 home-users with different usage-profiles. We discriminate the cases according to home-users' percentage that follows each of the three usage profiles: A) away for 8 hours, B) always away, C) periodically away (1-3 hours at home, then 1-2 hours away). Moreover, we simulated the cases where (A, B, C) percentages are: i) (0, 100, 0), ii) (20, 40, 40), iii) (10, 10, 80), iv) (0, 0, 100), while guest-users vary (10-100).

We conducted a series of experiments where increasing home users with usage profiles (i) and (iii), causes lack of connectivity, while increasing the number of guest-users allows for more routes and improved message delivery in terms of time. In these experiments, we observed that data remains stored at home-users available for: i) delivery to the server when connection will be up, ii) transmission to a guest-user in the vicinity, iii) transmission to a home-user in the vicinity. Fig. 3(b) presents average buffering time, which decreases as mobile nodes increase, while the four graphs coincide. Clearly, usage-profile has small impact on buffering time, since the number of home-users is sufficiently large. On the contrary, average Latency graphs vary, and their values increase when periodic nodes increase, while increasing guest-users decreases average Latency as depicted in Fig. 3(a). We report, although not present it here due to space limitations, that Overhead ratio is not influenced by usage-profile. Usage-profiles appear to have significant impact on average Latency, while *Epidemic* protocol manages to deliver messages, though with a high overhead.

4.3 Scenario 3: Impact of Guest-Users' Number

In this scenario, we aim to compare the functionality of all five protocols and highlight the most efficient strategy, in the extended opportunistic networking paradigm introduced herein. The topology consists of 118 HAPs constantly available, while mobile nodes vary (10-100).

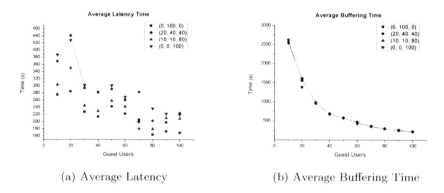

(a) Average Latency   (b) Average Buffering Time

Fig. 3. Scenario 2: Impact of Home-Users' Usage-Profiles

Spray and Wait introduces the highest average Buffering time (see Fig. 4(b)), which is not affected by the number of guest-users, while *Spray and Focus* achieves the lowest. Both algorithms were configured with 6 message copies, therefore their behavior at spraying phase is identical; consequently, the *focus* phase is responsible for the significant reduction of buffering time, as opposed to the *wait* phase. Fig. 4(a), depicts the average Latency, where *Spray and Focus* is again outperforming the rest of the protocols. *First contact* is the worst performing algorithm, since the first encountering node has no guarantee to deliver the message immediately. The Overhead ratio in Fig. 4(c) evinces the efficiency of *Spray and Focus* mechanism compared to the others. As expected *Epidemic* did not perform well with regards to overhead owing to mere flooding.

Therefore, increasing guest-users' number improves the average latency, except from *First Contact*. Furthermore, it also reduces average buffering time at the expense of overhead. In summary, regarding the impact of guest-users' number, *Spray and Focus* is the most efficient of the tested algorithms.

4.4   Scenario 4: Impact of Guest-Users' Speed

The speed of mobile nodes, together with connectivity opportunities, the message size and links' bandwidth are critical to protocol's efficiency. Increased speed allows for more encounters with other nodes, although it reduces the communication time. Using realistic settings, we evaluate the performance of the five protocols with regards to speed differentiation, for 10 guest- (maximum supported number for the specific configuration) and 118 home-users available.

Increasing speed (1 to 20 m/s) allows for increased data relaying due to more encounters and reduces the average buffering time (Fig. 4(e)). *Spray and Focus* has the best performance, even though it is the only algorithm whose buffering time increases with speed; this is due to utility function's inability to adapt to increased encounters. This result shows the potential improvement of the specific algorithm in this context. Average latency in Fig. 4(d) is highly decreased for

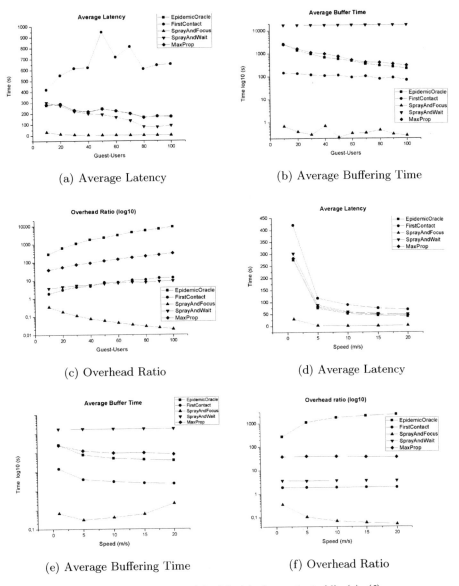

(a) Average Latency

(b) Average Buffering Time

(c) Overhead Ratio

(d) Average Latency

(e) Average Buffering Time

(f) Overhead Ratio

Fig. 4. Scenario 3: (a), (b), (c), Scenario 4: (d), (e), (f)

low speeds (5 m/s), while further speed increase does not affect the results. Fig. 4(f) depicts the overhead ratio, where *Epidemic* routing has the highest overhead ratio in contrast to *Spray and Focus*. In conclusion, *Spray and Focus* is the best performing algorithm in this scenario with regards to all evaluation parameters.

5   Conclusions

We have proposed and investigated a cooperative networking scheme, in the context of *User-Provided Networks*, where storage resources are offered to mobile users, until bandwidth at HAPs becomes available to transmit mobile users' data. Storage-enabled nodes and access points are a key feature of our opportunistic networking paradigm. We evaluated the impact of this scheme on the performance of opportunistic routing and compared the performance of five well-known DTN routing protocols in a realistic simulation setting. The proposed networking scheme avails in terms of latency and buffering time, although overhead ratio is sometimes increasing. Since mobile devices are involved, an efficient routing protocol that achieves high delivery ratio and low overhead is crucial. We have concluded that *Spray and Focus* [10] is the most suitable for the aforementioned scheme, amongst the evaluated protocols.

These preliminary results indicate that a new DTN routing protocol suitable for this environment can achieve improved overall performance. Its functionality should allow for reduced latency, communication and storage overhead, in conjunction with high delivery ratio, even in case of opportunistic routing (few and sparse HAPs). We argue that the basic guidelines for the design of the algorithm are: (i) Route data through HAPs with a higher probability than mobile nodes in order to alleviate the latter's storage and energy constraints. (ii) Exploiting HAP density and offloading sophistication or routing state info from mobile nodes to HAPs will further enhance performance e.g., via encounter prediction. (iii) Integration of *Spray and Focus* functionality in order to perform efficiently when mobile nodes are dominant in the topology. (iv) Dynamic configuration of message redundancy according to feedback from encounters and time scales [22], will allow for low overhead in conjunction with the desired delivery rate. As a next step we intend to integrate these observations in a new protocol.

References

1. Xu, T., Chen, Y., Fu, X., Hui, P.: Twittering by cuckoo: decentralized and socio-aware online microblogging services. SIGCOMM Computer Communication Review 40(4), 473–474 (2010)
2. Leavitt, N.: Network-Usage Changes Push Internet Traffic to the Edge. IEEE Computer Magazine 43(10), 13–15 (2010)
3. BT FON FON Wireless Ltd and British Telecommunications, http://www.btfon.com
4. Psaras, I., Mamatas, L.: On Demand Connectivity Sharing: Queuing Management and Load Balancing for User-Provided Networks. Elsevier Computer Networks (COMNET), Special Issue on Wireless for the Future Internet (2010) (accepted)

5. Mamatas, L., Psaras, I., Pavlou, G.: Incentives and Algorithms for Broadband Access Sharing. In: 1st ACM Sigcomm Workshop on Home Networks (HomeNets), New Delhi, India (August 2010)
6. Bychkovsky, V., et al.: A Measurement Study of Vehicular Internet Access Using in Situ Wi-Fi Networks. In: Proceedings of MobiCom, New York, USA, pp. 50–61 (2006)
7. Goodman, D.J., Borras, J., Mandayam, N.B., Yates, R.D.: INFOSTATIONS: a new system model for data and messaging services. In: IEEE VTC 1997, vol. 2, pp. 969–973 (May 1997)
8. Vahdat, A., Becker, D.: Epidemic routing for partially connected ad hoc networks. Technical Report CS-200006, Duke University (2000)
9. Fall, K.: A delay-tolerant network architecture for challenged internets. In: SIGCOMM 2003, pp. 27–34. ACM, New York (2003), http://doi.acm.org/10.1145/863955.863960, doi:10.1145/863955.863960
10. Spyropoulos, T., Psounis, K., Raghavendra, C.S.: Spray and Focus: Efficient Mobility-Assisted Routing for Heterogeneous and Correlated Mobility. In: Fifth Annual IEEE International Conference on Pervasive Computing and Communications (PerCom), White Plains, NY, March 19-23, pp. 79–85 (2007)
11. Spyropoulos, T., Psounis, K., Raghavendra, C.S.: Spray and wait: Efficient routing in intermittently connected mobile networks. In: Proceedings of ACM SIGCOMM Workshop on Delay Tolerant Networking, WDTN (2005)
12. Burgess, J., Gallagher, B., Jensen, D., Levine, B.N.: MaxProp: Routing for Vehicle-Based Disruption-Tolerant Networks. In: Proc. of IEEE INFOCOM (April 2006)
13. Sofia, R., Mendes, P.: User-provided Networks: Consumer as Provider. IEEE Communications Magazine 46(12), 86–91 (2008)
14. Thraves, C., et al.: Driving the Deployment of Citywide Ubiquitous WiFi Access. In: SimulWorks (2008)
15. Solarski, M., et al.: An Experimental Evaluation of Urban Networking using IEEE 802.11 Technology. In: Wireless Mesh, pp. 1–10 (2006)
16. Balasubramanian, A., Levine, B.N., Venkataramani, A.: DTN routing as a resource allocation problem. In: Proc. ACM SIGCOMM (August 2007)
17. Small, T., Haas, Z.: Resource and performance tradeoffs in delay-tolerant wireless networks. In: Proceedings of ACM SIGCOMM WDTN (2005)
18. Psaras, I., Wood, L., Tafazolli, R.: Delay-/Disruption-Tolerant Networking: State of the Art and Future Challenges Technical Report (2009), http://www.ee.ucl.ac.uk/~uceeips/dtn-srv-ipsaras.pdf
19. Pitkänen, M., Kärkkäinen, T., Ott, J.: Opportunistic Web Access via WLAN Hotspots. In: Proc. of PERCOM 2010, Mannheim, Germany (March 2010)
20. Han, B., et al.: Cellular traffic offloading through opportunistic communications: a case study. In: Proceedings of ACM CHANTS (2010)
21. Keränen, A., Ott, J., Kärkkäinen, T.: The ONE Simulator for DTN Protocol Evaluation. In: SIMUTools 2009, Rome, Italy (2009)
22. Karvo, J., Ott, J.: Time scales and delay-tolerant routing protocols. In: Proceedings of the 3rd ACM CHANTS 2008, pp. 33–40. ACM, New York (2008)

A Model to Improve the Accuracy of WSN Simulations

Óscar Gama[1], Paulo Carvalho[1], and P.M. Mendes[2]

[1] Informatics Dept.,
[2] Industrial Electronics Dept.,
University of Minho, Portugal
{osg,pmc}@di.uminho.pt, paulo.mendes@dei.uminho.pt

Abstract. Simulation studies have been extensively adopted in the networking research community. Nevertheless, the performance of the software components running within the network devices is often not modeled by generic network simulators. This aspect is particularly important in wireless sensor networks (WSN). As motes present very limited computing resources, the overhead of the software components cannot be ignored. Consequently, WSN simulation results may diverge significantly from the reality. After showing experimentally the validity of this assumption, the paper proposes a set of generic equations to model the performance of WSN software components. Validation tests using contention and multiplexing-based MAC protocols show that the inclusion of the proposed model in a WSN simulator improves the confidence degree in the simulation results significantly.

Keywords: wireless sensor network, simulation, real tests, parameterized model.

1 Introduction

Many studies within the WSN research community resort commonly to simulators. A review based on 151 wireless network articles from a five-year-period reported that 76% of those works used simulations [1]. The preference for simulators is justified by the difficulty of deploying real networks, as programming a large number of motes, gathering performance metrics, and managing the power sources is tedious and time consuming. Simulators allow building and modifying network scenarios easily, and tests are easily monitored. A comparison of simulators for WSNs is provided in [2].

WSN simulation studies use frequently unrealistic assumptions, such as, flat physical environment, circular radio transmission area, channel with bidirectional symmetry, and no fading or shadowing phenomena. These assumptions lead to simulation results that differ significantly from experimental results [3].

Since simulators can use different models to represent the same physical phenomenon, appreciable divergences in the results may be obtained using distinct simulators. The performance results of a simple algorithm using diverse simulators proved this fact [4]. Furthermore, models cannot represent reality with absolute accuracy [5]. Simulation scenarios can also ignore diverse hardware and software aspects that may influence the final results. An example is the time required by the base-station (BS) and the motes to process the incoming or outgoing packets.

X. Masip-Bruin et al. (Eds.): WWIC 2011, LNCS 6649, pp. 128–139, 2011.
© IFIP International Federation for Information Processing 2011

Aware of the difficulty that a simulator may have in presenting accurate results, this work studies software-related aspects of a WSN that contribute to the differences between simulation results and real measurements. This important topic is usually neglected in WSN simulations. First, within the IEEE 802.15.4 domain, the results obtained in a simulated WSN are compared to those obtained in an analogous physical scenario, and the causes of divergence in the results are identified. Then, a model using empirical software-related parameters to improve the accuracy of the simulation results is proposed. Instead of trying to present accurate values for the model parameters, which are necessarily specific to each testbed, this work intends to model software-related issues which have influence on the testbed results, and which may also occur in another WSN testbed. The main contribution of this paper is to present a model reflecting the impact of the software components on a physical WSN. The proposed model is generic to be easily implemented in current WSN simulators, being also an important contribute for future development of simulation tools.

2   Experimental Platforms

The physical and simulated experimental platforms as well as the test conditions used in this work are presented next. The reference testbed is composed of 16 ZigBit-A2 motes [7] placed statically in a semi-circle around the BS, about one meter away from the BS. To evaluate the impact of software components on the performance of a WSN, a static small-area WSN was adopted to minimize the effects of additional source of errors, such as nodes mobility and fading phenomena. The testbed is limited to sixteen motes due to the RAM memory constraints of the BS. Indeed, a minimum amount of memory in the BS is required to hold data for packet statistical analysis, and this memory is dependent on the number of active motes in the WSN.

The ZigBit-A2 mote is an IEEE 802.15.4/ ZigBee-compliant module operating in the 2.4 GHz band. It contains one AT86RF230 transceiver and one ATmega1281V microcontroller. Motes run TinyOS, an event-oriented operating system. The testbed uses the BS available from the manufacturer. As the BS is built-in around a ZigBit-A2 module, in terms of software performance the BS is identical to a mote.

To study the validity of the proposed model in a different test scenario, traffic from another IEEE 802.15.4 WSN is admitted in the channel used by the reference testbed. The reference WSN and the interfering WSN have distinct personal area network identifiers, and are close enough to sense the carrier signals mutually.

The physical testbed scenario was equally implemented in the Castalia-2.3b [6], an open-source, discrete event-driven simulator designed specifically for WSNs.

2.1   Test Conditions

In the reference WSN, each mote transmits a packet with 90 bytes (B) of MAC payload to the BS every 250 ms approximately. This traffic volume is typical in WSNs with high data rates, such as e-health WSNs monitoring electrocardiographic signals. In these scenarios, the influence of the software components on the overall network performance is not negligible. In the interfering WSN, one mote sends a packet with 100 B of MAC payload to its BS every 50 ms approximately.

The non-slotted CSMA-CA MAC protocol described in IEEE 802.15.4 standard was used in the reference WSN and interfering WSN. In the reference WSN, the CSMA-CA algorithm used the default parameters. The interfering WSN also used the default parameters apart from the maximum number of frame retries, which is zero to guarantee that the CSMA algorithm execution ends before 50 ms.

The reference WSN operated in a channel free of IEEE 802.15.4 traffic. For this purpose, a channel analyzer was used to find a free channel. To reduce the impact of spurious interferences, motes transmit at maximum power (3 dBm).

Tests were carried out in the physical testbed and in the simulator for an increasing number of motes in the WSN. The test duration was 16 minutes for each set of motes. Tests were run with and without 802.15.4 interfering traffic in the operating channel.

3   Experimental Results

The results for round-trip (RT) delay, and Delivery Error Ratio (DER) obtained both in the physical testbed and in the simulator are discussed next. Both metrics are considered from the perspective of the application layer. In the context of this study, RT delay is the time spent between sending an application data packet from a mote and the successful confirmation of the operation, which occurs after receiving the MAC ACK frame from the BS. DER expresses the probability of an application data packet sent from a mote to the application layer of the BS failing the delivery.

Fig. 1 and Fig. 2 present the results obtained *without the presence* of interfering traffic. Fig. 1 shows the simulation results for the DER when increasing the number of motes sending packets to the BS. The graphical bars correspond to the DER obtained in the physical testbed. For each number of active motes in the WSN, it is represented the maximum, average, and minimum DER values. Fig. 2 shows the maximum and average round-trip delays obtained in the simulator and in the physical testbed. In Fig. 1, while the simulation results reveal a WSN scaling up to 16 nodes with a maximum DER always below 1%, the physical testbed results show that above six active motes the maximum DER becomes higher than 1%. Fig. 2 reveals that the delays obtained in the simulator are significantly distinct from the real results.

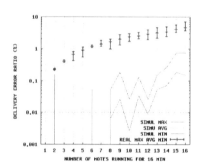

Fig. 1. DER without interferences

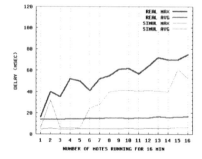

Fig. 2. RT delay without interferences

Fig. 3 and Fig. 4 present the DER and round-trip delay results obtained *with the presence* of interfering traffic. The results shown in both figures were obtained in the simulator and in the physical testbed. As expected, the network performance degrades before the presence of interfering traffic. The differences in the results registered in the physical testbed and in the simulator are considerably distinct.

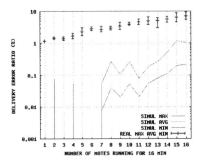

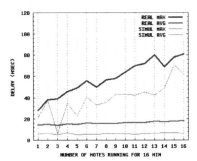

Fig. 3. DER with interferences   **Fig. 4.** RT delay with interferences

4   Model Parameters

The main causes for the divergence of the results obtained in the simulator and in the physical testbed are identified and discussed next. As result of this analysis, a parameterized model is proposed for the simulator to minimize the differences to the testbed results. This aspect is of particular relevance to bring simulation scenarios close to real environments, increasing the meaningfulness of simulations results.

4.1   Software Components

The first reason for the differences observed in the results is that the simulator does not take into consideration both the behavior of the operating system used in the network devices and the software processing time. As TinyOS can only schedule and handle single events and computing resources are very limited, significant delays may occur in scheduling and processing those events, as well as in processing the code of the protocol layers software. This overhead in terms of delay may be responsible for packet loss. To understand why, let us suppose that a packet has been received by the BS' transceiver. After processing it, the physical layer software triggers events to forward the payload to the upper protocol layers. Since the delivering time to the application layer is not null, another packet may be received by the BS' transceiver during this transactional phase. In this case, TinyOS does not attend the hardware interrupt from the transceiver indicating that a new packet is ready to be transferred to the microcontroller, and the new received packet is dropped. This situation was observed in the testbed. Yet, other operating system might attend the hardware interrupt from the transceiver indicating a new packet, and drop the packet in process previously received. In both cases, an incoming packet is completely processed by the application layer only if a time interval elapses without other packet being received by the mote's transceiver. Next, it is proposed a model to reflect this behavior in a simulator. Its parameterized nature makes the model generic and independent of the type of operating system and hardware used in the WSN.

The model uses the delivery time parameters $T_{BS\ mac \rightarrow app}(n)$ and $T_{BS\ phy \rightarrow mac}(n)$. The parameter $T_{BS\ mac \rightarrow app}(n)$ indicates the time required by the BS to process the packet received from mote n at MAC layer and deliver the data to the application layer. Therefore, this parameter reflects both the event scheduling delay and the packet processing delay imposed by the link, network, and transport layers. The delivery time parameter $T_{BS\ phy \rightarrow mac}(n)$ reflects the time required by the BS to process the packet received from mote n at physical layer and deliver the payload to the MAC layer. Note that MAC layer tasks can be split between the transceiver and the microcontroller. In Zigbit motes, for example, address filtering, FCS check, and ACK transmission operations of a receiving MAC frame are carried out in the transceiver, but the MAC frame de-encapsulation and upper layer delivering are accomplished in the microcontroller. As software components timings are very hard to be measured directly in the transceiver's firmware, the parameters $T_{BS\ mac \rightarrow app}(n)$ and $T_{BS\ phy \rightarrow mac}(n)$ are measured relatively to the MAC layer component in the microcontroller.

The process time parameter $T_{BS\ app}(n)$ indicates the time required for the application layer of the BS to process the received payload from mote n. So, an incoming packet from mote n is completely processed by the application layer of the BS after a time interval $T_{BS\ totRX}(n)$:

$$T_{BS\ totRX}(n) = T_{BS\ phy \rightarrow mac}(n) + T_{BS\ mac \rightarrow app}(n) + T_{BS\ app}(n) . \tag{1}$$

The delivery time parameter $T_{BS\ phy \rightarrow mac}(n)$ includes the following partial times: i) the time required to receive the packet from mote n, $T_{RX}(n)$; ii) the packet processing time in the physical and MAC layers of the transceiver, $T_{BS\ phyRX}(n)$; iii) the time required by the microcontroller to read the bytes from the transceiver reception buffer through the peripheral communication interface, $T_{BS\ pciR}(n)$:

$$T_{BS\ phy \rightarrow mac}(n) = T_{RX}(n) + T_{BS\ phyRX}(n) + T_{BS\ pciR}(n) . \tag{2}$$

For a packet received from mote n with a physical header size PHY_h bytes, a MAC header plus trailer size MAC_h bytes, a MAC payload length $MAC_d(n)$ bytes, and a nominal transmission rate R bits/s:

$$T_{RX}(n) = (PHY_h + MAC_h + MAC_d(n)).8/R . \tag{3}$$

The parameter $T_{BS\ phyRX}(n)$ is very hard to be measured directly as it is related with the firmware performance of the transceiver. However, it can be obtained indirectly from the $T_{BS\ phy \rightarrow mac}(n)$ measurement, because $T_{RX}(n)$ and $T_{BS\ pciR}(n)$ are known.

Usually the peripheral communication interface between the microcontroller and the transceiver is a serial peripheral interface (SPI). In this case,

$$T_{pciR}(n) = (B_C + MAC_h + MAC_d(n))*(8/S_{clk} + T_{sep}) , \tag{4}$$

where B_C is the number of bytes of a read command, S_{clk} is the SPI clock frequency, T_{sep} is the separation time between the less significant bit of the last byte and the most significant bit of the next byte. For Zigbit motes, $B_C=3$ B, $S_{clk}=4$ MHz, $T_{sep}=250$ ns.

If $T_{BS\ phy \rightarrow mac}(n)$ is lower than the Long Inter-Frame Spacing (LIFS) period (or Short IFS, if the received MAC frame size $\leq$ maxSIFSFrameSize), then it takes the respective IFS value. For an IEEE 802.15.4 WSN at 250 kbps, SIFS is 0.192 ms and LIFS is 0.640 ms, at least; the maxSIFSFrameSize is 18 B.

Analogously, $T_{totTX}(n)$ is the total time required for mote n to complete the transmission process of an application data packet. Hence, the application packet delay comes increased by the sum of $T_{totRX}(n)$ and $T_{totTX}(n)$, where

$$T_{totTX}(n) = T_{app}(n) + T_{app \rightarrow mac}(n) + T_{mac \rightarrow phy}(n) + T_{conf}(n) . \tag{5}$$

$T_{conf}(n)$ is the time required for the application layer to obtain the confirmation of the transmission request success, as required in common MAC protocols (e.g., IEEE 802.15.4); $T_{app}(n)$ is the time needed for the application layer of the mote n to prepare the data payload; $T_{app \rightarrow mac}(n)$ is the time required by mote n to deliver the data payload to the MAC layer, and prepare the MAC frame; $T_{mac \rightarrow phy}(n)$ is the time required by mote n to deliver the MAC frame to the physical layer, prepare the packet and transmit it. This last parameter includes the following partial times: i) the time required by the microcontroller to write the bytes in the transceiver's transmission buffer and registers through the peripheral communication interface, $T_{pciw}(n)$; ii) the packet preparing time in the physical layer (and MAC layer, if present) of the transceiver, $T_{phyTX}(n)$; iii) the listen state to transmission state switching latency, $T_{l \rightarrow tx}(n)$; iv) the time required to transmit the packet, $T_{RX}(n)$, which is equal to $T_{TX}(n)$.

$$T_{mac \rightarrow phy}(n) = T_{pciw}(n) + T_{phyTX}(n) + T_{l \rightarrow tx}(n) + T_{TX}(n) . \tag{6}$$

The parameter $T_{phyTX}(n)$ is very hard to be measured directly because it is related with the firmware performance of the transceiver. However, it can be obtained indirectly from the $T_{mac \rightarrow phy}(n)$ measurement, because $T_{TX}(n)$, $T_{BS\,pciw}(n)$, and $T_{l \rightarrow tx}(n)$ are known. $T_{l \rightarrow tx}(n)$ is read from the transceiver technical specifications of mote n.

If the peripheral communication interface between the microcontroller and the transceiver is SPI, then $T_{pciw}(n)$ can be calculated using Eq. 4, being B_C the number of bytes of a write command. For Zigbit motes, B_C is 2 B and $T_{l \rightarrow tx}$ is 0.18 ms.

After sending a packet, a mote must wait $T_{nextTX}(n)$ before sending another packet, where:

$$T_{nextTX}(n) = T_{totTX}(n) - T_{TX}(n) . \tag{7}$$

This equation is important since it may limit the performance of mote n regarding data throughput or retransmission trials.

Let us consider now that the application timers of mote a and mote b fire respectively at time $T(a)$ and time $T(b)$ to send application data, and that $T(b) > T(a)$. Also, let us assume that both motes use a MAC algorithm which does not perform any Clear Channel Assessment (CCA) to detect a clear channel or backoff contention procedures, i.e., once the timer fired, packets are directly sent to the wireless channel. This is a usual procedure in TDMA-based MAC protocols. In this context, mote a ends transmitting the physical packet a into the wireless channel at time $T_{endTX}(a)$:

$$T_{endTX}(a) = T(a) + T_{totTX}(a) - T_{conf}(a) . \tag{8}$$

Mote b starts sending the physical packet b into the channel at time $T_{startTX}(b)$:

$$T_{startTX}(b) = T(b) + T_{totTX}(b) - T_{TX}(b) - T_{conf}(b) . \tag{9}$$

If $T_{startTX}(b) < T_{endTX}(a)$ then a packet collision occurs and both packets are lost. To avoid this situation, $T_{startTX}(b)$ must occur after $T_{endTX}(a)$, which means that the application timer of mote b must trigger after $T(a)$ the following time:

$$T(b) - T(a) > \max\{0, T_{TX}(b) + (T_{totTX}(a) - T_{totTX}(b)) + (PT_{conf}(b) - PT_{conf}(a))\} . \quad (10)$$

In this case, if the condition

$$T_{startTX}(b) + T_{TX}(b) > T_{endTX}(a) + T_{BS\ totRX}(a) - T_{RX}(a) \quad (11)$$

holds ($T_{RX}(a)$ is subtracted because it is included in both $T_{endTX}(a)$ and $T_{BS\ totRX}(a)$), then mote b finishes the transmission after the BS having completely processed the packet a. In this case, the BS ends processing packet b at time $T_{BS\ end}(b)$, where:

$$T_{BS\ end}(b) = T_{startTX}(b) + T_{BS\ totRX}(b) . \quad (12)$$

However, if Eq.(11) is false, then mote b finishes the transmission while the BS is still processing the packet a, and consequently one of the packets is dropped (packet b in Zigbit motes). To guarantee that packet b is successfully processed by the BS, it must not collide with packet a, and it must be totally received after the BS finishes processing packet a. The first condition is expressed by Eq.(10). The second condition implies that $T(b)$ must be incremented by $T_{BS\ totRX}(a) - T_{RX}(a)$. Additionally, if $T_{BS\ totRX}(a) - T_{RX}(a) > T_{TX}(b)$, then $T(b)$ can be decremented by $T_{TX}(b)$, because the transceiver can receive packet b while the microcontroller processes packet a. So,

$$T_{endTX}(b) - T_{endTX}(a) > T_{BS\ totRX}(a) - T_{RX}(a) - (T_{BS\ totRX}(a) - T_{RX}(a) > T_{TX}(b)?T_{TX}(b):0) . \quad (13)$$

Let us consider that mote b is ready to transfer data from the microcontroller to the transceiver, and mote a is transmitting to the BS. The transceiver of mote b must listen for packet a to read its physical and MAC headers. In Zigbit motes, it was observed that the transceiver of mote b can only accept data from the microcontroller after its radio circuit has finished the listening for the whole packet a. No channel collision occurs between packet a and packet b. This phenomenon imposes an additional delay, $T_{hdrD}(b,a)$, when sending a packet b to the channel due to the influence of packet a, where $T_{hdrD}(b,a) \le T_{TX}(a)$. This delay must be added to $T_{totTX}(b)$, expressed in Eq.(5). As $T(b)$ cannot occur before $T(a)$, it results altogether that,

$$T(b) - T(a) > \max\{0, T_{TX}(b) + (T_{totTX}(a) - T_{totTX}(b)) + (PT_{conf}(b) - PT_{conf}(a)) +$$
$$T_{BS\ totRX}(a) - T_{RX}(a) - (T_{BS\ totRX}(a) - T_{RX}(a) > T_{TX}(b) ? T_{TX}(b) :0) - T_{hdrD}(b,a)\} . \quad (14)$$

If mote a and mote b are identical, run the same software, and send packets with the same size, then $T_{totTX}(a) = T_{totTX}(b)$, $PT_{conf}(b) = PT_{conf}(a)$, and Eq.(14) simplifies to,

$$T(b) - T(a) > T_{BS\ totRX}(a) - T_{TX}(a) - T_{hdrD}(b,a) . \quad (15)$$

In the ideal case of mote a and mote b presenting a null delay in all software components and sending equal size packets, Eq.(14) becomes $T(b) - T(a) > T_{TX}(a)$.

Let us assume now that mote a and mote b use a contention-based MAC protocol. Since random backoffs and CCA operations are carried out by the CSMA algorithm to find a clear channel, it is not possible to establish an equation relating $T(b)$ with $T(a)$. However, packet a and packet b are successfully processed by the BS only if the condition expressed in Eq.(13) holds.

Experimental tests with Zigbit motes revealed that the BS' transceiver is able to send a MAC ACK frame to a mote only if T_{ack} milliseconds have passed since the transmission of the MAC ACK frame of the last received packet.

MAC ACK frames sent by the BS' transceiver while the BS microcontroller is processing a received packet deteriorate the DER. To understand why, let us consider that the BS microcontroller is processing packet a when packet b is received by the BS' transceiver, and the respective MAC ACK frame arrives with success to mote b. As BS is processing packet a, packet b will be dropped. Since no retransmission will occur at mote b, packet b will not be delivered to the application layer of the BS. However, if the MAC ACK frame is not sent by the BS, packet b may be retransmitted and delivered successfully to the application layer of the BS, if meanwhile packet a has been completely processed.

4.2 Time Drift

The second reason for the differences in the results is that the motes present an appreciable time drift. The cause of this time drift is distinct of the CPU clock time drift, which is typically a few microseconds per second. While the latter is due to physical characteristics of the semiconductor components, the former is mainly due to the CPU internal software performance running under limited computing resources. To reflect this feature, the drift parameter D_{ab} was introduced in the simulator. To set this parameter correctly, measurements were carried out using the BS and pairs of motes. Generically, if the drift between mote a and the BS is D_a, and the drift between mote b and the BS is D_b, then the drift between mote a and mote b is $D_{ab} = D_a - D_b$. This means that if mote a and mote b start transmitting separated in time by T_{ab}, and if $D_a > D_b$, then both motes will contend for the wireless channel after sending T_{ab} / D_{ab} packets. The D_{ab} value can be calculated experimentally through the relation:

$$D_{ab} = ((Ta_{i+1} - Tb_{i+1}) - (Ta_i - Tb_i)) / (Tb_{i+1} - Tb_i), \qquad (16)$$

where Ta_i, Ta_{i+1}, Tb_i, and Tb_{i+1} express the local time of the BS when packet i and packet $i+1$ are received from mote a and mote b, respectively. It is assumed that packet i from mote b arrives after packet i from mote a, as well as all successive received packets from both motes during the period Tb_i and Tb_{i+1}. Since $T_{ab} < 125$ ms in the physical testbed, and assuming $D_{ab} = 0.1\%$, channel contentions between a pair of motes may occur whenever 125 packets are sent at maximum. However, no channel contention occurs if D_{ab} is zero and T_{ab} is above the full-loaded packet transmission time. In this situation, the simulator results presented a null DER in a WSN with more than sixteen active motes. To prevent this unrealistic situation, the simulation results in Figs. 1, 2, 3, 4 were taken using a D_{ab} equal to 0.005%.

4.3 Setting of the Model Parameters

Whenever possible, the tuning of the model parameters was accomplished from measurements performed in the physical testbed. Table 1 presents the values found for the defined parameters, expressed in milliseconds, which are specific to this physical testbed. MAC payloads of 30 B and 90 B were considered. These values were measured on an analogical oscilloscope, and may present an error of +/– 0.5 ms. The values in *italic* were calculated analytically: $T_{BS\ phyRX}$ derives from Eq.(2); T_{RX} and T_{TX} from Eq.(3), $T_{BS\ pciR}$ and T_{pciW} from Eq.(4), T_{phyTX} from Eq.(6); $T_{l_2 tx}$ was obtained from the transceiver technical specifications. Recall that the IEEE 802.15.4 protocol stack is implemented in the firmware of the nodes' transceiver.

Table 1. Values of the model parameters for: the BS (left) and the motes (right)

MAC_d	30 B	90 B	MAC_d	30 B	90 B
$T_{BS\ app}$	**1.8** ms	**1.8** ms	T_{app}	**1.8** ms	**2.0** ms
$T_{BS\ mac \to app}$	**1.0**	**1.3**	$T_{app \to mac}$	**1.2**	**2.0**
$T_{BS\ phy \to mac}$	$1.0+T_{RX}$	$1.4+T_{RX}$	$T_{mac \to phy}$	$1.4+T_{TX}$	$2.5+T_{TX}$
T_{ack}	**3.3**	**3.7**	T_{conf}	**4.0**	**4.0**
$T_{BS\ pciR}$	*0.10*	*0.23*	T_{pciW}	*0.10*	*0.23*
$T_{BS\ phyRX}$	*0.90*	*1.17*	T_{phyTX}	*1.12*	*2.09*
$T_{RX},\ T_{TX}$	*1.50*	*3.42*	$T_{l_2 tx}$	*0.18*	*0.18*
$T_{BS\ totRX}$	$3.8+T_{RX}$	$4.5+T_{RX}$	T_{totTX}	$8.4+T_{TX}$	$10.5+T_{TX}$

Measurements showed that the software time drift between motes may have values up to 0.3%, depending on the pair of motes used. The time drift between a pair of motes varies along the time. The simulator was programmed so that each mote at start-up chooses an average time drift D_{ab} up to 0.3% randomly.

The computing performance of the BS in the physical testbed is similar to a mote. This situation is not normally found in a WSN since a BS presents typically stronger computing resources and a more efficient operating system than motes. In this case, the value of T_{totRX} and T_{totTX} may be negligible. However, in a multi-hop WSN the packets may be routed through the motes, and so the value of these parameters can influence significantly the network performance.

5   Simulation Results with the Model

In order to validate the proposed model, tests were carried out in the physical and simulation platforms using both TDMA and CSMA-based MAC protocols. The motes used in the experiments are identical in terms of hardware, and run the same software.

5.1 TDMA Algorithm

Validation tests of the proposed model were carried out in the physical and simulation platforms using a simple TDMA-based algorithm. The BS sends a beacon every 100 ms. This value was chosen to minimize the effect of the time drift D_{ab}. In each superframe, two or three motes transmit once with the minimum time gap that guarantees a null DER. Table 2 compares the values obtained in both platforms. Simulation tests were accomplished with and without the proposed model implemented in the simulator. As illustrated, the inclusion of the proposed model in the simulator, brings the simulation outcome close to the real results, with differences below 0.5 ms. The registered differences are justified taking into account the accuracy error that affects the measured values. T_{hdrD} presented a null value in all tests, excepting the test marked with an asterisk, where T_{hdrD} was 1.0 ms.

An important conclusion taken from the real results is that slots should be allocated to the motes in accordance with the respective packet sizes to be transmitted. Whenever possible, smaller packets should be sent first, otherwise bandwidth waste occurs. This is shown in Table 2 when mote *a* sends 90 B and mote *b* sends 30 B.

Table 2. Results from the physical and simulation (with and without the model) testbeds

mote *a*	mote *b*	mote *c*	Real	Simul. w/ model	Simul. w/o model
30 B	30 B	30 B	**4.0**	3.8	1.5
30 B	30 B	-	**4.0**	3.8	1.5
90 B	90 B	90 B	**4.5**	4.5	3.4
90 B*	90 B*	-	**3.0**	3.5	3.4
30 B	90 B	-	**0.5**	0.0	1.5
90 B	30 B	-	**8.5**	8.5	3.4

5.2   CSMA Algorithm

Validation tests of the proposed model were also carried out in the physical and simulation platforms using the IEEE 802.15.4 MAC protocol. Fig. 5 and Fig. 6 show the simulation results using the proposed model when IEEE 802.15.4 interfering traffic was not present. It is observed that the DER simulation results approximate closely to the DER values found in the physical scenario (the corresponding physical testbed results are also replicated for better comparison). The results of the maximum and average delays also become close to those obtained in the physical scenario.

Simulations without using the proposed model showed that the average DER *improves* over 75% when the MAC payload decreases from 90 B to 30 B. As the channel occupation decreases, the number of collisions diminishes, and so the DER improves. However, tests on the physical platform revealed that the average DER *degrades* about 20% when the MAC payload decreases from 90 B to 30 B. The same degradation was observed in the simulations with the proposed model, confirming the validity of the model. As the packet size decreases, the probability of having multiple packets arriving without collisions to the BS during T_{totRX} becomes higher, and consequently the DER increases too. Fig. 7 and Fig. 8 present the simulation results when IEEE 802.15.4 interfering traffic was present. The DER results keep close to the DER values found in the physical scenario. The results of the average and maximum delays are also identical to those obtained in the physical scenario.

With the CSMA-CA algorithm, a mote may send a duplicate packet if it does not receive the MAC ACK frame from the BS. The average Duplicate Packets Ratio

(<DPR>) is defined as the percentage of the total number of data packets received in duplicate by the application layer of the BS comparatively to the number of application data packets received for the first time from all motes in the WSN.

Fig. 9 shows the <DPR> obtained with and without the presence of IEEE 802.15.4 interfering traffic, not using the proposed parameterized model. Fig. 10 presents de <DPR> using this model. In this latter case, the simulation results are very identical to those obtained in the physical testbed.

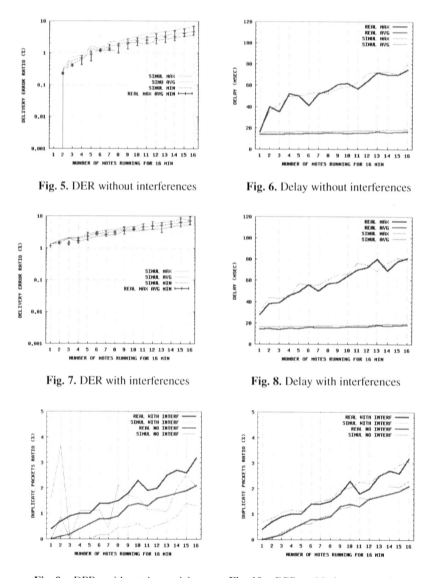

Fig. 5. DER without interferences   **Fig. 6.** Delay without interferences

Fig. 7. DER with interferences   **Fig. 8.** Delay with interferences

Fig. 9. <DPR> without the model   **Fig. 10.** <DPR> with the proposed model

6 Conclusions

Since motes present typically very limited computing resources, the performance of the operating system and high-level software running inside the motes impose significant constrains to the overall performance of a WSN. This paper showed that if the limitations of the software components are not considered, the simulation tests may produce results significantly more optimistic than those obtained in real conditions. Indeed, tests showed that it is difficult to obtain satisfactory simulation results using only the parameters of the wireless channel, the physical layer, and the MAC layer provided by the WSN simulator. This important aspect is often neglected in many works presenting WSN evaluation studies carried out on simulators.

In order to obtain satisfactory simulation results, a parameterized model was proposed, tuned, and included in the simulator. Simulation tests showed that the results obtained with the proposed model match satisfactory to those obtained in real conditions. Therefore, the inclusion of this model in a WSN simulator helps to improve the confidence on the simulation results. The model is generic enough to be also included in simulators running network scenarios other than WSNs.

References

1. Kurkowski, S., Camp, T., Colagrosso, M.: Manet Simulation Studies: the Incredibles. ACM Mobile Computing and Communications Review 9(4), 50–61 (2005)
2. Singh, C.P., Vyas, O.P., Tiwari, M.K.: A Survey of Simulation in Sensor Networks. IEEE, Computational Intelligence For Modelling Control & Automation, Washington (2008)
3. Kotz, D., Newport, C., Gray, R.S., Liu, J., Yuan, Y., Elliott, C.: Experimental Evaluation of Wireless Wimulation Assumptions. In: Intern. Conf. on Modeling, Analysis and Simulation of Wireless & Mobile Systems. ACM, New York (2004)
4. Cavin, D., Sasson, Y., Schiper, A.: On the Accuracy of Manet Simulators. In: Principles of Mobile Computing, pp. 38–43. ACM, New York (2002)
5. Banks, J., Carson, J., Nelson, B.: Discrete-Event System Simulation. Prentice Hall, Englewood Cliffs (1996)
6. Castalia: A Simulator for WSN, http://castalia.npc.nicta.com.au (accessed in March 2011)
7. ZigBit Modules,
   http://www.atmel.com/dyn/resources/prod_documents/doc8226.pdf
   (idem)

Terminal–Side QoE Estimations for Cross–Layer Network Control*

Towards a User–Centric Approach to Network Management

Martín Varela and Jukka–Pekka Laulajainen

VTT Technical Research Centre of Finland
{martin.varela,jukka--pekka.laulajainen}@vtt.fi

Abstract. While the layered OSI model for networks provides a very clean conceptual framework for network design, certain applications are not completely indifferent to what happens at the lower layers. This is particularly true for multimedia and other real–time applications, which usually have stringent constraints on network performance in order to deliver an acceptable Quality of Experience (QoE) to the user.

Several cross–layer approaches for optimizing application quality have been proposed in the literature. In this paper we show how by combining network QoS measurements and application–level knowledge, significant improvements can be made to current management solutions.

1 Introduction

Ubiquitous Internet access is no longer a nice idea, but a fact. Everyday devices such as phones, tablets and laptops keep users connected practically everywhere, over a variety of network technologies, and with relatively low costs. As a consequence, networked services, such as social networks, Internet telephony, video sharing, etc. have become an important part of users' activities on the Internet, every day, at all times, and anywhere.

As users become used to having these services available, and depend on them, the issue of how to ensure appropriate service levels, and a good user experience becomes very important. This is especially the case for media services, which not only require the availability of network access, but also have constraints on network performance.

The Quality of Experience (QoE) for media services depends on many factors, but generally it will be mainly defined by both the application's requirements (e.g. video, telephony, music streaming, all have different requirements vis–à–vis the network) and characteristics, and the actual performance of the underlying network. Other factors, such as equipment characteristics, along with user expectations and environmentalfactors also play an important role in defining the QoE; however, those are usually fixed and it is not possible to do much in order to improve on them.

---
* This work was partially supported by the CELTIC Easy Wireless 2 and CELTIC IPNQSIS projects, Tekes and VTT Technical Research Centre of Finland.

X. Masip-Bruin et al. (Eds.): WWIC 2011, LNCS 6649, pp. 140–149, 2011.

In this work we focus on media services and their quality from the users' point of view. In particular, we explore how QoE estimations on the terminal side can be used to perform cross–layer control actions at the network level, in order to better cope with performance issues commonly encountered in IP networks.

The rest of the paper is organized as follows. Section 2 describes how accurate QoE estimations can be obtained single–sidedly on the terminal, in real–time. In Section 3 we describe possible applications of the QoE measurements for network control purposes, and in Section 4 we provide an example of cross–layer QoE–based control. Finally, we conclude the paper and present future research ideas in Section 5.

2   Measuring QoE

Measuring the quality as perceived by the users – or QoE – is difficult since there is a very strong subjective component implicit in its definition. There is a large and long standing body of work dealing with methods for defining and measuring the quality of media and media services [3,27,5], ranging from qualitative approaches, to quantitative ones, and yet other, psychometrics–based ones [9,13]. The most commonly ones, however, consist of basically asking a panel of (usually *naïve*) test subjects to give ratings to media samples or live services under a very controlled environment (cf. ITU-T P.800 [20] for speech quality, ITU-R BT.500 [6] for video quality, ITU-T P.920 [23] for interactive services, etc.). These testing methods produce, in a way, a "true value" for quality, as they consider the subjective experience of a large enough panel of users[1]. They are, however, very expensive and cumbersome to implement, and hence other approaches to assessing quality have been developed.

In contrast to the aforementioned *subjective* methods, they are usually referred to *objective* or *instrumental* methods, and they do not rely on human subjects. These instrumental methods can be classified according to whether they are signal–based or parametric, or on whether they use a full–reference signal for comparison, a reduced reference, or no reference at all. For example, for speech applications, the most widely used instrumental metric is currently PESQ [21] (currently being superseded by P.OLQA [22]), which is a full–reference model. Full–reference models produce some of the most accurate assessments[2], but are by definition ill-suited for being used in any control mechanisms, since reference signals are not available in real–time for normal applications.

For control purposes, accurate, no–reference, single–sided models are needed in order to obtain QoE estimations in real–time. A metric such as Pseudo–Subjective Quality Assessment (PSQA) [17] lends itself well to this task. PSQA is a parametric methodology for estimating QoE, usually in the form of Mean

---

[1] Note that there is, within the QoE research community, a large push to move away from these types of tests towards more sophisticated ones. In practice, however, most subjective testing nowadays is carried out in this way.

[2] In terms of correlation with subjective assessment.

Opinion Score (MOS) values. It has been used successfully for VoIP quality assessment, both listening [25] and conversational [7], as well as video [15,8].

2.1 About PSQA

PSQA works by mapping, via a statistical estimator, network– and application–level parameters known[3] to affect perceptual quality to actual subjective scores. Some examples of such are the encoding used, the error protection and concealment, the loss rate, delay and jitter in the network, etc.

For each parameter π a range of possible values is identified, according to the expected usage context. This range lies between a minimal value π_{min}, and a maximal one, π_{max}. Within this range, a set of representative values is chosen.

Let $\mathcal{P} = \{\pi_1, \cdots, \pi_P\}$ be the set of selected parameters and $\{p_{i1}, \cdots, p_{iH_i}\}$ the set of possible values chosen for parameter π_i, with $p_{i1} < p_{i2} < \cdots < p_{iH_i}$. A *configuration* of the set of quality-affecting parameters, is any set of possible values for each one, i.e. a configuration γ is a vector $\gamma = (\gamma_1, \cdots, \gamma_P)$, where $\gamma_i \in \{p_{i1}, \cdots, p_{iH_i}\}$

For even a moderate number of parameters, the total number of possible configurations (that is, $\prod_{i=1}^{P} H_i$) is usually very large, and subjective testing is not feasible over the whole parameter space. Therefore, a small subset of this space is selected to be used as (part of) the input data for the chosen statistical estimator used in the learning phase. This is usually a 3–layer feed–forward Random Neural Network (RNN) [10], although it could, in principle, be any other suitable machine learning tool.

In order to generate a media database composed of samples corresponding to different configurations of the selected parameters, a simulation environment or a testbed must be implemented[4]. This is used to transmit media samples (or perform live tests, as needed) from the source to the destination and to control the underlying network. Every configuration in the defined input data must be mapped into the system composed of the network, the source and the receiver. The destination stores the transmitted media sample and associates it with the corresponding configuration.

Thus, for each media sample σ, and set of S configurations, a set $\mathcal{T} = \{\sigma_1, \cdots, \sigma_S\}$ of degraded samples is constructed. These samples have encountered varied transmission conditions. That is, the clip σ_s corresponds to the result of sending σ through the source-network system where the selected P parameters have the values of configuration γ_s.

Once the material (and/or testbed) is ready, a subjective assessment campaign is conducted. The MOS values obtained from the testing campaign are then mapped to each sample (and thus to the corresponding configuration); the value corresponding to sequence σ_s is denoted here by ψ_s.

Finally, a suitable RNN is trained and validated. The trained RNN can be seen as a function f having P real variables, such that

---

[3] Or at least strongly suspected.

[4] In the case of interactive assessment, a suitable testbed must be implemented.

(i) for any sample $\sigma_s \in \mathcal{T}$, $f(v_{1s}, \cdots, v_{P,s}) \approx \psi_s$,
(ii) and such that for *any other* configuration with values $(v_1, \cdots, v_P)$, $f(v_1, \cdots, v_P)$
     is close to the MOS that would be associated in a subjective evaluation with
     a media sample for which the selected parameters had those specific values
     $v_1, \cdots, v_P$.

As with any statistical learning tool, the performance of the resulting estimator is evaluated on validation data, which is not used during training. The
most relevant metric for this performance is the correlation of the MOS estimations produced by the PSQA implementation and subjective scores. PSQA can
achieve very high correlations for both voice (listening and conversational) and
video applications.

Once the RNN is trained, calculating the MOS estimations is computationally trivial, which makes PSQA a good choice for use in resource–constrained
devices, where signal–based estimations, such as the one described in ITU-T recommendation P.563 [19] might be too costly in both processing time and energy
consumption.

3 Possible Applications

When talking about network management and control mechanisms, it is commonly understood that these are issues dealt with by network operators, within
the network itself. In fact, access control mechanisms, traffic differentiation mechanisms, resource provisioning, etc. are mostly implemented on the network side,
and the terminal (and hence the user or the application) has little chance of
having any impact on them.

There are, however, some things that can be best done on the terminal side,
especially when it comes to end–to–end QoE, since at least one service end–point
resides on the terminal itself. One such application is mobility management. Be it
based on Mobile IP [11], IMS Service Continuity [1] (or VCC in older networks),
Media independent handover (MIH) [2], or Host Identity Protocol (HIP) [16], the
terminal is usually in the best position to determine when a handover is needed.

Another application is simultaneous multi–streaming of SVC streams. In this
context, a multi–access terminal could choose to have different layers of the
scalable video stream sent over different networks, depending on the available
networks and their QoS.

Packet marking for traffic differentiation, as proposed in [18] for intra–stream
marking, in [26] for LAN–level priority management for VoIP, or in [14] for QoS
management in wireless home networks, is also a good candidate application for
performing control on the terminal end.

Moving beyond the terminal itself, it is possible to exploit the QoE measurements when making network–side control decisions, if suitable signaling from
the terminal to the network is implemented. Similarly, terminal side QoE estimations could be used to adapt the operation of the application in use. For
this purpose, signaling QoE information between the terminal and applications
should be provided.

4 Case Study: Improving Mobility Management via QoE Estimations

In this section we present a case study on an application of QoE estimations to network–level control mechanisms. We have developed a prototype smart mobility management tool which significantly enhances the performance of Mobile IP (MIP) systems, by using PSQA–based QoE estimations for VoIP to signal when a handover is needed.

4.1 Mobile IP in a Nutshell

Mobile IP [11] allows users to attach to networks in different administrative domains while still being reachable through an address in their own network (called *home network*). Incoming traffic towards the home address of the mobile node is forwarded to a care–of address, to which the node is currently bound.

As the node roams through different networks, it creates mobility bindings, and these are used by a so–called *home agent* to reach the mobile node at any given time. If the mobile node has multi–homing capabilities, it is possible for it to seamlessly roam through different network technologies (for example, from Ethernet to WiFi to 3G).

Typically, in this multi-homing scenario, MIP solutions implement a priority–based policy mechanism for choosing an access network. The priorities are usually based on expectations of cost and performance of the different access networks, but do not usually consider actual performance of the network (beyond being able to reach the home agent), nor application–level performance. This leads to situations in which a mobile node will remain attached to a network with sub–par performance, even though other networks are available and might provide better quality levels.

4.2 Prototype Implementation and Experimental Setup

The proposed solution prototype improves on this situation by monitoring the QoE of the application being used (in this case VoIP, but it can trivially be extended to video or other applications where PSQA or a similar mechanism might be used), and making handover decisions when the quality is degraded below a configurable threshold.

Several strategies are available to make the handover decisions, depending on the desired "dynamism" of the solution. The most stable strategy considers a sliding weighted average of the MOS estimations over a configurable time window. The weighted average can be replaced with a simple, non-weighted average if a more "reactive" behaviour is desired. It is also possible to consider only the last estimation before deciding whether to perform a handover, although this strategy is likely to result in unwarranted handovers due to minor network impairments.

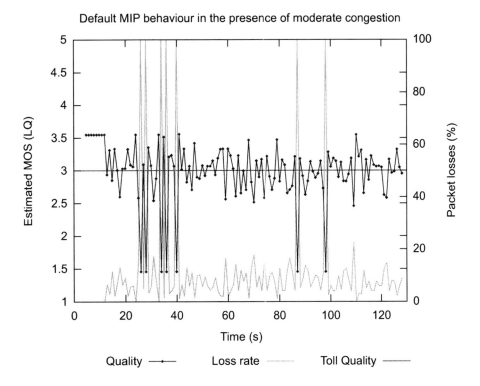

Fig. 1. When the QoE is not considered for handover decisions, the listening quality can significantly degrade in the presence of temporary network congestion

The prototype also allows for roaming back into the previous network after a configurable period, which is useful in the case of temporary impairments.

The current implementation of the prototype uses VTT's QoSMeT tool [24] to perform passive measurements of the network performance, and feed the obtained values to a PSQA implementation and the decision logic. The decision logic then interacts with Birdstep's[5] MIP solution to perform the actual handovers. In this way, the MIP solution is augmented with a user–centric view of network performance, namely, forcing a handover when the application quality (QoE) drops below acceptable levels.

The prototype has been tested in a variety of scenarios and it has yielded very promising results. In this paper, a simple, yet representative scenario for network congestion is presented. A mobile node with Ethernet and WiFi connections, is attached, via its Ethernet connection, to a Linux router running NetEm [12]. NetEm is then used to emulate the effects of network congestion on the link by introducing packet losses. We compare the behaviour of the plain MIP solution, and that of the QoE–based smart mobility management proposed.

---

[5] Formerly Secgo Mobile IP. `http://www.birdstep.com/Products/`

4.3 Performance Improvements

Figure 1 shows the degradation of listening quality for a VoIP stream using GSM and media–dependent FEC (as described in [4]). Since the impairment is not too severe, the mobility manager does not lose contact with the home agent, and no handover is performed, despite the call quality dropping below usable levels.

The improvements made by augmenting the handover decision–making with QoE estimations is visible in Figures 2 and 3. In these figures, the prototype was configured to consider a weighted average of the MOS estimations over a 10s sliding window. In Figure 2 the handover is triggered about 6s after the congestion period starts, and in another 3s the quality has once again reached acceptable levels.

In the case of Figure 3, the option to roam back to the previous network after a period of about 35s was enabled, and a second handover can be observed at about the 84s mark. In the same figure, some losses in the WiFi connection can also be observed (at 72s), but as the impairment was very small and of short duration, no action was taken.

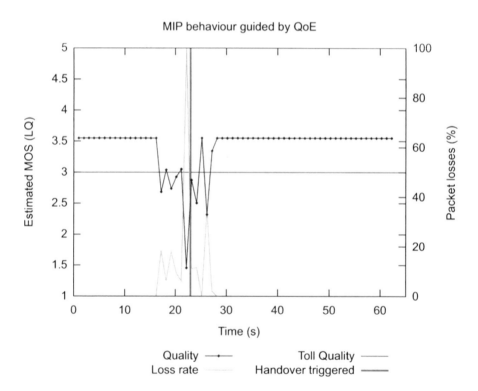

Fig. 2. Taking QoE into account when making the handover decision results in a fast recovery from a degradation in listening quality

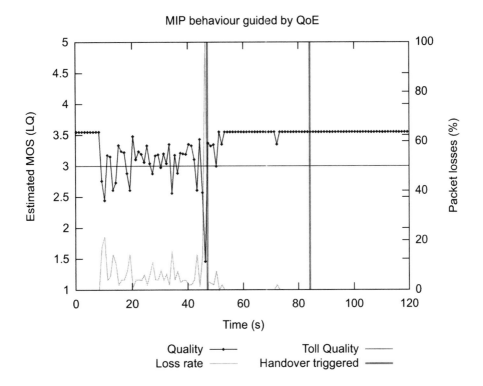

Fig. 3. It is possible to automatically roam back into the previous network after a period of time. This is useful in cases where occasional short congestion periods are common

5   Conclusions and Future Work

In this paper we have discussed possible applications of QoE estimations on the terminal side to achieve some degree of user–centric network control. While there are limits to the type of network–level control that can be implemented by the terminal itself, several interesting possibilities for improving the QoE of media services can be explored. We substantiated our claims by means of a case study in which a Mobile IP–based system was significantly improved by taking a cross–layer approach and considering application–level QoE estimations when deciding whether to perform a handover.

Further work on this area will include other applications of control on the terminal side, as discussed in Section 3, as well as network–side control mechanisms (such as access control, traffic marking and shaping, etc.). This last topic is one of the main targets of the ongoing CELTIC IPNQSIS project.

References

1. 3GPP TSG SA WG2. 3GPP TS 23.237: IP Multimedia Subsystem (IMS) Service Continuity; Stage 2 (2008)
2. IEEE 802.21. Std 802.21-2008 – IEEE Standard for Local and Metropolitan Area Networks – Part 21: Media Independent Handover Services (January 2009)
3. Allnatt, J.: Subjective rating and apparent magnitude. International Journal of Man-Machine Studies 7(6), 801–816 (1975)
4. Bolot, J., Vega Garcia, A.: The case for FEC-based error control for packet audio in the internet. In: ACM Multimedia Systems (1996)
5. Bouch, A., Sasse, M.A., DeMeer, H.: Of packets and people: A user-centered approach to quality of service. In: Proceedings of IWQoS2000, pp. 189–197 (2000)
6. ITU-R Recommendation BT.500-10. Methodology for the subjective assessment of the quality of television pictures (March 2000)
7. Couto da Silva, A., Varela, M., de Souza e Silva, E., Rubino, G.: Quality assessment of interactive real time voice applications. Computer Networks 52, 179–1192 (2008)
8. Couto da Silva, A., Rodriguez-Bocca, P., Rubino, G.: Optimal Quality-of-Experience design for a P2P Multi-Source video streaming. In: IEEE International Conference on Communications,ICC 2008, May 2008, pp. 22–26 (2008)
9. Durin, V., Gros, L.: Measuring speech quality impact on tasks performance. In: INTERSPEECH, pp. 2074–2077. ISCA (2008)
10. Gelenbe, E., Fourneau, J.–M.: Random neural networks with multiple classes of signals. Neural Computation 11(3), 953–963 (1999)
11. IETF Network Working Group. IP Mobility Support for IPv4 (RFC 3344) (August 2002)
12. Hemminger, S.: NetEm website, http://www.linuxfoundation.org/collaborate/workgroups/networking/netem
13. Jumisko-Pyykkö, S., Hannuksela, M.M.: Does context matter in quality evaluation of mobile television? In: Henri ter Hofte, G., Mulder, I., de Ruyter, B.E.R. (eds.) Mobile HCI. ACM International Conference Proceeding Series, pp. 63–72. ACM, New York (2008)
14. Laulajainen, J.-P.: Implementing qos support in a wireless home network. In: WCNC, pp. 3273–3278. IEEE, Los Alamitos (2008)
15. Mohamed, S., Rubino, G.: A study of realtime packet video quality using random neural networks. IEEE Transactions On Circuits and Systems for Video Technology 12(12), 1071–1083 (2002)
16. Moskowitz, R., Nikander, P., Jokela, Henderson, T.: RFC 5201 - Host Identity Protocol (April 2008)
17. Varela, M.: Pseudo-Subjective Quality Assessment of Multimedia Streams and its Applications in Control. PhD thesis, INRIA/IRISA, univ. Rennes I, Rennes, France (November 2005)
18. Orozco, J., Ros, D.: DiffServ-Aware streaming of h.264 video. In: Proceedings of the 14th International Packet Video Workshop (PV 2004) (2004)
19. ITU-T Recommendation P.563. Single ended method for objective speech quality assessment in Narrow-Band telephony applications (2004)
20. ITU-T Recommendation P.800. Methods for subjective determination of transmission quality (1996)
21. ITU-T Recommendation P.862. Perceptual evaluation of speech quality (PESQ), an objective method for End-To-End speech quality assessment of narrowband telephone networks and speech codecs (2001)

22. ITU-T Recommendation P.863. Perceptual objective listening quality assessment (2011)
23. ITU-T Recommendation P.920. Interactive test methods for audiovisual communications (2000)
24. Prokkola, J., Perälä, P.H.J., Hanski, M., Piri, E.: 3G/HSPA Performance in Live Networks from the End User Perspective. In: ICC, pp. 1–6 (2009)
25. Rubino, G., Varela, M., Mohamed, S.: Performance evaluation of real-time speech through a packet network: a random neural networks-based approach. Performance evaluation 57(2), 141–162 (2004)
26. Rubino, G., Varela, M., Bonnin, J.-M.: Controlling multimedia qos in the future home network using the psqa metric. Computer Journal 49(2), 137–155 (2006)
27. Watson, A., Sasse, M.A.: Evaluating audio and video quality in Low-Cost multimedia conferencing systems. ACM Interacting with Computers Journal 8(3), 255–275 (1996)

First Step in Cross-Layers Measurement in Wireless Networks
How to Adapt to Resource Constraints for Optimizing End-to-End Services?*

Philippe Owezarski[1,2], Rasha Ghassan Hasan[1,2],
Guillaume Kremer[1,2], and Pascal Berthou[1,2]

[1] CNRS; LAAS; 7 avenue du colonel Roche, F-31077 Toulouse Cedex 4, France
[2] Université de Toulouse; UPS, INSA, INP, ISAE; UT1, UTM, LAAS; F-31077
Toulouse Cedex 4, France
{owe,gkremer,berthou}@laas.fr, r.g.hasan@gmail.com

Abstract. Wireless networks are more and more popular, and more specifically as the access technology for all wireless devices generally used (laptops, smartphones, tablets, sensors, ...). It is then frequent to encounter at least one wireless network segment on a communication path. Because of the complexity and limits of the hertzian air medium, the end-to-end communication is impacted by the quality of such wireless networks which are not offering the same amount of resources or the same determinism in the quality of Service (QoS) level. Because of the complexity of the physical transmission mechanisms, and of the MAC layer, traffic observed at the network level can have unexpected characteristics and the network exhibits unexpected performances and QoS. At the opposite of wired network for which monitoring packets at network level is enough, monitoring wireless networks requires to look at physical, MAC and network layers all together and to analyze their correlation levels: this is called cross-layered monitoring in the related literature. This paper then proposes an overview of the monitoring of the quite unknown physical layers of wireless networks, and exhibits how the studies of the 3 layers are necessary for analyzing the wireless network behavior, and more generally of the end-to-end connections. As an example, this paper illustrates how the SNR impacts the delays and jitters in an unexpected way in wireless networks, thus impacting end-to-end delays and jitters.

Keywords: Measurement, Cross-layering, Wireless networks, SNR, E2E services, E2E delay.

1 Introduction

Network communications more and more rely on wireless technologies. But compared to wired technologies, they present some limitations because of the

---

* This work has been partially made in the framework of the RESCUE project granted by the French National Agency for Research (ANR).

X. Masip-Bruin et al. (Eds.): WWIC 2011, LNCS 6649, pp. 150–161, 2011.

hertzian support, for instance in terms of capacity limits. In addition, while the MAC layer is most of the time deterministic, and anyway quite simple, for wired network, it can be quite complex and indeterministic for wireless networks, leading to major issues for enforcing a stable performance or QoS level. In addition, because of the complexity inherent to each of the layers of significant importance in a wireless network, it is not easy to understand what happens, or to predict the service level that can be expected. For instance, interferences can impact the way the MAC layer is working, and at the end the final delivery of network packets. On the other side, a packet burst at the network level might dramatically impact the MAC performance by increasing the number of collisions, and might also induce many interferences. The convergence between wired and wireless networks and services is also of significant complexity because of differences between the technologies, as well as resources and services provided.

In such a context, connections have to cross several networks of various technologies. They therefore need to monitor the network performances and/or available resources to adapt accurately to network conditions, and getting the best possible Quality of Service (QoS). We argue that the worst conditions are almost always met in wireless networks, generally at the access point, as WLANs, GPRS, UMTS, or any other network technology used for interconnecting wireless devices (laptops, smartphones, tablets, sensors, ...) to the wired Internet infrastructure. As a consequence, the key difficulty deals with monitoring wireless networks to be encountered on Internet paths. This especially includes the very difficult task of monitoring the complex architectures of wireless networks. This is then one of the issues addressed in the framework of the French RESCUE project which aims at designing and prototyping new monitoring methodologies and tools specifically dedicated to wireless networks (WIFI, GPRS, UWB, UMTS). The originality of this work is the cross-layer monitoring approach which aims to jointly work at each of the layers involved for a wireless network, i.e. the physical, MAC and network layers. Indeed, mechanisms and protocols for each of these 3 layers are very different and then have an important impact on the way data are generated, and then on network characteristics. The idea then deals with combining and correlating measurement made and the information got from each layer in order to analyze the interdependencies that exist between the 3 layers depending on the sent traffic characteristics. By jointly analyzing the 3 layers of wireless networks altogether, it is expected to understand where and how wireless networks can experience lacks of performances and QoS. Based on such analysis results, it is also expected to find ways for adapting to wireless networks behaviors and limits for optimizing their performances and trying to guarantee the requested services.

The RESCUE project is at its very early stage. This paper then just addresses a limited scope in terms of parameters. It then focuses only on the impact of the Signal/Noise Ratio (SNR) on delays and jitters, two essential parameters for end-to-end services. Despite the scope of this study is not very broad, it nevertheless has the merit to exhibit unexpected results on the level of performance and QoS provided by wireless networks depending on the air access conditions.

The rest of this paper is organized as follows: section 2 presents the state of the art. Section 3 describes the different parameters, exclusively focusing on physic ones which are often unknown in the Internet research community. Based on this, this section also details the research problematic to be addressed in the remainder of the paper. Then section 4 starts presenting the contribution by describing the experimental platform and process. Section 5 presents the results, i.e. experiment results showing the impact of SNR on delays and jitters at network level. Finally, section 6 concludes this paper by presenting future work to be performed in the framework of the RESCUE project.

2   State of the Art in Wireless Networks Cross-Layered Monitoring

Wireless network monitoring has raised significant efforts these last years. It started with the monitoring of such wireless networks at the network (IP) level on WLANs (WIFI essentially) or on long distance Wireless networks as GPRS or UMTS [16]. This is of course of limited interest as the monitoring equipment is located at the Access Point (AP), but on the wired side. Other work, as [5], focuses on the wireless side of such networks and studies the MAC level. Another example is provided by Barrett et al. [4] which study the interaction existing between the performance of a peculiar MAC protocol and the upper-layer routing protocol used. It rigorously investigates and confirms the expectations that protocols performances at different logical layers (MAC and upper) have to be studied together. This confirms what we argued at the beginning of this paper about the need of developing cross-layered monitoring techniques for wireless networks. In particular, it has been then investigated that the physical layer has a strong impact on the performance and QoS provided by the upper layers. Let's quote a few papers illustrating this statement. Raghavendra et al. [14] analyze 802.11 traces and enlighten protocol and implementation flaws which led to problems such as packet losses. According to this paper the existence of adjacent channel leakage power, due to their small number, is as important as alien RF interferences. Verma et al. [17] present work done on a new passive method for estimating link quality based on SNR-BER mapping. It also extensively investigates the wireless cards to assess its calibration and thus ensuring correct precision. This highlights the importance of hardware to conduct RF measurements, thus pinpointing the lack of accurate monitoring tools at the wireless physical level (at least in the tools commonly used in the networking community). This is still true, despite effort by Feng et al. [11] who developed a 802.11 cross-layer measurement tool and cross-implications of layers from the application to the physical medium. This is however a good tool for whoever wants to get a grip on the cross-layer capture and analysis problematic. Sundaresan and Papagianaki [15] perfectly illustrate the need of cross-layered monitoring starting from the physical layer in wireless networks. In this paper, they investigate how clients willing to join a new 802.11 network may select the access point they want to communicate with. It more precisely compares metrics driving this choice. Contrary to previous methods, metrics used here get ground on cross-layer measurements; namely these metrics are the received signal strength (physical layer), a metric which characterizes the access point global throughput capacity (MAC layer) and another one which computes an estimation of response time from the AP when a client sends a request (MAC layer). They thus propose completely different methods than actual ones which are only based on the RSSI metric. In this paper, Sundaresan and Papagianaki exhibit the need to consider various parameters from any logical and physical layers. Lacage et al. [10] also highlight the fact that performances at different logical and physical layers have to be studied both singularly and plurally at the same time. They propose an extensive study of the influence of bit-rate parameters through 802.11 PHY automatic rate control over MAC protocol performances. Wang et al. [18] provide another example of the effect of PHY parameters on 802.11 MAC protocol. Many studies are also conducted to characterize the evolution of wireless medium parameters in time; for example Qiu et al.[13] and Jain et al. [7] are proposing models of interferences and wireless link behavior.

Based on this short overview on cross-layered monitoring, we want to alarm readers on the fact that most papers on wireless networks monitoring adopt the wired vision of networks and are taking aside the physical aspect of wireless communications [9]. It has to be strictly avoided, and it is understood that future tools should adopt a finer vision on what happen at the physical layer, and for the mechanisms involved at all layers of the communication stack, at the same time.

3   Problematic

Delay is a key parameter for characterizing and assessing the end-to-end QoS of network and distributed systems. This parameter is of real significance for users and their applications. Measured on a wired network, this dimension is quite similar at all levels of the communication architecture; it is generally measured at the network, transport or application level, but its evolution at the physical or data-link levels is pretty similar compared to upper layers. In wired networks, delays or jitters are mostly influenced by the congestion level of network devices as routers, switches, gateways, firewalls, etc.

The problematic in wireless networks is more complex. Delays and jitters are also influenced by the congestion level, but more generally, it seems that the traffic impact on the air medium is more complex, and it significantly influences the performance and QoS level of wireless networks. Depending on the traffic, it seems obvious that it can create interferences in the communication hertzian space or between adjacent communication channels, introduce noise, etc... At the physical level, it can merge some signals which are very close (the phases or periods of signals can appear the same), what makes difficult for wireless physical devices to extract the original signal. Because of that, the Physical reception algorithms and MAC access principle are adapted to the new traffic conditions on the air medium (i.e. degraded): the physical available throughput is significantly reduced, and, what we will show in the remainder of the paper, the delay is also impacted.

Physical parameters on the hertzian medium are then of key importance and must be considered and monitored for wireless networks (generally, computer scientists and engineers do not focus on so low layers requiring telecommunication skills, limiting their monitoring on layers 3 and upper (there are also some examples at layer 2 for some specific kinds of WLAN as WIFI). The rest of this section then aims at presenting the different parameters for characterizing and assessing the state of the hertzian medium for wireless communications.

The well known Signal to Noise Ratio (SNR or S/N) is the ratio between the amplitude of data signals over the amplitude of noise signals. It measures the corruption level of the original signal by noise.

A similar ratio called Signal to Noise plus Interference Ratio is an extension of the SNR. In addition of the Noise, it includes in its computing the level of interferences which are of major importance in wireless networking.

The $\frac{E_b}{N_o}$ ratio corresponds to the quantity of energy used to send one bit of data. It is also called the *energy per bit over noise spectral density ratio*. This value is often used as a normalization of the SNR value for a bit. Thus, the $\frac{E_b}{N_o}$ value is similar for the digital signals to the SNR for analogous signals.

The strength of the received signal is also a parameter of importance. it can be used in many applications as localization (e.g. trilateralization) [6] or link access (e.g. detection of ongoing transmissions on an emission channel) [8]. Several units exist for this parameter as the mW (milliWatt), the dBm, and the Received Signal Strength Indicator or Radio Signal Strength Indication (RSSI). The three units are similar and it exists methods for converting them into each other. As the strength of the received signal does not linearly decrease with distance, but in a logarithmic way, the most used unit is the dBm logarithmic unit. The mW and dBm are common measurement units instead, the RSSI only exists in the context of 802.11 standards which define it along with mechanisms for measuring Radio Frequency (RF) energy by electronic circuit. Standards also specify RSSI range between 0 (no signal) and 255 (maximal signal). Nevertheless, equipment designers are not forced to use 256 different values. Atheros devices measure RSSI between 0 and 60 while for CISCO, maximal RSSI value is 100 [3]. An important note about its use is that it is defined to be used only by microcodes present on hardware devices or by drivers, but not by higher level applications. Note also that, often, drivers of wireless 802.11 chips assimilate the measure of the received signal strength with a measure of the SNR.

Adjacent Channel Power Ratio - ACPR (also called sometimes Adjacent Channel Leakage Power - ALCR) is of significant importance for communication technologies which divide the frequency band or amplitude range in several channels centered on different frequencies, e.g. OFDM. Two adjacent channels can then interfere, i.e. one sending on a channel can cause interferences on an adjacent channel (Adjacent Channel Interference - ACI). The APCR is defined as the ratio between the intensity of the energy sent on a channel over the intensity of the whole set of inference energy sent from all adjacent channels. The units generally used for computing the ACPR are dBm, dBW or Watt.

The used bandwidth is a well known and very useful parameter measuring the width of the frequency band which contains a given percentage of the energy of a particular signal.

The Symbol Error Rate (SER) or Packet Error rate (PER) are also well known parameters defining at the receiver level the total number or erroneous symbols or packets over the total number of received symbols or packets.

The Error Vector Magnitude - EVM - measures the performance of digital communication systems. It is obtained by comparing the characteristics of the IQ modulation of a signal (signal properties in a complex space representation) with the one of a reference signal.

All the previously mentioned parameters are of significant importance for monitoring the wireless networks behaviors and performance levels. It is nevertheless not easy to make such physical measurement on the air interfaces or the hertzian medium. Such measurement needs, for being accurate, very specific and costly equipments generally used by specialists in electronics. At this stage of the RESCUE project, we are still in the study of existing equipments for performing such kinds of measurements very accurately. Thats is why in the remainder of the paper, we will focus our study on the single well known SNR parameter; many tools, and especially software and free ones, exist for measuring this parameter. The results we are presenting are not guaranteed to be accurate: they just show trends that we will check when we will have at our disposal better physical measurement equipments.

4   Experimental Platform and Process

4.1   The Test Environment

The experiment runs indoor, in the research laboratory LAAS (Laboratoire d'Analyse et d'Architecture des Systèmes) in Toulouse-France. The experiment field is a hallway inside the laboratory, rooms are located on its both sides, the walls are of concrete and the rooms furniture is mostly of wood, iron and glass. The experiment took place in a working day at the laboratory, so we can predict the existence of other experiments running at the same time, plus many users having wireless connectivity.

4.2   The Test Bed

The test bed consists of two laptops and three access points. The two laptops: PC1 with Unix OS and PC2 with Windows OS supported with Intel(R) PRO/Wireless card 3945ABG which is compatible with 802.11a, 802.11b and 802.11g wireless standards, can operate at 5 GHz or 2.4 GHz frequencies at speeds up to 54 Mbps. Both laptops are placed on fixed places on a mobile table which was moved to different measurement points in the hallway without changing its height (67.5 cm) or its direction. The three APs are 802.11g ones, they

Fig. 1. Test environment: hallway in research laboratory

are located as shown in figure 1 where AP1 is at the beginning of the vertical hallway, AP2 at its end and AP3 is in a lateral hallway that is orthogonal with the test hallway. All access points are at height 231 (cm) above the ground.

4.3   The Test Methodology

- Ten test points were considered in the hallway between AP1 and AP2 in a way that the first test point is located immediately under AP1, the second is further and so on. So, at each next test point we were getting further from AP1 and closer to AP2.
- The SNR at each test point was measured using NetStumbler open source measurement tool which was running on PC2.
- At each test point, we were sending 200 ICMP packets from PC1 to AP1, the ACK of these packets is sent back from AP1 to PC1, this last reports the packets' history.
- Computers' clocks were synchronized via ntpdate [1] which lets access an external server and gets actual hour and date, actualizing the local computer's

clock. Then through ntptrace [2] we examined the offset time in milliseconds from the external server consulted with ntpdate. We executed ntpdate and checked the offset with nptrace. This process was made several times until the offset obtained was less than 0.00008 seconds on each computer.
– Data was collected online, then analyzed offline.

5   Results

5.1   Exploring SNR

In our work, SNR was measured for the three APs at the ten test points described above. The SNR values corresponding to each test point are shown in table 1 where the values establish a minimum-maximum pattern.

Table 1. Min-max SNR values of the three APs measured at the ten test points

Test point	SNR(db) for AP1	SNR (db) for AP2	SNR (db) for AP3
1	47 - 60	13 - 37	0 - 11
2	44 - 52	11 - 33	0 - 18
3	34 - 45	16 - 39	14 - 25
4	34 - 42	0 - 37	21 - 32
5	27 - 39	25 - 39	25 - 41
6	16 - 37	23 - 45	27 - 46
7	16 - 33	20 - 44	36 - 41
8	14 - 30	31 - 46	18 - 32
9	12 - 31	35 - 57	13 - 26
10	0 - 27	50 - 62	11 - 20

We notice that in some ranges there are overlapped values. This overlapping is due to the natural unpredictable behavior shown by the wireless communications. This unstable behaviour derives in the possibility of obtaining different SNR measurements at the same location. For example: at test point 4, the minor SNR value for AP1 was 34 (db) while at test point 5 the SNR highest value for AP1 was 39 (db). In this example, we have the values in the range 34-39 (db) repeated at both points of measurements.

Figure 2 shows the SNR values range at each test point for each AP in third tile presentation to reflect as well the values distribution between the max and min SNR edges. In this figure we see that by stepping from test point 1 to test point 10 getting further from AP1 and closer to AP2, the SNR for AP1 was decreasing and for AP2 was increasing. In fact the correlation factor for SNR with distance for AP1 was -0,97 and for AP2 was +0,98. This lets us say that the value of SNR measured depends on the distance in a way that, the longest the distance to the AP the less the value of SNR measured is and vice versa.

Regarding SNR for AP3, we notice that between test point 1 and test point 6 it was increasing then between test point 7 and test point 10 it was decreasing.

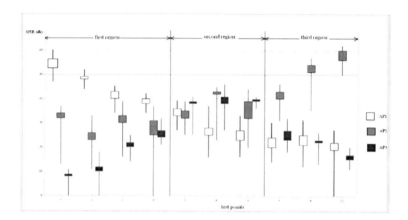

Fig. 2. SNR values in third tile representation for each AP at the ten test points

This is because while performing the experiment, we crossed the lateral corridor where AP3 is, which means that we approached it then went far from it, this resulted in making the picks of SNR values for this AP be at test point 6.

Figure 2 also illustrates that the laptop is not necessarily connected to the AP having the highest SNR. The figure can be divided into three regions according to SNR min-max values and distribution for the three APs:

1. First region: Covers 1-4 test points. AP1 SNR was the dominant. In fact, while running the experiment at those four test points, the portable computer was connected to LAAS network through AP1.
2. Second region: Covers 5-7 test points. AP3 SNR was the dominant. The portable computer was connected through AP3 at these test points while running the experiment.
3. Third region: Covers 8-10 test points. AP2 SNR was the dominant. While running the experiment at those three test points, the portable computer was connected to LAAS network through AP2.

We can say that there is a possibility that the client selects the AP of the best SNR to connect through. A better understanding of this situation can be reached by reading about roaming in the user guide of the wireless card embedded in the laptops [12] in order to know the roaming protocol that this card follows.

It is worth commenting that at test point 6; although SNR for AP2 is higher than of AP3 (figure 2), still the portable computer remained connected to AP3 while running the experiment at this test point. The reason might be that, since the portable computer has started connecting to the network through AP3 since test point 5, it remained connected to it at test point 6 because the SNR of AP3 at this test point was still sufficient to establish the connection even being less than the SNR of AP2.

5.2 SNR Impact on Upper Layers

The goal of this study is to determin how and when do the SNR changes on the physical layer propagate to upper layers, thus affecting the E2E connection. While running the experiment we noticed that the AP signal power was much over the level needed to establish a good connection, this was reflected through the frame loss parameter wich was 0,3% (non lossy paths). This results in masking the trends. So to have a meaningful study for the SNR impact on Delay and Jitter we chose the test point at which the average SNR value was the minimum, it was test point 3. We considered the time stamps for SNR values as a reference and shifted the Delay and Jitter traces with several time values up to a maximum shift of 1 second on millisecond scale. Table 2 shows the correlation values at each time shift.

Table 2. Correlation values for SNR with Delay and Jitter at test point 3

Time shift (ms)	Corr(SNR,Delay)	Corr(SNR,Jitter)
0	0,89	0,67
100	0,84	0,76
200	0,61	0,48
300	-0,88	-0,81
400	-0,69	-0,07
500	-0,37	0,49
600	0,21	0,14
700	0,46	0,6
800	0,25	-0,01
900	0,59	0,83

We notice that at time shift 300 ms, the impact of SNR on other both parameters appeared in a way that the decrease in SNR reflects in Delay and Jitter increase and vice versa. In other words, the decrease of SNR on the physical layer propagates to upper layers in term of Delay and Jitter increase. In our experiment the propagation happened with time delay of 300 ms where the correlation values were -0,88 and -0,81 respectively.

On the other hand, we notice that a small change in SNR values is strongly reflected on upper layers. For example, while running the experiment, an increase in SNR value from 43 db to 45 db made the Delay value falls from 124 ms to 59 ms after time shift of 300 ms, and a decrease in SNR value from 45 db to 44 db resulted in Delay increase from 3 ms to 91 ms.

6 Conclusion

This paper aims at motivating the use of cross-layered monitoring in wireless networks. For this purpose, it puts emphasis on the complexity of the largely unknown (in the networking community) physical layer and all its constraints.

The paper then makes a brief but significant presentation of the different parameters to be measured at the physical layer. It exhibits the inherent complexity of such parameters and emphasizes on the difficulty of accurately measuring them. A strong effort has to be provided to find suited monitoring equipments (we are currently taking advantage of the equipments own by researchers in electronics in our lab) or design and develop new ones. The paper then presents a very preliminary and illustrative study aiming at exhibiting the unexpected behaviors of the physical layers of wireless networks. It is shown that the SNR has a significant impact on the communication delay and jitter in a completely unexpected way in terms of intensity: a small change in the SNR causes huge changes in delay and jitters values. This is especially damageable for the global network performance, as well as for streaming or real-time applications which require stable jitter and low delays. It then appears clearly that the current evolution of wireless networks, especially devoted for favoring the integration of digital applications on wireless supports, is not completely fulfilling its objectives because of such unexpected sensitivity to SNR.

References

1. ntpdate, set the date and time via ntp, http://www.eecis.udel.edu
2. ntptrace, trace a chain of ntp servers back to the primary source, http://www.eecis.udel.edu
3. Bardwell, J.: Converting Signal Strength Percentage to dBm Values (November 2002), http://www.wildpackets.com/elements/whitepapers/Converting_Signal_Strength.pdf
4. Barrett, C., Drozda, M., Marathe, A., Marathe, M.: Analyzing interaction between network protocols, topology and traffic in wireless radio networks. In: 2003 IEEE Wireless Communications and Networking, WCNC 2003, vol. 3, pp. 1760–1766 (2003)
5. Claveirole, T., de AmorimMarcelo, D.: Wipal and wscout, two hands-on tools for wireless packet traces manipulation and visualization. In: ACM Mobicom Workshop on Wireless Network Testbeds, Experimental Evaluation, and Characterization, MobiCom 2008 (2008)
6. Hightower, J., Vakili, C., Borriello, G., Want, R.: Design and Calibration of the SpotON Ad-Hoc Location Sensing System (2001), http://citeseerx.ist.psu.edu/viewdoc/summary?doi=10.1.1.23.6231
7. Jain, K., Padhye, J., Padmanabhan, V.N., Qiu, L.: Impact of interference on multihop wireless network performance. In: Proceedings of the 9th Annual International Conference on Mobile Computing and Networking, MobiCom 2003, pp. 66–80. ACM, New York (2003), http://doi.acm.org/10.1145/938985.938993
8. Kolar, V., Bharath, K., Abu-Ghazaleh, N.B., Riihijarvi, J.: Contention in multihop wireless networks: model and fairness analysis. In: Proceedings of the 12th ACM International Conference on Modeling, Analysis and Simulation of Wireless and Mobile Systems, MSWiM 2009, pp. 21–29. ACM, New York (2009), http://doi.acm.org/10.1145/1641804.1641812
9. Kotz, D., Newport, C., Elliott, C.: The mistaken axioms of wireless-network research. Tech. rep., Dartmouth College (July 2003)

10. Lacage, M., Manshaei, M.H., Turletti, T.: "ieee 802.11" rate adaptation: a practical approach. In: Proceedings of the 7th ACM International Symposium on Modeling, Analysis and Simulation of Wireless and Mobile Systems, MSWiM 2004, pp. 126–134. ACM, New York (2004), http://doi.acm.org/10.1145/1023663.1023687

11. Li, F., Li, M., Lu, R., Wu, H., Claypool, M., Kinicki, R.: Tools and techniques for measurement of ieee 802.11 wireless networks. In: 2006 4th International Symposium on Modeling and Optimization in Mobile, Ad Hoc and Wireless Networks, pp. 1–8 (2006)

12. Parkway, E.Y., Hillsboro.: Intel(r) pro/wireless 3945abg network connection user guide. In: User Guide. Intel Corporation (2004-2005), ftp://download.intel.com/support/wireless/wlan/sb/3945abgug.pdf

13. Qiu, L., Zhang, Y., Wang, F., Han, M.K., Mahajan, R.: A general model of wireless interference. In: Proceedings of the 13th Annual ACM International Conference on Mobile Computing and Networking, MobiCom 2007, pp. 171–182. ACM, New York (2007), http://doi.acm.org/10.1145/1287853.1287874

14. Raghavendra, R., Belding, E., Papagiannaki, K., Almeroth, K.: Unwanted link layer traffic in large ieee 802.11 wireless networks. IEEE Transactions on Mobile Computing 9(9), 1212–1225 (2010)

15. Sundaresan, K., Papagiannaki, K.: The need for cross-layer information in access point selection algorithms. In: Proceedings of the 6th ACM SIGCOMM Conference on Internet Measurement, IMC 2006, pp. 257–262. ACM, New York (2006), http://doi.acm.org/10.1145/1177080.1177113

16. Svoboda, P., Ricciato, F., Hasenleithner, E., Pilz, R.: Composition of gprs/umts traffic: snapshots from a live network. In: 4th Int'l Workshop on Internet Performance, Simulation, Monitoring and Measurement, IPS-MOME 2006 (2006)

17. Verma, L., Kim, S., Choi, S., Lee, S.J.: Reliable, low overhead link quality estimation for 802.11 wireless mesh networks. In: 5th IEEE Annual Communications Society Conference on Sensor, Mesh and Ad Hoc Communications and Networks Workshops, SECON Workshops 2008, pp. 1–6 (2008)

18. Wang, L.C., Chen, A., Huang, S.Y.: A cross-layer investigation for the throughput performance of csma/ca-based wlans with directional antennas and capture effect. IEEE Transactions on Vehicular Technology 56(5), 2756–2766 (2007)

A Quality of Experience Based Approach for Wireless Mesh Networks[*]

Anderson Morais and Ana Cavalli

Télécom SudParis, France
{anderson.morais,ana.cavalli}@it-sudparis.eu

Abstract. Wireless Mesh Network (WMN) is an emerging technology that is gaining importance among traditional wireless communication scenarios. Wireless Mesh Networks are becoming a popular way of offering end-to-end services, such as Voice over IP (VoIP) and Video on Demand (VOD), in an inexpensive, practical, and fast manner. However, those applications require a minimum network performance level in order to provide an acceptable Quality of Experience (QoE) level to users. In this paper, we present a QoE based approach, which analyzes key QoS parameters like delay, jitter, and packet loss in a mesh network executing the Better Approach To Mobile Ad hoc Network (BATMAN) proactive routing protocol. The proposed mechanism evaluates the actual QoE level from the point of view of each mesh node taking into account the calculated QoS parameters, and then proposes a response in case of QoE degradation as reducing the node broadcasting rate.

Keywords: QoE, Wireless Mesh Network, QoS parameters.

1 Introduction

Wireless Mesh Network (WMN) has emerged in the wireless communication scenario as a new technology to fulfill the requirements of Next Generation Wireless Networks (NGWN), such as offering adaptive, flexible, and reconfigurable network architecture while providing cost-effective solutions to wireless Internet Service Providers (ISPs) [1]. ISPs are choosing Wireless Mesh Network (WMN) to offer Internet connectivity since it allows an easy, fast, and cheap network deployment.

WMNs are characterized by dynamic self-organization, self-configuration, and self-healing whereas the mesh nodes automatically establish an ad hoc network and maintain the connectivity among the nodes. The mesh nodes transmit traffic from others nodes to reach a destination that they could not reach by themselves. The mesh structure assures the availability of multiple paths for the node in the network. If a mesh node crashes or loses the connection, its neighboring nodes simply find another route and the network continues operating. Rather than traditional wireless networks, WMNs do not rely on dedicated wireless infrastructure, but the nodes count on each other to maintain the network entirely connected and transmit data traffic to the destination. As a result, the network is very reliable and has a good coverage because

[*] This work was funded by EUREKA/CELTIC project IPNQSIS as project number CP07-009.

X. Masip-Bruin et al. (Eds.): WWIC 2011, LNCS 6649, pp. 162–173, 2011.

there is often more than one route between a source node and a destination node. Wireless community networks and municipal wireless networks are good examples of real-life WMNs, which offer low-cost Internet access via Wi-Fi to large areas by using inexpensive IEEE 802.11 wireless mesh routers.

However, streaming multimedia applications including VoIP, Internet Protocol Television (IPTV), and multiplayer online games, require a minimum level of performance, for example, fixed bit rate, low latency, and low jitter, in order to provide an acceptable usability, reliability, and end-to-end quality level to users. Quality of Experience (QoE) is the user perceived service performance, or the required degree of satisfaction of the user. A typical QoE measurement method is the Mean Opinion Score (MOS) [2], which can be determined from subjective ratings by real subjects, for instance, subjective quality assessment of audio listening where a number of users judge the quality of the receive audio. Alternatively, the MOS can be predicted from objective analysis, which uses an original signal and the degraded received signal as input. The MOS provides a numerical indication of the perceived quality of received media after compression and/or transmission.

In this paper, we describe a QoE based approach, which analyzes key QoS parameters such as delay, jitter, and packet loss for a VoIP service. The aim of the proposed mechanism is to show how the current network performance level can impact on the service quality level. We assume the service is running in a mesh network, where each node executes BATMAN proactive routing protocol. The proposed mechanism calculates the objective QoS parameters for each mesh node by applying active and passive monitoring techniques. Then these parameters are used to calculate the MOS, which represents the user perceived performance, i.e., the QoE. The approach can also carry out responses in case of QoS and QoE degradation as reducing the broadcasting rate of the node to improve the network performance and bandwidth, or updating the node's routing table to redirect the data traffic to a different path and consequently avoid taking congested routes that provoke collisions.

The main contributions of the paper are: (i) a QoE based approach that analyzes performance metrics for a mesh network; (ii) a mechanism to calculate passively and actively the QoS parameters and the corresponding QoE level in a mesh network; (iii) a reaction mechanism in case of QoS/QoE deterioration for QoE adjustment.

The remainder of the paper proceeds as follows. Section 2 describes the related work. Section 3 introduces the QoE based approach composed of a monitoring module and a controlling module. Finally, Section 4 concludes the paper.

2 Related Work

Research efforts have been focused on obtaining QoE measures from objective metrics offered by QoS assessment in order to overcome the difficulties and drawbacks of performing a subjective QoE assessment. Those approaches can be classified in intrusive and non-intrusive methods. The Perceptual Evaluation of Speech Quality (PESQ) [3] is an intrusive method for automated assessment of speech quality, which predicts the subjective quality of speech codecs by comparing the source signal with the degraded received signal. PESQ was developed to model subjective tests commonly used in telecommunications to assess the voice quality by real users, thus using true voice samples as test signals.

The E-model [4] and the ITU-T Recommendation P.563 [5] are common examples of non-intrusive techniques. The E-model tool assess the voice quality taking into account telephony impairments, e.g., low bit-rate codecs, one-way delay, loss, noise, and echo, and outputs a "Transmission Rating Factor R". The ITU-T P.563 evaluates the voice quality executing three steps: (i) preprocessing of the voice signal, (ii) extraction of distortion and speech parameters from the voice signal parts, and (iii) determination of distortion class and generation of the MOS.

Moreover, new non-intrusive approaches for VoIP and Video over IP have been proposed to objectively estimate the QoE from QoS parameters. In [6], the authors propose a framework to provide online QoE estimates for Voice and Video over IP (VVoIP) on the network paths. The QoE model is expressed as a function of the measurable network factors: bandwidth, delay, jitter, and loss. In [7], a model that characterizes the relationship between packet loss and video distortion is developed. That model is used to develop a video quality evaluation method that is independent from the video content characteristics. The work [8] extends the E-model considering the effects of packet loss and delay jitter in VoIP scenarios. A new formula is proposed to quantify these effects and incorporated into the E-model.

However, approaches that perform subjective QoE assessment based exclusively on QoS analysis using real-time traffic in real network environments are hardly found, and even less for multimedia applications based on IPTV and VOD technologies.

3 The QoE Based Approach

The goal of the proposed mechanism is to monitor the performance level of a mesh network in order to ensure a stable and proper QoE level for each mesh node. Objective QoS parameters are measured, and then mapped to the user-perceived QoE, which is expressed through the *Mean Opinion Score* (MOS). Performance and service quality problems should be detected as quickly as possible by the approach, and a precise reaction should be provided to maintain a high QoS level and a good quality level for the services. Every relay mesh node is equipped with monitoring capacities, which evaluate the current network conditions, and provides a response accordingly.

The approach provides QoS support at MAC Layer by using BATMAN Layer 2 routing functionality. BATMAN protocol operates entirely on ISO/OSI Layer 2, so not only the routing information is transported using raw Ethernet frames, but also the data traffic is handled by BATMAN. BATMAN encapsulates and forwards all data traffic until it reaches the destination, thus emulating a virtual network switch of all mesh nodes. Hence, all nodes seem to be link local and not aware of the network's topology. The BATMAN algorithm [9] is detailed as follows.

Each node (also referenced as Originator) periodically broadcasts hello messages, known as Originator Messages (OGMs), to tell its neighbors about its existence. An OGM owns at least an Originator address, a Source address, a Time To Live (TTL), and a unique Sequence Number value. As a neighbor receives an OGM, it modifies the Source address to its own address and rebroadcast this OGM in accordance to BATMAN forwarding rules to tell its neighboring nodes about the existence of the node that originated the OGM, and so on and so forth. Hence, the mesh network is flooded with OGMs until every node has received it at least once, or until they got lost because of communication links packet loss, or until their TTL value has expired. The Sequence Number value of the OGM is utilized to verify how fresh the message is, i.e., to discern between new OGMs and duplicated OGMs in order to guarantee that each OGM is only counted once. The amount of OGMs, i.e., the total number of Sequence Numbers, received from an Originator via each neighboring node is utilized to calculate the route quality, i.e., the Transmission Quality (TQ). Thus, BATMAN chooses as next-hop to the Originator the neighboring node from which it has received the highest amount of OGMs from that Originator within a sliding window.

Basically, the proposed approach consists of two modules, the *Traffic Monitoring Module* that analyzes the network performance status from the node, and the *Routing Control Module* that offers different possibilities to influence on the traffic that goes through the node in order to provide appropriate QoS. These two components must communicate with each other in the node for QoS/QoE information exchange. Furthermore, all the *Routing Control Modules* throughout the network should be able to exchange QoE and performance information in a distributed way.

Figure 1 shows the general structure of the proposed approach. The main part is formed by the BATMAN Layer 2 protocol. Running BATMAN on every node enables all the nodes to connect to each other and to form a mesh cloud. The *Traffic Monitoring Module* is implemented as a hybrid probe in each node, which passively captures packets passing through to the BATMAN interface and actively injects BATMAN traffic in the network, when necessary, to collect measurements such as packet loss, and round trip time. In addition, the module is executed independently of network layer (ex.: IPv4, IPv6, and DHCP) and the transporting protocol. The *Routing Control Module* is implemented as an extension to BATMAN protocol. It can make use of BATMAN OGMs or generate specific messages to allow communication between different *Routing Control Modules*. The *Routing Control Module* and *Traffic Monitoring Module* are connected to each other via communication sockets. Sections 3.1 and 3.2 explain these two modules in more detail.

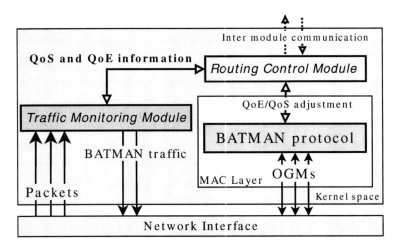

Fig. 1. Scheme for QoE/QoS control

3.1 Traffic Monitoring Module

The *Traffic Monitoring Module* is an active and passive network-monitoring tool that is customized for a BATMAN mesh network to monitor QoS parameters from the mesh network traffic.

The *Traffic Monitoring Module* obtains some basic information about a certain packet stream flow that it intercepts and analyzes. Table 1 illustrates the explicit information provided by the *Traffic Monitoring Module* that is extracted from BATMAN packets and from the node's routing table. For instance, the node receives an OGM from its neighbor `fe:fe:00:00:02:01` (Source address), which was originated by node `fe:fe:00:00:01:01` (Originator address) with a unique Sequence Number value. According to the node's routing table its neighbor `fe:fe:00:00:02:01` is the current best ranking neighbor towards the Originator. The routing table also provides a "Potential Nexthop" towards the Originator.

Table 1. Explicit information extracted from BATMAN packets and the routing table

BATMAN Packet			BATMAN Routing Table		
Source	Originator	Sequence Number	Best Nexthop	Potential Nexthop	Transmission Quality (TQ) to the Originator
fe:fe:00:00: 02:01	fe:fe:00:00: 01:01	125	fe:fe:00:00: 02:01	fe:fe:00:00: 03:01	245/255

Active Approach. Table 2 presents the statistical information obtained by the active monitoring mechanism. The Round Trip Time (RTT) is the length of time it takes for a packet to be sent plus the length of time it takes for an acknowledgment of that packet to be received.

Table 2. Statistical information obtained by the active monitoring mechanism

Active monitoring				
Packet Loss (%)	Minimum RTT (ms)	Maximum RTT (ms)	Mean RTT (ms)	RTT Standard Deviation (ms)
0.0	10.912	68.917	12.640	5.330

The active monitoring approach is applied to obtain the *Packet Loss*, the *Minimum RTT* (the shortest RTT), the *Maximum RTT* (the longest RTT), the *Mean RTT* (the average of measured RTTs), and the *RTT Standard Deviation* (an indication of how regular or varied the RTTs were). For that, BATMAN Advanced Control and Management tool (*batctl*) is employed [10]. The reason to use BATMAN *batctl* tool is since BATMAN operates on Layer 2, thus all nodes participating in the virtual switch are completely transparent for all protocols above Layer 2. Therefore, the common diagnosis tools do not work as expected in a BATMAN mesh network.

The *batctl* ping diagnostic tool is a useful way to determine if a network connection is of sufficient quality, for example, to carry out a VoIP call without voice quality degradation. For that, the *batctl* ping tool injects custom ICMP echo request packets into the data flow demanding an immediate response. Then it measures the time it takes for the response to be received. From this, the RTT is calculated. If a response is not detected, then a lost packet is recorded. Note that absolute values of RTT is of less importance since it does not matter at all to voice quality if the a RTT is 1ms or 100ms, what matters for VoIP calls are the following indicators [11]:

- If the *Mean RTT* is less than 150ms, then the latency itself will not be an issue to users. VoIP calls can still be carried on networks with RTTs as high as 500ms and above (satellite network frequently have RTTs higher than 700ms) but the delay is noticeable to callers.
- If the *Packet Loss* is less than 2%, then the voice quality is not affected. In fact, *Packet Loss* should to be close to 0%, but voice quality degradation will only become an issue as *Packet Loss* goes beyond 2%.
- If the *RTT Standard Deviation* is less than 10ms, then the voice quality is not deteriorated. The main problem with networks carrying voice is jitter [12], the variability in packet latency times. A network with constant latency has no variation, and consequently no jitter. If RTTs vary abruptly then voice quality will suffer from jitter. If *RTT Standard Deviation* goes beyond 20ms one will start to have problems with voice traffic because of jitter.
- If the difference between the *Minimum RTT* and *Maximum RTT* values is less than 20ms then jitter is not a problem. If it is above 20ms, then a more detailed analysis of the responses is required to determine if the *Maximum RTT* is an isolated anomaly or an indication of significant jitter. Frequent variation in the RTT values over a range greater than 20ms indicates jitter issues and voice quality problems.

The equations to calculate the RTT statistical information are given below.

- For a packet p_i that is generated by *batctl* tool, the RTT is defined as:

$$RTT_i = te_{p_i} - ts_{p_i}, \tag{1}$$

where ts_{p_i} is the start time, i.e., the time packet p_i is sent to destination, and te_{p_i} is the end time, i.e., the time packet p_i is received back on the sender.

- The *Mean RTT* is given by:

$$\overline{RTT} = \frac{1}{n} \sum_{i=1}^{n} RTT_i, \tag{2}$$

where n is the number of measured RTTs for n packets.

- The *RTT Standard Deviation* (or jitter) is calculated as:

$$RTTSD = \sqrt{\frac{1}{n} \sum_{i=1}^{n} RTT_i^2 - \overline{RTT}^2}. \tag{3}$$

- The *Packet Loss* is calculated as:

$$P_{Loss} = 1 - \frac{n}{N}, \tag{4}$$

where N is the total number of packets injected by *batctl* tool.

Passive Approach. Table 3 shows the statistical information that can be obtained by passive monitoring, which simply observes the packets passing through the BATMAN node interface. The *Packet Loss*, the *Mean Inter Packet Delay*, the *Inter Packet Delay Standard Deviation*, the *Bit Rate*, and the *Packet Rate* can be obtained.

Table 3. Statistical information obtained by the passive monitoring mechanism

Passive monitoring				
Packet Loss (%)	*Mean Inter Packet Delay* (ms)	*Inter Packet Delay Standard Deviation* (ms)	*Bit Rate* (bit/s)	*Packet Rate* (pkt/s)
0.2	20.640	5.330	120.5	130.0

For every BATMAN packet pkt_i that traverses the node the following implicit and explicit information can be obtained:

- seq_i, that is the unique sequence number of pkt_i generated by Originator O_j, for $i = \{0, ..., n\}$ and $j = \{0, ..., m\}$.
- t_i, the absolute arrival time of pkt_i.
- $\Delta t_i = t_i - t_{i-1}$, the relative arrival time of pkt_i compared to pkt_{i-1} expressed in seconds, for $0 < i \leq n$.
- len_i, the total length of pkt_i in bytes.

Using these definitions, the statistical information can be obtained as follows.

- The *Mean Inter Packet Delay* is defined as:

$$MIPD = \overline{\Delta t} = \frac{1}{n} \sum_{i=1}^{n} \Delta t_i \ , \tag{5}$$

where n is the number of the packets analyzed for Originator O_j.

- The *Inter Packet Delay Standard Deviation*, i.e., the jitter, is calculated as:

$$IPDSD = \sqrt{\frac{1}{n} \sum_{i=1}^{n} \Delta t_i^2 - \overline{\Delta t}^2} \ . \tag{6}$$

- The *Packet Loss* is defined as:

$$PKT_{Loss} = 1 - \frac{(n+1)}{seq_n - seq_0} \ , \tag{7}$$

where $(n + 1)$ is the number of the captured packets, seq_n is the maximum sequence number received from Originator O_j, and seq_0 is the minimum sequence number received from Originator O_j.

- The *Bit Rate* in kbit/sec (kbps) is defined as:

$$BR = \frac{1}{t_n - t_0} \sum_{i=0}^{n} len_i \ . \tag{8}$$

- While the *Packet Rate* in pkts/s is defined as:

$$PKT_{Rate} = \frac{(n+1)}{t_n - t_0} \quad .$$

(9)

3.2 Routing Control Module

The key part of the proposed approach is the *Routing Control Module*. It is in charge of evaluating whether the actual network situation is acceptable according to the performance measurements supplied by the *Traffic Monitoring Module*, and if this is not the case, it must decide how to react to the traffic QoS problems. To perform this task, certain thresholds are required.

Threshold Mechanism. Monitoring of the services alone is not enough to provide QoS/QoE enhancement. It is also necessary a mechanism that evaluates the monitored information and responds in the case of a possible performance quality decrease. To perform this task, a *threshold* mechanism is necessary which indicates a *good*, *medium*, or *bad* service quality level.

Moreover, key parameters have to be defined in order to establish the *thresholds* and attribute correct quality levels to them. The key parameters selected to evaluate the QoS and possible QoS impairment are the previously ones introduced for the active and passive approaches:

- Active approach: the *Mean RTT – $\overline{RTT}$* (latency), the *RTT Standard Deviation – RTTSD* (jitter), and the *Packet Loss – P_{Loss}*.
- Passive approach: the *Mean Inter Packet Delay – MIPD* (latency), the *Inter Packet Delay Standard Deviation – IPDSD* (jitter), and the *Packet Loss – PKT_{Loss}*.

In this work, *thresholds* are defined to evaluate the QoS level, which are based on key performance parameters, and should be configured according to each service. Each BATMAN packet transporting data for a specific service can be configured with 12 *thresholds* values, which 6 for the active approach and 6 for the passive approach, as shown in Table 4. The *thresholds* values for the active approach take into account a VoIP service, as explained in Section 3.1. For instance, if $0 \leq \overline{RTT} < Th_{RTT}^{m-g}$ the call service will not be affected, and the output of quality level is certainly a *good* rating. If $Th_{RTT}^{m-g} \leq \overline{RTT} \leq Th_{RTT}^{m-b}$ the delay will notably deteriorate the transmission quality, providing a *medium* quality level. If $\overline{RTT} > Th_{RTT}^{m-b}$ the user experience will be practically unacceptable, then providing a *bad* quality level.

Table 4. Thresholds defined for the key QoS parameters of the active and passive approaches

Active approach		Passive approach	
medium-good	*medium-bad*	*medium-good*	*medium-bad*
$Th_{RTT}^{m-g} = 150\text{ms}$	$Th_{RTT}^{m-b} = 500\text{ms}$	$Th_{MIPD}^{m-g} = 150\text{ms}$	$Th_{MIPD}^{m-b} = 400\text{ms}$
$Th_{RTTSD}^{m-g} = 10\text{ms}$	$Th_{RTTSD}^{m-b} = 20\text{ms}$	$Th_{IPDSD}^{m-g} = 10\text{ms}$	$Th_{IPDSD}^{m-b} = 20\text{ms}$
$Th_{P_{Loss}}^{m-g} = 0.4\%$	$Th_{P_{Loss}}^{m-b} = 2\%$	$Th_{PKT_{Loss}}^{m-g} = 0.4\%$	$Th_{PKT_{Loss}}^{m-b} = 2\%$

The *thresholds* of the passive approach are defined in accordance with ITU-T G.114 [13], which recommends that a one-way delay of 400ms should not be exceeded, although highly interactive services such as voice calls and video conferences can be affected by much lower delays. In addition, if delays are kept below 150ms, most applications, both speech and non-speech, will experience essentially transparent interactivity.

The *thresholds* could become less demanding in case of a larger number of services running in the network, which demand more bandwidth. Alternatively, they can be more claiming in an empty network, which means more bandwidth resource is available. The *threshold* adaptation process is based on the defined *Bit Rate BR* and *Packet Rate PKT*$_{Rate}$ values. Therefore, the *thresholds* can be adapted to different network situations. Moreover, they could assume dynamic values according to each type of service and taking into consideration the network load.

The monitored information calculated by the *Traffic Monitoring Module* is available to the *Routing Control Module* at any time. More precisely, the statistical information is computed and saved internally for the last n captured packets (for the passive approach) or for the last N injected packets (for the active approach). Thus, at the moment the *Routing Control Module* makes a request, the calculated statistical information (the key QoS parameters) is instantly provided to it.

In the active approach, the key parameters are calculated for N generated packets at every T seconds. These measurements provide an indication of the network quality at a single point in time. That frequency (N/T) can be configured by the user to provide more accuracy measurements of the network at more regular times. In the passive approach, the key parameters are calculated for n newer received packets. This value n can also be configured, so that the key parameters can be calculated using more fresh packets. Then, more importance is given to recently received packets because they can provide a more precise indication of the current network situation. Afterwards, the calculated key parameters are compared to the *thresholds*, which are in turn mapped to the QoE expressed as MOS.

In particular, we use the *Mean Opinion Score* (MOS) to represent the QoE of the VoIP service. In this approach, PESQ method is applied to compare an original audio file with the "received" audio file, which supposes suffered some deterioration in its route due to packet loss or other impairments factors. The PESQ algorithm provides raw scores in the range 0.5 – 4.5, which represent a prediction of the perceived quality that would be given to the received audio by real users in a subjective listening test. The resulting PESQ value is then mapped into a MOS objective listening quality value in the range 1 – 4.5 according to the mapping function in ITU-T P.862.1 [14]. The MOS values can assume the following interpretation: (1) bad; (2) poor; (3) fair; (4) good; (5) excellent.

In work [15], an exponential relation is established between the MOS and an impairment factor (QoS parameter) such as jitter, or packet loss, for VoIP services. The authors apply the PESQ method and the MOS mapping function respectively using audio files degraded by packet loss ratios along with the reference audio files. The following exponential function is retrieved from the obtained MOS values and the packet loss ratios used in the experiments.

$$QoE \cong MOS = 2.866 \cdot e^{-26.335 \cdot P_{Loss}} + 1.122 \ . \qquad (10)$$

We can use the Equation (10) to calculate the MOS values taking into the account the *thresholds* defined for *Packet Loss* P_{Loss}. Table 5 illustrates the calculated MOS *thresholds* representing the QoE level for the *Packet Loss threshold* – $Th_{P_{Loss}}$, which are mapped to the VoIP service quality level.

Table 5. MOS values for packet loss representing the QoE mapped to the service quality level

Quality level	MOS (1 – 4.5)	$Th_{P_{Loss}}$ (%)	P_{Loss} (%)
good	$4.0 \geq$ MOS > 3.7	0.4	$0 \leq P_{Loss} < 0.4$
medium	$3.7 \geq$ MOS > 2.8		$0.4 \leq P_{Loss} < 2$
bad	$2.8 \geq$ MOS ≥ 1.1	2	$2 \leq P_{Loss} \leq 100$

We can observe that MOS has maximum value of 4.0 when P_{Loss} is 0%, i.e., no packet loss is detected and VoIP call has a *good* quality level. As P_{Loss} reaches critical level of 2%, the MOS value drops to 2.8, then signaling a *medium* quality level. If P_{Loss} achieves the maximum 100%, MOS has the minimum value of 1.1, meaning that the quality level is *bad*.

Traffic Control Mechanism. Quality deterioration can occur for several reasons, for instance, packet loss, jitter, and long end-to-end delays. In particular, for WMNs, a cause to these impairment factors could be the high number of collisions between neighboring nodes. A possible reaction to collisions is reducing the amount of transmitted traffic, which causes interference between neighbor transmissions and congests the links. For example, by increasing the *OGM Interval* (the time that defines how often the node broadcasts OGMs, e.g., the default value is 1000ms) to a higher value but still acceptable for a mesh network (to allow BATMAN to recognize route changes in its near neighborhood), the frequency of possible colliding packets is automatically decreased, and the link interference as well.

New fields should be added to BATMAN OGMs, or specific messages should be exchanged between the *Routing Control Modules* of the affected nodes, in order to inform the disturbed nodes that the key QoS parameters and MOS *threshold* have been surpassed, and the respective QoE level has been deteriorated.

If the detected *Packet Loss* PKT_{Loss} is high between neighboring nodes, that means the *thresholds* $Th_{PKT_{Loss}}^{m-b}$ and $Th_{P_{Loss}}^{m-b}$ were exceeded, and also the corresponding MOS *threshold* was overpassed. Therefore, the *Routing Control Module* of those nodes can apply the following corrective actions.

- Increase the *OGM Interval* of the nodes. Consequently, the *Bit Rate BR* and *Packet Rate* PKT_{Rate} values (bandwidth) will automatically decrease for these nodes, and the delay *MIPD*, the jitter *IPDSD*, and the *Packet Loss* PKT_{Loss} should decrease subsequently. Nonetheless, altering the *OGM Interval* can have effects on the discovery process of the other nodes in highly mobile scenarios.
- Apply a Hop Penalty to the Transmission Quality (TQ) field of each OGM forwarded by the nodes. A high Hop Penalty (the maximum value is 255) will make it more unlikely that other nodes will choose this node as the "Best Nexthop"

towards any given destination. Thus, the data traffic will diminish on the nodes' interface. As a result, the inter node interference and collisions will be attenuated on the communication links, and *Packet Loss* PKT_{Loss} should decrease.

- Force the nodes to update its routing table to change the actual "Best Nexthop" to the alternative "Potential Nexthop" towards the Originator. That would force the node to redirect the current data traffic to other route via other neighbor, then possibly avoiding collisions and interference with the problematic neighboring node. Hence, the *Packet Loss* PKT_{Loss} would eventually decrease.

As the delay *threshold* Th_{MIPD}^{m-g} and the jitter *threshold* Th_{IPDSD}^{m-g} have been exceed, the quality level is possibly turned *medium*. If we are dealing with a bandwidth sensitive service, the QoE must be restored to the *good* level. Thus, we apply a bit rate based approach to overcome that issue. The *Routing Control Module* of the node will use the calculated *Bit Rate BR* and *Packet Rate* PKT_{Rate} as a quality metric to select the best route towards the destination (Originator), i.e., the rote that offers the highest throughput. For example, in Figure 2 node O_1 will choose O_2 as "Best Nexthop" to node O_3 since this path has the best TQ. Nevertheless, the route that provides the most bandwidth to node O_1 is through neighbor O_4.

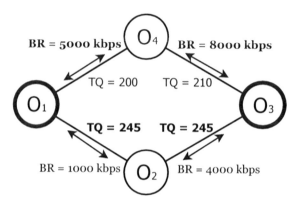

Fig. 2. Bit Rate approach to increase the QoE level

Therefore, the *Routing Control Module* will update the node's routing table using as "Best Nexthop" neighbor node O_4, which offers the route toward the destination with the highest *Bit Rate BR*. Using this route will certainly decrease the delay *MIPD*, and the jitter *IPDSD* values, then improving the quality level.

4 Conclusion

In this paper, we presented an approach that provides the required Quality of Experience (QoE) level for a VoIP service in a BATMAN mesh network. The approach is comprised of two modules, the *Traffic Monitoring Module* and the *Routing Control Module*. The *Traffic Monitoring Module* measures the status of the network situation by calculating key QoS parameters, which are then mapped to a

QoE level. If the QoS performance and the corresponding QoE level are degraded, the *Routing Control Module* executes a response in the node to recover the QoE level.

In a future work, we envisage to implement the proposed monitoring and control modules in a real mesh network environment to evaluate the approach effectiveness for IPTV and VoIP services. We also plan to design a QoE model for IPTV service taking into account the key QoS parameters presented in this work.

References

1. Zhang, W., Wang, Z., Das, S.K., Hassan, M.: Security issues in wireless mesh networks. In: Book Wireless Mesh Networks: Architectures and Protocols. Springer, New York (2008)
2. ITU-T, Methods for subjective determination of transmission quality. ITU-T Recommendation P.800 (1998)
3. ITU-T, Perceptual evaluation of speech quality (PESQ): An objective method for end-to-end speech quality assessment of narrow-band telephone networks and speech codecs. ITU-T Recommendation P.862 (2001)
4. ITU-T, The E-model, a computational model for use in transmission planning. ITU-T Recommendation G.107 (2009)
5. ITU-T, Single-ended method for objective speech quality assessment in narrow-band telephony applications. ITU-T Recommendation P.563 (2004)
6. Calyam, P., Ekici, E., Lee, C.-G., Haffner, M., Howes, N.: A "GAP-Model" based framework for online VVoIP QoE measurement. Journal of Communications and Networks 9(4), 446–456 (2007)
7. Tao, S., Apostolopoulus, J., Guerin, R.: Real time monitoring of video quality in IP networks. IEEE/ACM Transactions on Networking 16(5), 1052–1065 (2008)
8. Ding, L., Goubran, R.A.: Speech Quality Prediction in VoIP Using the Extended E-model. In: Proceedings of the IEEE Global Telecommunications Conference, Globecom 2003 (2003)
9. Neumann, A., Aichele, C., Lindner, M., Wunderlich, S.: Better approach to mobile ad-hoc networking (B.A.T.M.A.N.). IETF Internet-Draft, expired October 2008 (April 2008)
10. Open-Mesh.net, B.A.T.M.A.N. (better approach to mobile ad-hoc networking), http://www.open-mesh.net/
11. Interpreting Ping Response Times, http://wiki.netvoice.ca/ doku.php?id=trouble:ping-interpretation
12. RTP: A Transport Protocol for Real-Time Applications, RFC 3550 (2003), http://tools.ietf.org/html/rfc3550
13. ITU-T, One-way transmission time. ITU-T Recommendation G.114 (2003)
14. ITU-T, Mapping function for transforming P.862 raw result scores to MOS-LQO. ITU-T Recommendation P.862.1 (2003)
15. Fiedler, M., Hoßfeld, T., Tran-Gia, P.: A Generic Quantitative Relationship between Quality of Experience and Quality of Service. In: IEEE Network Special Issue on Improving QoE for Network Services (2010)

Knowledge Base for an Autonomic Transport Layer

Ernesto Exposito[1,2], Christophe Chassot[1,2], and Michel Diaz[1,2]

[1] CNRS; LAAS; 7 av. du Colonel Roche, F-31077 Toulouse, France
[2] Université de Toulouse; UPS, INSA, INP, ISAE; LAAS; F-31077 Toulouse, France
{ernesto.exposito,christophe.chassot,michel.diaz}@laas.fr

Abstract. The accelerated development of Internet and mobile devices has lead to new QoS-demanding distributed applications and new QoS-providing communication services, particularly at the transport level. The diversity of transport services and underlying networks environments asks for a novel design of the transport layer, able to provide in a transparent and autonomous way the most adapted service to the application. With this aim in mind, this paper presents a methodology based on a model-driven architecture (MDA) approach specialized using ontologies. It provides a QoS ontology model integrating standard and QoS-oriented transport services, protocols and mechanisms aimed at characterizing the entities, concepts and relationships composing this complex domain. This semantic model is intended to facilitate the integration of future mechanisms and protocols extensions. It offers the required properties to implement the knowledge base of an autonomic manager enabling transport service discovery, selection and composition based on application requirements and network constraints.

Keywords: Model-driven architecture, ontology-driven architecture, transport protocols, autonomic computing.

1 Introduction

With the accelerated development of Internet and the diversity of mobile devices (smart-phones, tablets, netbooks and laptops), a new large family of networked distributed applications and communication services are available today. Multi-platform instances of a same application are available at home, at work, in our mobile devices or more recently within the Cloud. These applications present heterogeneous needs in terms of Quality of Service (QoS) mainly related with time, bandwidth and reliability requirements. Moreover, networked applications are constantly changing from high-speed and high-bandwidth networks (e.g. ADSL networks at home), to variable bandwidth and high delay networks (e.g. when operating over WiFi or 3G mobile wireless networks).

For traditional applications offering file transfer, web navigation or email functionalities, a fully ordered and fully reliable transport service such as the one offered by TCP over a Best-Effort network is well suited. However, time-constraint applications such as multimedia and interactive applications could prefer a partially reliable and partially ordered service able to offer a more suited lower end-to-end

X. Masip-Bruin et al. (Eds.): WWIC 2011, LNCS 6649, pp. 174–185, 2011.

delay. Likewise, current heterogeneous network environments lead to more complex scenarios from the transport layer point of view. Even if traditional protocols such as TCP perform well over classical wired IP networks, their performances are suboptimal under new network technologies. Actually, current high speed, wireless and mobile networks deeply modify the QoS characterization of the network layer by providing more complex service models in terms of bandwidth, losses, delay or jitter.

These new models of the current heterogeneous network layer, as well as the complex requirements demanded by the new generation application layer, have deeply impacted the traditional transport layer. Classical TCP [1] and UDP [2] protocols are not able to provide an optimal transport service in this new context. This explains the trends for transport protocols creation and extensions proposals during the last decades. Examples of the transport layer evolution are the specializations proposed by the IETF aimed at enhancing traditional transport protocols (e.g. TCP congestion control and error control extensions [3], TCP extensions for mobile wireless networks [4], TCP fast retransmission and recovery strategies [5], TCP satellite enhancements [6], UDP-lite [7], Reliable UDP [8], etc). Likewise, completely new transport protocols such as the Stream Control Transmission Protocol or SCTP [9] and the Datagram Congestion Control Protocol or DCCP [10] have also been developed. Recently, a new IETF group has been created in order to propose an important extension to TCP called MPTCP [11] in order to take advantage of the new network capabilities of end-terminals (i.e. multi-homing and multi-paths). We believe that the current diversity of transport services as well as the complexity resulting from the deployment of a particular transport protocol or transport mechanism over the different services provided by heterogeneous networks ask for a novel design of the transport layer. The next generation transport layer must be able to cope with the diversity and complexity of this new family of transport protocols. Moreover, current and future applications will only be able to take advantage of the most adapted and available transport service if they are able to efficiently interact with this advanced transport layer.

In this paper a methodology based on a model-driven architecture (MDA) approach aimed at guiding the design of such a new generation transport layer is proposed. The approach proposed is based on the specialization of the MDA paradigm by using ontologies (i.e. ontology-driven architecture or ODA approach). The main contribution of this paper consists in a QoS ontology model integrating standard transport services, protocols, functions and mechanisms aimed at characterizing the entities, concepts and relationships composing this complex domain. This semantic model is intended to facilitate the integration of future mechanisms and protocols extensions resulting from the transport layer evolution. This semantic model offers the required properties to implement the knowledge base of an autonomic manager enabling transport service discovery, selection and composition based on application requirements and network constraints. Furthermore, this model also integrates the required knowledge to guide self-managing strategies in order to cope with dynamic and heterogeneous environments.

This paper is structured as following. Section 2 presents the state of the art of model-driven architecture design approaches. Section 3 presents the ontology-driven architecture design of a knowledge base representing the different features of a QoS-oriented transport layer. Section 4 illustrates how this knowledge base may be used to guide self-configuring properties of an autonomic transport layer. Finally, the conclusions and perspectives of this paper are presented.

2   Model-Driven and Ontology-Driven Architecture

This section introduces the model-driven architecture approach aimed at guiding the design and development of complex and evolving systems such as the transport layer protocols. This approach guarantees the portability, the interoperability and the reusability of the final system. A methodology based on this approach and using semantic models will be proposed in order to design the architecture of a new generation QoS-oriented transport layer. In the next paragraphs, the model-driven architecture and the various models used to represent different abstract level views of the designed system will be presented. An extension to this approach named ontology-driven architecture will also be presented.

2.1   Model-Driven Architecture

The Model Driven Architecture or MDA approach is based on the separation of the specification of a system from its implementation in any specific platform [12], [13], [14]. Model-driven approach allows the use of models to understand, design, develop and maintain a system architecture. The primary goals of MDA are portability, interoperability and reusability.

The MDA approach follows a process based on abstractions by viewpoints. It means that a system can be modeled by abstracting a set of selected architectural concepts and structuring rules. In this way, simplified viewpoints of the system can be constructed. MDA specifies three viewpoints on a system, a computation independent viewpoint, a platform independent viewpoint and a platform specific viewpoint. Each one of these viewpoints is represented or specified using models.

- Computation Independent Model: a computation independent viewpoint focuses on the requirements of the system and its environment, hiding the details related to its structure and internal behavior. The Computation Independent Model or CIM represents this viewpoint. The CIM is also known as the domain model and is built using the semantic associated to the system domain.
- Platform Independent Model: a platform independent viewpoint focuses on the operation of the system, hiding the details related to specific platforms. This viewpoint should be the same for different platforms. The Platform Independent Model or PIM represents this viewpoint. Platform independence can be obtained by representing the system as operating in a technology neutral virtual machine.
- Platform Specific Model: a platform specific viewpoint results from adapting the platform independent viewpoint to specific details of platform. The Platform Specific Model or PSM represents a system at this viewpoint. A PSM combines the specifications in the PIM with the details of using a particular platform.

2.2 Ontology-Driven Architecture

The Ontology Driven Architecture or ODA has been proposed by the W3C in order to promote the use of semantic models or ontologies in the framework of the MDA methodology [15]. The use of Semantic Web technologies is intended to naturally extend the MDA framework by defining unambiguous domain vocabularies and by providing model consistency checking and validation capabilities [16]. Semantic web technologies are mainly based on implementations following the RDF and OWL languages specifications.

Ontologies can be used to represent services allowing declarative functionalities to be deployed, discovered and reused. The use of ontologies can facilitate software development by enabling discovering and composition of existing functions to provide a new functionality rather than construct a completely new solution.

ODA may also facilitate dynamic service composition by enabling the definition of semantic models integrating the agreements that software components expose via their interfaces. These semantic models should include preconditions, post-conditions, and invariant rules aimed at specifying the behavior of components and composition of components. ODA can be used to build semantic models aimed at supporting specification and design phases. These models can also be integrated within the system implementation by including components identification and descriptions and thus enabling discovering and reuse then during design-time and runtime. These ontology models capture semantic related to properties, relationships, and behavior of components. As an ontology is an explicit conceptual model with formal logic-based semantics, the descriptions of components may be queried or may be checked to avoid inconsistent compositions.

The large set of mechanisms and services available at the transport layer, make hard or even impossible to applications' programmers to select the most adequate service (or composition of mechanisms) during design-time, based on application requirements and all the possible network environments while integrating current and future transport solutions. This paper proposes to follow model-driven and ontology-driven architecture approaches to allow application programmers to design distributed systems able to use a common knowledge base enabling self-configuration and self-adaptation autonomic properties of transport services. Next section presents the CIM and PIM level models of a QoS ontology aimed at guiding the design and development of an autonomic transport layer.

3 QoS Transport Ontology for an Autonomic Transport Layer

As previously introduced, the constant evolution of application and network layers has produced an important impact at the transport layer. As a consequence a large diversity of extensions and enhancements to the traditional protocols as well as the design and implementation of new transport protocols have deeply complexified the transport layer, making the selection of the adequate transport services a difficult task to be programmed at the application layer. For instance, traditional hard-coded strategies for transport socket selection (e.g. static selection of UDP or TCP service) are not well suited anymore in this dynamic context.

A novel approach is required to easily integrate the dynamicity required for a transport layer of next generation. This new approach should facilitate the selection of services and could allow the dynamic deployment of the required transport mechanisms and functions. Due to the complexity related with the diversity of services, protocols, functions and mechanisms, an important effort of semantic characterization and representation is required. In order to apply the Model Driven Architecture approach, next paragraphs introduce a standard framework aimed at providing a CIM-level model for the quality of service. Based on this referential model, we have defined a PIM-level QoS ontology transport model integrating the semantic of transport requirements, services, protocols, functions and mechanisms for the next generation transport layer.

3.1 ITU-T X.641 QoS Framework

The ITU-T recommendation X.641 has proposed a QoS framework intended to develop standards related to QoS in the area of information technology [17]. The X.641 framework provides definitions and inter-relationships between these definitions in order to supply a common context for defining, representing and expressing QoS. This framework introduces the concepts of service, service user, service provider, QoS characteristic, QoS requirement, QoS parameter, QoS management function and QoS mechanism. Figure 1 illustrates the main concepts introduced by X.641.

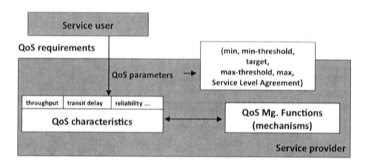

Fig. 1. ITU X.641 QoS framework

- Service: in the ITU-T X.641 framework, service is a very general term that can be applied to the provision of functions such as processing, storing, transmitting, delivering, etc. A service is provided by a service provider to a service user.
- Service user: a service is delivered to the service user. This user may have QoS requirements such as the maximum delay tolerated to transmit data. These QoS requirements are expressed as QoS parameters conveyed to the service provider.
- Service provider: a service provider is the entity responsible to deliver a service to the service user. The QoS parameters describing the QoS requirements of the

service user are conveyed to the service provider. The service provider analyzes the service user requirements and determines the management functions and mechanisms that are required to meet them. The QoS parameters can be conveyed to other entities involved in providing the service. These parameters could be used to produce more detailed QoS requirements to be conveyed to other entities.

• QoS characteristic: a QoS characteristic is defined as a quantifiable aspect of QoS of a system, service or resource that is defined independently of the means by which it is represented or controlled. QoS characteristics are intended to be used to model the actual, rather than the observed, behavior of the systems that they characterize. QoS characteristics definitions include name, description, quantification unit and optionally statistical derivations and specializations. Examples of QoS characteristics related to communication services are throughput, delay, jitter, order or reliability.

• QoS requirement: a QoS requirements expresses part of or all the user requirement expected on one or several QoS characteristics.

• QoS parameter: a QoS parameter is a vector of scalar values describing a QoS requirement in terms of:

 − A desired or target level of characteristic
 − A maximum or minimum level of a characteristic
 − Threshold values enabling warning or alert signals to be triggered or operations to be executed
 − A measured value, used to convey historical information
 − A service level agreement concerning the parameter. The term service level agreement is used to describe the nature of the commitment of the service provider to deliver the service required by the service user. The agreement nature determines the actions that the service provider and/or the service-users agree to take to maintain agreed levels of QoS:

  · Best effort is the weakest agreement indicating that there is no assurance that the agreed QoS will be provided.
  · Compulsory agreement indicates that the service must be aborted if the QoS degrades below the agreed level.
  · Guaranteed agreement indicates that the service provider must guarantee the QoS required by the service user, and that the service will not be initiated unless it can be maintained within the specified QoS parameters.

• QoS function: QoS management refers to the activities related to the control and administration of QoS within a system or network. QoS management functions are designed to assist in satisfying one or more user QoS requirements. QoS functions are composed by one or several QoS mechanisms.

• QoS mechanism: QoS mechanisms are intended to support establishment, monitoring, maintenance, control, or enquiry of QoS. QoS mechanisms are driven by users' QoS requirements expressed as QoS parameters. These mechanisms commonly operate in collaboration with other QoS mechanisms.

Based on these definitions, Figure 2 represents a CIM-level QoS ontology model of the X.641 framework. This basic QoS ontology will be extended in order to incorporate requirements, mechanisms, functions, protocols and service concepts from the transport layer point of view.

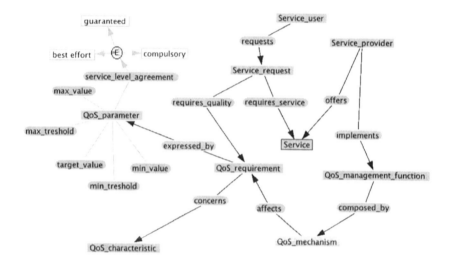

Fig. 2. QoS ontology model

3.2 QoS Transport Semantic Model

Based on the previous CIM model, a QoS transport ontology integrating requirements, parameters, services, protocols, functions and mechanisms has been defined. This ontology is aimed at providing consistent transport layer semantic model aimed at enabling managing different levels of representation and validation. This model will be presented in the next paragraphs.

3.2.1 QoS Transport Requirements
The expression of application requirements in terms of QoS parameters at the transport layer is built based on the following QoS characteristics:

- Reliability: packet loss rate (PLR) tolerance
- Order: out of sequence tolerance
- Throughput: transmission capacity per time unit
- Delay: end-to-end transmission time
- Jitter: variation of the delay

Based on these characteristics, QoS requirements can be expressed in terms of QoS parameters. For instance, for interactive video conferencing applications, examples of parameters expressions for QoS transport requirements are:

- Minimum and target values: reliability requirements could be expressed by a minimum value of 97% (or 3% of PRL tolerance) and a target value of 100%.

• Maximum and target values: delay requirements could be expressed by a maximum delay of 400 ms and a target value of 150 ms.

• Service level agreements: best effort agreements could be expressed for all or part of the requirements. For instance, best-effort agreement for reliability and compulsory agreement for delay (e.g. the service should be stopped when the delay exceed the maximum value).

3.2.2 QoS Transport Mechanisms, Functions and Protocols

Based on the RFC specifications of standard transport protocols, the various mechanisms implemented by TCP, UDP, SCTP, DCCP and MPTCP protocols have been integrated in the QoS transport ontology. Likewise, transport functions including basic functions (e.g. connection management, multiplexing/demultiplexing, etc.), advanced functions (e.g. multi-streaming and multi-path management), error control functions (e.g. ARQ or FEC) and flow and congestion control functions (e.g. window-based congestion control, TFRC, etc.) have also been integrated in this ontology. Likewise, the various mechanisms implementing these functions have also been incorporated. Figure 3 represents the QoS transport ontology integrating application requirements as well as the transport mechanisms, functions and protocols.

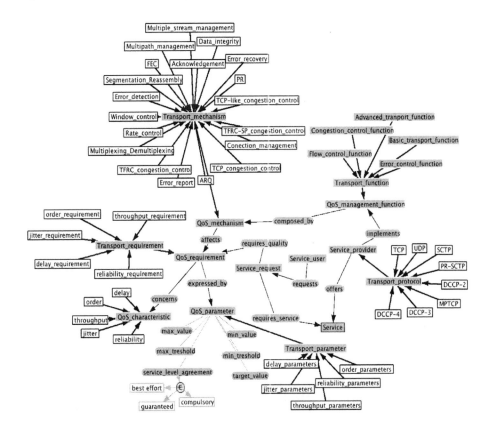

Fig. 3. QoS transport ontology model

4   Evaluation of the Ontology-Based Autonomic Knowledge Base

Based on the previous QoS transport ontology model, this section is aimed at illustrating how a knowledge base, composed of this semantic model, can be used to guide self-configuring properties of an autonomic transport layer.

4.1   QoS Transport Services Characterization

Based on the main functions provided at the transport layer, the following characterization of transport services has been defined:

• Error controlled: integrating fully reliable, partially reliable, fully ordered and partially ordered.
• Throughput controlled: includes congestion, flow and rate controlled services.
• Time controlled services: integrates delay and jitter controlled services. This class integrates the services implemented by QoS-oriented transport functions based on specializations of error-control and throughput control functions.
This classification allows to characterize the service offered by the transport protocols as following
• TCP: fully reliable, fully ordered, congestion-controlled and flow-controlled, time-uncontrolled
• UDP: error-uncontrolled (unreliable, unordered), throughput-uncontrolled, time-uncontrolled
• SCTP: fully reliable, fully ordered and unordered, congestion-controlled, flow-controlled, time-uncontrolled. As SCTP offers a multi-stream transport service, it can be considered as intra-stream fully ordered as TCP but inter-stream unordered service.
• PR-SCTP: partially reliable, fully ordered and unordered, congestion-controlled, flow-controlled, time-uncontrolled
• MPTCP: fully reliable, fully ordered, congestion-controlled, flow-controlled, time-uncontrolled
• DCCP-2, DCCP-3 and DCCP-4: error-uncontrolled (unreliable, unordered), congestion-controlled, time-uncontrolled.

Figure 4 illustrates this transport service classification for error-based and throughput-based service classifications. This service classification can largely facilitate the dynamic selection of the adequate transport service based on application requirements and following a service-oriented design approach. Moreover, this selection can be performed by integrating both functional and non-functional properties of the expected transport service. Furthermore, this semantic model can easily be enhanced in order to integrate future mechanisms and services. In this way, applications designed following this approach will be able to dynamically discover and use future services.

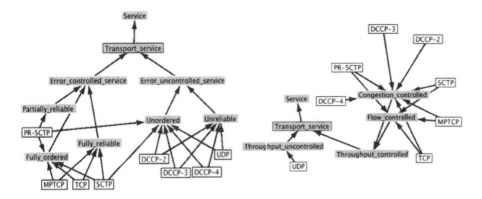

Fig. 4. Error-based and throughput-based transport services classification

4.2 Transport Components and Transport Composite Characterization

Most of the previously presented transport protocols are based on implementations where mechanisms offering different functionalities (i.e. error control or congestion control) are merged within a same monolithic implementation. However a component-based approach can be followed to characterize them. Figure 5 illustrates this composite approach in the representation of the TCP transport protocol functions.

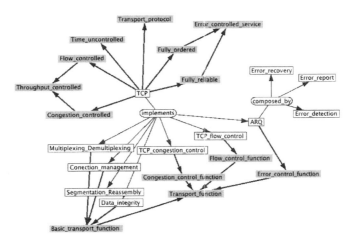

Fig. 5. Example of composite-based approach for the TCP transport functions

Actually, each transport protocols can be represented as the implementation of one or several transport functions. The composition relationship between functions has been integrated in this ontology. Likewise, transport functions can be represented as the implementation of one or several transport mechanisms. The composition relationship between functions and mechanisms has also been integrated in the ontology. Figure 6 illustrates how the ARQ error control function and the TFRC congestion control function are implemented as a composition of mechanisms. Both functions share common transport mechanisms (i.e. error detection and error report). However, the specificities of each function are achieved by the addition of an error recovery mechanism for ARQ and a rate control mechanism for TFRC.

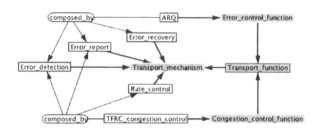

Fig. 6. Example of a component-based approach for ARQ and TFRC functions

The use of such component-based approach could widely facilitate the design and development of new transport protocols. Indeed, new transport services could result of the dynamic combination of pluggable components offering the services properties required by the applications. Further information about the classes, individuals and properties definitions of this ontology can be found in [18]. Likewise, the semantic description of standard (TCP, UDP, SCTP, DCCP and MPTCP) and component-based (FPTP) protocols including the assertions about their mechanisms and the inferences characterizing their services and aimed at verifying the consistency of this semantic model (verified using the Pellet reasoner) can be found in [18].

5   Conclusions and Perspectives

This paper has presented a methodological approach based on model-driven and ontology-driven architecture design principles and aimed at building a knowledge base well suited to self-manage an autonomic transport layer.

In order to better characterize the diversity and complexity involved within the transport layer, a Computation Independent Model (CIM) providing an abstract and high-level service model has been presented. The QoS basis for the CIM model has been provided by the ITU X.641 framework. Based on this abstract model, a Platform Independent Model (PIM) of the transport layer has been elaborated and its semantic representation based on ontologies has been presented. This PIM model is intended to characterize and classify the large diversity of available transport services, protocols, functions and mechanisms. Likewise, this model provides an unambiguous transport layer vocabulary and enables model consistency checking and validation capabilities.

This ontology model offers the required semantic basis for managing different levels of representation and for integrating current and future services to be offered by the next generation transport layer.

The proposed methodology also provides the basis for developing a service-oriented and component-based architecture for transport protocols. Systems designed and developed following MDA and ODA approaches will gain major benefits in terms of flexibility and extensibility by integrating a service oriented approach. Indeed, Service Oriented Architecture (SOA) approach can be used for designing applications focused on services composition and coordination which is the specification level required by PIM models. Likewise, component-based approach facilitates the discovery and dynamic composition of reusable components, which can satisfy the service specification required for platform specific models. Current works targeting the use of this semantic model to design and develop the self-adapting functionalities of autonomic transport protocols based on the observed network conditions and the application preferences and requirements are being carried out.

References

1. Jon, P.: Transmission Control Protocol, DARPA Internet Program Protocol Specification, RFC 793 (September 1981)
2. Jon, P.: User Datagram Protocol (UDP), RFC 768 (August 1980)
3. Duke, M., Braden, R., Eddy, W., Blanton, E.: A Roadmap for Transmission Control Protocol (TCP) Specification Documents, RFC 4614 (September 2006)
4. Inamura, H., Montenegro, G., Ludwig, R., Gurtov, A., Khafizov, F.: TCP over Second (2.5G) and Third (3G) Generation Wireless Networks, RFC 3481 (February 2003)
5. Stevens, W.: TCP Slow Start, Congestion Avoidance, Fast Retransmit, and Fast Recovery Algorithms, RFC 2001 (January 1997)
6. Allman, M., Glover, D., Sanchez, L.: Enhancing TCP Over Satellite Channels using Standard Mechanisms, RFC 2488 (January 1999)
7. Larzon, L.-A., Degermark, M., Pink, S., Jonsson, L.-E., Fairhurst, G.: The Lightweight User Datagram Protocol (UDP-Lite), RFC 3828 (July 2004)
8. Bova, T., Krivoruchka, T.: RELIABLE UDP PROTOCOL, INTERNET-DRAFT (February 1999)
9. Stewart, R. (ed.): Stream Control Transmission Protocol, RFC 4960 (September 2007)
10. Kohler, E., Handley, M., Floyd, S.: Datagram congestion control protocol (DCCP), RFC 4340 (March 2006)
11. Ford, A., Raiciu, C., Barre, S., Iyengar, J.: Architectural Guidelines for Multipath TCP Development, IETF Internet-draft (June 2010)
12. MDA Guide Version 1.0.1, OMG (June 2003)
13. Mellor, S.J., Scott, K., Uhl, A., Weise, D.: MDA Distilled: Principles of Model-Driven Architecture. Addison-Wesley Professional, Reading (2004)
14. Kleppe, A., Warmer, J., Bast, W.: MDA Explained: The Model Driven Architecture: Practice and Promise. Addison-Wesley Professional, Reading (2003)
15. Ontology Driven Architectures and Potential Uses of the Semantic Web in Systems and Software Engineering, W3C Working Draft (April 2006)
16. Lassila, O., Hendler, J., Berners-Lee, T.: The Semantic Web. Scientific American (May 2001)
17. ITU-T Information Technology - Quality of Service Framework, ITU-T X.641 (ISO/IEC IS13236) (December 17, 1997)
18. QoS transport ontology,
   http://homepages.laas.fr/eexposit/hdr/QoSTransportOntology.htm

Traffic Monitoring for Assuring Quality of Advanced Services in Future Internet

A. Cuadra[1], F. Mata[2], J.L. García-Dorado[2], J. Aracil[2], J. López de Vergara[2],
F.J. Cortés[3], P. Beltrán[3], E. de Mingo[3], and A. Ferreiro[4]

[1] Indra Sistemas - Valladolid, Spain
[2] Universidad Autónoma de Madrid – Madrid, Spain
[3] Telnet Redes Inteligentes – La Muela, Spain
[4] Telefónica I+D – Madrid, Spain
acuadra@indra.es,
{felipe.mata,jl.garcia,javier.aracil,
jorge.lopez_vergara}@uam.es,
{fcortes,pbeltran,edemingo}@telnet-ri.es,
olivo@tid.es

Abstract. Services based on packet switched networks are becoming dominant in telecommunication business and both operators and service providers must evolve in order to guarantee the required quality. Increasing bandwidth is no longer a viable solution because of the business erosion for network operators which cannot expect revenues due to the large investments required to satisfy new applications demand of bandwidth. This paper presents devices and a specific architecture of services monitoring platform that allows network operators and service providers to analyze the perceived quality of service and check their service level agreements. Thus, a cost-effective service management, based on direct IP traffic measuring, can be supported on integrated monitoring systems to provide network-centric mechanisms for differentiated quality of service, security and other advanced services.

Keywords: QoS, network monitoring, Future Internet.

1 Introduction

Future Internet must tackle the lack of built-in facilities to support non-basic functionalities in order to offer service-aware functionality [1]. Traditionally, the growth of the Internet and convergent services in the IP layer has been solved, as far as performance concerns, by increasing bandwidth and computational power in the edge devices. However, this trend is reaching its limits to provide Quality of Service (QoS); furthermore security and differentiated QoS, namely QoS as a service beyond the "best effort" packet delivery, which also takes into account specific applications characteristics, requires a new network-centric management architecture. Among their goals, the Future Internet service-aware architecture should include a cost-effective QoS management based on direct IP traffic monitoring so that network operators and service providers can verify their Service Level Agreement (SLA).

X. Masip-Bruin et al. (Eds.): WWIC 2011, LNCS 6649, pp. 186–196, 2011.
© IFIP International Federation for Information Processing 2011

Besides, combining traffic measurement systems with on-line analysis will help detecting malicious users or unintended configuration errors even in multi-operator scenarios and render Internet governance plausible. In summary, the transition from specific circuit-switched (CS) networks towards convergent packet-switched (PS) networks supporting real-time applications and numerous new broad-band services in a disaggregated market must be based on powerful yet intelligent traffic monitoring systems in order to guarantee cost-effective QoS, security and privacy protection.

The objective is to keep the old CS networks facilities in the multiplexed Service Centric (SC) transport networks by means of additional control elements inside the network. So far only client devices and applications tackled these issues considering the operator could just offer them end-to-end (E2E) connectivity without any additional service. However, the required analysis to improve service architectures and diagnose configuration failures or critical dimensioning lacked significant traffic data from commercial networks. Numerous projects have developed measurement infrastructures to track Internet functioning [2] and several research groups have actively participated in these efforts [3], [4]. Recent proposals to use such measurement facilities for network management have raised relevant problems such as privacy protection, leading to the development of anonymization solutions [5]. Besides, the access to heterogeneous traffic monitoring data is very challenging; thus, a semantic tool (mediator) has been developed [6], and standardization initiatives [7] have been carried out in order to establish interoperable data formats, as well as KPI (key Performance Indicator) and other measurements to support QoS monitoring. This paper presents an architecture for service-aware networking compatible with Future Internet paradigms like resources virtualization and autonomic management within a network-centric approach. After a brief presentation of measurement devices developed by the authors, their application to service monitoring platforms and QoS-driven network management design are presented. Due to space limitations, results are rather given by reference so that a holistic view can be reached.

2 QoS Datasources

Monitoring systems can be categorized according to the measuring devices. In fact, KPI can be derived from active or passive probes: The first ones inject packets into the network with explicit control of timing, scheduling and sizes [8], while the second ones just capture traffic in order to analyze it in terms of protocol performance and application modeling. Active methods are used to measure delay, packet loss, jitter, available capacity and connectivity. Passive methods are useful to measure network parameters like data rate, most-used services, traffic matrix, routing, etc. and derive traffic modeling or supervise specific applications, as well as to detect fraud or hacking. Deep Packet Inspection (DPI) systems analyze traffic in detail by decoding application protocol headers; thus their exploitation allows characterizing network traffic in detail and differentiated QoS analysis can be performed. Active and passive methods can be considered complementary since they provide information about different network characteristics and parameters [9] [10].

Active probes are intrusive and overload the network with their traffic but are simple, can reproduce users behavior and may be distributed throughout the network for different tests simulating different devices (access ADSL / FTTH terminals GSM / GPRS / UMTS, etc..). A smart planning of tests, placement of probes and knowledge of the service to analyze is required to obtain a clear insight into end to end services by this means.

Passive probes are non-intrusive equipment but analyze the whole traffic in the section of network considered (access point, for instance, or a core link). Their hardware must cope with the connection bandwidth and need a great amount of computational power to analyze the data they extract. Some network elements incorporate passive monitoring facilities, such as STP (signaling transfer point) probing its own SS7 links, DWDM multiplexers or port span switches with monitoring capabilities. Thus, these deployed network elements (WDM equipment line, HLR and MSC in GSM and UMTS SGSN and GGSN in GPRS and UMTS, IP Routers, etc) provide traffic information to the network operator: The data collection is mainly done through OMCs (Operation and Maintenance Center) developed by each provider, but is sometimes reached through a mediation device. The principal drawback is that the measures provided are defined by the supplier because of lack of standardization.

Embedded agents are software pieces that can be introduced in a network element, such as a softswitch in an OLT (Optical Line Terminator), or in the customer's equipment, like a Set-Top-Box or a mobile terminal. These agents can act as active or passive probes and may be useful to monitor the perceived quality of service or QoE (Quality of Experience). Their main obvious drawback is the difficulty of deployment since they require the approval of manufacturer, service provider and end user.

In general, we can assume that an intelligent combination of probes would set up a platform for service providers, network operators and authorities to monitor traffic and supervise applications performance. Obviously, the availability of universal interfaces and standard KPI is a requirement to progress in this way.

As a first diagnosis tool, operators and big clients look after point-to-point (p2p) links, then operators and service providers watch end-to-end (e2e) connections so as to check QoS at IP layer and supervise applications performance. In the following, some examples of products designed as probes to accomplish the corresponding measurements are given.

3   P2P Traffic Monitoring Systems

Point-to-point (p2p) measurements include throughput, latency, jitter and packet loss detected in the network layer. As it turns out, the operators have interest in supervising critical links in order to react quickly to any performance loss. One of the authors implemented a probe of high flexibility by means of a FPGA that allows generating and measuring Ethernet traffic [11] without using expensive equipment (fig. 1). Besides, the monitoring system built on them can be used to set demarcation between operator and client network.

Fig. 1. Equipments developed for Ethernet transport networks checking and operation

These are active probes normally configured in loop: The Origin device (source MAC address) sends test packets and the results are processed when they are returned. The tests are SNMP based and can be controlled by the user through a dedicated administration application that allows for specific parameters definition: Length Frame, data Rate, number of test packets, VLAN Identifier, source and destination MAC Address and test Interface. Similarly the operator can choose the type of test to execute: Single Burst Test, Continuous Burst Test or Timed Burst Test, for which the duration of the test and the time between bursts can be defined.

The user also obtains reports by means of the provided administration application: Measure, Complete and Summary Report. All of them include values of: Latency (1 μs accuracy) with maximum and medium Roundtrip value, packet loss, jitter (1 μs accuracy), maximum and medium value for each one-way and throughput.

The applications of these devices in OAM (Operations, Administration & Maintenance) systems to support IP Network and Performance Monitoring include, but are not limited to, STP (Spanning Tree Protocol) management: Regarding optical link protection issues, it is possible to set an alternative path based on real-time measurements defined by the operator as switching criteria. The whole carrier class Ethernet improvements for PTT (Packet Transport Technology) rely in devices like these ones.

Furthermore, a whole range of line cards have been added to satisfy specific customers demands and should be submitted to standardization process; for example, to monitor QoS in master-slave fashion networks (master is at the operator's domain and the slave in the customer premises) as a kind of VIP service for corporations, government and large customers. These devices are known as Ethernet Demarcation Devices (EDD). They are gaining interest for L2- VPN and new PTT-based networks [11]. Their interfaces can be either optical or electrical. The EDD equipments developed by the authors (and tested in a public Spanish network) permit to extend optical gaps (up to 80Km) between two user switches, using the dark fiber property of the telecom operator and, allow setting alternative paths or simply determining the responsibility of eventual failures (packet loss, latency, etc.).

4 One Way P2P Systems Measurements

To measure the IP services performance in terms of bandwidth availability and eventual differences between one way and return packet travelling, one can inject test packets and accurately timestamp the capture instant of such packets. One of the authors has developed a high-precision timestamping probe based on GPS synchronization. Its design was developed taking as a base the NetFPGA card, which provides a cost-effective, yet powerful solution with four 1-Gbps interfaces (see fig. 2).

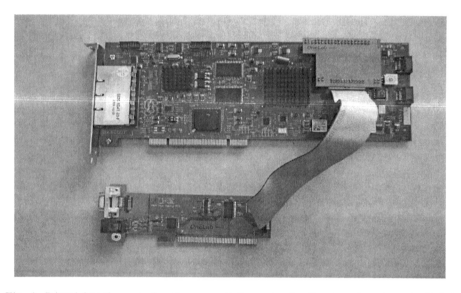

Fig. 2. Printed board composing the core of the probe for timestamping through Global Positioning System (GPS)

The application of this system to measure OWD (One Way Delay) was presented in the CELTIC event (Paris, 2009) for a connection Madrid-Paris and has also been partially funded by the ONELAB FP7 project. The OWD measurement tool sent trains of UDP packets while other (streaming) applications were delivered e2e through the public networks. The OWD measurements are statistically analyzed in order to give an accurate mean value for the OWD. Accuracy of tens of nanoseconds is achieved by means of this simple device, which can be easily plugged in a PCI bus in the measurement device. At the operating system, the card can be accessed through a standard socket interface, which makes it possible to analyze packet-by-packet from any user application.

On the other hand BART platform [12] (Bandwidth Available in Real Time) is an active measurement method for estimating path available capacity and other capacity-related parameters in real time over multi-domain packet-switched network paths. BART sends traffic over a network path in order to determine at which rate the path shows signs of congestion. This rate defines the path available capacity. A BART sender is transmitting IP packets at randomized inter-packet separations towards a receiver; the separation is affected by other IP traffic sharing the network path. The receiver timestamps each incoming IP packet and calculates the new inter-packet separation. The inter-packet separations at the receiver are analyzed by a Kalman filter, a statistical method for tracking not directly observable properties in real time. Combining measurements from different segments for a given end-to-end connection gives rise to a powerful tool to operate the network and find bottlenecks.

5 Service Monitoring Architecture

A service monitoring platform has an architecture composed by probes distributed in different segments of the network depending on its topology, the remote pre-processors, physically close to the probes, and the central repository and analyzer system (fig.3).

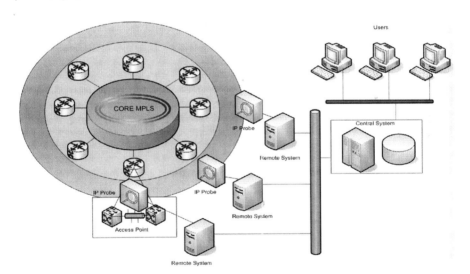

Fig. 3. Architecture of a service monitoring platform

The Remote pre-processors are able to calculate specific KPI; in fact, the captured frames are stored in these remote locations during a reasonable time in order to analyze anomalies "post mortem". In the central process unit, those KPI are further processed (grouped and correlated) in order to analyze the whole service platform performance and produce periodic reports for administrative and technical purposes.

Service monitoring platforms must provide capabilities for analysis, service assurance and monitoring support. Furthermore, they must support tools for diagnosing problems, such as protocol analyzers and call tracers. A wide number of functionalities must be fulfilled in order to support QoS management. These functionalities can be grouped in two areas: Traffic measures and quality measures. The first ones offer an overview of the network load (volume) and traffic characteristics along specific time periods (charged hour, cycling holiday, etc) similar to the traffic modeling mentioned above. Quality measures are targeted towards obtaining a thorough overview of how users perceive the service and how network services (offered by the operator) match service demands by applications (offered by the service providers). The traffic measures are grouped in a few parameters every hour to get a statistical estimate of the network evolution; the quality measures are taken more often (every few minutes) so that anomalies can be detected before users complain. The traffic measures cover all the protocols of the OSI tower, covering the range from level to level Liaison Implementation, and also distinguishing the particularities of each plane. As a natural nomenclature, these measures are referred to:

- Origin (probe side, close to a remote site): This range would be implicitly associated with a particular geographical area, such as a network access node.
- Destination (end opposite site towards traffic is driven): Core network elements such as application servers or control nodes.

Quality measures are obtained from statistics of failure in the protocol, number of errors in connections made and other parameters that indicate degradation in service quality.

The QoS monitoring platform (called OMEGA-Q, fig. 4) developed in Telefónica Group (Spain, Brazil, Venezuela, etc.) supports three categories of services so far: Broadband for mobile access, VoIP provision in the framework of next generation networks (NGN) and IPTV. It monitors voice-PLMN, mobile services (SMS, MMS, roaming, CAMEL...), VoIP/IMS/NGN, IPTV/MobileTV, etc. The main parameters monitored are:

- For Internet data transmission: Effectiveness of the service rate, Time to establish a connection and Loss rate information
- For VoIP quality: Effectiveness of the service rate, Call setup time
- For IPTV: Effectiveness of the service rate, Average time to swap channels and Loss of signal reception.

There are several experimental initiatives for Future Internet monitoring fostered by the European Commission, each of them devoted to extend the current state of the art in different topics. See a list of referred infrastructures and traffic measurement test-beds in [10].

The European Traffic Observatory Measurement InfrastruCture (ETOMIC) was launched in 2004 to provide the scientific community with an Internet measurement platform that was fully open and reconfigurable, extremely accurate and uses GPS synchronization for timing. Now more than 20 nodes are distributed throughout Europe, with specific monitoring hardware that is integrated with the Planetlab [10] infrastructure. ETOMIC automatically performs periodic measurements that provide general network performance parameters like routes and one-way delay between all nodes of the system.

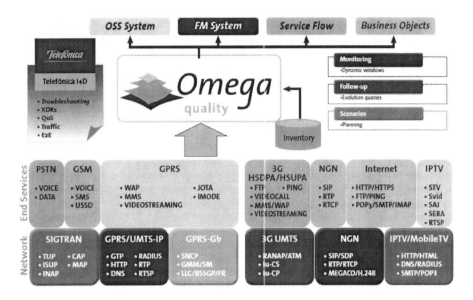

Fig. 4. Network and Services monitored by OMEGA-Q

DIMES [10] uses a dedicated community of software "agents", installed by thousands of volunteers around the Globe. Using these agents, DIMES manages to measure from roughly 200 VPs on a weekly basis since 2005 and from over 350 different VPs overall since the beginning of 2009. Once installed by the user, the agent operates at a very low rate so as to have minimal impact on the machine performance and on its network connection. The project intends to explore possible relationships between the data gathered on the Internet's growth with geographical and socio- economic data, in particular for fast developing countries, to see if they can provide a measure of economic development and societal openness. The project is committed to openness and thus publishes period maps at several aggregation levels on the web. It also includes web interfaces for running remote coordinated measurements, which is used by researches around the world.

Other relevant projects are PerfSonar, a FP7 effort that serves to integrate different measurement probes in a single measurement infrastructure, and OneLab / OneLab2 IP projects that have also provided the PlanetaLab community [10] with monitoring tools.

These projects have pursued rather different objectives, and have involved a large number of research groups across Europe but most of the research groups have been involved in only one project thus being unaware of the rest.

6   QoS Management and Network Management

Monitoring platforms link a series of precedent monitoring systems, some of them developed from previous circuit-switched network maintenance systems or ad-hoc operation platforms and management systems provided by manufacturers. Others were specifically designed and implemented for managing QoS of new services. From the point of view of pure operator, it is also interesting to obtain information from the service providers´ premises through SNMP access to extract basic statistics about network behavior. Then operators and service providers may overlap their respective platforms and integrate systems to manage QoS. This effort of integration is really important (fig. 5) in setting up Future Internet management and renders benefits to both agents since the final objective of such integration is achieving a QoS-driven network management. In practice, this approach leads to close the loop of "service provision – traffic monitoring - QoS monitoring – adaptive service provision" by means of cognitive systems acting on the network operation systems. Whether this loop requires a central operation mechanism or it is performed by autonomic agents is a further development issue although one can imagine parallel improvements following both approaches, for different scenarios, namely MANET (Mobile Ad hoc Networks), home networks, corporative virtual private networks, public networks of general purpose, etc.

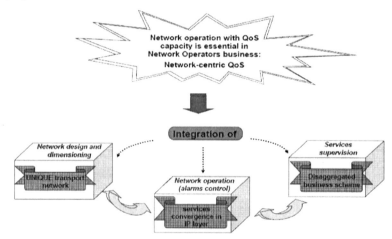

Fig. 5. Conceptual representation of a network-centric approach for QoS-driven network management architecture in future Internet

This management architecture will be able to cope with the increasing demands to offer bundled multi-services (Multi-play with IPTV/VoD/mobile), which is an important way to attract and retain customers and complies to NGN paradigms, namely convergent transport infrastructures. From a rather economic point of view, such integration is the only cost-effective solution to fulfil future Internet expectations, like operating upon virtualized resources and satisfy the "four anies", namely any access, anywhere, any time for any service users may demand.

7   Conclusions

This paper has presented several tools for service monitoring and QoS management including recently developed devices for traffic monitoring and a complete operating platform. All these elements should converge towards the objectives of extending Internet services with guaranteed quality, coping with NGN paradigms, in a cost-effective way for both service providers and network operators. Improved active and passive probes to measure traffic parameters were used to verify connectivity performance of public networks. Point-to-point measurement products were included as OAM tools for networks over packet transport technology. End-to-end measurement devices demonstrated their ability to detect network congestion and feed repositories for bottleneck analysis. Besides, an enhanced algorithm for analysis of traffic data was used to achieve traffic modeling and anomalies detection. The performance of the systems achieved is self-explained by the applications of the service monitoring world-wide deployed, as described, for IPTV, VoIP and ISP among other services.

Thus a solid base of devices, algorithms and architecture design is available for achieving network monitoring and service monitoring although other instruments, like DPI (deep packet inspection) not presented in this paper, must complete the toolbox. A further work to develop cognitive agents that perform real-time actions to correct network bottlenecks or protect it from attacks will be next step.

Acknowledgments. This work has been partially developed in the framework of the Celtic and EUREKA initiative IPNQSIS (IP Network Monitoring for Quality of Service Intelligent Support).

References

[1] Galis, A., Abramowicz, H., Brunner, M.: Management and Service-aware Networking Architectures (MANA) for Future Internet System Functions, Capabilities and Requirements. In: Position paper in Future Internet Assembly meeting, Prague, Czech Rep., May 11-13 (2009)

[2] Ferreiro, A., et al.: IP traffic monitoring for Future Internet management and governance (pending to be published in JNSM)

[3] Cooperative Association for Internet Data Analysis (CAIDA), http://www.caida.org/home/

[4] The Traffic Monitoring and Analysis (TMA), http://www.tma-portal.eu/

[5] See, for instance the PRISM (PRIvacy-aware Secure Monitoring) project, http://www.fp7-prism.eu/

[6] Ferreiro, A., et al.: Semantic Unified Access to Traffic Measurement Systems for Internet Monitoring Service. In: ICT-MobileSummit, Santander, Spain (2009)

[7] Ferreiro, A.: Standardizing ontologies for the IP traffic measurement: A first step in QoS standardization at ETSI. In: The workshop "Future Internet Design: Aspects of network monitoring, privacy and security", Brussels, Belgium (September 2009)

[8] Paxson, V.: End-to-End Internet Packet Dynamics. In: ACM SIGCOMM, Cannes, France (September 1997)

[9] Lindh, T.: A new approach to performance monitoring in IP networks combining active and passive methods. In: Proceedings of Passive and Active Measurement Workshop, Colorado, USA (March 2002)

[10] FP7-MOMENT (Monitoring and Measurement in the Next Generation Technologies), http://www.fp7-moment.eu
[11] TRAMMS (Traffic Measurements and Models in Multi-Service Networks) project measurement devices are describe in its document D4.3, executive summary available in http://projects.celticinitiative.org/tramms/files/ TRAMMS_D4.3_ExecutiveSummary.pdf
[12] Ekelin, S., et al.: Real-time measurement of end-to-end available bandwidth using Kalman filtering. In: Proceedings to the IEEE/IFIP Network Operations and Management Symposium, Vancouver, Canada (April 2006)

End-to-End Adaptive Framework for Multimedia Information Retrieval

Maria Sokhn[1], Elena Mugellini[1], Omar Abou Khaled[1], and Ahmed Serrrouchni[2]

[1] University of applied sciences of western Switzerland
[2] Telecom ParisTech France
{maria.sokhn,elena.mugellini,omar.aboukhaled}@hefr.ch,
ahmed.serrrouchni@telecom-paristech.fr

Abstract. The evolution of the web in the last decades has created the need for new requirements towards intelligent information retrieval capabilities and advanced user-oriented services. The current web integrates heterogeneous and distributed data such as XML database, relational database, P2P networks etc. leading to the coexistence of different data models and consequently different query languages. In this context, effective retrieval and usage of multimedia resources have to deal with the issues of creating efficient content based indexes, developing retrieval tools and improving user-oriented visualization interfaces. To that end we put forward an end-to-end adaptive framework based on an ontological model. This framework aims at enhancing the management, retrieval and visualization of multimedia information resources based on semantic techniques.

Keywords: knowledge management, querying, visualization, ontology, P2P network.

1 Introduction

We witnessed in the last decades a massive growth of the available multimedia information on the web. This information presents several challenges in the information retrieval process. This is caused by the dynamic nature of the medium and the lack of advanced and precise methods that handle non-textual features [1]. This multimedia information lacks semantic content annotation, giving place to the so-called semantic gap. This gap was defined by Smeulders [2] and other papers such as [3] as "the lack of coincidence between the information that one can extract from the visual data and the interpretation that the same data has for a user in a given situation". In recent years, semantic techniques such as ontologies have been adopted to enhance content based annotation services and, accordingly, retrieval and visualization of multimedia resources [1, 4, 5]. Indeed, as argued in Hare [6], the use of ontologies improves both automatic annotation and retrieval process. Using ontologies to describe multimedia resources provides methods to define well structured and related concepts facilitating the burden of annotation and retrieval [7]. Ontologies are also very useful for visual representation of resources [8, 9], and may considerably enhance browsing, navigation

X. Masip-Bruin et al. (Eds.): WWIC 2011, LNCS 6649, pp. 197–206, 2011.
© IFIP International Federation for Information Processing 2011

and data accessibility. In our work we aim at handling the scientific conference multimedia information. We propose an end-to-end scalable solution that meets the needs of massively distributed and heterogeneous multimedia information produced by different services along a scientific conference.

This paper presents an end-to-end framework for multimedia retrieval based on semantic techniques. The remaining parts of the paper are structured as follows: In section 2, we present some of the related works. In section 3, we describe the framework CALIMERA. In section 4 and 5, we describe the use of the CALIMERA framework. Finally, in the section 6 we conclude the paper and present future works.

2   Related Work

The semantic approach to existing web resources is one of the major challenges for building the semantic web. Few tools among those we found use systems that exploit the power of millions of users every day seeking information on the web. Today, many applications of file sharing peer-to-peer exist. These applications do not have a major characteristic: the semantic search. Although most applications of peer-to-peer sharing offer a keyword search based on indexing data, few are actually accessing the data content and use powerful annotation systems that provide detailed information on data. This situation is due to lack of use of metadata information generated by annotations and ontology models that describe the data content rather than a general description of the file.

Many publications and projects have been designed to manage multimedia information retrieval [7, 10–14]. Some of them, such as VIKEF [10], were developed in order to provide support for advanced semantic information, content production and knowledge acquisition, processing, annotation and sharing by empowering information and knowledge environments for scientific and commercial communities. MATTERHORN [14] produces recordings of lectures, manages existing videos, distribution channels and provides user interfaces for students with educational videos. These projects did not use the possibilities of a distributed system such as the P2P architecture, whereas other projects such as PHAROS[11] and SAPIR [13] use the power of P2P. However these projects do not make use of semantic techniques. In our work we propose a novel end-to-end adaptive framework named CALIMERA that takes advantage of semantic techniques and exploit the power of the peer to peer network.

3   CALIMERA Framework

CALIMERA stands for Conference Advanced Level Information ManagemEnt and RetrievAl. This framework based on a ontological conference model and aims at facilitating the management and retrieval of the multimedia information generated within the scientific conferences [15]. The figure 1 outlines the global view of the framework architecture.

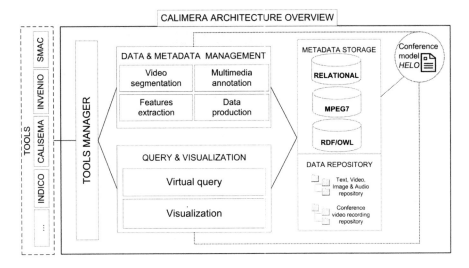

Fig. 1. CALIMERA architecture overview

3.1   Architecture Overview

(1) Tools manager: CALIMERA is a tool independent framework. The tool manager allows any user to integrate a tool that may be used for data and metadata management, query and visualization or both. For a proof of concept we integrated four principal tools. 1.INDICO a tool developed by the CERN [22] that manages the administrative part of a conference (such as the conference planning, logistics, etc.). 2.SMAC is a tool we developed, to record conference talk and automatically segment the recording of this talk based on slide change detections. 3.CALISEMA is a tool for semi-manual and manual video annotation based on semantic techniques. 4.INVENIO is a set of modules for automatic features extraction, information indexing and retrieval.

(2) Data and metadata management module: It consists on handling the conference high-level information, such as recording talks, segmenting video recordings, annotating video segments, managing the context information of these talks, etc.

(3) Data and Metadata storage: It integrates existing data and metadata formats such as MPEG-7 [23] which is one of the most widely used standard for multimedia description, and RDF [24] and OWL [25], which are a more semantically oriented standards.

(4) Query and visualization module: It queries the data and metadata storage in order to return the video or the set of video sequences of the recorded talks that the users are seeking for.

(5) Conference model, HELO: It is an ontological model that describes and structures the information conveyed within a conference life cycle. the model has been designed to enhance the multimedia information retrieval and more precisely the scientific conference recordings. It is based on the effort made in

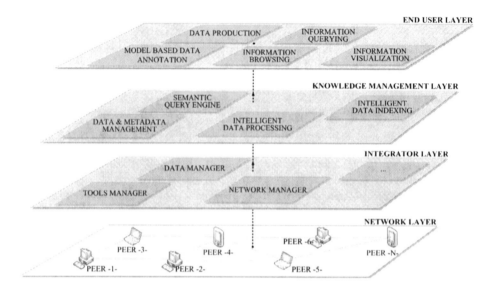

Fig. 2. CALIMERA layered model overview

ESWC2006, ISWC2006 and SWC [26] and a study we conducted on user' needs and requirements when searching for scientific recorded talks. The work is detailed in the paper [16].

3.2   Layered Model Overview

In this section we introduce the proposed layered model (Figure 2) that maps the architecture of the framework presented in the previous section. The layered model describes the adaptive approach offered by the framework aiming to guarantee an end-to-end service. The model is composed of four main layers, the **Network layer**, the **Integrator layer**, the **Knowledge Management layer** and the **End User layer**. Each layer uses performed actions of the underneath layer. The Network layer deals with the P2P protocols and network. The Integrator layer manages the peer integration within the network on one hand and the communication between the peers and the knowledge database on the other hand. The Knowledge Management layer handles the data and metadata management (processing, indexing, querying, extracting, etc.). This layer is a key point for the End User top layer which focuses on the users needs and performs modules such as data semantic annotation and information browsing and visualization.

4   Heterogeneous Information Retrieval

Multimedia information retrieval, more precisely scientific conference data retrieval, is enhanced by using a conference ontology model throughout the three main activities of an information retrieval process: the modal based annotation (section 4.1), the semantic querying process (section 4.2) and the multimedia results rendering/visualization (section 4.3).

4.1   Model Based Annotation

The Semantic web initiative seeks to add semantics to web resources in order to enhance their management, retrieval and access. In order to add semantics, web resources should move from *machine-readable* to *machine-understandable*. For that, effort should be provided to create content based description for these resources. This description is called annotation. Annotations are an important key-success in the emergence of the semantic web. Since manual annotation is a laborious task, it is important and required to develop annotation tools that facilitate this task. In our work we developed CALISEMA, a tool for video annotation: manually with a model based interface and automatically through a speech to text plug-in module. What characterizes it from other existing tools is that it is fully integrated and adapted to conferences. In fact CALISEMA is based on the conference model HELO and is integrated in the information management process of the framework CALIMERA. This enables the annotator to -automatically- collect information (e.g. name of the speaker, duration of the video, etc.) from other tools used in our framework as well as peers annotation. Moreover, it integrates several video segmentation algorithms (such as slide change detection algorithm) allowing users to choose the one that most meets their requirements. The annotation is exported in MPEG-7 format, OWL format or both.

4.2   Semantic Query Engine

CALIMERA allows the integration of heterogeneous data sources such as the output of the manual or automatic annotation, etc. These resources (may) have different data storage models. This leads to the coexistence of different models and scheme and therefore different query languages. The structural and semantic heterogeneity of data makes the development of custom solutions for querying these data time-consuming and complex. This issue can be divided into three main parts: dispatching important search information depending on the data sources, creating database-specific queries and merging results from several sources. To handle this issue we designed a query system named Virtual-Q. Virtual-Q aims to provide users transparent and easy access to retrieve data from heterogeneous sources. This system is a novel approach based on a virtual-query engine. This engine integrates concepts such as query analysis or sub-queries formulation, which facilitate transparent access to heterogeneous data. More details about this approach can be found in the paper [17].

4.3   Model Based Browsing and Visualization

As mentioned earlier, using ontology is a powerful key in multimedia information retrieval. Still, to be effective the rendering of the query result has to be

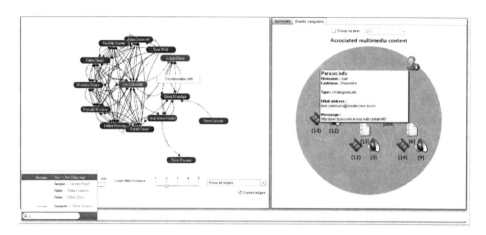

Fig. 3. NAVIR - Scientific community graph (left), Associated multimedia resources (right)

easy to read and simple to navigate through. To address this issue and further enhance the retrieval of scientific recordings of the talks, we designed a set of graphical renderings of information based on the semantic model HELO. Using this model for visualization, provides the users with an interface where the descriptions are grouped based on their use (the multimedia information can be searched by person, by date, by topic, etc.)), offering them the ability to explore the information content in an interactive way. These features become essential in multimedia retrieval which has a complex content hardly searched by "traditional" keyword-based searching. We implement a proof-of-concept prototype named NAVIR which focuses on information related to the scientific community member relationships and their associated multimedia data such as scientific publications, recorded talks, etc. (Figure 3). Once the media is retrieved, users have the possibility either to play the video within the search interface (Youtube-like visualization) or to get redirected to a new window where the video of the recorded talk is played within a conference based visualization interface using our prototype SMAC. This visualization interface presents three distinct blocks (Figure 4): the recorded talk block on the left, the slides set block on the right and the information block on the bottom. The recorded talk is synchronized with the slides extracted from the presentation slides set. The navigation banner at the bottom of the slide set block allows the user to navigate through the slides. When the user chooses a slide the corresponding talk video sequence is played. Using SMAC to replay the recorded talks provides users with simple navigation through the different sequences of the talk, in addition to the display of information provided by the framework such as the annotations coming from the annotations of the peers or the output of the automatic metadata extraction modules.

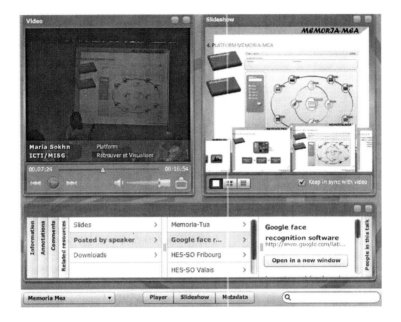

Fig. 4. SMAC visualization - Recorded talk replay interface

5 Distributed Information Retrieval

The advances in wireless communication technology and the increasing number of mobile users networks brought a shift from the traditional client-server computing model to the P2P computing model. In this type of model, each peer takes both roles, client and server. In our work we addressed the issue of the distributed information retrieval. Every peer of the Network layer (Figure 2) may host a database to be shared with its peers in the network. Through the Network Manager of the Integrator layer every peer can access the P2P network. Each peer can make use of the Integrator layer to push information (through the Data Manager) into the Knowledge database of the framework and can integrates knowledge management tools into the framework. The peers make use of the End User layer to perform tasks such as the information browsing and visualization.

5.1 P2P Network

We based our work on the JXTA framework [27], into which we introduced the RDF technology as a descriptor for available multimedia information. The JXTA platform is a series of classes and methods for managing and transmitting application and control data between JXTA compatible peer platforms. Using our platform the user can annotate the data to be shared, based on the designed conference model HELO and can initiate traditional keyword search: The query is performed over the neighbors that search in turns for information related to the concerned keyword. The application is composed of the following modules: **Graphic User Interface** (GUI): It allows the user to interact with the application by sharing and managing the files and performing search queries. **Controller**: It collaborates with the user interface to send the query to the query manager and manage the ontology using Jena, a Java framework for building Semantic Web applications [28]. **Query Manager**: The intermediate module between the application modules (GUI, Controller, Jena) and the network modules (JXTA manager, Download manager). **JXTA Manager**: It is responsible of the connections and the discovery of new peers in the network. **Jena**: The programming toolkit that manages tasks related to the semantic annotation. **Download Manager**: It is responsible of uploading and downloading the shared files.

5.2   Process Over the P2P

We used in our work a decentralized network architecture. When the application is launched, the peer connects to the JXTA net peer group then sends advertisements to the peers on the network to exchange some information about their respective sockets. The classes and functions of the JXTA framework provide these functionalities. The class JXTAManager is responsible for connecting the peer to the network. It uses the NetworkManager class provided by JXTA framework and creates a multicast JXTA socket on each peer, allowing it to send and receive requests and responses. The application makes use of the Discovery Service offered by JXTA in order to periodically detect the new peers in the network and connect to them.

Data annotation: When the users want to share/annotate a file, they choose the type of file they want to share in the annotation tab of the interface (Figure 5). According to the choice, the fields to annotate are shown dynamically in the tab. The user may also be redirect to a specific annotation tools such as CALISEMA. Once the user submits the annotation, the Knowledge Management layer takes the lead to make the necessary updates.

Information retrieval: Our application allows any peer to join the network. In our scenario, we have two *types* of peers: the *normal* peers that represent the users that might want to share/annotate files and search for information and the *INVENIO servers* peer that acts like a super peer integrating the Metadata Storage and Data Repository of CALIMERA (ref. Figure 1). The search is performed over all the connected peers through the semantic query engine. The address of the results is mention in the search interface: Resources coming from the super peer are designated by "'invenio:IPadress"', resources coming from a *normal* peer are designated by the "'IPadress"' only (Figure 5).

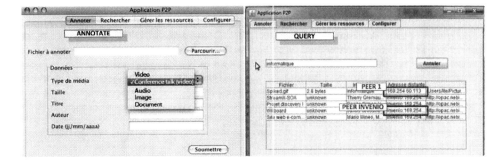

Fig. 5. Distributed data annotating and querying

6   Conclusion and Future Work

In this paper we presented an end-to-end adaptive framework that meets the needs of massively distributed multimedia information produced by different services along a conference life cycle. This end-to-end solution is supported by the framework CALIMERA. A framework for multimedia information retrieval based on the ontological model HELO and a layered approach model. HELO was built on the base of a study that analyses the user's needs and requirements when searching for videos of recorded talks. The model is used over the layered model to perform and build efficient content based annotations and to enhance browsing, navigation and data accessibility. As next steps, we intend to evaluate the proposed frameworks with its different modules. This evaluation focuses mainly on four axes: 1- The ontological model HELO: This evaluation should validate the adaptability of the scopes and their coherence from different users point of view. It should also measure the facility of learning and using this model.2- The semantic search interface: This interface should be evaluated in a set of experiments to verify both its expressiveness and its effectiveness. 3- The multimedia rendering and browsing interfaces: This evaluation should compare the proposed interfaces versus the existing ones in different retrieval situations. 4- The information retrieval over the P2P network: This evaluation should analyze the results efficiency and pertinence and the added value compared to the use of the framework without the P2P network.

References

1. Andrew, D., et al.: Semantic annotation and retrieval of video events using multi-media ontologies. In: ICSC, pp. 713–720 (2007)
2. Smeulders, A., et al.: Content-based image retrieval at the end of the early years. IEEE Transactions on Pattern Analysis and Machine Intelligence (2000)
3. Liu, Y., et al.: A survey of content-based image retrieval with high-level semantics (2007)
4. Hollink, L., et al.: Building a visual ontology for video retrieval. In: 13th Annual ACM International Conference on Multimedia, Singapore (2005)

5. Knud, M., et al.: The ESWC and ISWC Metadata Projects. In: Aberer, K., Choi, K.-S., Noy, N., Allemang, D., Lee, K.-I., Nixon, L.J.B., Golbeck, J., Mika, P., Maynard, D., Mizoguchi, R., Schreiber, G., Cudré-Mauroux, P. (eds.) ASWC 2007 and ISWC 2007. LNCS, vol. 4825, pp. 802–815. Springer, Heidelberg (2007)
6. Hare, J.S., et al.: Bridging the semantic gap in multimedia information retrieval - top-down and bottom-up approaches. In: Sure, Y., Domingue, J. (eds.) ESWC 2006. LNCS, vol. 4011, Springer, Heidelberg (2006)
7. Bertini, M., et al.: Soccer Video Annotation Using Ontologies Extended with Visual Prototypes. In: CBMI 2007, Bordeaux (2007)
8. Vladimir, G., et al.: Visualizing the Semantic Web: XML-based Internet and information visualization (2006)
9. Heiko, P., et al.: Ontology-based information visualization in integrated UIs. In: IUI 2011. ACM, New York (2011)
10. An advanced software framework for enabling the integrated development of semantic-based information, content, and knowledge management systems, http://cordis.europa.eu/ist/kct/vikef_synopsis.htm
11. Laurier, C., et al.: Pharos: an audiovisual search platform using music information retrieval techniques (2009)
12. Huang, W., et al.: Conkmel: A contextual knowledge management framework to support multimedia e-learning (2006)
13. SAPIR - Search In Audio Visual Content Using Peer-to-peer IR, http://www.sapir.eu/
14. MATTERHORN - Platform to support the management of educational audio and video content, http://www.opencastproject.org/project/matterhorn
15. Sokhn, M., et al.: Knowledge management framework for conference video-recording retrieval. In: SEKE 2009, Boston (July 2009)
16. Sokhn, M., et al.: Conference Knowledge modelling for conference-video-recording querying and visualization. Journal of Multimedia Processing and Technologies 1(2) (June 2010)
17. Sokhn, M., et al.: Virtual-Q: Querying over heterogeneous and distributed data sources. In: AWIC 2011. Advances in Soft Computing Series. Springer, Heidelberg (2011)
18. AKT, http://www.aktors.org/publications/ontology/
19. Conference ontology by Jen Golbeck, http://www.mindswap.org/~golbeck/web/www04photo.owl/
20. eBiquity Conference Ontology, http://ebiquity.umbc.edu/ontology/conference.owl/
21. Semantic Web Technologies ESWC 2006, http://www.eswc2006.org/technologies/ontology-content/2006-09-21.html
22. CERN, Centre Europeen de Recherche Nucleaire, http://www.cern.ch
23. General introduction to MPEG-7, http://mpeg.chiariglione.org/standards/mpeg-7/mpeg-7.htm
24. RDF, Resource Description Framework, http://www.w3.org/RDF/
25. OWL, Web Ontology Language, http://www.w3.org/TR/owl-features/
26. Semantic Web Conference Ontology, http://data.semanticweb.org/ns/swc/swc_2009-02-27.html
27. The Language and Platform Independent Protocol for P2P Networking, Semantic Web Conference Ontology, http://jxta.kenai.com/
28. Jena – A Semantic Web Framework for Java, http://jena.sourceforge.net/index.html

Optimizing the Delivery Chain in Heterogenous Networks

Xavier Sanchez-Loro[1,2], Josep Paradells[1,2],
Jordi Casademont[1,2], and José Luís Ferrer[1,2,*]

[1] Wireless Networks Group - Telematics Department,
Universitat Politècnica de Catalunya,
Mod. C3 Campus Nord, C/ Jordi Girona 1-3, 08034 Barcelona, Spain
[2] i2CAT Foundation,
Gran Capita 2-4 (Nexus I building), 08034 Barcelona, Spain
{xsanchez,josep.paradells,jordi.casademont}@entel.upc.edu,
jlferrer@i2cat.net
http://www.i2cat.net/en
http://wireless.upc.edu/en/index.html

Abstract. Herein, we will focus on proposing a service taxonomy and classification for RBA/SOA architectures aiming to model a common framework for the description and composition of possible Atomic Services or networking functions valid for architectures coping with heterogenous environments. The final objective is fine-tuning the delivery chain to optimize application and delivery performance and behaviour in heterogenous networks. Although our work takes the TARIFA architecture as the basis model for our contribution, we think it can be helpful for other architectures dealing with protocol modularization and service composition.

Keywords: Heterogenous Networks, Ubiquitous and Pervasive Computing, Service Composition, Future Internet, Context-Awareness, Functional composition.

1 Introduction

In previous work [5], we explored the possibilities of context-awareness, service discovery and negotiation as the basis to deploy ubiquitous services in heterogenous environments. First, we explored the concept of delivery context in the Ubiquitous Web, seeking ways to acquire context data from user devices and enhancing the available mechanisms for negotiation and context acquisition across the delivery chain. This way we worked with proxies to enhance server and client negotiation in heterogeneous web environments, allowing proxies to

---

* This work is partially funded by MECD and FEDER project TEC2009-11453 and I2Cat Foundation Project TARIFA[1]. The authors would like to express their thanks for contributions from the TARIFA project and the participating research groups: NETS, MediaEntel, GXO, ANA, Cols and GTM.

X. Masip-Bruin et al. (Eds.): WWIC 2011, LNCS 6649, pp. 207–219, 2011.

transparently detect device capabilities and personalizing context distribution and content negotiation according to user preferences, device capabilities and network environment. Furthermore, we explored the possibilities of using intermediaries to optimize web traffic by means of header reduction. One conclusion of this piece of work is that e-2-e principles of current Internet are not valid in heterogeneous environments. With such different underlying computing and networking technologies, we need more intelligence and autonomy in the network and means to adopt different protocol behaviours depending on underlying network environment and context. Using a model of autonomic proxies/middleboxes performing local adaptations at required network segments provides better results than plain-old e-2-e negotiation across the delivery chain.

All this work give us with enough insight in the field to conclude that Ubiquitous and Pervasive Computing requires more level of control and adaptation granularity than current networking models offer. We cannot made the network more pervasive and invisible at the Application level, indeed we need that the network stack itself becomes ubiquitous and pervasive. Thus, on further efforts [7,6,10] we have worked in designing from scratch a semantic context-aware network architecture focused on the provision of ubiquitous services. This Future Internet (FI) architecture expands the concept of delivery context to support any type of service traffic, not just web traffic. So, we propose that intermediate nodes participate in the discovery, negotiation and adaptation of services. Hence, integrating service discovery, negotiation and adaptation as core features of the architecture. Besides, another important divergence of the architecture from TCP/IP stack is its layer-less modular nature, since it is based on SOA principles, and follows the model of RBA instead of OSI's one. Hence we designed a flow-oriented context-aware network architecture where communications are composed on the fly (using reusable components) according to the needs and requirements of the consumed service.

1.1   New Networking Models for the Future Internet

The Internet is facing an architectural crisis as the load and stress on the Network increase with new users and applications. Current Internet architecture is becoming more and more ossified and complex; with lots of patches aimed to amend different issues that have arisen during its almost 40 years of existence. This patching has been done outside the core of the architecture, increasing its complexity and blurring -and sometimes even contradicting- the neat principles behind the original design of the Internet. Furthermore, new services and computing paradigms require new modes of interaction, new features (identification, context-awareness, seamless service discovery and composition, etc.) and clean solutions to known issues (mobility, security, flexibility, etc.); but it is not clear how the current Internet architecture will be able to cope with all these new requirements. In the research community, there are two approaches to solve this crisis: evolutionary and disruptive (clean-slate). Most of the initiatives fall in the category of clean-slate redesign, where the network architecture is designed anew from scratch. These initiatives exhibit some clear lines of research and similar approaches for certain issues. The main common lines of research are:

1. **Redefinition of the layering concept and protocol design**. These lines imply a complete redefinition of the network architecture. Most of the initiatives follow this trend in one-way or the other. Some approaches:
   (a) *Questioning of the end-to-end principles of communication.* e-2-e principles are not taken for granted and many initiatives depart from this communication paradigm.
   (b) *Changes from host/interface-centric paradigm to information/service centric paradigms.* Two main approaches:
      i. Content-centric architectures
      ii. SOA/RBA architectures
   (c) *Protocol modularization and protocol custom composition.* Some common goals
      i. Flexibility: overcome current protocol stacks rigidness in their design and restricted inter-layer communication.
      ii. Adaptability: to changes in communication environments and application requirements, including different nodes, links and applications
      iii. Loose-coupling and evolution: current protocols are ossified by its tight-coupling design, they can't naturally evolve. Protocols need means to evolve by loose-coupling principles.
      iv. Autonomic: protocols (and networks) must be autonomic and self-*.
      v. Custom protocols for dealing with network heterogeneity and meet new application requirements. Two main trends, composed from scratch (e.g. SONATE, TARIFA) and template-based (e.g. Netlets, ANA, SILO)
      vi. Context-awareness. Current protocols are oblivious of context conditions, being unable to adapt or even detect changes in environment conditions.
      vii. Time of composition: run-time or design-time.
2. **Changes in the routing and addressing paradigm**. These initiatives take into account that most of the transactions in the Internet are for accessing to content not to hosts. Although minor in number compared to initiatives following trend 1, a good deal of FI solutions imply changes in the routing paradigm. In some cases, these lines may coexist and/or work with legacy technologies like IP networking. Some approaches:
   (a) *Redefinition of what to address.* From hosts to content and/or services.
      i. Location/Identifier split
      ii. Self-certifying content identifiers
      iii. Content-centric addressing and naming
      iv. Semantic discovery of services and data: service-oriented paradigms usually involve mechanism for discovering and negotiating services. Similarly, content-centric networking needs some way to discover and locate requested content

(b) *Changes in forwarding paradigms.* Route by data content not by host.

(c) *Publish/Subscribe paradigm for locating data.*

3. **Network virtualization as a means to deploy multiple concurrent architectures and networks**. Although not a new solution, research on network virtualization is critical to the deployment of FI technologies since with all probability no one architecture will be the final solution and many of them will coexist in the future thanks to virtualization.

Herein, we will focus on proposing a service taxonomy and classification for RBA/SOA architectures aiming to model a common framework for the description and composition of possible Atomic Services (ASs)[1] or networking functions valid for architectures coping with heterogenous environments. The final objective is the fine-tuning the delivery chain to optimize application and delivery performance and behaviour. The paper is structured as follows: first we will introduce the concept of RBA in section 1.2 and how this model is key to understand the philosophy behind some of the most disruptive FI architectures. In section 2 we will analyze the available service definition in the field and propose a "common" service definition, valid for any type of networking service regardless the granularity, thus including support both for Atomic Services (ASs) and Composed Services (CSs). Once we have a clear definition of what a service is, we can propose a taxonomy in section 3 useful for classifying services for composition and allocation purposes in heterogenous environments. With this taxonomy at hand, we propose a service classification in section 4 which is suitable for our needs[2]. In section 5 we discuss some strategies fro the allocation of services along the delivery chain. Finally, section 6 concludes the paper.

1.2   RBA

From an architectural point of view, the most ground-breaking (and influential for our own research) proposal was, and still is, the RBA [2], a non-layered and modular architecture built around the concept of roles. A role represents a communication building block that performs some specific function relevant to forwarding or processing packets. Therefore, new relations amongst network components are established by defining a set of roles to be played by each component involved. In this way, nodes implement the different roles required for a certain communication (i.e., "packet forwarding", "fragmentation", "flow rate control", "byte-stream packetization", "request web page", or "suppress caching"). The protocol stack in this architecture is replaced by a protocol "heap" in which each node's realm of execution in the protocol heap is restricted to the roles it exercises. Non layering thus implies new rules for modularity, header structure and ordering for the processing of metadata, as well as encapsulation. These new rules and relationships were (and still are) not fully investigated and unexpected

---

[1] Other terminology for ASs are roles, building blocks, functions...

[2] Any service classification will be subject of controversy and lack of exhaustiveness. We think the proposed classification covers most of the aspects for optimizing service provisioning and connection performance, but it by no means an exhaustive list.

synergies and incompatibilities may appear in implementing RBA-based architectures. This kind of micro-modularization, breaking existing protocols into small modules with a definite function, is common practice in most clean slate proposals [4]. While they are all aimed at improving flexibility, their key difference is the way in which modularization is approached (in terms of scope, focus, purpose and module granularity) and how network architecture and protocols are abstracted, defined and built on the basis of these modules, that is, how the architecture and communications are composed with these modules. All these synergies between different initiatives concentrate around the concept of service/role. Nevertheless there is no unified or commonly agreed service definition and taxonomy although there are some isolated approaches [8,9].

Since RBA proposes a conceptual model, it can be implemented in different terms: disruptive or evolutionary. On one hand, a pure RBA architecture may be implemented with no layers at all and roles scope ranging from application all the way through to physical layers or perhaps just above a virtualized link layer. This would be the disruptive or clean-slate approaches, and it is the main trend for RBA-based architectures. On the other hand, it can be deployed as an evolutionary enhancement on top of the network layer or even just at the application level. The scope and definition of roles will be directly derived from the implementation scenario. Hence, a common definition of basic roles would be useful both for FI architectures and evolutionary solutions applying the concept at the Application layer.

2   Service Definition: What Constitutes a Service?

If we take a look on the literature of service discovery, Service-Oriented Architectures, protocol modularization and service/functional composition fields[4], we can found different definitions of what is a service.

- RFC 2165-SLPv1: The service is a process or system providing a facility to the network. The service itself is accessed using a communication mechanism external to the the Service Location Protocol.
- ATIS: Something of value being provided to and consumed by end-users of communications networks. A function that is performed by software whose output is used by some other entity. It may be, for example, a presence engine, or a routing function, or a number translation capability, or protocol interworking. 'Service' may also refer to the software itself.
- W3C
  - Web Service: A service is an abstract resource that represents a capability of performing tasks that form a coherent functionality from the point of view of providers entities and requesters entities. To be used, a service must be realized by a concrete provider agent.
  - An application that provides computational or informational resources on request. A service may be provided by several physical servers operating as a unit.

– OASIS: The performance of work (a function) by one for another. Services
are the mechanism by which needs and capabilities are brought together.

All these definitions stress that a service is performing some type of networking
or computational function, task or process at request of other entities (users, services, applications...). Although they differ in specific terms, the basic meaning
is very similar. Therefore, we can generalize and infer the following definition:

*"A service is a process, function or task that provides networking, com-
putational or informational resources on request"*

With this definition we abstract that the service can be provided by any type
of entity regardless their characteristics (e.g. hardware, software, distributed,
virtual, physical,etc.) and that the service itself can be of very different natures,
ranging from computing a function or storing data to providing resources and
tasks to interconnect different entities. Thus, covering from low-level services
like MAC, ACKs and sequencing to end-services or applications like PBS, file
transfers or web services.

3   Service Taxonomy

The following independent categories define a taxonomy valid for different types
of services, regardless their granularity (see figure 1). This taxonomy aims to
organize and ease role/service definition in SOA/RBA solutions and is inferred
from our initial proposal of AS, published in [6]. Figure 1 illustrates graphically
this taxonomy.

– **Granularity**: atomic, molecular, composed.
   • *Atomic Services* are the core of our architecture. They are the building
     blocks (roles) used to establish communications and to deliver data in a
     self-adaptable, self-configurable and context-aware way. Each atomic ser-
     vice provides one concrete and well-defined networking function (along
     with the reverse function, if any). Different algorithms and implemen-
     tations of an atomic service may exist (i.e. different congestion control
     algorithms), and co-exist in the same node, using attributes to both de-
     scribe the different possibilities and to tune/configure the atomic service
     in order to use it to fulfill specific workflows needs.
   • *Molecular Services* are common compositions for small sets of ASs that
     usually work together to perform a more complex function than just
     a single ASs (e.g. sequencing and retransmission may be composed as
     two independent ASs, but they are often composed together in form of
     a molecular service). Using this intermediate abstractions can ease and
     simplify the composition process of bigger composed services.
   • *Composed Services* are network applications with a wider scope than
     just establishing communications (e.g. sensing service, directory service,
     file transfer, instant messaging, presence, etc.). Each composed service
     or application implies consuming different atomic and sometimes other

composed services, with possible dependences appearing between them. In addition, they can involve one or more nodes, depending on the complexity of the service.

- **Execution/Distribution**:
  - *Isolated*: local execution of the service
  - *Distributed*: execution distributed between two nodes, regardless their location. It includes support for e-2-e, section and hop-by-hop distribution/allocation of services.
- **Scope**: services can be applied with different scopes or considerations depending on the desired result.
  - *Network*: services are executed to optimize communication according network context.
  - *Application*: services are executed to optimize application behaviour and interconnection to meet application requirements according to context characteristics.
- **Usage**: rules governing the service usage.
  - *Mandatory*: usage of this service is mandatory as it i basic for establishing a communication (e.g. forwarding).
  - *Optional*: usage of this service is optional, its usage will depend on application requirements and context characteristics
- **Purpose**: which is the purpose of the service.
  - *Delivery*: to deliver data between two different entities involved in the delivery chain (they can be adjacent or non-adjacent nodes or they can be two end applications, depending on the scope of the service)
  - *Mobility*: services related to application, user and node mobility.
  - *Storage*: services dealing with the storage of data.
  - *Security*: services dealing with security issues.
  - *Data Adaptation*: services dealing with adapting and transforming data for different objectives, interoperability, customization and optimization of data.
  - *Addressing*: services dealing with the identification and labeling of resources.
  - *Management*: services dealing with the management of the different entities in the network (nodes, applications, services, etc.).
  - *Signaling*: services dealing with interchange of signaling and control data.
  - *Presentation*[3]: services dealing with the presentation of contents and user/application interfaces
- **Order**: order/existence of the AS in workflow composition may be dependent of another service.
  - Dependent.
  - Independent.

---

[3] This category is only available for services with application scope.

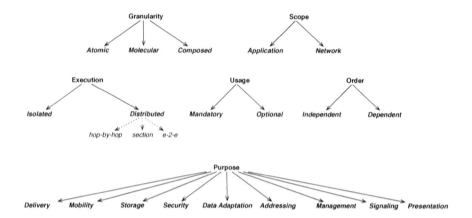

Fig. 1. Service taxonomy

4   Service Classification

The following tables (see table 1 and table 2) show the different services that can be applied according to different purposes: Application and Network.[4,5]

5   Allocation Strategies

One critical process during the negotiation of a composed service is the composition and allocation of AS to obtain a feasible workflow for each node involved in the communication; one that allows the fulfillment of the service requirements according to the context constraints. Thus, this process must perform the following analysis:

- Analysis of context constraints Vs QoS Requirements. Requirements should be checked against context constraints in order to obtain sets of possible AS.
- Analysis of possible feasible AS configurations for the whole path (not for just isolated individual nodes) to fulfill service requirements with these context constraints. Obviously, this analysis implies knowing where the different AS are allocated in each configuration. For this analysis, we can adopt some techniques proposed in the field (see section 5).

Hence, as we can see, service composition and allocation are two interleaved processes that cannot be feasibly decoupled.

Implementing this process implies knowing two variables for each AS implementation: the cost and the benefit/effect of using it. Costs should be checked

---

[4] Each service includes the reverse function if any.
[5] Transcoding is a coupled pair of Decoding/Encoding. Includes any data transformations, i.e. data transcoding, cyphering, compression, etc.

Table 1. Service Classification for Application domain

Purpose	Service
Delivery	Flow control/Rate control
	Error Control
	Object Control
	Flow Multiplex/Joining
	Monitoring
Mobility	Portability
	Nomadism
Storage	Cache
	Directory
	Store
Security	Authorization
	Authentication
	Access Control
	Token Exchange
Data Adaptation	Encoding/Transcoding
Addressing	Labeling
Management	Configuration
Signaling	Session control
	Service Discovery
	Service Announcement
	Negotiation
Presentation	Rendering
	Adaptation
	Encoding/Format
	Content Negotiation
	Interaction (Modality)

against context constraints, whilst effects should achieve QoS requirements. Therefore, metrics should be researched to measure the cost of executing an AS in different terms (e.g. CPU/RAM utilization, affected bandwidth, delay, etc.), although in the end all these metrics should be unified/normalized to use the same units in order to be suitable for expressing a cost function. Even it must be thoroughly investigated, at a first glance expressing costs in terms of delay with time units seems a good starting approach. However, our first impressions is that the benefits of using a certain AS have not a straightforward translation to a common unit, and it should be investigated even if it is possible.

When deciding which is the best workflow configuration for a composed service path, it is needed some tools to analyze the effect and the cost of using each configuration. After some research on the field, we have found some techniques and references that may be suitable for our purposes. This is the case of Wolf's layered graph approach [3], this technique allows to compute the cost of service allocation inside a network, by transforming it in a shortest-path problem, which can be easily computed using Dijkstra's algorithm. The key idea is to transform the network in a graph with multiple layers, where each layer represents the

Table 2. Service Classification for Network domain

Purpose	Service
Delivery	Congestion control
	Flow control/Rate control
	Forwarding
	Joining/Multiplex
	Forking/Splitting
	Aggregation
	Framing/Encapsulation
	Fragmentation
	Medium Access Control
	Acknowledgement
	Retransmission
	Sequencing
	Monitoring
	Negotiation
Mobility	Inter-domain
	Intra-domain
	Handover
	Point of Attachment (Multi-path)
Storage	Cache
	Buffering
Security	Authorization
	Authentication
	Access Control
	Token Exchange
Data Adaptation	Encoding/Transcoding
	Rate adaptation
	Channel adaptation
Addressing	Labeling (flow, packets, etc.)
Management	Configuration
	Network management
	Node management
Signaling	Session control
	Route discovery
	Route setup
	Circuit setup
	Session Negotiation

execution of a service. Then, the optimal path is found executing Dijkstra's algorithm for finding the shortest path in the transformed graph. Finally, the multi-layered graph is mapped back to the original network. This approach has some real good pros and some cons we discuss:

- *It is suitable for computing the placement of multiple services.* But services are allocated in sequential order, thus not suitable for parallel service execution. In our virtual circuit model, for the purposes of allocation, services may be deployed sequentially.

- *Session-oriented*. The algorithm assumes that the intermediate nodes and the network links used for communication are selected. This is the case of our architecture, since we use a virtual circuit model with a fixed path.
- *Bandwidth alteration awareness*. The algorithm can be extended to be aware of the influence on bandwidth of using one service. For instance some services like compression have a cost, but decrease the required bandwidth. In the opposite site, FEC increases overhead and, thus, the required bandwidth. This effect is reflected with bandwidth scaling factor. It should be investigated, but probably this extension of the algorithm (or a very similar one) may be applied for services affecting other network metrics like delay, probability error, etc.
- *Optional processing*. The algorithm can be used to incorporate the possibility of optional services, services that are not necessary for the correct data communication but can enhance the quality of the connection.
- *Multicast sessions*. Multicast sessions may also be computed using this approach, but instead of a shortest-path problem, the resulting problem is a standard Steiner tree problem.
- *Capacity constraints*. Although taking into account capacity constraints is clearly a NP-hard Hamiltonian path problem, which cannot be assured to find an efficient solution, least the lowest-cost path; the authors have proposed modification to Dijkstra's algorithm to incorporate capacity constraints, so that in most situations they can find low cost session configurations with the required resources.
- *Decided and ordered set of services*. In this technique, services to be placed are decided beforehand. For purposes of adapting it to our proposal, we must decide first which sets of AS will be tested, so we can check the feasibility of a certain set of AS; but the algorithm cannot decide for us which are the services to be allocated.
- *Knowing costs and benefits*. In order to be able to use this technique, we must envision a method to obtain the correct values for costs and effects of using the services. However, this is not a problem of this technique alone, whatever method we use to compute the allocation of services will require to know the cost and the benefit of using a service.

It seems quite obvious that this technique can help to compute the cost of a service allocation with a reasonable computation cost, but it is not straightforward how to use it for expressing effects. It must be investigated but one possibility to be researched is integrating the effects of services as a means to modify the cost, and thus, just checking if the modified cost complies with the context constraints and the service requirements. This can be feasible for those services where the cost and the benefit can be easily related; but this is not always the case (e.g. FEC increases delay and required bandwidth, but decreases PER). For those metrics that cannot be incorporated in the graph as a scaling factor, the benefit may be calculated with a new layered-graph where the benefit is computed as a cost, but inverted in order to keep the problem as a Dijkstra's shortest-path problem.

Some of the shortcomings of these approaches for our case study is that they cannot take into account capacity constrains [3]; the exact services that will be used and the ordering of execution of these services are known before-hand, since they work with high-level and application level services and not with basic network services like ASs. So, in order to make these solutions work with our proposal we must devise ways to:

1. Compute the cost of using each AS in terms of computing and network usage
2. Decide what are the most appropriate ASs (and their configuration) to obtain a certain performance and behavior. This implies finding ways to infer the benefits of using a certain service. This may be a simple problem when dealing with independent services, but it can become complex when working with inter-dependent services (i.e. ACK and CRC). Furthermore, many ASs imply allocating two services, one at the input node and one at the output node, which further complicates the problem.
3. Determine the correct ordering of execution of ASs.

We are currently working on simple scenarios with a small subset of ASs, researching for interdependences and the cost and the benefit of using these services, both alone and in combination. We expect to obtain results in the following months.

6   Conclusion

Protocol modularization and functional composition are key to overcome the limitations in performance of traditional e-2-e transport protocols in heterogeneous networks. In order to provide and consume (composed) networked services in a truly ubiquitous fashion (according to desired functionality, behavior and QoS constraints), ASs must be suitably allocated along the communication path where they are actually needed, and tuned/configured accordingly to accomplish the application requirements and resource availability. With this objective in mind, we have proposed a service definition and taxonomy generic enough to cover both low-level services and end-user applications. We have also provided a list of basic ASs for composing protocols for heterogeneous networks. Obviously, this list isn't exhaustive, but in our opinion is complete enough to build protocols for interconnecting different heterogenous networks in most of the application environments. And new services can be added to the list whenever a new functionality is required. As mentioned in allocation section weare currently working on simple scenarios with a small subset of ASs, researching for interdependences and the cost and the benefit of using these services, both alone and in combination. We expect to obtain results in the following months.

Acknowledgments. This work is partially funded by MECD and FEDER project TEC2009-11453 and I2Cat Foundation Project TARIFA. The authors would like to express their thanks for contributions from the TARIFA project[1] and the participating research groups: NETS, MediaEntel, GXO, ANA, Cols and GMT.

References

1. TARIFA: The Atomic Redesign of the Internet Future Architecture, http://www. i2cat.net/en/projecte/tarifa-1
2. Braden, R., Faber, T., Handley, M.: From protocol stack to protocol heap: role-based architecture. SIGCOMM Comput. Commun. Rev. 33, 17–22 (2003), http:// doi.acm.org/10.1145/774763.774765
3. Choi, S., Turner, J.: Configuring sessions in programmable networks with capacity constraints. Proc. of IEEE International Conference on Communications (ICC), Anchorage, AK (February-May 2003)
4. Henke, C., Siddiqui, A., Khondoker, R.: Network functional composition: State of the art. In: Telecommunication Networks and Applications Conference (ATNAC), Australasian, 31-November 3, pp. 43–48 (2010)
5. Sanchez-Loro, X., Casademont, J., Ferrer, J.L., Beltran, V., Catalan, M., Paradells, J.: Dynamic content negotiation in web environments. In: Context-Aware Computing and Self-Managing Systems, March 25. Chapman and Hall/CRC Studies in Informatics Series (2009), http://www.crcpress.com/product/isbn/ 9781420077711
6. Sanchez-Loro, X., Ferrer, J.L., Casademont, J., Paradells, J., Vidal, A.: Proposal of a Clean Slate Network Architecture for Ubiquitous Services Provisioning. In: IEEE First International Conference on Future Information Networks ICFIN 2009, Beijing, China, October 14-17 (2009)
7. Sanchez-Loro, X., Ferrer, J.L., Gomez, C., Casademont, J., Paradells, J.: Can Future Internet be based on constrained networks design principles?. Computer Networks (2010) (In Press, Corrected Proof), http://www.sciencedirect.com/ science/article/B6VRG-51S25P9-5/2/ad39433134291a948e7f5555d583d3df
8. Schwerdel, D., Siddiqui, A., Reuther, B., Müller, P.: Composition of self descriptive protocols for future network architectures. In: Proceedings of the 2009 35th Euromicro Conference on Software Engineering and Advanced Applications, SEAA 2009, pp. 571–577. IEEE Computer Society. Washington (2009), http://dx.doi. org/10.1109/SEAA.2009.75
9. Sifalakis, M., Louca, A., Bouabene, G., Fry, M., Mauthe, A., Hutchison, D.: Functional composition in future networks. Computer Networks 55(4), 987–998 (2011) (special Issue on Architectures and Protocols for the Future Internet), http://www.sciencedirect.com/science/article/B6VRG-51RJDC4-2/ 2/a962d026b7c97716aa39b585f9e75e4f
10. Sanchez-Loro, X., Gonzalez, A., de Pozuelo., R.M.: A Semantic Context-Aware Network Architecture. In: Cunningham, P., Cunningham, M. (eds.) Future Network and Mobile Summit 2010, June 2010, IIMC International Information Management Corporation, Florence, Italy (2010)

Energy-Efficient Internetworking with DTN

Dimitris Vardalis[1] and Vassilis Tsaoussidis[2]

[1] Space Internetworks Ltd., 12 Rethymnou, 10682 Athens, Greece
[2] Space Internetworking Center, Dept. of Electrical and Computer Engineering,
Demokritos University of Thrace, Xanthi 67100, Greece

Abstract. We claim that Delay-Tolerant Networking has the potential to form an internetworking overlay that shapes traffic in a manner that exploits the capacity of last hop wireless channels and allows for energy-efficient internetworking. We demonstrate DTN potential for energy-efficient internetworking through an overlay-architecture and a tool we have developed that captures the required state transitions of the mobile device WNIC. We show experimentally that the DTN overlay can re-shape traffic in a manner that allows the receiver to exploit the energy-throughput tradeoff better: it may condense sporadic packets into a burst and, in return, prolong sleep and power-off duration without risk to miss incoming packets and without degradation in throughput.

Keywords: DTN, energy efficiency, internetworking.

1 Introduction

Mobile devices became a useful every-day tool for communication, storage and entertainment. They are equipped with increasingly more powerful CPUs, larger memory capacities, faster wireless network adapters, and a set of applications that require internetworking capabilities. However, advances in battery technology have not been able to match the increased energy demand.

So far, the main focus of attention was the energy-efficient administration of device components, the selection of routing with energy capacity to route packets, or the capacity of battery itself. The (inter-) network *per se* has never attested its vital role in energy efficiency. The Internet, due to its probabilistic nature constitutes a major reason for the lack of end-device energy control. Its scheduling uncertainty forces a receiver on continuously waiting for random contacts and, inevitably, enforces an energy-wasting policy; as a result, the device cannot incorporate energy-efficient modes of operation, such as *sleep*, into its transition state diagram. Therefore, a main reason for the inability to optimize end-device operations is the inherent inability of the internetwork to deliver data tactically, due to its store-and-forward and statistical multiplexing characteristics. Practically, what imposes the limitation to schedule transmission with accurate precision is the variation of delay, along with the potential lack of sufficient resources to store packets in transit, albeit having such a capacity could have, instead, permitted the network to shape traffic and corroborate a scheduling policy among the devices *and* the network.

X. Masip-Bruin et al. (Eds.): WWIC 2011, LNCS 6649, pp. 220–233, 2011.
© IFIP International Federation for Information Processing 2011

In this work, we attempt to demonstrate the potential of Delay Tolerant Networking (DTN) ([1], [2]) to shape internetwork traffic in a manner that allows mobile devices to balance their energy expenditure with minimal cost on throughput. In this context, we design and deploy an internetworking overlay that exploits two major DTN properties: (i) to store packets for as long as it is necessary, regardless of disruptions in communications; and (ii) to enhance the edge nodes with functionality to wait for sufficient amount of packets to arrive, prior to transmitting to the end node. We then develop scenarios and weigh our expectations using a broad set of experiments that reflect potential variations in traffic characteristics, error probabilities and disruptions.

In order to evaluate the proposed scheme we use the ns-2 network simulator. Since there is no established and reliable DTN implementation for ns-2 we opted for emulating the behavior of the bundle protocol by introducing a proxy application at the base station. The energy expenditure model of ns-2 was also not sufficient for this work, since the whole state transition diagram for the WNIC had to be recorded. Hence, energy expenditure calculations involved hacking into the physical layer of the wireless node and adding tracing for the state transitions. Our results show that (i) energy expenditure can be reduced drastically and (ii) clearly, DTN appears as an appropriate tool to construct such overlay: it allows for permanent storage and, in addition, it does not require full, but instead, partial deployment on top of IP; in fact, even a minimal deployment of DTN nodes can satisfy the architectural requirements of energy-saving overlay as soon as the edge nodes deploy such service.

The rest of the paper is organized as follows: In section 2 we discuss related work, focusing on more recent approaches to save energy on mobile devices. In section 3 we discuss our proposal and in section 4 we detail our experimental tools and methodology, including parameters for evaluation, metrics and scenarios developed. In section 5 we discuss the results and, finally, in section 6 we summarize our conclusions.

2 Related Work

The research literature on energy efficiency for mobile devices includes two broad categories that correspond to the device optimization and communication optimization. In [3], the authors identify as the main sources of energy expenditure the various subsystems of a handheld device, such as: the processor, the memory, the display, the audio system and the wireless networking. For network intensive applications, the power consumption of the Wireless Network Interface Controller (WNIC) can reach up to 60% of the total power necessary for the operation of the mobile device [4]. In [5] Jones et al. provide a comprehensive survey on the design principles of efficient network protocols. The authors focus on the specific mechanisms that can be employed in each of the layers in the network protocol stack (i.e. Physical, Data Link, Network, Transport, OS/Middleware and Application).

In [6], Adams et al. propose a buffering technique that exploits the inherent power-saving mode of 802.11. Data destined to a certain mobile node is hidden and thus, not made available to it for multiple beacon intervals. Mamatas and Tsaoussidis in [7] monitor the state transition of the WNIC and introduce two metrics for energy potential and unexploited available resource, to capture the energy performance potential of various protocols. The authors in [8] present a theoretical and empirical study of the impact of packet transmission interval and burst length on observed network performance characteristics, with or without use of a proxy service. They propose an adaptive, energy-saving streaming mechanism that adjusts the burst length. By the same token, however now focusing generally on TCP traffic, Anastasi et al. [9] introduce at the base station a proxy service that employs regular TCP on the wired network side and the novel Power-Saving Transmission Protocol on the wireless side. Authors in [10] expand on the proxy idea by introducing a scheduler service at the base station and a proxy at the mobile terminal. The scheduler incorporates a novel algorithm, called priority-based bulk scheduling (PBS). In [11] the proxy idea is again implemented at the base station introducing the novel RT_PS protocol for the communication between the base station and the mobile node. The RT_PS protocol includes *idle* intervals information so that the client can put the WNIC into *sleep* mode when applicable. By the same token, Batsiolas and Nikolaidis [12] propose a regulation of ACKs for TCP in a manner that allows the sender to predict with some accuracy when ACKs are expected; and meanwhile the sender enters a *sleep* mode.

3 Energy-Efficient Internetworking Overlay

We depart from the mobile device *modus operandi*: at any given moment, a WNIC can be in one of five operation states, each with different power requirements: *transmit, receive, idle, sleep* (or doze) and *power-off*. The *transmit, receive* and *idle* state of the WNIC constitute the active states, whereas the *sleep* and *power-off* constitute the inactive states. The power requirements of active states are comparable with each other [3]. In the *transmit* state maximum power is consumed, while in the *receive* state slightly more power is required than in the *idle* state. In the *sleep* state the energy expenditure is an order of magnitude less than that of the *idle* state, and finally, in the *power-off* state no power is required. The IEEE 802.11 [13] protocol provides an inherent mechanism for allowing client devices to manage the power requirements of their WNICs. The mechanism relies on the central role played by the Access Point when the network is in the PCF (Point Coordination Function) operation mode (in this paper we do not consider the ad-hoc or Distributed Coordination Function of 802.11).

It becomes apparent that the challenge in energy-saving strategies now translates into how to maximize the duration that the WNIC spends in either the *sleep* or the *power-off* state. It is obvious, however, that the AP has a limited buffer and therefore, the scheduling precision and flow control of the AP determine the efficiency of each strategy. Otherwise, the risk of entering a *sleep* mode may lead to costly retransmissions and throughput degradation due to buffer overflow or receiver inactivity. Data buffering essentially shapes traffic in bursts so that periods of inactivity are prolonged, allowing the WNIC to stay in a low-power state longer, while at the same time minimizing the performance trade-off with throughput. Hence, it makes sense to design an overlay that buffers at least a Delay X Bandwidth product (DxB) between the edge node and the receiver (prior to transmitting) and distributes data storage among nodes in a manner that packet dropping is avoided. This sort of sophistication has not been developed or analyzed in our present work. We construct a rather demonstrative overlay where buffers have enough space; the disruptions never go beyond the storage capacity, so the possibility to cause buffer overflow is cancelled, in practice. In this context, we evaluate only the ability of the overlay to shape traffic in a manner that optimizes the transitions of the mobile device; and we evaluate the characteristics of the tradeoff with throughput.

The pseudo-code of the algorithm at a DTN node of the overlay is as follows:

```
ReceiveIncomingData
If IsBaseStationNode
{
        If receivedData Is lastSetOfData OR receivedData > bufferingThreshold
                If (HasConnectivityToMobileEndNode)FlushData
                Else
                {
                        If (BufferAvailable) StoreData
                        Else RejectDataCustody
                }
}
Else
{
                If (HasConnectivityToNextHop) ForwardData
                Else
                {
                        If (BufferAvailable) StoreData
                        Else RejectDataCustody
                }
}
Go Back to the Beginning
```

What we also consider as novel in our proposal is the ability of the edge node (i.e. the last DTN node) to make a decision locally, with better precision than the sender of a typical end-to-end application. The architecture has the potential to exploit further the custody property of the DTN protocol, which leads to an automated balancing of storage as a result of the operation to shift data towards the destination only when the accepting nodes do have storage availability.

4 Experimental Methodology

We emulated the behavior of the bundle protocol by introducing a proxy application at the base station. Measuring the energy expenditure was made possible by directly monitoring the physical layer of the receiver and making log entries for each state change of the WNIC. The proxy application is associated with an incoming TCP connection originating from some source on the wired part of the network and an outgoing TCP connection that ends at the wireless receiver. The proxy application buffers data coming in from its receiving end and flushes it out to its sending end as soon as the desired amount of data is collected. This setup emulates the functionality of a DTN overlay on an IP network, when using TCP as the convergence layer.

The proxy application was implemented as a subclass of the Application class in ns-2, adding the required extra functionality. Additional functionality implemented within the new class includes: an agent that receives data from the wired source, an option for the buffer size and an option for the total size of the transfer. The proxy needs to be aware of the total transfer size so that, when the specified amount of data is received, the buffer is immediately flushed without waiting for the buffering threshold to be reached.

In order to facilitate the energy expenditure calculations we modified the physical layer of the wireless node. Code that traces the duration the WNIC spends in each of the three states (i.e. *send*, *receive* and *idle*) was added. By having an accurate picture of state transitions we are able to carry out post simulation calculations and find the potential energy savings if there was in place a mechanism that would switch the WNIC into the *sleep* state during *idle* intervals. In this paper we aim at emphasizing the energy saving potential that a DTN-based protocol can have for mobile devices. Addressing various optimization aspects, including the inherent load balancing capability of DTN custody transfer, is part of our future work plans.

4.1 Energy Expenditure Calculations and Comparison

During the post-simulation analysis a multi-purpose script identifies the energy-related log entries in the ns-2 trace file and calculates the energy expenditure based on certain input parameters. The script takes the following input parameters: transmit power (txPower), receive power (rxPower), idle power (idlePower), sleep power (sleepPower), transition power (transPower) and transition time (transTime). For the *transmit* and *receive* intervals the energy expenditure is calculated as the duration of the interval multiplied by the transmit and receive power respectively. Energy conservation can be achieved by exploiting the *idle* intervals and switching into the *sleep* state. The transition is considered feasible only if the time it takes to fall into the *sleep* state and then back to the *idle* state (i.e. transTime) is less than the duration of the *idle* interval itself. The transition is considered meaningful if the energy required for switching back and forth to the *sleep* state, plus the energy spent during the *sleep* state is less than the energy expenditure if the WNIC had remained in an *idle* state for the whole interval duration. If idleDuration is the duration of the *idle* interval, the decision is based on the following formula:

$$2 * \text{transPower} * \text{transTime} + (\text{idleDuration} - 2 * \text{transTime}) * \\ \text{sleepPower} < \text{idleDuration} * \text{idlePower}$$

It becomes obvious that the longer the duration of the *idle* intervals the greatest the opportunity for conserving energy. The power figures for the various WNIC states are set as follows [14]: txPower = 1.400 Watts, rxPower = 0.950 Watts, idlePower = 0.805 Watts and sleepPower = 0.060 Watts. As reported in [15] transition time from *sleep* to *idle* and vice versa, is in the order of tens of milliseconds. However, when switching back to the active state, the controller needs to wait for the next beacon in order to start receiving the buffered data. If we assume that it takes 50ms to switch states and another 100ms for the next beacon signal to be broadcast (a rather pessimistic estimation since 100ms is the default beacon interval for 802.11) the total for the transition amounts to 200ms. Therefore, we set the transition delay at 100 ms for both state transitions. Finally, based on measurements in [16] we can safely consider the energy expenditure in the transitive state to be the same as that of the *idle* state (i.e. transPower = 0.805).

4.2 Model Description

Figure 1 depicts the network topology that was implemented in order to evaluate the energy conservation that could be achieved by employing a DTN-like protocol in wired-cum-wireless scenarios. Network nodes are named as N1 – N6. N4 is the base station node that is connected to both the wired and the wireless networks and node N6 is the wireless receiver. Links L13, L23, L34 and L45 are wired, while WL is the wireless link between the base station and the receiver.

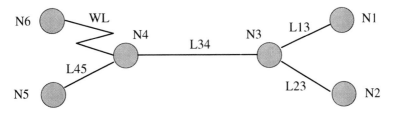

Fig. 1. Network Topology

The data transfer studied in this experiment follows the N1→N3→N4→N6 route, while the competing flow follows the N2→N3→N4→N5 route. The bandwidth of the backbone link (L34) is changed so that the desired congestion is introduced into the network. The rest of the links are kept at the same delay and bandwidth values for all the experiments.

The bandwidth and delay values for all the links are as follows: L13 - 2Mb, 100ms, L23 - 3Mb, 100ms, L34 – 300ms delay and varying bandwidth depending on the desired network characteristic, L45 - 3Mb, 100ms, WL - 802.11 with a data rate of 11Mb and a basic rate of 1Mb. Stochastic Fair Queuing is applied on all queues, the file transfer size is 10MB and, when present, the competing flow sends a 1000 byte packet every 3 ms. TCP packet size is 1460 and maximum window size 100 packets.

The resulting energy expenditure values are in Joule. In the End-to-end (E2E) scenarios there is an end-to-end connection between N1 and N6, whereas in the Split scenarios there is a splitting application on the base station acting as a transport layer mediator. In order to measure the delay of the wireless connection between the base station and the mobile receive we employed a ping agent. The delay was found to be around 2ms. The DxB is thus: 0.002 x 11 000 000 / 8 = 2.750 KB. Except otherwise noted, the splitting application buffers 30KB (around 10 x the DxB) before forwarding them to the mobile device. In case the wireless connection is the bottleneck and data piles up at the base station we make the assumption that there is no limit in the available memory used for buffering data and, therefore, no data is dropped.

Finally, experiments are carried out both for an FTP connection transferring 10 MB of data as well as CBR traffic that flows for a specified amount of time. In certain experiments we are introducing a packet error rate on the wireless LAN. The error follows a uniform distribution and is applied on the outgoing interface of both the base station interface as well as the WNIC of the mobile node.

5 Results

In this section we present the experimental results, organized in five subsections of experimental setups. Due to limited space we only present a subset of the available results. A full version of the results can be found in [17]. The setups presented in this paper are as follows: FTP and varying wired bandwidth (with and without a competing flow), FTP and varying wireless error (with and without a competing flow), FTP and varying buffering threshold (with and without a competing flow), CBR and varying buffering threshold.

5.1 Varying Bandwidth FTP Transfer

In this set of experiments the backbone link is assigned a constant delay of 300ms, while the bandwidth varies from 0.5Mb to 2.5Mb in steps of 0.5Mb. The total transfer duration (Table 1) is virtually the same for both the E2E and the Split case, and it is greatly affected by the bandwidth of the backbone link because of network congestion. Since the upstream link (L13) has a 2Mb bandwidth, setting the backbone bandwidth to values greater than 2Mb does not affect simulation results (L13 becomes the bottleneck of the connection and the backbone is uderutilized). Because of this, the transfer duration is equal for bandwidth values of 2Mb and 2.5Mb.

In terms of the energy efficiency, it is obvious from the chart of Figure 2 that smaller bandwidth values for the bottleneck link lead to greater energy gains of the Split approach. In the extreme setting of the 0.5Mb bandwidth, the energy conservation achieved in the Split case is approximately 44% of the energy expenditure in the E2E case.

As the network congestion is eased, due to the increase of the bottleneck link capacity, the energy conservation becomes less dramatic and it reaches the 5 Joule value. When severe network congestion is present on the network TCP introduces considerable overhead in its effort to achieve reliable transmission. In the E2E case, the mobile node at the receiving end is involved in this extra effort and, consequently, does not frequently have the opportunity to switch to *sleep* mode. Conversely, in the Split case the base station absorbs the effects of the network congestion (lost packets that lead to out-of-order data reception) and only transmits to the mobile host when consequent, buffer-sized chunks of data are available. In DTN terms, the base station will be receiving the incoming bundle without engaging the receiving node in the process. Upon successful bundle reception forwarding to the mobile node would start. In the meantime, the WNIC of the mobile host can switch to *sleep* mode and save significant amounts of energy. The higher the congestion level the greater the energy gains achieved by the Split approach. In the case where Power Saving Mode (PSM) is not employed, the energy expenditure is again related to the transfer duration. In the 0.5Mb bandwidth setting the No PSM energy expenditure is twice as much as that of the Split case, dropping to about 50% more than the Split case in the 2.5Mb setting.

Table 1. FTP, Varying Bandwidth, No Competing Flow Transfer Duration

L34 bandwidth (Mb)	Duration E2E (sec)	Duration Split (sec)
0.5	216.85	216.05
1	145.59	144.88
1.5	111.65	111.17
2	90.48	90.18
2.5	90.34	90.04

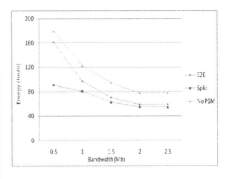

Fig. 2. FTP, Varying Bandwidth, No Competing Flow Energy Expenditure

In the previous scenario we added cross traffic and rerun the experiments. In this set of experiments the maximum bandwidth value for the backbone link was increased to 3.5, since beyond that capacity the measurements remain unchanged.

Table 2. FTP, Varying Bandwidth, Competing Flow Transfer Duration

L34 bandwidth (Mb)	Duration E2E (sec)	Duration Split (sec)
0.5	364.61	357.91
1	225.85	194.47
1.5	159.32	158.63
2	125.39	124.53
2.5	107.72	107.21
3	90.04	89.73
3.5	90.74	90.25

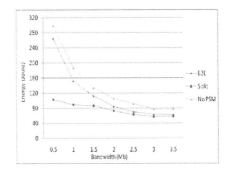

Fig. 3. FTP, Varying Bandwidth, Competing Flow Transfer Duration

As expected, the transfer duration, shown in Table 2, is significantly longer for both the E2E and the Split approaches when a competing flow is present. Nevertheless, unlike the previous scenario, small bandwidth values (i.e. 0.5 and 1 Mb) result to a slightly shorter transfer duration for the Split case.

Regarding the energy consumption, it can be observed in Figure 3 that despite the significantly longer time it takes for the transfer to complete for the 0.5Mb setting (around 60% more in both cases), in the E2E approach the additional energy requirement is 62%, while in the Split approach the additional energy requirement is only around 10%. As the bandwidth increases and the network is relieved from congestion, the energy conserved by the Split approach is limited to around 5 Joule (a value that was observed in almost all congestion-free experiments).

Figure 4 depicts the state transitions for the first 14 seconds of the file transfer in both the E2E and the Split cases when the backbone bandwidth is 1Mb. It is obvious from the chart that in the E2E case, the WNIC needs to switch to active more frequently than in the Split case. For example, between 2 and 6 seconds, in the E2E case the WNIC needs to switch to active 4 times, while in the Split case it remains in the *sleep* state for the whole duration. Also, even when a switch to the active state is necessary the time needed to remain in this state is shorter for the Split than for the E2E scenario (i.e. at 6, 7, 11 seconds).

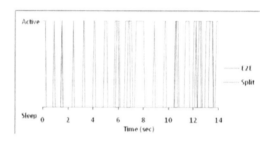

Fig. 4. FTP, 1Mb Bandwidth, Competing Flow State Transitions

5.2 Varying Wireless Error FTP Transfer

The purpose of this scenario is to reveal the effect of packet error on the wireless part of the network both on the transfer duration as well as the energy efficiency of the E2E and the Split approaches. The backbone link was assigned a 300ms delay and a 1Mb bandwidth. The delay was selected so that it is considerably longer than the delays of the rest of the links in the topology and the bandwidth was selected so that the backbone is also the bottleneck link of the transfer route (i.e. network congestion is present).

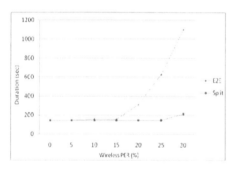
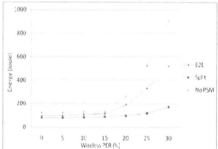

Fig. 5. FTP, Varying Wireless PER, No Competing Flow Duration

Fig. 6. FTP, Varying Wireless PER, No Competing Flow Energy Consumption

At first glance, it may be striking that as the wireless packet error rate (PER) increases the duration of the E2E transfer increases as well (Figure 5), reaching in the 25% case more than three times the duration of the 0% case, whereas the duration of the Split case transfer remains almost the same across all runs. Part of the explanation to this, seemingly bizarre, result can be found in the Indirect-TCP solution proposed in [18]. In the E2E scenario, it takes very long for TCP to recover from packets lost due to the wireless error, because of the long RTT of the connection (around 800ms). On the contrary, the RTT of the wireless link is measured to be around 6-7 ms, and, therefore, a TCP connection between the base station and the mobile host can be very swift in recovering the lost packets. Additionally, since the RTT of the wired part of the route is very long, when compared to that of the wireless part, the time it takes for the base station to buffer the required data is enough for the TCP of the last hop to recover from any packet losses. This observation is not true only for the 30% PER case, in which it is evident that the last hop TCP cannot serve the incoming data, delaying the overall transfer time. In such a case, data could be dropped at the base station if the buffer capacity is depleted. We plan to include monitoring of packets dropped due to limited buffer capacity in future experiments. The performance gains of a solution along the lines of Indirect-TCP that isolates the wireless error in the short-delay part of the transfer route come naturally as additional benefit when using DTN.

The energy consumption chart in Figure 6 shows that up to an error rate of 10% the energy savings achieved by the Split approach are approximately 16% - 20%. As the error rate increases so does the conserved energy, reaching as much as 66% for an error rate of 30%. At this error rate the energy required for the completion of the data transfer in the E2E case is 520.78 Joule, while in the Split case the required energy is 174.09 Joule. The energy expenditure in the No PSM case for the 30% error rate is as much as 910.49 Joule.

The state transitions for an indicative 15 second interval when the wireless PER is 20% are plotted in the chart of Figure 7. It can be observed that, for the whole duration covered in the chart, the WNIC switches to the active state 14 times in the E2E case, while it only switches 6 times in the Split case. The state transition frequency for the two cases is similar during the rest of the data transfer, resulting in the significant energy expenditure difference observed in Figure 6 for a 20% PER.

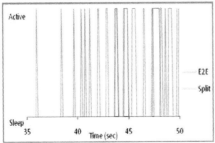
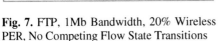
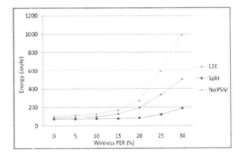

Fig. 7. FTP, 1Mb Bandwidth, 20% Wireless PER, No Competing Flow State Transitions

Fig. 8. FTP, Varying Wireless PER, Competing Flow, Energy Consumption

The experiments in the previous section were repeated with a competing flow present on the network. Because of the huge transfer times that would otherwise be necessary, the bandwidth of the backbone link was set to 2Mb (as opposed to the 1Mb value that was used in the previous section). Even though we cannot directly compare the resulting figures for the cases with or without a competing flow, we can still draw meaningful conclusions for the relative performance of the E2E vs. the Split case. The most significant observation in this scenario as depicted in Figure 8 is that when a competing flow is present, the energy expenditure of the E2E approach exhibits higher increase rates for smaller error rates. For higher error rates both the competing and the non-competing flow cases exhibit similar behavior.

5.3 Varying Buffer Threshold FTP Transfer

In this set of experimental runs the delay is set to 300ms, the bandwidth of the backbone link is set to 1Mb (rendering it as the bottleneck link of the transfer route) and the buffering size varies from 0 up to 200 KB. For the 0 buffering case we used the E2E approach, while for the rest of the runs we used the Split approach with the corresponding buffer size. The transfer duration is, reasonably, identical for all buffer sizes. The energy expenditure, however, drops significantly as the buffer size increases (Figure 9). Since the wireless link of the transfer route is consistently underutilized, buffering more data allows the WNIC of the receiver to switch to a *sleep* state for longer periods, while at the same time not getting penalized for waiting. Increasing the buffer size beyond a certain value could cause congestion problems on the wireless LAN and/or prolong the transfer duration. Such problems could become more severe in case multiple mobile clients are present and download data using the Split approach. With the increase in the buffering capacity the traffic on the wireless LAN becomes more bursty and consequently more prone to congestion. The size of the buffer, in case DTN is employed, can be thought of as the size of the bundle size that the base station would forward to the last hop of the transfer connection.

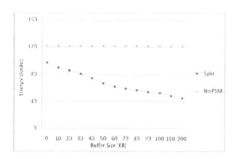

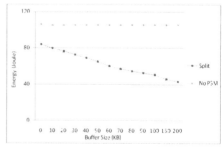

Fig. 9. FTP, Varying Buffering Threshold, FTP, No Competing Flow, Energy Consumption

Fig. 10. FTP, Varying Buffering Threshold, Competing Flow, Energy Consumption

The experiments of the previous scenario were repeated with the introduction of cross traffic caused by a competing flow. In order to compensate for the higher network traffic the bandwidth of the backbone link was increased to 2Mb. In both sets of experiments the transfer duration remains constant for all runs. With respect to the energy expenditure, shown in Figure 10 it is observed that while for small buffer sizes the amount of energy required by the no competing flow scenario is significantly higher, as the buffer size increases the two values converge to a common Joule value in the low 40s. This shows that increasing the buffer size can alleviate differences in the energy expenditure caused by varying congestion conditions in the wired part of the network.

5.4 Varying Buffer Threshold CBR Transfer

In this last set of experiments a CBR traffic flow of 10MB is considered in a network with no contending traffic. As in most of the previous scenarios the delay of the backbone link was set to 300ms and the bandwidth to 2Mb. The transfer duration does not convey any important information as it merely refers to the time the last packet is received by the mobile node and it depends solely on the end-to-end network delay.

This scenario can be mostly considered as a placeholder for future work, since the side effects of delaying CBR traffic are not taken into account. When measuring the service quality of a file transfer the time for completion can be an adequate metric. The sooner the file transfer finishes the better it is for the end user. In all the experiments, so far, the transfer duration was not affected by the buffering mechanism, rendering the mechanism acceptable from a user standpoint. However, CBR traffic is, in most cases, related to multimedia streaming. Extra delays introduced by the buffering mechanism can lead to unacceptable service quality, a factor which is not captured by our current experimental setup. Nevertheless, the experiments in this scenario reveal the potential a DTN-based Split approach can have for reducing the energy consumption for CBR traffic.

It becomes apparent from the chart in Figure 11 that even for a buffer size of 20KB, the energy saving potential is 33% compared to the case where no power saving is used (No PSM). As the buffering size increases the conserved energy increases as well, reaching almost 85% of the energy spent in the No PSM case. Although large buffering in multimedia streams can cause long delays and, thus, unacceptable user experience, if used with caution it can deliver significant energy conservation with little or no quality degradation.

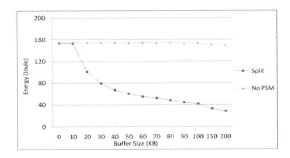

Fig. 11. CBR, Varying Buffering Threshold Energy Consumption

6 Conclusions and Future Work

We evaluated the potential of DTN to shape Internet traffic in a manner that allows mobile devices to utilize energy-conserving modes of operation, without risk to lose packets or degrade their throughput. Our results are based on a post-simulation analysis of the recorded transition state diagram of the mobile device, as this was determined by the communication between the end-device and the edge network node. The most conclusive results of our experiments capture the huge gain in useless transitions and uncover the energy potential of DTN properties.

We briefly discussed the property of DTN to balance network traffic as well. This is not peripheral to energy-saving strategies: Load balancing within the network, unlike typical end-to-end approaches, cancels the risk of packet dropping but also forwards information towards the destination as soon as possible. Application data, instead of waiting at the source, it is pushed at some network nodes closer to the destination. This latter becomes particularly important in environments, such as space for example, where a contact graph is predetermined and the penalty for losing a contact opportunity may delay communication significantly. Hence, load balancing strictly associates with less retransmissions and shortened communication time: two tactics with energy-conserving consequences. We plan to focus on this dimension of energy-saving strategies by extending our present evaluation framework with load balancing algorithms.

Finally, taming uncertainty allows for more sophisticated signaling techniques that deploy a hybrid Time Division and Statistical Multiplexing strategy. This sort of sophistication is under progress.

References

[1] Cerf, V., Burleigh, S., Hooke, A., Torgerson, L., Durst, R., Scott, K., Fall, K., Weiss, H.: Delay-Tolerant Networking Architecture. RFC 4838, IETF (2007)
[2] Scott, K., Burleigh, S.: Bundle Protocol Specification. RFC 5050, IETF (2007)
[3] Viredaz, M., Brakmo, L., Hamburgen, W.: Energy Management on Handheld Devices. ACM Queue Magazine - Power Management 1(7) (2003)
[4] Acquaviva, A., Simunic, T., Deolalikar, V., Roy, S.: Remote power control of wireless network interfaces. In: Proceedings of International Workshop on Power and Timing Modeling, Optimization and Simulation (2003)
[5] Jones, C., Sivalingam, K., Agrawal, P., Chen, J.: A Survey of Energy Efficient Network Protocols for Wireless Networks. ACM Journal on Wireless Networks 7(4) (2001)
[6] Adams, J., Muntean, G.M.: Adaptive-Buffer Power Save Mechanism for Mobile Multimedia Streaming. In: Proceedings of IEEE International Conference on Communications 2007 (2007)
[7] Mamatas, L., Tsaoussidis, V.: Exploiting Energy-Saving Potential in Heterogeneous Networks. International Journal of Parallel, Emergent and Distributed Systems (IJPEDS) 23(4) (2008)
[8] Korhonen, J., Wang, Y.: Power-efficient streaming for mobile terminals. In: Proceedings of ACM International Workshope on Network and Operating Systems Support for Digital Audio and Video (2005)
[9] Anastasi, G., Conti, M., Lapenna, W.: A Power-Saving Network Architecture for Accessing the Internet from Mobile Computers: Design, Implementation and Measurements. The Computer Journal 46(5) (2003)
[10] Zhu, H., Cao, G.: A Power-Aware and QoS-Aware Service Model on Wireless Networks. In: Proceedings of IEEE INFOCOM 2004 (2004)

[11] Anastasi, G., Conti, M., Gregori, E., Passarella, A., Pelusi, L.: A Power-Aware Multimedia Streaming Protocol for Mobile Users. In: Proceedings of the IEEE International Conference on Pervasive Services 2005 (2005)

[12] Batsiolas, I., Nikolaidis, I.: Selective Idling: Experiments in Transport Layer Energy Conservation. The Journal of Supercomputing 20(2) (2001)

[13] IEEE Standard for Information technology - Telecommunications and information exchange between systems - Local and metropolitan area networks - Specific requirements, Part 11: Wireless LAN Medium Access Control (MAC) and Physical Layer (PHY) Specifications (2007)

[14] Shih, E., Bahl, P., Sinclair, M.J.: Wake on Wireless: An Event DrivenEnergy Saving Strategy for Battery Operated Devices. In: Proceedings of the ACM International Conference on Mobile Computing and Networking (2002)

[15] Simunic, T., Boyd, S.: Managing power consumption in networks on chips. In: ACM DATE (2002)

[16] Xiao, Y., Savolainen, P., Karppanen, A., Siekkinen, M., Ylä-Jääski, A.: Practical power modeling of data transmission over 802.11g for wireless applications. In: Proceedings of the ACM International Conference on Energy-Efficient Computing and Networking (2010)

[17] Vardalis, D., Tsaoussidis, V.: Energy-efficient internetworking with DTN, Technical Report: TR-DUTH-EE-2011-4,
http://www.intersys-lab.org/pages/publications.php

[18] Bakre, A., Badrinath, B.R.: Implementation and Performance Evaluation of Indirect TCP. IEE Transaction on Computers 6(3) (1997)

DESC: Distributed Energy Efficient Scheme to Cluster Wireless Sensor Networks

Peyman Neamatollahi[1], Hoda Taheri[1], Mahmoud Naghibzadeh[2],
and Mohammad Hossein Yaghmaee[2]

[1] Dept. Computer Engineering, Young Researchers Club,
Mashhad branch, Islamic Azad University, Mashhad, Iran
{neamatollahi,taheri}@ieee.org
[2] Dept. Computer Engineering, Ferdowsi University of Mashhad, Mashhad, Iran
naghibzadeh@um.ac.ir
[3] Dept. Computer Engineering, Mashhad branch, Islamic Azad University, Mashhad, Iran
yaghmaee@ieee.org

Abstract. Organizing sensor networks into clustered architectures is an effective approach for load balancing, and prolonging the network lifetime. This paper proposes a Distributed Energy Efficient Scheme to Cluster Wireless Sensor Networks (DESC). This protocol achieves energy efficiency using two techniques: on demand clustering and a multi-criteria cluster formation. Whenever a cluster head consumes a prespecified part of its energy, it indirectly informs other nodes to hold cluster head elections for the upcoming round. Therefore, clustering is performed sporadically (in contrast to performing it every round). In DESC, a node with higher amount of remaining energy is considered a more eligible candidate for election as a cluster head. Besides, each node computes a multi-criteria cost, and a regular (non-cluster head) node elects the cluster head with the most cost to connect to. Simulation results show that the protocol outperforms HEED and LEACH protocols in terms of network lifetime and energy savings.

Keywords: Sensor networks, clustering, network lifetime, energy efficient protocols, distributed algorithms.

1 Introduction

Wireless sensor networks (WSNs) provide reliable monitoring from very long distances [1]. The main task of a sensor node in a sensor field is to detect events, perform quick local data processing, and then to transmit the data [2]. As mentioned in [3] and [4], nodes have typically low mobility and are limited in capabilities, energy supply and bandwidth. Therefore, all aspects of the sensor node, from the hardware to the protocols, must be designed to be extremely energy efficient.

In direct communication WSN, the sensor nodes directly transmit their sensing data to the Base Station (BS) without any coordination between the two. However, in Cluster-based WSNs, the network is divided into clusters. Each sensor node exchanges its information only with its cluster head (CH), which transmits the aggregated

X. Masip-Bruin et al. (Eds.): WWIC 2011, LNCS 6649, pp. 234–246, 2011.

information to the BS. In this way, clustering achieves a significant improvement in terms of energy consumption. Research on clustering in WSNs has focused on developing centralized and distributed protocols to compute sets of CHs and to form clusters. Centralized approaches (e.g. [5]) are rather inefficient in the case of large scale networks since collecting the entire amount of necessary information at the central control (BS) is both time and energy consuming. Distributed approaches are more efficient for large scale networks. In these approaches, a node decides to become a CH or to join a cluster based on the information obtained solely from neighbors within its proximity. Several distributed clustering protocols have been proposed in literature (e.g. [1], [3], [6], [7], and [8]). As mentioned in [9], most of these protocols are either iterative or probabilistic. In probabilistic protocols (e.g. [7], [8], and [10]), the decision to become CH is reached probabilistically. On the other hand, in iterative protocols (e.g. [3]), the nodes perform an iterative process to decide whether to become a CH or not. From another point of view, clustering protocols are considered as being static and dynamic. In static clustering, the clusters are permanently formed (e.g. [5], [6]), while in dynamic clustering (like [1], [3], [7], [8], and [11]), protocol operation is divided into rounds; clusters are formed for a round and then should be formed again for the next round. In doing so, extra overhead is imposed on the system.

This paper presents a distributed dynamic clustering protocol named DESC. The protocol is distributed as each node has a partial view of the network and can, therefore, makes it own decision as to whether become a CH or join a cluster based on local information. Clustering is dynamic as the clusters are not formed a priori nor are fixed during the network lifetime. In this protocol, each node employs an iterative process to decide its status. For each node, this repetition phase finishes when the node either elects itself as a CH or finds a CH to join. Compared to famous protocols, HEED [3] and LEACH [1], the goal of DESC is to achieve significant energy saving results in extending network lifetime. This proposed clustering approach does not make any assumptions regarding the distribution of the nodes or node capabilities, e.g., location-awareness. The protocol only assumes that sensor nodes can vary their transmission power. Compared to many previously presented protocols (e.g. [1] and [3]), DESC decreases both the overhead caused by the clustering's message complexity and the number of CH elections. Clustering is performed when at least one CH has consumed a significant part of its residual energy. With the assistance of its transferred data packet, the CH node informs the BS of its status. Then, the BS scatters special synchronization pulses in a multi-hop fashion throughout the area. Upon receiving these pulses, each node prepares to perform clustering for the upcoming round. In the protocol, CH selection is based on cost and remaining energy. Therefore, each node must compute a multi-criteria cost. The cost is proportional to node degree and node centrality. The regular nodes elect the most cost CH in their respective close proximity in order to connect to. Simulation results demonstrate that the benefits of DESC over HEED and LEACH protocols, in terms of improving network lifetime and energy savings are noticeable.

The rest of the paper is organized as follows: Section 2 describes the network model and clustering problem. A new energy efficient clustering scheme is outlined in Section 3. Section 4 presents the simulation results by comparing energy consumption, network lifetime, and the number of CH elections with other well known algorithms. Finally, the conclusion is presented.

2 Preliminaries

2.1 Network Model

The following properties are assumed in regard to the sensor network being studied:

- The nodes can use power control to change the amount of transmit power.
- The sensor nodes are quasi-stationary.
- Nodes are not equipped with GPS-capable antennae.
- Nodes are energy constrained and are left unattended after deployment.
- Distance can be measured based on the wireless radio signal power.

T_{CP} and T_{NO} are defined as follows:

- T_{CP} (the period of the clustering process) is the time interval used by the clustering protocol to cluster the network.
- T_{NO} (the network operation interval) is the time between the end of a T_{CP} interval and the start of the subsequent T_{CP} interval.

In order to reduce overhead, it must be ensured that $T_{NO} \gg T_{CP}$. Note that, in contrast with other dynamic clustering protocols that perform clustering in each round, DESC clusters the nodes on demand rather than at each round. Therefore, it is possible that some rounds do not include T_{CP}; instead T_{NO} is extended during these rounds. As a result, the length of the T_{CP} interval is fixed but the length of the T_{NO} interval varies throughout the network lifetime. In DESC, node readings are periodically reported to the BS. Therefore, a TDMA frame is created in each CH to remove interference within a cluster. The protocol uses special synchronization pulses to alert the sensor nodes that clustering will be triggered in the beginning of the next round. These pulses are propagated in a multi-hop fashion (as approach presented in [12]).

2.2 The Clustering Problem

Suppose the above assumptions hold and that n nodes are distributed in a field. In consideration of energy saving issues, the goal is to identify a collection of CHs which cover the entire area. Each node v_i, where $1 \leq i \leq n$, must be mapped to exactly one cluster c_j, where $1 \leq j \leq n_c$, and n_c is the number of clusters ($n_c \leq n$). L_i shall denote the lifetime of node i. The network lifetime will be defined as follows:

- F is the time elapsed until the First Node Dies (FND). In other words, $F = min\ (L_1, L_2, \ldots, L_n)$.
- H is the time elapsed until only one Half of Nodes remain Alive (HNA). Therefore, $H = median\ (L_1, L_2, \ldots, L_n)$.
- L is the time elapsed until the Last Node Dies (LND) or, $L = max\ (L_1, L_2, \ldots, L_n)$.

The major purpose here is to maximize F, H, and L, which requires using the energy of all nodes uniformly. A node must have the ability to directly communicate with its CH and by a single-hop fashion. A CH has two critical responsibilities: (1) intra-cluster coordination and (2) inter-cluster communication. Multi-hop routing is used for inter-cluster communication. CHs can utilize a routing protocol to compute inter-cluster paths for communicating in a multi-hop fashion with the BS, e.g. the power-aware routing protocol in [13].

Note that, in the clustering process, every iteration takes time, t_c. Period t_c should be long enough to receive messages from any neighbor within the cluster radius. Because the nodes are quasi-stationary, neighbor discovery is not required every time clustering is performed. Hence, the neighbor set of every node does not vary very frequently. In multi-hop networks, the nodes automatically update their neighbor sets by periodically sending and receiving heartbeat messages.

3 The DESC Protocol

In this section, the DESC protocol and its pseudo code are illustrated. The operation of DESC is divided into rounds and each round is comprised of two phases:

- The setup phase, which includes CH election and consequently cluster formation. In addition, in this phase, every CH coordinates with its members to send sensing data during the following phase.
- The steady state phase, which is broken up into TDMA frames. During each frame, every regular node, at the time of its respective time slot, sends sensing data to its CH (similar to [1]). At the end of each TDMA frame, every CH forwards the aggregated data to the BS through the CHs.

This protocol has the following characteristics which resemble [3]'s:

- The steady state phase is similar.
- The clustering process is iterative.
- A chosen CH advertises only to its neighbors.
- The clustering procedure ends in $O(1)$ iterations.
- Each node can directly communicate with its CH.
- During the clustering process, a node can be either a *tentative_CH* or a *final_CH* or it can be covered.
- At the end of the setup phase, CHs form a network backbone, such that packets are routed from the CHs to the BS in a multi-hop fashion over CHs.

3.1 On Demand Clustering

A novelty of DESC is that it decreases overhead by performing the setup phase on demand instead of in each round. To do so, when the clustering process finishes (at the end of each setup phase), every CH saves its residual energy in its memory, for example in its E_{CH} variable. During the steady state phase, whenever a CH finds that its $E_{residual}$ falls below αE_{CH} (α is a constant number and $0 < \alpha < 1$), the CH sets a prespecified bit in a data packet which is ready to be sent to the BS in the current TDMA frame. Upon receiving the forwarded CH data packet (sent in a multi-hop fashion), the BS informs the sensors to hold the setup phase at the beginning of the upcoming round. This could be achieved by having the BS send out, in a multi-hop fashion, specific synchronization pulses to nodes. These pulses are quickly dispersed throughout the network. When every node receives a pulse, it prepares itself to perform clustering. Therefore, CH election and consequently cluster formation are performed on demand. As a result, the overhead created by consecutive setup phases is tremendously reduced. Consequently, there is a decrease in the energy dissipation of nodes and an increase in network lifetime.

3.2 Multi-Criteria Cost

In the DESC protocol, each node computes a cost according to an equation (2). The nodes with the greater cost have a higher priority of being elected as CH. On the other hand, every regular node joins the CH which has the highest cost in its vicinity.

$$\text{cost}_v = \sum_{j=1}^{\text{num of neighbors}} \frac{1}{\text{dist}^2(v,j)} \qquad (1)$$

The combination of two main features, node centrality (the centrality of a node among its neighbors) and node degree (the number of neighbors), are considered when computing the cost:

- The lower the value of the neighbors' distances from node v, the higher the value of the cost_v. This means that the location of node v is more central among its neighbors and is, thus, more suitable for election as a CH. The node centrality feature in CH election has some advantages for consideration:
    - Member nodes can communicate with their respective CH node by consuming less energy.
    - Radio wave interferences between CHs are reduced.
- The greater the number of node v's neighbors, the higher the value of cost_v. In other words, node v is more suitable for election as a CH and so, dense clusters are constructed in the area. In many applications, dividing the network into dense clusters is an important goal to group spatially close sensor nodes. The aim is to exploit the correlation and eliminate the redundancies that often exist in the sensor readings.

3.3 Clustering Process

The clustering process of DESC is divided into three phases:

- *Initialization Phase*: In the beginning of this phase, neighbor information must be updated. Afterwards, each node may compute its cost independently. This cost will not be broadcasted to neighbors as it is exchangeable through *CH_msg* messages. As previously mentioned, note that updating the neighbor information and computing costs are not required every time clustering is triggered. At first, the protocol sets an initial percentage of CHs among all sensor nodes, C_{prob}. Here, C_{prob} is set to 0.05. Each sensor node sets its own probability of becoming a CH, CH_{prob}, (the same as [3]):
    •

$$CH_{prob} = MAX \left(C_{prob} * \left({E_{residual}}/{E_{max}} \right), p_{min} \right).$$

In the above, $E_{residual}$ is the current energy of the sensor node and E_{max} is the maximum energy corresponding to a fully charged battery. CH_{prob} is not allowed to fall below a certain threshold p_{min}, which has been selected to be inversely proportional to E_{max}. The threshold p_{min} limits the number of iterations of the *Main processing phase* to $O(1)$. See the *Initialization phase* in Fig. 1.

- *Main Processing Phase*: S_{CH} shall be defined as follows: $S_{CH} = S_{final\_CH} \cup S_{tentative\_CH}$, where $S_{final\_CH} = \{$All *final_CHs* from iteration 1 to iteration $i\}$ and $S_{tentative\_CH} = \{$All *tentative_CHs* from iteration 1 to iteration $i\}$. At the beginning of this repetitive phase, a node with higher amount of residual energy has a greater chance,

CH_{prob}, of becoming a *tentative_CH*. If a node becomes a *tentative_CH*, it broadcasts a message announcing its new status to all other sensor nodes within its cluster range. In the next iterations, if this particular node has the highest cost among the *tentative_CHs* in its proximity and its CH_{prob} reaches one, it will become a *final_CH* and shall broadcast a *final_CH* message within its cluster range. On the other hand, if a node receives a *final_CH* message, it can no longer be elected as a CH. Therefore, in the following phase, it must choose to connect to one of the *final_CHs* in its cluster radius, based on the cost of that *final_CH*. Finally, each sensor node doubles its CH_{prob} value and continues to the next iteration of the repetitive phase. When its $CH_{previous}$ reaches one, the sensor node stops executing this phase. As a result, the nodes with a higher amount of remaining energy will finish the execution of DESC earlier than nodes with a lower amount of remaining energy. This permits the nodes with lower amount of energy to join their clusters. Observe that, in this phase, each *tentative_CH* (or *final_CH*) node can send a *CH_msg* only once. See the *Main processing phase* in Fig. 1.

- *Finalization Phase*: During this phase, each sensor node makes a final decision about its status. If the node is not a *final_CH* and has received at least one *final_CH* message, it will elect the *final_CH* with the highest cost to join it. If a node completes the clustering process and has not yet received any *final_CH* message, it will find itself uncovered and so shall introduce itself as the *final_CH*. See the *Finalization phase* in Fig. 1.

Phase I. Initialization

$S_{nbr} \leftarrow \{v: v$ lies within my cluster range$\}$

$cost \leftarrow \sum_{v=1}^{num\ of\ neighbors} \frac{1}{dist^2(me,v)}$

$CH_{prob} \leftarrow MAX\ (C_{prob} \times (E_{residual}/E_{max}), p_{min})$

$is\_final\_CH \leftarrow FALSE$

Phase III. Finalization

IF $(is\_final\_CH = FALSE)$

  IF $((S_{final\text{-}CH} \leftarrow \{v: v$ is a $final\_CH\}) \neq \emptyset)$

    $my\_CH \leftarrow MOST\_COST\ (S_{final\text{-}CH})$

    $JOIN\_CLUSTER\ (my\_CH, NodeID)$

  ELSE

    $CH\_msg\ (NodeID, final\_CH, cost)$

Phase II. Main Processing

REPEAT

  IF $((S_{CH} \leftarrow \{v: v$ is a $tentative\_CH$ or $final\_CH\}) \neq \emptyset)$

    IF $((S_{final\text{-}CH} \leftarrow \{v: v$ is a $final\_CH\}) = \emptyset)$

      IF $(NodeID = MOST\_COST\ (S_{CH})$ AND $CH_{prob} = 1)$

        $CH\_msg\ (NodeID, final\_CH, cost)$

        $is\_final\_CH \leftarrow TRUE$

  ELSE IF $(CH_{prob} = 1)$

    $CH\_msg\ (NodeID, final\_CH, cost)$

    $is\_final\_CH \leftarrow TRUE$

  ELSE IF $(Random(0,1) < CH_{prob})$

    $CH\_msg\ (NodeID, tentative\_CH, cost)$

  $CH_{previous} \leftarrow CH_{prob}$

  $CH_{prob} \leftarrow MIN\ (CH_{prob} \times 2, 1)$

UNTIL $CH_{previous} = 1$

Fig. 1. Pseudo code of DESC protocol

4   Simulation Results

In this section, a comparison between the simulation results in DESC, LEACH and HEED protocols is performed via Matlab software. The following assumptions and system parameters (similar to [1]) are used:

- The nodes always have data to send to the end user and the nodes situated in close proximity to others have correlated data.
- The CHs perform ideal data aggregation.

- A simple model for the energy dissipation of radio hardware is assumed, in which the receiver dissipates energy to run the radio electronics and the transmitter dissipates energy to run the power amplifier and radio electronics. Thus, for transmitting a k-bit message over distance d, the radio expends:
  •

$$E_{Tx}(k,d) = \begin{cases} kE_{elec} + k\epsilon_{fs}d^2, & d < d_0 \\ kE_{elec} + k\epsilon_{mp}d^4, & d \geq d_0 \end{cases}$$

For receiving this message, the radio expends:

$$E_{Rx}(k) = E_{Rx-elec}(k) = kE_{elec}.$$

- The rest of the parameters are listed in Table 1.

Table 1. Parameter Settings

Parameter	Value
ϵ_{fs}	10 pJ/bit/m^2
ϵ_{mp}	0.0013 pJ/bit/m^4
E_{elec}	50 nJ/bit
E_{DA}	5 nJ/bit/signal
Idle power	13.5 mW
Sleep power	15 μW
Threshold distance (d_0)	75 m
Initial energy per node	2 J
Round time	20 sec
Round	5 frame
Data packet size	100 byte
Control packet size	25 byte
p_{min}	10^{-4}

In the simulation experiment, node sizes of 100, 200, 300, and 400 are chosen. The simulations for two scenarios are conducted:

- Scenario 1. A network with nodes deployed randomly over an area of size 100×100 m^2. The BS is located at the coordinate (50, 175).
- Scenario 2. A network with nodes deployed randomly over an area of size 200×200 m^2. The BS is located at the coordinate (100, 275).

For each of these scenarios with different numbers of nodes, the cluster range is chosen such that approximately five percentages of nodes are being elected as CH. In the following, the proper value of α is discussed, and then energy consumption, network lifetime, and the number of CH elections are evaluated.

4.1 Setting α Variable

As mentioned before, CH election (clustering execution) is performed on demand. When a CH consumes a prespecified part of its energy (i.e. $E_{residual} \leq \alpha E_{CH}$), it indirectly informs the other nodes that clustering must be performed for the upcoming round. In order to obtain the proper α, DESC was run for the two scenarios described above (here, initial energy per node is assumed to be 0.2 Joule). In Fig. 2, α differs from 0 to 1 and each plot demonstrates the average of three executions for 100, 200, 300, and 400 number of nodes, until the first node dies (FND). Also plotted is an average of the four mentioned plots.

When α is equal to zero, no clustering is performed during the network lifetime (i.e. the static clustering approach that considers fixed CHs). In homogenous networks in which nodes have similar capabilities and the same amount of energy, CHs quickly deplete respective energies. Therefore, when a CH dies, the respective cluster becomes dysfunctional. When α equals one, this signifies that clustering is performed in each round, similar to the LEACH and HEED protocols. Considering the plot, which is the average of the four different numbers of nodes, figures 3-9 are plotted using $\alpha = 0.7$ as it approximately results in better network lifetime.

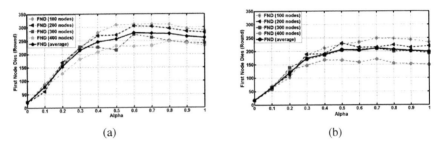

(a)   (b)

Fig. 2. α diagram in DESC for different numbers of nodes and their average. (a) Scenario 1 and (b) Scenario 2.

4.2 Energy Consumption Comparisons

In this subsection, the energy dissipation to cluster the WSN and the energy consumption to transmit the sensed data to the BS are evaluated. Note that in the figures belonging to this subsection, the vertical axis does not have an equal range of data because of the high energy dissipation of LEACH in Scenario 2. In Fig. 3, the average energy dissipation of protocols clustering the WSN per election is evaluated. The DESC protocol performs better because its clustering's message complexity is low and, similar to HEED, its messages are sent in the range of a cluster radius. The LEACH protocol reports the highest dissipation of energy because it does not apply a cluster radius to limit the range of message distribution. Therefore, the value of clustering's energy dissipation for LEACH depends on the network diameter. This evaluation is depicted in the difference found among the values of the LEACH protocol in Fig. 3 (a) and Fig. 3 (b).

Fig. 4 demonstrates the average energy dissipation per round of protocols clustering the WSN. The average for DESC is much lower than that of two other protocols.

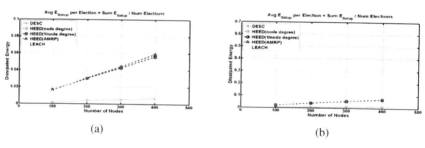

(a)   (b)

Fig. 3. Average energy dissipated to cluster WSN per election. (a) Scenario 1 and (b) Scenario 2.

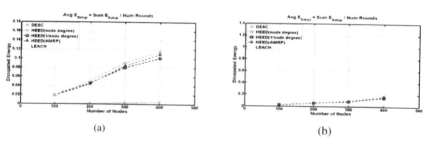

(a)   (b)

Fig. 4. Average energy dissipated to cluster WSN per round. (a) Scenario 1 and (b) Scenario 2.

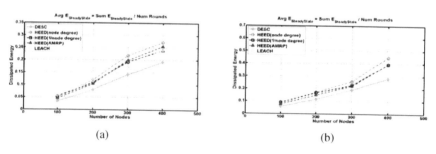

(a)   (b)

Fig. 5. Average energy consumption for data transmission in WSN per round. (a) Scenario 1 and (b) Scenario 2.

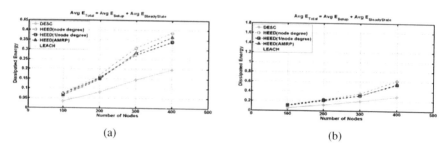

(a)   (b)

Fig. 6. Total average energy consumption in WSN per round. (a) Scenario 1 and (b) Scenario 2.

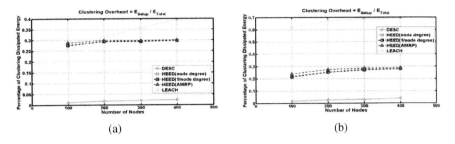

Fig. 7. Clustering overhead. (a) Scenario 1 and (b) Scenario 2.

This difference is caused by 1) low clustering message complexity and 2) not performing the CH election in each round. The average energy consumption for data transmission is depicted in Fig. 5. DESC consumes less energy in the steady state phase because it forms better clusters using a multi-criteria cost compared to the other protocols. HEED uses three different communication costs separately, but here a multi-criteria cost combining the node degree and node centrality is presented. Therefore, DESC forms better clusters than HEED and, of course, better than LEACH. In Fig. 5 (b), LEACH consumes the most energy in intra-cluster communication and also in the transferring of data to the BS. Its intra-cluster communication is not energy efficient because there is no guarantee of a fair distribution of CHs in the field. Therefore, it is possible that some CHs are located far away from their respective members. To sum up Fig. 4 and 5, the total average energy consumption per round for the three protocols is evaluated in Fig. 6. It is noticeable that DESC is an energy efficient protocol regardless of the network diameter.

Fig. 7 illustrates the ratio of energy dissipation when clustering the WSN to the total energy consumption for each protocol. Note that, in both scenarios, DESC achieves a tremendously lower clustering overhead compared to the HEED and LEACH protocols. From the figures provided in this subsection, it can be concluded that DESC is an energy efficient protocol.

4.3   Network Lifetime Comparisons

This paper compares the network lifetime of the discussed protocols for different numbers of nodes with the scenarios presented in Fig. 8. The round of FND, HNA, and LND are summarized in this figure. Because a simple multi-hop routing [13] is implemented to simplify the simulation, the value of FND for nodes 100-400 is in descending order in DESC and HEED protocols (Fig. 8 (a) and (b)). This power-aware routing chooses the minimum energy routes to transfer the data over CHs. Using the minimum energy path during the entire steady state phase will deplete the energy of the CHs on that path. Instead, one of the multiple paths with a certain probability can be used so that the whole network lifetime increases (similar to [14]). Fig. 10 shows that DESC clearly acts better in any definition of network lifetime than the HEED and LEACH protocols without any dependency on network diameter. Consecutively, DESC is a scalable clustering protocol in terms of the number of nodes and the network size.

4.4 Comparison of Number of CH Elections

By not performing the setup phase in all rounds of DESC, the total number of CH elections until LND for these protocols can be compared in Fig. 9. Both the LEACH

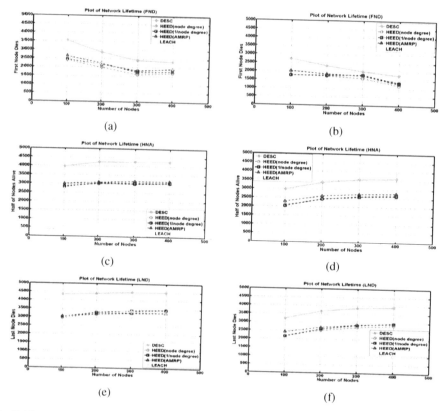

Fig. 8. The network lifetime. (a) FND with Scenario 1, (b) FND with Scenario 2, (c) HNA with Scenario 1, (d) HNA with Scenario 2, (e) LND with Scenario 1, and (f) LND with Scenario 2.

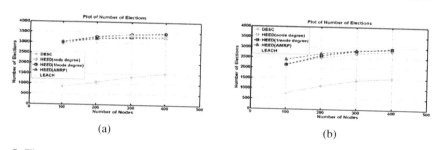

Fig. 9. The number of CH elections in the DESC, HEED, and LEACH protocols. (a) Scenario 1 and (b) Scenario 2.

and HEED protocols perform the setup phase in each round. As shown in this figure, the number of CH elections in DESC is much lower than this value in the other two protocols. As shown in this figure, adding to the number of nodes increases the number of elections. The reason for this is that, by increasing the number of nodes, the value of LND increases (see Fig. 8 (e) and (f)). The number of CH elections in the LEACH protocol decreases in Scenario 2, when compared to Scenario 1. The reason for this is because the value of LND for LEACH in Scenario 2 is much lower than that of Scenario 1.

5 Conclusion

This paper proposes an energy efficient, distributed clustering protocol for WSNs, termed DESC. In this protocol, the clustering's message overhead is low and cluster heads are distributed fairly across the network. Quasi-stationary networks are assumed in which the nodes are location-unaware and have equal significance. In DESC, the CHs are elected based on the residual energy of the node and multi-criteria cost. On the other hand, the regular nodes join the highest cost CH. Also, (after the first setup phase) clustering is not performed until at least one of the CHs consumes a prespecified part of its energy; performing the setup phase in each round imposes much overhead on the network. The efficiency of DESC was evaluated by using Matlab to compare it with the well known protocols, HEED and LEACH. The simulation results demonstrate that DESC outperforms the other two protocols in terms of network lifetime. The main reasons for this are as follows: (1) the clustering process is performed on demand, (2) cluster formation is based on multi-criteria cost, and (3) clustering message complexity is negligible. Although we provided algorithm to cluster homogenous nodes in the area, a future work can be an extension on the protocol to cluster the heterogeneous nodes.

References

1. Heinzelman, W.B., Chandrakasan, A.P., Balakrishnan, H.: An application-specific protocol architecture for wireless micro sensor networks. IEEE Trans. Wireless Commun. 1(4), 660–670 (2002)
2. Akiyldiz, I., Su, W., Sankarasubramaniam, Y., Cayirci, E.: A survey on sensor networks. IEEE Commun. Mag. 40(8), 102–114 (2002)
3. Younis, O., Fahmy, S.: HEED: A Hybrid, Energy-Efficient, Distributed clustering approach for Ad Hoc sensor networks. IEEE Transactions on Mobile Computing 3(4), 366–379 (2004)
4. Akkaya, K., Younis, M.: A survey on routing protocols for wireless sensor networks. Elsevier Journal of Ad Hoc Networks 3(3), 325–349 (2005)
5. Kaur, T., Baek, J.: A Strategic Deployment and Cluster-Header Selection for Wireless Sensor Networks. IEEE Trans. on Consumer Electronics 55(4) (2009)
6. Zhu, X., Shen, L., Yum, T.P.: Hausdorff Clustering and Minimum Energy Routing for Wireless Sensor Networks. IEEE Trans. Vehicular Technology 58(2) (2009)
7. Thein, M.C.M., Thein, T.: An Energy-Efficient Cluster-Head Selection for Wireless Sensor Networks. In: International Conference on Intelligent Systems, Modeling and Simulation, pp. 287–291 (2010)

8. Bandyopadhyay, S., Coyle, E.J.: An energy efficient hierarchical clustering algorithm for wireless sensor networks. In: INFOCOM 2003, vol. 3, pp. 1713–1723 (2003)
9. Younis, O., Krunz, M., Ramasubramanian, S.: Node Clustering in Wireless Sensor Networks: Recent Developments and Deployment Challenges. IEEE Network 20(3), 20–25 (2006)
10. Heinzelman, W.B., Chandrakasan, A.P., Balakrishnan, H.: Energy-Efficient Communication Protocol for Wireless Microsensor Networks. In: Proc. of the Hawaii International Conference on System Sciences (2000)
11. Soro, S., Heinzelman, W.: Cluster head election techniques for coverage preservation in wireless sensor networks. Ad Hoc Networks 7(5), 955–972 (2009)
12. Greunen, J., Rabaey, J.: Lightweight Time Synchronization for Sensor Networks. In: WSNA (2003)
13. Singh, S., Woo, M., Raghavendra, C.: Power-aware routing in mobile ad hoc networks. In: MobiCom (1998)
14. Shah, R., Rabaey, J.: Energy aware routing for low energy ad hoc Sensor Networks. In: WCNC (2002)

Analysis of Client Relay Network with Opportunistic Cooperation

Sergey Andreev[1], Olga Galinina[1],
Alexandra Lokhanova[2], and Yevgeni Koucheryavy[1]

[1] Tampere University of Technology (TUT), Finland
sergey.andreev@tut.fi, olga.galinina@tut.fi, yk@cs.tut.fi
[2] St. Petersburg Speech Technology Center (STC), Russia
alokhanova@yandex.ru

Abstract. In this work, we consider a client relay wireless system, where users cooperate to send uplink data packets. We focus on the simplest, but realistic network topology and derive the primary performance metrics, including throughput, mean packet delay, and energy efficiency. Importantly, our model enables opportunistic reception and transmission of relay packets thus allowing for many useful insights into realistic network performance. We conclude that opportunistic behavior is crucial for both spectral efficient and energy efficient system operation.

Keywords: client relay, wireless network, throughput, packet delay, energy efficiency, opportunistic cooperation.

1   Introduction and Motivation

Recent advances in wireless cellular networking are being shaped by the next-generation telecommunication standards [1] and [2]. For the emerging wireless systems, the concept of client quality-of-service becomes cornerstone, as diverse end user requirements should be satisfied simultaneously given limited network resources and variable wireless channel conditions [3].

Consequently, the concept of spectral efficiency maximization has long been dominant in wireless cellular network design [4]. However, recent research efforts tend to shift toward energy efficiency improvement [5], [6] primarily for battery-driven mobile devices [7]. We argue that accounting for spectral and energy efficiency is equally important for novel communication technologies [1], [2], which is in turn crucial for advanced resource management [8].

Recently, cooperative networking receives increasing attention from the research community [9], [10]. Typically, some network clients with favorable channel conditions transmit data more reliably and spend less power [11]. These users may help others by relaying some data packets on behalf of the users with poor communication link [12]. Previously, we demonstrated that spectral and energy efficiency may be improved if uplink cooperation among neighboring clients is forced [13]. Cooperative gain from a relay may also decrease packet transmission delays and reduce inter-cell interference. Therefore, client relay technique

X. Masip-Bruin et al. (Eds.): WWIC 2011, LNCS 6649, pp. 247–258, 2011.

is believed to be an effective solution to improve performance of future wireless cellular networks.

In this paper, we extend our earlier client relay research [13], [8] to a more practical scenario enabling opportunistic cooperation and include the relevant control parameters into consideration. As such, the relay may balance its extra energy expenditure and cooperative benefits for the network by reasonably choosing a client relay policy. In what follows, we detail the system model and analytically establish the primary performance metrics of cooperative networking, such as throughput, mean packet delay, energy expenditure, and energy efficiency. Finally, we conclude with some guidelines on choosing the client relay strategy.

2   Opportunistic Cooperative System

In this section, we briefly refresh the basic client relay system model from our previous work [13] and then extend it to the more realistic opportunistic scenario with non-mandatory reception and transmission of relay packets. For the sake of analytical tractability, we study the simplest but practical network topology (see Figure 1) and summarize our main assumptions below.

1. **The system**
    - System time is slotted
    - All communicated data packets have equal size
    - Transmission of each packet takes exactly one slot
    - Source node A is termed the originator. It generates new data packets with the mean arrival rate of λ_A packets per slot
    - Source node R is termed the relay. It generates new data packets with the mean arrival rate of λ_R packets per slot
    - Node R may eavesdrop on the transmissions from node A and store the packets from node A for the subsequent retransmission

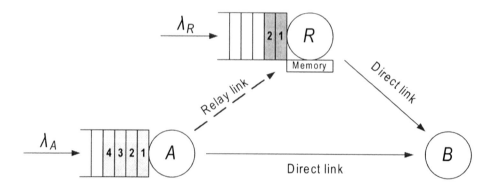

Fig. 1. Considered client relay system

  – Node R is incapable of simultaneous reception and transmission
  – Sink node B is termed the base station. It controls the system and re-
    ceives data packets from both node A and node R
  – Fair stochastic round-robin scheduler operates at node B. It alternates
    source nodes accessing the wireless channel
  – Scheduling information is immediately available to both source nodes
    over a separate channel. In practice, this information is typically avail-
    able in the downlink channel and this assumption only simplifies the
    understanding of the model
2. **The traffic**
  – Numbers of new data packets arriving to either node A or node R dur-
    ing consecutive slots are i.i.d. random variables. For simplicity, Poisson
    arrival flow is assumed. Node B has no outgoing traffic
  – Both node A and R have unbounded queues to store own data packets
  – Node R has an extra memory location to keep a single relay packet from
    node A
See Figure 2 as an example operation of the system in Figure 1, without
additional packet arrivals. Here light gray is a packet from A, whereas dark
gray is a packet from R, and the numbers correspond to sequential packet
numbers in Figure 1.
3. **The channel**
  – Communication channel is error-prone. It is based on the multi-packet
    reception channel model [10]
  – A data packet is received by the destination successfully with the con-
    stant probability. It depends only on the link type (direct or relay) and
    on which nodes are transmitting simultaneously
  – The following non-zero success probabilities are defined: p_{AB}, p_{RB}, p_{AR},
    and p_{CB}. It is expected that $p_{AR} > p_{AB}$, as well as $p_{CB} > p_{AB}$
  – Feedback information is immediately available to both source nodes over
    a separate channel. In practice, this information is typically available in
    the downlink channel and this assumption only simplifies the under-
    standing of the model
  – If the packet is not received successfully, it is retransmitted by its source.
    The maximum number of allowable retransmission attempts is unlimited

Table 1 summarizes the main system parameters. It comprises three parts: the
input parameters discussed in this section, the auxiliary parameters introduced
during the analysis, and the output parameters derived in the following section.
    The client relay network operation is summarized by Algorithm 1. Accord-
ingly, a single memory location for the eavesdropped data packets at the relay
suffices for the considered client relay system operation. Importantly, the originator is unaware of the cooperative help from the relay and the relay sends
no explicit acknowledgments to the originator by contrast to the approach from
[10]. This enables tailoring the proposed client relay model to the contemporary
cellular standards [1], [2].
    The relay improves the throughput of the originator by sacrificing its own
energy efficiency. Extra energy is spent by the relay on the eavesdropping, as

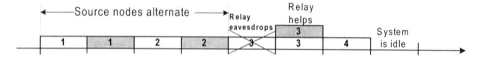

Fig. 2. Example client relay system behavior

Table 1. Input, auxiliary, and output system parameters

Notation	Parameter description
λ_A	Mean arrival rate of packets in node A
λ_R	Mean arrival rate of packets in node R
p_{AB}	Probability of successful reception from A at B when A transmits
p_{RB}	Probability of successful reception from R at B when R transmits
p_{AR}	Probability of successful reception from A at R when A transmits
p_{CB}	Probability of successful reception from A at B when A and R cooperate
p_{rx}	Probability of eavesdropping by node R
p_{tx}	Probability of cooperative transmission by node R
τ_{AR}	Mean service time of a packet from node A
τ_{RA}	Mean service time of a packet from node R
ρ_{AR}	Queue load coefficient of node A
ρ_{RA}	Queue load coefficient of node R
q_A	Mean queue length of node A
q_R	Mean queue length of node R
δ_A	Mean packet delay of node A
δ_R	Mean packet delay of node R
η_A	Mean departure rate of packets from node A (throughput of A)
η_R	Mean departure rate of packets from node R (throughput of R)
ε_A	Mean energy expenditure of node A
ε_R	Mean energy expenditure of node R
φ_A	Mean energy efficiency of node A
φ_R	Mean energy efficiency of node R

well as on the simultaneous packet transmissions with the originator. To save
some of its energy, the relay may act opportunistically. As such, in each time slot
the relay may decide not to eavesdrop on the transmissions from the originator
with probability $1 - p_{rx}$ and/or not to relay a packet with probability $1 - p_{tx}$.
The probabilities p_{rx} and p_{tx} correspond to a particular client relay policy and
may be used to trade overall system throughput for total energy expenditure.

3   Performance Evaluation

3.1   Previous Results

Our analytical approach to the performance evaluation of the client relay system
[13] is based on the notion of the packet service time. The service time of the

Require: A new slot starts
 1: Generate new packets for A and R with λ_A and λ_R
 2: {Fair stochastic round-robin scheduling}
 3: **if** both queues at A and R are not empty **then**
 4:        Slot is given to either A or R with probability 0.5
 5: **else if** queue at A is not empty **then**
 6:        Slot is given to A
 7: **else if** queue at R is not empty **then**
 8:        Slot is given to R
 9: **else**
10:        Slot is idle
11: {Packet transmission}
12: **if** slot is given to A **then**
13:        **if** current packet from A is not stored at R **then**
14:               Packet from A is successful at B with p_{AB}
15:               **if** R has decided to eavesdrop with p_{rx} **then**
16:                      Relay eavesdrops on the packet from A
17:                      Eavesdropping is successful with p_{AR}
18:               **else**
19:                      Relay stays idle
20:               **if** packet from A is successful at R **then**
21:                      Packet from A is stored at R
22:        **else**
23:               **if** R has decided to cooperate with p_{tx} **then**
24:                      Relay transmits stored packet simultaneously
                        with A (trying to improve its performance)
25:                      Packet from A is successful at B with p_{CB}
26:               **else**
27:                      Relay stays idle
28:                      Packet from A is successful at B with p_{AB}
29:        **if** packet from A is successful at B **then**
30:               Relay empties its single memory location
31:        **else**
32:               Originator retransmits in the next available slot
33: **else if** slot is given to R **then**
34:        Packet from R is successful at B with p_{RB}
35: **else**
36:        Slot is idle

Algorithm 1. Client relay network operation

tagged packet from a node starts when this packet becomes the first one in the queue of this node and ends when its successful transmission ends. We denote the service time of a packet from node A as $T_{AR}(\lambda_A, \lambda_R) \triangleq T_{AR}$, where '$\triangleq$' reads as "equal by definition". Additionally, we introduce the mean service time of a packet from node A as $\tau_{AR}(\lambda_A, \lambda_R) \triangleq \tau_{AR} = E[T_{AR}]$ (see Table 1). Further, we denote by $\tau_{AR}(\lambda_A, 0) \triangleq \tau_{A0}$ the mean service time of a packet from node A conditioning on the fact that $\lambda_R = 0$. Symmetrically, we introduce respective characteristics T_{RA}, τ_{RA}, and τ_{R0} for node R.

We established in [13] that for both system with cooperation (when $p_{AR} > 0$) and system without cooperation (when $p_{AR} = 0$) it holds that $\tau_{R0} = p_{RB}^{-1}$, whereas only for the system without cooperation it holds that $\tau_{A0} = p_{AB}^{-1}$. The derivation of τ_{A0} for the system with cooperation is a more complicated task and will be addressed below. Denote the numbers of data packets in the queues of the nodes A and R at the beginning of a particular slot t by $Q_A^{(t)}$ and $Q_R^{(t)}$ respectively. As we observe the client relay system in stationary conditions, we omit the upper index t of variables $Q_A^{(t)}$ and $Q_R^{(t)}$.

Finally, we denote the queue load coefficient of node A as $\rho_{AR}(\lambda_A, \lambda_R) \triangleq \rho_{AR}$. By definition, we have $\rho_{AR} = \Pr\{Q_A \neq 0\} = \lambda_A \tau_{AR}$. In particular, queue load coefficient of node A conditioning on the fact that $\lambda_R = 0$ may be established as $\rho_{AR}(\lambda_A, 0) \triangleq \rho_{A0} = \lambda_A \tau_{A0}$. For the system without cooperation ρ_{A0} further simplifies to $\rho_{A0} = \lambda_A / p_{AB}$. The queue load coefficients ρ_{RA} and ρ_{R0} of node R are introduced analogously. For both systems with and without cooperation ρ_{R0} further simplifies to $\rho_{R0} = \lambda_R / p_{RB}$.

Consider now the queue at node A and set $\rho_{A0} > \rho_{R0}$ as an example. The following propositions may thus be formulated [13].

Proposition 1. For the queue load coefficient of node A it holds:

$$\rho_{AR} \leq \frac{\rho_{A0}}{1 - \rho_{R0}}.$$

Proposition 2. For the queue load coefficients of nodes A and R it holds:

$$\rho_{AR} - \rho_{RA} = \rho_{A0} - \rho_{R0}.$$

Proposition 3. For the queue load coefficient of node R it holds:

$$\rho_{RA} = \rho_{AR} - \rho_{A0} + \rho_{R0} \leq \frac{\rho_{A0}}{1 - \rho_{R0}} - \rho_{A0} + \rho_{R0}.$$

The established upper bounds on ρ_{AR} and ρ_{RA} hold for both systems with and without cooperation. Below we list our previous results for the system without cooperation (when $p_{AR} = 0$) and then extend the proposed analytical approach to the system with opportunistic cooperation. Firstly, our approach is applicable for establishing the exact mean departure rate of packets from (throughput of) nodes A and R. In particular, the throughput of A is given by:

$$\eta_A = \begin{cases} \lambda_A, \text{ no saturation} \\ (1 - \lambda_R \tau_{R0})\tau_{A0}^{-1}, \text{ saturation for } A \\ (2\tau_{A0})^{-1}, \text{ saturation for } A,\ R. \end{cases}$$

The throughput of R may be derived similarly. Here, the saturation conditions are defined as follows:

- For A: $(\lambda_A \tau_{A0} + \lambda_R \tau_{R0} > 1)$ and $(\lambda_R \tau_{R0} < 0.5)$.
- For R: $(\lambda_A \tau_{A0} + \lambda_R \tau_{R0} > 1)$ and $(\lambda_A \tau_{A0} < 0.5)$.
- For both A and R: $(\lambda_A \tau_{A0} > 0.5)$ and $(\lambda_R \tau_{R0} > 0.5)$.

Secondly, we study the behavior of node A within the framework of the queueing theory. Due to the fact that the queues of nodes A and R are mutually dependent, the notorious Pollazek-Khinchine formula may not be used to obtain the exact mean queue length of node A. We, however, apply this formula to establish the approximate value of the mean queue length of node A as:

$$q_A \cong \rho_{AR} + \frac{\lambda_A^2 E[T_{AR}^2]}{2(1 - \rho_{AR})}.$$

We introduce the following auxiliary probability:

$$\gamma_A \triangleq \Pr\{Q_R \neq 0 | Q_A \neq 0\} = \frac{\Pr\{Q_R \neq 0, Q_A \neq 0\}}{\Pr\{Q_A \neq 0\}}.$$

Clearly, the scheduler either assigns the subsequent slot to node R with probability $0.5\gamma_A$ or assigns it to node A with the complementary probability $1 - 0.5\gamma_A$. After some derivations and accounting for the above propositions, we establish:

$$0.5\gamma_A = 1 - \frac{\rho_{A0}}{\rho_{AR}}.$$

We may obtain the following distribution for the service time of a packet from node A:

$$\Pr\{T_{AR} = n\} = p_{AB}(1 - 0.5\gamma_A)(1 - p_{AB}(1 - 0.5\gamma_A))^{n-1}.$$

The above expression accounts for the fact that out of n slots spent to serve a packet from node A the last slot was assigned to node A and its transmission in this slot was successful. The previous $n - 1$ slots were either not assigned to node A or its transmissions in these slots were unsuccessful.

Calculating the first and the second moment of the service time ($E[T_{AR}]$ and $E[T_{AR}^2]$), accounting for Pollazek-Khinchine formula and also using Little's formula in the form $q_A = \lambda_A \delta_A$, it is now easy to approximate the mean packet delay of node A as:

$$\delta_A \cong \frac{\rho_{AR}}{\lambda_A} + \frac{\lambda_A(2 - p_{AB}(1 - 0.5\gamma_A))}{2(1 - \rho_{AR})p_{AB}^2(1 - 0.5\gamma_A)^2}.$$

The performance metrics of node R may be calculated analogously, due to the symmetric nature of the respective direct links. Additionally, we may obtain the exact value of the mean energy expenditure of e.g. node A as:

$$\varepsilon_A = P_{TX}\eta_A\tau_{A0} + P_I(1 - \eta_A\tau_{A0}).$$

Here P_{TX} is the average power that is spent by a node in the packet transmission state, whereas P_I is the average power that is spent by the same node in the idle state. As such, the mean energy efficiencies of nodes A and R readily follow as $\varphi_A = \eta_A/\varepsilon_A$ and $\varphi_R = \eta_R/\varepsilon_R$ respectively.

3.2   Opportunistic Cooperative System

Studying the system with opportunistic cooperation, we firstly consider an important special case when the queue at node R is always empty. We establish the distribution of the number of slots required to serve a packet from node A. By using the obtained distribution, we then generalize the proposed approach for the case of non-empty queue at node R. All the respective performance metrics for the system with opportunistic cooperation are marked by symbol '*' in the rest of the text.

The queue at the relay is always empty. ($\lambda_R = 0$). Similarly to the derivations from the previous subsection, we may establish the sought distribution for the service time of a packet from node A as:

$$\Pr\{T^*_{A0} = n\} = X(1 - \tilde{p}_{CB})^{n-1} - Y[(1 - p_{AB})(1 - p_{AR} \cdot p_{rx})]^{n-1},$$

where $\tilde{p}_{CB} = p_{CB} \cdot p_{tx} + (1 - p_{tx})p_{AB}$,

$$X = \frac{p_{AR} \cdot p_{rx}(1 - p_{AB})\tilde{p}_{CB}}{1 - \tilde{p}_{CB} - (1 - p_{AB})(1 - p_{AR} \cdot p_{rx})}, \quad \text{and } Y = X - p_{AB}.$$

Coming now to the mean service time, we have the following:

$$\tau^*_{A0} = \frac{\tilde{p}_{CB} + (1 - p_{AB})p_{AR} \cdot p_{rx}}{\tilde{p}_{CB}[p_{AB} + (1 - p_{AB})p_{AR} \cdot p_{rx}]}.$$

The queue at the relay is not always empty. ($\lambda_R > 0$).

Omitting lengthy derivations, we give the respective distribution for the service time of a packet from node A as:

$$\Pr\{T^*_{AR} = n\} = X(1 - 0.5\gamma^*_A)(1 - \tilde{p}_{CB}(1 - 0.5\gamma^*_A))^{n-1} - \\ -Y(1 - 0.5\gamma^*_A)(1 - p_A(1 - 0.5\gamma^*_A))^{n-1},$$

where $0.5\gamma^*_A = 1 - \rho^*_{A0}/\rho^*_{AR}$ and also $p_A = p_{AB} + p_{AR} \cdot p_{rx}(1 - p_{AB})$ for brevity.

Queue load coefficients of nodes A and R (ρ^*_{AR} and ρ^*_{RA}) may be calculated similarly to the respective parameters for the system without cooperation accounting for the fact that $\rho^*_{A0} \triangleq \lambda_A \tau^*_{A0}$, where the expression for τ^*_{A0} is given above.

Finally, calculating the second moment of the service time, we derive the resulting expression for the approximate mean packet delay of node A as:

$$\delta^*_A \simeq \frac{\rho^*_{AR}}{\lambda_A} + \frac{\lambda_A}{2(1 - \rho^*_{AR})(1 - 0.5\gamma^*_A)^2} \times \\ \times \left[X \cdot \frac{2 - \tilde{p}_{CB}(1 - 0.5\gamma^*_A)}{\tilde{p}^3_{CB}} - Y \cdot \frac{2 - p_A(1 - 0.5\gamma^*_A)}{p^3_A} \right],$$

where X and Y were also given above.

Accounting for τ^*_{A0}, the resulting approximation for the mean packet delay δ^*_R of node R, as well as expressions for the throughput η^*_A and η^*_R of nodes A

and R in the system with cooperation are similar to the respective metrics in the system without cooperation from the previous subsection.

Analogously, the mean energy expenditure of node A in the considered case is given by:

$$\varepsilon_A^* = P_{TX}\eta_A^*\tau_{A0}^* + P_I(1 - \eta_A^*\tau_{A0}^*),$$

whereas the mean energy expenditure of node R may be calculated as:

$$\varepsilon_R^* = P_{TX}\left(\eta_R^*\tau_{R0} + \eta_A^* p_{tx} \cdot \frac{1-p_{AB}\tau_{A0}^*}{\tilde{p}_{CB}-p_{AB}}\right) + P_{RX}p_{rx}\left(\eta_A^*\tau_{A0}^* - \eta_A^* \cdot \frac{1-p_{AB}\tau_{A0}^*}{\tilde{p}_{CB}-p_{AB}}\right) +$$
$$+P_I\left(1 - \eta_R^*\tau_{R0} - \eta_A^*\tau_{A0}^* p_{rx} - (p_{tx} - p_{rx})\eta_A^* \cdot \frac{1-p_{AB}\tau_{A0}^*}{\tilde{p}_{CB}-p_{AB}}\right)$$

Here P_{RX} is the average power that is spent by a node in the packet reception state. As before, the mean energy efficiencies of nodes A and R are given by expressions $\varphi_A^* = \eta_A^*/\varepsilon_A^*$ and $\varphi_R^* = \eta_R^*/\varepsilon_R^*$ respectively.

4   Numerical Results and Conclusions

In this section, we validate our analytical model derived in the previous section. We use our own time-driven simulator described in [14] and [15]. Partly following [10], the simulation parameters are set as: $p_{AB} = 0.3$, $p_{RB} = 0.7$, $p_{AR} = 0.4$, $p_{CB} = 0.5$, $\lambda_R = 0.15$, whereas λ_A is varied across the system stability region. Additionally, we normalize power consumption values from [16] by P_{TX} to obtain $P_{TX} = 1.00$, $P_{RX} = 0.85$, and $P_I = 0.70$.

With respect to opportunistic cooperation, we fix the probability of cooperative transmission $p_{tx} = 1$ and study the influence of the probability of eavesdropping p_{rx}. In practice, it is more reasonable to control the opportunistic cooperation via p_{rx} as whenever a packet is eavesdropped by the relay, it is transmitted together with the originator in the next available slot. Thus, the time spent by the relay packet in the memory location of node R is minimized.

The three cases are contrasted: no cooperation ($p_{rx} = 0$), conventional mandatory cooperation ($p_{rx} = 1$), and opportunistic cooperation ($p_{rx} = 0.5$). Firstly, we study the mean packet delay in Figure 3. We notice that the proposed approximation demonstrates excellent accordance with the simulation results. Additionally, mandatory cooperation leads to the maximum delay reduction for the originator, whereas opportunistic cooperation shows moderate mean packet delay decrease.

By contrast, Figure 4 demonstrates the drawback of the mandatory cooperation. Despite considerable delay improvement, using it results also in the highest relay energy expenditure. The relay may thus choose to cooperate opportunistically by falling back to e.g. $p_{rx} = 0.5$ and save its power. Consequently, this will lead to some energy expenditure growth for the originator, as it would have to transmit more packets on its own. As such, opportunistic cooperation makes an important practical mechanism to balance extra relay energy expenditure and cooperative benefits for the entire system.

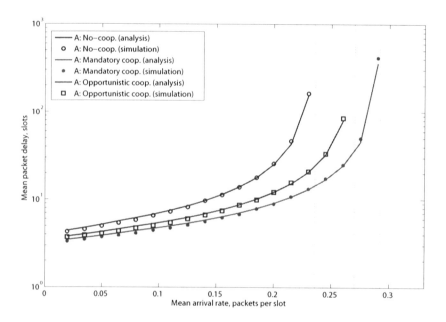

Fig. 3. Mean packet delay dependence

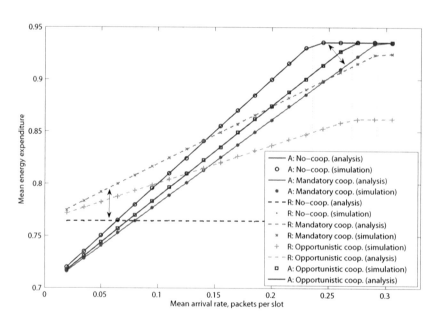

Fig. 4. Mean energy expenditure dependence

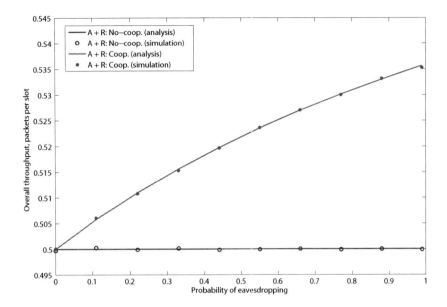

Fig. 5. Overall system throughput dependence

Finally, in Figure 5 we address the maximum throughput gain of the cooperative system by varying p_{rx} across its feasible range in saturation. We plot the overall throughput of both nodes A and R to conclude that client relay technique may considerably improve the performance of cellular wireless networks.

The proliferation of wireless networks introduces novel important research directions, including client cooperation, energy efficient communication, multi-radio co-existence, spectrum aggregation techniques, and others. These directions are insufficiently addressed by the conventional simulation methodology and existing analytical models, which only cover static or semi-static cellular environments [3]. In this paper, we developed a tractable dynamic model that may be useful to study the basic trade-offs of the cooperative networking. Its development toward more realistic traffic arrival patterns is the direction of our future work.

References

1. IEEE Std 802.16m (D9), Amendment to IEEE Standard for Local and metropolitan area networks. Advanced Air Interface
2. LTE Release 10 & beyond (LTE-Advanced)
3. Andreev, S., Koucheryavy, Y., Himayat, N., Gonchukov, P., Turlikov, A.: Active-mode power optimization in OFDMA-based wireless networks. In: Proc. of the IEEE BWA Workshop of Globecom (2010)
4. Song, G., Li, Y.: Asymptotic throughput analysis for channel-aware scheduling. IEEE Transactions on Communications 54(10), 1827–1834 (2006)

5. Benini, L., Bogliolo, A., de Micheli, G.: A survey of design techniques for system-level dynamic power management. IEEE Transactions on VLSI Systems 8, 299–316 (2000)
6. Schurgers, C.: Energy-Aware Wireless Communications. PhD thesis, University of California, Los Angeles (2002)
7. Miao, G., Himayat, N., Li, G.Y.: Energy-efficient link adaptation in frequency-selective channels. IEEE Transactions on Communications 58(2), 545–554 (2010)
8. Andreev, S., Galinina, O., Vinel, A.: Performance evaluation of a three node client relay system. International Journal of Wireless Networks and Broadband Technologies (to appear, 2011)
9. Tannious, R., Nosratinia, A.: Spectrally efficient relay selection with limited feedback. IEEE Journal on Selected Areas in Communications 26(8), 1419–1428 (2008)
10. Rong, B., Ephremides, A.: On opportunistic cooperation for improving the stability region with multipacket reception. In: Proc. of the NET-COOP Conference, pp. 45–59 (2009)
11. Stuber, G.L.: Principles of Mobile Communication. Kluwer Academic Publishers, Norwell (2001)
12. Cui, S., Goldsmith, A., Bahai, A.: Energy-efficiency of MIMO and cooperative MIMO techniques in sensor networks. IEEE Journal on Selected Areas in Communications 22(6), 1089–1098 (2004)
13. Andreev, S., Galinina, O., Turlikov, A.: Basic client relay model for wireless cellular networks. In: Proc. of the ICUMT Congress (2010)
14. Pyattaev, A., Andreev, S., Vinel, A., Sokolov, B.: Client relay simulation model for centralized wireless networks. In: Proc. of the EUROSIM Congress (2010)
15. Pyattaev, A., Andreev, S., Koucheryavy, Y., Moltchanov, D.: Some modeling approaches for client relay networks. In: Proc. of the IEEE CAMAD Workshop (2010)
16. Turck, K.D., Andreev, S., Vuyst, S.D., Fiems, D., Wittevrongel, S., Bruneel, H.: Performance of the IEEE 802.16e sleep mode mechanism in the presence of bidirectional traffic. In: Proc. of the IEEE ICC Conference (2009)

Enhanced OFDM Distributed Antenna Systems through Power Redistribution

Wei-Peng Chen, Chenxi Zhu, and Takao Naito

Fujitsu Laboratories of America
1240 East Arques Ave, Sunnyvale, CA 94085, U.S.A
{wei-peng.chen,chenxi.zhu,Takao.Naito}@us.fujitsu.com

Abstract. Distributed antenna systems (DAS) have the advantages of achieving low system costs in deployment, operation, and management. While a simple blanket transmission scheme in DAS shows poor performance, several practical limitations prevent the beamforming scheme in DAS from being adopted in the existing systems. By taking advantages of spatial proximity and diversity between different radio equipments (REs) and mobile stations in DAS, we propose a novel approach to enhance the system capacity of orthogonal frequency division multiplexing (OFDM) DAS through power coordination between REs. In comparison with standalone base station deployment, blanket transmission scheme, and beamforming scheme, our proposal achieves higher system capacity by 35.9%, 82.2% and 14.2%, respectively.

Keywords: DAS, LTE, OFDM, power redistribution.

1 Introduction

A Distributed antenna systems (DAS) is "a network of spatially separated antenna nodes connected to a common source via a transport medium that provides wireless service within a geographic area or structure" [1]. DAS has been broadly adopted in the current wireless cellular communication systems to fulfill numerous challenging deployment requirements [2][3]. In DAS, Radio Equipments (RE) are distributed to different locations and connected to a central control unit, Radio Equipment Control (REC) over optical fiber. Common Public Radio Interface (CPRI) [4] is the industry de facto standard of the interface between REC and RE and the data communicated over CPRI link are in-phase/quadrature (I/Q) samples of baseband signals. REC is the same as a standalone base station (BS) except without the antenna functionalities, whereas the basic functionalities of RE include digital-to-analog (D/A) and analog-to-digital (A/D) conversions, and radio frequency (RF) operations.

The main reason for adopting DAS is to reduce the operation and deployment costs through reduction of radiated power and flexible deployment strategy. To achieve satisfactory coverage, either the sheer number of low power BSs or a few high power BSs are deployed. The total radiated power to cover the same area by many antenna elements (e.g. DAS) rather than a single antenna is actually reduced [5]. In addition, compared to the traditional BS architecture where REC and REs are co-located, operators can adopt a more cost-effective strategy to deploy DAS such that massive

X. Masip-Bruin et al. (Eds.): WWIC 2011, LNCS 6649, pp. 259–271, 2011.

RECs can be located at a central office and light-weighted REs can be easily installed at desired locations [6]. The cost of site acquisition to install an RE instead of a BS is much relieved. Yet more benefits of the DAS with multiple REs in contrast with a single RE controlled by an REC are as follows: First, the system cost becomes lower since only one costly REC is used along with multiple inexpensive REs to cover a wide range of area. Second, less frequent inter-cell handovers are expected because the area covered by different REs under the same REC is considered as the same cell. Third, the management cost is reduced due to less number of cells covering the same area. The amount of control packets exchanged between radio access networks and core networks decreases accordingly with the reduced number of cells and handovers.

The simplest transmission strategy in DAS with multiple REs is called **blanket transmission** [3] where a single set of I/Q samples are transmitted/received by REC to/from different REs on the downlink/uplink (DL/UL) connection, respectively. However, its drawback is that the system capacity is not improved in comparison to distributed standalone BSs because the array gain of multiple antennas in DAS is not fully exploited. On the other hand, in the **beamforming** scheme [8][9], REC exchanges different sets of I/Q samples with different REs. In the ideal beamforming scheme with the knowledge of detailed channel state information (CSI), the signals received from different antennas can be combined coherently to acquire better SINR (signal to interference-plus-noise ratio). Nevertheless, its main drawback is that the detailed CSI at transmitter, receiver, or both is required. Although detailed CSI is assumed available in the previous works [2][3][7][8][9][10], the assumption does not always hold true. RE-specific reference signal is not designed in most standard specifications of cellular radio networks such as 3GPP Long Term Evolution (LTE) [11] or IEEE 802.16 [12] to support multiple REs in DAS. Without RE-specific reference signals, MSs are not aware of the existence of multiple REs. Therefore, estimating each channel response between individual REs and MS is not feasible at MS. Even if RE-specific reference signals are allowed, the overheads of additional reference signals on the control channel are considerable.

In this paper, we propose a novel approach to redistribute power of subcarriers in each RE without the requirement of detailed CSI at either the transmitter side or receiver side. The concept of our proposal is similar to the waterfilling power allocation [16] such that more power is allocated to a subcarrier when its channel quality is good. However, unlike the waterfilling scheme which requires the detailed CSI to decide the power allocations for all the antennas located at the same location, our proposal needs only the approximate estimate of channel response rather than the detailed CSI and it is applicable to DAS with multiple REs. Since REs in DAS are usually placed far apart, there exists a significant difference between the channel gains from different REs to an MS. Therefore, by exploiting the spatial proximity between REs and MS, it is sufficient to estimate the dominant part of channel response, i.e. slow fading, in order to capture the differences of channel responses in different links. In other words, it is no longer critical to learn the volatile component of the channel response, i.e. fast fading, and consequently RE-specific reference signals are not needed in our proposal. Lastly in this paper we focus on orthogonal frequency division multiplexing (OFDM) systems by virtue of the fact that OFDM has become the fundamental technology in the next generation wireless systems such as LTE, IEEE 802.16, and IEEE 802.11n [13].

The rest of the paper is organized as follows. In Sec. 2, we describe the problems and motivations behind the proposal. An overview of the procedures in the proposal is introduced in Sec. 3 followed by the detailed analysis of the baseline schemes and our proposal presented in Sec. 4. Simulation results and performance comparison based on system level simulation are shown in Sec. 5.

2   Problems and Motivation

2.1   Problems in Blanket Transmission and Beamforming Schemes

In the blanket transmission scheme the same set of I/Q samples is transmitted between REC and REs. In the DL, each RE simply relays the received DL I/Q samples to the next hop RE. In the UL, a RE adds its own I/Q samples to those received from the upstream RE and then send the combined data to its downstream RE (towards the REC). A delay is inserted to compensate for the CPRI propagation and processing delay at each RE. However, a drawback of the blanket transmission is that the array gain of multiple REs in DAS is not fully exploited because the received DL and UL signals are not added up coherently at MS and BS, respectively. In the DL, the channel experienced by an MS is the sum of the channel responses of each individual RE to the MS because the MS cannot estimate the individual CSI between each RE to itself. This is an incoherent operation because no calibration is performed to synchronize the phases of different channel responses. Similarly, the processing of UL signals here is not a coherent operation because REs only compensate the delays caused by both CPRI propagation delay and processing time at REs but not the differences in both magnitude and phase of channels. Consequently the UL array gain of multiple REs in the blanket transmission scheme is not fully exploited.

In the beamforming schemes, different sets of I/Q samples are exchanged between REC and REs. The transmit beamforming scheme [8][9] includes the linear precoding before signals are sent out from the transmitter while the receive beamforming scheme applies the equalization to the received signals at the receiver. The idea of the beamforming schemes is to maximize the array gains of multiple antennas by combining signals of different antennas in a coherent manner. Nevertheless, if each RE does not broadcast its exclusive RE reference signals, the receiver is unable to estimate the individual channel response from different REs. Therefore, the equalization operation cannot be applied at MSs and receiver beamforming is not feasible. Similarly, it is difficult to adopt transmit beamforming in practical systems because the detailed DL CSI is not available at transmitters to compute the precoding matrix. This motivates us to develop solutions not dependent on the detailed CSI.

2.3   Motivation of the Proposal

Three key components to determine channel response are path loss, shadowing, and multipath fading [14]. While the first two elements, path loss and shadowing, are considered as slow fading or large scale fading, multipath fading is called fast fading or small scale fading since it can change rapidly in both time and spatial domains. Besides, the magnitude of fast fading is much smaller than that of slow fading [15]. In contrast with the effects of shadowing and multipath fading which are random processes, path loss is the most dominant component in channel response. Moreover, it is a deterministic function of the locations of the transmitter and receiver, and the properties of the antennas and environment. Under the system of DAS with multiple REs, the distances between an MS and different REs are usually different and so are their corresponding channel responses. The differences in the path losses from different REs are even more significant compared to the system with multiple co-located antennas. As the magnitude of the channel gain is dominated by the effect of path loss, higher channel gain is seen between an MS and a closer RE. The main idea behind our proposal is to take advantage of spatial proximity and diversity by applying different power allocations at different REs based on the estimation of slow fading components rather than detailed CSI. The RE closer to an MS uses higher power in the subcarriers allocated to this MS, whereas the RE further away from the MS reduces the power of these subcarriers and saves the unused power to the subcarriers allocated to other MSs. The traditional OFDM systems adopt uniform power distribution to all subcarriers because there is a limited gain to apply non-uniform power distribution in cellular systems. On the contrary in the system with multiple REs, non-uniform power distribution could enhance DL SINR at MSs because the gain of the power amplification from a closer RE outweighs the loss of the reduced power from a distant RE.

3   Overview of the Procedures in the Proposal

The proposed power redistribution scheme consists of 4 stages of procedures.

Stage 1 - Channel Estimation: The first stage of our proposal is to estimate the magnitude of DL channel response from the measured magnitude of UL channel response based on the reciprocity principle. The estimation is robust since slow fading does not change rapidly. In FDD systems, the difference in the magnitude of DL and UL path loss is a constant term which is a deterministic function of carrier frequency and antenna settings. Similarly in TDD systems, by assuming that an MS's position does not dramatically change in DL and UL subframe, the difference in the DL and UL path loss is a constant term which is a deterministic function of antenna settings. In our proposal, each RE measures the average received power of the subcarriers allocated to the same MS and deliver this information to REC over CPRI control channel [4].

Stage 2 - Scheduling: REC executes a scheduling algorithm to allocate subcarriers in a channel to MSs. Here we decouple the decision of scheduling subcarriers from the problem of subcarrier power redistribution because the joint power and subcarrier assignment problem is NP-hard. Any scheduling algorithm can be used.

Stage 3 – Power Redistribution Computation: Based on the measured UL power, REC redistributes the DL power to subcarriers applied in each RE to maximize the system capacity. There could be several strategies to apply power redistribution. One possibility based on maximum ratio combination (MRC) is that the DL power of the subcarriers assigned to an MS at an RE is proportional to the magnitude of the UL channel gain of the same MS measured at that RE. Our proposal is based on maximizing the system capacity. The details of the optimization formulation are presented in Sec. 4.4. A simple example illustrating the main idea of power redistribution is shown in Fig. 1. Suppose that one REC controls two cascaded REs and there are two MSs located in the area served by these two REs. To simplify the scenario, the scheduling algorithm at REC allocates the equal number of subcarriers to these two MSs in a frame. We further assume that the relationship of the magnitudes of channel gain between two REs and two MSs are as follows:

RE1↔MS1 : RE1↔MS2 = 2 : 1 and RE2↔MS1 : RE2↔MS2 = 1 : 2

Then based on the principle of MRC, the power allocated to MS1's subcarriers by RE1 is boosted from 1/2 to 2/3 of total power while the power allocated to MS2's subcarriers by RE1 is reduced from 1/2 to 1/3 of RE1's total output power. Similarly, the power allocated to MS2's subcarriers by RE2 is increased from 1/2 to 2/3 of RE2's total output power while the power allocated to MS1's subcarriers by RE2 is decreased from 1/2 to 1/3 of RE2's total output power.

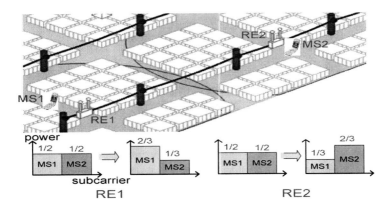

Fig. 1. An example showing the idea of power redistribution

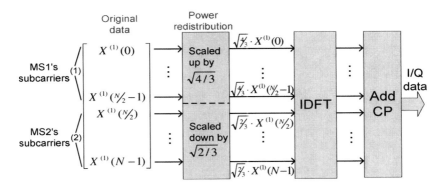

Fig. 2. Power amplification or attenuation at RE1

Stage 4 – Applying Power Redistribution: After REC computes each RE's power allocation, power amplification or attenuation is applied to the data in the frequency domain before inverse discrete Fourier transform (IDFT) operation. Traditional OFDM systems apply the same power to each subcarrier. By contrast, in our proposal after DL power redistribution, the signal ($X^{(i)}$) is scaled up or down proportionally subject to the constraint that the total transmission power from each RE remains the same. In the example of Fig. 1, RE1 scales up the signal $(X^{(1)})$ carried on MS1's subcarriers by $\sqrt{4/3}$ while the signal carried on MS2's subcarriers is scaled down by $\sqrt{2/3}$ to maintain the same total output power at RE1. Fig. 2 illustrates the operation of power amplification/attenuation.

4   Detailed Analysis of the Baseline Schemes and Our Proposal

The analysis in this paper is based on OFDM systems. In particular we focus on LTE [11]. The DL LTE is based on OFDMA (orthogonal frequency division multiple access) while the UL is based on SC-FDMA (single-carrier frequency division multiple access). We focus on the analysis on the DL in this paper. The detailed analysis on the basic LTE DL processing as well as two baseline schemes of blanket transmission and beamforming will be compared with the proposed scheme.

4.1   LTE DL Processing

LTE DL processing is shown in Fig. 3. The left and right hand side are the processing at the transmitter (i.e. BS) and receiver (i.e. MS), respectively. REC's DL data at each symbol are $X[0], ..., X[N-1]$. IDFT is applied fist to obtain the time domain data: $x[0], ..., x[N-1]$. Then REC sends the time domain data along with the cyclic prefix (CP) in the format of I/Q samples to RE. Then RE transmits the time domain I/Q data over the air to MSs. On the MS side, first $N+G$ samples are received at each symbol: $y^{cp}[0]$, $y^{cp}[1], ..., y^{cp}[N+G-1]$ where G is the length of CP. After removing CP and applying N-point FFT (Fast Fourier Transform), N point frequency domain data, $Y[0], ..., Y[N-1]$, are obtained at MS. Next a frequency domain equalizer (FDE) is applied to N-point frequency domain data in order to offset the effect of channel response caused to the transmitted data and we obtain: $\hat{X}[0], \cdots, \hat{X}[N-1]$.

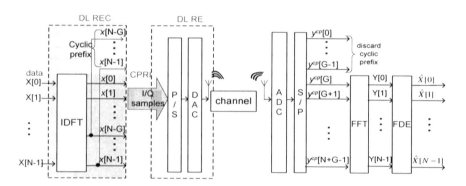

Fig. 3. LTE DL processing

4.2   Analysis of DL Processing for Blanket Transmission Scheme

In the blanket transmission scheme the same set of signals is sent from N_R REs to a MS where N_R is the number of REs controlled by an REC in a cell. The signal of subcarrier k received at MS consists of the signals coming from N_R REs as:

$$Y[k] = \sum_{r=1}^{N_R} \sqrt{\frac{P_{r,k}}{N_T}} H_r(k) \cdot X[k] + \sum_{i=1}^{N_I} \sqrt{\frac{P_{i,k}}{N_T}} H_i(k) \cdot X_i[k] + N[k] \tag{1}$$

where N_I is the number of interference BSs (including both intra-cell and inter-cell interference) and N_T is the number of transmitting antennas at each RE. $N[k]$ is the noise power of subcarrier k. $P_{r,k}$ is the received power of the subcarrier k at the r-th RE by considering path loss and shadowing:

$$P_{r,k} = P_{r,k}^T \cdot G_r \cdot 10^{X_r/10} / L(d_r) \tag{2}$$

where $P_{r,k}^T$ is the transmission power assigned to subcarrier k at r-th RE, G_r is the antenna gain (excluding shadowing) between the MS and r-th RE, X_r is the lognormal shadowing between the MS and r-th RE, $L(d_r)$ is the path loss from r-th RE to MS at distance d_r. $H_r(k)$ in Eq. (1) is the channel response between r-th RE and MS with inclusion of multipath fading only because both path loss and shadowing have been incorporated into the expression of $P_{r,k}$.

As the MS is unaware of the existence of multiple REs, the channel response it sees is the combined channel responses from all REs. Thus, the corresponding FDE for subcarrier k is:

$$FDE[k] = \Phi[k]^H = \sum_{r'=1}^{N_R} H_{r'}[k]^H \tag{3}$$

Lastly, the SINR, the ratio of signal power to interference-plus-noise power, of subcarrier k can be represented as:

$$SINR(k) = \frac{\sum_{r=1}^{N_R} \frac{P_{r,k}}{N_T} \cdot \left\| \Phi(k)^H \cdot H_r(k) \right\|^2}{\sum_{i=1}^{N_I} \frac{P_{i,k}}{N_T} \cdot \left\| \Phi(k)^H \cdot H_i(k) \right\|^2 + \left\| \Phi(k) \right\|^2 \cdot \sigma^2} \tag{4}$$

Note that the numerator of SINR can be decomposed into two terms: in-phase component $\sum_{r=1}^{N_R} \frac{P_{r,k}}{N_T} \cdot \left| H_r(k) \right|^2$ and out-of-phase component $\sum_{\substack{j,j=1 \\ i \ne j}}^{N_R} \frac{P_{r,k}}{N_T} H_i(k) \cdot H_j(k)^H \cdot$ The first term is the sum of Frobenius norm of individual channel responses while the second term is the sum of the interactions between different channel responses of different REs. Since in the blanket transmission scheme MS lacks the information of individual CSI, signals from different REs received at MS cannot be added up coherently. Because the phases of different channel responses, $H_i[k]$ and $H_j[k]$, are not synchronized, the second term causes the destruction of the overall SNR. That is, the transmitter array gain of multiple transmitting antennas at REs is not fully exploited.

4.3 DL Processing Equation for Beamforming Scheme

Even though beamforming scheme [8][9] is not considered as a practical method in DAS, for comparison purpose, in this subsection we analyze the DL performance of the beamforming scheme by assuming that the detailed DL CSI and UL CSI are available. The first step in the beamforming scheme is that the transmit weighting coefficient (or precoding) vector $W_{tr}(k)$ of subcarrier k at RE r is applied to input data, $X[k]$, before IDFT operation: $\tilde{X}_r[k] = W_{tr}(k) \cdot X[k]$. The vector of the precoding coefficients for all the REs, $W_t(k) = [W_{t_1}(k), \dots, W_{t_{N_R}}(k)]$, can be obtained by computing first N_R eigenvectors of the matrix $\Psi_k^H \cdot R_{Z,k}^{-1} \cdot \Psi_k$ where $R_{z,k} = \sum_{i=1}^{N_I} P_{i,k} H_i(k) H_i^H(k) + N_0 \cdot I$ and $\Psi_k = [\sqrt{P_{1,k}} \cdot H_1(k) \quad \sqrt{P_{2,k}} \cdot H_2(k) \quad \cdots \quad \sqrt{P_{N_R,k}} \cdot H_{N_R}(k)]$. Ideally in the transmit beamforming scheme, both the magnitude and phase are amplified coherently. MS computes the receiver spatial equalizer matrix $W_r(k)$ as:

$$W_r(k) = \frac{\sum_{r=1}^{N_R} \sqrt{P_{r,k}} H_r(k) W_{1,r}^H(k)}{\sum_{r=1}^{N_R} P_{r,k} H_r(k) H_r^H(k) + \sum_{i=1}^{N_I} P_{i,k} H_i(k) H_i^H(k) + N_0 \cdot I} \quad (5)$$

The SINR of subcarrier k in the beamforming scheme is:

$$SINR(k) = \frac{\sum_{r=1}^{N_R} \frac{P_{r,k}}{N_T} \cdot \left\| W_r(k)^H \cdot H_r(k) \right\|^2}{\sum_{i=1}^{N_I} \frac{P_{i,k}}{N_T} \cdot \left\| W_r(k)^H \cdot H_i(k) \right\|^2 + \left\| W_r(k) \right\|^2 \cdot \sigma^2} \quad (6)$$

Note that the beamforming method considered here is **carrier non-cooperative** approach. That is, each subcarrier is *independently* processed. Therefore, it does not adjust the power allocation similar to waterfilling power allocation [16] across different subcarriers. In DAS, there exists a significant difference in the magnitude of the channel gains of different subcarriers allocated to different MSs. Therefore, the optimization within one subcarrier like the carrier non-cooperative beamforming scheme is not an optimal solution. On the other hand, the carrier corporative method by considering all subcarriers is computationally prohibitive.

4.4   Analysis of the Proposal

The goal of our proposal is to maximize the system capacity of DAS via properly assigning power of subcarriers at different REs. The coefficients of power amplification/attenuation of subcarriers are determined by solving an optimization problem of maximizing the system capacity. The input of the optimization problem is based on the magnitude of UL power without the requirement of detailed CSI. The output of the optimization problem is the magnitude of power amplification/attenuation of all subcarriers, expressed as $g_{r,k}$ for subcarrier k at the r-th RE. The received signal at MS after FFT operation can be expressed as:

$$Y[k] = \sum_{r=1}^{N_R} \sqrt{\frac{P_{r,k}}{N_T}} H_r(k) \cdot g_{r,k} \cdot X[k] + \sum_{i=1}^{N_I} \sqrt{\frac{P_{i,k}}{N_T}} H_i(k) \cdot g_{i,k} \cdot X_i[k] + N[k] \quad (7)$$

The corresponding FDE at MS side is:

$$F\,DE\,[k] = \Phi[k]^H = \sum_{r'=1}^{N_R} g_{r',k} \cdot H_{r'}[k]^H \quad (8)$$

Finally the DL SINR of subcarrier k in the proposed scheme is:

$$SINR(k) = \frac{\sum_{r=1}^{N_R} \frac{P_{r,k}}{N_T} \cdot \left\| \Phi(k)^H \cdot g_{r,k} \cdot H_r(k) \right\|^2}{\sum_{i=1}^{N_I} \frac{P_{i,k}}{N_T} \cdot \left\| \Phi(k)^H \cdot g_{i,k} \cdot H_i(k) \right\|^2 + \left\| \Phi(k) \right\|^2 \cdot \sigma^2} \quad (9)$$

By comparing the SINR equation of the proposed scheme with that of the blanket transmission scheme shown in Eq. (4), the only difference is the coefficient of power gain $g_{r,k}$ exists in both numerator and denominator. Based on the information theory, the system capacity of subcarrier k can be estimated as a function of SINR: $C(k) = \ln(1 + SINR(k))$. The objective of the optimization problem is to find out the power amplification gain $g_{r,k}$ (or square of gain, $G_{r,k} = g_{r,k}^2$) such that the overall system capacity is maximized. Note that the power gain cannot be amplified indefinitely since the total transmission power per RE is limited to its maximum output power, P_T. Therefore, the constraint function in the optimization problem is that the total transmission power from each RE is less than or equal to P_T. Besides P_T, the given inputs of the optimization problem also include $P_{r,k}^{UL}$, the received UL power of subcarrier k at r-th RE. The DL received power at MS, $P_{r,k}^{DL} = c \cdot P_{r,k}^{UL}$, is proportional to the UL received power at RE, $P_{r,k}^{UL}$, where c is a constant factor to calibrate the differences between the antenna gains of DL and UL connections. Thus, the DL SINR formula shown above can be presented as a function of UL received power. Finally, the capacity of subcarrier k with power amplification can be expressed as:

$$C(k) = \ln(1 + \frac{\sum_{r=1}^{N_R} \frac{c \cdot P_{r,k}^{UL}}{N_T} \cdot \left\| \Phi(k)^H \cdot g_{r,k} \cdot H_r(k) \right\|^2}{\sum_{i=1}^{N_I} \frac{c \cdot P_{i,k}^{UL}}{N_T} \cdot \left\| \Phi(k)^H \cdot g_{i,k} \cdot H_i(k) \right\|^2 + \left\| \Phi(k) \right\|^2 \cdot \sigma^2}) \tag{10}$$

To simplify the problem, in this paper we only consider the optimization problem without inter-cell interferences:

$$\max_{\{g_{r,k}\}} \sum_{k=1}^{N} c(k) = \sum_{k=1}^{N} \ln(1 + \frac{\sum_{r=1}^{N_R} \frac{c \cdot P_{r,k}^{UL}}{N_T} \left\| \Phi(k)^H \cdot g_{r,k} \cdot H_r(k) \right\|^2}{\left\| \Phi(k) \right\|^2 \cdot \sigma^2})) \tag{11}$$

$$s.t. \sum_{k=1}^{N} g_{r,k}^2 \cdot P_{r,k}^{TX} \leq P_T \quad \forall r = 1, \ldots, N_R$$

We can further simplify the objective and constraint functions in Eq. (11) based on the following two arguments:

• First we restrict that the same power amplification gain, $g_{r,u(k)}$, is applied to the subcarriers associated with the same MS u, where $u(k)$ is the mapping function (i.e. scheduling) of the subcarrier k to the MS u. Such an assumption is reasonable because the path loss between the BS and the MS would not change much in these subcarriers. With this simplification, the number of variables, $g_{r,k}^2 (= G_{r,k})$, in the optimization problem is reduced from $N_R \cdot N$ to $N_R \cdot N_{MS}$ where N_{MS} is the number of MSs scheduled to receive data in one frame. Thus, the power gain control parameter for subcarrier k assigned to MS u can be represented as $g_{r,u}$. Furthermore, before power amplification, uniform power assignment is set to all subcarriers. That is, $P_{r,k}^{TX} = P_T/N$. Then the constraint function can be simplified as:

$$\sum_{u=1}^{N_{MS}} S_u \cdot G_{r,u} \leq N \quad \forall r = 1, \ldots, N_R \tag{12}$$

where S_u is the number of subcarriers allocated to MS u and $G_{r,u} (= g_{r,u}^2)$ is the square of the power amplification at r-th RE for all the subcarriers allocated to MS u.

• Second, we further assume $H_r(k) = 1$ for all subcarriers. This is equivalent to ignoring the effects of multipath fading in the formulation of optimization problem.

With this simplification, $\Phi(k)$ appearing on both numerator and denominator of the objective function can be cancelled out with each other.

With considering these two simplifications, the optimization formulation becomes a non-linear programming problem which can be solved fast:

$$\max_{\{G_{r,u}\}} \quad \sum_{u=1}^{N_{MS}} S_u \cdot \ln(1 + \frac{\sum_{r=1}^{N_R} \frac{c \cdot P_{r,u}^{UL}}{N_T} \cdot G_{r,u}}{\sigma^2}))$$

$$s.t. \quad \sum_{u=1}^{N_{MS}} S_u \cdot G_{r,u} \leq N \qquad \forall\, r = 1,\ldots,N_R \qquad (13)$$

$$G_{r,u} \geq 0 \qquad \forall\, r = 1,\ldots,N_R\,; u = 1,\ldots,N_{MS}$$

Because both the objective function and constraint functions are convex (or concave) functions, there exists a global optimization solution by solving the equations of Karuch-Kuhn-Tucker optimality conditions [20].

5   Performance Evaluation

In this section we evaluate the DL system performances via a system level simulator which simulates the models of path loss, shadowing, and multipath fading based on system evaluation methodology in [17] and [18]. Both intra-cell and inter-cell interferences are considered in the simulations. Exponential Effective SINR Mapping (EESM) based abstraction [17] of LTE physical layers is implemented in the system level simulator. We compare the performance in two system configurations: macrocell and DAS. In the traditional macrocell deployment (called "macrocell" in the following description), each BS is placed at the center of three hexagons in each cell [18]. On the other hand, in the configuration of DAS we consider, one RE is deployed at the center of three hexagons in each cell, same as the position of BSs. Fig. 4 shows the area of one cell where an REC controlling a set of 3 REs is placed at the center of 9 hexagons. BSs (in the case of macrocell) or REs (in the case of DAS) are located 1 km apart from each other. Mobile stations (MSs) are uniformly distributed in 50 m apart. We focus on a center cell that is surrounded by two tiers of adjacent cells. Frequency reuse 1/3/1 (i.e. the system channel of 10MHz is reused in each of three sectors of each cell) [17] is considered in the simulation. Furthermore, the MIMO setting in the simulation is 2x2 MIMO with Alamouti transmit diversity [19]. The important system level parameters that we use are summarized in Table 1.

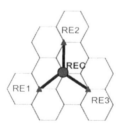

Fig. 4. Layout of one cell area in DAS controlled by one REC

Table 1. Important system parameters [17]

Parameter	Value	Parameter	Value
BS (RE) Tx antenna Gain	16 dBi	MS terminal height	2 m
BS (RE) height	32 m	MS noise figure	7 dB
BS (RE) Tx antenna power	43 dBm	Channel bandwidth	10 MHz
BS noise figure	5 dB	FFT size	1024

We compare the proposed power redistribution scheme in Sec. 4.4 against two other DAS schemes, blanket transmission in Sec. 4.2 and beamforming in Sec. 4.3 as well as the setting of macrocell. The effects of the inter-cell interferences are included in the simulation. Table 2 shows the DL sector capacity of these four schemes based on the results of the average of 30 runs (i.e. 30 frames) when the effects of shadowing and multipath fading could be changed at different frames. Note that the cell capacity is three times of sector capacity. Different number of N_{MS} (= 2, 3, 4, or 5) are simulated in our proposal. Besides, the set of MSs to be scheduled in the same frame is randomly chosen. As the performance of the schemes of macrocell, blanket transmission, and beamforming scheme is invariant under different N_{MS} settings, only one number of these schemes is shown in Table 2. In addition, the proposal with $N_{MS} = 1$ is equivalent to the blanket transmission scheme.

Table 2. Comparison of DL sector capacity (unit: Mbps)

Scheme	macrocell	Blanket	Beamforming	Proposal			
N_{MS}	1~5	1~5	1~5	2	3	4	5
Sector Capacity	10.82	8.07	12.87	12.03	13.69	14.45	14.70

The simulation results first show that in comparison with macrocell setting, the performance of the blanket transmission scheme is degraded by 34.1% which indicates the great impact of the non-coherent operations in the blanket transmission scheme. The simulation results also show that the performance of the proposed scheme improves as N_{MS} increases. This is because when N_{MS} increases, more freedom in the optimization problem of power distribution is created to maximize the system capacity. Our proposal under all the cases of N_{MS} outperforms the case of macrocell. In addition, the proposed scheme outperforms the beamforming scheme when $N_{MS} \geq 3$. As explained in Sec. 4.3 the beamforming scheme evaluated here is a *carrier non-cooperative* approach where each subcarrier is independently processed without the power adjustment across different subcarriers. The result indicates the effectiveness of non-uniform power allocation over carrier non-cooperative beamforming schemes in the DAS environment. In the case of $N_{MS}=5$, our proposal improves the DL system capacity by 35.9%, 82.2%, and 14.2% compared to macrocell, blanket transmission scheme and beamforming scheme, respectively.

Fig. 5 compares the coverage performance of various modulation and coding scheme (MCS) shown by the indices on the x-axis. In our study, we define the coverage for a given MCS as the percentage of MSs which have a higher SINR than the required SINR of that MCS over a long duration. It represents the average percentage of MSs that are supported by that MCS level. The system coverage is defined as the coverage on the most reliable MCS. The results in Fig. 5 show the superior coverage performance of our proposal over the other schemes. Not only the system capacity but also the system coverage are improved in our proposal.

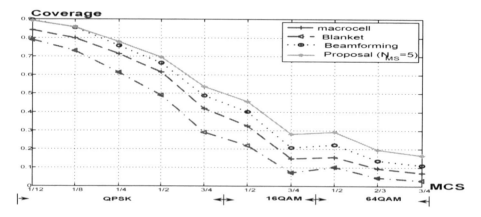

Fig. 5. Comparison of DL coverage

Fig. 6 shows the pictorial presentation of DL coverage of macrocell, blanket transmission, beamforming, and our proposal (N_{MS}=5). Each small square inside the hexagon indicates the MCS used by the MS located at the position at this square. The yellow color in a square indicates no coverage while the blue color indicates the highest order of MCS, 64QAM with code rate of ¾. The results show the same trend as the results of DL system capacity. In particular, the coverage of edge user is much enhanced in our proposal.

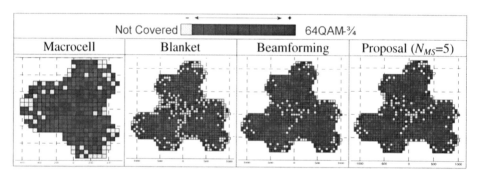

Fig. 6 Comparison of visual presentation of DL coverage

6   Conclusion

In this study we propose a novel approach to enhance the system capacity in distributed antenna systems through redistributing the powers of OFDM subcarriers in the REs. The proposed solution not only maintains the advantages of DAS, which include both low system costs of deployment, operation, and management, and less frequent inter-cell handover, but also improves the performances of system capacity and coverage in DAS compared to other baseline schemes such as the traditional BS with a single pair of REC and RE, as well as DAS with either blanket transmission or beamforming schemes. The proposal can be easily implemented in the existing OFDM wireless systems such as LTE, WiMAX, or WiFi as well as the next generation wireless systems such as LTE-A and 802.16m. In the future works, we will focus more on optimizing the deployment strategy of the proposal.

References

[1] The DAS Forum, http://thedasforum.org/
[2] Zhou, S., Zhao, M., Xu, X., Wang, J., Yao, Y.: Distributed wireless communication system: a new architecture for future public wireless access. IEEE Communications Magazine 41(3) (March 2003)
[3] Choi, W., Andrews, J.G.: Downlink performance and capacity of distributed antenna systems in a multicell environment. IEEE Transactions on Wireless Communications 6(1) (January 2007)
[4] Common Public Radio Interface (CPRI); interface specification, V4.1 (February 2009), http://www.cpri.info/downloads/CPRI_v_4_1_2009-02-18.pdf
[5] Wikipedia, Distributed Antenna System, http://en.wikipedia.org/wiki/Distributed_Antenna_System
[6] Leavey, G.: Enabling distributed base station architectures with CPRI, http://www.pmc-sierra.com/whitepaper-processor-mips-sonet-ethernet/enabling-distributed-base-station-architectures-cpri/index.html
[7] Feng, W., Li, Y., Zhou, S., Wang, J., Xia, M.: Downlink capacity of distributed antenna systems in a multi-cell environment. In: IEEE Conference on Wireless Communications & Networking Conference (April 2009)
[8] Sun, L., McKay, M.R., Jin, S.: Analytical performance of MIMO multichannel beamforming in the presence of unequal power cochannel interference and noise. IEEE Transactions on Signal Processing 57(7) (July 2009)
[9] Palomar, D.P., Cioffi, J.M., Lagunas, M.A.: Joint Tx-Rx beamforming design for multicarrier MIMO channels: A unified framework for convex optimization. IEEE Trans. Signal Process. 51(9) (September 2003)
[10] Rong, Y., Hua, Y., Swami, A., Swindlehurst, A.L.: Space-time power schedule for distributed MIMO links without instantaneous channel state information at the transmitting nodes. IEEE Trans. Signal Processing 56(2) (February 2008)
[11] 3GPP TS 36.300: Evolved Universal Terrestrial Radio Access (E-ULTRA) and Evolved Universal Terrestrial Radio Access Network (E-ULTRAN); overall description (2008)
[12] IEEE standard for local and metropolitan area networks part 16: Air interface for fixed and mobile broadband wireless access systems, IEEE Std 802.16e-2005 (2005)
[13] IEEE standard for local and metropolitan area networks part 11: Wireless LAN medium access control (MAC) and physical layer (PHY) specifications amendment 5: Enhancements for higher throughput. IEEE Std 802.11n-2009 (2009)
[14] Goldsmith, A.: Wireless communications. Cambridge University Press, Cambridge (2005)
[15] Tranter, W., Shanmagan, K., Rappaport, T., Kosbar, K.: Principles of communication systems simulation with wireless applications. Prentice Hall, Englewood Cliffs (2004)
[16] Tse, D., Viswanath, P.: Fundamentals of Wireless Communications. Cambridge University Press, Cambridge (2005)
[17] WiMAX System Evaluation Methodology, Version 2.1, WiMAX Forum (July 2008)
[18] 3GPP TS 36.942, Evolved Universal Terrestrial Radio Access (E-ULTRA); Radio Frequency (RF) system scenarios (2009)
[19] Alamouti, S.M.: A simple transmit diversity technique for wireless communications. IEEE Journal on Selected Areas in Communications 16(8) (October 1998)
[20] Bertsekas, D.P.: Nonlinear programming. Athena Scientific (1999)

NeuroCast: Adaptive Multi-source P2P Video Streaming Application for Wireless Networks

Carlos Gañán, Juan Caubet, Sergi Reñé
Jorge Mata-Díaz, Juan J. Alins, and Óscar Esparza

Universitat Politècnica de Catalunya, Departament Enginyeria Telemàtica
1-3 Jordi Girona, C3 08034 Barcelona, Spain
{carlos.ganan,juan.caubet,sergi.rene,jmata,jalins,oesparza}@entel.upc.es

Abstract. Streaming consists in distributing media to large audiences over a computer network. Providing a streaming service for wireless mobile nodes presents many challenges. A peer-to-peer (P2P) solution has the big advantage of seamlessly scaling to arbitrary population sizes, as every node that receives the video, while consuming resources, can at the same time offer its own upload bandwidth to serve other nodes. In this paper we present the design and implementation of NeuroCast: an unstructured P2P application for video streaming. NeuroCast implements a robust scheduling algorithm which minimizes the scheduling delay. Moreover, given heterogeneous contents, delays and bandwidths. Thus, NeuroCast becomes suitable for wireless scenarios due to its capability to adapt to changing network conditions.

Keywords: Video streaming, P2P networks, multi-source, wireless.

1 Introduction

During the last decade, the growth of popular web sites serving multimedia contents has led to the increase of video streaming applications. However, video streaming over a wireless network has to deal with several challenges: 1) nothing is guaranteed about bandwidth, delay, and packet loss rate; 2) it is difficult to predict the bandwidth, delay, and loss rate information, since it is unknown and time-varying; 3) the heterogeneity of receiver capabilities is a significant problem when video streams are distributed over a multicast network; and 4) a congestion/flow control mechanism has to be employed to prevent congestion epochs in the wireless network.

There have been proposed several ways to approach these challenges. The traditional client-server model is suitable for streaming, but it presents scalability problems and a loss of efficiency in resource exploitation. In fact, a server has a limit bandwidth and cannot serve more than a limited number of clients at the same time. The best way to distribute multimedia content from a source to a group of hosts at the same time is the IP multicast. However the deployment of IP multicast has been limited due to several reasons. First of all it requires changes in the network devices increasing the complexity and the overhead at

X. Masip-Bruin et al. (Eds.): WWIC 2011, LNCS 6649, pp. 272–284, 2011.

the routers. But also, it presents commercial problems since a lot ISPs disable it. Another possibility is to use peer-to-peer networks for the streaming. In these networks, the stream receivers act as clients and servers at the same time (i.e. servent) replicating packets they receive. The aim for these techniques is to allow bandwidth-consuming streaming media to be delivered to a large number of consumers in a scalable, robust and efficient manner. In this sense, we present NeuroCast, a P2P open-source solution to video streaming over wireless networks.

P2P streaming systems strive to optimize three important metrics: i) start-up delay, ii) end-to-end delay, and iii) playback continuity index. Most of the systems may be classified based on the type of distribution graph they implement: mainly tree and mesh, though a lot of hybrid solutions have been implemented already. Tree-based overlays implement a tree distribution graph, rooted at the source of the content [1–4]. In principle, each node receives data from a parent node, which may be the source or a peer. If peers do not change too frequently, such a system requires little overhead; in fact, packets can be forwarded from node to node without the need for extra messages. However, in high churn environments (i.e. fast turnover of peers in the tree), the tree must be continuously destroyed and rebuilt, a process that requires considerable control message overhead. As a side effect, nodes must buffer data for at least the time required to repair the tree, in order to avoid packet loss. Mesh-based overlays [5–7] implement a mesh distribution graph, where each node contacts a subset of peers to obtain a number of chunks. Every node needs to know which chunks are owned by its peers and explicitly pulls the chunks it needs. This type of scheme involves overhead, due in part to the exchange of buffer maps between nodes (nodes advertise the set of chunks they own) and in part to the pull process (each node sends a request in order to receive the chunks). Thanks to the fact that each node relies on multiple peers to retrieve content, mesh based systems offer good resilience to node failures. On the negative side, they require large buffers to support the chunk pull, as large buffers are needed to increase the chances of finding the missing chunks in the playback sequence. In this sense, NeuroCast evolves the Peercast [2] tree network to a mesh-based overlay.

Peercast is an open source streaming media multicast tool which is generally used for streaming audio and makes use of a bandwidth distributing approach where users can choose the relay to connect in the downstream. NeuroCast extends Peercast in order to enhance its capabilities making it possible to watch videos even in a wireless scenario. Moreover, NeuroCast adds the necessary design to allow any user to become a *broadcaster*. Among the different improvements made in NeuroCast, it is worth to mention the multi-source streaming capability. In contrast to Peercast, NeuroCast solves the typical asymmetry of the link by using multiple sources. Therefore, it allows to video stream over a wireless network.

In this paper, we first approach the problem of media streaming from a practical point of view. We present the design of NeuroCast, a P2P streaming for wireless networks, that: 1) supports very high levels of churn, 2) supports strongly heterogeneous distributions of peer upload capacity, 3) has multi-source capabilities to use efficiently the available upload capacity, and 4) employs fast adaptation and recovery from abrupt changes in network conditions. Due to this fast adaptation, NeuroCast can operate in a wireless scenario where nodes are prone to suffer from disconnections.

The rest of the paper is structured as follows. Section 2 introduces the basics of Peercast. Section 3 describes the NeuroCast system. Section 4 presents a analysis of NeuroCast, carried out by way of emulation on medium-scale network testbeds. Finally, section 5 concludes this work.

2   Peercast

The multimedia streaming application Peercast is a multi-thread application, so that different processes can be executed at the same time concurrently. The number of processes in Peercast is variable and depends on the amount of connections that are established. The main thread deals with the creation of its child threads. In addition to these tasks, this thread becomes passive waiting for incoming connections. In general, for each request that it receives, a thread is created which will serve the request till its death.

2.1   PCP: Packet Chain Protocol

PCP is the protocol used in Peercast to allow communication among different clients. The main goal of this protocol is to reuse the same data-flow which is used to send the multimedia information, to send the control information too. PCP chaining allows users to 'piggy back' a download from another user.

The first packet of a group indicates the type of the packets that are being sent and the number of packets that come after it. These packets that indicate the type of the group are called *parent packets*. The great potential of this protocol lies in the way the packets are chained, as each one of the packets inside a group can be at the same time parent of another type of packets.

2.2   Entities

Peercast uses the Oriented Object programming, i.e., it has several classes that represent the different system entities. Therefore, Peercast consists of *servent, channel, buffer* and *root* classes.

Servent. This class becomes essential for the performance of the Peercast application. As any real-time P2P application, the application depends on the network conditions, so the packets can arrive out of order. Hence, it is basic to have a good system to order and store packets efficiently. The servent class manages the channel transmission and listens to requests coming from the network or from the same host. Servents exert the server and the client at the same time. Servents are classified according to the transmission type. Thus, the most used servents are:

- **Server**: It is the server of the main thread which handles any request. This subclass creates new server classes to manage the different requests.
- **Relay**: This class manages the retransmission of a channel among different NeuroCast instances. In this mode, the data are sent using the PCP protocol.
- **Direct**: This class is used to retransmit the multimedia file directly without packing the data. This class is used to handle the packet transmission to a player.

Channel. A channel is originated when a user starts to retransmit new multimedia information to the Peercast network. This user, the first one in uploading the channel to the network, is named the *emitter* or *broadcaster*, and it becomes the unique contact between the original source and the Peercast network. The channel is shared among the different peers.

Buffers. It is obvious the necessity of a buffer in Peercast due to the fact that each node can perform as client as well as server, so it needs to store in memory the information in order to be capable of retransmitting it. Without a buffer, a node can only reproduce the received packets in a player but cannot send them to any other client in the network.

Root Nodes. Despite the fact that Peercast was designed to run in a decentralize way, the actual situation is centralized. The developers implemented Peercast in order to create a network without servers. Thus, Peercast only has clients. If a group of users want to share a video among them, they only need to know the IP address of some of them and the channel identifier. Hence, they will create a download tree. On the other hand, if a user wants a video but it does not know any user from the sharing group, that user cannot see the video. Therefore, this situation makes the tree model of Peercast unfeasible for real scenarios. Peercast deals with this issue with the concept of *root nodes*. For every broadcasting network, one node will act as root, being the primary source of the data flow, while the others will receive it and possibly retransmit it. Root nodes gather information about other clients in order to create an information directory.

3   NeuroCast

Analyzing the evolution of P2P application for file distribution, it has been noted a leading trend to move from the typical tree/forest topologies to the mesh topology. This evolution allows NeuroCast to use the bandwidth of N users which cannot broadcast the video by themselves, but together they are able to achieve the broadcasting. NeuroCast is a multi-thread application, each network user is able to receive a stream from different peers, and at the same retransmit it to any other user.

Users interact with NeuroCast through a web interface quite simple and friendly. By means of these web pages, the user can manage the application as well as get information about the retransmission taking place or about the peers from where the stream is being downloaded.

Apart from the broadcasters who perform as stream sources, there is another type of clients in NeuroCast: the *trackers*. These clients deal with the gathering of information about the peers that are sharing a particular channel. Thus, when a user starts a session the tracker will provide to that user a list with the peers that are offering the requested channel. These peers that are sharing the channel are named *hits*. Therefore, it becomes essential that the trackers have an updated hit list. NeuroCast has been implemented in such a way that all the users perform as trackers. Hence, any peer can share with another their hit list.

On the other hand, using a mesh approach forces us to introduce a new concept: *substreaming*. Substreaming appears as consequence of the need of receiving a stream from several sources at the same time. In this way, substreaming consists in dividing the original stream in N parts, which are delivered from the different sources that are available following certain criteria that are explained later. Moreover, it could be interesting to receive more packets from one source than from another. Therefore, there are new issues to take care of, such as the arrival packet order or the packet distribution among the available sources. All the packets that the substream consists of are called *chunks*.

The actions that take place while joining the NeuroCast network are:

- *Getting the Hit List.* During the initialization, the NeuroCast application connects to the tracker, and it sends back a hit list of the requested channel.
- *Peer Selection.* Once a peer has the hit list, then it has to select the best set of peers from the list.
- *Packet Allocation.* NeuroCast sends the packets grouped in specific chunk numbers which are assigned to the peer transmitting the stream.
- *Network and load adaptation.* NeuroCast monitors the network status permanently while downloading the channel.

3.1   Entities

The number of processes in NeuroCast is variable and depends on the amount of established connections. As in Peercast, NeuroCast has a main thread which deals with the incoming requests and creates the children processes that handle these requests. In this section we briefly present the two main NeuroCast entities.

Servent. A servent handles requests from the system and sends the stream either to another NeuroCast instance or to the player. It acts as a server as well as a client. As in Peercast, there exists three different type of servents: direct, relay and server.

Channel. The channels are the main elements in NeuroCast. They are used to handle the different multimedia flows which are being shared in the network. Each flow uses a different channel. NeuroCast only distributes parts of the stream not the whole stream. Every channel has its original source. In general, this source is a user (*broadcaster*) who creates the channel and becomes the only physical link among the NeuroCast clients and the original multimedia file. The channel has two main elements.

- *The buffer*: It manages and stores the incoming packets temporally to allow a retransmission posterior. The maximum number of packets that the buffer can contain is 64.
- *The channel stream*: It deals with the handshaking and the channel reception. Channel stream class allows controlling the incoming packets.

NeuroCast also introduces the possibility of using several peers concurrently, dividing the stream among these, and making the network structure look like a grid. The subchannels are the application elements that allow to identify the stream fragments. Thus, each one of the sources will be associated to a subchannel.

3.2 Load Balance

As mentioned in the previous section, NeuroCast allows to balance the load according to the network conditions. In this way, NeuroCast implements different algorithms to optimize the peer selection among the hits of the requested channel and the load distribution among the chosen ones. In the following we show how NeuroCast is able to adapt to the network conditions and redistribute the load according to these conditions.

Peers selection. One of the most critical parts in any player based on a P2P network is the selection of peers. Unlike conventional P2P applications for file distribution, the fact of working with video creates a hard and direct dependence on the peers that are transmitting the stream.

Once the hit list has been received from the tracker, it is necessary to calculate which is the subset of peers that will allow to download the stream with the best conditions regarding the network. NeuroCast will always try to prioritize those peers with a high available bandwidth, with the lower packet loss rate, and with a high availability. NeuroCast peer selection algorithm is based in CollectCast algorithm [5]. The strengths of this algorithm are the sources selection, the network status monitoring and the periodic source redistribution in order to adapt to the time-varying network conditions. The selection process can be split up into three phases:

1. Obtaining the hit list associated to the requested channel.
2. Enumerating the sets of hits that satisfy the constraints imposed by:

$$R_l \leq \sum_{P=\bar{P}_{act}} R_p \leq R_u, \tag{1}$$

   where Rp is is the maximum *sending rate* that a peer can contribute anytime during the session, Rl is the lower limit of the total sending rate of a set of peers, and Ru is the upper limit of the total sending rate of a set of peers.
3. Selecting the best set of peers among the solutions obtained previously.

When requesting a new channel, NeuroCast obtains a set of parameters from each source. Thus, the requesting peer obtains the peerRp of each source, i.e., the maximum *sending rate* that a peer can contribute with. Then, NeuroCast calculates the throughput and the losses of the link with each one the hits. In order to do these measurements, NeuroCast takes advantage of a modified version of the Iperf [8] application.

Apart from the bandwidth that a specific peer is willing to share, it is also interesting to know the availability of the set of hits. In any P2P network, it is impossible to determine the expected lifetime of the network, as it is not possible to predict when a node will be disconnected from the network, or the congestion of the network with the subsequent massive packet loss. A possible implementation to calculate the availability in our environment is carried out in the following way. A parallel process to NeuroCast runs to check the status of the hits during a limited period of time. With these measurements, it is generated a probabilistic function for each instant of the day, allowing to know the probability that a peer is connected at that time.

Packet Allocation. Unlike the CollectCast algorithm, in this first version of NeuroCast the final application is simplified and does not use FEC codes to distribute the load among the different hits that have been selected to retransmit the channel.

The active peers ($\bar{P}_{act}$) collectively send the media file segment by segment: they all cooperate in sending the first segment, then the second one, and so on. The media file is divided into equal-length data segments. Peer p is assigned a number of packets D_p to send in proportion to its actual streaming rate:

$$D_p = \left\lceil \Delta \cdot \frac{R_p}{\sum_{x \in P_{act}} R_x} \right\rceil. \tag{2}$$

where Δ is the size of original packets in which the media file is divided into. The D_p value is used to distribute the chunks among the different peers of the set. Delta is the number of chunks into which the stream is divided in order to work per groups with subchannels.

Network adaptation. To accommodate the maximum load of the network, NeuroCast adds a new functionality so that it is able to adapt at any moment the number of chunks that a peer is downloading. The variable used to determine the most appropriate chunk-distribution is the time between arrivals of packets. Thus, controlling the time between packet arrivals during the session, NeuroCast sets a threshold that allows to redistribute the number of chunks that each peer retransmits. This threshold is calculated following next equation:

$$threshold = \frac{\frac{buffer\_length}{bitrate} \cdot FACTOR\_SEP\_PACKETS \cdot numChunks}{numSubChannelChunks}. \tag{3}$$

As seen in equation 3, the threshold depends on different parameters:

1. It depends on the bitrate of the played video.
2. The `FACTOR_SEP_PACKETS` (maximum allowed delay between packet arrivals).

3. `numChunks` is related to the number of chunks into which the stream is divided among the different hits.
4. The `numSubChannelChunks` is the number of chunks that this subchannel retransmits.

To alert the rest of hits of the load redistribution the requesting peer sends to each one of the hits the message `CHANGE_PEER_CHUNKS` through it. Next, a NeuroCast server in the target machine reads the request and enables the flag associated with the redistribution, so that the `Relay` server that broadcasts the channel is ready to receive.

Once the subchannel is ready for the load redistribution, the peer performs the following steps:

1. Notifies the others subchannels about the redistribution.
2. Decreases by one the number of chunks that is downloading from its hit.
3. Searches for a subchannels with a lower `time_between_arrivals` in order to send the chunk it has you just subtracted.
4. Waits until the subchannel with lower `time_between_arrivals` has redistributed the chunks.

Once the rest of subchannels have been informed that a load redistribution is going to take place, they also enter into the process of redistribution. At this point, two different situations must be distinguished: on one hand the subchannels with lower `time_between_arrivals` and on the other hand the rest of subchannels. The latter simply expect that the redistribution is done, to continue with the download of the new allocated chunks.

And regarding to the subchannel with the lowest `time_between_arrivals`, it follows these steps:

1. Checks that the channel has more than one subchannel currently. If that hit is the only active subchannel it must start to download the full stream from that hit.
2. If there are more subchannels, it increases by one the number of chunks of the subchannel.
3. Finally, it redistributes the load among all the hits from the list according to their number of chunks.

A different case from the one presented above, but that also requires load redistribution occurs when a peer does not receive packets from a certain subchannel. In these situations the load redistribution is forced immediately.

Another of the new features that have been introduced in NeuroCast is to get rid of the hits that are only sending a single chunk, and despite that, they still send packets with delay. In these cases, the peer removes that hit from its list of hits and downloads the latest chunk from another peer, leaving the subchannels on standby until the channel becomes unavailable or it decides to leave the network.

4   Performance Evaluation

In this section, we present emulation results by which NeuroCast capabilities are evaluated. Two different environments are configured in order to check Neuro-Cast's performance in heterogeneous network conditions. The reference scenario for our emulations is created using VNUML [9] as shown in Figure 1. In this virtual network, the *Host* serves the video to $E0$, and the latter sends the stream to 3 machines ($E1$, $E2$ and $E3$).

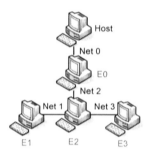

Fig. 1. Network topology used for the tests

The main features of the virtual network and the virtual machines are shown in Table 1. Using this configuration, we change the network conditions where these peers are operating to recreate two different environments. These environments will emulate the conditions of a peer operating in a wireless network.

Table 1. Initial parameters of the virtual network and the virtual machines

	Type	Bw
Net0	lan	2 Mbps
Net1	ppp	1 Mbps
Net2	ppp	1,5 Mbps
Net3	ppp	750 Kbps

	Host	E0	E1	E2	E4
maxRelays	1	4	4	4	4
peerRp	2 Mbps	1 Mbps	1 Mbps	700 Kbps	1 Mbps
minRp	100 Kbps	100 Kbps	100 Kbps	100 Kbps	100 Kbps
delta	0	10	10	10	15
factor_sep_pack	1	1.3	1.3	1.3	1.3
delay_margin	0	4	4	4	3
buffer_sep_pack	0	30	30	30	16
Rl	100 Kbps	100 Kbps	100 Kbps	100 Kbps	100 Kbps
Ru	2 Mbps	2 Mbps	3 Mbps	3 Mbps	3 Mbps

4.1   Impact of Topology Changes

In a wireless scenario, it is common to have highly changing topologies. In this section, we evaluate how NeuroCast achieves to adapt to these changing conditions without disrupting the quality of the multimedia service.

Thus, when downloading a video from more than one source, if one of these sources leaves the network, then the requesting peer redistributes the load and continues downloading the subchannels from other sources. The process that takes place consists in:

1. Checking if there is a free peer in the cached list of hits. That is, a hit from which the peer is neither downloading any chunk nor sending any part of the stream.
2. Requesting a new list of hits to the tracker and check again if there are any free hits.
3. Downloading the "missing" chunks from one of the hits that the peer is already using.

In the latter case it requires a reallocation of subchannels. Depending on the situation, NeuroCast carries out a series of changes:

- If the client is downloading more than one subchannel from the same hit, then it groups the chunks in the same subchannel.
- If a subchannel that is not at the end of the list is deleted, then this position is filled with the last subchannel, so there are no empty spaces in the list.
- If a subchannel downloads all the chunks into which the stream is divided, then the value of numChunks is set to 1 and the stream is no longer divided into different parts.

Next, we show an example of a peer leaving the network. Initially we have the following configuration (see Table 2):

Table 2. Initial List of Hits and chunks distribution among the 3 subchannels

Hit List	
Hit	**IP**
0 (tracker)	10.0.0.1
1	10.0.0.2
2	10.0.1.2
3	10.0.2.2

Subchannels List			
	IP address	**Number of Chunks**	**Chunks**
Subchannel 0	10.0.0.2	6	0 2 4 6 8 10
Subchannel 1	10.0.1.2	3	1 3 5
Subchannel 2	10.0.2.2	3	7 9 11

After some time, source 10.0.0.2 leaves the network. The requesting peer checks that there are no-free hits in its hit list, so it requests a new hit list to the tracker (see Table 3).

Table 3. New List of Hits and final chunks distribution among 2 subchannels

Hit List	
Hit	**IP**
0 (tracker)	10.0.0.1
1	10.0.1.2
2	10.0.2.2
3	10.0.3.2

Subchannels List			
	IP address	**Number of Chunks**	**Chunks**
Subchannel 0	10.0.2.2	3	7 9 11
Subchannel 1	10.0.1.2	9	0 1 2 3 4 5 6 8 10

As the only new addition to the list of hits is its own IP address, it has only the possibility of reusing the hits which were already transmitting the stream. In this example, as shown in Table 3 it is selected the 10.0.1.2 peer. Summarizing, NeuroCast is able to adapt to any change in the topology of the network no matter if the peer has left because it lost connectivity or because it decided to stop streaming.

4.2   Impact of Traffic Interferences

Another situation that is prone to happen in a wireless scenario is to suffer interferences from another peer in the network. To show how NeuroCast works under these conditions, continuing with the network topology of figure 1, we evaluate the situation where we have 4 machines running NeuroCast and playing a video: *Host*, *E0*, *E1* and *E2*. As we have seen in previous cases, in a "stable" situation machine *E0* downloads the stream from *Host*, machine *E0* downloads it from *E1*, and finally *E2* downloads it from *E0* and *E1* simultaneously.

In this section, we focus on studying the performance of machine *E2* while suffering from traffic interferences. To achieve that environment, we introduce traffic interference in link *Net1* using Distributed Internet Traffic Generator (D-ITG) [10] in *E3*.

Prior to the injection the traffic interference, *E2* is downloading 6 chunks from each source as the conditions of *Net1* and *Net2* are virtually identical. However, when we introduce a traffic of 800 kbytes/s in *Net1* link, this balance is broken. Thus, chunks coming from the *E1* are affected, and consequently, the time between packet arrivals is increased. Precisely this is reflected in the graphs of figure 2(a) and 2(b).

Figure 2 shows, apart from the mean time between packet arrivals, the theoretical limit that the program uses to determine when a redistribution of chunks is necessary. It is worth noting that the redistribution occurs when that limit is exceeded 3 times, because this is the value of the parameter `delay_margin` defined in the NeuroCast configuration file running in *E2*.

As we have seen previously, some parameters in the configuration file directly affect the behavior of the application during variations of the network conditions. In the following we carry out several setups, varying two parameters such as `delta` and `buffer_sep_packets`, and we observe in each case the time needed to redistribute the chunks.

To force the redistributions, we use Network Emulator (NetEm) [11] to change the link capacity of one of the hits that is retransmitting the stream. Thus we switch from the 1000 Kbps available at the beginning of the session, to 112 Kbps. Analyzing the results in Table 4 we observe that the parameter `Delta`, i.e. the number of chunks into which the stream is divided, does not affect significantly the obtained time, while the parameter `buffer_sep_packets` is decisive.

Table 4. Performance with a traffic interference of 90% of the link capacity

	Test1	Test2	Test3	Test4	Test5
Delta	20	5	20	20	5
buffer_sep_packets	20	20	50	5	5
Time to redistribution	90s	86s	173s	31s	31s

Consequently, as it can be inferred from these results, any peer running NeuroCast even while suffering from interferences is able to operate without major quality of service degradation.

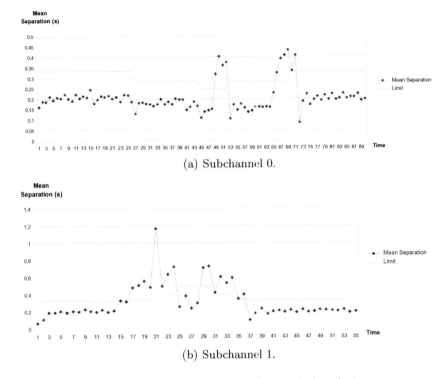

(a) Subchannel 0.

(b) Subchannel 1.

Fig. 2. Mean time between packets arrival evolution

5   Conclusions

P2P technology gives novel opportunities to define an efficient multimedia streaming application but at the same time, it brings a set of technical challenges and
issues due to its dynamic and heterogeneous nature. We must make a balance
between the breadth and depth of a live streaming overlay tree. At the same
time, the robustness issue must be considered carefully, as the dynamic feature
and freedom of P2P network itself. In this this work we have presented the implementation of NeuroCast, an unstructured P2P system for video streaming
that is able to adapt to wireless network conditions. NeuroCast design is based
on an unstructured mesh-based architecture. It intends to optimize bandwidth
allocation and combine dynamic peer selection strategies that rely on implicit
feedback from data reception.

NeuroCast's performance is evaluated in emulated network environments. The
experiments indicate that NeuroCast is capable of operating in a harsh environment taking into account network conditions. Our results also confirm the ability
of unstructured mesh-based systems to withstand the high levels of transience
that can result from user and network dynamics (churn, failures, congestion,
etc.).

References

1. Deshpande, H., Bawa, M., Garcia-Molina, H.: Streaming live media over a peer-to-peer network. Technical Report 2001-30, Stanford InfoLab (2001)
2. Peercast: P2p broadcasting for everyone, `http://www.peercast.org` (accessed on January 2011)
3. Castro, M., Druschel, P., Kermarrec, A., Nandi, A., Rowstron, A., Singh, A.: Split-stream: High-bandwidth multicast in cooperative environments. In: 9th ACM Symposium on Operating Systems Principles (2003)
4. Rowstron, A., Druschel, P.: Pastry: Scalable, decentralized object location, and routing for large-scale peer-to-peer systems. In: Liu, H. (ed.) Middleware 2001. LNCS, vol. 2218, pp. 329–350. Springer, Heidelberg (2001)
5. Hefeeda, M., Habib, A., Xu, D., Bhargava, B., Botev, B.: Collectcast: A peer-to-peer service for media streaming. ACM Multimedia 11, 68–81 (2003)
6. Gnutella, `http://rfc-gnutella.sourceforge.net` (accessed on January 2011)
7. Zhang, X., Liu, J., Li, B., Yum, T.: Coolstreaming/donet: A data-driven overlay network for efficient peer-to-peer live media streaming. In: Proceedings of IEEE Infocom (2005)
8. Tirumala, A., Gates, M., Qin, F., Dugan, J., Ferguson, J.: Iperf: The (tcp/udp) bandwidth measurement tool, `http://iperf.sourceforge.net/` (accessed on January 2011)
9. Virtual network user-mode-linux (vnuml), `http://www.dit.upm.es/vnuml` (accessed on January 2011)
10. Avallone, S., Guadagno, S., Emma, D., Pescapè, A., Ventre, G.: D-itg distributed internet traffic generator. In: International Conference on Quantitative Evaluation of Systems, pp. 316–317 (2004)
11. Hemminger, S.: Network emulation with netem. In: Linux Conf. Au, `http://linux-net.osdl.org/index.php/Netem` (accessed on January 2011)

Scheduler-Dependent Inter-cell Interference and Its Impact on LTE Uplink Performance at Flow Level

D.C. Dimitrova[1,*], G. Heijenk[1], J.L. van den Berg[1,2], and S. Yankov[3]

[1] University of Twente, Enschede, The Netherlands
Neubruckstrasse 10, CH 3012 Bern, Switserland
`dimitrova@iam.unibe.ch`
[2] TNO ICT, Delft, The Netherlands
[3] Technical University Sofia, Bulgaria

Abstract. The Long Term Evolution (LTE) cellular technology is expected to extend the capacity and improve the performance of current 3G cellular networks. Among the key mechanisms in LTE responsible for traffic management is the packet scheduler, which handles the allocation of resources to active flows in both the frequency and time dimension. This paper investigates for various scheduling scheme how they affect the inter-cell interference characteristics and how the interference in turn affects the user's performance. A special focus in the analysis is on the impact of flow-level dynamics resulting from the random user behaviour. For this we use a hybrid analytical/simulation approach which enables fast evaluation of flow-level performance measures. Most interestingly, our findings show that the scheduling policy significantly affects the inter-cell interference pattern but that the scheduler specific pattern has little impact on the flow-level performance.

1 Introduction

A key feature of packet scheduling in LTE networks is the possibility to schedule not only in time (as in UMTS/EUL) but also in frequency. The latter is enabled by the orthogonality between sub-carriers in SC-FDMA (Single Carrier Frequency Division Multiple Access) - the radio access technology chosen in LTE uplink. The smallest scheduling unit is termed a resource block (RB), see [6], and is the intersection between the frequency and time domain scheduling units. Due to the organisation of the spectrum into resource blocks and the various allocation approaches of these over the users, each resource block may experience different inter-cell interference. Hence, we can observe multiple inter-cell interference processes each of which behaves as a stochastic process.

Inter-cell interference for LTE networks has been widely researched. Interestingly most studies concentrate on performance evaluation of packet scheduling mechanisms with interference mitigation either based on inter-cell interference

---

* Corresponding author.

X. Masip-Bruin et al. (Eds.): WWIC 2011, LNCS 6649, pp. 285–296, 2011.
© IFIP International Federation for Information Processing 2011

coordination, see [7,10,12], or based on pre-existing knowledge of the interference, see [2,9,11]. Still, they do not provide insights on the inter-cell interference process itself. We argue however that such insights are valuable for the design of an optimal allocation strategy. Therefore, in this study we take a step back and build an understanding of the mutual interaction between scheduling and interference. This is done in the context of LTE uplink with special focus on flow-level behaviour.

Studies that are closely related to our research are [5] and [8]. In [5] two allocation schemes for LTE downlink with distinct frequency allocation approaches are compared taking into account flow-level dynamics. Despite being very insightful the research does not provide information on how the inter-cell interference pattern is affected by the type of allocation. It also does not discuss flow-level performance in terms of throughput (only SINR is evaluated). The authors of [8] provide a valuable study on basic scheduling schemes and their impact on inter-cell interference. Unfortunately, the study considers only averaged metrics to describe the flow-level performance. The research inspired us to study the inter-cell interference process in an LTE uplink in more detail, including both scheduler's specifics and user behaviour.

The novelty of our research lays in two aspects. On the one hand, in the context of LTE uplink, we determine the dependency of the inter-cell interference on the scheduling strategy and, in particular, on the various ways to order users for service. On the other hand, user performance is evaluated at flow level taking into account the continuously changing number of ongoing flows in a system.

Previously, see [4], we showed that flow-level evaluation reveals important performance trends in the context of UMTS/EUL. We expect this general observation to hold for an LTE network as well; however we expect different outcomes. On the one hand, additional complexity is introduced by the new freedom to schedule in the frequency domain. On the other hand, due to the orthogonality of sub-carriers in LTE intra-cell interference is no more an issue. In order to investigate that we applied a significantly extended version of the hybrid analysis approach developed in [4]. The basic separation between packet level (to capture specifics of the scheduler and the radio environment) and flow level (to model the random user behaviour) is preserved. However, we introduce additional means at packet level to capture the changes in inter-cell interference in both time and frequency. Further, at flow level the generation and completion of finite-sized flows is modelled by Markov chains from whose steady-state distribution performance measures, e.g. mean flow transfer times, were derived. Detailed discussion of the current research can be found in [3].

The paper continues with Section 2, which elaborates on the investigated scheduling aspects. The system model is presented in Section 3, while Section 4 discusses the applied analysis approach. The discussion on numerical results is split over Section 5 (a study on the inter-cell interference process) and Section 6 (discussion of performance results). Finally, we conclude with Section 7.

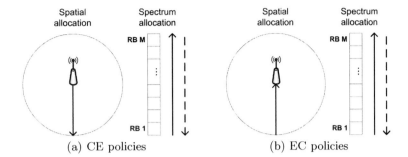

Fig. 1. User ordering policies for scheduling in LTE uplink. (a) CE-begin (solid arrow) and CE-end (dashed arrow) and (b) EC-begin (solid arrow) and EC-end (dashed arrow).

2 Interference-Aware Scheduling

In LTE we have the freedom to schedule in both time and frequency domain with the smallest scheduling unit being a resource block (RB). In particular, we denote by a resource block[1] a unit of bandwidth of 180 kHz and duration of 1 ms. If we denote by M the total number of RBs within the available system bandwidth during a single TTI, the scheduler can distribute at most M resource blocks over the active users. The total bandwidth that can be allocated to a single MS depends on the resource availability, the radio link quality and the terminal's transmit power budget. Although intra-cell interference is hardly an issue due to the sub-carrier orthogonality in SC-OFDM, situations are still possible when transmissions of users (allocated the same resource blocks) in neighbouring cells interfere with each other.

The **scheduling scheme** studied in our analysis is a resource fair scheduling scheme, which assigns equal resource shares to all active users, independently of their respective channel conditions. We consider the case of single resource block allocation and thus, given a total of M RBs in the total LTE uplink bandwidth, there are at most M users that can be served in one TTI. As a consequence there are M inter-cell interference processes - one for each RB.

An aspect of the scheduling is the **ordering policy**. The ordering policy dictates in which sequence users are selected for service and in which order the RBs are allocated to the selected users. We base the user selection on the location of the user in the cell. This spatial aspect is important since users at different locations generate different inter-cell interference values at the base station of a neighbour cell. Users close to the base station tend to generate similar levels. On the contrary, the interference levels from users located towards the cell edge vary significantly depending on their relative position to a neighbour cell. A user close to the neighbour cell generates high interference while a user on the opposite end (farthest from the neighbour cell) generates low interference levels.

---

[1] In standards a resource block refers to the intersection of 180 kHz and 0.5 ms.

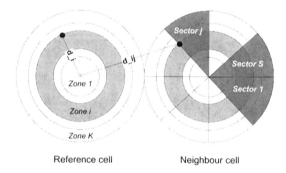

Fig. 2. System model - reference cell and neighbour cell

We have defined five distinct ordering policies accounting for both the spatial and frequency aspect of ordering. The first policy, which is also our reference case, is termed *random* and as the name suggests the selection of users and the allocation of RBs is based on a random principle, i.e. independently of the user's location. The other four policies have a more 'structured' approach. The *CE-begin* policy starts allocating RBs from the low end of the used spectrum to users closest to the base station and proceeds with farther located ones, see Figure 1(a) solid arrow. The *CE-end* policy, presented also in Figure 1(a), but dashed arrow, adopts the same spatial order but starts assigning first RBs from the high end of the spectrum. The *EC-begin* (see Figure 1(b), solid arrow) and *EC-end* (see Figure 1(b), dashed arrow) policies both start serving first the users located farthest from the base station; the former starts assigning RBs from the beginning of the spectrum while the latter starts from the high end of the spectrum. Note that the CE-begin and EC-end policies in fact differ since not at all times the total spectrum is occupied.

3   Model

We consider a two cell system - one cell (neighbour cell NC), where the interference originates, and one cell (reference cell RC), where its effect on user performance is observed. Such model, see Figure 2, suffices to observe the impact of the scheduler on the inter-cell interference pattern. The reference cell is divided in K zones of equal area which allows us to distinguish in user's performance depending on its location in the cell, i.e. distance to the base station. Each zone is characterised by a distance d_i to the base station, $i = 1, ..., K$, measured from the outer edge of the zone. Additionally, to model the effect of user location on interference, the neighbour cell is divided in S sectors of equal area. The intersection of a zone and a sector is termed a segment, which is characterised by a distance d_i to the base station of the NC and a distance d_{ij} to the base station of the RC, $j = 1, ..., S$. The number of users in a cell and their distribution is given by the system state $\underline{n}$. Given the chosen cell model the RC is characterised by $\underline{n} \equiv (n_1, n_2...n_K)$ and the NC by $\underline{n} \equiv (n_{11}, n_{12}, ..., n_{1S}, n_{21}, n_{22}, ..., n_{KS})$. We assume that the NC depends independently and is does not experience interference from the RC.

Further, users are uniformly distributed over the cell(s) and initiate new flow transfers according to a Poisson arrival process with rate λ. Flow size is exponentially distributed with mean F. Given the equal size of zones and sectors we can define arrival rate per zone (for the RC) $\lambda_i = \lambda/K$ and arrival rate per segment (for the NC) $\lambda_{ij} = \lambda/(KS)$. The number of active users is limited to the maximum number of resource blocks M that fit in the LTE uplink bandwidth. This is a reasonable assumption, which significantly eases analysis without biasing results[2]. Note that the assumption holds only for the scheduling schemes that we study; for other schemes it might not be applicable. Users apply a maximum transmit power P_{max}^{tx} unless lower level suffice. The signal received at the base station is affected by path loss and inter-cell interference. We apply the COST 231 Hata propagation model, see [6], giving the path loss in logarithmic scale as:

$$L(d_i) = L_{fix} + 10a \log_{10}(d_i), \tag{1}$$

where L_{fix} is a system parameter and a is the path loss exponent.

4   Analysis

The analysis of the two-cell model described in Section 3 needs to account for three aspects - (i) the inter-cell interference from the neighbour cell, (ii) modelling the inter-cell interference in the reference cell and (iii) user performance at flow level in the reference cell. The proposed analysis approach to tackle these issues is described in Section 4.2. Before that Section 4.1 discusses the user behaviour within a single cell (NC or RC), which is the basis for the two-cell system modelling.

4.1   Individual Cell Analysis

Since a user applies a P_{max}^{tx} even if a lower power would be sufficient to achieve the highest possible data rate, we are looking at a worst-case interference scenario. Accounting for thermal noise N and inter-cell interference I_{oc}, the signal-to-interference-plus-noise ratio (SINR) is given as:

$$SINR_i = \frac{P_i^{rx}}{N + I_{oc}}, \tag{2}$$

where i indicates the zone number, $i = 1, ..., K$, and the received power P_i^{rx} is calculated according to $P_i^{rx} = P_i^{tx}/L(d_i)$. Note that the I_{oc} component depends on whether the reference or the neighbour cell is modelled. In the calculation of

---

[2] Our observations show that situations with more than M users form 10% of all observations for very high load but are below 1% for medium and low loads.

the $SINR$ we have considered an upper and lower bound set by the technically feasible modulation and coding schemes (MCSs) and the minimum required level for successful reception respectively.

The data rate realised by a user (from zone i) when it is scheduled is what we term *instantaneous rate* r_i. It is determined by the SINR as derived above, the possible MCSs and the receiver characteristics related to that MCS. In our analysis we use the Shannon formula modified with a parameter σ to represent the limitations of implementation, see Annex A in [1]. Hence, for the instantaneous rate we can write:

$$r_i = (m \cdot 180\text{kHz})\sigma \log_2(1 + SINR_i), \qquad (3)$$

where 180 kHz is the bandwidth of a single RB and m is the number of RBs allocated to a user (in our case one). Note that both $SINR_i$ and r_i are calculated over the same RB allocation.

Flow dynamics, i.e. the changing number of active users over time, are incorporated in our analysis by means of a continuous time Markov chain. A state in the model corresponds to the state $\underline{n}$ and the transitions rates are determined as follows: the forward transition rates are taken from the Poisson arrival rate λ; the backward transition rates are derived from the instantaneous rate r_i taking into account the mean flow size F resulting in r_i/F. The form of the Markov chain of a single cell depends on the modelling, e.g. the Markov chain of the RC has K dimensions corresponding to the K zones while The Markov chain of the neighbour cell is $K \times S$ dimensional (due to the division in segments). From the steady-state distribution of the Markov chains performance metrics such as mean flow transfer times can be derived. Generally, the steady-state distribution can be found either analytically or, when necessary, by simulation. More elaborate description of the model can be found in [3].

4.2   Two-Cell System Performance

Applying the analysis from Section 4.1 to both the RC and NC we are able to evaluate the performance of the two-cell model, see Section 3. The evaluation goes through three phases.

Phase 1. In phase one we study the inter-cell interference generated by the neighbour cell towards the reference cell as a stochastic process. We are particularly interested in the observed interference levels and their probability distribution, reflected by the cumulative distribution function and the entire interference process. Generally, each segment in the NC corresponds with a different interference level. This since the inter-cell interference is in fact the received power at the base station of the reference cell from a user in the neighbour cell. Hence, the inter-cell interference from a segment ij can be derived as:

$$I_{oc}^{ij} = \frac{P_{max}^{tx}}{L(d_{ij})}, i = 1, ..., K, j = 1, ..., S. \qquad (4)$$

The probability distribution is determined by how often each particular value exhibits for a specific observation period. Hence, it depends on the traffic load and on the chosen scheduling (and ordering) policy. By applying the single-cell analysis for the neighbour cell we can derive the probability of each I_{oc} level.

Phase 2. At this phase we account for the inter-cell interference at the base station of the reference cell. This is easily done due to the assumption that there are at most M users in the system. As result, given a state $\underline{n}$, a user is always assigned the same RB, i.e. in the RC each user always experiences the same inter-cell interference. The exact interference value per RB per state and the duration for which it exhibited (how long the NC stayed in each state) are taken from a trace file generated at phase one.

Phase 3. The third and last phase of the evaluation is determining the user performance in the reference cell at the flow level. For this again the single-cell analysis is used but applied to the RC. In building the Markov model we dynamically account for the inter-cell interference measured as described in phase two. By simulating the Markov chain of the reference cell we derive its steady-state distribution and subsequently the mean flow transfer time for each zone.

5 Numerical Results - Inter-cell Interference

In this section we present a discussion on the inter-cell interference levels and probability distribution for each of the ordering policies described in Section 2. Before that we give the applied parameter settings.

5.1 Parameter Settings

An LTE system with 10 MHz bandwidth is studied, which, given that a RB has 180 kHz bandwidth, results in 50 RBs available per TTI (including control overhead). Cell radius is set to 1 km. Cell division in ten zones, i.e. $K = 10$, and ten sectors (for NC), i.e. $S = 10$, is applied[3]. For the path loss we have used $PL_{fix} = 141.6$ dB considering height of the mobile station 1.5 m, height of the eNodeB antenna 30 m and system frequency 2.6 GHz; and a path loss exponent of $a = 3.53$. The thermal noise per sub-carrier (180 kHz) is -121.45dBm and with a noise figure of 5 dB the effective noise level per resource block is $N = -116.45$ dBm. The attenuation of implementation σ is taken at 0.4 flows/sec, see [1]. Mobile stations have a maximum transmit power $P_{max}^{tx} = 0.2$ Watt. The lower bound on the $SINR$ is -10 dB while the upper bound on performance is determined by a 16QAM modulation, which corresponds to a $SINR$ of 15 dB. The average file size F is 1 Mbit and the rate λ at which users become active changes depending on the discussed scenario.

---

[3] Finer division increases the differentiation ability in interference values but also the complexity of the model and simulation time. Tests with finer granularity did not show a significant change in the results.

292   D.C. Dimitrova et al.

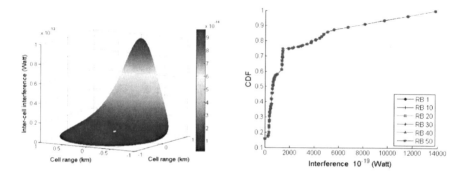

Fig. 3. Inter-cell interference levels

Fig. 4. CDF of inter-cell interference levels for the *random* ordering policy

5.2   Inter-cell Interference Process

We start with a discussion on the inter-cell interference values that a user in the neighbour cell generates at the base station of the reference cell. The results are shown in Figure 3. The x and y axes specify the location of the user in the NC while the z axis indicates the values of the inter-cell interference. The base station of the RC in located at coordinates (2,0). Users close to the RC generate the highest interference levels as visible in the sharply increasing values for locations close to the RC, i.e. coordinates (1,-1:1). Furthermore, users from the cell centre generate interference levels close in values, i.e. with low variance, while the interference from users towards the cell edge can differ significantly, i.e. has high variance.

A cumulative distribution function (CDF), although hiding the chronological development of the inter-cell interference, can provide valuable insights. Note that for each ordering scheme there are 50 inter-cell interference processes, one for each RB, see Section 2. We present the CDFs of the processes observed at RBs numbers 1, 10, 20, 30, 40 and 50. In all figures the x-axis indicates the observed inter-cell interference levels, while the y-axes plots the CDF function for each of the selected RBs. The arrival rate λ per cell is 4 flows/sec, which is close to the maximum of what the system can support, i.e. $\lambda = 4.8$ flows/sec with zero inter-cell interference.

Figure 4 presents the CDF curves observed in the case of a random ordering policy. As we can see the plots coincide, which can be explained by the random manner in which users are selected for service and are assigned RBs. For example, while at one time instant on RB1 a user from the centre can be served at the next instant a user from the cell edge can be chosen. Hence, each possible inter-cell interference level has equal chance to exhibit at any RB. The steep initial part of the curves is determined by the many segments with similar low I_{oc} levels, see Figure 3.

Let us now consider the policies with strictly defined order of service shown in Figure 5. We notice that the graphs of the CE-begin and the CE-end policies

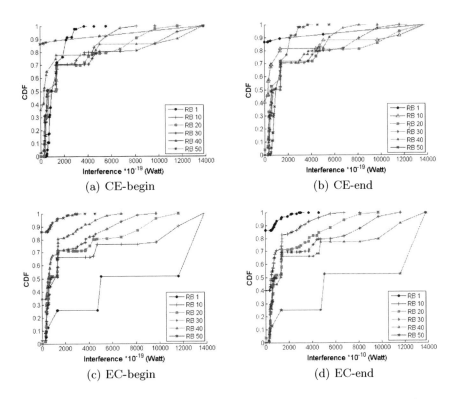

Fig. 5. CDFs of the inter-cell interference for the four pre-set ordering policies

are mirror images, as well as the graphs of the EC-begin and EC-end policies. This is the result of the same spatial ordering of users that each set of policies applies but starting from the opposite ends of the spectrum.

Focusing on the CE-begin policy, presented in Figure 5(a), we observe that the CDF curves for different RBs differ significantly. As we move towards the end of the spectrum, initially (from RB1 to RB30) the probability that high inter-cell interference values occur increases. Subsequently however low (including zero) interference values are more often observed, i.e. have higher probability towards the end of the allocated spectrum (e.g. for RB40 and RB50). This behaviour is the combined result of two factors. On the one hand, with the particular spatial ordering (centre to edge), edge users receive RBs towards the end of the spectrum. These users, when located close to the reference cell, have much higher interference levels than centre users, which explains the initial increase in the probability of high interference levels. On the other hand, RBs at the high end of the spectrum are occasionally left unused when $n < M$ holds, resulting in zero interference. Due to the similarities in behaviour, as already mentioned, the same observations hold for the CE-end scheme but in reverse order, see Figure 5(b).

The CDF curves for the EC-begin ordering policy are shown in Figure 5(c). Immediately we notice that the CDF curves of RBs towards the end of the

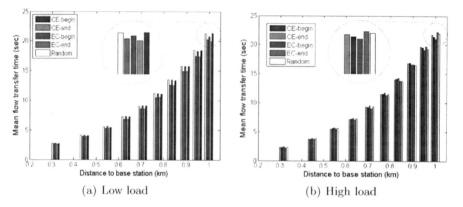

Fig. 6. Mean flow transfer times for lightly (arrival rate $\lambda = 0.7$ flows/sec) and heavily (arrival rate $\lambda = 4$ flows/sec) loaded system

spectrum are characterised with decreasing probability of high inter-cell interference levels and increasing probability of zero interference. We reason that cell edge users (with potentially high I_{oc}) are served first at the beginning of the spectrum, e.g. at RB1. Subsequent resource blocks are assigned to users located steadily closer to the cell centre, which have (on the average) lower induced interference levels. Finally, RBs at the end of the spectrum, e.g. RB40 and RB50, additionally experience the effects of a non-full system. The observations made for the EC-begin policy also apply for the EC-end policy taking into account the 'reverse' order of RB allocation, see Figure 5(d).

In summary we can say that (i) in a random ordering the inter-cell interference does not depend on the part of spectrum where it exhibits; (ii) a centre to edge ordering results in intersecting CDFs of different RBs, making the final effect on performance difficult to predict; and (iii) policies with edge to centre spatial ordering show potential for interference mitigation. The latter is based on the assumption that neighbour cells apply opposite spectrum allocation, e.g. EC-begin and EC-end, such that the interference experienced by the opposite ends of the spectrum is minimised.

6   Numerical Results - Flow-Level Performance

In this section we address five evaluation scenarios. In each scenario the NC adopts one of the five ordering policies (CE-begin, CE-end, EC-begin, EC-end or random) while the RC always adopts a CE-begin policy; this provides us a common base for comparison. We have evaluated performance in terms of mean flow transfer times for lightly and highly loaded system.

The user performance for each of the evaluation scenarios is presented in Figure 6. Two situations are shown - a lightly (arrival rate $\lambda = 0.7$ flows/sec) and a heavily (arrival rate $\lambda = 4$ flows/sec) loaded system. In order to ease interpretation of the results, for each situation, we have also shown a zoom in view of the last zone for which the differences in performance are most articulated. The general conclusion from Figure 6 is that the particular choice of ordering does not influence significantly the flow-level performance. This may be slightly surprising recalling the big difference in CDF's of the inter-cell interference. We explain this behaviour by the specific choice of scheduling policy, namely a single RB per user. Under this condition relatively many users (50 with total system bandwidth of 10 MHz) can be served during one TTI and thus increasing the arrival rate does not lead to drastic changes in performance. We should also account for the fact that under low load the scheme is inefficient in the resource use, i.e. artificially keeps data rates lower than the potentially possible.

Although performance is similar there is a clear change between a lightly and heavily loaded system. In a lightly loaded system ordering from the high end of the spectrum in the NC, e.g. CE-end or EC-end, delivers better results (Figure 6(a)). In a system with low load mainly the RBs close to the spectrum end, where allocation starts, are used; RBs from the middle of the spectrum and further are often not allocated. Hence, starting RB allocation in neighbour cells from the opposite ends of the spectrum leads to zero interference for the majority of RBs in the RC. Starting RB allocation in neighbour cells from the same end of the spectrum results in interfering transmissions. In a highly loaded system however, see Figure 6(b), the CE-begin and EC-begin policies perform better. Under high load the majority of RBs are allocated and inter-cell interference appears in the bigger part of the spectrum. Hence, applying ordering policies in neighbour cells that start from the opposite ends of the spectrum allows to exploit the few interference free RBs occasionally left out due to insufficient users.

We can conclude that (i) the type of ordering policy does not impact flow-level performance significantly, regardless of the system load, and (ii) some performance gains, mainly for low system load, can be achieved if the ordering policies in neighbour cells are carefully chosen. The former behaviour is explained by two factors - with a single RB allocation 50 users can be served in parallel in 10 MHz band and having 50 users in the system (even under high load) is rare. Hence, flow changes only cause minor redistribution in the inter-cell interference over the spectrum, suggesting mostly constant interference levels in the long run.

7   Conclusions

This paper discussed the mutual influence scheduling and inter-cell interference have on each other. On the one side, we showed that the inter-cell interference pattern depends on the particular service policy used by the scheduler. On the other side, the study examined the impact of the inter-cell interference on user performance at flow level. The investigations were done for an access-fair scheduling policy with five different approaches of service allocation. Flow-level evaluation was enabled by the use of a hybrid analytical/simulation approach which benefits from providing insights on the performance while supporting quick evaluation.

The results show that the type of the ordering policy significantly affects the inter-cell interference pattern but that this scheduler-specific pattern has little impact on the flow-level performance. By including flow-level behaviour in the analysis we were able to show that certain factors that exhibit strongly at packet level do not affect the eventual performance on a longer time scale (at flow level). This conclusion should be drawn with care since it holds for the particularly studied scheduling scheme. Other schemes may show other behaviour. Still, knowledge on scheduler-dependent inter-cell interference can be used when studying scheduling schemes with interference mitigation.

References

1. 3GPP TS 36.942. LTE; Evolved Universal Terrestrial Radio Access (E-UTRA); Radio Frequency (RF) system scenarios (2010)
2. Bonald, T., Hegde, N.: Capacity gains of some frequency reuse schemes in OFDMA networks. In: Proc. of Globecom 2009, Honolulu, Hawaii, USA, pp. 1–6 (2009)
3. Dimitrova, D.C.: Analysing uplink scheduling in mobile networks. A flow-level perspective. PhD thesis, Wöhrmann Print Service (2010)
4. Dimitrova, D.C., van den Berg, H., Heijenk, G.: Scheduler dependent modelling of inter-cell interference in UMTS EUL. In: Proc. of NGMAST 2008, Cardiff, UK (2009)
5. Fodor, G., Telek, M.: Performance analysis of the uplink of a CDMA cell supporting elastic services. In: Proc. of Networking 2005, Waterloo, Canada (2005)
6. Holma, H., Toskala, A.: LTE for UMTS: OFDMA and SC-FDMA based radio access. John Wiley & Sons Ltd., Chichester (2009)
7. Mao, X., Maaref, A., Teo, K.H.: Adaptive soft frequency reuse for inter-cell interference coordination in SC-FDMA based 3GPP LTE uplinks. In: Proc. of Globecom 2008, New Orleans, Louisiana, USA, pp. 1–6 (2008)
8. Racz, A., Reider, N., Fodor, G.: On the impact of inter-cell interference in LTE. In: Proc. of Globecom 2008, New Orleans, USA, pp. 1–6 (November 2008)
9. Xiang, X., Liu, F., Ji, Y.: Simulation based performance evaluation of ICI mitigation schemes for broadband wireless access networks. In: Proc. of CNS 2008, Montreal, Canada, pp. 181–187 (2008)
10. Xiangning, F., Si, C., Xiaodong, Z.: An inter-cell interference coordination technique based on users' ratio and multi-level frequency allocations. In: Proc. of WiCom 2007, Shanghai, China, pp. 799–802 (2007)
11. Xie, Z., Walke, B.: Resource allocation and reuse for inter-cell interference mitigation in OFDMA based communication networks. In: Proc. of WICON 2010, Singapore-city, Singapore, pp. 1–6 (2010)
12. Zhang, T., Zeng, Z., Feng, C., Cheng, J., Song, L.: Uplink power allocation for interference coordination in multi-cell OFDM systems. In: Proc. of ChinaCom 2008, pp. 716–720 (2008)

Transport over Heterogeneous Networks Using the RINA Architecture*

Eleni Trouva[1], Eduard Grasa[1] John Day[2], Ibrahim Matta[2],
Lubomir T. Chitkushev[2] Steve Bunch[3] Miguel Ponce de Leon[4],
Patrick Phelan[4], and Xavier Hesselbach-Serra[5]

[1] i2CAT Foundation, Jordi Girona, Barcelona, Spain
[2] Computer Science, Boston University, Massachusetts, USA
[3] TRIA Network Systems, LLC, Illinois, USA
[4] TSSG, Waterford Institute of Technology, Ireland
[5] Technical University of Catalonia, UPC, Barcelona, Spain
{eleni.trouva,eduard.grasa}@i2cat.net,
{day,matta,ltc}@bu.edu,
steve.bunch@ieee.org,
{miguelpdl,pphelan}@tssg.org,
xavierh@entel.upc.edu

Abstract. The evolution of various wireless technologies has greatly increased the interest in heterogeneous networks, in which the mobile users can enjoy services while roaming between different networks. The current Internet architecture does not seem to cope with the modern networking trends and the growing application demands for performance, stability and efficiency, as the integration of different technologies faces many problems. In this paper, we focus on the issues raised when attempting to provide seamless mobility over a hybrid environment. We highlight the shortcomings of the current architecture, discuss some of the proposed solutions and try to identify the key choices that lead to failure. Finally, we introduce RINA (Recursive Inter-Network Architecture), a newly-proposed network architecture that achieves to integrate networks of different characteristics inherently and show a simple example that demonstrates this feature.

Keywords: Recursive Inter-Network Architecture (RINA), heterogeneous networks, data transport, mobility, hand-offs.

1 Introduction

The Internet originated from and still is primarily a wired network. However, with the years several wireless technologies evolved to meet the growing need for mobility. Users have come to expect access from anyplace, anywhere. In order to make this vision a reality, in the future users will have a greater choice between

---

* The work of Ibrahim Matta and John Day was supported in part by NSF grant CNS-0963974.

X. Masip-Bruin et al. (Eds.): WWIC 2011, LNCS 6649, pp. 297–309, 2011.

a wide range of services from various access networks, wired and wireless, giving a new meaning to the Internet as an heterogeneous network. In the effort to migrate the current Internet architecture to a hybrid environment, the research community has encountered many problems. One of the main difficulties arose in providing seamless mobility, while achieving the best utilization of the resources.

As transport over heterogeneous networks must be one of the main features of the future network, it should be faced as a chance to re-evaluate the current Internet architecture. In this paper, we review the challenges encountered, examine the proposed solutions and analyze their inability to provide a global solution that addresses all the problems. Next, we explore how these issues are handled when based on fundamental principles as in the Recursive Inter-Network Architecture (RINA), a clean-slate architecture and present a realistic example of RINA over different physical media.

2   Challenges in Mobility over Heterogeneous Networks

2.1   Characteristics of the Hybrid Paths

Hybrid paths exhibit varied behavior across different physical media and technologies as we move from one end of the network to the other. A plethora of available hardware technologies that carry the signal exist and can be classified into guided (wired) or unguided (wireless). In wireless communications, many physical phenomena, such as fading, shadowing, path loss, affect transmission and put impairments in the propagation of the electromagnetic waves. As a result, wireless channels are characterized by higher bit error rates (BER), lower bandwidth and longer round trip times (often variable) comparing to the wired ones.

TCP's performance over hybrid environments has been extensively studied and proven inefficient with the wireless media [2, 5, 8–10]. Specifically, the congestion control mechanisms of TCP are the main reason why TCP fails to adapt to an heterogeneous environment. As already mentioned, BER is high in wireless links, whilst negligible in wired. In addition, wireless links are characterized by interrupted connectivity and frequent hand-offs. Media related losses that happen in wireless links are falsely interpreted by TCP for losses due to congestion in the network and trigger congestion control mechanisms. Each "false alarm" forces a reduction in the TCP window size, which results in a severe drop in throughput. This assumption leads to degradation of performance. In essence, TCP has network congestion control, rather than Internet congestion control.

Another issue occurs from the default behavior of TCP to increase the window size proportionally to the rate of the incoming acknowledgments (ACKs). In hybrid paths, the wireless nature imposes high delays, which implies a slower rate in opening the window compared to pure wired links, although the channel might have the capacity for higher throughput. Most of the operations performed from a mobile terminal (e.g. e-mail, web browsing) require the transmission of small amounts of data on short-lived flows. In TCP a sender starts to transmit data in slow start phase and gradually increases the window and thus, the throughput. For short-lived flows, there is high possibility that the operation will be completed while the sender is still in slow start. This is another case in which the native TCP congestion control mechanisms lead to poor use of the available resources.

To alleviate the problems of traditional TCP new implementations have considered additional mechanisms for congestion control: Congestion Avoidance (Tahoe, Reno, Vegas), Fast Retransmit (Tahoe, New Reno), Fast Recovery (Reno, New Reno) and Selective Acknowledgment (SACK) are some of the algorithms introduced. Nashiry et al. [6] and Henna [7] show results of performance measurements of the TCP variants. However, the problem of opening the window according to the received ACKs rate has remained. Moreover, many TCP modifications were proposed to address the problem, such as TCP SAK, TCP FACK and TCP Santa Cruz.

Apart from these proposals, other approaches tried to address the unsatisfactory performance in heterogeneous environments. One of the ideas proposed was to split a connection over a hybrid path to wired and wireless part, for example at the base station. In this way, the base station has the role of acknowledging every packet back to the source. This solution breaks the end-to-end reliability. It is possible that an ACK arrives to the source without the packet actually has arrived to the destination. Another approach is to perform actions in the data link layer and hide it from the transport layer in order to avoid the problems with TCP. Modifications outside TCP were also proposed. Explicit Congestion Notification (ECN) is an example, in which explicit notification for congestion is signaled by the routers. In addition, some new transport layer protocols were designed with the wired/wireless environment in consideration (e.g. WTCP). Pentikousis [5] provides an extended review of the proposed solutions.

Many of the proposals mentioned above managed to improve the performance of TCP over heterogeneous networks. Yet, none of them manages to address all the problems caused by the characteristics of the hybrid paths, as TCP was not originally designed for such an environment. However, some of the proposed solutions provide some insight on what is the root of the problem. Splitting the hybrid path to wired and wireless for example, underlines the necessity of having a way to treat parts of the network differently, depending on their characteristics, e.g. wired versus wireless links. TCP does not provide us with this functionality as it acts in a global scope, not allowing any further configuration. Taking action in the data link layer and hiding the problem from the transport layer points to the radical idea of explicitly recognizing in its structure that the Internet is a network of networks and points to an architecture of layers that perform the same functions over different scopes. For example, a layer could manage a wired network, another layer could manage a wireless network, and a layer on top of them managing the end to end inter-network.

2.2 Mobility and Hand-offs

As a user moves away from the Access Point (AP) that attaches him to the network, the link quality drops gradually, but with luck another AP is getting closer and can attach to it. Mobility over heterogeneous networks involves hand-offs, as usually the last part of the path before the users terminal is a wireless link. The whole hand-off procedure can be divided in phases: a) discovery, b) selection, b) de-attachment, c) authentication (if required), d) re-attachment. Whether the de-attachment phase precedes or follows the re-attachment to the new AP is a matter of policy or availability. In the case that the de-attachment follows the re-attachment, the mobile node will be multi-homed by two APs for a period of time.

There are two kinds of hand-offs, horizontal and vertical. In an horizontal hand-off, the mobile terminal performs a switch between two wireless APs that belong to the same technology. In a vertical hand-off, APs of different technologies are involved. The switch from one Point of Attachment (PoA) to another might happen while transferring data to another node of the network. The challenge is to allow the user to roam freely between different networks without interruptions or degradation of performance due to hand-offs. The current Internet architecture does not provide a way to address mobility that involves vertical hand-offs. The problem originates from the choice to provide names only for PoAs (IP addresses) and not for the nodes in the naming schema. If the new AP, to which the mobile node attaches, belongs to the same domain with the previous AP, the same IP address may be used. But if the APs belong to different domains (usually the case in vertical hand-offs), the mobile node will be assigned a new IP address and the connection will break due to the infamous TCP pseudo header, which contains the source and the destination IP addresses. The inevitable change of IP address means loss of the nodes identity. Another problem is that during a switch from a fast network to a slow network (and vice versa), the TCP sender does not have a fast way to adapt to the new characteristics of the channel and update accordingly parameters such as the transmission rate, the congestion window and the RTO (retransmission timeout) estimate in order to achieve the best utilization of the resources. Adaptation to the parameters takes place slowly, after several round trips, as the transport layer learns the characteristics of the new channel implicitly by probing it.

TCP was not designed with hand-offs in mind nor is it clear that it should have been. Again, several solutions have been proposed to deal with the problems occurring during a hand-off. The Internet Engineering Task Forces (IETF) Mobile IP uses a foreign agent to update the location of the mobile node at its home agent, thus allowing the mobile node to keep its IP address even when moving. When a mobile node leaves its home router and is attached to a foreign router, the foreign router informs the home router of a care-of address (CoA) to which all packets with destination the mobile node should be sent. An IP tunnel is created between the home agent and the foreign agent with a direct connection to the mobile node. When PDUs are sent to the mobile node with the old IP address, they are routed to the home agent. The home agent knows the mobile node has changed its location. The PDUs are encapsulated and sent down the IP tunnel to the foreign network. There the PDUs are forwarded on the CoA address that connects the mobile node to the foreign agent. Mobile IP achieves mobility, although several issues arise from the use of tunnels. IP tunnels are hard to configure, create various security problems and represent single points of failure (if the home or the foreign agent fail, communication is lost). Traffic going through the home agent distorts the RTT estimates. In addition, extra cost and overhead is added due to the necessary location update messages and registration messages to the home agent. Propagation of the new position of the mobile node will increase the delay perceived by the user and during this location update, some packets may get dropped. As TCP cannot be aware that the loses are a consequence of the hand-off, it will handle the dropped packets as loses due to congestion. A decrease in the TCP window will be forced, resulting in a drop in throughput. The sender will have to wait for the retransmission timeout to expire, to be able to send packets again. The probability of packets re-ordering at the destination will increase.

Several modifications and enhancements to the TCP protocol have been proposed [5, 12] in an attempt to deal with the packet losses and the performance degradation of TCP during a hand-off. One of the ideas is to perform a make-before-break hand-off [13], in which the connection to the old AP breaks after the connection to the new AP has been established to avoid losses. Another proposal is to make TCP aware of the path change due to a vertical hand-off. This information is signaled to the TCP sender from the lower layers of the stack by setting a new TCP option. After the hand-off the sender sets parameters such as the congestion window, RTO as specified for a new connection. To avoid the long delay caused by waiting for the retransmission timeout to expire, the Fast Retransmit algorithm [14] has been introduced. A similar proposal is the use of a TCP retransmission trigger option, which notifies the TCP sender to retransmit packets immediately after the connection to the new AP has been established. Another solution relies on the fact that the TCP receiver on the mobile node explicitly notifies the TCP sender that a hand-off has just taken place and thus, the receiver can take appropriate actions. Packet buffering at the base station [11] is another approach to avoid losses (split-connection protocol, snoop). Again many of the proposed solutions achieve improvement in TCP hand-off performance. However, it seems that once again we miss the root of the problem that needs to be addressed, which is the incomplete naming schema of the current Internet architecture.

3 Recursive Inter-Network Architecture (RINA) over Heterogeneous Networks

Reviewing the proposals made, it is clear that mobility over heterogeneous networks is a very active research area. However, each proposal offers an improvement to one or some of the existing issues but does not address all the problematic points. Several of the solutions work well under specific circumstances and under-perform when the parameters change. None attempts to solve the fundamental problem. As it was already implied, mobility over hybrid environments is incompatible with the current Internet architecture. Trying to stretch the capabilities of the current architecture, does not seem to provide an answer. In the following sections of the paper we present RINA, a clean-slate network architecture that inherently manages to integrate networks of different physical media.

3.1   Main Principles of RINA

RINA is a network architecture proposed by John Day in his book 'Patterns in Network Architecture: A Return to Fundamentals" [1]. RINA is based on the view that networking is only inter-process communication (IPC). The core element of the architecture is a Distributed IPC Facility (DIF). A DIF is a distributed application that provides IPC for a given range of QoS. Any two application processes[1] in different systems are able to communicate using the services provided by a DIF. DIFs of higher levels are able to use the services provided by DIFs of lower levels, forming a recursive structure. A DIF is a layer, but not in the same sense as in the current Internet architecture[2]. In RINA all layers use the same protocols to perform a coordinated set of policy managed functions and achieve the desired IPC service. A detailed description of the RINA model, as well as its features, can be found in [1, 4]. In this paper we intend to explore the way RINA deals with transport over heterogeneous networks by examining how mobility and hand-offs are handled.

3.2   Hybrid Paths in RINA

RINA provides a recursive architecture formed by different layers stacked one on top of the other. Each layer is self-contained, and operates a complete set of mechanisms to provide data transport services to the client layers, the layers above. These mechanisms include data transport, relaying and multiplexing of data packets, transmission control, flow control, congestion control, authentication and others. A key feature of RINA is that the protocols implementing these mechanisms are the same in each layer, but operate under different configurations (policies) in order to make their operation optimal for certain conditions. The structure provided by RINA perfectly suits the requirements of transport over heterogeneous paths, as with RINA there is no need for mechanisms or algorithms that work well for all types of physical media. Each physical medium has its own dedicated DIF, tailored to the specific medium characteristics. In fact, the configuration of the lower level DIFs aims to match the best way possible the QoS requirements set by the higher level DIFs. Applications that use the transport services provided by DIFs still can have end-to-end mechanisms, such as end-to-end error, flow, and congestion control, as they typically use a DIF that is sitting on top of multiple lower level DIFs, which in turn operate on top of different physical media. Examples of this recursive structure are illustrated in Fig(s). 2, 3 and 4.

---

[1] For clarity, we refer to application processes that are members of a DIF as IPC Processes and users of a DIF as application processes or simply applications.

[2] To compare to the Internet, (MAC, LLC) are one layer; Network and Transport are one layer. They are complete units of IPC.

3.3   Mobility and Hand-offs in RINA

RINA provides names for applications/nodes rather than interfaces (PoAs). This choice permits routing on the node level and not on the interface level, as in the current Internet architecture and thus, multihoming is supported. In fact, it is provided as a consequence of the structure without the need of any special protocols.

Mobility can be seen as a dynamic version of multihoming with "expected failures". As the mobile node moves, it acquires new points of attachments that connect it to the network. In RINA each new PoA means that the mobile system joins a new DIF. Thus, while moving, the mobile node joins new DIFs and drops its participation in the old ones, a procedure that is equivalent to the attachment and de-attachment to APs during a hand-off. At times, the mobile node might be a member of more than one DIF (multi-homed), which is analogous to a mobile terminal that is in range of several APs and is connected to the network by more than one of them.

To better understand how mobility works, a closer look to the naming and addressing schema used in RINA is required. Figure 1 shows an example of the RINA architecture with two levels of DIFs. A DIF maps the source and the destination application names to node addresses (IPC processes) through the directory function. Then, the route from a source application to a destination application is computed as a sequence of (N)-addresses (the blue line in Fig.1), where the next hop is a node address. Each IPC process knows how to map (N)-addresses to (N-1)-addresses for all nearest neighbors to determine the path to the next hop. Having the addressing schema of RINA in mind, multihoming could now be expressed as an IPC process having more than one (N-1) mapping and mobility as acquiring new (N-1) mappings to use and maybe losing some others. Thus, in any hand-off scenario, vertical or horizontal, indifferent of the technology of the physical media, connecting to a new AP means that an IPC process acquires a new (N-1) binding. For the incoming flows, this new binding is the last binding in the translation of a route to a path connecting a source IPC process to a destination IPC process, while for the outgoing flows

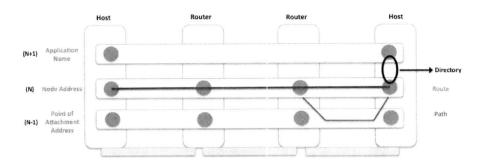

Fig. 1. Translating a route to a path in RINA naming and addressing schema

is the first binding. The cost for updating this new binding is small, since the update is done locally during the route to path translation. Ishakian et al. [3] provide further analysis on this cost. Acquiring or dropping (N-1) bindings may modify the graph (topology) at the (N)-layer. These changes are disseminated through routing updates, which will trigger the recalculation of the local forwarding tables of the affected IPC-processes of the N-layer. It is important to note that routing updates carry information about changes in the graph only regarding IPC process addresses ((N)-addresses). The bindings of (N)-addresses to (N-1)-address are a local matter of each IPC process.

4   An Example of Hand-off in RINA Architecture

In this section, we present a simple hand-off scenario in order to explain how transport over heterogeneous networks is handled in RINA architecture. Our scenario involves a user moving around with a mobile terminal causing hand-offs (Fig. 2). The mobile terminal has two different interfaces active (e.g. Wi-Fi and GPRS). An application process running on the user's terminal has opened a connection with an application process running on a server and data transfer is taking place (e.g. the user is streaming live video). While the connection is open and packets are in transit, the user moves physically, forcing a hand-off from the one AP to the other. In our example this is vertical hand-off, as the first AP is a WLAN router (e.g. Wi-Fi) and the second AP is a router of some technology belonging to the Long Term Evolution (LTE) standard (e.g. GPRS, WiMAX).

Having both APs connected to the same router that the server is connected to is unlike to happen in reality, but we are pointing to a simplified scenario that can be easily pictured and understood by the reader. However, this choice does not spoil the generality, since the number of the possible intermediates does not affect the way mobility and hand-offs are treated in RINA.

Figure 2 depicts the case in which the user is in the range only of the Wi-Fi and the terminal is attached to the network through the first AP. In the lower part of figure we can see the RINA architecture for this case. We illustrate as "source" the system of the server that shares content to the mobile user and as "destination" the system of the mobile terminal. "Intermediate" is an intermediate router that connects through a wired link the server from the one side and the two APs (WLAN and LTE routers) from the other. The oval shapes are the IPC application processes residing in each system. In different colors and numbered from 1 to 7 are the DIFs formed, which are the layers of the RINA architecture. The DIFs numbered 1 - 6 are lower level DIFs (0-level or 0-DIFs), while the larger DIF, numbered 7, is an upper level DIF (1-level or 1-DIF). We can see that the whole architecture involves only application processes that communicate with each other (IPC).

Although it is possible to have multiple layers of DIFs to achieve further configuration through policies, in our example we have chosen to describe a 2-layer RINA architecture for simplicity. The reader should keep in mind that a

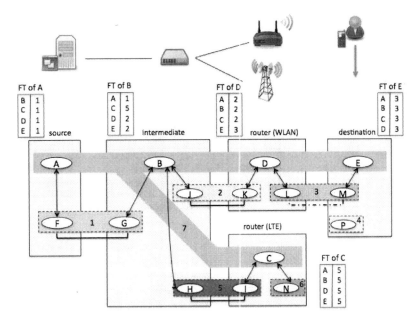

Fig. 2. The mobile terminal is connected to the first AP

0- level DIF for each media AP with a 1-level DIF for networks of a given type, i.e. technology dependent and a 2-level DIF for the technology independent service would be the norm.

The letter in each IPC process denotes its address. Every IPC process has a forwarding table with entries that map addresses of IPC processes to lower level DIFs, so that an IPC process knows where to forward an incoming PDU with a specific destination address. At the lower parts of the 0-DIFs we can see the physical links. The wireless links are denoted with dotted lines, while the wired ones are with continuous lines. As we can see in Fig.2, 0-level DIFs are sitting on top of every physical link, wired or wireless. These 0-level DIFs allow to perform different configurations through policies analogous to the characteristics of each medium. In this way the 0-level DIFs, although configuring different kind of media, provide the 1-level DIF service with certain properties (e.g. loss, delay), so that, transport at the N-DIF can operate more effectively. The 1-DIF can be seen as an "overlay" to which the source, the intermediate router, the Wi-Fi router, the LTE router and the destination have subscribed and it can be used by the applications of the source and the destination systems to request IPC services. The DIF numbered 4, which consists only of one IPC process, denotes that a second interface is operative in the user's mobile terminal but without a connection to an AP.

The upper DIF maps the source and destination application process names (applications running on the server and the mobile terminal respectively) to IPC process addresses (A and E). For the data transfer between the server and the mobile terminal, the route from A to E is computed as a sequence of intermediate

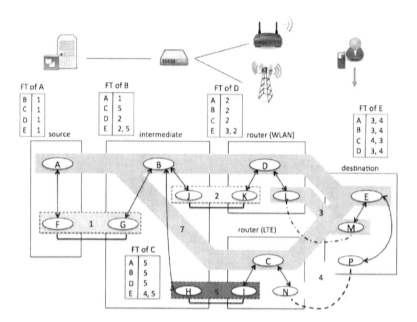

Fig. 3. As the user moves, gets in the range of the second AP and connects to it through the second interface on his terminal (multi-homing)

addresses of the 1-level DIF (A, B, D, E). Using its forwarding table, each IPC process has mappings of (N)-DIF addresses to DIFs of the (N-1)-layer, in order to determine the next hop. For example, for a PDU to reach to destination IPC process E, A will forward it to DIF 1, B to DIF 2, etc.

The next figure (Fig. 3) illustrates the changes that happen when the user enters in the range of the second AP and connects to it through an other interface of his terminal. At this moment the mobile node is multi-homed, having the two interfaces on his terminal connected to the two different APs. The IPC processes P and N form a new DIF numbered 4, which is configured according to the characteristics of the wireless link connecting the LTE router and the mobile terminal. A new binding that points to the 0-DIF is added to the forwarding table of IPC process E. This new binding causes changes to the topology of the 1-layer, since the IPC processes A, B and D are now reachable from E through C. These changes are disseminated using routing updates, which trigger re-calculation of the forwarding tables in each IPC process of the 1-layer (DIF 7). Fig. 3 shows the entries of the forwarding tables after the end of this re-calculation process.

Figure 4 describes what happens when the user moves out of the range of the first AP, but remains connected to the second one, completing the hand-off process. The IPC process M departs from DIF 3 and the (N-1)-binding between the processes E and M is dropped. This removal will cause changes to the graph of the 1-DIF, which will be advertised to the rest 1-layer processes through routing updates. In turn, re-calculations of the forwarding tables will take effect to reflect the current bindings.

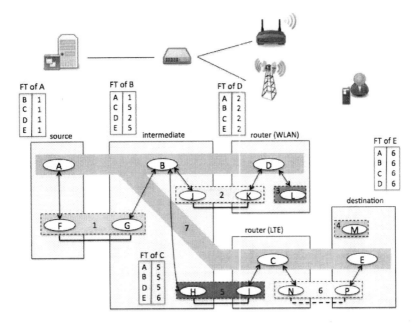

Fig. 4. The user gets out of the range of the first AP and remains connected only through the second one

5   Conclusions, On-Going and Future Work

Despite all the work carried out in many years, transport over heterogeneous networks is still a challenge today. In this paper we indicated that the architectural choices in the current Internet architecture lie at the root of the problem. Specifically, we observed two flaws: The first one is that the current Internet architecture does not recognize that it is operating over more than one network. Although, the network and transport layers operate on top of networks with very different characteristics, the functions they provide apply on a global scope. Trying to perform the same function over different physical networks will always lead to inefficiencies, as it allows for a single configuration, which makes it impossible to adapt to the specific requirements each network imposes. A structure that allows different instances of the same functions to operate independently over different scopes will provide a better framework to achieve transport over hybrid networks. The second flaw we noted is that the current Internet architecture has an incomplete naming and addressing schema, which makes mobility hard, expensive and inefficient. An architecture that provides different names for its basic entities (nodes, PoAs and applications) supports mobility and multi-homing inherently. Following the above observations, we presented RINA, a Recursive Inter-Network Architecture that provides the two features missing from the

current architecture, along with many more (support for QoS, multicast, enhanced security). Adopting RINA as the architecture for future networks would
make it much easier to support transport over heterogeneous networks.

Currently we are developing a prototype that implements the RINA. Future
work includes experimentation with the developed prototype over networks of
different physical media and further research, measurements and performance
comparisons of RINA versus the current Internet architecture.

References

1. Day, J.: Patterns in Network Architecture: A Return to Fundamentals (2008)
2. Tsaoussidis, V., Matta, I.: Open issues on TCP for mobile computing. Wireless
   Communications and Mobile Computing 2(1), 3–20 (2002)
3. Ishakian, V., Matta, I., Akinwumi, J.: On the cost of supporting mobility and multihoming. In: GLOBECOM Workshops, pp. 310–314. IEEE, Los Alamitos (2010)
4. Day, J., Matta, I., Mattar, K.: Networking is IPC: A Guiding Principle to a Better
   Internet. In: Proc. of ReArch 2008, Madrid, Spain (2008)
5. Pentikousis, K.: TCP in wired-cum-wireless environments. IEEE Communications
   Surveys and Tutorials 3, 2–14 (2000)
6. Nashiry, M.A., Abdullah-Al-Mahmud, M., Rahman, M.M., Anjum, M.N.: Evaluation of TCP performance over mobile IP wired-cum-wireless networks. In: 11th
   International Conf. on ICCIT, pp. 150–155 (2008)
7. Henna, S.: A Throughput Analysis of TCP Variants in Mobile Wireless Networks.
   In: NGMAST Third International Conf., pp. 279–284, 15–18 (2009)
8. Balakrishnan, H., Seshan, S., Amir, E., Katz, R.H.: Improving TCP/IP Performance over Wireless Networks. In: Proc. of 1st ACM Conf. on Mobile Computing
   and Networking (1995)
9. Caceres, R., Iftode, L.: The Effects of Mobility on Reliable Transport Protocols.
   In: Proc. 14th Conf. Distributed Computing Systems, pp. 12–20 (1994)
10. DeSimone, A., Chuah, M.C., Yue, O.C.: Throughput Performance of Transport-
    Layer Protocols over Wireless LANs. In: Proc. GLOBECOM (1993)
11. Eom, D.S., Lee, H.S., Sugano, M., Murata, M., Miyahara, H.: Improving TCP
    handoff performance in Mobile IP based networks. In: Computer Communications,
    pp. 635–646 (2002)
12. Ben-Othman, J., Nait-Abdesselam, F., Mokdad, L., Ramirez, O.: Performance
    evaluation of TCP handoffs over mobile IP connections. In: Proc. of the 2008
    IEEE/ACS (2008)
13. Daniel, L., Kojo, M.: Adapting TCP for Vertical Handoffs in Wireless Networks.
    In: Proc. 31st IEEE LCN, pp. 151–158 (2006)
14. Caceres, R., Iftode, L.: Improving the performance of reliable transport protocols
    in mobile computing environments. IEEE Journal on In Selected Areas in Com-
    munications 13(5), 850–857 (1995)

An Adaptive Resource Control Mechanism in Multi-hop Ad-Hoc Networks

Yimeng Yang[1,*], Geert Heijenk[1], and Boudewijn R. Haverkort[1,2]

[1] CTIT, University of Twente, P.O. Box 217,
7500 AE Enschede, Enschede, The Netherlands
yangy@ewi.utwente.nl
[2] Embedded Systems Institute, Eindhoven, The Netherlands

Abstract. This paper presents an adaptive resource control mechanism for multi-hop ad-hoc network systems, which avoids bottleneck problems caused by the node-fairness property of IEEE 802.11. In our proposal, the feedback information from the downstream bottleneck, derived from Request-To-Send (RTS) and Clear-To-Send (CTS) messages is utilized to control the Transmission Opportunity (TXOP) limit of the upstream nodes for traffic balancing. The proposed mechanism is modelled control-theoretically using the 20-sim control system modelling tool, which has the advantage that results can be obtained in a fast and efficient way. Compared to systems without resource control, a higher throughput and lower delay can be achieved under a variety of traffic load conditions as well as in dynamic network environments.

Keywords: resource control; multi-hop; 802.11; RTS/CTS; TXOP.

1 Introduction

IEEE 802.11 [1] based Wireless Local Area Networks (WLANs) are in widespread deployment nowadays. In the 802.11 Medium Access Control (MAC), the Distributed Coordination Function (DCF) is the key mechanism to provide shared access in an ad-hoc mode. In most scenarios, the equal access as provided by the DCF is desirable. However, in certain multi-hop wireless networks, the fairness among contending nodes will lead to undesirable situations where packets may get lost at bottlenecks even after having gone through the initial hops already. In this paper, we consider multi-hop ad-hoc network scenarios, in which certain nodes happen to function as bottlenecks, forwarding packets received from a number of upstream nodes towards other stations. In 802.11 DCF ad-hoc network systems, a certain bottleneck obtains an equal capacity share as any one of its upstream nodes in the same interference domain; however, it has to support the traffic from all of them. This leads to a very high queue length of the bottleneck, eventually also buffer overflow, and in any case, long delays.

In order to combat this packet loss problem in multi-hop ad-hoc networks, an adaptive resource control mechanism is proposed to provide efficient use of the limited channel capacity by applying controlled access differentiation. The mechanism utilizes

---

* Corresponding author.

X. Masip-Bruin et al. (Eds.): WWIC 2011, LNCS 6649, pp. 309–322, 2011.

information in the Request-To-Send/Clear-To-Send (RTS/CTS) message exchange, and is generally applicable to access mechanism using RTS/CTS. The proposed resource control mechanism is modelled with a control-theoretic modeling approach, and the system performance is evaluated using the 20-sim tool [15].

The contributions of this paper are as follows: (i) We introduce an adaptive resource control mechanism, in which there is no modification to the IEEE 802.11 standard frames, no control overhead in the frame structure, and no need for a centralized controller. (ii) The designed mechanism is modelled in a control-theoretic way. The control model is hierarchically structured and formalized, and results can be obtained much more quickly and efficiently compared to an ns-2 simulation. (iii) Experimental results show that the new mechanism is able to provide fair and efficient capacity use, avoids packet loss at intermediate bottlenecks, achieves fairly low queuing delay, and quickly adapts to network environmental changes.

The remainder of the paper is organized as follows. Section 2 introduces background and related work. Section 3 discusses the objectives of the TXOP control, and describes the new control mechanism for multi-hop ad-hoc networks. Section 4 presents a control-theoretic model for the proposed mechanism modeling. Section 5 shows experimental results, and in Section 6 the paper is concluded.

2 Background and Related Work

RTS/CTS is an optional four-way handshaking mechanism adopted by the 802.11 DCF to reduce data frame collisions caused by the hidden terminal problem. The RTS and CTS are short frames exchanged prior to data transmission between a pair of source and destination nodes. Before transmitting a packet, an RTS will be broadcasted comprising the destination address and the expected data duration information. Besides the intended destination, this RTS packet can also be received by all other nodes in reach of the source node, so that they will refrain from accessing the medium during the period that the source will be transmitting. To acknowledge the receipt of an RTS, the destination node replies with a CTS packet, which is also a broadcast packet including the data duration information. Therefore, with the RTS/CTS mechanism applied, other nodes within the range of both the source and the destination will not disturb the medium for the intended packet transmission time until the following acknowledgement (ACK).

In order to support Quality of Service (QoS) in WLANs, an Hybrid Coordination Function (HCF) has been proposed and incorporated in [1]. The TXOP limit is one of the QoS differentiation parameters specified in 802.11 HCF, which is defined as the time interval during which multiple packets are allowed to be transmitted consecutively by one station per successful channel access. However, the problem is how to set the TXOP for good performance and fairness trade-off. To overcome the problem of selecting a fixed TXOP setting, in this paper the TXOP limit is made adaptive.

In [2], a control-theoretic model has been designed for 802.11 ad-hoc networks, in which a chosen TXOP limit is studied to improve the system performance. However, the dynamic adaptation of the TXOP parameter according to the current network situation is not done. An adaptive TXOP allocation is achieved in [3,4] to improve the system efficiency. However, in [3,4] a <u>centralized</u> controller, known as the Hybrid Coordinator

(HC) is required, which is not applicable in distributed wireless ad-hoc networks. A resource allocation protocol has been described in [5] to provide a QoS service in 802.11 networks, which allows each individual node to adjust its TXOP limit when it wins a channel contention. However, each node has to monitoring the MAC-level queue continuously in order to obtain the queue length and packet arrival information. The work [6] proposed an adaptive resource control mechanism in 2-hop ad-hoc networks, which can not be applied in multi-hop network scenarios, because the TXOP limit of the bottleneck node is set to a fixed value.

Our proposed resource control is based on an improved Additive Increase Multiplicative Decrease (AIMD) algorithm, in which the TXOP decrease ratio can be dynamically adapted according to the current network condition. A lot of work has been done in order to provide solutions for the AIMD improvement. Yang and Lam [7] presented a relationship between the increase rate and decrease ratio parameters to produce TCP-friendly flows. These parameters can be further dynamically adjusted based on current network condition for smooth multimedia streaming [8]. However, all their work is limited to TCP congestion control. In TCP, each sender limits its sending rate as a function of perceived network congestion in order to resolve the packet loss problem; this leads to underutilization of the limited channel resource in wireless environment [9]. There are different techniques proposed to adapt the standard TCP to wireless networks [10,11]. However, TCP modifications or other link layer solutions are required. In [12], a congestion control mechanism combined with random access MAC has been proposed to improve network utilization in multi-hop wireless networks. However, an enhanced carrier-sensing technique is required to provide full awareness of a link's neighbor set.

In this paper a new resource control mechanism based on TXOP adaptation is proposed. It is able not only to avoid congestion at bottleneck nodes, but also to ensure high network throughput. Furthermore, our mechanism requires no modification to the IEEE 802.11 frames and no control overhead as well.

3   Resource Control Objectives and Designed Mechanism

Section 3.1 discusses the objectives of resource control. Section 3.2 presents our resource control strategy for multi-hop ad-hoc networks, and in Section 3.3, the TXOP value assignment method is introduced.

3.1   Resource Control Objectives

The objectives of the resource control design for multi-hop ad-hoc networks are as follows:

(1) *Fairness:* Ideally, a fair capacity sharing among all flows, regardless of the number of hops is desired. However, in wireless ad-hoc network systems, only local information can be utilized by each node since global knowledge of the entire network is not available. With our resource control mechanism applied, an equal sharing of the channel capacity among all the nodes on each individual hop can be achieved.

(2) *Maximizing the network throughput:* It has been shown in [14] that higher network throughput can be achieved by adopting a larger TXOP limit, leading to less frequent channel competition. However, in multi-hop ad-hoc networks, packet loss

occurs at bottlenecks if all the nodes transmit with the maximum TXOP value. As a result, the resource capacity consumed on the initial hops will be wasted. Therefore, TXOP control is required to provide more efficient use of the channel capacity, meanwhile ensuring the network throughput.

(3) *Avoiding bottleneck overflow:* All incoming packets can be fully forwarded by each bottleneck node, i.e., no packet loss at bottlenecks.

(4) *Minimizing the queuing delay:* The queue lengths at each node within the network should be as small as possible.

(5) *Being adaptable in dynamic network environments:* The resource control system should react on network changes quickly.

3.2   Resource Control Strategy

The key idea of our TXOP control is that upstream nodes transmitting through the same downstream bottleneck adjust their TXOP limits based on the feedback information obtained from the bottleneck node. Note that in the following, we will express the TXOP value in terms of number of packets that can be transmitted within the chosen TXOP (as alternative notion of time).

For simplicity, the proposed TXOP control mechanism will be presented by considering a simple 2-hop network scenario, as depicted in Fig.1. A bottleneck node B forwards packets received from a number of n sources towards other destinations. Sources and the bottleneck are all within reach of each other; hence, share the same bandwidth capacity during communication.

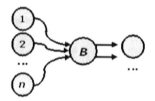

The detailed TXOP control procedure is illustrated in Fig.2. We see in Fig.2(a) that in case one of the source nodes i $(i = 1, 2, \ldots, n)$ wins a channel competition, an RTS packet will be sent including its current expected Packet Transmission Duration information, PTD_i, from which the number of packets intended to transmit, T_i can

Fig. 1. Bottleneck in a 2-hop ad-hoc network

be computed, relying on a fixed data rate assumption. Note that T_i is determined by the number of queued packets in the buffer of node i, q_i and its TXOP limit, i.e., $T_i = \min(q_i, TXOP_i)$. After receiving this RTS, a CTS packet will be broadcast by B, also including the PTD_i. Therefore, all the source nodes that have seen this CTS are informed about the number of packets that will arrive at B, A_B, in source i's current channel access. By this means, the source nodes can accumulate all the A_B based on a number of consecutive CTS received from B in order to obtain the total number of packets arrived at B, $\sum A_B$, until B wins a channel access. As soon as the bottleneck B obtains a chance to transmit, the number of packets that will be transmitted by B, T_B, can be calculated by the sources as well according to the broadcasted RTS from B, as shown in Fig.2(b). After comparing $\sum A_B$ with T_B, the TXOP limit of each source i, $TXOP_i$, can be adapted accordingly. If the total number of packets that arrived at B is equal to the amount that can be currently transmitted, i.e., $\sum A_B = T_B$, the bottleneck B is considered to be lightly loaded, so that each source will try to increase the $TXOP_i$. As a result, more packets are sent to B, which leads to a larger $\sum A_B$. In case

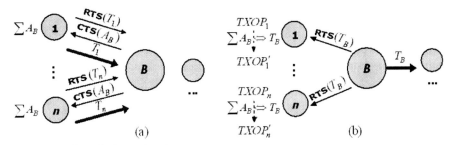

A - Num. of packets arrived;
T - Num. of packets transmitted;

Fig. 2. TXOP control procedure

the overall feedback value $\sum A_B$ is larger than T_B, $TXOP_i$ will be decreased, leading to fewer packet arrivals at B, so that the queue of the bottleneck will be emptied, during which each source will keep its current $TXOP_i$ until the bottleneck B becomes lightly loaded again. The specific algorithm proposed for TXOP value assignment will be discussed in Section 3.3.

With this feedback TXOP control strategy applied, fairness between two consecutive hops will be achieved, regardless of the number of nodes competing for bandwidth at each hop. The use of the RTS/CTS message for feedback realizes this control strategy at no additional cost in terms of bits to be transmitted and no protocol changes!

3.3 TXOP Value Assignment

In order to provide fairness among the nodes on each individual hop in multi-hop ad-hoc networks, a variation on the Additive Increase Multiplicative Decrease (AIMD) mechanism known from TCP congestion control is used to adapt each source i's TXOP value. AIMD has been proven in [13] to be able to provide fairness among sources. The $TXOP_i(\alpha, \beta)$ control algorithm is expressed as follows:

$$TXOP'_i = \begin{cases} TXOP_i + \alpha, & \sum A_B = T_B \text{ (lightly loaded at } B), \\ TXOP_i \cdot (1 - \beta), & \sum A_B > T_B \text{ (over loaded at } B), \\ TXOP_i, & \sum A_B < T_B \text{ (queue emptying at } B), \end{cases} \tag{1}$$

where α and β are control gains used to determine the increase rate and decrease ratio of $TXOP_i$, respectively, and $TXOP'^1_i$ denotes the value of source i's TXOP limit after control. Note that in order to drain the queue of the bottleneck B, the current $TXOP_i$ will be kept unchanged in case $\sum A_B < T_B$. We only increase $TXOP_i$ when $\sum A_B = T_B$, since B's queue can then be perceived to be emptied.

The problem now focuses on how to choose proper control gains α and β. We assign α to 1 to achieve a slow increase of the TXOP value, so that large system variation can be avoided. As an improvement on the original AIMD, an adaptive control gain $\hat{\beta}$ is

---

[1] $TXOP'_i$ can be a real number if fragmentation is applied during packet transmission in practice.

dynamically computed according to the current traffic load condition of the bottleneck B, leading to a more efficient use of the channel capacity. In case $\sum A_B$ is larger than T_B, the following total number of packets that may arrive at B, $\sum A'_B$ will be controlled to be equal the number of packets that can be transmitted by B minus the amount currently stuck in B's queue, that is,

$$\sum A'_B = T_B - \left(\sum A_B - T_B\right). \tag{2}$$

Moreover, the TXOP limit of each source i determines the number of packets that will arrive at B, therefore, the control gain $\hat{\beta}$ used to control $TXOP_i$ is applied to $\sum A_B$ as well:

$$\sum A'_B = \sum A_B \cdot (1 - \hat{\beta}). \tag{3}$$

According to (2) and (3), the control gain $\hat{\beta}$ can then be calculated as follows:

$$\hat{\beta} = \frac{2 \cdot \left(\sum A_B - T_B\right)}{\sum A_B}. \tag{4}$$

In most cases, each source i can determine its TXOP limit using the derived $\hat{\beta}$. However, in dynamic network environment the bottleneck B may become overloaded when a group of source nodes join into the network simultaneously. As a result, the $TXOP'_i$ for the following packet transmission will be controlled to be smaller than 1 or even be negative according to the adopted $\hat{\beta}$. In this case, we assign $TXOP'_i$ to 0, so that the transmission of the sources can be temporary suspended until all packets arrived at B are perceived to be successfully transmitted ($\sum T_B = \sum A_B$), and then the $TXOP'_i$ will be reset to 1. Note that with this source nodes' transmission suspension method applied, the bottleneck can also obtain more opportunities to access the medium to empty its queue.

4   Resource Control System Modeling

In ad-hoc network systems, all the nodes within reach of each other compete for medium access in a distributed manner without any central coordination function. We abstract from this random access method, and implement the proposed resource control mechanism in a basic control-theoretic way. To model the TXOP control process, we adopt a discrete (integer) time scale as presented in Fig.3, in which t represents a discrete time instant, and the following time interval is denoted by $I_t = [t, t+1]$. It is assumed that all the nodes within the network may get a chance to transmit once in each time interval I_t for simplicity.

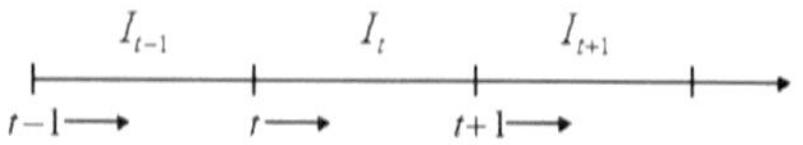

Fig. 3. Timing scheme for control system modeling

According to the discrete timing scheme, a basic control-theoretic modeling framework is designed and illustrated in Fig.4. The TXOP control mechanism described in Section 3 is modelled in the "TXOP control" module. It is clear that the number of packets transmitted by B in current time interval I_t, $T_B(t)$ and the accumulated packet arrivals $A_B(t)$ are used by each source

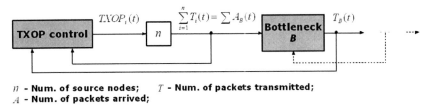

n - **Num. of source nodes;** T - **Num. of packets transmitted;**
A - **Num. of packets arrived;**

Fig. 4. The basic control-theoretic modeling framework

i to control its TXOP value. Note that the TXOP adaptation behaviour of n homogeneous source nodes is identically controlled by the feedback from B, therefore, we only model it once using the "TXOP control" module, as shown in Fig.4. By multiplying the adapted $TXOP_i(t)$ with n, we obtain the total number of packets transmitted by n sources in the current interval I_t, $\sum_{i=1}^{n} T_i(t)$ (assuming saturated sources). It is equal to $\sum A_B(t)$, which will further impact the bottleneck B's following packet transmission.

Note that our control-theoretic model can be easily extended by adding more steps in terms of hops, and then the TXOP limit of the bottleneck B will also be controlled by its downstream node. Moreover, we can also have more source and bottleneck nodes on each individual hop. Therefore, using the control-theoretic model the presented TXOP control mechanism can be studied under various network topologies.

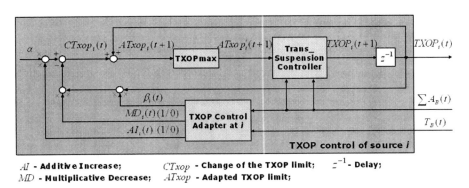

AI - **Additive Increase;** $CTxop$ - **Change of the TXOP limit;** z^{-1} - **Delay;**
MD - **Multiplicative Decrease;** $ATxop$ - **Adapted TXOP limit;**

Fig. 5. Source i's "TXOP control" module

The detail of each source i's "TXOP control" module is depicted in Fig.5. Following the control rule presented in (1), the TXOP Control Adapter function block activates either the TXOP Additive Increase (AI) or the Multiplicative Decrease (MD) process by setting the corresponding output, i.e., $AI_i(t)$ or $MD_i(t)$, to 1 according to the perceived $\sum A_B(t)$ and $T_B(t)$ at t. Note that if the TXOP limit of source i is determined to be unchanged in the following time interval I_{t+1}, both $AI_i(t)$ and $MD_i(t)$ will be set to 0. Furthermore, in case the current $MD_i(t)$ is 1, the current $\hat{\beta}_i(t)$ will be calculated based on (4), otherwise, it is assigned 0. The change of $TXOP_i(t)$ after control, $CTxop_i(t)$, can then be derived as follows:

$$CTxop_i(t) = \begin{cases} \alpha, & \sum A_B(t) = T_B(t), \\ -\hat{\beta}_i(t) \cdot TXOP_i(t), & \sum A_B(t) > T_B(t), \\ 0, & \sum A_B(t) < T_B(t). \end{cases} \quad (5)$$

Based on the $CTxop_i(t)$, the adapted TXOP limit of source i for the following interval I_{t+1}, $ATxop_i(t+1)$, can be expressed as:

$$ATxop_i(t+1) = TXOP_i(t) + CTxop_i(t). \quad (6)$$

In addition, a general TXOP upper limit, $TXOP_{max}$, has to be applied to restrict each source i's channel occupancy in time interval I_{t+1}, $ATxop_i'(t+1) = \min(ATxop_i(t+1), TXOP_{max})$.

The transmission suspension method described in Section 3.3 is implemented in the Trans_Suspension Controller function block, as shown in Fig.5. If the value of $ATxop_i'(t+1)$ is not smaller than 1, the output TXOP limit of source i in I_{t+1}, $TXOP_i(t+1)$, is equal to the input $ATxop_i'(t+1)$, otherwise, it will be assigned to 0, that is:

$$TXOP_i(t+1) = \begin{cases} ATxop_i'(t+1), & ATxop_i'(t+1) \geq 1, \\ 0, & ATxop_i'(t+1) < 1. \end{cases} \quad (7)$$

Note that in case of $ATxop_i'(t+1) < 1$, $TXOP_i(t+1)$ will be kept to 0 until all the packets arrived at B in I_t, $\sum A_B(t)$, have been successfully transmitted, and then $TXOP_i(t+1)$ will be reset to 1, following (5).

The queue dynamics of the bottleneck B is illustrated in Fig.6. The queue length of

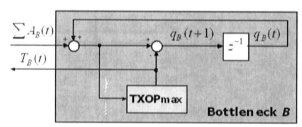

q - Queue length;

Fig. 6. The bottleneck module

B at $t+1$ is equal to that at the current t plus the total number of packets arrived, and minus those can be transmitted within I_t:

$$q_B(t+1) = q_B(t) + \sum A_B(t) - T_B(t). \quad (8)$$

Note that to ensure the current $T_B(t)$ to be no more than the adopted $TXOP_{max}$, the TXOP$_{max}$ function block is applied as well.

Using the described basic TXOP control model, the introduced TXOP control mechanism can be studied in a simple and explicit way. As a further step, this basic model is embedded into the control-theoretic framework introduced in [2] in order to include random access behaviour, in order to be able to also do the performance evaluation of the TXOP control in IEEE 802.11 DCF applied multi-hop ad-hoc network systems. The corresponding experimental results are presented in Section 5.2.

5   Experimental Results

The adaptive resource control mechanism introduced in Section 3 is studied using the software package 20-sim [15]. A multi-hop network scenario is designed, as shown in Fig.7. There are two intermediate bottleneck nodes IB_1 and IB_2, each of which forwards packets received from a number of n sources towards other stations via the same

bottleneck B. Note that we model intermediate bottlenecks using the bottleneck module presented in Fig.6, in which the TXOP control module presented in Fig.5 is embedded instead of the TXOPmax function block. We assign the system parameter $TXOP_{max}$ to 10, which is used for B's packet transmission per successful channel acquisition. Note that the value of the $TXOP_{max}$ can be chosen according to the delay and delay jitter requirements of different network systems. Furthermore, a saturated network condition is assumed, so that the TXOP limit of each source node will always be reached per channel access.

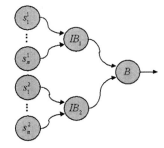

Fig. 7. Designed multi-hop network scenario

Note that the proposed mechanism is also applicable in many other network topologies, e.g., more nodes functioning as the second-hop bottlenecks instead of just B. In case there are more downstream nodes available, multiple TXOP adaptation processes can be maintained at a node based on feedback information from the corresponding receivers.

5.1   Results without Random Access

The performance of the resource control mechanism is evaluated using the basic control model without random access, as explained in Section 4. We consider a non-static network situation in which the intermediate bottleneck IB_2 with n sources joins the network after time interval 200. Note that in what follows, we denote the group of all sources sending to IB_j as $S_j = \{s_1^j, \ldots, s_n^j\}$ ($j = 1, 2$). For the parameter setting $n = 3$, the corresponding system response is depicted in Fig.8, where the performance shows the adapted TXOP limits of IB_1 and its sources S_1 at each time epoch t.

Since in the first 200 time intervals there is only one intermediate bottleneck in the network, all packets from IB_1 can be forwarded by the bottleneck B, hence, the TXOP value of IB_1 always reaches $TXOP_{max}$. After n sources of IB_2 joining into the network, the $TXOP_{IB_1}$ will be controlled to be smaller, leading to a decrease of the TXOP

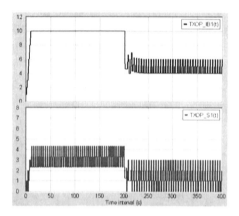

Fig. 8. TXOP limit as a function of time under non-static network conditions

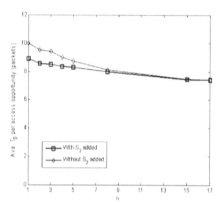

Fig. 9. Average T_B per access opportunity

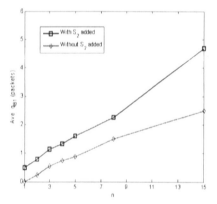

Fig. 10. Average queue length at IB_1

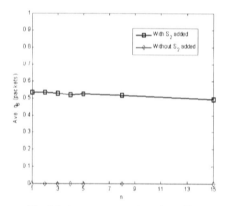

Fig. 11. Average queue length at B

limit of s_i^1 ($i = 1, 2, \ldots, n$). It can also be observed in Fig.8 that the TXOP control system reacts on network condition changes quickly, so that the system becomes stable again within a few time intervals. Note that the TXOP values of all the sources and intermediate bottlenecks are adapted based on the algorithm presented in Section 3.3.

We continue now to study the average number of packets transmitted by the second-hop bottleneck B, T_B, per access opportunity for varying number of sources of each intermediate bottleneck, n. Simulation results in Fig.9 show that the average throughput T_B decreases when the group of sources S_2 are added into the network. This is due to the fact that the adding of the sources and the corresponding node IB_2 increases the variation of the TXOP control. We also see in Fig.9 that the average throughput T_B decreases slightly with increasing n, however, it can still remain above 7 in both cases with and without S_2 added, because the source nodes' transmission suspension method (described in Section 3.3) plays a key role under larger n settings. Note that in Fig.9-13, only discrete data points have been computed; lines are drawn to ease interpretation.

nodes can be avoided, meanwhile ensuring fairly low queuing delay. Furthermore, the resource control is adaptive in dynamic network environments, and the system is re-stabilized quickly.

The current work can be further extended by considering varying data rates and varying channel and traffic load conditions. Scenarios, in which certain downstream nodes are generating or taking in packets, will be considered as future work as well. Besides these, we will investigate a control-theoretic modeling approach for multi-hop ad-hoc networks in which each node is contending for channel access with only a subset of the set of nodes, i.e., each node has its own interference domain. Furthermore, the control model will be validated using the simulation platform OPNET, and different network topologies will be studied. Finally, we will do a number of comparative studies, thereby also including higher layer protocols, in order to investigate overall system behaviors.

References

1. IEEE 802.11 WG, Part II: Wireless LAN Medium Access Control (MAC) and Physical Layer (PHY) specifications. IEEE (June 2007)
2. Yang, Y., Haverkort, B.R., Heijenk, G.: A Control-theoretic Modeling Approach for Service Differentiation in Multi-hop Ad-hoc Networks. In: Proceedings of 5th International Conference on the Quantitative Evaluation of Systems, pp. 7–16. IEEE CS Press, France (2008)
3. Majkowski, J., Palacio, F.C.: Enhanced TXOP Scheme for Efficiency Improvement of WLAN 802.11e. In: Proceedings of 64th IEEE Vehicular Technology Conference, pp. 1–5. IEEE Press, Canada (2006)
4. Choi, Y., Lee, B., Pak, J., Lee, I., Lee, H., Yoon, J., Han, K.: An Adaptive TXOP Allocation in IEEE 802.11e WLANs. In: Proceedings of 6th WSEAS International Conference on Electronics, Hardware, Wireless and Optical Communications, pp. 187–192. ACM Press, Greece (2007)
5. Ksentini, A., Nafaa, A., Gueroui, A., Naimi, M.: ETXOP: A Resource Allocation Protocol for QoS-sensitive Services Provisioning in 802.11 Networks. Performance Evaluation 64(5), 419–443 (2007)
6. Yang, Y., Heijenk, G., Haverkort, B.R.: Adaptive Resource Control in 2-hop Ad-Hoc Networks. In: Proceedings of International Conference on Ultra Modern Telecommunications 2009, IEEE CS Press, Russia (2009)
7. Yang, Y.R., Lam, S.S.: General AIMD Congestion Control. In: Proceedings of International Conference on Network Protocols 2000, pp. 187–198. ACM Press, Japan (2000)
8. Huang, Y., Xu, G., Huang, L.: Adaptive AIMD Rate Control for Smooth Multimedia Streaming. In: Proceedings of 12th International Conference on Computer Communications and Networks, pp. 171–177. IEEE Press, USA (2003)
9. Xylomenos, G., Polyzos, G.C., Mähönen, P.: TCP Performance Issues over Wireless Links. IEEE Communications Magazine 39(4), 52–58 (2001)
10. Balakrishnan, H., Padmanabhan, V., Seshan, S., Katz, R.H.: A Comparison of Mechanisms for Improving TCP Performance over Wireless Links. IEEE/ACM Transactions on Networking 5(6), 756–769 (1997)
11. Floyd, S., Jacobson, V.: Random Early Detection gateways for Congestion Avoidance. IEEE/ACM Transactions on Networking 1(4), 397–413 (1993)

12. Gao, Y., Kumar, P.R.: Joint Congestion Control and Random Access MAC in Multi-hop Wireless Networks via a Simplified Model. In: Proceedings of 48th IEEE Conference on Decision and Control, pp. 7119–7124. IEEE Press, China (2009)
13. Kurose, J.F., Ross, K.W.: Computer Networking: A Top-Down Approach Featuring the Internet, 3rd edn. Addison-Wesley Longman, Amsterdam, 0-321-26976-4
14. Remke, A., Haverkort, B.R., Heijenk, G., Cloth, L.: Bottleneck Analysis for Two-hop IEEE 802.11e Ad Hoc Networks. In: Al-Begain, K., Heindl, A., Telek, M. (eds.) ASMTA 2008. LNCS, vol. 5055, pp. 279–294. Springer, Heidelberg (2008)
15. http://www.20sim.com/

Utility-Based Analytical Model for Representing User QoE

Manzoor Ahmed Khan[1], Jie Lu[2], and Muhammad Amir Mehmood[3]

[1] DAI Labor, Technical University Berlin, Germany
manzoor-ahmed.khan@dai-labor.de
[2] Technical University, Berlin, Germany
[3] Deutsche Telekom Laboratories, Technical University, Berlin, Germany

Abstract. Next Generation Mobile Networks (NGMNs) together with smart phones evolution have opened new opportunities to deliver mobile services, including voice, data and multimedia applications to the users. However this conflation has brought several challenges in terms of Quality of Experience – *QoE* of users. Mainly due to degradations with time-varying characteristics in the presense of link heterogeneity, varying packet loss and codec switching. In this paper we propose an analytical quality prediction model which predicts user QoE for conditions that are typically occurring in NGNMs such as network handovers, codec switching and different packet loss rates due to adverse wireless networking conditions. We augment our model with service price as another key factor in QoE representation. We validate quality prediction of our model with subjective tests. Our results show that the quality prediction by our model has correlation of $r = 0.923$ with subjective ratings.

Keywords: Utility function, NGMN, QoE, VoIP.

1 Introduction

Wireless internet access has grown significantly over the last decade from, a barely sufficient bandwidth provided by GRPS and EDGE, to the medium sized UMTS/HSDPA, UMTS/HSPA+, WiFi, WiMax and towards the high speed envisaged by LTE. Also smart phones such as *iphone* and *Android* are equipped with multiple wireless network interfaces e.g. 3G UMTS or WiFi. This has given users an opportunity to be always connected to the Internet anywhere and anytime. Moreover, it has provided users a choice to select the best network according to their own preference driven by their network choice, quality acceptance and cost effectiveness [1].

While bandwidth offered by these technologies is increasing, the link layer properties are also exhibiting time-varying characteristics. These factors may force users to react according to the network conditions. For instance, due to adverse nature of wireless medium it is imperative to change speech bandwidth inorder to maintain a certain quality of service. This action sometimes results in changing of speech codec during the ongoing call i.e., *codec changeover* and/or change of network point of attachment i.e., *network handover*. The study of the these new conditions and modeling the impact on speech quality prediction for NGMN is the key focus of this work.

X. Masip-Bruin et al. (Eds.): WWIC 2011, LNCS 6649, pp. 323–337, 2011.
© IFIP International Federation for Information Processing 2011

On one hand, the availability of these high-speed access technologies have encouraged the users to use Mobile VoIP while they are on the move, on the other hand the physical layer implementation of these wireless technologies have different impact on real time applications. For instance, HSDPA link exhibits more fluctuations than WiFi due to shared downlink. The primary reasons for this is base station scheduling which allocate resources only to the users having good wireless link conditions. WiFi is also interference limited technology and link transmission is greatly dependent on the simultaneous demand of the wireless channel resources. However WiFi as compared to HSDPA performs better in terms of throughput and latency. These differences in access technologies are the key factor of different quality of experience of users for different services. Due to this fact, network service providers which are offering superior quality VoIP services by employing wideband codecs sampled at 16kHz in their network require service adaptation to narrowband codec at 8kHz when facing adverse network conditions.

The usage of voice services over IP networks has grown significantly. Skype for instance dominates the market with its over 521 Million accounts and over 40 million active users that generate most amount of international traffic. Mobile VoIP is also becoming popular and it is being incorporated into the mobile phones using SIP protocol. This protocol allows exchange of SIP messages into the device and then RTP may be used to manage voice path. Mobile VoIP demands high-speed wireless communications such as WiFi, WiMax or HSDPA. Also these access networks open opportunities to deliver new services to the mobile users.

Mobile service adoption is clearly dependent on quality received by the users as users expect same quality of fixed phone while on roaming. Thus call quality monitoring is really crucial for NGMN service providers. The call quality monitoring may be based on network transmission metrics, but also on the evaluation of the transmitted audio signal arriving at the user end terminal. This information can be further mapped into the quality experienced by the end user. Real user perception measurement requires time-consuming and expensive subjective tests but also provide the ground truth and most accurate Mean Opinion Score (MOS), which express the mean quality score of a group of users according to ITU-T Rec. P.800 [2]. The test complexity limits the applicability of such a quality measurement. These limitations form the basis and serve as the driving force for an alternate approach of instrumental quality prediction.

The functional principle of quality prediction models can rely on evaluation of transmission parameters measured in networking layer e.g. E-model [3], or on the analysis of the signal waveform measured at the output of the transmission system e.g. Perceptual evaluation of speech quality – PESQ [4]. These approach allow to derive the quality index without performing subjective tests and is based on either parametric approach or signal-based approach. However, these models have been tested for only certain conditions related to fixed networks and their applicability for NGMN typical networking conditions are still limited. This underscore the stark need of another modeling approach which can capture NGMN effects along with external factors such as service price. Our model is premised on the fact that along with typical conditions in NGMN's e.g., network handovers, codec switchovers and packet loss, service price offered by a particular provider plays a major role in mobility management based on QoE.

In this paper, we present analytical quality prediction model based on the *utility function* of a user, that predicts quality for NGMN typical conditions.Our main contributions are as follows:

- Analytical representation of user satisfaction using utility function specifically concentrating on impact of handover and codec switchover on the user satisfaction for heterogeneous services.
- Validating the estimated satisfaction values attained from the proposed utility function for different scenarios (by comparing the estimated satisfaction values of utility function to the values attained from the experimental work).

We structure rest of the paper as follows. In Section 2, we discuss related work, next in Section 3 we present user satisfaction function. We continue with discussion on satisfaction criteria in Section 4. In Section 5 we show our experimental methodology and we compare experimental and model results in Section 6. We conclude the paper in Section 7.

2   Related Work

Speech quality assessment has been the subject of many researchers [5]. Various different models and their modifications have been proposed for signal based speech quality prediction model such as PESQ and WB-PESQ [6][7]. Similarly many efforts have been made in parametric based model such as ITU-T E-model [3] and its various extensions. In the context of speech quality assessment when network handovers and codec switchover are prevalent, a comprehensive quality assessment study has been carried out by Möller et al. [8], which encompasses the changes in the user quality of experience for various different roaming scenarios. Their study highlight the fact that packet loss is the most dominant factor in NGMN conditions and network handover (only) has minimal impact compared to packet loss and codec switching. Another interesting fact from that study reveals that when packet loss is high, changing codecs does not impact quality much. However, when the packet loss is low, changing codec has high impact on the quality.

   In another recent study by Mehmood et al. [9] authors show that WB-PESQ model failed to predict quality under some NGMN conditions. It was shown with experimental evidence that WB-PESQ underestimates quality due to (i) wideband-narrowband speech codec switching, (ii) speech signal fading during codec switching, and (iii) talkspurt internal time-shifting due to jitter buffer instabilities. This highlights the fact that current signal based models are still not tuned for NGMN typical conditions and needs enhancement. Similar studies of NGMN conditions carried by Blazej et.al. [10] pointed out that the parametric model such as E-model was unable to predict the quality where narrowband and wideband codecs are present in a single call. Their suggested codec-switching impairment factor to E-model improved the correlation of the E-model prediction to auditory tests to $r = 0.937$. Chen et.al. [11] have tried to find out user satisfaction index of voip user, however their work is limited to Skype user satisfaction only.

Utility theory, basically a concept from economics has been greatly used in wireless communication. [12,13] modeled network selection using utility functions, Das et al. [14] helps users take decision over service price by modeling users' utility that captures data delay considerations. A number of utility models with numerous technical / non-technical parameters such as QoS degree, service pricing, security, power consumption, throughput/bandwidth, delay, etc. are existent in the literature. The utility modeling and selection of parameters are basically driven by the scalability and their application to a specific problem. Expecting users as the center of all services in future wireless land-scape, utility theory is a natural candidate that can be used to translate user satisfaction. Utility function answers the basic question, how much does a user value the service? Utility, when defined as the function that captures user satisfaction for communication service, user keeps on consuming services as long as the user's satisfaction is met [15]. The failure of signal-based and parametric-based models has prompted the need of an alternate model which could cover NGMN typical conditions and provide accurate pre-diction as compared to the existing models. Therefore in this paper, we endeavor to bridge this gap by taking advantage of analytical tools and present an analytical model. However, to the best of our knowledge, there are no current analytical quality models to estimate quality level fluctuations as a consequence of time-varying conditions such as network handovers and codec switchovers which are typical conditions in NGMN environments.

Why Is QoS $\sim$ QoE Mapping Needed?

The arguments justifying the QoS~QoE mapping also serve to be the motivation force for this work. We now briefly list few of the arguments as follows; i) Owing to the short term contractual agreements of users with operators, the objective of network operators will be driven by the satisfied user pool. To attain this objective, network operators will be interested in knowing the user behavior towards service in different context. This provisions analytical function that can estimate user satisfaction for different services for online optimization. Having estimated the user QoE for any service, an operator is in better position to select the optimal strategy(ies) to increase its objective function both in competitive and cooperative market settings.

3 User Satisfaction Function

In this section, we present the primer on utility function and real-time applications followed by the proposed utility function.

3.1 Background on Utility Function

The concept of utility function is defined by the notation " $\succeq$ ", which comes from the field of Economics. It is an abstract concept and is derived largely from Von Neumann and Morgenstern(1947). Utility function is designed to measure the user's satisfaction, which is subjective in nature. A satisfaction function measures users' relative preference for different levels of considered parameter values. For instance, given a number of items characterized by various parameters, a user decision of selecting any of these items will be based on relative values item specific parameters. Thus preference relation can be defined by the function, $U : X \rightarrow \Re$, that represents the preference $\succeq$ for all x and $y \in X$, if and only if $U(x) \geq U(y)$. Here the concept of marginal satisfaction is worth mentioning, that represents the additional satisfaction gained from each extra unit of attribute. This concept is basic to demand theory which states that marginal satisfaction diminishes as the consumption of an item increases. Basically a satisfaction function should satisfy non-station and risk aversion properties [16].

Definition 1. *Let $u(\rho_i)$ represent the satisfaction function for attribute i, from the attribute space $\Sigma = \{\rho_1, \ldots, \rho_m\}$, then non-station property states that satisfaction $u(\rho_i)$ increases with attribute value (given that attribute value has the expectancy the greater the better) i.e. $u'(\rho_i) > 0$.*

Definition 2. *Risk-aversion property states that satisfaction function is concave meaning thereby marginal satisfaction decreases with increasing value of attribute (provided that attribute value has the expectancy the greater the better),i.e. $u''(\rho_i) < 0$.*
The proposed satisfaction function can capture the user-preferences over multiple attributes including those having major influence on user QoE. In the broader sense, these attributes may be categorized in three different expectancies, i) the larger the better, ii) the smaller the better, and iii) the nominal the better. The combined effect of these attributes dictate the user satisfaction level.

3.2 Background on Real-Time Applications

Streaming and conversational traffic classes can be combined in real-time applications, which are commonly termed as inelastic or rigid applications. Examples of real-time symmetric applications include teleconferencing, Videophony and VoIP. Generally real-time applications are constrained by minimum amount of bandwidth i.e., application is admitted only when the demand for minimum required bandwidth is met. Such stringent requirement on bandwidth are typically represented by a step function, which means that as soon as the demand for application required bandwidth is met, users' maximum satisfaction is reached, and for a slight reduction in this bandwidth below the minimum required bandwidth, users satisfaction is *zero*. In our case, bandwidth offers may be defined by different codecs. However, bandwidth is not the only factor that affects the satisfaction of user, factors like packet loss, delay, handover, and codec switchover costs are important parameters to be considered specifically for mobile users.

3.3 Environment Assumptions

Heterogeneous applications have differing preferences over QoS parameters, such as delay, packet loss, and jitter etc. Values of these parameters can in turn be translated into consumer satisfaction. In this research work, we focus on real-time applications i.e., voice application. Basically as all other services real-time voice application can also be defined in terms of delay and packet loss rate, and its sensitivity to these parameters pose service quality requirements. We term application preferences as *minimum application required QoS*, whereas user preferences are represented by user-profile. Thus the lower bound on user preferences is set by the minimum application required QoS. We assume that different user profiles define user types. Such user distinction is an attractive solution of adaptive applications, however for real-time applications we assume that all users are equally treated. We further assume that delay impact is negligible, this assumption is strengthened by the fact that we are considering non-interactive speech, and also the assumption is in line with E-model, where below a certain delay threshold (<177ms) non-interactive communication is not affected. However, we assume that packet loss rate deteriorates the user satisfaction, as it varies in time and such time varying conditions are the consequence of varying wireless channel conditions, which in turn is influenced by the interference caused by users in the cell and other medium characteristics. We also assume that user experiences vertical handovers and codec switch overs during the life time of a call. We consider network technologies of different characteristics, let these be represented by the set W, that contains as elements the *broadband* and *cellular network* technologies. It is also assumed that handover execution delay is within permissible bounds, however we do capture its impact on the user satisfaction.

3.4   Utility Function Representation of User Satisfaction

In this section, we take into consideration the handover costs and codec switching costs in the formulation of the utility function. The proposed user utility function (satisfaction function) is the function of packet loss, handover, codec switchover costs but also reputation and security and reputation indexes of the operator. We summarize in Table-1 the notations and their description used in the paper. Let $u_j(.)$ be the utility function of user j, and is given by

Table 1. Notations and their description

Notation	Description
$u_j(.)$	Utility function of user j
k	Index of service type
c	The class of service (VoIP in this case)
co	Index of codec
w	Index of network technology
π	the price user pays against the service
$n_{o,k,c,co,w}$	Number of users (k, c, co, w) with operator o
b	Bandwidth
pl	Packet loss
σ	Measures the rate of decay of user's satisfaction.
ζ	*Handover* costs.
r_0	Index of operator reputation
s_o	Index of operator offered security
φ	*Codec-switchover* costs respectively.

$$u_{j,k,o,c,co,w}(pl, \psi\zeta, \varphi) = \tilde{u}_o\left(\frac{b_{k,o,c}}{n_{o,k,c}}\right)\mu^{\bar{c}o}_{\bar{w},k,o,c} e^{-\sigma(pl^{\bar{c}o}_{\bar{w},k,o,c}+\psi(\frac{b_{k,o,c}}{n_{o,k,c}})\zeta^{\bar{w}}_w)}$$

$$-\psi\left(\frac{b_{k,o,c}}{n_{o,k,c}}\right)\tilde{\mu}^{co\longrightarrow\bar{c}o}_{w\longrightarrow\bar{w}} e^{-pl^{co}_{w,k,o,c}\varphi^{\bar{c}o}_{co}} - \pi_{k,o,c,co,w} - f(r_o, s_o) \qquad (1)$$

where $\mu^{\bar{c}o}_{\bar{w},k,o,c}$ represents the maximum achievable MOS value in the network technology $w \in W = \{WLAN, HSDPA\}$ using codec $co \in \{G722, G722.2, G711\}$ for operator o, pl represents the packet loss rate. Here ψ takes the value of 1, when the call handsover from *high bandwidth* to *lower bandwidth* technology or from *wideband* codec to *narrowband* codec, and -1 otherwise. $\tilde{\mu}^{co\longrightarrow\bar{c}o}_{w\longrightarrow\bar{w}}$ represents the constant gain or loss of MOS value when codec switch over takes place and their values are dictated by the network and codec characteristics. The function π represents the pricing function to the users. The term $\tilde{u}_{j,o}\left(\frac{b_{o,k,c}}{n_{o,k}}\right)$ is a function of network state $n = (n_{o,k,co,w})_{o,k,c,co,w}$ and the offered bandwidth $b_{o,k,c}$ by the operator o. The collection n is the vector that represent the total number of users those request the service of specific class under specific codec and handover. The function f is a generic function that takes into consideration the reputation and the security of the operator (an increasing function in each of the component).

It is noted that $\mu^{\bar{c}o}_{\bar{w},k,o,c} \neq \mu^{co}_{w,k,o,c}$, where $(co, w) \neq (\bar{c}o, \bar{w})$, it shows that users quality rating is dependent on the networking conditions e.g., WiFi with stable network bandwidth along with a superior quality wideband codec sampled at $16kHz$ provides best results, whereas HSDPA with its fluctuating bandwidth due base station based scheduling and high link layer retransmissions is expected to provide lesser quality even if superior quality codecs are used [8]. Value of ζ is dictated by the handover type i.e., $\zeta_{bm} > \zeta_{mb}$, where bm, and mb represents the *break before make*, and *make before break* approaches respectively. Generally the value of σ is dictated by the application type and the underlying network technology.

Since the proposed utility function is monotonically decreasing in all the considered parameters i.e., with increase in a considered parameter value the user gets more irritated. We therefore, introduce the term *cost value* that represent the aggregated effect of different parameter values. Let L represents the set of considered parameters, then $L = \{pl, \zeta, \varphi\}$. We define the cost value as: $\mathcal{K} = \sum_{z_m \in L} z_m$, where z_m is the individual cost contribution of parameter m. Thus the function can now be written as:

$$u_j(\mathcal{K}, pl, \psi\zeta, \varphi) = \begin{cases} 0 & \text{if} \quad \mathcal{K} \geq \mathcal{K}_{max} \\ \mu^{co}_w + \psi\tilde{\mu}^{\bar{c}o}_w & \text{if} \quad \mathcal{K} < \mathcal{K}_{ac} \\ \mu^{co}_w e^{-\sigma(\mathcal{K}-pl\varphi)} - \psi\tilde{\mu}^{\bar{c}o}_w e^{\mathcal{K}-(pl+\psi\zeta)} & \text{if} \quad \mathcal{K}_{ac} < \mathcal{K} < \mathcal{K}_{max} \end{cases}$$
$$(2)$$

where $\mu^{co}_w + \psi\tilde{\mu}^{\bar{c}o}_w$ represents the maximum achievable utility depending on the user context and users association with a technology and codec for the voice call, $\mathcal{K}_{max}$ is the maximum tolerable cost by the user j , it can also be interpreted as cost threshold, above which user is no more satisfied. $\mathcal{K}_{ac}$ represents the acceptable cost of the user, and it is taken as the ideal cost threshold for maximum satisfaction of user.

Consider the $u_j(\mathcal{K})$ of user j, where $\mathcal{K}$ is the aggregated cost computed from the technical characteristics of operators' offers. This dictates that there always exists an upper bound for the considered parameters due to technological constraints or user preferences / requirements. Such bounds define different regions of utilities as shown in Equation-2. Where the two obvious regions are translated as fully satisfied and fully irritated regions bounded by $\mathcal{K} < \mathcal{K}_{ac}$ and $\mathcal{K} \geq \mathcal{K}_{max}$ respectively. Third region bounded by $\mathcal{K}_{ac} < \mathcal{K} < \mathcal{K}_{max}$ shows the satisfaction behavior of user following the function given in Equation 2. All the three regions define the user satisfaction of users. Let us scale the user satisfaction on the same lines as the ITU standard for QoE measurements. We scale the satisfaction function between $0 \sim 5$, where 5 represents the maximum and 0 minimum user satisfaction, i.e. $u_j(\mathcal{K}) \in [0,5]$.

The region of proposed utility function represented by $\mu_w^c e^{-\sigma(\mathcal{K}+pl\varphi)} - \psi\tilde{\mu}_w^{\tilde{c}} e^{\mathcal{K}-(pl+\psi\zeta)}$ should be twice differentiable on interval $[\mathcal{K}_{ac}, \mathcal{K}_{max}]$. Fulfilling this requirement guarantees that the user satisfaction level does not change drastically with a small change in the $\mathcal{K}$ value and marginal satisfaction is regular. Similarly, increase in value of considered parameter, say packet loss ratio above certain threshold results in near zero user satisfaction, therefore user behaves indifferently for parameters values above some threshold value. This implies the convexity of the satisfaction curve.

In addition the utility function should also satisfy the following requirements:

$$u_j(\mathcal{K}) = 0 \qquad \vee \mathcal{K} \geq \mathcal{K}_{max} \qquad (3)$$
$$u_j(\mathcal{K}) = \mu_{max} \qquad \forall \mathcal{K} < \mathcal{K}_{ac} \qquad (4)$$

where μ_{max} represents the maximum user utility.

3.5   User Equilibrium Characterization

We denote the second term in Equation 1 by ν_j, which is expressed as function of pl, ψ, ζ, φ and the type, the class, the codec and the handover. We assume that the performance index pl decreases with the number of users $n_{o,k,c}$. We propose the following form:

$$\nu_{j,o,k,c,co,w}(pl, \psi, \zeta, \varphi) = \mu_{\tilde{w},k,o,c}^{\tilde{c}o} e^{-\sigma(pl_{\tilde{w},k,o,c}^{\tilde{c}o} + \psi(\frac{b_{k,o,c}}{n_{o,k,c}})\zeta_w^{\tilde{w}})}$$
$$-\psi(\frac{b_{k,o,c}}{n_{o,k,c}})\tilde{\mu}_{w \longrightarrow \tilde{w}}^{co \longrightarrow \tilde{c}o} e^{-pl_{\tilde{w},k,o,c}^{co} \varphi_{co}^{\tilde{c}o}} \qquad (5)$$

Now, we formulate the user problem based on the utility functions. Each user j optimizes u_j depending on its codec, handover, type, class of services, and operator. By fixing the operators offer (prices, technology, network availability etc), we analyze the interaction between the users in an autonomous and self-optimizing manner. We use the notion of equilibrium (Cournot, Nash, correlated, sequential, hierarchy etc.) which characterizes the outcomes. Here we restrict our attention to the packet loss pl component but the delay function can be incorporated as well.

1. The equilibria in absence of handover: In this case, we omit the index w. A pure equilibrium is a configuration of choices of users, the total number of user profiles

with specific codec, type, class represented by $(n_{o,k,c,co})_{o,k,c,co}$ such that if user j moves to $(\bar{o}, \bar{co})$

$$u_{j,o,k,c,co}(n_{o,k,c,co}) \geq u_{j,\bar{o},k,c,\bar{co}}(n'_{\bar{o},k,c,\bar{co}})$$

where $n'_{o,k,c,co} = n_{o,k,c,co} - 1$ if user j has moved from (o, co), $n_{o,k,c,co} + 1$ if user moves to (o, co) and equal to $n_{o,k,c,co}$ if user does not move.

2. The equilibria in absence of codec switchover: In this case, we omit the index co. A pure equilibrium is a configuration of choices of users, the total number of user profiles with specific handover, type, class represented by $(n_{o,k,c,w})_{o,k,c,w}$ such that if user j moves to $(\bar{o}, w)$

$$u_{j,o,k,c,w}(n_{o,k,c,w}) \geq u_{j,\bar{o},k,c,\bar{w}}(n'_{\bar{o},k,c,\bar{w}})$$

where $n'_{o,k,c,w} = n_{o,k,c,w} - 1$ if user j has moved from (o, w), $n_{o,k,c,w} + 1$ if user moves to (o, w) and equal to $n_{o,k,c,co,w}$ if no moves.

3. The equilibria in presence of both handover and codec switchover:
In this case, we take on both indexes w, co. A pure equilibrium is a configuration of choices of users, the total number of user profiles with specific codec, type, class represented by $(n_{o,k,c,co,w})_{o,k,c,co,w}$ such that if user j moves to $(\bar{o}, \bar{co}, \bar{w})$

$$u_{j,o,k,c,co,w}(n_{o,k,c,co,w}) \geq u_{j,\bar{o},k,c,\bar{co},\bar{w}}(n'_{\bar{o},k,c,\bar{co},\bar{w}})$$

where $n'_{o,k,c,co,w} = n_{o,k,c,co,w} - 1$ if user j has moved from (o, co, w), $n_{o,k,c,co,w} + 1$ if user moves to (o, co, w) and equal to $n_{o,k,c,co,w}$ if no move.

For the mixed equilibria of the selection problem with strict support are characterized by the *indifference* conditions. This means that one needs the solve the system $u_{j,o,k,c,co,w}(x^*) = \max_{\bar{o},\bar{co},\bar{w}} u_{j,\bar{o},k,c,\bar{co},\bar{w}}(x^*)$ where x^* the vector with component $x^*_{o,k,c,co,w}$ of probabilities of being in the configuration (o, k, c, co, w).

In real world scenarios user satisfaction is influenced by different technical and non-technical parameters, however non-technical parameters are out of the scope of this paper. Concentrating further on technical parameters, the effect of these parameters can either be dependent on each other or independent of each other. In the scope of this research work, we consider the parameters that are mutually independent in terms of its impact on the users satisfaction. We model the utility function so that it captures the codec switch over handover costs independently, and their independent impact is added to the degradation caused by the packet loss costs. Such utility function modeling can be understood following lemma-1.

Lemma 1. *The proposed satisfaction function is invariant under various independent parameters.*

Proof. Assume that user $i's$ satisfaction is the function of packet loss only. Let it be represented by $U_i(pl)$, and is given by $U(pl) = e^{-\sigma(pl)}$, then for any constant parameter x it is straight forward to prove $U(x + pl) = e^{-\sigma(pl+x)}$, which results in $U(x + pl) = U(pl)e^{-\sigma(x)}$.

Remark 1. *Having known the expected MOS value of a user in different user contexts, a decision maker is provided with suitable and necessary information for policy making, taking different quality improvement measures, and adopting certain service price offering strategies that in turn increases the operators' payoffs. Given the utility function the proportion of MOS degradation by different parameters can also be estimated.*

Remark 1 is true for both the scenarios, i) where individual MOS effecting parameters are considered, ii) combined impact of various MOS effect parameters are considered. However when it comes to the later case, the proposed satisfaction function can be generalized for a number of dependent and independent parameters by introducing the relevant functions of newly introduced parameters and associating it to the satisfaction function using additive sum concept. In this case associating weights to parameters is intuitive, which takes into account the sensitivity of the parameter.

Remark 2. *The satisfaction function can be replaced by an equivalent satisfaction function for*

$$u(y) = Au(y) + B \tag{6}$$

where $A > 0$ and B is arbitrary. Hence it is possible to standardize the satisfaction function for a particular point ς.

Example 1. Let the the standardization of satisfaction function is required for $\varsigma = 0$, the for the satisfaction (simplified form of equation-1).

$$u(y) = \mu.e^{-\sigma(y)} \tag{7}$$

It can be noted that for $y \to \infty$, the satisfaction is bounded and tends to the finite value zero.

4   Satisfaction Criteria

In this section, we investigate the performance of proposed utility function for single and multiple criteria.

4.1   Single Attribute Utility Function

In a single criterion utility function, the utility function captures user satisfaction for the possible degradation effect introduced by the criterian. Consider an ideal scenario, where a static user experiences *zero* delay, no vertical handover and no codec switchovers. In such a case users satisfaction is fully dependent on the packet loss rate.

$$u_i(pl) := \mu_w^{co} e^{-\sigma.pl} \qquad \forall pl \in [pl_{ac}, pl_{max}] \tag{8}$$

Let us consider that user the is associated to a specific codec say $co = G711$, and with network technology $w = HSDPA$, here μ_w^{co} represents the maximum achieveable MOS value in this scenario, which is achievable for packet loss less than pl_{ac}. We plot the MOS curve for this scenario in Fig 1a. In addition we also investigate single attribute utility function for a different network technology $w = WLAN$, and broadband codec

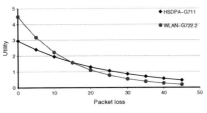 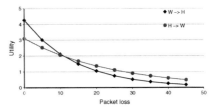

(a) Plot of utility values considering single attribute (packet loss)

(b) Plot of utility values considering multiple attributes (packet loss & handover cost)

Fig. 1. Impact of various attributes on user satisfaction

$G722$, and plot the user satisfaction curve for this scenario as well 1a. As can be observed that $\mu_{WLAN}^{G722} > \mu_{HSDPA}^{G711}$, this strengthens the argument presented in section 3. One more point to be noticed here is that $\sigma-$value in WLAN is greater than in HSDPA, which results in greater decay of MOS value with increasing packet loss. The proposed utility function behavior is validated for various scenarios in later sections; i.e., keeping the mentioned setting for experiments we obtain values for different values of packet loss ($0\%, 10\%, 20\%$).

4.2   Multiple Attributes Utility Function

In a multiple attribute utility function, the utility function captures user satisfaction for the possible degradation effect introduced by the combined effect of multiple criteria. Now we consider a scenario, where a user experiences vertical handovers, and his satisfaction is influenced by both packet loss and handover costs, which is represented by:

$$u_i(pl) := \mu_w^{co} e^{-\sigma.(pl+\psi\zeta)} \qquad \forall pl \in [pl_{ac}, pl_{max}] \qquad (9)$$

Let us consider a specific scenario, where a user is initially associated with network technology WLAN and codec $G722.2$. The maximum achieveable MOS value for this user is $\mu_{WLAN}^{G722.2}$, now that user experiences a vertical handover to $HSDPA$, he experiences a further degradation (this degradation is represented by $\psi\zeta$, in this case $\psi = -1$). We plot the MOS curve for this scenario as shown in Fig 1b.

The plot resembles exactly the one shown in Fig 1a for different value of packet loss, but shifted by a small value representing the handover cost. In the similar fashion, we plot MOS curve for users initially associated to HSDPA network technology and handsover to WLAN network technology, such handover introduces a gain to users satisfaction (therefore $\psi = 1$). Equation 9 captures user satisfaction for both mentioned scenarios for multiple attribute utility function. In general Fig 1b presents somewhat similar behavior as in Fig 4 shifted by the cost of handover cost in either direction depending on the value of ψ.

5   Experiments

In this section, we discuss our experimental methodology for carrying out the controlled experiments and then conduct auditory tests for NGMN conditions.

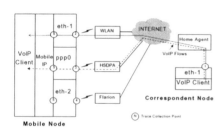

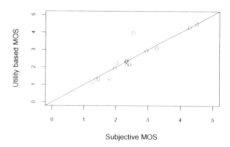

Fig. 2. Mobisense experimental setup for VoIP services in NGMNs

Fig. 3. Relationship of Model quality estimation and user quality ratings (correlation $r = 0.923$)

5.1   Mobisense Testbed

In order to perform quality of experience study, we rely on Mobisense testbed which was designed to investigate user perceived quality in NGMN using VoIP as the primary application. The testbed depicted in Figure 2 allows mobile clients to perform network handovers and voice codec changeover while keeping on-going calls. The testbed uses Mobile IPv4 as a solution to enable seamless handovers between different radio access technologies [17]. Thus, the main network elements of the testbed are the Mobile Node (MN), the Corresponding node (CN) and the Mobile IPv4 Home Agent (HA). The setup includes various different access technologies such as WLAN/WiFi, UMTS/HSDPA and Flash-OFDM (pre-WiMax release) that are used to emulate an integrated NGMN environment.

The CN and MN were deployed on laptops with linux 2.6.18.2 and HA was configured on a *Cisco 2620XM* router with *Cisco IOS 12.2(18r)*. Based on SIP protocol we choose PJPROJECT [18] framework as voip client to play speech files. We employed seamless codec switching scheme by Wältermann et al. [19]. The detailed description of design and the capabilities of Mobisense testbed are outlined in [20].

5.2   Methodology

We pre-selected NGMN conditions with the combination of (i) Network handovers between different technologies, (ii) Codec-switching between narrowband codec and wideband codec, and (iii) Different packet loss rates. We use ITU-T G.711 log PCM codec at 64 kb/s for narrowband (NB) with native packet loss concealment and ITU-T G.722.2 (AMR-WB) codec at 23.05 kb/s for wideband transmission. For benchmarking purposes we select few conditions with a single network, a single codec and 0% packet loss. We establish the quality bounds by using these benchmark conditions. Of course one could argue why not to test all combinations but carrying out a full factorial combination of subjective tests is practically infeasible. We use netem packet shaper for degrading VoIP packets as shown in Figure 2.

All calls were initiated at CN and terminated at MN. During on-going calls network conditions were imposed depending upon the requirements of network handovers or codec switching. At MN, speech samples were collected and processed for subjected

Table 2. Comparison of Analytical Model estimates and Auditory Judgments (MOS)

No.	Network	Codec	Ppl	Subj.	Model	Diff.
1	W→H	722.2	0	4.27	4.27	0.00
2	W	722.2	0	4.49	4.49	0.00
3	W→H(b.)	722.2→711	0	2.34	2.35	-0.01
4	H→W(a.)	711→722.2	0	2.55	3.98	-1.43
5	H→W	711	10	2.42	2.158	0.26
6	W	722.2	10	2.02	2.23	-0.21
7	H→W(b.)	711→722.2	20	1.81	1.339	0.47
8	W→H(a.)	722.2→711	0	2.32	2.33	-0.01
9	W→H	722.2	10	2.34	2.12	0.22
10	H	711	0	2.95	2.95	0.00
11	H→W	711	0	3.28	3.10	0.18
12	H	711	10	1.96	1.95	0.01
13	W→H(b.)	722.2→711	20	1.38	1.28	0.1
14	W	722.2	20	1.27	1.11	0.16
15	H	711	20	1.45	1.3	0.15

Ppl: Packet loss in %; Diff.: Difference of subjective MOS & Utility-based Model MOS; W: WLAN; H: HSDPA; →: Handover/Changeover, a./b. : Changeover before/after handover.

tests according to ITU-T P.800 [2]. Further we select speech samples for both male and female speakers to obtain a balance set of speech samples. These samples were then presented to 24 subjects for quality assessment. For the quality rating, 5-point Mean Opinion Score (MOS) scale was used. More details of these tests can be found in [8]. The overall assessment along with conditions is listed in Table 2.

6   Results and Model Validation

In this section, we compare subjective ratings with our model predictions. In principle the model should be able to predict estimations for most of the conditions. We first check correlation of the predicted values of our model with the subjective test ratings obtained in Table 2. The results are shown in Figure 3. The concentration of most of the points around the diagonal line is an indicator of a good match between model predicted values and the actual ground truth obtained from the subjects. There is a correlation of 0.923 between model predicted values and the subjective ratings.

We note that for the conditions # 1, 2, 3, 8 10 and 12 in Table 2, our model perfectly match the subjective ratings. For conditions #5, 9, 11, 14 and 15 model is off by maximum of 0.26 MOS value. However, inspite the fact that we see a high correlation we have certain conditions e.g., condition #4 and 7 where our model deviates from the subjective ratings. We plot different curves for both the utility function and experimental data in different scenarios so that behavior of utility function for different parameters can be investigated. In Figure-5, we consider the scenario where the user is associated to WLAN and G722.2, in this scenario we study the impact of packet loss rate. As evident from the Figure-5 proposed utility function almost overlaps the experimental results for low packet loss values, very small deviation is observed, when packet loss

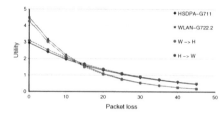
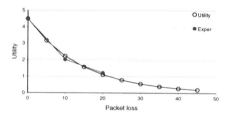

Fig. 4. Plots of Utility for single and multi-attribute scenarios

Fig. 5. User associated with WLAN & G722.2(No Handover/codec switchover)

rate approaches 20%. Although experimental results are not available for greater packet loss than 20%, the proposed model can confidently estimate the behavior for higher packet loss values. A number of similar curves were obtained for scenarios like i) user associated to HSDPA and G711 with experiencing no handover and codec switch over, ii) user associated to WLAN, G722.2 and experiencing handover to HSDPA, iii) user associated with HSDPA and handsover to WLAN, iv) Codec switchover, v) Simultaneous codec switchover and network handover etc. In all the mentioned scenario user utility function was validated against the experimental results.

7   Summary and Future Work

The emergence of new access technologies along with evolution of smart phones have paved a way of any time anywhere connectivity for mobile users. However this new paradigm has brought along many challenges for network service providers. The biggest of them is to maintain a certain level of quality for multimedia streams of their customers.

With this context, in this paper we propose a utility-based analytical quality prediction model which predicts user QoE for conditions that are typical to NGNMs such as network handovers, codec switching and different packet loss rates due to adverse wireless networking conditions. We validate quality prediction of our model with subjective tests. Our results show that the quality prediction by our model has correlation of $r = 0.923$ with subjective ratings.

In future, we plan to include more NGMN typical conditions and to extend our model for new services e.g. IPTV, video conferencing and video telephony.

References

1. Ganchev, I., Morabito, G., Narcisi, R., Passas, N., Paskalis, S., Friderikos, V., Jahan, A.S., Tsontsis, E., Bader, C., Rotrou, J., Chaouchi, H.: Always best connected enabled 4g wireless world (2003)
2. ITU-T Rec. P.800. Methods of Subjective Determination of Transmission Quality. ITU (1996)
3. ITU-T Rec. G.107. The E-model, a Computational Model for Use in Transmission Planning. ITU (2009)

4. ITU-T Rec. P.862. Perceptual Evaluation of Speech Quality(PESQ): An Objective Method for End-to-End Speech Quality Assessment of Narrow-Band Telephone Networks and Speech Codecs,ITU (2001)
5. Raake, A.: Speech Quality of VoIP: Assessment and Prediction. John Wiley & Sons, Chichester (2006)
6. Möller, S., Raake, A., Kitawaki, N., Takahashi, A., Wältermann, M.: Impairment Factor Framework for Wideband Speech Codecs. IEEE Transactions on Audio, Speech, and Language Processing 14(6), 1969–1976 (2006)
7. Côté, N., Möller, S., Gautier-Turbin, V., Raake, A.: Analysis of a Quality Prediction Model for Wideband Speech Quality, the WB-PESQ. In: Proceeding of the 2nd ISCA/DEGA Tutorial and Research Workshop on Perceptual Quality of Systems, pp. 115–122 (2006)
8. Moller, S., Waltermann, M., Lewcio, B., Kirschnick, N., Vidales, P.: Speech quality while roaming in next generation networks (2009)
9. Mehmood, M.A., Lewcio, B., Vidales, P., Feldmann, A., Moeller, S.: Understanding signal-based speech quality prediction in future mobile communications (2010)
10. Lewcio, B., Wältermann, M., Möller, S., Vidales, P.: E-model supported switching between narrowband and wideband speech quality. In: Proceedings of First International Workshop on Quality of Multimedia Experience (QoMEX 2009), San Diego, CA, United States (2009)
11. Chen, K.T., Huang, C.Y., Huang, P., Lei, C.L.: Quantifying Skype user satisfaction. ACM SIGCOMM Computer Communication Review 36(4), 399–410 (2006)
12. Winkler, R.L.: Decision modeling and rational choice: Ahp and utility theory. Manage. Sci. 36(3), 247–248 (1990)
13. Ormond, O., Murphy, J.: Utility-based intelligent network selection. In: IEEE International Conference on Communications in Beyond 3G Systems (2006)
14. Buyya, R., Abramson, D., Giddy, J., Stockinger, H.: Economic models for resource management and scheduling in grid computing, pp. 1507–1542. Wiley Press, Chichester (2002)
15. McNair, J., Zhu, F.: Vertical handoffs in fourth-generation multinetwork environments (2004)
16. Neumann, V.: Theory of games and economic behavior. Manage. Sci. (1954)
17. Perkins, C.: IP Mobility Support for IPv4. RFC 3344 (Proposed Standard), Updated by RFC 4721 (August 2002)
18. Prijono, B.: Open Source SIP Stack and Media Stack for Presence, Instant Messaging, and Multimedia Communication, http://pjsip.org/
19. Wältermann, M., Lewcio, B., Vidales, P., Möller, S.: A Technique for Seamless VoIP-Codec Switching in Next Generation Networks. In: Proceedings of IEEE International Conference on Communications, ICC 2008 (2008)
20. Vidales, P., Kirschnick, N., Steuer, F., Lewcio, B., Wältermann, M., Möller, S.: Mobisense Testbed: Merging User Perception and Network Performance. In: Proceedings of the 4th International Conference on (TRIDENTCOM), Innsbruck, Austria (2008)

An Approach to a Fault Tolerance LISP Architecture*

A. Martínez, W. Ramírez, M. Germán, R. Serral, E. Marín
M. Yannuzzi, and X. Masip-Bruin

Advanced Network Architectures Lab (CRAAX),
Universitat Politècnica de Catalunya (UPC)
Neàpolis Building, Rbla. Exposició, 59-69 – 08800 Vilanova i la Geltrú, Spain
{anny,wramirez,mgerman,rserral,eva,yannuzzi,xmasip}@ac.upc.edu

Abstract. Next Generation Internet points out the challenge of addressing "things" on both a network with (wired) and without (wireless) infrastructure. In this scenario, new efficient and scalable addressing and routing schemes must be sought, since currently proposed solutions can hardly manage current scalability issues on the current global Internet routing table due to for example multihoming practices. One of the most relevant proposals for an addressing scheme is the Locator Identifier Separation Protocol (LISP) that focuses its key advantage on the fact that it does not follow a disruptive approach. Nevertheless, LISP has some drawbacks especially in terms of reachability in the border routers. In face of this, in this paper we propose a protocol so-called LISP Redundancy Protocol (LRP), which provides an interesting approach for managing the reachability and reliability issues common on a LISP architecture, such as those motivated by an inter-domain link failure.

Keywords: Internet Routing Scalability, LISP, Fault Tolerance.

1 Introduction

In the past years, early forms of ubiquitous communication have arisen and become more evident, as society expectations towards technology increases. These facts seem to prove that current Internet will naturally evolve to an Internet of Things (IoT) as a new dynamic communication scheme where objects, services, spaces and even people may be given a unique number, almost avoiding barriers for re-cognizing, locating, addressing, reaching, controlling and enjoying almost anything via the Internet, through a mix of heterogeneous wired and wireless network infrastructures.

The current Internet semantic overloading of addresses, where addresses are simultaneously referred to identifiers and locators of a node, is an important constraint over mobility and scalability concerns. In a world where a huge volume of objects can be uniquely identified and also where objects capacity of mobility increases over time, decoupling of naming and location seems to be one of the first steps towards the evolution to a IoT. Several factors, such as the rise of multihoming sites, semantic

---

* This work was partially funded by the Spanish Ministry of Science and Innovation under contract TEC2009-07041, and the CIRIT (Catalan Research Council) under contract 2009-SGR1508.

overloading of IP addresses, among others, affect the scalability of the global Internet routing table, fueling its size and dynamics. Several proposals have emerged to solve these issues: SHIM6 [1], Six/One Router [2], HIP [3], Multipath TCP [4], GSE [5] and LISP [6] are just a few to name. The latter seems to be one of the strongest as already considered by the Internet Engineering Task Force (IETF).

The LISP concept is based on the idea of decoupling host identifier (Endpoint identifier, EID) and host localization (Routing locator, RLOC). The main benefit from using LISP is that while locators are AS-level distributed (allocated to the external interfaces of the border routers) the identifiers are only locally distributed, therefore reducing the overall routing load throughout the network. While from a deployment perspective LISP is a non-disruptive approach, the existing control plane proposals have some drawbacks especially in terms of reachability in the border routers. Since these border routers are responsible for carrying out the mapping between EIDs and RLOCs, these issues may hinder its possible deployment. In this paper, we conceptually propose the basics of a new protocol, so-called LISP Redundancy Protocol (LRP) which is designed for managing the reachability and reliability issues, such as those motivated by either an inter-domain link failure, a border router failure, an intra-domain link/node failure or an intra-domain TE action.

The rest of this paper is organized as follows. First, section 2 presents the current Internet architecture and its scalability problems; section 3 introduces LISP basics; section 4 presents the LRP as a potential solution for the control plane problems; section 5 discusses future work related issues. Finally, section 6 presents conclusions.

2   Background and Problem Statement

The Internet architecture is organized into Autonomous Systems (ASes). The ASs interconnections generate a hierarchy between different Internet Service Providers (ISPs). In this hierarchical network structure, the Internet routing system is largely based in the Border Gateway Protocol (BGP) [8], a long lived path-vector protocol which is used to exchange reachability information between ASes. Being a policy-routing protocol, it provides operators with the freedom to express their enterprise requirements and policies, allowing the attachment of several attributes for each route or network prefix. However, it has been largely demonstrated in the literature that the currently deployed Internet architectural model suffers from some weaknesses, mainly on the terms of routing scalability issues that along with the specific problems on the Internet addressing scheme require the deployment of new solutions. Next subsections detail most relevant aspects limiting routing performance on the overall Internet. It is worth highlighting that any solution proposed for end-to-end addressing must consider a completely heterogeneous network scenario consisting of different wired and wireless network segments distributed along the route, where some user (e.g., quality) and network (e.g., physical attributes) requirements must be met.

2.1   Internet Routing Scalability Problems

Recent studies including the Internet Architecture Board (IAB) report [9], reveal that Internet routing is facing serious scalability problems, all involving both the size and dynamics of the global routing table in the Internet's Default Free Zone (DFZ).

The global routing table size in the DFZ has been growing at an alarming rate in recent years [10], till reaching now a total of 36.717 ASes that originate 355.262 IPv4 prefixes (see Figure 2) despite several limitations such as lack of IPv4 addresses, strict address allocation and routing announcement policies. Although IPv6 deployment would remove the problem of lack of IPv4 addresses, there is a strong concern that the deployment of IPv6 on a large scale could result in a significant growth of the routing table.

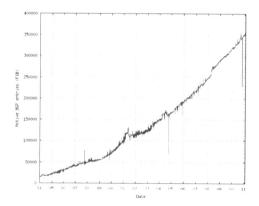

Fig. 1. Growth of the BGP Tables at DFZ Routers

The IAB report [9] identified the following factors as the main reasons behind the rapid growth of the global routing table in the DFZ:

- Multihoming.
- Traffic engineering.
- Non-aggregable address allocations

In [11] authors conclude that address fragmentation, caused by multi-homing and load balancing is the major reason of BGP table growth.

2.2   Dynamics of the BGP Control Plane Information

In [12], a systematic study of highly active prefixes is presented, concluding that a small fraction of advertised prefixes are responsible for a relevant amount of churn in BGP; furthermore, they found that some generators of BGP beacons, used for active monitoring of BGP updates, appear as highly active. Despite the big amount of related work, the dynamics of the BGP control plane information (i.e., the exchanging of updates messages due to the advertisement of new prefixes) remains unknown, but certain evidence exists of Long Range Dependence [13]. As BGP propagates changes to the best path, a single router may send multiple updates based on one triggering event, and further, cause induced updates at other locations; examples of such events are link failures, newly added networks, prefix deaggregation and policy changes, among others. Moreover, it is important to notice that, since the routing information is subject to successive filtering by internal ASes policies, any route view of the network is always partial, determined by the local point of observation. On the other hand, a relatively small number of ASes are responsible for a disproportionately large fraction of the update churn that is observed today. In turn, another problem motivated by the growing of the BGP updates is the BGP convergence time, since as the larger the topology complexity is the longest the convergence time, hence motivating the network to take longer to recover from failures.

2.3   Multihoming Sites

Another factor related to the growth of the routing table refers to the multihoming sites. For a network edge to be reachable by any service provider, the network-edge address-prefixes should be visible in the global routing tables. Meaning that no service provider can aggregate these address prefixes within their own address prefix, even if the network edges have addresses that belong to the provider-assigned address block. In addition, the network edges are increasingly obtaining provider-independent addresses from the Regional Internet Registries (RIRs), in order to avoid the renumbering every time a change of service provider happens. In summary, the topological information based on prefix-aggregation per provider is badly altered by multihoming, and in turn, leads to rapid growth of the global routing table.

2.4   Semantic Overloading

Another critical problem is the semantic overloading of IP addresses. This is because an IP address identifies a host (in fact its interface), and also serves to locate the host on the network. In this addressing scheme when a host changes of network provider, its IP address changes, therefore changing not only the network providing host access but also the host identifier. For upper layer applications that have IP addresses hard-coded for a host, this represents a severe mobility constraint. In short, the semantic overloading of IP addresses is the main problem when talking about renumbering a network.

3   LISP Overview

LISP uses IP-over-IP tunnels deployed between border routers located at different domains. The IP addresses allocated to the external interfaces of the border routers act as Routing Locator (RLOC) addresses for the end systems in the local domain. Since an AS usually groups several border routers, the local Endpoint Identifier (EID) addresses can be reached through multiple RLOC addresses. Hence, LISP separates the overall address space into two parts, where only addresses from the RLOC address space are assigned to the transit Internet. Therefore, only RLOC addresses are routable through the Internet, that is, EID addresses are considered routable only within their local domain. In addition, a number of scaling benefits would be realized by separating the current IP address into two different spaces; among them are:

- Reduction of the routing table size in the Default Free Zone (DFZ)
- More cost-effective multihoming for sites that connect to different service providers

- Easy renumbering when clients change providers
- Traffic engineering capabilities
- Mobility without address changing

The basic idea is that an EID represents an end-host IP address, while RLOCs represent the IP addresses where end hosts are located. At border routers EIDs are mapped into RLOCs, following a map-and-encap scheme, a basic mechanism of a LISP architecture. The scaling benefits arise when EID addresses are not routable through the Internet — only RLOC addresses are globally routable, allowing efficient aggregation of the RLOC address space. Recent studies show that LISP offers some key advantages. For instance, authors in [14] show that the size of the global routing table can be reduced by roughly two orders of magnitude with LISP. Next subsection details how LIST performs on both the data and control planes.

3.1   Data Plane

Data plane performance is described on the example shown in Figure 3[1]. When the local end host S with EID address 190.1.1.1 wants to communicate with end host D with EID address 200.1.1.2 in a different domain, the following sequence of events occur in LISP:

1) The first step is the usual lookup of the destination address ED in the DNS.
2) Once ED is obtained, the packets sourced from ESource traverse the domain and reach one of the local border routers. In LISP the latter are referred to as Ingress Tunnel Routers (ITRs).
3) Since only RLOC addresses are globally routable, when an ITR receives packets toward ED, it queries the control plane to retrieve the EDestination-to-RLOC mapping.
4) After the ED-to-RLOC mapping resolution, the ITR encapsulates and tunnels packets between the local RLOC address (ITR address 3.3.3.2 in the example) and the RLOC address retrieved from the mapping system, the Egress Tunnel Router (ETR) address in LISP terminology (either 4.4.4.2 or 10.0.0.2 to ED depending on the mapping).
5) At the destination domain, the ETR decapsulates the packets received through the tunnel and forwards them to ED — which, as mentioned above, is locally routable within the domain. From the first packet received, the ETR caches a new entry, solving in this way the reverse mapping for the packets to be tunneled back from EDestination to ESource.

3.2   Control Plane

Despite the benefits of using LISP described in section above, the proposals for the LISP control plane present some major challenges. These challenges lie in the fact that since EIDs are not globally routable through the Internet, a mapping system is

---

[1] This example is extracted from "The Locator Identifier Separation Protocol (LISP)", by David Meyer, published in Internet Protocol Journal, vol 11, n°:1.

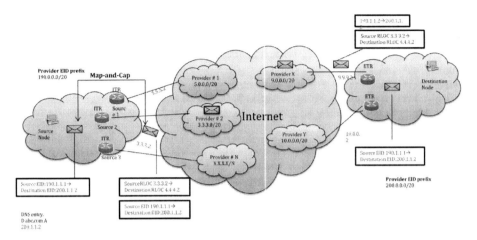

Fig. 2. The basics of LISP

necessary between EIDs and RLOCs. LISP does not specify a mandatory mapping system, and as a consequence, different proposals can be found in the recent literature, such as ALT [15], NERD [16] or Map Server [17].

Besides, in [18] we introduced a new control plane for LISP; the new control plane presents an improvement on three aspects respect to the existing solutions; (i) firstly, "First packets drop problem" when an ITR does not have a mapping for an EID-prefix; (ii) secondly, potential increase in the latency to start a communication due to the mapping resolution; and (iii) in order to avoid a two-way mapping resolution, the ITR is used as the local ETR for the packets sent from D to S. The latter introduces limitations in terms of inbound Traffic Engineering, especially, when outbound and inbound traffic policies do not match. Despite these improvements there are other issues relating to reachability and reliability that have not been resolved, such as those motivated by an inter-domain link failure.

4   Making the Way to a Fault Tolerance LISP

In [18] authors propose a new LISP control plane, aimed to overcome the issues derived by current mapping systems such as ALT, CONS or NERD. The main issue behind these approaches is related to the first packet drop problem, which refers to the mapping resolution for a prefixed EID for the first outgoing packet, this also derives in the potential increase in the latency to start a communication. This newly proposed control plane is based on the idea of retrieving EID-to-RLOC mappings within the DNS Resolution time. A major shortcoming of the solution proposed in [18] is that the mappings between EIDs and RLOCs are replicated in all of the edge routers within the same AS. Despite the fact that this option ensures improved reachability, unfortunately it may bring scalability problems since each router must store mapping information that rarely needs to use (i.e. the mapping table size), thus increasing the latency time to find a mapping. This new issue directly affects the memory component within the router, which is currently a bottleneck in the computer system compared with processing capacity. In order to minimize the mapping information managed by a router, hence minimizing the latency time, and in turn, ensuring the highest possible reachability, the LISP Redundancy Protocol (LRP) is proposed, which is inspired by the Cisco's Hot Standby Routing Protocol (HSRP) [19]. This architectural approach essentially permits to configure two routers for mapping purposes, so that before a failure on one of them, the other can supplant it (Master-Slave model). The contribution of the LRP is that it extends HSRP functionalities by creating different logical groups. In this scenario, border routers can be members of different groups, and the "key" difference between LRP and HSRP focuses on the fact that LRP enables a router to be Slave in a group and Master in another (see Figure 4). By implementing this feature all routers can be in forwarding mode, hence overcoming the limitation present in [18], namely to avoid the need of replicating the entire mapping on all the border routers. In case of either a link or border router failure, the last one will interchange his mapping with the border router that is now responsible of handling the traffic in this logical group.

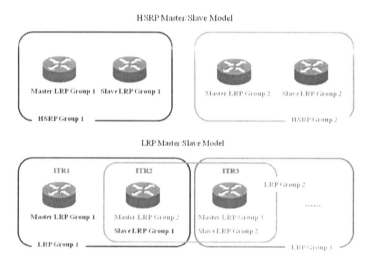

Fig. 3. Master/Slave Model HSRP vs. LRP

In summary, the main features offered by LRP are:
- The xTRs can be clustered into different LRP groups or pairs.
- The Mappings are pushed onto the LRP groups or pairs.
- All the xTRs in the group can carry traffic (active rather than standby).
- No need for data-probes when the xTR does not have a mapping.
-

In the following subsections we consider different scenarios that may originate reachability and/or reliability problems and require solutions to be managed by the current proposed protocol

4.1   Inter-domain Link Failure in an ITR

In the following we will discuss and describe the actions that are executed in order to solve the failure of an inter-domain link. In step 1 of Figure 5, the traffic is sent to the edge router (ITR1), which is responsible for encapsulating the traffic and send it through its international links to the destination. When the international link fails (step 2) the ITR1 automatically detects this event and in real time forwards all the incoming traffic to the other ITR belonging to its LRP group (step 3). ITR2 has the correspondent mapping since it shares the LRP Group with ITR1 and now is in charge of encapsulating and sending this traffic to its destination (step 4). On the other hand, by means of the internal routing protocol (running in the AS), the failure of the international link is notified to update the routing tables and hence the traffic is rerouted (step 5). In time, the LISP Control Box (LCB) would be responsible for reconfiguring the mapping of the different ITRs with the purpose of load balancing the outbound traffic (step 6). Finally, the traffic is rerouted according to internal routing policy (step 7). In conclusion, in this scenario our border architecture prevents packet loss and in particular the sending of data-probes.

4.2   ITR Failure or Unexpected Shutdown

If one ITR fails or is shutdown, gigabits of data would be lost. To overcome this situation the LISP control plane must converge to the IGP running in the AS to send back first gigabits of data-probes and then after successful mapping, send data according to the normal procedure. The following describes the step followed by the LRP to prevent any loss of data and to avoid sending data-probes. In step 1 in Figure 6, the traffic is sent to edge router (ITR1), which is responsible for encapsulating the traffic and send it through its international link to destination. When ITR1 fails (step 2) the HSRP that runs between ITR2 and ITR1 converges, and automatically ITR2 assumes the role of Master of the LRP group and forwards all traffic that arrives (step 3) in real time. The convergence of HSRP (HSRP detected in about 3 seconds the router failure) is much faster than any IGP, such as Open Shortest Past First - OSPF. In turn, the internal routing protocol that is running notifies the failure of ITR1 (step 4) to update the routing tables and hence allowing the traffic to be rerouted. On the other hand, the LCB would be responsible for reconfiguring the mapping of the different ITR to balance the outbound traffic load (step 5). Finally, the traffic is rerouted according to the IGP (step 6). In conclusion, in this scenario our border architecture minimizes the packet loss and in particular the sending of data-probes.

4.3   ITR Mapping Miss

In this scenario, an action of Traffic Engineering or an internal failure (step 1 in Figure 7) makes the traffic to be rerouted. When the packet reaches a border router (step 2) that has no corresponding mapping, this router makes a broadcast to other LRP Groups of the packets that are arriving (step 3), and in turn, the LRP Group sends a Map-Request to the LCB (step 4) that is responsible for handling all mappings within an AS. A LCB (LISP Control Box) is an entity introduced in [18] responsible

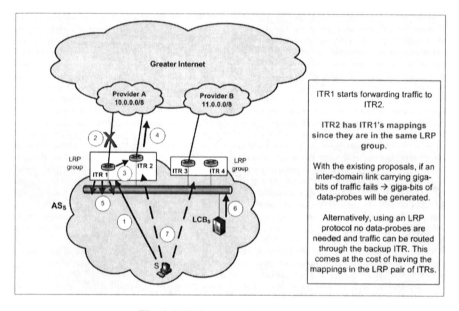

Fig. 4. LRP: Inter-domain link failure

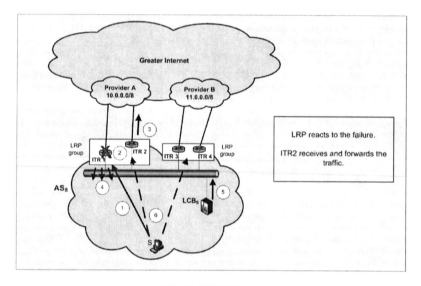

Fig. 5. ITR Failure

of all mappings within an AS which might be a standalone device or run as an instance of a PCE. The LRP Group that owns the required mapping, sends it via unicast to the LRP Group responsible for these packages (requester) (step 5), and encapsulates and forwards the traffic. While traffic is derived from the LRP Group mapping holder (step 6), the LCB sends to the LRP Group who sent the Map-Request the mapping necessary to encapsulate the packages (step 7). Finally, the LRP Group can now encapsulate packets and, therefore, makes the package forwarding through the LISP data plane (step 8). In conclusion, in this scenario our border architecture prevents packet loss and in particular the sending of data-probes.

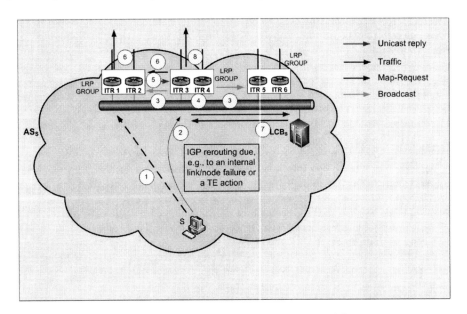

Fig. 6. ITR has no mapping from EID-to-RLOC

5   Future Work

In our network scenario we assume that LRP nodes are all part of a broadcast domain. In today's ISP core networks this is not always the case, with the introduction of new technologies like MPLS, where edge routers reach each other using LSP (Label switched Path) across an MPLS core. In this network scenario a single broadcast domain does not exist anymore.

Another similar problem can occur when BGP confederations are introduced. To overcome these challenges, extensions to LRP have to been made and configurations in edge routers have to be carefully taken into account.

We expect to present simulations of our proposal with measures of improvement of a response to a EID-RLOC mapping in a future article.

6   Conclusions

In this paper we present the concepts of a new protocol aimed to overcome the scalibility issues that surround the new control plane approach presented in [18], in order to improve reachability and reliability for an Autonomous System. LISP Redundancy Protocol is built based on the HSRP protocol with the addition of new features. In turn, this new proposed architecture deals with two problems. Firstly, the sending of data-probes which involves sending a lot of information without knowing where is to be sent. Secondly, it avoids packet losses in the presence of a failure in the network, what is achieved in all scenarios except when the failure occurs at the edge router of the network (in this case, LRP only minimizes packet loss).

Currently, we are working on an implementation of the LRP Protocol, in order, to obtain measurements on the convergence time in the network, considered as a primary metric for determining the scalability and efficiency of routing schemes.

References

1. Nordmark, E., Bagnulo, M.: Shim6: Level 3 multihoming shim protocol for ipv6, RFC 5533 (Draft Standard) (June 2009)
2. Vogt, C.: Six/One Router: A Scalable and Backwards Compatible Solution for Provider-Independent Addressing. In: MobiArch 2008: Proceedings of the 3rd International Workshop on Mobility in the Evolving Internet Architecture, Seattle, WA, USA, August 22, pp. 13–18 (2008)
3. Yang, X., Sheng Ji, X.: Host Identity Protocolrealizing the Separation of the Location and Host Identity. In: International Conference on Information and Automation, ICIA 2008, Changsha, June 20-23, pp. 749–752 (2008)
4. Handley, M., Wischik, D., Bagnulo, M.: Multipath Transport, Resource Pooling, and implications for Routing, RRG, August 1 (2008),
   http://www.ietf.org/proceedings/72/slides/RRG-2.pdf
5. Massey, D., Wang, L., Zhang, B., Zhang, L.: A Proposal for Scalable Internet Routing & Addressing. Internet Draft, draft-wang-ietf-efit-00.txt (February 2007)
6. Farinacci, D., Fuller, V., Meyer, D., Lewis, D.: Locator/ID Separation Pro-tocol (LISP). Internet Draft, draft-ietf-lisp-09.txt (October 2010)
7. Hawkinson, J., Bates, T.: Guidelines for creation, selection, and registration of an Autonomous System (AS). RFC 1930 (Best Current Practice) (March 1996)
8. Rekhter, Y., Li, T., Hares, S.: A Border Gateway Protocol 4 (BGP-4). RFC 4271 (Draft Standard) (January 2006)
9. Meyer, D., Zhang, L., Fall, K.: Report from the IAB Workshop on Routing and Addressing. IETF, RFC 4984 (Draft Standard) (September 2007)
10. Houston, G.: The growth of the BGP table - 1994 to present (1994),
    http://bgp.potaroo.net (last visit: January 2011)
11. Bu, T., Gao, L., Towsley, D.: On characterizing BGP routing table growth. In: IEEE Global Telecommunications Conference 2002 (GLOBECOM 2002), Taipei, Taiwan, R.O.C. (November 2002)
12. Oliveira, R., Izhak-Ratzin, R., Zhang, B., Zhang, L.: Measurement of highly active prefixes in BGP. In: IEEE Global Telecommunications Conference 2005 (GLOBECOM 2005), St. Louis, Missouri, USA (November 2005)
13. Flavel, Roughan, M., Bean, N., Maennel, O.: Modeling BGP Table Fluctuations. In: 20th International Teletraffic Congress, Ottawa, Canada (June 2007)
14. Quoitin, et al.: Evaluating the Benefits of the Locator/Identifier Separation. In: Proc. ACM SIGCOMM MobiArch, Kyoto, Japan (August 2007)
15. Farinacci, Fuller, V., Meyer, D.: Lisp alternative topology (lisp+alt). Internet Draft, draft-ietf-lisp-alt-05.txt (October 2010)

16. Lear: Nerd: A not-so-novel eid to rloc database. Internet Draft, draft-lear-lisp-nerd-08.txt (March 2010)
17. Fuller, V., Farinacci, D.: LISP Map Server. Internet Draft, draft-ietf-lisp-ms-06.txt (October 2010)
18. Yannuzzi, M., Masip-Bruin, X., Grampin, E., Gagliano, R., Castro, A., German, M.: Managing interdomain traffic in Latin America: a new perspective based on LISP [Topics in Network and Service Management]. IEEE Commun. Mag. 47(7), 40–48 (2009)
19. `http://www.cisco.com/en/US/tech/tk648/tk362/tk321/tsd_technology_support_sub-protocol_home.html`

Quality of Experience Adaptation Controllers for Voice and Video in Wireless Networks

David Rodrigues[1], Eduardo Cerqueira[2], and Edmundo Monteiro[1]

[1] University of Coimbra, Pinhal de Marrocos, 3030-290 Coimbra, Portugal
`{drod,edmundo}@dei.uc.pt`
[2] Federal University of Para, Rua Augusto Correa, 01, 66075-110 Belem, Brazil
`cerqueira@ufpa.br`

Abstract. Real-time multimedia will be among the most important applications in next generation mobile networks. However, the efficient delivery of these applications to guarantee Quality of Experience (QoE) to fixed and mobile users in multimedia-aware networks is still a research challenge. This paper proposes new approaches to keep voice and video applications with an acceptable quality level in mobile wireless networks with scarce resources and investigates the impact of different video coding parameters on the QoE of voice sessions and real video sequences. Simulation experiments were carried out in a mobile multimedia system to show the benefits of the proposed QoE optimizations, by analyzing well-known QoE objective and subjective metrics.

Keywords: Quality of Service, Quality of Experience, Multimedia, Wireless.

1 Introduction

In recent years, the advancement of mobile communications and the popularization of multimedia services have emerged to offer a novel and comfortable living style for costumers. In this context, it is expected the delivery of mobile multimedia content anytime, anywhere and with an acceptable quality level. In mobile systems, the IEEE 802.11, which defines a Medium Access Control (MAC) and several Physical Layers (PHYs), is the most popular wireless technology used in Wireless Local Area Networks (WLANs). However, due to the lack of Quality of Service (QoS) and Quality of Experience (QoE) support, the scientific community and the industry are researching new approaches to improve the quality level of multimedia delivery and user perception, while optimizing the usage of wireless network resources.

To cope with QoS issues in WLANs, the IEEE 802.11e working group was created, where the draft version [1] brought new MAC improvements incorporated in the IEEE 802.11 standard in 2007 [2]. To provide QoS assurance, eight User Priorities (UPs) were defined. Each packet is assigned to an UP and mapped to an Access Category (AC). Each AC is directly mapped to a queue, where several queues have different priorities and applications must be put to them according to requirements, policies, content characteristics, among other parameters.

Regarding multimedia video and voice encoding, several Coder-Decoders (CODECs) were developed to reduce the bandwidth required to distribute multimedia

X. Masip-Bruin et al. (Eds.): WWIC 2011, LNCS 6649, pp. 350–361, 2011.

content. This improvement is specially needed in mobile networks with limited resources. The Moving Picture Experts Group (MPEG) codifier is widely used and employs a structure composed of 3 frame types named *I*, *P* and *B* as shown in Figure 1 [3][4]. *I* frames are encoded using spatial compression and without reference to other frames in the sequence. To achieve temporal compression, *P* frames (predicted frames) are reconstructed using motion prediction from the last *I* or *P* frame. As a result, *P* frames have a better compression ratio than *I* frames but depending on the amount of motion present in the sequence. *B* frames (bidirectional frames) archive the better compression ratio using prediction from the last and next *I* or *P* frame. The sequence of frames that depend on an I frames is called Group of Pictures (GOP).

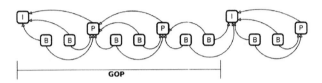

Fig. 1. MPEG Structure

To ensure end-to-end quality level control for multimedia content, new QoS schemes and metrics were created and developed to provide information about the network conditions, such as loss, delay and jitter. However, these QoS metrics only provide information from the network (packet) point of view, as well as, QoS control solutions fail in subjectivity aspects related with human perception. To cope with these limitations and to assess the quality level of multimedia applications at the user-level, QoE metrics and controllers were introduced [5]. QoE metrics provide a deeper analysis of the flows, taking into account the specificity of each multimedia application, as for example, CODEC type, luminance and contrast, as well as, loss and delay tolerance [6-7].

This paper proposes and evaluates new QoE-based multimedia packet control approaches for IEEE 802.11e mobile networks. The proposed mechanisms were designed to optimize multimedia content delivery according to multimedia content characteristics, user perception and frame importance and dependence. In order to show the benefits of the proposed solutions on the user perception, simulation experiments were carried out in multimedia wireless scenarios. The results presented the efficiency of each QoE-aware approach when used in mobile environments with different audio flows and real video sequences, and network conditions.

The remainder of this paper is organized as follows. Section 2 presents the related work. Section 3 details the advanced QoE control mechanisms. Section 4 presents the simulation environment and the performance evaluation for each mechanism. Finally, Section 5 concludes the paper and describes the future work.

2   Related Work

Several voice and video-related solutions were proposed to work in systems with different Coder-Decoders (CODECs) and different wired/wireless QoS models. An

IEEE 802.11 system to improve multimedia quality is proposed and tested in [8]. This proposal adds a second queue to Distributed Coordination Function (DCF) in order to give priority to multimedia streams, and therefore reduces their delay. However, this approach is obsolete and does not focus on the new Hybrid Coordination Function (HCF) operation mode introduced by the IEEE 802.11e draft, which already includes several classes and queues that allow different priorities. Furthermore, few details are provided about the simulations results and environments. The conclusions are only based on network performance measurements, such as delay and losses, and no user level assessments were accomplished.

Another approach uses a cross-layer architecture to map packets with different priorities to different Enhanced Distributed Channel Access (EDCA) queues of IEEE 802.11 [9]. However, this proposal is not in accordance with the recommendations of the IEEE 802.11 standard, as well as, additional traffic placed into the highest priority class may damages voice flows and no scenario related to this problem was analyzed. Furthermore, the mapping of packets from the same flow into different queues increases the jitter and generates losses. Finally, the simulations only take into accounting QoS metrics and no user-based measurements are performed.

A cross-layer video quality proposed approach is deployed in [10]. The signaling from the MAC layer to the upper layers provides further information to the encoder to adjust the video rate and quality to the current network conditions. Thus, in a major interference scenario, the encoder adapts its flows to a lower rate in order to reduce the loss and delay. However, because only local information from the MAC layer is used for video rate adaptation, adjustment cannot be done according to end-to-end path conditions. Therefore, it is not suitable for heterogeneous next generation mobile networks with different requirements and mobile devices.

In [11] a framework for MPEG video delivery over heterogeneous networks (Differentiated Service (DiffServ) and IEEE 802.11e) is analyzed. However, the proposed solution only uses QoS metrics and PSNR in the evaluation process and no HVS-based metrics are measured, failing in human perception assessments. Moreover, the mapping of packets from the same flow into different queues increases the jitter and generates losses

Video streaming traffic delivery in an IP/UMTS network is studied in [12]. In IP networks, video quality is enhanced by mapping video packets, according to their importance, to different traffic classes in a DiffServ environment. Packets with lower importance are mapped to queues with higher drop probability. When packets arrive to the UMTS network, DiffServ traffic classes are mapped to UMTS traffic classes. The evaluation was carried out taking into account a MPEG-4 scalable video stream. However, the paper only assumes the existence of a fixed and simple scenario and is only suitable for scalable MPEG-4 CODEC over DiffServ and UMTS networks, which reduce the implementation in Emerging Wireless Networks.

Other proposals aim to provide QoE-aware assessment in wireless systems for video and voice applications [13-16]. However, they are focused on fixed or/and wired scenarios, do not consider intra-frame dependence neither mobile IEEE 802.11 environments in their approaches.

The analysis of the related work has shown that QoE is a key topic for the success of next generation wireless systems, but current packet control approaches do not assure quality level support based on user perception in IEEE 802.11e networks neither mobility situations. Furthermore, the dependency of each frame of a sequence during the adaptation has rarely been addressed. Existing solutions also fail in capturing QoE metrics during their evaluation processes.

3 Advanced QoE Control Mechanisms

Traditional QoS traffic conditioners, as supported in current DiffServ, IEEE 802.11e and IEEE 802.16 QoS model, provide unfair and poor QoE-aware support for video and voice applications. For example, video streams are encoded so that different frame types have different importance in the final quality from the user point of view. Therefore, by taking into account this property, traffic conditioner elements (i.e., classifier, marker and dropper) can be configured to improve the user experience without increasing the usage of network resources or damaging other ongoing flows.

Multimedia flows are different in terms of encoder parameters, intra-frame dependence, as well as other QoS and QoE requirements. Hence, new mechanisms need to be used to improve the quality level of multimedia sessions and optimize network resources. In this context, multimedia QoE-based approaches are required to operate also in IEEE 802.11e that will be one of the most important access network technology in emerging wireless networks. The mechanisms need to be implemented taking into account the impact of multimedia flow on the end-user perception in congestion situations and to adapt traffic controllers according to the current network conditions, user experience, frame importance and dependence.

In order to satisfy these requirements, this section presents three mechanisms to improve video and voice quality level in wireless system, where the first two mechanisms are focused on advanced drop schemes based on intra-flow packet control, without changing the mapping of the different flows to the IEEE 802.11e access categories. The last mechanism improves the application quality, by mapping the different video frames to the existing queues in order to assure higher priority to frames with higher importance in congestion periods.

As illustrated in Figure 1, the MPEG encoding structure turns some frames more important than others. Because all frames in a GOP depend on I frames, these are the most important ones. P frames are also important, since part of the GOP depends on them. Finally, B frames can be dropped with minimal impact on the other frames as well as on the user experience.

Considering these proprieties, the Advanced Mechanism Priority Drop (AMPD) includes an advanced packet drop scheme that performs its multimedia quality level management based on the importance of each frame of CODECs. If a packet containing an I frame is marked to be dropped, it will be beneficial to check whether a packet corresponding to a P or B frame is currently in the buffer. Since the number of frames that depends on a P or B frame is reduced, the loss of these frame types will have a reduced impact on the final quality and therefore on the user perception. The same process happens when a P frame is marked to be dropped and a B frame is in the queue. It will be beneficial to drop the B frame that is already in the buffer and enqueue the incoming P frame.

Another mechanism, called The Advanced Mechanism Broken Drop (AMBD) aims to keep multimedia applications with an acceptable quality level, while reducing the waste of network resources based on the management of intra-frames dependency and user perception. AMBD recovers a packet marked to be discarded if there is a packet in the queue containing a frame with broken dependencies, that is, a frame that cannot be completely reconstructed on the receiver side. As shown in Figure 2, if the *P2* frame is lost, then *B3, B4, B5* and *B6* cannot be totally reconstructed by the receiver and will waste scarce wireless resources. Therefore, if the *P3* frame is marked to be drop and the *P2* frame has been dropped before, it is preferable to verify if there is a packet in the queue that contains a *B2, B3, B4, B5* or *B6* frame to be discarded and enqueue the incoming packet with the *P3* frame.

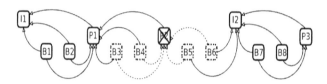

Fig. 2. MPEG Structure with broken dependences

Taking the frame dependence into account, when a packet is marked to be dropped, it is checked if it has broken dependencies. If so, it is dropped. If not, a packet with broken dependencies is searched in the queue. If it is found, the packet from the queue is dropped and the incoming packet is enqueued. Otherwise, the incoming packet is rejected.

Finally, The Advanced Mechanism Split Flow (AMSF) mechanism offers an approach to improve the video streams quality using an enhanced multimedia mapping process, which enqueues different packets to distinct ACs according to the different frames importance. At least, the high priority applications and frames will be allocated into most important classes. The remainder frames are mapped to a less significant class. This method can be used when the packet re-ordering is not crucial. For instance, it can be suitable for scheduled video and audio, where it is more important to ensure an intelligible audio flow than a perfect video.

As suggested in Table 1, priority packets containing *I* frames are mapped to AC_VO, intermediate priority packets carrying *P* frames are mapped to AC_VI and packets with *B* frames, and therefore less important, are mapped to AC_BE. The mapping of other flows remains as defined in the IEEE 802.11e standard.

Table 1. Flows & Queues Mapping in AMSF

Priority	Flow	Access Category
Highest	VoIP and I-Frames	AC_VO
	P-Frames	AC_VI
	Best-Effort and B-Frames	AC_BE
Lowest	Background	AC_BK

Depending on local policies, agreements and available wireless resources in each class, the mapping of frames can be configured to operate in a different way to avoid the session blocking and the re-ordering of packets, for example, by mapping all frames of a multimedia application to a less suitable class in congestion periods.

4 Performance Evaluation

This section presents the simulation scenarios, results and discussions of the proposed QoE-aware control mechanisms. First, an overall comparison of the mechanisms is performed. Afterwards, a depth analysis of the mechanism with the best performance, i.e. AMPD, is performed. The objective of the experiments is to verify the impact of each mechanism on the user experience in mobile networks, by measuring objective (Peak Signal to Noise Ratio (PSNR) and Structural Similarity (SSIM)) and subjective QoE metrics (Mean Opinion Score (MOS))

The PSNR is the most traditional objective metric and compares frame by frame the quality of the video received by the user with the original one. The value of PSNR is expressed in dB (decibels). For a video to be considered with good quality according to the MOS scale, it should have an average PSNR of at least 30dB. The SSIM is a measurement of the video structural distortion, trying to get a better correlation with the user's subjective impression where values vary between 0 and 1, where 1 is the best value.

In order to define a scenario similar to a real system, simulations were carried out, where the Network Simulator 2 (NS2) with real video sequences in IEEE 802.11e environments. Experiments with Mobile IP (MIP) were used to verify the overall improvements of each mechanism on the performance of the mobile network. In each scenario, four flows were used: VoIP, video, best-effort and background traffic. Each flow type was mapped to a different IEEE 802.11e AC in accordance with its priority: VoIP flow to AC_VO, video stream to AC_VI (except for AMSF), best-effort traffic to AC_BE and background traffic to AC_BK.

Two well-known Common Intermediate Format (CIF) video sequences, News and Foreman, were used with 30 frames per second (fps), 2 *B* frames between each *P* frames, a bitrate of 320 kbps and a GOP size of 10. These values were changed for the AMPD analysis. Additionally, the Evalvid video control tool [17] was used to add real video sequence support to NS2. Regarding VoIP flows, they were encoded using the ITU-T G.729 standard, with a rate of 8 kbps and without Voice Activity Detection (VAD). Audio file support for NS2 was included using the VoIP packet trace module implemented by the Technical University of Berlin [18]. Best-effort and background flows were simulated with Constant Bit Rate (CBR).

QoE-aware simulation results for the video flows with different wireless congestion rates are depicted in Figures 3(a) and 3(b), for PSNR and SSIM assessments, respectively.

Regarding IEEE 802.11e, the packet loss rate remains low despite of high values of congestion generated by background traffic in the network, which aims to assure quality level support for video flows. Only flows with lower priority, this is, background and best-effort traffics, are strongly affected. Therefore, the QoE assessments reveal a good quality of video for all values of congestion. However, the IEEE 802.11e quality of service controller does not distinguish between I, P and B frames and random values of loss exist for the different frames types. Therefore, video quality improvements can be achieved if the importance of each frame type is taken into consideration.

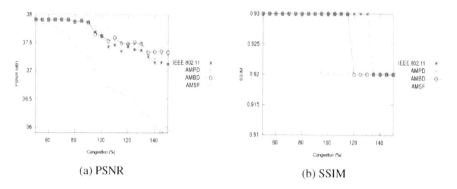

(a) PSNR   (b) SSIM

Fig. 3. QoE assessment for the video flows with different congestion rates

AMPD achieves a better I frame protection owing to the advanced drop mechanism. Thus, for all values of congestion, no I frame packets have been discarded and the best values of PSNR for all values of congestion are achieved. Despite a large number of dropped frames, including I frames, AMBD shows intermediate values of quality thanks to the discard of packets with broken dependencies, this is, packets that contain frames which cannot totally be reconstructed by the decoder on the mobile device. Finally, AMSF shows no loss in terms of I and P frames due to low congestion values achieved by the frames division over different queues. However, because B frames are mapped to a queue with less priority and in concurrence with best-effort traffic, loss rates for this type of frames raise, reaching values up to 80% when the congestion is of 150%. User experience is highly affected by such values, presenting lower quality assessments than those achieved with traditional IEEE 802.11e quality of service support. Based on the mapping of PSNR values to MOS, AMPD keeps multimedia applications with excellent quality level during all experiments.

Regarding VoIP flows, E-Model and PESQ evaluations are depicted in Figures 4(a) and 4(b), respectively. Because no packet loss occurs in the VoIP traffic, as it has the highest priority and enough network resources, IEEE 802.11e only shows a small decrease in VoIP quality level due to the delay and jitter increase with the network load. Moreover, because AMPD and AMBD only affect video traffic, VoIP quality for these mechanisms is equal to IEEE 802.11e. However, besides the video quality degradation for AMSF, VoIP quality is also affected for this mechanism. Because I frames are mapped to AC_VO, the delay and jitter for voice traffic increase, leading to a degradation in VoIP quality.

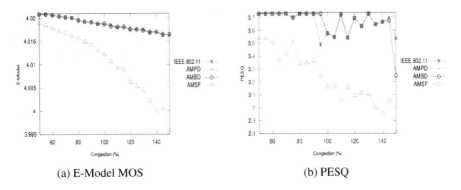

(a) E-Model MOS   (b) PESQ

Fig. 4. QoE assessment for the VoIP flows

For all values of GOP size used for video encoding and network congestion, no packet loss occurs in the VoIP traffic, as it has the highest priority and enough network resources. However, Figures 5(a) and 5(b) show a decrease in the quality assessed with the increase of the congestion. This decrease occurs only due to the increase of the delay and jitter with the network load. However, the quality decrease is minimal due to the protection achieved by the IEEE 802.11e QoS support. Different values of GOP size do not affect the voice perception either. Because video traffic is separated from VoIP, a change in video encoding does not affect the voice quality.

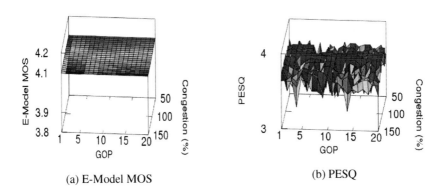

(a) E-Model MOS   (b) PESQ

Fig. 5. QoE assessments for VoIP for different values of GOP and congestion for AMPD

The same conclusions are achieved for different numbers of B frames and bitrate used for video encoding, as shown in Figures 6 and 7, respectively. Only the increase in congestion leads to a decrease in the voice quality due to the increase of delay and jitter.

Regarding the video quality level, it varies according to the GOP size, the number of B frames used and bitrate. In Figures 8(a) and 8(b), the GOP size impact in user's experience is visible. For GOP values less than 5 the video quality is low, as it is

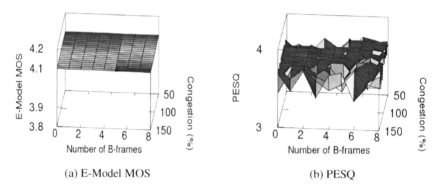

(a) E-Model MOS

(b) PESQ

Fig. 6. QoE assessments for VoIP flows for different values of B-frames and congestion for AMPD

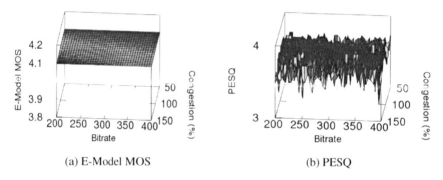

(a) E-Model MOS

(b) PESQ

Fig. 7. QoE assessments for VoIP for different values of bitrate and congestion for AMPD

evidenced by PSNR and SSIM evaluations. When small GOP size values are used, the quantity of P and B frames generated is low and therefore compression too. Thus, for the same data rate and lower compression, the video quality achieved by the encoder is lower. This is visible when the video quality is low despite the low network congestion. When large values of GOP size are used, and therefore when the number of P and B frames is high in relation to the number of I frames, the number of dropped packets with I frames reaches zero, because the advanced drop mechanism protects this important frame type. The same happens with the number of packet dropped with P frames. By increasing the GOP size, the number of B frames is increased and the drop of other frames becomes less probable. Evaluation results demonstrate best results for GOP sizes higher than 10. Because the most important frames are protected there are less broken dependencies and therefore quality values keep high even for large values of GOP size.

Regarding the number of B frames used for encoding, the impact in quality can be seen in Figures 9(a) and 9(b). Because the GOP size is always 10, the I frames loss rate is always zero. However, for low values of B frames used, the number of P

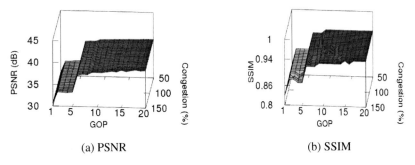

(a) PSNR   (b) SSIM

Fig. 8. QoE assessments for videos for different values of GOP and congestion for AMPD

frames discarded is high. Because the loss of a P frame is more harmful compared to the loss of a B frame, the video quality is low for very small values of B frames used. Finally, for values higher than 2 B frames between each P frame, the encoding quality is degraded due to the increase of predictions.

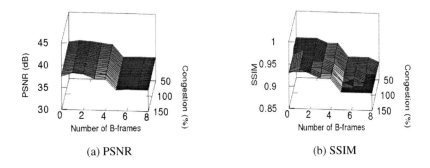

(a) PSNR   (b) SSIM

Fig. 9. QoE assessments for video flows for different values of B-frames and congestion for AMPD

Based on the simulation results, it is possible to conclude that for low GOP size values the mechanism has generally worst performances. Small GOP values lead to large number of I frames and turn the discovery of less important frames to be discarded less probable. On the other hand, large GOP values lead to higher numbers of dependencies. Therefore, a frame loss can induce a high number of discarded frames on the receiver side if broken dependencies exist. However, AMPD keeps a good quality due to the protection of most important frames.

Regarding the number of B frames, simulation results show that small values lead to a reduction in the quality level. A small number of B frames leads to a higher number of P frames. Since the number of P frames increases, the loss rate for these frames also increases.

Concerning the bitrate, simulation results present that different values do not have a visible impact on the proposed mechanisms. The quality variation is only related to the video quality achieved by the encoder when using different compression schemes. Overall simulations results show better quality when GOP size values higher than 10 and a maximum of 2 B frames between each P frame are used.

6 Conclusion

The usage of multimedia applications, such as voice and video streaming, is increasing in the Internet and will be very popular in next generation networks. However, existing wireless networking systems are not prepared to optimize resources and the quality level of current and new multimedia applications according to the user perception. Throughout this paper, various QoE advanced mechanisms to improve video flows were analyzed, compared, discussed and evaluated. Performance evaluation results show better video experience, without degrading VoIP flows quality, in IEEE 802.11e environments when advanced mechanisms are used. As demonstrated by simulations, AMPD presents the best video quality ratio.

Due to the mechanism simplicities, they can be implemented easily in real networking systems. Information about the frame types can be placed in the Real Time Protocol (RTP) header and acquired by any node through packet inspection. Service providers, such as mobile and multimedia markets, who increasingly provide audio-visual content, can increase their portfolio and revenue, by using QoE-aware packet controller mechanisms, which combine improvement in user perception, video and voice quality level, and wireless resources.

As future works, the proposed mechanisms will be adapted and evaluated in IEEE 802.11s, IEEE 802.16 and Long Term Evolution (LTE) systems. A test-bed environment will also be setup to confirm the simulation results and show the efficiency of the proposed solution in real scenarios.

Acknowledgment

The work is supported by FCT UBIQUIMESH project (PTDC/EEATEL/105472/2008) – Portugal and by National Council for Scientific and Technological Development (CNPq) and FAPESPA - Brazil.

References

1. IEEE standard for local and metropolitan area networks part 16: Air interface for fixed and mobile broadband wireless access systems amendment 2: Physical and medium access control layers for combined fixed and mobile operation in licensed bands and corrigendum 1 (2006)
2. IEEE standard for information technology - telecommunications and information exchange between systems - local and metropolitan area networks specific requirements - part 11: Wireless LAN medium access control (MAC) and physical layer (PHY) specifications (2007)

3. Moussa, N., Soudani, A., Tourki, R.: Performances evaluation and enhancement of MPEG4 transmission over IEEE 802.11 WLAN. In: International Conference on Design and Test of Integrated Systems in Nanoscale Technology, DTIS 2006, Tunis, pp. 341–344 (September 2006)
4. Eichhorn, A.: Modelling dependency in multimedia streams. In: Proceedings of the 14th Annual ACM International Conference on Multimedia, pp. 941–950. ACM, Santa Barbara (2006)
5. Mu, M., Cerqueira, E., Boavida, F., Mauthe, A.: Quality of experience management framework for real-time multimedia applications. Int. J. Internet Protoc. Technol. 4(1), 54–64 (2009)
6. Cerqueira, E., Janowski, L., Leszczuk, M., Papir, Z., Romaniak, P.: Video artifacts assessment for live mobile streaming applications. In: Mauthe, A., Zeadally, S., Cerqueira, E., Curado, M. (eds.) FMN 2009. LNCS, vol. 5630, pp. 242–247. Springer, Heidelberg (2009)
7. Serral-Gracia, R., Cerqueira, E., Curado, M., Monteiro, E., Yannuzzi, M., Masip-Bruin, X.: An Overview of Quality of Experience Measurement Challenges for Video Applications in IP Networks. In: Osipov, E., Kassler, A., Bohnert, T.M., Masip-Bruin, X. (eds.) WWIC 2010. LNCS, vol. 6074, pp. 252–263. Springer, Heidelberg (2010)
8. Liang, H.M., Ke, C.H., Shieh, C.K., Hwang, W.S., Chilamkurti, N.K.: Performance evaluation of 802.11e EDCF in the ad-hoc mode with real audio/video traffic. In: 2006 IFIP International Conference on Wireless and Optical Communications Networks (April 2006)
9. Ngoc, D.M., Tan, P.A., Lee, J.S., Oh, H.: Improvement of IEEE 802.11 for multimedia traffic in wireless LAN. In: Wireless Telecommunications Symposium, WTS 2007, Pomona, CA, pp. 1–4 (April 2007)
10. Ksentini, A., Naimi, M., Gueroui, A.: Toward an improvement of h.264 video transmission over IEEE 802.11e through a cross-layer architecture. IEEE Communications Magazine 44(1), 107–114 (2006)
11. Haratcherev, L., Taal, J., Langendoen, K., Lagendijk, R., Sips, H.: Optimized video streaming over 802.11 by cross-layer signaling. IEEE Communications Magazine 44(1), 115–121 (2006)
12. Ke, C.-H., Chilamkurti, N.: A new framework for MPEG video delivery over heterogeneous networks. Computer Communications 31(11), 2656–2668 (2008)
13. Pliakas, T., Kormentzas, G., Skianis, C.: End-to-End QoS issues of MPEG4-FGS video streaming traffic delivery in an IP/UMTS network. In: Autonomic Management of Mobile Multimedia Services, pp. 247–255 (2006)
14. Ameigeiras, P., Ramos-Munoz, J.J., Navarro-Ortiz, J., Mogensen, P., Lopez-Soler, J.M.: Qoe oriented cross-layer design of a resource allocation algorithm in beyond 3g systems. Computer Communications (October 2009)
15. Liu, L., Zhou, W.-A., Song, J.-D.: Quantitative and qualitative research on service quality evaluation system in ngn, vol. 16, pp. 71–77 (2009)
16. Binzenhöfer, T.H.A.: Analysis of Skype VoIP traffic in UMTS: End-to-end QoS and QoE measurements. Computer Networks 55(3), 650–666 (2008)
17. EvalVid Tool. A video quality evaluation tool-set (February 2011), http://www.tkn.tu-berlin.de/research/evalvid/
18. Predicting the perceptual service quality using a trace of VoIP packets (February 2011), http://www.tkn.tu-berlin.de/research/qofis/

User to User QoE Routing System

Hai Anh Tran and Abdelhamid Mellouk

Image, Signal and Intelligent Systems Lab-LiSSi Lab
University of Paris-Est Creteil Val de Marne (UPEC)
122 rue Paul Armangot 94400, Vitry sur Seine
{hai-anh.tran,mellouk}@u-pec.fr

Abstract. Recently, wealthy network services such as Internet proto-col television (IPTV) and Voice over IP (VoIP) are expected to become more pervasive over the Next Generation Network (NGN). In order to serve this purpose, the quality of these services should be evaluated sub-jectively by users. This is referred to as the quality of experience (QoE). The most important tendency of actual network services is maintaining the best QoE with network functions such as admission control, resource management, routing, traffic control, etc. Among of them, we focus here on routing mechanism. We propose in this paper a protocol integrating QoE measurement in routing paradigm to construct an adaptive and evolutionary system. Our approach is based on Reinforcement Learning concept. More concretely, we have used a least squares reinforcement learning technique called Least Squares Policy Iteration. Experimental results showed a significant performance gain over traditional routing protocols.

Keywords: Quality of Service (QoS), Quality of Experience (QoE), Network Services, Inductive Routing System.

1   Introduction

The theory of quality of experience (QoE) has become commonly used to repre-sent user perception. For evaluating network service, one has to measure, moni-tor, quantify and analyze the QoE in order to characterize, evaluate and manage services offered over this network. For users, also for operators and Internet ser-vice providers, the end-to-end quality is one of the major factors to be achieved. Actually the new term of QoE has been introduced to make end-to-end (e2e) QoS more clearly captures the experience of the users, which attempts to objec-tively measure the service delivered, QoE also takes in account the needs and the desires of the subscribers when using network services. Furthermore, the main challenge lies in how to take the dynamic changes in the resources of communi-cation networks into account to provide e2e QoS for individual flows. Developing an efficient and accurate QoS mechanism is the focus of many challenges; mostly it is the complexity and stability. In reality, e2e QoS with more than two non correlated criteria is NP-complete [1]. Both technologies and needs continue to develop, so complexity and cost become limiting factors in the future evolution of networks.

X. Masip-Bruin et al. (Eds.): WWIC 2011, LNCS 6649, pp. 362–373, 2011.
© IFIP International Federation for Information Processing 2011

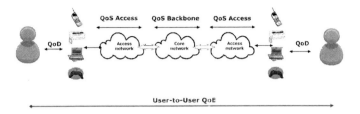

Fig. 1. Quality chain in an e2e service

In order to solve a part of this problem, one has integrated QoE in network systems to adapt decision control in real-time. In fact, QoE does not replace QoS, but improves it. As an important factor of the end-to-end user perception, the QoE is an key metric for the design of systems and engineering processes. In addition, with QoE paradigm, we can reach a better solution to real-adaptive control network components.

Many people think that QoE is a part of QoS but it is a wrong perception. In reality, QoE covers the QoS concept. In order to demonstrate this theoretical point, we observe a quality chain of user-to-user services in Fig. 1. The quality perceived by end-user when using end-devices is called QoD (Quality of Design). The quality of network service including core network and access network is determined by QoS access and QoS backbone. QoE is satisfied only in the case that QoD and QoS are satisfied. So we can see that the user-to-user QoE is a conjunction of QoD and QoS.

In fact, there are many of network functions through which we can implement QoE concept to improve system quality such as admission control, resource management, routing, traffic control, etc. Among of them, we focus on routing mechanism. Our purpose is to construct an adaptive routing method that can retrieve environment information and adapt to the environment changes. This adaptive routing mechanism maintains the required QoE of end-users. It is very necessary with network systems that have great dynamics (i.e. unreliable communication) and multiple user profiles where the required QoE levels are different. Most of the actual adaptive routing mechanisms that focus on optimizing simultaneously more than two non-correlated QoS metrics (i.e. e2e delay, jitter, response time, bandwidth) meet NP-complete problem we have mentioned above.

That is why in this paper we want to present a novel approach that integrates QoE measurement in a routing paradigm to construct an adaptive and evolutionary system.

Our approach is based on Reinforcement Learning (RL). More concretely, we based our protocol on Least Squares Policy Iteration (LSPI) [2], a RL technique that combines least squares function approximation with policy iteration.

The paper is structured as follows: Section 2 surveys briefly related works. In section 3, some preliminaries of reinforcement learning for routing paradigm are expressed. In section 4 we focus on our approach based on reinforcement learning. The experimental results are shown in section 5. Paper is ended with conclusion and some future works in section 6.

2   Related Work

Routing mechanism is key to the success of large-scale, distributed communication and heterogeneous networks. The goal of every algorithm is to direct traffic from source to destinations maximizing network performance while minimizing costs. We cannot apply a static routing mechanism because network environment changes all time. So most existing routing techniques are designed to be capable to take into account the dynamics of the network. In other word, they are called adaptive routing protocol.

[3] presents a dynamic routing algorithm for best-effort traffic in Integrated-Services networks. Their purpose is to improve the throughput of high-bandwidth traffic in a network where flows exhibiting different QoS requirements are present. In this algorithm, one of two approaches is captured: either performing hop-based path computation, or evaluating the available bandwidth on a specific path. The problem is that the authors just focus on QoS requirements. Furthermore, this approach lacks learning process for an adaptive method.

The idea of applying RL to routing in networks was firstly introduced by Boyan and Littman [4]. Authors described the Q routing algorithm for packet routing. Reinforcement learning module is integrated into each node in network. Therefore, each router uses only local communication to maintain accurate statistics in order to minimize delivery times. However, this proposal is a simple reinforcement learning approach. It just focus on optimizing one basis network metric (delivery times).

AntNet, an adaptive, distributed, mobile-agents-based algorithm is introduced in [5]. In this algorithm, each artificial ant builds a path from its source to destination node. Collecting explicit information about the time length of the path components and implicit information about the load status of the network is realized in the same time of building the path. This information is then back-propagated by another ant moving in the opposite direction and is used to modify the routing tables of visited nodes.

In [6], authors proposed an application of gradient ascent algorithm for reinforcement learning to a complex domain of packet routing in network communication. This approach updates the local policies while avoiding the necessity for centralized control or global knowledge of the networks structure. The only global information required by the learning algorithm is the network utility expressed as a reward signal distributed once in an epoch and dependent on the average routing time.

In [7], KOQRA, a QoS based routing algorithm based on a multi-path routing approach combined with the Q-routing algorithm, is presented. The global learning algorithm finds K best paths in terms of cumulative link cost and optimizes the average delivery time on these paths. The technique used to estimate the end-to-end delay is based on the reinforcement learning approach to take into account dynamic changes in networks.

We can see that all of these approaches above do not take into account the perception and satisfaction of end-users. In other word, they ignored QoE concept. In order to solve this lack, other proposals are presented:

In [8], authors propose to use an overlay network that is able to optimize the e2e QoE by routing around failures in the IP network. Network components are located both in the core and at the edge of the network. However, this system has no adaptive mechanism that can retrieve QoE feedback of end-users and adapt to the system actions.

[9] presents a new adaptive mechanism to maximize the overall video quality at the client. This proposal has taken into account the perception of end-users, in other words, the QoE. Overlay path selection is dynamically done based on available bandwidth estimation, while the QoE is subjectively measured using Pseudo-Subjective Quality Assessment (PSQA) tool. After receiving a client demand, the video server chooses an initial strategy and an initial scheme to start the video streaming. Then, client uses PSQA to evaluate the QoE of the received video in real time and send this feedback to server. After examining this feedback, the video server will decide to keep or to change its strategy. With this adaptive mechanism, all is done dynamically and in real time. This approach has well considered end-users perception. However this adaptive mechanism seems to be quite simple procedure. One should add learning process to construct much more user's profile.

In [10], authors proposed a routing scheme that adaptively learns an optimal routing strategy for sensor networks. This approach is based on LSPI, the same way on which we base our approach. However, in [10], the feedback information is gathered on each intermediate node along the routing path, that is not applicable for integrating the QoE feedback that we just obtain until data flux reach the destination. In our approach, we have changed LSPI technique such that we only require the feedback from the end node of the routing path.

3   Preliminaries

3.1   Reinforcement Learning Model

In a reinforcement learning (RL) model [11] [12], an agent is connected to its environment via perception and action (Fig. 2). Whenever the agent receives

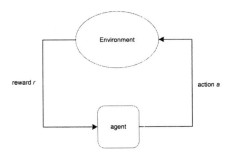

Fig. 2. Reinforcement Learning model

as input the indication of current environment state, the agent then chooses an action, a, to generate as output. The action changes the state of the environment. The new value is communicated to the agent through a reinforcement signal, r. Formally, the model consists of:

- a discrete set of environment states: S;
- a discrete set of agent actions: $\mathcal{A}$;
- a set of scalar reinforcement signals: $\mathcal{R}$;

So the agent's goal is to find a policy π, mapping states to actions, that maximizes some long-run measure of reinforcement. In RL paradigm, one uses two types of value functions to estimate how good is for the agent to be in a given state:

- State-Value function $V^\pi(s)$: expected return when starting in s and following π thereafter.

$$V^\pi(s) = E_\pi\{R_t|s_t = s\} \tag{1}$$

- Action-Value function $Q^\pi(s, a)$: expected return starting from s, taking the action a, and thereafter following policy π

$$Q^\pi(s, a) = E_\pi\{R_t|s_t = s, a_t = a\} \tag{2}$$

where: t is any time step and R is the return.

Regarding policy iteration notion, the reason for computing the value function for a policy is to find better policies. Once a policy, π, has been improved using V^π to yield a better policy, π', we can then compute $V^{\pi'}$ and improve it again to yield an even better π''. We can thus obtain a sequence of monotonically improving policies and value functions:

$$\pi_0 \xrightarrow{E} V^{\pi_0} \xrightarrow{I} \pi_1 \xrightarrow{E} V^{\pi_1} \xrightarrow{I} \pi_2 \xrightarrow{E} \dots \xrightarrow{I} \pi^* \xrightarrow{E} V^* \tag{3}$$

where E denote a policy evaluation and I denotes a policy improvement.

The goal is to find an optimal policy that maps states to actions such that the cumulative reward is maximized, which is equivalent to determining the following Q function (Bellman equation):

$$Q^*(s, a) = r(s, a) + \gamma \sum_{s'} P(s'|s, a) max_{a'} Q^*(s', a') \tag{4}$$

In our approach, we don't apply directly this basic Q function. In fact, this basic Q-Learning value function requires a large number of tries before being able to converge to the optimal solution, furthermore it is sensitive to the parameter setting. So we must approximate it using a technique called Function Approximation that is presented in the next section.

3.2   Function Approximation

The table representing the estimate of value functions with one entry for each state or for each state-action pair is limited to tasks with small numbers of states and actions. Time and data needed to accurately fill them is a problem too. In routing system to which we applied reinforcement learning, most states encountered will never have been experienced exactly before. Generalizing from previously experienced states to ones that have never been seen is the only way to learn anything at all on these tasks.

We require a generalization method called *function approximation* [12] because it takes examples from a desired function (e.g., a value function) and attempts to generalize from them to construct an approximation of the entire function. Function approximation is a combination between reinforcement learning methods and existing generalization methods. One of the most important special cases in function approximation is *Linear method* that is the method we have applied to our approach.

4   Proposed Approach

Our idea to take into account end-to-end QoE consists to develop adaptive mechanisms that can retrieve the information from their environment (QoE) and adapt to initiate actions. These actions should be executed in response to unforeseen or unwanted event as an unsatisfactory QoS, a negative feedback or malfunctioning network elements.

The purpose of this approach consists of:

- Integrate parameters from the terminal application (or user) in terms of QoE metrics in the decision loop system.
- Taking into account the feedback of QoS and QoE metrics as input for autonomy in the adaptive model.
- Developing a viable model of a knowledge plane enabling scaling on equipment located in different parts of the network.
- Taking into account a propagation model of dysfunction and stable algorithms.

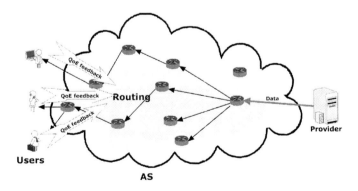

Fig. 3. Integration of QoE measurement in routing system

Concretely, the system integrates the QoE measurement in an evolutionary routing system in order to improve the user perception based on the choice of the
best optimal QoE paths (Fig. 3). So in that way, the routing process is build
according to the improvement of QoE parameters. The system is based on adaptive algorithms that simultaneously process an observation and learn to perform
better.

In this section, we describe in detail our proposal in order to integrate QoE
measurement in an adaptive routing system. We first present our mapping of
reinforcement learning model to our routing model. Then we describe Least-
Squares Policy Iteration technique on which we based our approach. Finally the
learning procedure is depicted.

4.1 Reinforcement Learning Based Routing System Including QoE Measurement

In order to integrate reinforcement learning notion into our routing system, we
have mapped reinforcement learning model to our routing model in the context
of learning routing strategy (Fig. 4). We consider each router in the system as a
state. The states are arranged along the routing path. Furthermore, we consider
each link emerging from a router as an action to choose. The system routing
mechanism corresponds to the policy π.

After data reach end-users, QoE evaluation is realized to give a QoE feedback
to the system. We consider this feedback as environment reward and our purpose
is to improve the policy π using this QoE feedback. Concretely, the policy π is
chosen so that it is equal to $argmax$ of action value function Q in policy π:

$$\pi_{t+1}(s_t) = argmaxQ^{\pi_t}(s_t, a) \tag{5}$$

4.2 Least-Squares Policy Iteration

Least-Squares Policy Iteration (LSPI) [2] is a recently introduced reinforcement
learning method. Our choice is based on the fact that this technique learns the
weights of the linear functions, thus can update the Q-values based on the most

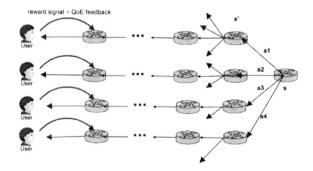

Fig. 4. Routing system based on reinforcement learning

updated information regarding the features. It does not need carefully tuning initial parameters (e.g., learning rate). Furthermore, LSPI converges faster with less samples than basic Q-learning. In this technique, instead to calculate directly action-value function Q (Equation 4), this latter is approximated with a parametric function approximation. In other words, the value function is approximated as a linear weighted combination:

$$\hat{Q}^{\pi}(s,a,\omega) = \sum_{i=1}^{k} \phi_i(s,a)\omega_i = \phi(s,a)^T \omega \tag{6}$$

where $\phi(s,a)$ is the basis features vector and ω is weight vector in the linear equation. The k basis functions represent characteristics of each state-action pair.

We have to update the weight vector ω to improve system policy.

Equation 4 and 6 can be transformed to $\Phi\omega \approx R + \gamma P^{\pi}\Phi\omega$, where Φ represent the basis features for all state-action pairs. This equation is reformulated as:

$$\Phi^T(\Phi - \gamma P^{\pi}\Phi)\omega^{\pi} = \Phi^T R \tag{7}$$

Basing on equation 7, the weight ω of the linear functions in equation 6 is extracted:

$$\omega = (\Phi^T(\Phi - \gamma P^{\pi}\Phi))^{-1} \times \Phi^T R \tag{8}$$

4.3 Learning Procedure

For a router s and forwarding action a, s' is the corresponding neighbor router with $P(s'|s,a) = 1$. Our learning procedure is realized as follows: when a packet is forwarded from node s to s' by action a, which has been chosen by current Q-values $\phi(s,a)^T\omega$, a record $< s,a,s',\phi(s,a) >$ is inserted to the packet. The gathering process (Fig. 5) is realized until the packet arrives at the destination (end-users). Thus with this way, one can trace the information of the whole routing path. At the end-users, a QoE evaluation process is realized to give a QoE score that is the value of R vector in equation 8. Furthermore, with the gathered information, the new value of ω is determined using equation 8. Then this new weight value ω' is sent back to the system along the routing path in order to improve policy procedure in each router on the routing path. With the

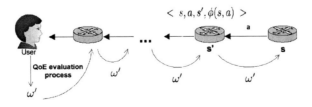

Fig. 5. Learning procedure

new weights ω', policy improvement is realized in each router on the routing path by selecting the action a with the highest Q-value:

$$\pi(s|\omega') = argmax_a \phi(s,a)^T \omega' \qquad (9)$$

The next section presents some experiment results in comparing our approach with other routing protocols.

5   Simulation Results

We have used Opnet simulator version 14.0 to implement our approach in an autonomous system. Regarding network topology, we have implemented an irregular network with 3 separated areas including 38 routers, each area is connected to each other by one link, all links are similar (Fig. 6). For QoE evaluation method,

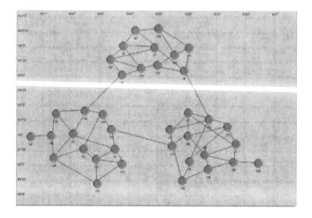

Fig. 6. Simulated network

we have used a reference table represents human estimated MOS[1] function [13] of loss packet rate based on real experiment.

To validate our results, we compare our approach with two kinds of algorithm:

- Those based on Shortest Path First (SPF) technique where routing in this family used the only best path based on delay constraint.
- The Routing Information Protocol (RIP), a dynamic routing protocol used in local and wide area networks. It uses the distance-vector routing algorithm. It employs the hop count as a routing metric. RIP prevents routing loops by implementing a limit on the number of hops allowed in a path from the source to a destination.

---

[1] Mean Opinion Score (MOS) gives a numerical indication of the perceived quality of the media received after being transmitted. MOS is expressed in one number, from 1 to 5, 1 being the worst and 5 the best. The MOS is generated by averaging the results of a set of standard, subjective tests where a number of users rate the service quality.

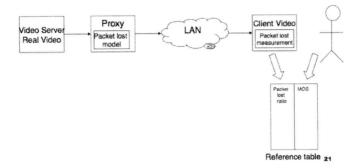

Fig. 7. QoE evaluation model

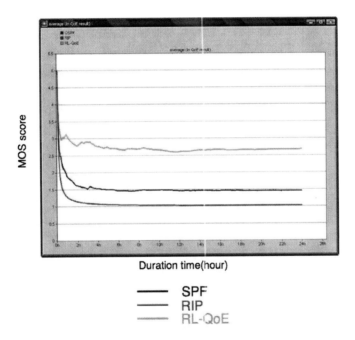

Fig. 8. Simulation results

In order to have QoE evaluation results, we have implemented a measurement model that is depicted in Fig. 7. The video server provides video streaming to the client through a proxy into which we have integrated a packet lost model. In the destination, in order to construct the reference table, the Client Video realizes packet lost measurement and the end-users give a MOS score. Thus we have an equivalent MOS score for each packet lost ratio. Our simulation results are based on this reference table to give MOS scores equivalent to packet lost ratio. Fig. 8 illustrates the result of average MOS score of three protocols: SPF, RIP and our approach. With the three protocols we have implemented in the simulation, we can notice that each is based on a different criteria. The SPF focuses on minimizing the routing path. On the other side, RIP focuses on the hop-count of routing packages. As our protocol, we rely on user perception. As shown in Fig. 8, we can see that our approach gives better results than two other algorithms in the same delay. So with our approach, despite network environment changes, we can maintain a better QoE without any other e2e delay.

6 Conclusion

In this paper, we present a novel approach for routing systems in considering the user-to-user QoE, which has integrated QoE measurement to routing paradigm for an adaptive and evolutionary system. The approach is based on a least squares reinforcement learning technique. The simulation results we obtained with OPNET simulations demonstrates that our proposed approach yields significant QoE evaluation improvements over traditional approaches using the same e2e delay.

Some future works includes applying our protocol to real testbed to verify its feasibility, using standard QoE evaluation methods and implementing protocol on IPTV flows.

Acknowledgment

The work is carried out in the framework of the Celtic and EUREKA and was done in IPNQSIS project.

References

1. Wang, Z., Crowcroft, J.: Quality of service routing for supporting multimedia applications. IEEE Journal on selected areas in communications 14(7), 1228–1234 (1996)
2. Lagoudakis, M.G., Parr, R.: Least-squares policy iteration. Journal of Machine Learning Research 4, 1149 (2003)
3. Casetti, C., Favalessa, G., Mellia, M., Munafo, M.: An adaptive routing algorithm for best-effort traffic in integrated-services networks. Teletraffic science and engineering, 1281–1290 (1999)
4. Boyan, J.A., Littman, M.L.: Packet routing in dynamically changing networks: A reinforcement learning approach. In: Advances in Neural Information Processing Systems, p. 671 (1994)
5. Caro, G.D., Dorigo, M.: Antnet: A mobile agents approach to adaptive routing. In: The Hawaii International Conference On System Sciences, vol. 31, pp. 74–85 (1998)
6. Peshkin, L., Savova, V.: Reinforcement learning for adaptive routing. In: Intnl. Joint Conf on Neural Networks (2002)
7. Mellouk, A., Hoceini, S., Zeadally, S.: Design and performance analysis of an inductive qos routing algorithm. Computer Communications 32(1371-1376) (2009)

8. Vleeschauwer, B.D., Turck, F.D., Dhoedt, B., Demeester, P., Wijnants, M., Lamotte, W.: End-to-end qoe optimization through overlay network deployment. In: International Conference on Information Networking (2008)

9. Majd, G., Cesar, V., Adlen, K.: An adaptive mechanism for multipath video streaming over video distribution network (vdn). In: First International Conference on Advances in Multimedia (2009)

10. Wang, P., Wang, T.: Adaptive routing for sensor networks using reinforcement learning. In: IEEE International Conference on Computer and Information Technology (2006)

11. Kaelbling, L.P., Littman, M.L., Moore, A.W.: Reinforcement learning: A survey. Journal of AI Research 4, 237–285 (1996)

12. Sutton, R.S., Barto, A.G.: Reinforcement learning: An introduction. IEEE transactions on neural networks 9 (1998)

13. I.-T. R. P.801. Mean opinion score (mos) terminology. International Telecommunication Union, Geneva (2006)

Link-Layer Based Anycast Routing for a Dynamic and Distributed Portal Selection in Wireless Mesh Networks

A. Ariza-Quintana, A. Triviño-Cabrera, and E. Casilari

Dpto. Tecnología Electrónica, E.T.S.I. Telecomunicación, University of Málaga
Campus Teatinos 29071 Málaga, Spain
{atc,aarizaq,ecasilari}@uma.es

Abstract. Wireless mesh networks may be equipped with multiple Portals that offer access to external networks such as the Internet. These Portals are provided with two interfaces: one to a wired network (to communicate with other Portals and Gateways) and another one to the wireless network. In the current 802.11s standard, the interaction between these two interfaces is not defined. By connecting both interfaces in a seamless way, this paper addresses and solves the problem of dynamically selecting multiple Portals in a Wireless Mesh Network. In particular, the proposal is supported by the definition of an anycast group formed by the Portals in the network. Any data frame whose destination is an external host is routed to any Portal in the network. The route is selected depending on the instantaneous network conditions (e.g. path availability, number of hops, delay or losses). To make this selection a distributed process, a link-layer based forwarding scheme is employed. By means of simulations, we state that the application of the proposed technique yields to significant improvements concerning the network performance.

Keywords: Mesh Portal, Wireless mesh network, Multiple Mesh Portal, Anycasting.

1 Introduction

Wireless communications have become a common mechanism to connect machines. This expansion of wireless technologies has prompted the more popular mobile devices (smartphones, electronic pads, tablets and laptops) to be equipped with one or multiple built-in radio interfaces: one interface to connect to a telecommunication operator and another one to communicate in the free unlicensed spectrum. In order to facilitate their integration into the Internet in a cost-effective way, some cities, organisms and business have opted for the development of their own wireless mesh network [1] [2]. Due to this popularity, IEEE 802.11s has been released as an experimental standard amendment for wireless mesh networks [3]. According to these specifications, a wireless mesh network is formed by a set of dedicated, static nodes which are wirelessly interconnected leading to a multihop backbone [4]. These nodes, which are called Mesh Points (MP), act as static relays for other mesh nodes by executing a link layer based routing protocol called HWMP (Hybrid Wireless Mesh Protocol) [5]. However, some MPs offer additional features. In this sense, the Mesh

X. Masip-Bruin et al. (Eds.): WWIC 2011, LNCS 6649, pp. 374–385, 2011.

Access Points (MAP) provide access to mobile devices or stations (STA). On the other hand, the Mesh Portals (MPP) are MPs which are outfitted with an Internet connection. MPPs fulfill a similar role to a gateway in a typical IP-based access network. In order to communicate with the Internet, the STA or mobile client (user) has to connect to any MAP in the backbone. Then, the MAP discovers and selects the best path (composed of a sequence of MPs) to route the messages to a certain MPP.

In a wireless mesh network with multiple MPPs, the selection of the MPP to be used by the traffic flowing from/to a STA can impact on the network performance. In this sense, some policies have already been published for 802.11s based and IP-based access networks. In order to describe the particularities of the existing proposals in a generic way, MPPs and Gateways will be called connection nodes. The connection nodes are provided with different functionalities which depend on the proposals. Basically, a scheme in this context can be characterized by the five following features: (i) how the connection node is discovered, (ii) whether the discovery is supported by an anycast transmission, (iii) the capability to use multiple connection nodes simultaneously, (iv) the selection of the connection node and (v) whether the connection nodes collaborate in the intra-mesh routing (i.e. the routing between two MPs belonging to the same wireless mesh network). Concerning the anycast transmission, the related works restrict this capability to the discovery of the connection nodes. Once they are identified, the data transmission is forwarded to a fixed destination node. This setting prevents the flexibility of having multiple connection nodes from being fully exploited so that the instantaneous radio characteristics could be also taken into account in the data transmissions. In order to overcome this limitation, we propose that the MAC addresses of the MPPs can be interchangeable in both phases (discovery and transmission). Moreover, we have incorporated the capability of benefiting from the wired connection among the MPPs for the intra-mesh traffic. We have conducted extensive simulations in OMNeT++ [6] and the results confirm the performance enhancements of our proposal.

The rest of the paper is organized as follows. Section 2 describes the related work proposed in this area. Section 3 details the proposal. The proposed algorithm is evaluated in Section 4. Finally, Section 5 draws the main conclusions of our work.

2 Related Work

Several research works analyze the use of multiple connection nodes (a MPP in a 802.11s based network or a Gateway in an IP-based access network) in a wireless mesh network. These proposals can be classified according to the following issues:

- Timing of the procedures to discover the connection nodes. This characteristic refers to the instant when the procedures to discover the connection nodes are triggered. In this sense, the proposals can be divided into reactive, proactive or hybrid. Under the reactive or on demand mechanism, a node willing to get access to the Internet emits a message to become aware of the routes to the connection nodes. The message is broadcast to the condition that the source does not keep in their routing tables any information about a path to the connection nodes or when this information is assumed to be stale. Examples of this kind of implementation can be found in [7] [8]. On the other hand, the proactive schemes are accomplished by the periodic emission of announcements generated by the connection nodes. The sources receiving the messages acquire the routing information to transmit their data to the external hosts. Some examples of this kind of schemes are described in [9] [10]. Finally, in the hybrid schemes, the periodic announcements generated by the connection nodes are propagated to an area around them and defined by the maximum number of times (hops) that the messages can be retransmitted. The nodes outside this area employ a reactive approach. Authors in [11] present a hybrid scheme. There also exist some hybrid approaches that employ the proactive or the reactive mechanism depending on the functionality of the nodes. HWMP (Hybrid Hybrid Wireless Mesh Protocol) defines two alternatives to establish the paths: one for intra-mesh traffic and another one for the external (Internet) traffic [5]. For the Internet traffic, spanning trees rooted at the MPP are periodically updated. Towards this goal, the MPP emits Root Announcements (RANN). The work in [12] proposes to selectively retransmit the RANN in order to allow the use of multiple MPP in the network. An enhanced version of HWMP is presented in [13] to support Quality of Service.

- Capability to perform the discovery of the connection nodes by an anycast transmission. Some proposals define an anycast group to which the connection nodes attach. Then, the discovery is supported by messages to the anycast group. In IP-based access networks, this capability is incorporated in [7] [11]. On the other hand, the 'One Laptop Per Child' (OLPC) networking solution proposes MPPs to be discovered by means of a link layer anycast MAC address [14]. This discovery is mainly prompted to simplify the HWMP by avoiding its proactive behavior.

- Capability to associate to multiple connection nodes. When multiple connection nodes are available, some research works suggest that Internet flows use them simultaneously. A multipath routing protocol may support this capability so this kind of schemes is often termed as multi-gateway, multipath or multiple-association. Works in [8] and [12] are examples of proposals holding this capability.

- Selection of the connection node. Once that the reachable connection nodes are discovered, a decision about which one to employ is required. The decision may consider diverse parameters such as the radio link rate, the Gateway load [15] or the number of hops [16]. For instance, a novel metric which combines the gateway load, the route interference and the link quality is presented in [9]. Alternatively, the work in [17] proposes a mathematical formulation to enable the construction of a Spanning Tree rooted at the Gateway. In this way, the paths from any node to the Gateway are composed of nodes which have selected the same Gateway as the best one. The selection of the connection node could also affect the retransmission of the announcements generated by these Internet-connected nodes as portrayed in [12].

- Participation of the connection nodes in the intra-mesh routing. In some schemes, the intra-mesh routing benefit from the routing information acquired by the connection nodes. In [12], the MPPs also collaborate in the discovery of paths among nodes in the same network. With this intention, in order to create a route, a MP sends the frames targeted to another MP towards the MPP, which retransmits them to the intended MP. Once the first frame is received by the final MP, it triggers a mechanism to set a bidirectional path to the source.

3 Link-Layer Based Anycast Routing for 802.11s Networks

Our proposal is intended for wireless networks where routing procedures are executed at the link layer. In this kind of networks, 802.11s based networks outstand. The proposal provides three fundamental features. Firstly, the MPPs are discovered by means of an anycast-like scheme. Moreover, this anycast-like procedure is not restricted to the MPP discovery but it is also employed in the data transmission. An additional contribution of this work relies on the fact that the routing information for both interfaces (wired and wireless) is combined in the MPPs. In this way, the communication between MPs could take advantage of the wired connection among the MPPs. The details about these characteristics are described next.

3.1 Anycast-Like Discovery of the MPPs

In the link layer addressing scheme, an anycast MAC address is not defined. OLPC proposes to set a particular MAC address as an anycast address [14]. The problem of this approach is that all the MPs in the network should be configured to properly work with this address. In order to avoid this configuration in all the MPs, we propose a novel mechanism that emulates the anycast discovery in 802.11s networks. The mechanism is supported by the proactive discovery of the MPPs. In this sense, a MPP becomes aware of all the mesh nodes acting as MPPs through the wired network. One of them is periodically selected to 'represent' the group. The representation involves the emission of periodic messages in the wireless network. This specific message informs about all the available MPPs in the wireless mesh network. Alternatively, the MPs may trigger the procedures to discover the MPP when its corresponding routing information has become stale. In this way, the MP node emits a message in the neighborhood so that a directly-connected node can respond to it with the information associated to the MPPs. This mechanism is usually performed when a new node enters the network.

Upon reception of the MPP announcements, a MP becomes aware of the MAC addresses of the MPPs in the network. The anycast transmission is emulated in this work by setting the MPP MAC addresses as interchangeable. With this goal, the management of the interchangeable addresses is supported by a data structure called Equivalent Address Table (EAT). This structure is created and maintained by the nodes.

In this phase, the routing information is not completed. A routing protocol needs to be executed to determine the communication costs to every MPP. A routing metric to assess the communication cost will be used to decide about the preferable MPP to which the frames must be transmitted. The present approach does not require any specific communication cost to decide about the suitability of an MPP to be used. In our experiments, we have opted for the number of hops as the route metric.

One of the main advantages of the proposal is that it can be gradually incorporated to the mesh network as it can be executed even when there exist some mesh nodes that do not implement it. These MPs will ignore the additional information contained in the MPP announcements and, in turn, will not be able to work with the EAT. An additional pro of the presented approach relies on the fact that the Equivalent Address Table could be also employed for other kind of groups or clusters. Thus, the technique provides a flexible mechanism to emulate the anycast transmission for any group in the network.

3.2 Anycast-Like Data Forwarding

Once the EAT is configured, the anycast support is extended to the frame retransmissions. Although the source sets the preferable MPP in the destination field of the frame, a relaying node in the route to this MPP may decide that an alternative MPP is more appropriate for the transmission. This is the case of a relaying node that has detected that the MPP set in the destination field has become unreachable or when the forwarding node has updated the communication costs, which make the use of another MPP to be more cost-effective. Under these circumstances, the relaying node changes in the frame the destination MPP. The change is supported by the EAT and the routing table. Fig. 1 illustrates an example about how this procedure works. The dashed lines represent wireless links whereas the solid lines symbolize the wired connections. In this case, MP-A generates a frame to the Internet. To make a routing decision, MP-A looks up at its routing table and decides that the best MPP to send the frames is MPP3. According to this routing entry, MP-A retransmits the frame to MP-B. The destination field of the frame is set to MPP3 by the node MP-A. When MP-B receives the frame, it detects that the destination defined in the corresponding field is included in its EAT. Thus, it is an interchangeable address. MP-B evaluates the convenience of continuing sending the frame to MPP3. With this purpose, it analyzes the routing entries of those addresses included in its EAT. The communications costs perceived by MP-B reveal that transmitting the frame to MPP2 is more convenient since the cost (in this case, set in terms of number of hops) to MPP2 is 1 whereas the cost to MPP3 is 3. Under these circumstances, MP-B decides to change the MAC address of the destination field to MPP2. Consequently, MP-B will retransmit the frame according to the routing information related to the MPP2 entry.

The retransmission based on the EAT is able to consider the instantaneous communication costs (path availability, number of hops, losses, delay or any valid metric) associated to the alternative nodes and the current destination. Furthermore, a dynamic selection of the routing path is established for every frame. The MP can use multiple MPPs so the scheme allows a multi-association. Additionally, the use of interchangeable addresses is also employed to forward control frames such as Route Requests.

3.3 Combination of the Routing Information in the MPPs

Mesh Portals (MPPs) are usually connected by means of a high-rate wired infrastructure such as a Gigabit-Ethernet or a FastGigabitEthernet. Thus, MPPs are provided with two interfaces: one for the Ethernet and another one for the wireless mesh network. In our proposal, these two modules are connected so that the routing information in both networks is combined.

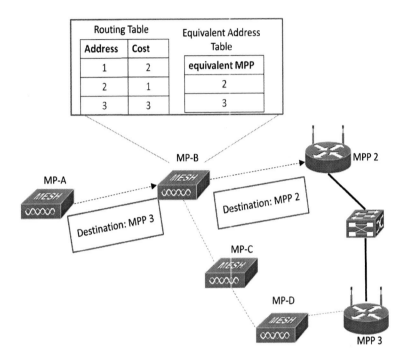

Fig. 1. Illustration of the anycast-like retransmission of a frame. A redirection occurs in MP-B.

By combining both types of information, the MPPs could participate in the routing between two MPs belonging to the same wireless mesh network. Conversely to other previous proposals, the collaboration of the MPPs is not restricted to the route discovery but MPPs may also participate in the retransmission of the frames. Fig. 2 shows how this new functionality works. In this case, MP-A needs to transmit a frame to MP-B. MP-A is not directly connected to MP-B while the links in the wireless mesh network do not offer any route to connect the nodes. The unique (and optimal) route is composed of some MPPs. Since MP-A is connected to a MPP, the selected route uses the wired infrastructure to transmit the frame to the destination. The arrows represent the sequence of retransmissions for the frame.

Due to the interworking of the link layer and the Ethernet modules in the MPPs, the number of hops that the packets traverse in the network will be considerably reduced. Besides, the use of the wired links (instead of the wireless mesh links) also avoids packet collisions and minimizes the congestion in the radio channel, which improves the behavior of the mesh communications.

On the other hand, the combination of the two interfaces in the MPPs also affects the portal discovery. As previously said, the MPPs are represented by one of the nodes in the EAT. This role rotates between the MPPs periodically. When representing the

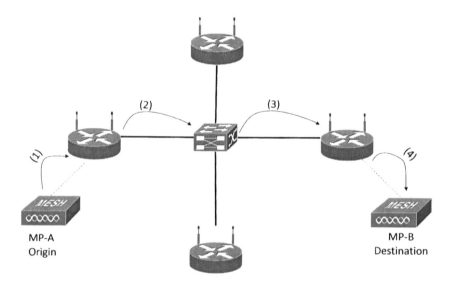

Fig. 2. Illustration of the collaboration of the MPP for the transmission of intra-mesh traffic

group, the MPP emits an announcement containing all the MAC addresses of the group. This announcement is transmitted through the two network interfaces in the MPP. Thus it is received by both the wireless mesh nodes as well as by the others wired MPPs. In this way, all the MPPs regularly announce their presence to the two networks. In a similar way, Route Request messages in the mesh network demanding the route to any MP are also derived by the MPPs and propagated through the wired infrastructure. Thus, multihop communications between two mesh nodes can benefit from the wired links.

4 Evaluation

The performance of our proposal is evaluated by means of simulations carried out in OMNeT++ [6]. The simulated scenario employs an area representing the Teatinos Campus of the University of Málaga. The campus and, consequently, the simulation area are 1245×630 m^2. In order to evaluate our proposal, we have placed one MAP (i.e. nodes giving access to the mesh network) in every place where the access to the Internet is expected to be more demanded, that is, in libraries, exposition halls and cafés. This has led to a network composed of 77 MAPs. In addition, 5 connected MPPs are also incorporated in the mesh architecture in order to enable the Internet connection. Four of these 5 MPPs are placed in the corners of the campus area while another one is located in the center of the simulation area. The 5 MPPs are wired connected by means of a Giga Ethernet network. 40 users (mobile nodes with Wi-Fi interfaces) can access to the network by connecting to a MAP. We have conducted two set of experiments varying the mobility model and the traffic load. Concerning the mobility, the two considered mobility patterns are the model presented in [18] which is an obstacle-based mobility model and the well known Random WayPoint

Mobility Model [19]. In both cases, the speed is chosen by means of a Uniform probability distribution from 1 to 2 m/s and the pause time is set to 0 seconds. Over 3000 seconds, 12 out of the 40 mobile nodes perform as traffic sources. The conducted experiments include some tests where only Internet traffic is present and some other tests that also incorporate intra-mesh traffic (i.e.: traffic between users). In this last case, 50% of the injected uplink traffic is for another MP in the network while the resting 50% of the uplink traffic is routed through the Internet (a MPP is needed). In all the experiments, downlink and uplink traffic loads are equivalent. In this way, the MPPs inject the data transmitted from external Internet hosts. The transmission rate is varied in our experiments to analyze the performance of the proposal. For every transmission rate, 5 simulation runs with different seeds have been executed.

This work aims at evaluating a simplified 802.11s based network. Consequently, the routing protocol supporting the communication is AODV, which is the reactive scheme included in the HWMP [5]. Concerning the propagation model, a Two Ray has been selected. The antennas of the MPs are assumed to be at a height of 1 meter. The transmission range is fixed to 100 meters. Other simulation parameters are summarized in Table 1.

Table 1. Simulation parameters

Simulation parameters	Value
Simulation area	1245x630 m^2
Simulation time	3000 seconds
Number of experiments for a transmission rate	5
Number of MPPs	5
Number of MAPs	77
Number of mobility nodes	40
Number of sources	12
Period of the MPP announcements	100 s
Propagation model	Two Ray
Coverage area	100 m
Ethernet connection between MPPs	10Giga Ethernet

The network performance is quantified with two metrics: the frame delivery ratio and the end-to-end delay (delay in the section of the routes within Internet is not emulated). In the first set of experiments, we aim at evaluating the impact on the performance when using the anycast discovery and transmission, which are two of three fundamental features of our proposal. By exclusively generating Internet traffic, the redirection of the routing information (Route requests) through the MPPs does not affect this analysis. The mobility model used in these tests is the Random WayPoint. The results are represented in Fig. 3 and Fig. 4. The results represent the mean value of the measured metric and the associated 95% confidence interval.

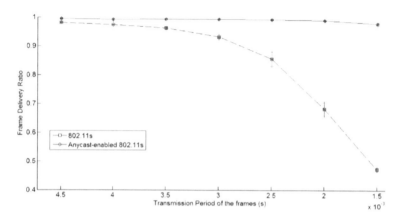

Fig. 3. Frame delivery ratio versus the transmission period for Internet traffic

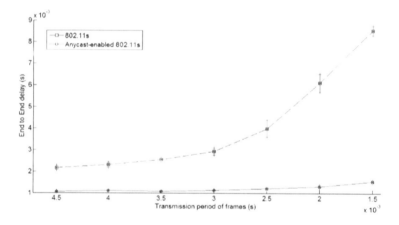

Fig. 4. End-to-End delay versus the transmission period for Internet traffic

As it can be observed, the frame delivery ratio clearly improves when the anycast-based scheme is used. The use of the MPPs as an anycast group can support high transmission rates without perceiving any significant degradation neither in the frame delivery ratio nor in the delay. On the other hand, the benefits of combining the routing information in the MPPs are evaluated by a second set of experiments. In these experiments, we divide the traffic generated by the MPs into intra-mesh traffic and Internet-traffic. The proportion of the traffic load injected by each type is equivalent. Fig. 5 and Fig. 6 show the frame delivery ratio and the delay obtained under these circumstances. The use of this capability reduces the number of hops that the frames traverse. The reduction also implies a clear decrement in the wireless interferences. In turn, the frame delivery ratio increases (up to practically 100%). On the other hand, the route lengths are also decremented. Consequently, the delay diminishes.

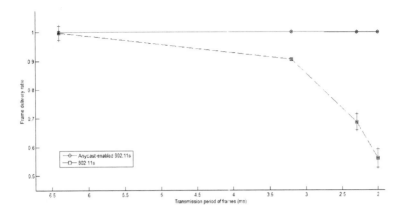

Fig. 5. Frame delivery ratio versus the transmission period for Internet and intra-mesh traffic

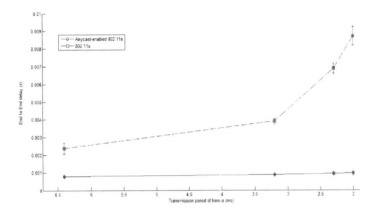

Fig. 6. End-to-End delay versus the transmission period for Internet and intra-mesh traffic

5   Conclusions

This paper has presented a mechanism by which anycast-type transmission is enabled in 802.11s mesh networks. The anycast transmission is employed to communicate with the external hosts through an MPP (Mesh Portal). By means of the anycast implementation, a dynamic selection of the MPP can be performed. Additional, the two radio interfaces in the MPP are combined so that the intra-mesh traffic can be diverted and supported by the wired connections between the MPPs. The proposal allows the use of customized communication costs and it can be also applied in other link-layer based networks. The simulation results show that the frame delivery ratio is clearly improved while the end-to-end delay is reduced.

Acknowledgment

This work has been partially supported by the National Project No. TEC2009-13763-C02-01.

References

1. Aguayo, D., Bicket, J., Biswas, S., Morris, R.: RoofNet, experimental mesh network, http://pdos.csail.mit.edu/roofnet/doku.php
2. Freifunk, International Project for free wireless networks and frequencies, http://start.freifunk.net/
3. 802.11s IEEE Draft Standard for Information Technology-Telecommunications and information exchange between systems-Local and metropolitan area networks-Specific requirements-Part 11: Wireless LAN Medium Access Control (MAC) and Physical Layer (PHY) specifications-Amendment 10: Mesh Networking
4. Hiertz, G.R., Denteneer, D., Max, S., Taori, R., Cardona, J., Berlemann, L., Walke, B.: IEEE 802.11s: The WLAN Mesh Standard. IEEE Wireless Communications 17, 104–111 (2010)
5. Bahr, M.: Proposed Routing for IEEE 802.11s WLAN Mesh Networks. In: 2nd Annual International Wireless Internet Conference (WICON). ACM, Boston (2006)
6. Varga, A.: OMNeT++ User Manual, http://www.omnetpp.org/
7. Pal, A., Nasipuri, A.: GSQAR: A Quality Aware Anycast Routing Protocol for Wireless Mesh Networks. In: IEEE Global Communications Conference (Globecom), pp. 1–5 (2010)
8. Lakshmanan, S., Sivakumar, R., Sundaresan, K.: Multi-gateway association in wireless mesh networks. Ad Hoc Networks 7(3), 622–637 (2009)
9. Ashraf, U., Abdellatif, S., Juanole, G.: Gateway Selection in Backbone Wireless Mesh Networks. In: IEEE Conference on Wireless Communications & Networking Conference (WCNC), Budapest (2009)
10. Isabwe, G.M.N., Kim, K.-S.: A Novel Approach to WLAN Mesh Interworking with Multiple Mesh Portals. In: 5th IEEE International Conference on Mobile Ad Hoc and Sensor Systems (MASS), Atlanta, pp. 641–646 (2008)
11. Sharif, K., Cao, L., Wang, Y., Dahlberg, T.: A Hybrid Anycast Routing Protocol for Load Balancing in Heterogeneous Access Networks. In: 17th International Conference on Computer Communications and Networks (ICCCN), St. Tomas, pp. 1–6 (2008)
12. Hu, Y., He, W., Yang, S., Zhou, Y.: Multi-Gateway Multi-Path Routing Protocol for 802.11s WMN. In: IEEE 6th International Conference on Wireless and Mobile Computing, Networking and Communications (WiMob), Niagara Falls, pp. 308–315 (2010)
13. Ben-Othman, J., Mokdad, L., Cheikh, M.O.: Q-HWMP: improving end-to-end QoS for 802.11s based mesh networks. In: IEEE Global Communications Conference (Globecom), Miami (2010)
14. The One Laptop per Child project, http://laptop.org/en/
15. Ancillotti, E., Bruno, R., Conti, M.: Load-balanced routing and gateway selection in wireless mesh networks: Design, implementation and experimentation. In: IEEE International Symposium on A World of Wireless, Mobile and Multimedia Networks (WoWMoM), Montreal (2010)

16. Song, W., Fang, X.-M.: Design and Simulation of Fairness-aware Routing Algorithm in Wireless Mesh Networks. In: System Simulation, pp. 4320–4325 (2007)
17. Papadaki, K., Friderikos, V.: Joint Routing and Gateway Selection in Wireless Mesh Networks. In: IEEE Conference on Wireless Communications & Networking Conference (WCNC), Las Vegas, p. 2325 (2008)
18. Triviño-Cabrera, A., Morales-Berrocal, R., Casilari, E.: Simulation of realistic mobility patterns for mobile ad hoc networks. In: 7th Conference on 7th WSEAS International Conference on Applied Computer Science, Venice, pp. 227–231 (2007)
19. Yoon, J., Liu, M., Noble, B.: Random WayPoint considered harmful. In: 22nd Annual Joint Conference of the IEEE Computer and Communications Societies (INFOCOM), San Francisco, pp. 1312–1321 (2003)

Using Buffer Space Advertisements to Avoid Congestion in Mobile Opportunistic DTNs

Jani Lakkakorpi, Mikko Pitkänen, and Jörg Ott

Aalto University, Department of Communications and Networking
P.O. Box 13000, FI-00076 AALTO, Finland
{jani.lakkakorpi,mikko.pitkanen,jorg.ott}@aalto.fi

Abstract. This paper investigates congestion control in opportunistic networks that use delay-tolerant networking (DTN) as a basis for communication. We propose a mechanism that advertises buffer occupancy information to adjacent nodes and avoids forwarding through nodes with high buffer occupancy. The nodes then achieve global congestion avoidance simply based on locally available information. The proposed mechanism works independent of the routing protocol and is thus applicable to wide array of scenarios. Extensive simulations, with different node mobility models and radio modeling, indicate that the proposed mechanism improves message delivery ratio and decreases end-to-end delay.

Keywords: DTN, congestion control, ns-2, opportunistic network.

1 Introduction

Opportunistic wireless networks dynamically created between mobile nodes are able to function without supporting infrastructure (such as base stations and the core network). While traditional Mobile Ad-hoc Networks (MANETs) use packet-based routing to establish end-to-end paths between communicating nodes, opportunistic networks allow for store-(carry-)and-forward operation based upon hop-by-hop message exchanges. Relaxing the need for an end-to-end path following the ideas of Delay-tolerant Networking (DTN) allows nodes to communicate in challenged networking environments, characterized, e.g., by sparse node population, high mobility, high delays, or unstable (short-lived) links. However, this advantage comes at a cost: Lacking an end-to-end path makes it difficult for the originator of a message to get feedback on the transmission progress of a message and thus to protect against congestion in the nodes that the messages traverse on their way towards the destination. In this paper we explore a simple local scheme for congestion control for mobile opportunistic networks. While congestion control in connected packet networks usually provides feedback to the sender to (instantaneously) throttle communication, we cannot rely on such feedback and hence seek to a) distribute and b) limit resource consumption within the network.

DTN routing protocols often attempt to protect communication against unreliable network conditions by creating multiple copies of message to deliver at least a single instance to its destination [1,2]. Multiple copies can lead to congestion in networks that are typically characterized by scarce resources. To avoid harmful effects of congestion, such as message drops and retransmissions, message copies can be removed once a copy

X. Masip-Bruin et al. (Eds.): WWIC 2011, LNCS 6649, pp. 386–397, 2011.

has reached its destination [3]. Without feedback mechanisms it is difficult to adjust the number of messages copies while the message is still in its way towards the destination.

This paper introduces a simple mechanism to avoid congestion in opportunistic networks that operates proactively before congestion-induced message drops occur. The proposed mechanism locally advertises a node's buffer occupancy to adjacent nodes based upon which the latter can take local decisions and avoid sending messages to nodes whose buffers are nearly full. The proposed congestion control mechanism enables to maximize resource utilization when resources are available. When resources are scarce, however, the mechanism prevents congestion from occurring by postponing message transfers until sufficient resources are available. As our congestion control mechanism performs load reallocation inside the network, there is no need to return explicit feedback to the message source. Implicitly, any source will learn the degree of congestion inside a (region of a) network based upon the buffer state notifications it receives from its neighbors.

To evaluate the congestion control mechanisms we conduct extensive simulations. The model is novel in compared to different previous DTN routing algorithms since it models also the effect of congestion in physical radio layer, which is often omitted in DTN simulations. The simulations model the proposed usage scenarios closely and provide results with both synthetic and real life mobility traces.

This paper is organized as follows. Section 2 begins with an overview of congestion control (starting with IP networks), explains the IRTF DTN architecture and protocol, and covers related work. Section 3 introduces the proposed congestion control mechanism for mobile DTNs. Section 4 describes the models and parameters used in our simulations. Section 5 presents variety of simulation results. Finally, Section 6 concludes the paper with a summary and a brief discussion.

2 Background and Related Work

The foundations of congestion control in the Internet date back to 1988 when suitable mechanisms were devised for TCP [4]. In TCP, sender controls rate based on acknowledgments from the receiver that can be used to deduce that some packets are lost or delayed too much, and rate can be accordingly decreased at sender. To avoid synchronized buffer overflows in the network, Floyd and Jacobson [5] introduced random early detection (RED) in 1993. RED is applied to router queues and drops IP packets in a randomized fashion already before the buffers are full, thereby implicitly providing early feedback to senders. RED can lead to lower packet delays and increased TCP goodput; yet, despite being well-known and widely implemented in routers, it is not broadly deployed in the Internet. In another approach, called explicit congestion notification (ECN) [6], routers mark packets when congestion is imminent and thereby signal to the endpoints that they reduce their sending rate.

2.1 DTNs and Congestion Control

The DTN [7] architecture introduces a *bundle* protocol [8], which offers transport services for applications. The bundles are often significantly larger than IP packets in order to allow creation of self-contained messages that enable complete application interactions with a single message exchange. The architecture is designed for networks where an end-to-end path may not exist, thus the bundles are transmitted based only on hop-by-hop reliability. Any suitable convergence layer (such as TCP, UDP or LTP [9]) can be used for transferring a bundle over a single hop. Bundle spreading is limited by its lifetime, also known as time-to-live (TTL), after which the bundle expires and is removed from the network. Bundle retransmission can take place either at the originating node or at an intermediate node.

Numerous routing protocols have been proposed for DTNs. Most of them create multiple copies of the bundle in order to increase the probability of reaching the destination. *Epidemic* routing [1] creates unlimited number of messages by copying the message to all nodes that do not yet have a copy. The large number of message copies created by epidemic routing has been shown to cause congestion, which decreases message delivery probability. *Spray and wait routing* [2] explicitly limits the number of bundle copies to a fixed value. *MaxProp* uses explicit acknowledgments to remove delivered messages from intermediaries [10] .

Independent of the DTN routing protocol, the destination node may generate a return receipt to the source node when the bundle is received. The return receipts can also act as antipackets like in VACCINE antipacket mechanism [3], which deletes the bundles and gives immunity to nodes upon seeing a return receipt. Whatever the bundle routing scheme, antipackets are always sent using epidemic routing [11]. Antipackets will eventually expire, just like the bundles. Seligman *et al.* [12,13] propose a solution to congestion for DTN custody transfer, in which a node is not allowed to drop a message to make room if it has accepted custody for this message. They suggest resolving congestion in individual nodes by moving bundles temporarily to other non-congested nodes and taking them back again later (somewhat similar to swapping in operating systems). However, their approach relies on nodes being able to reach non-congested nodes predictably (for both "swapping" messages out and back in) and cannot be applied to an opportunistic network with unpredictable contact patterns.

Burleigh *et al.* [14] implement DTN congestion control by propagating buffer utilization stress back to the bundle sources. This is accomplished by declining to take custody of bundles, forcing the source to retain the bundles and thereby increasing source node's demand for buffer space, forcing it in turn to refuse custody of bundles. A financial model of buffer space management is suggested. Zhang *et al.* [15] propose a rather similar approach.

2.2 Congestion Avoidance in Opportunistic Networks

Krifa *et al.* [16] present different bundle buffer management policies for DTNs showing that traditional buffer management policies, such as drop tail, are sub-optimal. An optimal buffer management policy, based on global knowledge about the network, is proposed using the theory of encounter-based message dissemination. The proposed policy can be tuned either to minimize the average delay or to maximize the average delivery ratio. Moreover, they propose a distributed algorithm that uses statistical learning to approximate the global knowledge.

Radenkovic and Grundy [17] propose a congestion approach for social opportunistic networks. They suggest a combination of routing and congestion avoidance that uses heuristics to infer shorter paths to destinations from social information and use buffer information to avoid areas of the network that are congested. Pujol *et al.* [18] introduce a routing algorithm for delay tolerant networks, where messages are preferably forwarded to users that have a stronger social relation with the target of the message. The aim of the approach is to balance the message load in the network.

Ryu *et al.* [19] present a back-pressure routing and rate control algorithm for intermittently connected networks. In back-pressure routing, per-destination queues are maintained at each node. A message for destination d can be forwarded to a neighbor node only if the backlog for destination d is smaller at the neighbor node. In the modified back-pressure routing algorithm, the queue lengths are advertised to other nodes and advertised gateway node queue lengths are scaled down first. They consider applying the approach so that periodic and predictable mobile movement patterns are exploited in order to obtain throughput-optimal performance. However, this is not applicable in many opportunistic scenarios where replication-based algorithms are used to secure against unpredictable events in the network.

Thompson *et al.* [20] propose a congestion control algorithm for intermittently connected networks (later used for performance comparison in Section 5). In their scheme, message replication is dynamically limited based on local information. In order to determine congestion level in the network, the nodes exchange information about message drops and message replications upon encountering other nodes. This information is then used in calculating the replication limit. Similarly to our approach, they use local information in order to prevent congestion. However, their approach seems more prone to message drops, since the individual reception capacity of the next hop node is not known.

3   Using Buffer Space Advertisements to Avoid Congestion

With long message lifetime in DTNs, an effective congestion control mechanism should not be based on network conditions at the message creation time, but it should instead make congestion control decisions adaptively during the message lifetime in the traversed nodes. Thus, we propose a congestion control mechanism, where a message can be transferred only to such intermediate nodes who advertise sufficient available buffer capacity at the time of message forwarding. The proposed mechanism spreads buffer occupancy information in *Hello* packets that nodes periodically broadcast to each other (nodes use the same packets to discover each other). Nodes forwarding messages use the advertise buffer availability to infer how much data the the next hop node accepts for forwarding.

Our congestion control mechanism works with heterogeneous buffer and message sizes. The mechanism can be used with any DTN routing scheme and does not rely on specific routing information, support for custody transfer [14,15], or antipackets [3].

Figure 1 illustrates the variables in our model. The advertised buffer size B_a is simply calculated from total buffer size B_s by multiplying it by a congestion threshold T_C (safety margin) and subtracting the current buffer occupancy B_o as follows:

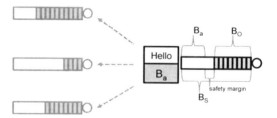

Fig. 1. Adaptive node model for congestion avoidance

$$B_a = T_C \times B_s - B_o. \tag{1}$$

The key benefit of using the above formula to advertise the available buffer space is that each node can locally define safety margin for amount of data they want to receive. When congestion is likely to occur, e.g., the node has larger probability to experience message drop, the safety margin can be increased to accommodate larger number of unexpected message arrivals. In sparse network conditions, and when message drops have not occurred recently, the node can advertise available capacity with small safety margin. Without safety margin any concurrent transmissions from adjacent nodes could lead to message drops.

Algorithm 1. Adapt buffer space advertisement B_a

---

if $D = 0$ AND $T_C < T_{Cmax}$ then
    set $T_C \Leftarrow T_C + ai$
else
    if $D > 0$ AND $T_C > T_{Cmin}$ then
        set $T_C \Leftarrow T_C \times md$
    end if
    set $D \Leftarrow 0$
end if
set $B_a \Leftarrow T_C \times B_s - B_o$

To adapt the advertised value to varying network conditions, we propose to adjust the advertised buffer capacity based on message drops D according to Algorithm 1. It uses the additive increase and multiplicative decrease (AIMD) approach to adapt the congestion threshold T_C based on message drops. If there are message drops between two consecutive Hello messages (interval of 100 ms), the congestion threshold is reduced. Otherwise, the congestion threshold is increased. This leads to an adaptive approach that backs off exponentially when congestion occurs, and conservatively increases when more capacity appears available. We apply the following default parameters that we determined experimentally: $ai = 0.01$ and $md = 0.8$. Variable T_C is initialized with a value of 0.8. The minimum and maximum values for T_C are 0.5 and 0.9, correspondingly. After having calculated B_a, node appends the value to Hello messages that it sends to its immediate neighbors as shown in Figure 1.

Algorithm 2. Forward message to intermediate node

---

select message from message storage
if routing protocol allows **then**
   get $B_a(i)$
   if $B_a(i) > M_s$ **then**
     forward message
     set $B_a(i) \Leftarrow B_a(i) - M_S$
   end if
end if

Upon sending messages to another intermediate node for forwarding, each node executes Algorithm 2. If the advertised buffer space B_a at the neighbor node (or message creator node) is less than message size (M_s), the message cannot be forwarded to this particular neighbor (or created). This approach maintains two properties that are typical to DTN routing protocols. First, if a node receives a message that is destined for it, full buffers do not matter. Second, the message is not sent to a node that already holds a copy of it.

The congestion control mechanism is executed immediately after node encounter occurs, i.e., prior to forwarding to next hop node. Thus, the approach is interoperable with any mechanism used by the known DTN routing protocol making it applicable to wide variety networks. For example, with spray and wait, when the node runs out of message tokens, the approach allows forwarding the message only to final destination.

Our congestion control algorithm requires only minimal state because it uses only information about the neighbors per current contact. The approach is somewhat similar to back-pressure mechanisms, since information about full buffers is propagated, albeit not explicitly beyond a single hop into the direction of the message originator. The mechanism operates clearly using only a local scope, with the information it requires and the interactions it performs restricted to nodes in its local proximity. However, in Section 5 we show that it is effective across the network.

4   Simulation Model

Our simulations use several extensions to the *ns2* simulator that allow us to study DTN routing together with accurate models for radio links. Our simulations build on top of synthetically generated random waypoint (RWP) model, more realistic yet synthetic pedestrian mobility model, and real-world vehicular traces.

4.1   Traffic and Mobility Models

We apply a relatively simple traffic model in which each node sends a (fixed or variable size) message at a random time with 200 second intervals $[t, t + 200s]$ to another, randomly selected, node. Before sending to MAC layer, the bundles are fragmented into 1500-byte datagrams. A retransmission mechanism, providing reliable delivery of datagrams is implemented, so that messages will not be lost due to transmission errors.

392 J. Lakkakorpi, M. Pitkänen, and J. Ott

Random waypoint is our first mobility model since this model is well understood and it is easy to generate scenarios with different network densities and node velocities. We generate random waypoint node mobility using the setdest program, which is part of the ns-allinone package [21]. We have 40 mobile nodes that select a random direction and a random (uniformly distributed) speed at random times. Maximum speed is 20 m/s and pause length is two seconds. We always pause before choosing a new direction and a new speed. In our RWP scenarios, area size ranges from 10 m times 10 m to 2000 m times 2000 m, and the simulation time is always 5000 seconds.

In both of our trace-based mobility models the number of mobile nodes is 116 and the simulation time is 3600 seconds. In the first mobility trace, the San Francisco taxi cab trace [22], the area size is 5700 m times 6600 m. The whole data set contains GPS coordinates of approximately 500 taxis collected over 30 days in the San Francisco Bay area. We choose to use this trace due to its high resolution, node positions are recorded frequently enough to provide location information for the used radio models.

The second mobility trace was obtained in a synthetic fashion: the map of Helsinki city center (area dimensions: 4500 m times 3400 m) is used as input for the ONE simulator [23] and the nodes are configured to move between selected points of interest. Node velocity is uniformly distributed between 0.7 m/s and 1.4 m/s and pause length between 0 and 120 s. This model provides a more dense network scenario in comparison to the aforementioned taxi cab scenario, which is relatively sparse.

4.2 DTN Model

In the simulator, DTN nodes advertise their buffer content to each other every 100 ms by sending Hello messages. In our simulations, this message has enough room for the identifiers of buffered bundles and return receipts. A bundle can be generated only if the node has sufficient buffer space available. When the bundle lifetime expires, all copies of that bundle are deleted. If the sender does not receive a return receipt within retransmission timeout, it will retransmit the bundle. Return receipts may also serve as antipackets; their lifetime is the minimum of retransmission timeout (1000 seconds) less bundle forwarding time and bundle lifetime (750 seconds). Antipackets and Hello messages are small in size. The selected routing protocol is either epidemic routing or binary spray and wait, the latter if uses 16 message copies.

Return receipts are forwarded first. When the head-of-line receipt has been forwarded to all current neighbors, one by one, we put that receipt to the tail of the receipt queue and dequeue the next receipt. Then, we forward regular bundles to their destinations, in a similar manner as return receipts. After this, the bundles are re-ordered so that the least forwarded bundles are put to the head of the queue. Finally, regular bundles are forwarded to neighboring, non-destination nodes.

4.3 Wireless Channel Model

We use a realistic wireless channel model from the dei80211mr library [24], which is now a part of the *ns-allinone* package. There is support for different transmission rates, modulation methods and coding schemes that are defined in the IEEE802.11b/g standards.

A signal-to-interference-and-noise ratio (SINR)[1] based packet level error model is introduced that is calculated using pre-determined curves of packet error rate (PER) vs. SINR and packet size. The reception threshold (RXThresh_) variable, which has been used in the default *ns2* 802.11 implementation, has been removed. SINR, in turn, is calculated using received signal strength, noise, and interference. Interference is calculated using a Gaussian model to account for all transmissions that happen simultaneously to the one which is considered for reception. Noise strength is fixed in all simulations. The IEEE 802.11g simulation parameters are the same as in [25].

The capture model, that is, the determination of whether a packet can be received when there are other concurrent transmissions, is embedded in the interference model.

5   Simulation Results

5.1   Random Waypoint Mobility

Figure 2 compares routing performance in the random waypoint scenario, showing plain epidemic, spray and wait, and epidemic routing enhanced with congestion control (CC). For each protocol, performance figures are also provided with the antipacket (AP) mechanism. Node buffer sizes are randomly chosen to be 250 KB or 2 MB so that both occur with equal probability. The size of the individual bundles is uniformly distributed between 1 Byte and 20 KB, and the (static) congestion threshold (T_C) is 0.8.

An initial (expected) observation is that reducing congestion by means of antipackets improves message delivery probability with all routing protocols. A significant improvement is also gained by applying congestion control or explicitly limiting the number of copies per message. Combining both we find that antipackets dominate the performance gain, irrespective of congestion control. But for sparse scenarios (1000 m and above), congestion controlled epidemic routing does as well as antipackets.

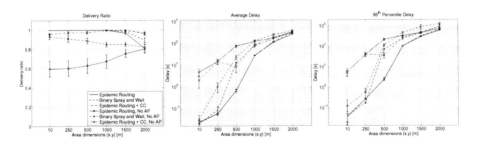

Fig. 2. Heterogeneous nodes, RWP mobility

The message delivery delay plot shows that the antipacket mechanism is very efficient in reducing the message delivery delay. This is expected behavior since removing

---

[1] Noise is set according to $Pn = kTB$, where k = 1.38e-23 J/K, T = 290 K, and B =2.437 GHz. With the selected parameters, the node transmission range will be 66-130 m, depending on the modulation and coding scheme (MCS). The better the MCS, the higher the transmission rate (and smaller the transmission range).

copies of delivered messages from buffers prevents them from blocking the undelivered ones. Explicitly limiting number of message copies (spray and wait) yields the smallest delivery delays, since the other approaches do not minimize queuing in intermediaries, but rather only avoid increasing it too much. With antipackets, congestion control adds a marginal improvement and only for sparse scenarios. Without antipackets there is notable gain but the main advantage is clearly on the delivery ratio—which is expected because our congestion control algorithm delays forwarding.

Further simulations (graphs omitted) with homogeneous buffer size (400 KB) and uniform bundle size (10 KB) show largely similar results.

5.2   Trace-Based Mobility

Figure 3 illustrates the performance evaluation with more realistic conditions. The top row shows performance with vehicular mobility derived from the San Francisco cab trace and the bottom row with pedestrian mobility created using the Helsinki City Scenario. In both cases, the message size is uniformly distributed and varies between 10 KB and 100 KB with 10 KB granularity. In the San Francisco case, the node buffer size is either 1.375 MB or 11 MB (both occur with 50% probability) whereas in the Helsinki case the node buffer size is always 6 MB.

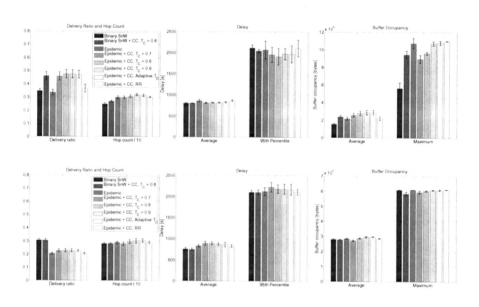

Fig. 3. Real (top) and synthetic mobility trace (bottom)

The results of the two simulation scenarios are quite similar. With both mobility models, using congestion control leads to better delivery ratios. However, in the (more dense) Helsinki city scenario, this gain is marginal and it seems that bandwidth is a bottleneck, too, so that spray and wait outperforms epidemic routing. Larger hop counts indicate that using congestion control allows (partly forces) messages to travel further through the network. This is a positive observation, since using congestion control prevents the message replication (also towards destination) in the intermediary nodes under heavy traffic.

The delay plot indicates largely similar behavior across all routing approaches. With congestion control, on the one hand, queues are kept a shorter by means of the threshold value, as also indicated by the maximum queue sizes. On the other hand, messages may take longer routes (leading to larger delay) because well-connected ("central") nodes, which would enable shorter paths, may have already full buffers and thus cannot be chosen as next hops. A reduction of the (maximum) delivery delay is achievable in some scenarios (as visible for the taxi trace), but not in others. In the RWP scenario above and in the HCS scenario, node mobility and frequent but shorter contacts lead to higher buffer fill ratio and thus more queuing. Overall, the performance gain for delay is scenario-dependent and improved delivery rate may or may not come with reduced delay.

The right side of figure 3 shows the buffer occupancy of the nodes. To some extent, this reflects the operation of the congestion control algorithm. For the sparser taxi scenario, the maximum and mean buffer levels are correlated with the respectively chosen threshold (see below) whereas, for the denser HCS scenario, the fill levels are roughly equal and above the threshold. We attribute this to the dense nature: frequent contacts and parallel transfers lead to the congestion control algorithm making active use of its safety margin. Overall, this shows that, despite explicitly limiting message replication, our congestion control is able to make use of forwarding capacity in the network.

Figure 3 also illustrates a performance comparison of different congestion control schemes. Congestion threshold (T_C) is either static (0.7, 0.8, 0.9) or adaptive. We can see that a congestion threshold of 0.9 leads to best message delivery ratio. However, we believe that static congestion threshold may not be suitable for all traffic and mobility scenarios and, therefore, we prefer an adaptive congestion threshold. The first adaptive case is our own algorithm (adaptive increase, multiplicative decrease of T_C) while the second one (RR) is from Thompson et al. [20]. As described earlier, our minimum and maximum values for T_C are 0.5 and 0.9.

The results show that our adaptive algorithm (congestion threshold fluctuates between 0.5 and 0.9) gives as good results as the best static case. However, the algorithm from Thompson et al. does not seem to work as expected. We think that this may be the result of different mobility and wireless models as in [20]. We implemented the latter algorithm exactly as described in [20] with the exception that congestion value CV was updated periodically (every ten seconds) and not every time a given node meets another node. The latter alternative (according to [20]) lead to very low delivery ratios; the time between two contacts could be either very short or very long and thus there could be no or tens of received/dropped messages between two contacts.

Summarizing we find that the proposed congestion control variants improve delivery performance with both mobility scenarios while not negatively impacting any of the central performance metrics. This suggests that even a very simple congestion control approach with only minimal knowledge can be effective in opportunistic networks.

6   Conclusion

We have presented a simple congestion control mechanism for mobile opportunistic
networks that operates using only instantly available local information from itself and
its current contacts. Moreover, the algorithm is independent of the chosen routing protocol. Our simulation results using the random waypoint model as well as real-life and
synthetic mobility traces show that our simple congestion control enhancement (implemented for epidemic routing and spray and wait) performs well across our diverse
scenarios: applying this congestion control scheme generally leads to higher message
ratios and may additionally yield lower delivery delays. We did not come across cases
in which our algorithm harms performance. Exploring additional mobility scenarios
and studying the interaction with other routing protocols (especially such using utility
functions) are subject to our ongoing work.

In contrast to well-connected networks, our algorithm focuses on distributing the
load inside the network and provides only indirect backpressure to the sender: a sender
refuses to create new messages if there is not enough buffer space locally available;
this allows the congestion control algorithm to pace message generation. This decision
is taken as a function of its own buffer occupancy (and thus implicitly) the past immediate surroundings rather than of the path towards the destination; this assumes that
transitive propagation of congestion information about a region occurs. Moreover, the
feedback may—naturally—arrive with quite some delay and relies on sufficient interactions between the nodes. One interesting avenue of future research is understanding how
congestion signals spread in time and space, how congestion regions can be identified,
and how such knowledge can be exploited for refining congestion control mechanisms.

Finally, the indirect way feedback is provided causes all applications on a node (in
fact all nodes in a region) being treated equally: if some of them generate a dispro-
portionally high load all others might suffer, too, so that additional mechanisms for
segregating traffic inside the buffers (e.g., as discussed in [26]) may need to be applied.

Acknowledgments

This work was partly funded by the Academy of Finland in the RESMAN project (grant
no. 134363).

References

1. Vahdat, A., Becker, D.: Epidemic routing for partially connected ad hoc networks. Tech. rep.,
   Duke University (April 2000)
2. Spyropoulos, T., Psounis, K., Raghavendra, C.S.: Spray and wait: an efficient routing scheme
   for intermittently connected mobile networks. In: ACM SIGCOMM Workshop on Delay-
   Tolerant Networking, Philadelphia, PA, USA, August 2005, pp. 252–259 (2005)
3. Haas, Z.J., Small, T.: A new networking model for biological applications of ad hoc sensor
   networks. IEEE/ACM Trans. Netw. 14(1), 27–40 (2006)
4. Jacobson, V.: Congestion avoidance and control. In: ACM SIGCOMM, Stanford, CA, USA,
   August 1988, pp. 314–329 (1988)

5. Floyd, S., Jacobson, V.: Random early detection gateways for congestion avoidance. IEEE/ACM Trans. Netw. 1(4), 397–413 (1993)
6. Ramakrishnan, K., Floyd, S., Black, D.: The Addition of Explicit Congestion Notification (ECN) to IP. RFC Standards Track 3168, IETF (September 2001)
7. Delay Tolerant Networking Research Group, http://www.dtnrg.org
8. Scott, K., Burleigh, S.: Bundle Protocol Specification. RFC Experimental 5050, IETF (November 2007)
9. Ramadas, M., Burleigh, S., Farrell, S.: Licklider Transmission Protocol - Specification. RFC Experimental 5326, IETF (September 2008)
10. Burgess, J., Gallagher, B., Jensen, D., Levine, B.N.: Maxprop: Routing for vehicle-based disruption-tolerant networks. In: IEEE INFOCOM, Barcelona, Spain, pp.1–11 (April 2006)
11. Walker, B., Glenn, J., Clancy, T.: Analysis of simple counting protocols for delay-tolerant networks. In: CHANTS 2007, Montréal, Québec, Canada, September 2007, pp. 19–26 (2007)
12. Seligman, M., Fall, K., Mundur, P.: Alternative custodians for congestion control in delay tolerant networks. In: CHANTS 2006, Pisa, Italy, September 2006, pp. 229–236 (2006)
13. Seligman, M., Fall, K., Mundur, P.: Storage routing for DTN congestion control. Wirel. Commun. Mob. Comput. 7(10), 1183–1196 (2007)
14. Burleigh, S., Jennings, E., Schoolcraft, J.: Autonomous congestion control in delay-tolerant networks. In: SpaceOps (2006)
15. Zhang, G., Wang, J., Liu, Y.: Congestion management in delay tolerant networks. In: WICON 2008, Maui, Hawaii, USA, pp. 1–9 (November 2008)
16. Krifa, A., Barakat, C., Spyropoulos, T.: Optimal buffer management policies for delay tolerant networks. In: SECON, San Francisco, CA, USA, July 2008, pp. 260–268 (2008)
17. Randkovic, M., Grundy, A.: Congestion aware forwarding in delay tolerant and social opportunistic networks. In: WONSk, Bardonecchia, Italy, January 2011, pp. 60–67 (2011)
18. Pujol, J., Toledo, A., Rodriguez, P.: Fair routing in delay tolerant networks. In: IEEE INFOCOM, Rio de Janeiro, Brazil, pp. 837–845 (April 2009)
19. Ryu, J., Bhargava, V., Paine, N., Shakkottai, S.: Back-pressure routing and rate control for icns. In: ACM MobiCom, Chicago, Illinois, USA, September 2010, pp. 365–376 (2010)
20. Thompson, N., Nelson, S., Bakht, M., Abdelzaher, T., Kravets, R.: Retiring replicants: congestion control for intermittently-connected networks. In: IEEE INFOCOM, San Diego, California, USA, March 2010, pp. 1118–1126 (2010)
21. UCB/LBNL/VINT, Network Simulator - ns (version 2), http://www.isi.edu/nsnam/ns
22. Cabspotting, http://cabspotting.org
23. Keränen, A., Ott, J., Kärkkäinen, T.: The ONE Simulator for DTN Protocol Evaluation. In: SIMUTools 2009, Rome, Italy (March 2009)
24. U. of Padova, dei80211mr: a new 802.11 implementation for NS-2, http://www.dei.unipd.it/wdyn/?IDsezione=5090
25. Lakkakorpi, J., Pitkänen, M., Ott, J.: Adaptive routing in mobile opportunistic networks. In: ACM MSWIM 2010, Bodrum, Turkey, October 2010, pp. 101–109 (2010)
26. Solis, J., Asokan, N., Kostiainen, K., Ginzboorg, P., Ott, J.: Controlling resource hogs in mobile delay-tolerant networks. Comput. Commun. 33(1), 2–10 (2010)

Urban-X: A Self-organizing Cognitive Wireless Mesh Network for Dense City Environments

Wooseong Kim[1], Andreas J. Kassler[2], Marco Di Felice[3],
Mario Gerla[1], and Luciano Bononi[3]

[1] Department of Computer Science, University of California, Los Angeles, USA
[2] Department of Computer Science, Karlstad University, Karlstad, Sweden
[3] Department of Computer Science, University of Bologna, Bologna, Italy

Abstract. The practical deployment of Wireless Mesh Networks (WMNs) using unlicensed ISM band within dense urban scenarios is difficult due to the increasing number of wireless devices operating in those licensed exempt frequencies. For this reason, current research on WMN is directed towards novel and more flexible network paradigms which would allow the WMN to dynamically adapt to the environmental interference conditions. Here, we propose Urban-X, which is a novel cross-layer architecture for self-organizing WMNs over urban scenarios. Urban-X combines elements from classical Multi-Radio Multi-Channel (MC-MR) technology with novel Dynamic Spectrum Access (DSA) mechanisms. The self-organizing behavior is achieved through a novel distributed channel assignment scheme, an adaptive multi-path routing scheme and a flexible layer 2.5 channel and path scheduler algorithm. Based on the current interference on each channel, Urban-X performs channel allocation among the nodes of the WMN, updates the available paths towards the gateways and distributes the internal traffic among the paths/channels in order to maximize the network throughput while minimizing interference to the external networks. Simulation results demonstrate the effectiveness of our cross-layer approach in terms of increased throughput compared to traditional routing schemes for WMNs, and its adaptiveness to the variation in channel conditions and external user traffic.

Keywords: Wireless Mesh Networks, Multi-Radio, Multi-Channel, Cross-Layer Design, Performance Evaluation.

1 Introduction

Wireless Mesh Networks (WMNs) have emerged as a key technology for next generation wireless networks, mainly due to the possibility to provide broadband Internet access over urban scenarios at higher performance and lower cost than other wireless access technologies, e.g the 3G Mobile Internet [1]. Nowadays, several deployments of WMNs demonstrate the possibility to build multihop wireless networks which can cover highly dense urban areas (e.g Vienna, Frankfurt, etc) and serve thousands of users (e.g. the Chaska project [4]). However, the performance of WMNs is still not comparable with the wired Internet, due to interference problems in highly dense urban environments.

X. Masip-Bruin et al. (Eds.): WWIC 2011, LNCS 6649, pp. 398–409, 2011.
© IFIP International Federation for Information Processing 2011

Multi-Radio Multi-Channel (MC-MR) technology constitutes a well-investigated approach to alleviate the interference problem in WMNs, by multiplying the spectrum resources available to each mesh Access Point (AP) [3,15]. However, most of the previous works address the problem of *self-interference* (i.e. interference between the nodes of the WMN) by assigning adjacent APs to orthogonal channels. We highlight here that the interference problem becomes much more serious when the WMN nodes must share the spectrum with external devices, such as residential Wi-Fi networks, which belong to different organizations [11]. In this paper, we call such devices *Primary Nodes* (PNs) to distinguish from the nodes of the WMN. In such a case, Channel Assignment (CA) schemes should consider the dynamic changes of the PN interference. Moreover, a more flexible network design is required to dynamically reconfigure the CA and traffic forwarding process based on the actual environmental conditions [19].

In this paper, we combine elements from classical MC-MR technology with Dynamic Spectrum Access (DSA) [2] mechanisms to deploy self-organizing WMNs in high dense city environments. To this aim, we propose a novel cross-layer architecture, called *Urban-X*, which allows a WMN to co-exist with other PNs, and to dynamically adapt its configuration in order to (*i*) maximize its performance while (*ii*) minimizing the impact to the PNs. In Urban-X, self-organization is achieved through the mutual integration of four main components:

- *Spectrum Sensing:* In contrast to classical cognitive radio networks [2], Urban-X is deployed in ISM band. Thus, a WMN node does not need to vacate its channel even if PN traffic is detected. However, we use sensing techniques to implement novel collaborative load estimation mechanisms, through which the WMN nodes can estimate the PN workload on each channel.
- *Channel Assignment:* While existing CA algorithms mainly consider intra-mesh interference [12], Urban-X CA (UCA) uses input from the collaborative spectrum sensing to balance the impact of interference caused by PNs with intra- and inter-flow interference to achieve robustness and high performance.
- *Multipath Routing:* Urban-X leverages the availability of multiple paths towards the gateways by maintaining a forwarding mesh centered around the best metric path. The routing protocol extends AODV by maintaining a set of candidate forwarders at each node for each source/destination pair. In contrast to previous works [6][9], our approach can dynamically change individual path segments on a per-packet basis to effectively cope with interference caused by variation in PN traffic and intra-mesh congestion.
- *Forwarding and Scheduling:* Urban-X develops novel packet scheduling algorithms for selecting a route and a channel in the multipath WMN. Although a practical approach based on back-pressure scheduling [5][10][18] has been developed in a single radio WMN [14], Urban-X is the first work that extends it to MC-MR WMNs by also taking into account the channel switching cost.

Using a detailed evaluation of Urban-X in the ns-2 simulator, which has been extended in [7] to model MC-MR operation and PN traffic, we demonstrate that Urban-X is able to dynamically adapt the WMN configuration to the variation of channel conditions and external user traffics, thus achieving higher performance than classical CA and single-path routing schemes for MR-MC WMNs.

The paper is organized as follows. In Section 2, we review existing CA and routing schemes for MR-MC WMNs. Section 3 describes our Urban-X architecture, along with our channel assignment, routing and scheduling algorithms. Evaluation results are shown in Section 4. The paper concludes in Section 5.

2   Related Works

Most of the current research on WMNs focuses on techniques to enhance the network capacity through channel diversity in the 2.4-5 GHz bands and multi-radio technology [12][17]. Generally speaking, Channel Assignment (CA) for multiple radio interfaces on a conflict graph is a NP-hard problem, and several CA schemes have been proposed in the literature, usually based on static, semi-dynamic or hybrid approaches. In static CA approaches, the binding between channel and radio interface is decided during the network setup [10]. In semi-dynamic CA approaches, the nodes change a static assignment over time (e.g. on a minute or hour timescale) to cope with changes in environment [3][15]. However, both the static and the semi-dynamic approaches are not feasible for urban environments where traffic demands and interference conditions can change rapidly like in Urban-X. To avoid the ripple effect of dynamic and semi-dynamic channel assignment, hybrid solutions have been proposed (e.g. NetX [12]). Here, each node is equipped with a receiving interface using a fixed channel and a switchable interface which dynamically change channel to send data to the neighbours' fixed interfaces. However, the CA scheme in [12] does not address asymmetric traffic and interference caused by PNs.

At network layer, many interference-aware routing metrics have been proposed for WMNs, e.g. the expected transmission count (ETX) [6], the expected transmission time (ETT) [8] and the weighted cumulative expected transmission time (WCETT) [9], among others. The main drawback of these metrics is that a given minimum metric path might become suboptimal over time due to varying traffic and link quality conditions. In addition, it is hard to quantify the impact of external PN traffic using such metrics. In this paper, we develop routing and channel switching scheduling schemes which use local information to approach the performance of the centralized schemes as an upper bound. The scheduling scheme is based on a back-pressure algorithm with differential backlogs [18] of the multiple paths, which solves a network utility maximization problem [5][10]. For multi-channel, multi-radio (MC-MR) WMNs, the authors of [13][16] proposed heuristic algorithms of maximal weight scheduling in a distributed manner but requiring heavy signaling traffic for its implementation. Horizon [14] proposed a simplified system model which allows to estimate the path quality for back-pressure scheduling with less probing overhead. However, it works for single radio WMNs and considers only congestion delay for the path cost. Here, we extend the framework in [14] for MC-MR WMNs, taking also into account the impact of channel switching overhead in the scheduling process.

3   Urban-X Architecture

3.1   System Model

The Urban-X architecture is shown in Figure 1(a). Urban-X consists of Mesh
Clients (MCs) and Cognitive Mesh Nodes (CMNs) that coexist with PNs. The
PNs can be residential 802.11 Access Points (APs) as well as Bluetooth or Zigbee
devices. In dense urban areas, experimental results show that these devices already occupied most of the spectrum in ISM bands [11]. The CMNs are wireless
routers equipped with three WiFi radio interfaces (i.e. R1, R2 and R3), through
which they form a forwarding backbone as in Figure 1(a). R1 and R2 are used
to receive or transmit packets simultaneously on different ISM channels, while
R3 is used for exchanging control messages. The R1 is tuned to a semi-dynamic
channel that changes according to PN activity and mesh network traffic. The
CA strategy for R1 is described in Section 3.3. The R2 is dynamically switching
among the channels of the neighbor CMNs with a predefined switching interval
(e.g. 40 msec). In current platforms, switching delay is the overhead to switch
channels on a per-packet basis [12], and it is approximately 1 msec. Compared
to existing MC-MR solutions [3,15], the hybrid multi-radio approach of Urban-X
provides two main benefits: *(i)* it achieves high throughput using a CA strategy
which takes into account the impact of both internal and external interference
(Section 3.3), and *(ii)* it preserves the network connectivity through the switchable transmitting interface. In addition, we use a designated interface for control
(R3), which is fixed to a common control channel (CCC) to disseminate routing
information and updates of the CA protocol. Such a control interface introduces
an additional cost which can be justified by the overhead reduction for broadcast messages, which otherwise would require to send multiple copies of the same
packets on all the available channels, as in [12]. The channel selection for the
CCC is out of the scope of this work. An example of operations of the Urban-X
CA scheme in a three-nodes chain topology is shown in Figure 1(b).

3.2   Spectrum Sensing and Primary Traffic Load Estimation

An important aspect of Urban-X is the effective avoidance of external interference due to PN traffic. This is achieved by the interference aware CA scheme
described in Section 3.3, which requires information on external interference.
Therefore, the CMNs sense the spectrum periodically and estimate the channel
workloads of PN traffics (ω), defined as the ratio of time the channel is used by
an active PN. In Urban-X, each CMN performs spectrum sensing through an
energy detector scheme, which detects a signal during a single symbol duration
(e.g. 4 μsec in case of 802.11a). The reliability of the estimated results depends
on the sensing period and on the sampling rate. As the sensing period is longer
and the sampling rate is high, the result is more reliable. According to our simulation study, more than 300 msec for the sensing period is required to get an
approximated workload value with 10% error. In addition, estimating the busy or
idle durations needs a sampling rate that at least is higher than the Nyquist sampling rate (e.g. 0.3, 0.5 msec). Thus, each CMN calculates the channel workload

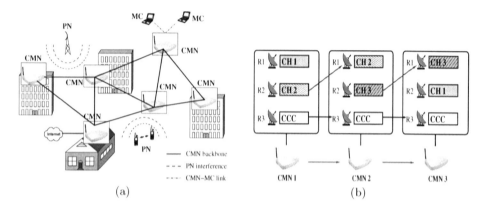

(a)   (b)

Fig. 1. The Urban-X architecture is shown in Figure 1(a). An example of operations of the Urban-X CA scheme is shown in Figure 1(b).

as: $\omega = \frac{T_{busy}}{T_{busy}+T_{idle}}$ where T_{busy} (T_{idle}) represents the average time the channel is detected busy (idle) during the sensing period. The estimation of ω poses at least three important issues to be solved for its practical implementation. First, a CMN is not allowed to send packets during the second period because it cannot distinguish between PN and CMN traffics. Second, a long sensing period for each channel (e.g. 50, 100, 200 msec) would significantly reduce the network performance. Third, with increasing number of available channels, a significant time would be required for each CMN to estimate the PN traffics on all the channels. To solve the first issue, we assume that sensing is synchronously performed by the CMNs, leveraging the CCC for synchronization issues [2]. To reduce the impact of sensing interval on network performance, we use collaborative sensing techniques, i.e. each CMNs exchange sensing information with neighbors to enhance the measurement performance. Since channel status is asymmetric in receive and transmit nodes, measuring PN workload should be executed on both the fixed channel used by R1 and on the transmitting channel of R2. The details of our collaborative sensing scheme can be found in [20].

3.3   Interference Aware Channel Assignment

In Urban-X, the CA scheme defines the channel to be used on the fixed radio R1. In our CA scheme, we take into account the impact of *external* interference (caused by PNs) and *internal* interference (caused by other CMNs). For this purpose, each CMN chooses the channel which has the least impact by PN traffics while at the same time minimizing internal interference caused by CMN traffics along the path to the receiver node (intra- and inter flow interference). Algorithm 1 shows the operations of the Urban-X CA scheme (UCA).

From the results of channel workload measurement ω in the previous section, we can approximately derive an expected capacity of channel i as: $C_i = C_{n_0} \cdot (1 - \omega)$ where C_{n_0} denotes the non-interfered channel capacity as given by

---

Algorithm 1. Fixed channel allocation under primary traffic

---

for each channel i in K **do**

    $C_i = C_{n_0} \cdot (1 - \omega)$, $C_i = C_i / N(i)$

    $C_{CPF,i} = C_i / N(Flows)$

    $Q1 = C_{CPF,i} \bigcup Q1$

end for

$C_{LCPF} = $ EXTRACT-MIN(Q1)

$i_{R1} = $ EXTRACT-MAX(Q1)

$C_{min} = $ MIN(Q2), $C_{max} = $ MAX(Q2)

$C_{CR} = C_{max} - C_{min}$

$P_s = 1 - C_{LCPF} / C_{CR}$

if $P_s \geq Random[0,1]$ **then**

    Select i_{R1} as a fixed channel, i.e. i_{Rx}, for R1

end if

Broadcast HELLO with C_{LCPF} and i_{Rx}

Q2= Q2 $\bigcup C_{LCPF}$ received from neighbor nodes

Update $N(i_{Rx})$

Shannon under Additive White Gaussian Noise (AWGN). For each channel i, the CMNs estimate the available Capacity per Flow, i.e. $C_{CPF,i}$, by dividing C_i first for the the number of nodes selecting channel i within two hop neighborhoods, i.e. $N(i)$, and then for the number of active flows i.e. $N(Flows)$. Then, the maximum capacity channel i_{R1} is chosen for the R1 interface with a probability P_s. As shown in Algorithm 1, the value of P_s is a function of the Least Capacity per Flow, i.e. C_{LCPF}, of the neighbor nodes, so that a node serving many flows compared to its link capacity or suffering heavy external interference from PNs gets prioritized in the CA. Then, each CMN periodically broadcasts an HELLO messages including the C_{LCPF} value and the selected channel for R1 (i.e. i_{Rx}) on the R3 interface. When receiving an HELLO message from other nodes, each CMN stores the received information in a neighborhood information table.

3.4   Multipath Based Forwarding Mesh Structure

Multipath routing protocols enable CMNs to discover multiple paths towards the gateway and to use alternate paths when the current one is no longer available or congested due to PNs or CMNs traffic. In addition, load-balancing schemes allow to distribute the traffic among the available paths, considering the performance of each path. Multipath routing is therefore an efficient method to cope with varying PN traffic dynamics. However, the existing routing metrics for WMN, e.g. ETX [6], ETT [8] or WCETT [9] are not appropriate for *Urban-X* since an established path could rapidly change its quality due to the dynamic PN activities. For this reason, *Urban-X* creates an adaptive forwarding mesh structure in which a forwarding node maintains multiple next hop candidates for a given destination. Packets are distributed over the next-hop candidates

based on the individual path and link conditions, through the scheduler scheme
described in Section 3.5. Thus, a packet will traverse just one path that however
may change dynamically at every hop. A detailed procedure of our multipath
routing protocol is illustrated in Figure 2(a). We have extended the popular
AODV routing scheme for multipath operations. In our scheme, a source node
broadcasts a route request (RREQ) message through the CCC on the R3 interface. The intermediate nodes rebroadcast the RREQ messages received from
different upstream nodes. Unlike AODV, an intermediate node can forward duplicate RREQ messages if they contain a lower metric value than the one stored
in the routing table. We will discuss the routing metric (Cumulative ETT) in the
next section separately. After receiving multiple RREQ messages, a destination
node replies with multiple route reply (RREP) messages by unicasting. In order
to limit the forwarding mesh structure, the forwarding mesh is constructed of
individual paths that are not longer than a certain hop count. The destination
node calculates the Threshold hop count, $ThresholdHC = \alpha \cdot hop_{min}$ for the
RREP message in which $\alpha \geq 1$ and hop_{min} is the hop count of the shortest path
that has the lowest metric among the multiple RREQ messages. Intermediate
nodes become forwarders of a given flow only when the hop count from them
to the source is less than the $ThresholdHC$ value. Otherwise they discard the
RREP message and remove the routing entry of the flow. While a broader mesh
structure (by e.g. setting $\alpha=2$) enhances spatial diversity, it also leads to longer
paths and inter-flow interference. Figure 2(a) depicts an example with $\alpha=1$. The
details of the Urban-X routing scheme can be found in [19].

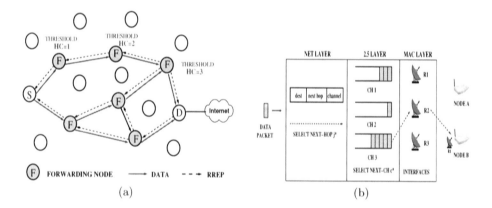

(a)   (b)

Fig. 2. The Urban-X forwarding mesh is shown in Figure 2(a). The packet and channel
scheduler operations are shown in Figure 2(b).

3.5   Routing and Channel Switching Scheduling

Since in *Urban-X* each CMN can choose among multiple next hop candidates,
we have developed a *routing scheduler*, which decides the next hop candidate

for every packet to be transmitted. To this aim, we have proposed a new layer 2.5 which maintains channel queues that hold packets to be sent on the corresponding channels of the switchable interface R2. Moreover, we have developed a *channel scheduler* at the layer 2.5 that decides the channel of the interface R2 for the next switching interval. Figure 2(b) shows the operations of the packet and channel scheduler. The channel scheduler is based on the Horizon framework [14], which defines a simplified model for back-pressure scheduling in a single channel WMN. In Urban-X, we have extended the model in a MR-MC environment also considering the channel switching cost. We have formulated the channel scheduling problem as an optimization problem where each CMN must determine the best channel which maximizes the utility function, i.e. throughput. Due to space shortage, we omit the details of the optimization framework, which can be found in [19]. Instead, we report here only our heuristic solutions to the scheduling problem. As shown by Figure 2(b), our scheduling algorithm selects the next hop j^* which is the minimum cost path in the routing layer and the channel c^* which has the largest number of flow packets, P_c^f to maximize the packet transmission in layer 2.5:

$$j^* = arg \min_{j \in G} C_{rate,j}^f, \quad c^* = arg \max_{c \in K} \frac{P_c^f}{R} \tag{1}$$

The path and channel costs for the scheduling algorithms are derived in Eq.(2) and (3).

$$C_{ch,i}^f = \max \frac{P_i^f}{z_c} + C_{rate,j}^f \tag{2}$$

$$C_{rate,j}^f = \max_{c \in K} \frac{Exp(P_c^f)}{R} + C_{ch,j}^f \tag{3}$$

where the path cost, $C_{rate,j}^f$ refers to the packet transmission delay of a flow via a node j to a destination. In addition to the path cost, channel cost, $C_{ch,i}^f$ at node i denotes the additive delay from channel switching under the virtual link rate in Eq.(2). The total path cost, $C_p^f = C_{ch,s}^f$ from a source node is utilized for the routing metric ($CETT_{p(s,d)} = C_p^f$) in the multipath routing protocol as well. The virtual link rate can be derived as $R \cdot T_{slot,c}/T_{super}$ in which $T_{slot,c}$ is the number of slots for the corresponding channel c in a single super frame T_{super} that has at least one time slot for every active channel to prevent starvation. Moreover, virtual data rate includes the additional delay D_{sw} for channel switching when the currently transmitting channel is not c. As shown in Eq.(3), the path cost considers the actual data rate R and the expected number of queued packets, $Exp(P_c^f) = P_c^f \cdot (1 - PER_{i,j})$ for depressing queueing over the link to node j on channel i, which has an estimated Packet Error Rate $PER_{i,j}$. Assuming a steady state configuration, our heuristic can be proved to maximize the network utility by showing that it satisfies the optimality conditions defined in [14]. Details of the proof and of the scheduler implementation can be found in [19].

4   Performance Evaluation

We have implemented Urban-X in ns2 with extensions from [7] to model the
PN activity and MC-MR operations. Each CMN is equipped with three radio
interfaces using 2 Mbps data rate without rate adaptation. Each radio interface
can use in total 11 orthogonal channels, but channel 1 is designated for the implementation of the CCC. We plan to extend the analysis to cope with adjacent
channel interference (ACI) as future work. The sensing period for the workload
measurement is 70 msec per second. We report here the results for a random
topology scenario, composed by 50 CMNs randomly placed inside an area of
1000m by 1000m. Three CBR flows transmit data with varying data rates from
200 to 1000 Kbps between random source-destination pairs. We varied the number of active PNs in the scenario, and the workload θ produced by each PN.
The PN traffic is modeled through a classic birth-death Markovian model [2]
with parameters λ and μ. Based on such model, the Cumulative Distribution
Functions (CDFs) for the expected idle duration, i.e. T_{idle}, and busy duration,
i.e. T_{busy}, can be derived as:

$$P(T_{idle} < t) = 1 - e^{-\lambda t}, \quad P(T_{busy} < t) = 1 - e^{-\mu t}$$

In the following, we propose a modular evaluation of Urban-X. In Section 4.1,
we analyze the performance of our CA scheme under different PN workloads
and CMNs traffic [19]. In Section 4.2, we investigate the benefit provided by
the multi-path forwarding mesh over a single-path approach. We compute the
network throughput and the end-to-end delay as performance metrics [20].

4.1   Channel Assignment Analysis

In Figures 3(a), 3(b) and 3(c) we compare the performance of the Urban-X
CA scheme (UCA) described in Section 3.3 against the performance of the Distributed Channel Assignment (DCA) scheme described in [12]. In DCA, the

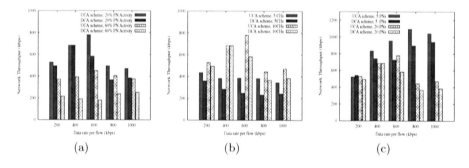

Fig. 3. The UCA and DCA throughputs as a function of the system load produced by
the CMNs are shown in Figures 3(a), 3(b) and 3(c)

number of neighbor nodes on a given channel is balanced within the two hop neighborhood. However, DCA does not consider the impact of external PN traffic on the channel selection process. Figure 3(a) shows the aggregated network throughput as a function of the load produced by each flow (on the x-axis). We consider a scenario with 20 active PNs distributed on 10 channels, and two configurations of PN workload (20% and 60%). As shown in Figure 3(a), the throughput of UCA and DCA is close under low traffic load and PN workload, while UCA can achieve higher performance when the PN interference increases. Under high system load (i.e. 1000 Kb/s), UCA provides a performance improvement of 20% for $\theta=20\%$, and of more than 60% for $\theta=60\%$, thus confirming the importance of PN detection. Figure 3(b) shows the aggregated network throughput when we vary the system load (on the x-axis) and the number of channels (i.e. 5 or 10). We consider a scenario with 20 active PNs with 20% workload. We observe that the number of occupied channels due to PN activity is more critical to network performance than workload of a given PN population since throughput difference between workloads in Figure 3(a) is smaller compared to Figure 3(b). Figure 3(c) confirms that UCA is able to achieve higher throughput than DCA also when we vary the number of active PNs in the scenario.

4.2 Routing Analysis

In order to evaluate the ability of our architecture to cope with dynamic variation of the PN traffic, we have considered two different configurations of *Urban-X*:

- Urban-X with single-path routing (UCA-SP): we consider the basic Urban-X architecture with the CA scheme described in Section 3.3, but with the multipath (Section 3.4) and channel scheduling (Section 3.5) modules disabled. A single path is used between the source and destination nodes.
- Urban-X with multi-path routing (UCA-MP): we consider the full Urban-X architecture, with the multipath and channel scheduling modules enabled. Multiple paths are used between the source and destination nodes.

The main goal of the simulation analysis is to show that UCA-SP cannot maximize network throughput because of fluctuations in PN traffics, while UCA-MP can increase robustness and thus achieve higher performance through the adaptive path and channel scheduler over the multipath mesh. Figure 4(a) shows the aggregated network throughput as a function of the load produced by each flow (on the x-axis), for two configurations of the PN workload (20% and 60%), produced by 5 PNs. Figure 4(b) shows the same analysis when we vary the system load and the number of active PNs (5 and 20), with a PN workload of 20%. UCA-MP outperforms UCA-SP in almost every scenario under varying number of PNs and workloads as shown in Figure 4(a) and Figure 4(b) except for the configuration with 200 Kbps data rate where the advantages of the multi-path are penalized by the higher overhead and the additional self interference effect.

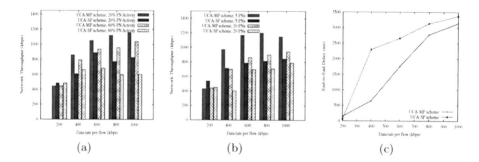

Fig. 4. The UCA-SP and UCA-MP throughputs as a function of the system load produced by the CMNs are shown in Figures 4(a), 4(b) and 4(c)

Interestingly, the aggregated throughput of UCA-MP increases with increasing data rate, which indicates that UCA-MP can effectively reduce the inter-flow interference. Figure 4(c) shows the end-to-end delay as a function of the system-load (on the x-axis) for 5 PNs , PN workload of 20%. and 10 channels. For low data rate, switching delay becomes more critical since network congestion is not severe and the number of PNs are scarce in the network. As a result, UCA-MP shows longer delay at 200 Kbps compared to UCA-SP. However, as the number of PNs and data rate of flows increases, UCA-MP considerably reduces the end-to-end delay compared to UCA-SP.

5   Conclusions

In this paper, we have presented *Urban-X*, a novel cross-layer architecture which combines elements from classical MC-MR technology with Dynamic Spectrum Access principles to deploy self-organizing WMNs over urban environments. To this purpose, we have proposed a novel CA scheme which takes into account the impact of external interference on each channel and we have integrated it with a multipath routing scheme and a back-pressure channel/packet scheduler, through which we are able to dynamically distribute the traffic inside the WMN based on actual channel conditions. The simulation results reveal that Urban-X can increase robustness and performance significantly under a wide range of scenarios. Future works include: the implementation of the UCA scheme on a testbed and the analysis of TCP performance over Urban-X.

Acknowledgments

This research is supported by grant YR2009-7003 from Stiftelsen för internationalisering av högre utbildning och forskning (STINT).

References

1. Akyildiz, I.F., Wang, X., Wang, W.: "Wireless Mesh Networks: A Survey,". Computer Networks Journal 47(4), 445–487 (2005)
2. Akyildiz, I.F., Lee, W.Y., Vuran, M.C., Mohanty, S.: NeXt Generation/Dynamic Spectrum Access/Cognitive Radio Wireless Networks: A Survey. Computer Networks Journal 50(1), 2127–2159 (2006)
3. Alicherry, M., Bhatia, R., Li, L.E.: Joint channel assignment and routing for throughput. optimization in multi-radio wireless mesh networks. In: Proc. of ACM MOBICOM (2005)
4. Chaska wireless solutions, http://www.chaska.net/
5. Chen, M., Low, S., Chiang, M., Doyle, J.: Cross-layer congestion control, routing and scheduling design in ad hoc wireless networks. In: Proc. of IEEE INFOCOM (2006)
6. Couto, D., Aguayo, D., Bicket, J., Morris, R.: A high-throughput path metric for multi-hop wireless routing. In: Proc. of ACM MOBICOM (2003)
7. Di Felice, M., Chowdhury, K.R., Bononi, L.: Modeling and performance evaluation of transmission control protocol over cognitive radio ad hoc networks. In: Proc. of ACM MSWIM (2009)
8. Draves, R., Padhye, J., Zill, B.: Comparison of routing metrics for static multi-hop wireless network. In: Proc. of ACM SIGCOMM (2004)
9. Draves, R., Padhye, J., Zill, B.: Routing in multi-radio, multi-hop wireless mesh networks. In: Proc. of ACM MOBICOM (2004)
10. Georgiadis, L., Neely, M., Tissiulas, L.: Resource allocation and cross-layer control in wireless networks. Foundation and Trends in Networking 1(1), 1–144 (2006)
11. Gokhale, D., Sen, S., Chebrolu, K., Raman, B.: On the feasibility of the link abstraction in (rural) mesh networks. In: Proc. of IEEE INFOCOM (2008)
12. Kyasanur, P., Vaidya, N.: Routing and link-layer protocols for multi-channel multi-interface ad hoc wireless networks. ACM MC2R 10(1), 31–43 (2006)
13. Merlin, S., Vaidya, N., Zorzi, M.: Resource allocation in multi-radio multi-channel multi-hop wireless networks. In: Proc. of IEEE INFOCOM (2008)
14. Radunovic, B., Gkantsidis, C., Gunawardena, D., Key, P.: Horizon: Balancing tcp over multiple paths in wireless mesh network. In: Proc. of ACM MOBICOM (2008)
15. Raniwala, A., Chieueh, T.: Architecture and algorithms for an ieee 802.11-based multi-channel wireless mesh network. In: Proc. of IEEE INFOCOM (2005)
16. Rasool, S., Lin, X.: A distributed join channel assignment scheduling and routing algorithm for multi-channel ad hoc wireless networks. In: Proc. of IEEE INFOCOM (2007)
17. So, J., Vaidya, N.: Multi-channel mac for ad hoc networks: handling multi-channel hidden terminals using a single transceiver. In: Proc. of ACM MOBIHOC (2004)
18. Tassiulas, L., Ephremides, A.: Stability properties of constrained queueing systems and scheduling policies for maximum throughput in multihop radio networks. IEEE Transaction on Automatic Control 37(12) (1992)
19. Kim, W., Kassler, A.J., Di Felice, M., Gerla, M.: Cognitive multi-radio mesh networks on ISM bands: a cross-layer architecture. In: Proc. of IEEE IPCCC (2010)
20. Kim, W., Kassler, A.J., Di Felice, M., Gerla, M.: UrbanX: towards distributed channel assignment in cognitive multi-radio mesh networks. In: Proc. of IFIP Wireless Days (2010)

Always Best (dis-)Connected: Challenges to Interconnect Highly Heterogeneous Networks

Daniel Rodríguez-Fernández[1], Isaias Martinez-Yelmo[1,2],
Ellen Munthe-Kaas[1], and Thomas Plagemann[1]

[1] Department of Informatics, University of Oslo
Gaustadalléen 23 D, N-0373, Oslo, Norway
{dani,imyelmo,ellenmk,plageman}@ifi.uio.no
[2] Universidad Carlos III de Madrid
Av. Universidad 30, 28911, Leganés, Madrid, Spain
imyelmo@it.uc3m.es

Abstract. Wireless networks enable mobility, multihoming, and Delay Tolerant Networks. In such networking environments, the principles of the Internet, i.e., the end-to-end principle and the combination of location and identification in IP addresses, cannot be applied. In this paper, we propose a scalable application centric approach for mobility and multihoming that is able to interconnect highly heterogeneous networks where the networks may belong to different networking paradigms, e.g., IP based and Delay Tolerant Networks. Applications and users that aim to communicate, form communities. Community members might together have several network technologies available, and the community layer manages internetworking information for the members to seamlessly integrate these. Networking adaptation layers are used to provide a common interface for the different networks to the community layer. Addressing is based on names, cryptographic identifiers, and network locators and such that identifiers can also be created in infrastructure-less and disconnected situations.

1 Introduction

Mobile devices with multiple wireless networking capabilities, like IEEE 802.11, 3G and Bluetooth, have become mainstream devices in the recent years, and their popularity will increase also in the future. Applications running seemingly smoothly over these different networks give the impression that the Internet architecture is well suited for future wireless and mobile computing. Unfortunately, this impression is not correct. Basic mobility support required a patch to the Internet architecture, i.e., Mobile IP. Mobile IP enables the user to be reachable via the same IP address while roaming, through the help of a Home Agent. Since the Home Agent is a part of the network it conflicts with the fundamentals of the Internet architecture, i.e., the end-to-end principle. The basic problem that causes this conflict is the fact that IP addresses are used as locators and identifiers at the same time. The combination of identification and location causes also substantial problems for seamless integration of different networking technologies at the end host, i.e., for multihoming, because each network interface requires its own IP address. There are several ongoing efforts in the IETF to develop new patches to the

X. Masip-Bruin et al. (Eds.): WWIC 2011, LNCS 6649, pp. 410–421, 2011.

Internet architecture to handle multihoming, but so far no solution has been adopted and is mature enough.

Another challenge to the Internet architecture is introduced by Mobile Ad Hoc Networks (MANETs) and Delay Tolerant Networks (DTNs). DTNs are infrastructure-less networks, which are so sparse that end-to-end connections cannot be established. Therefore, DTNs apply the store-carry-forward principle, i.e., nodes carry messages for some time until they meet other nodes that can be used to forward the message one hop. Obviously, such an approach is contradicting to the end-to-end principle and IP cannot be used in DTNs. Thus, DTNs represent a new networking paradigm and are clearly separated from MANETs. MANETs are also infrastructure-less networks, but they obey the end-to-end principle and are based on IP. In MANETs, it is assumed that route breaks caused by mobility can be quickly fixed through discovery of new routes and re-routing. We believe that the strong separation between MANETs and DTNs is wrong, because both network types are infrastructure-less and are used either due to necessity, i.e., no network infrastructure exists, or due to the explicit choice of the user. Examples for the first case include sensor networks for wildlife and environmental monitoring, emergency and rescue operations in areas with destroyed infrastructure, and also military applications. Examples for the second case include Vehicular Networks which do not want to rely on cellular networks like 3G due to the unacceptable end-to-end delay between neighbouring vehicles, and social content distribution networks that either want to save money (roaming costs) or want to establish a network that nobody can control, like floating content [1]. The question whether MANETs or DTNs should be deployed in a certain setting depends on the density and mobility of the nodes. MANETs might become quickly partitioned and nodes in DTNs might be close enough to each other to form a MANET with end-to-end connection. Multihoming and a seamless integration of the different networking paradigms would enable applications that are always best (dis-)connected in highly heterogeneous networks. Therefore, full advantage and resource optimisation of available communication capabilities from underlying layers could be obtained for applications and services in any network (dis-)connected node.

The contributions of this work comprise the identification of the challenges introduced by mobility, multihoming and different network paradigms and a proposal to address these challenges. One of the main characteristics of our proposal is that it is application and user centric compared to related network centric solutions.

The rest of the paper is structured as follows. In Section 2, we detail the challenges that mobility and multihoming over highly heterogeneous networks present. The state of the art in mobility, multihoming and heterogeneous internetworking is discussed in Section 3. In Section 4, we present our proposal for solving the aforementioned problems. Section 5 concludes the paper, discussing the differences between the proposed approach and related work, and pointing out our future work.

2 Challenges

The proliferation of wireless technologies has broken many of the assumptions made in the design of the current Internet. On the one hand, the Internet was designed with a much more reliable wired network in mind, so some protocols as TCP may be inefficient for wireless communication. On the other hand, wireless technologies have facilitated node mobility and multihoming through the access to different network technologies, such as e.g. IEEE 802.11, Bluetooth, and 3G. These two novelties have revealed a fundamental problem in the design of IP, i.e. the dual role of the IP address, which acts as node identifier and network locator. Due to this design issue, IP cannot provide native support for node mobility and multihoming. In Section 3, we present several approaches for identifier and locator split, which in turn introduce many new problems.

The application of wireless technologies has pushed to the limits the utilisation of networking technologies. In so-called challenged networks [2], it is necessary to deal with long delays and network disruptions, breaking some of the fundamental assumptions made during the Internet protocol suite design. In such networks, it is not possible to rely on the classical end-to-end principle widely used in the Internet. This has caused the apparition of a new networking paradigm, i.e. DTN. In this section we describe the challenges that arise from the conjunction of mobility and multihoming support when internetworking highly heterogeneous networks that might be based on different networking paradigms.

Wireless technologies have inherent problems which are not usually observed in wired networks. The transmission medium causes a higher probability of transmission errors due to interferences or collisions when several nodes try to transmit in a free transmitting slot. These effects are caused by the existing limitations in the wireless medium and can consequently not be removed. In addition, such undesirable effects might be increased by other phenomena such as hidden nodes. Since these effects were not taken into account in the design of the Internet protocol suite, the usage of TCP/IP on wireless technologies leads to a suboptimal utilization of the available resources. The current layered approach of the Internet does not offer enough flexibility to take full advantage of the available resources. This has resulted in a number of different cross-layering optimisation proposals [3].

Wireless technologies have enabled device mobility. At the same time, the diversity of wireless technologies has caused the proliferation of multihomed devices, i.e., devices which can use more than one wireless technology to communicate. Neither host mobility nor host multihoming are supported in the current IP. This is due to a fundamental architectural problem of the current Internet, where IP addresses have a dual role as both host identifiers and network locators. At the application and transport layers, IP addresses are used to identify a host, so all information flows are attached to them. At the network layer, IP addresses are network locators, indicating points of attachment to the network. In order to achieve global scalability, IP addresses are aggregated reflecting the hierarchical organisation of the network. Therefore, if host mobility causes a change in the point of attachment to the network, the host appears as a different node to the rest of the network. In this case, the host should reset the information flows in order to continue with the communication. A similar problem comes from multihoming, where a host appears as different nodes to the network. The hosts should decide upfront which IP addresses to use for communication. In order to provide native support in the network layer for mobility and multihoming, there are many proposals that rely on the separation of the roles that the current IP address possesses. In Section 3, we describe some of those approaches.

The Internet was designed to interconnect sub-networks, which may have different underlying networking technologies. During the design of the Internet, the end-to-end principle was proposed, where complexity is moved to the hosts, while the network is kept as simple as possible. The end-to-end principle works fine in presence of constant end-to-end connectivity, low probability of error, and small end-to-end delays. However, the end-to-end principle cannot be successfully applied in all kinds of networks, e.g. in challenged networks [2]. Such networks require a different networking paradigm, i.e. DTN. This is based on the store-carry-forward principle, where the intermediate nodes need to play a much more important role than in the Internet. It should be noted that from the DTN perspective, node mobility and multihoming could be considered more as an opportunity than as a challenge, since they allow new alternative paths to deliver information if they are properly handled.

The internetworking of heterogeneous networks is a complex problem that poses many issues. According to [4], networks can vary in type of service, routing and forwarding protocols, addressing scheme, packet size, support for QoS, flow and congestion control, security, accounting, etc. An internetworking solution needs to take into account all the differences. In this paper, we also consider the integration of different networking paradigms, i.e. IP networks and DTNs, which adds additional challenges. The internetworking should be aware of the networking paradigm of the underlying networks and perform according to them. For example, in order to provide interoperability between the Internet and a DTN, the internetworking system should be able to work in DTN mode, avoiding or replacing the usage of the end-to-end principle.

Current mobility and multihoming solutions relying on IP may not work properly over DTNs since IP assumptions are incompatible with the DTN paradigm. Any solution should nonetheless take into account all challenges that emerge when the identifier-locator split is done. The mapping between identifiers and locators must also work in DTN mode. One issue is that, at times, it may not be possible to update the mapping information due to network partitions. Thus, the mapping system should be able to work with partial knowledge. On the other hand, the mobility of nodes could be beneficial since node mobility may allow communication among otherwise isolated partitions (akin to message ferrying).

In the following section, we present the state of the art of solutions that consider some of the aforementioned challenges.

3   State of the Art

In Section 2, we introduced the problems that the current IP has due to the dual role of the IP address. Unfortunately, IPv6 does not offer a native solution, having the same problems as IPv4. There has been an effort at the IETF to give solutions to issues like mobility, multihoming, security, etc. However, instead of providing a general solution, each of these solutions focuses on a specific challenge, leading to incompatible partial solutions. A network based solution for multihoming is LISP [5]. LISP does not require modifications on the hosts, only on network routers. The problem with LISP is that it presents scalability issues when deployed on the Internet. Other proposals are host based, requiring modifications only on hosts and a few nodes in the network. This is the case of Mobile IP (MIP) [6,7], SHIM6 [8], and HIP [9], which target mobility, multihoming and security, respectively, but with extensions that can be used to solve other issues. HIP provides a clear solution, not just to security but also to mobility and multihoming. HIP adds a new layer between network and transport, and introduces a new cryptography-based identity namespace. Identities are composed by a public-private key pair, where the public key is used as host identifier (HI). Upper layers use HIs, while IP continues using IP addresses which maintain their topological information. All these approaches are designed to solve problems of IP (IPv4 or IPv6), trying to patch the current Internet rather than giving new architectural designs. All assume that IP is used as network protocol. Thus, they are making the same assumptions as IP.

In parallel, the IETF DTN-RG has proposed the Bundle Protocol (BP) [10,11], which aims to provide a general solution to DTN. The bundle protocol creates an overlay composed by BP agents that interconnect different DTN regions. A convergence layer is used to encapsulate the native network stack of each region. Security is an optional extension defined in [12]. The naming proposal is intentional naming [13]. It is very flexible, but it is unclear how to do routing and how to support multihoming and mobility. BP has been criticised that it lacks reliability and error detection support, relies on synchronised time among BP agents, lacks a clear naming scheme, and lacks support for application requirements [14].

There has also been a significant amount of effort on the definition of the Future Internet. Many of the proposals give a clean slate design, reviewing the fundamental principles of the Internet. A general survey in the area can be found in [15]. Due to space limitations we can mention only a few of them. The Ambient Networks [16] propose a flexible framework to create the so-called ambient networks, which are formed spontaneously by the nodes that have some access to networking technology. The project aims to fulfil the always best connected vision [17]. The proposal of SpoVNet is also interesting, by providing a generic framework to create overlays. The internetworking functionality is provided by the Underlay Abstraction, described in [18]. However, neither Ambient Networks nor SpoVNet consider the problems that may arise from the integration of DTN. Despite the large amount of work, there are not many proposals that consider the problem of internetworking of highly heterogeneous networks, where different networking paradigms need to be integrated.

PONA [19] proposes a separation layer that performs the ID-locator split at different levels, allowing host, user, and data IDs. It proposes a hierarchy of realms that reflects logical organisations, e.g. administrative or commercial organisations. A hierarchy of connectivity zones reflects the physical network connectivity. PONA does not propose a specific ID definition, allowing different types depending of the type of realm. It also allows users to specify requirements by providing policies. This vision also allows the possibility of supporting DTN relying on the realm structure.

MEDEHA/HENNA [20,21] is a proposal for internetworking of highly heterogeneous networks. It can interconnect infrastructure networks and MANETs, and also can work in a DTN-like mode. MEDEHA was originally designed to work over IPv4. However, HENNA provides an ID-locator split which can be used to enhance MEDEHA. HENNA provides support for IPv4, IPv6 and DTN network locators. It works in a similar way to MIP, extending it to support DTN. The Location and Management Server

(LMS) plays a similar role to the Home Agent on MIP. HENNA has two main problems: (1) its lack of support for multihoming, allowing just one network locator for each node identifier, and (2) the construction of the identifiers. Node IDs are constructed by concatenating the LMS locator on the Internet and a local label managed by the LMS. This causes many security and scalability problems. HENNA makes many assumptions about the LMSs, which should be static and publicly available at all times. Furthermore, the node IDs depends on a specific locator (IP address) of the LMS. Thus, the ID-locator split problem still remains at the LMS level (e.g. making impossible to exploit LMS multihoming).

The Phoenix architecture [22] aims to fulfil the communication requirements after a disaster, on a so-called Day After Network (DAN). The idea of such networks is to integrate all available communication means after a disaster and use them to offer services to the rescue team, victims of the disaster, etc. The proposal relies on two protocols: the Phoenix Interconnectivity Protocol (PIP) which enables the creation on islands of connectivity though heterogeneous networks, and the Phoenix Transport Protocol (PTP) which enables delay tolerant communication between partitions. The proposed naming system is based on roles, such as firemen, police, etc. However, apart from the project description, there is not much information available about these two protocols.

4   Community Internetworking

In this section we present our proposal to solve the challenges presented in Section 2. In order to take full advantage of present and future networking heterogeneity, it is necessary to consider the following requirements. Firstly, it is vital not to make strong a priori assumptions about the underlying networks. Consequently, the internetworking system needs to be aware of the characteristics of these networks, by some kind of network description and corresponding ontology. The internetworking further needs to be aware of the changing status of the network and the nodes resources. It is also necessary to support node multihoming and mobility. An application should be allowed to influence the internetworking, describing the service that it expects from the network. Finally, security should be a main concern of the internetworking system.

Taking into account the aforementioned requirements, we propose community internetworking. The basic idea behind our proposal is to provide internetworking to a set of nodes that want to communicate with each other. This set of nodes is called *community* in our proposal. The nodes that compose a community may have access to several heterogeneous networks, so the community should handle this heterogeneity in order to perform the internetworking. Multihoming over highly heterogeneous networks can cause an explosion in routing information management, since nodes may be accessible though several networking interfaces. In order to avoid scalability issues, we propose that instead of managing all nodes in each network, just the community members are taken into account in each community. This allows performing a more sophisticated internetworking, because much less information needs to be managed. The communities are created to reflect a permanent or temporal relationship among the nodes that form them. The relationship can, e.g., reflect an organisation or a social network. It also can be created to support requirements of an application, as, e.g., a video streaming community or a content sharing community. Another example can be a Personal Area Network,

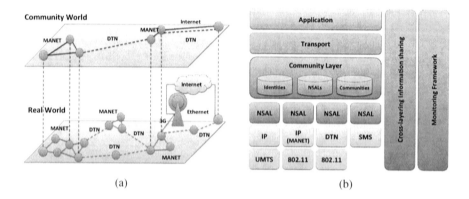

Fig. 1. (a) Community Internetworking example, and (b) Community Layer scheme

where the community integrates all the communicating devices currently used by a user (laptop, phone, PDA, etc.). We assume that the community receives a set of policies that reflects the requirements of the application and user. These policies determine the behaviour of the community. Node mobility and multihoming are supported through an identifier-locator split described in Section 4.1. Figure 1(a) illustrates how community internetworking reduces the size of the problem, as just the nodes that are members of the community are considered in the internetworking.

Our proposal relies on three main abstractions: *node*, *networking substrate*, and *community*. The *node* represents a device that has access to one or more networking substrata, and can be member of one or more communities.

The *community* abstraction represents a group of nodes that cooperate in order to fulfil some common objectives. Communities are formed to support the high level requirements of applications and users. These policies will be used to manage the community internals. Each community should perform the internetworking of its members over different networking substrata.

Finally, the *networking substrate* represents any kind of legacy or future network. Our proposal aims for minimising the assumptions about the internal characteristics of the networking substrata, which is just assumed to be able to provide some basic networking functionalities, such as transmission of packets and some kind of addressing. Thus, this abstraction can wrap many different types of networks, ranging from complex network overlays to simple communication services such as SMS, including direct communication over link layer protocols. The current Internet is one possible instance of a networking substrate. In order to be able to use the different networking substrata, we place on top of each of them a Networking Substrate Adaptation Layer (NSAL). The NSALs provide a common API to the communities by using the native primitives of each networking substrate. NSAL is further described in Section 4.4. However, the common NSAL API is not enough to perform a proper internetworking, it is also necessary to know the internal properties (addressing scheme, type of service, etc.) of each networking substrate. We obtain such knowledge from a self-description of the networking substrate, which is one of the key services provided by the NSAL.

4.1   Name-Identifier-Locator

Our approach for ID-locator split identifies three main entities: *name*, *identifier*, and *network locator*. Names constitute a high level abstraction, which can be resolved into identifiers, which are used to uniquely identify nodes and communities. Identifiers are mapped to the network locators that the nodes have on each of the networking substrata. The namespaces for names, identifiers and network locators are independent of each other.

Our proposal does not require names to be of a specific type. We believe that depending on the specific situation, different name systems might be used. The only requisite is that it must be possible to resolve names into identifiers. Two examples of name systems could be the fully qualified domain names provided by DNS, or the role based naming proposed in [22].

Network locator spaces are defined by each networking substrate. They may have meaning only inside the network substrate. For example, IPv4 and IPv6 would use IPv4 and IPv6 addresses respectively, while a DTN may use another type of network locators such as, e.g. GPS coordinates in geographic based DTN routing.

The common namespace for all the communities and nodes is the identifier namespace. We propose the usage of cryptographic based identifiers similar to what HIP proposes [9]. The identifiers are the public part of an *identity*, which is a public-private key pair. In our proposal, both nodes (hosts) and communities are associated with at least one identity, and therefore an identifier. Cryptographic identifiers have the following advantages: (1) They offer support for security and (2) can be auto-generated by each entity. In addition, (3) they are totally independent of names and network locators.

At the same time, they introduce some challenges since such identifiers do not provide any information about the location of the entities in the network substrata. Hence, we need a system that maps the identifiers to network locators in order to be able to start any communication with a node or community. An issue that arises from the usage of identifiers is privacy. In our proposal, nodes can have one or more identities. A node with two identities would appear to the rest of nodes as two different nodes.

4.2   Community Layer

The implementation of the community internetworking functionality is done in the community layer. As shown in Figure 1(b), this layer is introduced between layer 3 and layer 4. Nevertheless, the network substrate definitions allow the coexistence of very different networking substrata, ranging from link layer network technologies to complete protocol stacks. The community layer maintains on each node a registry that contains information about: (1) its identities, (2) its NSALs, and (3) the communities that the node is member of. The community layer is also responsible for coordinating the utilisation of shared resources on the node by different communities. The communities may, for example, have a priority that could be used to organise the usage of these resources.

As shown in Figure 1(b), a cross-layering information sharing component gives access to information from other components of the system. In order to achieve awareness, nodes, communities and networking substrata should be able to give a description of their characteristics. In addition to this description, information about the status of the networking substrata and the node internal resources is needed. For this purpose, a monitoring framework component will be used. The monitoring framework is in charge of performing measurements about the status of nodes and networking substrata. This component is shared by all communities, leading to an efficient utilisation of the resources. For instance, if several communities require the same type of measurements, they need to be performed only once.

4.3   Community Management

Each node can create communities. We assume that, when a community is created, it is provided with a set of policies that reflects the preferences of an application or user. Community management and internal routing will be done according to those policies. The ownership of a community is given by the ownership of the private key of the community identity. The node that creates a community is therefore its owner. The owner may either delegate to other community members management responsibilities, or share the private key with other members of the community. This is decided by the community policies.

Another way to become member of a community is joining an existing community. Nodes can apply for joining a community, or they can be invited to join it. In both cases, community membership policies are checked before membership is granted.

The communities maintain the mapping between the identifiers of its members and their network locators within the different networking substrata. This mapping is performed by the mapping manager component. The implementation of this component depends of the community. For instance, in a small size community that should deal with disruptions, each node may maintain its own local copy. In a larger community where nodes are accessible through stable networks, the mapping manager may be implemented in a different form, e.g. by a distributed hash table, in order to achieve better scalability.

The inter-community routing is performed according to the community topology. This can be extracted from the mapping manager of each community. The selection of the next hop inside of the community is done by using the routing policies of the community. In this process, the NSAL and the network locators that will be used are selected. This last process might be too heavy for a per-packet processing. Thus, it may be possible to use a per-flow processing, where a temporal state about the open communication flows is used. This state may react to changes in the community topology and modify the next hop of the flow. Each hop at the community level may be done in a different networking substrate. This hop inside of a network substrate may potentially require more than one internal hop, which will be managed by the native routing and forwarding mechanisms of the networking substrate.

Communities might also consider the case when none of the available networking substrata can be used to send data to the destination. This could for example occur when nodes do not have a DTN substrate. In this case the community might decide, based on the community policies, to provide some basic DTN support, e.g. buffering data. The behaviour of this DTN support would be managed by the community policies.

4.4   Networking Substrate Adaptation Layer

The networking substrate provides a generic abstraction for any kind of legacy network. This allows the community layer to handle highly heterogeneous networks. There may be large differences between the technology, protocols, addressing, and even networking paradigm of the networking substrata. In order to reduce the complexity required at the community layer, we introduce the Networking Substrate Adaptation Layer, which wraps a particular networking substrate and provides a set of services though a common API to the community layer. One of the key elements is the networking substrate description. We assume a network definition language that can be used to communicate the networking substrate properties to the community layer. The last may be done by a network definition ontology.

The services provided by the NSAL API include services to (1) send data and (2) receive data, (3) resolve names to identifiers, and (4) resolve identifiers to network locators. These two functions can be combined to find communities by using a networking substrate. The first is used to, given a name, resolve the identifier of a node or a community, while the second is used to, given an identifier, resolve network locators to a node or a community in the networking substrate. And finally, (5) request a description of the properties of the path to the destination in the network substrate. The path description is used by the community layer to identify the best network substrate to forward data to. To implement the name-to-ID and ID-to-locator resolve services, the adaptation layer will use the native services offered by the network substrate, if available. For example, an IP NSAL could use DNS, while a DTN NSAL may use an epidemic dissemination. The send and receive services are mapped to the native send and receive primitives of the network substrate.

5   Conclusions

In this paper we present community internetworking, which is our proposal to support mobility and multihoming in highly heterogeneous internetworking. The basic idea behind our proposal is to provide internetworking just to the nodes that need to participate in a communication, following an application and user centric approach compared to other networking centric approaches. This decision reduces the size of the problem, allowing a better scalability. In our approach, we define three main abstractions: *node*, *community*, and *networking substrate*. A node may be member of several communities and have access to different networking substrata. Communities manage the internetworking among the nodes that are members of the community. The behaviour of a community is driven by a set of policies that reflects the preferences of an application and user. Finally, the networking substrate represents any kind of legacy or future network. It is integrated into the community internetworking by a Networking Substrate Adaptation Layer (NSAL) that offers a common API to the communities. In order to deal with the networking substrata heterogeneity we propose that each NSAL provides a description of the networking substrate that it wraps.

There have been several proposals to support mobility and multihoming, and to perform heterogeneous internetworking. However, just a few approaches consider the integration of Delay Tolerant Networking (DTN).

The DTN Bundle Protocol presents a set of problems as indicated in [14]. The current naming system [13] is quite imprecise about how mapping and routing should be done. Neither is there a clear way to support mobility and multihoming. Finally, the support for the application requirements is very limited.

The vision of the Future Internet provided by PONA [19] presents many similarities with community internetworking. For instance, the user requirements are specified though policies. Realms and zones have a similar function as communities and networking substrata. However, our concept of community is more general since it is not necessarily attached to an organisation. The same is the case of the networking substrata, which can be used to describe, not just the connectivity structure, but almost any kind of network, ranging from the Internet to a DTN, including MANETs. In our proposal we also present a clear identity system and a mechanism to support legacy or future networks by using NSAL and its network description functionality.

The MEDEHA/HENNA [20,21] proposal for highly heterogeneous networks internetworking does not provide support for multihoming. Its ID-locator split scheme relies on the locators of a global Internet (LMS locator + a local label) and introduces the same ID-locator problems (mobility, multihoming, security) at the LMS level. Our proposal fully separates the identifier namespace from the specific network locator namespaces, in a similar fashion as HIP. MEDEHA/HENNA provides a limited support for the application requirements. There is no concept similar to the community, and therefore all the nodes need to be considered for the routing, which can lead to scalability issues.

The Phoenix architecture [22] targets DAN scenarios, while we propose a more general internetworking approach that covers a larger type of networks. Another difference is that Phoenix has a role based naming, whilst we propose the concept of community. Both role and community based approaches have as a goal to provide routing scalability. The community abstraction can be used to create role based communities, e.g. a police community. In our approach, application requirements are specifically supported through policies. Finally, [22] does not describe how node and network heterogeneity is managed, while our proposal relies on the node, community and networking substrate description, the last one provided by NSAL.

The ANA framework [23] provides very generic abstractions that can be used to implement different communication paradigms. It does not define how addressing, routing, etc. should be done, leaving this to the system designers.

Our ongoing and future work is to refine the design of the community internetworking presented in this paper and to implement a proof-of-concept prototype, for which we are considering to use the ANA framework. We plan to focus our first experimental studies on the integration of MANETs and DTNs.

Acknowledgements

This work has been funded by the VERDIKT Programme of the Norwegian Research Council through the DT-Stream project (project number 183312/S10).

References

1. Ott, J., Hyytiä, E., Lassila, P., Vaegs, T., Kangasharju, J.: Floating content: Information sharing in urban areas. In: Proceedings of the 2011 IEEE International Conference on Pervasive Computing and Communications (PerCom), PERCOM 2011, IEEE Press, Los Alamitos (2011)
2. Fall, K.: A delay-tolerant network architecture for challenged internets. In: Proceedings of the 2003 conference on Applications, technologies, architectures, and protocols for computer communications, SIGCOMM 2003, pp. 27–34. ACM, New York (2003), ACM ID: 863960
3. Srivastava, V., Motani, M.: Cross-layer design: a survey and the road ahead. IEEE Communications Magazine 43(12), 112–119 (2005)
4. Tanenbaum, A.S.: Computer Networks, 3rd edn. Prentice-Hall Inc., Englewood Cliffs (1996)
5. Farinacci, D., Fuller, V., Meyer, D., Lewis, D.: Locator/ID separation protocol, LISP (2011)
6. Johnson, D., Perkins, C., Arkko, J.: Mobility support in IPv6. RFC 3775 (2004)
7. Perkins, C.: IP mobility support for IPv4, revised. RFC 5944 (2010)
8. Nordmark, E., Bagnulo, M.: Shim6: Level 3 multihoming shim protocol for IPv6. RFC 5533 (2009)
9. Nikander, P., Gurtov, A., Henderson, T.R.: Host identity protocol (HIP): Connectivity, mobility, multi-homing, security, and privacy over IPv4 and IPv6 networks. IEEE Communications Surveys Tutorials 12(2), 186–204 (2010)
10. Cerf, V., Burleigh, S., Hooke, A., Torgerson, L., Durst, R., Scott, K., Fall, K., Weiss, H.: Delay-tolerant networking architecture. RFC 4838 (2007)
11. Scott, K., Burleigh, S.: Bundle protocol specification. RFC 5050 (2007)
12. Symington, S., Farrell, S., Weiss, H., Lovell, P.: Bundle security protocol specification (2011)
13. Basu, P., Brown, D., Polit, S., Krishnan, R.: Intentional naming in DTN (2009)
14. Wood, L., Eddy, W., Holliday, P.: A bundle of problems. In: IEEE Aerospace conference, pp. 1–17 (2009)
15. Paul, S., Pan, J., Jain, R.: Architectures for the future networks and the next generation internet: A survey. Computer Communications 34, 2–42 (2011)
16. Niebert, N., Schieder, A., Abramowicz, H., Malmgren, G., Sachs, J., Horn, U., Prehofer, C., Karl, H.: Ambient networks: an architecture for communication networks beyond 3G. IEEE Wireless Communications 11(2), 14–22 (2004)
17. Gustafsson, E., Jonsson, A.: Always best connected. IEEE Wireless Communications 10(1), 49–55 (2003)
18. Bless, R., Hübsch, C., Mies, S., Waldhorst, O.: The underlay abstraction in the spontaneous virtual networks (SpoVNet) architecture. In: Next Generation Internet Networks, NGI 2008, pp. 115–122 (2008)
19. Paul, S., Jain, R., Pan, J., Bowman, M.: A vision of the next generation internet: A policy oriented perspective. In: British Computer Society (BCS) International Conference on Visions of Computer Science (2008)
20. Rais, R.N.B., Mendonca, M., Turletti, T., Obraczka, K.: Towards truly heterogeneous internets: Bridging infrastructure-based and infrastructure-less networks. In: 2011 Third International Conference on Communication Systems and Networks, COMSNETS (2011)
21. Rais, R.N.B.: Communication Mechanisms for Message Delivery in Heterogeneous Networks Prone to Episodic Connectivity. PhD thesis, INRIA/University of Nice, Sophia Antipolis (2011)
22. Luo, H., Kravets, R., Abdelzaher, T.: The-Day-After networks: A First-Response Edge-Network architecture for disaster relief (2007)
23. Bouabene, G., Jelger, C., Tschudin, C., Schmid, S., Keller, A., May, M.: The autonomic network architecture (ANA). IEEE Journal on Selected Areas in Communications 28(1), 4–14 (2010)

Channel Assignment Based on the End-to-End Throughput in Multi-hop Wireless Networks[*]

Vasilios A. Siris[**], George Stamatakis, and Elias Tragos

Institute of Computer Science, FORTH
P.O. Box 1385, GR 711 10 Heraklion, Crete, Greece
{vsiris,gstam,etragos}@ics.forth.gr

Abstract. We define a utility-based framework for joint channel assignment and topology control in multi-rate multi-radio wireless mesh networks, and present a greedy algorithm for solving the corresponding optimization problem. The proposed approach can support different target objectives, which are expressed as utility functions of the end-to-end throughput from the gateways to the mesh nodes. The latter accounts for the 802.11 MAC sharing model and rate diversity. The model can be extended to the case of multipath routing, where there are multiple paths from the same or different gateways to the mesh nodes, and for performing joint channel assignment, topology control, and routing.

Keywords: end-to-end throughput, 802.11 MAC, multi-rate.

1 Introduction

Channel assignment in wireless mesh networks (WMNs) influences the contention among wireless links and the network topology or connectivity between mesh nodes. There is a trade-off between minimizing the level of contention and maximizing connectivity [1–3]. Moreover, channel assignment affects the interference between adjacent channels; such interference exists not only for 802.11b/g, but - contrary to common belief - also for 802.11a when the distance of antennas is small [4, 5], which occurs when they are located in the same mesh node. Finally, channel assignment influences the connectivity of mesh nodes with wired network gateways, which is a key application of wireless mesh networks.

Prior work on channel assignment considered minimizing the interference [6–8]. On the other hand, the channel assignment procedure proposed in this paper considers an optimization objective that is a function of the end-to-end (e2e) throughput, which accounts for the 802.11 MAC sharing of the wireless channel. The works of [2, 9–14] consider the throughput for channel assignment.

---

[*] This work was supported in part by the European Commission in the 7th Framework Programme through project EU-MESH (Enhanced, Ubiquitous, and Dependable Broadband Access using MESH Networks), ICT-215320, http://www.eu-mesh.eu

[**] V.A.Siris is also with the Department of Informatics, Athens University of Economics and Business.

X. Masip-Bruin et al. (Eds.): WWIC 2011, LNCS 6649, pp. 422–433, 2011.

[13–15] also consider a utility-based framework: [15] for joint congestion control and channel assignment, assuming a known network topology, [13] for joint congestion control and channel assignment, and [14] for joint congestion control, channel allocation, and scheduling, for which a greedy heuristic assuming orthogonal channels is proposed. Our work differs in that we present a utility-based optimization framework for joint channel assignment and topology control which is based on the e2e throughput. The application of a utility-based framework to congestion control is fundamentally different than the application to channel and topology control, since the latter is a discrete problem.

The work of [10] considers the problem of joint channel assignment and routing, while satisfying fairness constraints. Our work differs in that we investigate joint channel assignment and topology control, and our model supports rate diversity and different target objectives. [16] investigates topology control, and proposes a channel assignment procedure to minimize the aggregate interference, while satisfying a minimum node connectivity. Our approach differs in that we consider utility-based objectives for topology control, which are functions of the e2e throughput. Other works assume full connectivity between nodes that are within range [1, 2, 8], or assign a common channel to one interface of all mesh nodes [6]. The former approach can lead to low transmission rates, which significantly reduce the network's performance. On the other hand, assigning a common channel to all nodes reduces the available interfaces and the chance for more intelligent channel assignment, which is significant since practical mesh networks contain nodes with a few (typically 3-4) interfaces. The work in this paper also differs from our previous work [17] where channel assignment considered the per link throughput, rather than the e2e throughput of flows.

The channel assignment problem in mesh networks with multi-radio nodes is known to be NP-hard [18]. For this reason, channel assignment is typically based on heuristics which assign channels to interfaces or links based on some order or rank; the rank can depend on traffic load, distance to gateway, interference level, etc. In order of decreasing rank, interfaces are assigned the "best" channel according to some criteria [2, 3, 6, 18, 19]. The procedure proposed in this paper also considers assigning channels in some order; however, the order is not fixed or a priori known, but rather is determined during the execution of the channel assignment procedure, and is based on the target objective.

In summary, the proposed channel assignment and topology control approach has the following key features:

- Channel assignment can be performed with different target objectives, which reflect different operator-dependant requirements.
- Target objectives are expressed as utility functions of the end-to-end throughput of flows from gateways to nodes, which captures the MAC layer sharing and rate diversity.
- The node connectivity is not known a priori. Rather, the node connectivity (network topology) is determined together with channel assignment.
- The approach efficiently utilizes multiple wired network gateways, and ensures that for every mesh node there exists at least one path to a gateway.

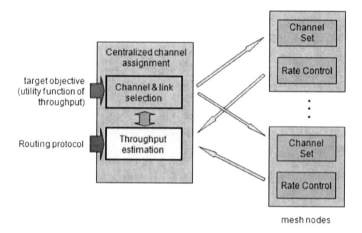

Fig. 1. The channel assignment and topology control procedure consists of two modules: the end-to-end throughput estimation and the channel and link selection module

Support for different objectives is motivated by the fact that network operators can have different operation and performance requirements, hence value differently the aggregate throughput achieved by the network and the distribution of throughput across flows. Such flexibility in operating a network is significant for the cost-effectiveness of future wireless access networks, enabling them to adapt to different operator and application requirements.

The remainder of the paper is structured as follows: In Section 2 we present an overview of the proposed channel assignment and topology control procedure, and in Section 3 we present the mathematical formulation of the problem, and its extension for multiple paths and for joint channel, topology, and routing control. In Section 4 we present more details for the channel and link selection algorithm, and the end-to-end throughput estimation algorithm. In Section 5 we present and discuss simulation results, and finally, in Section 6 we conclude the paper.

2   Channel Assignment and Topology Control Model

The proposed channel assignment and topology control procedure consists of two modules: the throughput estimation module, and the channel and link selection module, Figure 1. The throughput estimation module estimates the throughput of all end-to-end flows, for a specific channel assignment and node connectivity; this estimation considers the paths for all flows, which are determined by the routing protocol, and the transmission rate, which depends on the rate control algorithm at the transmitters. The channel and link selection module takes as input the target objective, expressed as a utility function, and selects the channel assignment and node connectivity that optimizes the specific objective. Note that the channel selection and throughput estimation modules are independent, hence the proposed channel and link selection procedure can work with some other throughput estimation module. Of course, the performance of the channel assignment depends on the joint operation of the two modules.

3   Problem Formulation

We consider a wireless mesh network with a set of nodes N. Each mesh node has multiple radio interfaces. Some nodes, which are referred to as gateway nodes, have wired network connections. The problem we address is to assign channels to mesh nodes and define node pairs that have a communication link, while ensuring that all nodes have a path to at least one gateway. Channel assignment alone does not fully define the node connectivity. Also, an interface's transmission rate depends on the destination interface it communicates with; the transmission rate in turn influences the throughput that is achieved by that link, as well as all other links in the same transmission range that operate on the same channel. Let L be the set of links between nodes, which contains elements of the form $(i, j; k)$, denoting a link between nodes i and j operating on channel $k \in C$; C is the set of available channels. X_i denotes the end-to-end throughput of the flow from a gateway to node i. Note that there can exist multiple links between two mesh nodes, operating on different channels and different nodes can communicate with the same node on the same channel.

The channel assignment and topology control problem can be written as

$$\text{Maximize} \quad \sum_{i \in N} U(\{X_i, i \in N\}) \tag{1}$$
$$\text{over} \quad L = \{(i, j; k) : i, j \in N, k \in C\}$$
$$\text{such that} \quad \exists \text{ path from a gateway to node } i, \forall i \in N \text{ and}$$
$$K_i \leq I_i, \forall i \in N$$

The path of a flow is determined by the routing protocol.

The aggregate utility $U(\cdot)$ in (1) encodes different operator-dependent requirements and objectives. Next we discuss different target objectives that correspond to different expressions for $U(\cdot)$.

Aggregate throughput objective: This objective corresponds to the following aggregate utility:

$$U(\{X_i, i \in N\}) = \sum_{i \in N} X_i, \tag{2}$$

i.e., the aggregate utility is equal to the sum of the end-to-end throughput of all flows from the gateways to the nodes.

Fairness objective: This objective corresponds to the following utility:

$$U(\{X_i, i \in N\}) = \sum_{i \in N} \log (X_i). \tag{3}$$

This objective tries to achieve fairness among the various end-to-end flows.

Load balancing objective: This objective tries to balance the load across gateways. Let G be the set of gateway nodes, F_m be the set of flows that traverse gateway m. The load balancing objective corresponds to the following utility:

$$U(\{X_i, i \in N\}) = \sum_{m \in G} \log \left(\sum_{i \in F_m} X_i \right). \tag{4}$$

3.1   Extensions

Multi-path: The formulation in Section 3 assumes that there is a single flow from a gateway to every node $i \in N$. The formulation can be extended to more than one flows to every node, possibly from different gateways. Multiple paths increase the network's redundancy, enabling it to overcome link failures.

Joint Channel Assignment, Topology Control, and Routing: The formulation in Section 3 assumes that a flow's path is determined by the routing protocol. The following modification corresponds to a joint channel assignment, topology control, and routing problem.

$$\text{Maximize } \sum_{i \in N} U(\{X_i, i \subset N\})$$
$$\text{over } L = \{(i, j; k) : i, j \in N, k \in C\}, P$$
$$\text{such that } \exists \text{ path from a gateway to node } i, \forall i \in N \text{ and}$$
$$K_i \le I_i, \forall i \in N$$

where P is the set of paths for all flows to nodes $i \in N$. In the above formulation, a flow's path is not determined externally by the routing protocol, but is determined by the optimization problem.

4   Utility-Based Channel Assignment Using the End-to-End Throughput Estimation

Next we discuss the functionality of the channel and link selection module, and the end-to-end throughput estimation module.

4.1   Channel and Link Selection Algorithm

The proposed channel assignment procedure implements a greedy heuristic that tries to maximize the aggregate utility of the mesh network, given by (1). The order in which flows are created is based on the utility the corresponding channel assignment yields, which is estimated during the execution of the algorithm and not known a priori. The pseudo-code for the channel selection procedure, which is executed in some central location, is shown in Algorithm 1. L is the set of links, which contains elements $(i, j, ; k)$ that denote a link between nodes i and j, operating on channel k. $U(L)$ is the aggregate utility for the link set L.

Algorithm 1. Greedy utility-based channel and link selection based on e2e throughput

---

1: **Variables:**
2:     $N_{unassigned}$: set of nodes that have not been assigned an end-to-end flow from a gateway
3:     L: set of links, which contains elements of the form $(i, j, ; k)$, denoting there is
       a link between nodes i and j operating on channel k; initially empty
4:     $U(L)$: aggregate utility for set of links L
5:     p_i: ordered set of nodes in the path from a gateway to node i as determined by
       the routing algorithm
6:     $M(i)$: set of links, which contains elements of the form $(i, j, ; k)$, for forming the
       path from a gateway to link i
7:     $U'(i)$: aggregate utility if channels are assigned to the links along the path from
       a gateway to link i
8: **Algorithm:**
9: **repeat**
10:     **for all** $i \in N_{unassigned}$ **do**
11:         p_i = ordered set of nodes from gateway to node i, as determined from
            routing algorithm
12:         **for all** $(i, j) \in p_i$ in order from closest to farthest from gateway **do**
13:             **select** channel k that yields largest utility **then**
14:                 $M_i = M_i + \{(i, j; k)\}$
15:             **end select**
16:         **end for**
17:         $U'(i) = U(L + M_i)$
18:     **end for**
19:     **select** $i \in N_{unassigned}$ with highest $U'(i)$ and smallest number of hops from gateway **then**
20:         $L = L + M_i$ {Assign channels to form a flow from gateway to i}
21:         Remove i from $N_{unassigned}$
22:     **end select**
23: **until** $N_{unassigned}$ not empty

The algorithm considers paths from a gateway to all nodes, as determined by the routing algorithm. The paths, and subsequently the links forming the paths, are created in order of increasing aggregate utility: For all possible paths, channels are assigned in a greedy manner, starting with links in the path that are closest to the gateway (line 12). The path whose assignment would yield the highest utility is then selected (line 19), and the corresponding channel assignments are made (line 20). The procedure ends when all paths are created.

4.2   End-to-End Throughput Estimation

In this section we describe a simple model for estimating the end-to-end throughput of flows in a multi-radio, multi-channel and multi-rate wireless mesh network (WMN) with non-saturated traffic conditions. The WMN is represented as a graph $G = (V, E)$, where V is the set of wireless interfaces and E is the set of directional links between them.

   Traffic is generated by UDP senders, which limit their rate to the end-to-end throughput with which the WMN is able to forward their traffic. Each UDP flow has a single, known path that originates at a source interface and is destined to a sink interface of the WMN. Let F be the set of flows in the network. The end-to-end throughput of a flow $f \in F$ will be $x_f = \frac{b_f}{T}$, where b_f is the number of bits served by flow f over a period of time T. Let $N(v)$ be the set of wireless interfaces whose transmissions can conflict with interface v's transmissions, due to the CSMA-based access protocol, and includes v. Hence, $N(v)$ contains all interfaces that are inside v's carrier sense range, and use the same channel as v. Transmissions from the interfaces in $N(v)$ determine the aggregate channel occupation time T_v seen by v, including the channel occupation time due to its own packet transmissions. T_v can be estimated from

$$T_v = \sum_{u \in N(v)} \sum_{f \in F_u} b_f T_{u,f},$$ (5)

where F_u is the set of flows whose packets are forwarded by interface u, and $T_{u,f}$ is the time needed for interface u to forward a single bit from flow f. Each pair (u, f) uniquely determines the link e over which interface u transmits flow f's packets; $T_{u,f}$ depends on the link e's transmission rate [20].

We use an iterative, water-filling procedure for calculating the values of b_f. Initially each flow f has zero b_f and is in a non-bottlenecked state. In every round of the procedure [21]:

- We increment the number of bits sent by all source interfaces that have at least one non-bottlenecked flow originating from them, by the same amount S. This reflects the fair channel access among contending interfaces in 802.11. Interfaces may belong to the same or different multi-radio nodes. If more than one non-bottlenecked flows have the same source interface, then the amount S is equally shared among these flows, which increase b_f by the same amount.
- We calculate the aggregate channel occupation time seen by each interface $v \in V$ using (5). If for some interface $v \in V$ holds that $T_v \geq T$, then all non-bottlenecked flows that either originate, terminate, or traverse the interface are marked as bottlenecked and in case $T_v > T$ their b_f values are decreased equitably so that either $T_v = T$ of $b_f = 0$. This reflects the fact that for any directional link of the WMN we may not increase the total number of bits transmitted over the link if either the transmitter or the receiver of the link perceives a fully occupied channel. Furthermore, the reduction of b_f values so that either $T_v = T$ of $b_f = 0$ models successfully throughput reduction or even flow starvation in well-known problematic scenarios of CSMA-based protocols like 802.11 DCF, such as information asymmetry, flow-in-the-middle, and near/far hidden terminal scenarios [22].

The above iterative procedure terminates when all flows are marked as bottlenecked; the derived values of b_f are used to calculate each flow's throughput.

5   Performance Evaluation

In this section we present simulation results for the proposed channel assignment algorithm, using the network simulator OMNET++. The simulations used the IEEE 802.11b network model. Traffic was generated by UDP senders, which limited their rate to the end-to-end throughput supported by the network. We present results that compare the proposed channel assignment algorithm for the

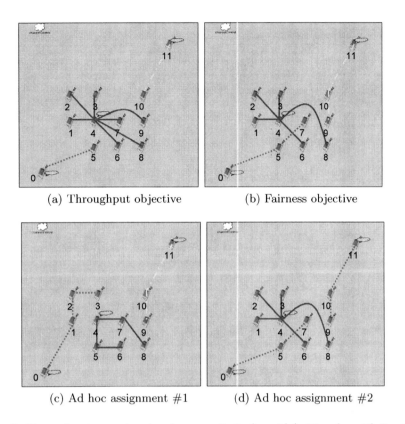

(a) Throughput objective   (b) Fairness objective

(c) Ad hoc assignment #1   (d) Ad hoc assignment #2

Fig. 2. Channel assignment and node connectivity for grid A: 11 nodes with 3 gateways (nodes 0,4,11). Available channels: 1, 6, 11.

aggregate throughput objective defined by (2), and the fairness objectives defined by (3), with an ad hoc channel assignment and node connectivity. The results also include the fairness index given by Fairness Index $= \frac{\left(\sum_{i=1}^{N} X_i\right)^2}{N \sum_{i=1}^{N} X_i^2}$, where X_i is the e2e throughput for the flow to node i and N is the total number of nodes.

Figure 2 depicts the channel assignment for a grid topology with 11 nodes and 3 gateways, for the proposed algorithm using the aggregate throughput and fairness objective, and for two ad hoc channel assignments. Gateway nodes in this and the other topologies investigated have three interfaces, whereas the other mesh nodes have two interfaces. Table 1 shows the corresponding results. The table shows that the throughput objective achieves the highest aggregate throughput, and the highest maximum flow throughput; this is achieved at the cost of fairness, since the aggregate throughput objective achieves the lowest fairness index and the lowest minimum flow throughput. On the other hand, the fairness objective achieves the highest fairness, at the cost of lower aggregate throughput. The two ad hoc channel assignments achieve worst aggregate throughput and fairness compared to the proposed channel assignment algorithm, for both the aggregate throughput and the fairness objective.

Table 1. Results for grid A

	Aggregate throughput objective	Fairness objective	Ad hoc assign.#1	Ad hoc assign.#2
Aggregate throughput	19,11	14,88	11,95	10,77
Fairness index	0,491	0,989	0,899	0,983
Fairness utility	1,478	1,814	0,930	0,665
Min flow throughput	0,836	1,150	1,051	0,939
Max flow throughput	6,169	2,174	2,238	1,449

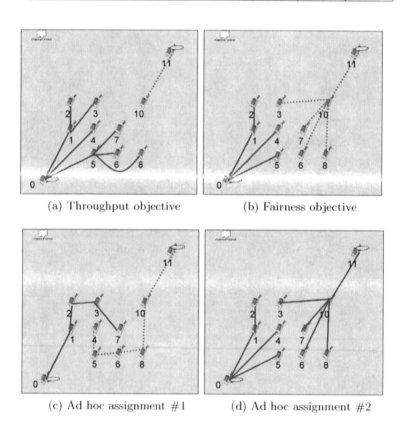

(a) Throughput objective

(b) Fairness objective

(c) Ad hoc assignment #1

(d) Ad hoc assignment #2

Fig. 3. Channel assignment and node connectivity for grid B: 11 nodes with 2 gateways (nodes 0,11). Available channels: 1, 6, 11.

Figure 3 shows the channel assignment and node connectivity for the grid B topology, which contains 11 nodes and 2 gateways. Table 2 shows the corresponding simulation results. As in the previous grid topology, the aggregate throughput objective achieves the highest aggregate throughput, at the cost of lower fairness. Also, the aggregate throughput is more than two times the aggregate throughput achieved with the first ad hoc channel assignment, and more

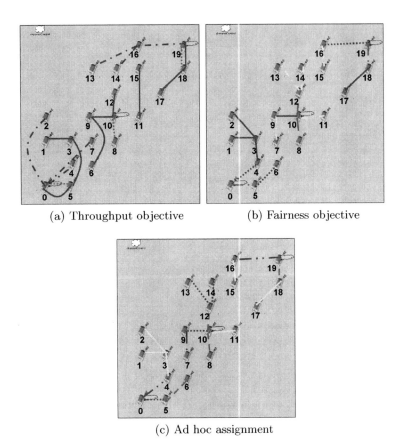

(a) Throughput objective   (b) Fairness objective

(c) Ad hoc assignment

Fig. 4. Channel assignment and node connectivity for grid C: 20 nodes with 3 gateways (nodes 0,10,19). Available channels: 1, 4, 7, 10.

than four times the aggregate throughput achieved with the second ad hoc channel assignment. Moreover, in this scenario the lowest minimum flow throughput is achieved with the second ad hoc channel assignment. The fairness objective achieves the highest fairness utility, given by (3) and a high fairness index which is close to the fairness index achieved by the first ad hoc channel assignment. Observe, however, that the fairness objective achieves a significantly higher aggregate throughput compared to the first ad hoc channel assignment.

Figure 4 depicts the channel assignment for a grid with 20 nodes and 3 gateways. Table 3 shows that, as in the previous two topologies, the aggregate throughput objective achieves the highest aggregate throughput, and the highest maximum end-to-end flow throughput. Also, the fairness objective achieves the highest fairness. Comparing the results for this topology, with the results for the previous two grid topologies, we note that the fairness achieved in this grid topology is significantly smaller than the fairness achieved in the previous two topologies; this occurs because this topology has a larger number of nodes, hence has higher contention for channel access, which results in flows having

Table 2. Results for grid B

	Aggregate throughput objective	Fairness objective	Ad hoc assign.#1	Ad hoc assign.#2
Aggregate throughput	10,16	8,93	4,17	2,98
Fairness index	0,287	0,932	0,954	0,915
Fairness utility	-1,627	-0,172	-3,096	-4,464
Min flow throughput	0,479	0,706	0,358	0,239
Max flow throughput	6,165	1,333	0,582	0,602

Table 3. Results for grid C

	Aggregate throughput objective	Fairness objective	Ad hoc assignment
Aggregate throughput	27,99	23,68	21,73
Fairness index	0,326	0,529	0,498
Fairness utility	-9,478	-0,514	-2,734
Min flow throughput	0,009	0,217	0,002
Max flow throughput	6,161	4,519	5,818

significantly different end-to-end throughput values; this is also the reason that some flows achieve a very small throughput, as indicated by the minimum flow throughput in Table 3. For the aggregate throughput objective, a few flows achieve very high throughput, while the other flows achieve very low throughput, and some of these achieve throughput that is almost zero.

6   Conclusion

We have presented a utility-based framework for joint channel assignment and topology control in multi-rate multi-hop wireless networks. The framework supports different target objectives, expressed as utility functions of the end-to-end throughput of flows from gateways to nodes. Simulation results show the performance in terms of aggregate throughput and fairness achieved by the proposed approach, and illustrate the influence of the target objective.

References

1. Marina, M.K., Das, S.R.: A Topology Control Approach for Utilizing Multiple Channels in Multi-Radio Wireless Mesh Networks. In: Proc. of Broadnets (2005)
2. Das, A.K., Alazemi, H.M.K., Vijayakumar, R., Roy, S.: Optimization Models for Fixed Channel Assignment in Wireless Mesh Networks with Multiple Radios. In: Proc. of IEEE SECON (2005)
3. Skalli, H., Ghosh, S., Das, S.K., Lenzini, L., Conti, M.: Channel Assignment Strategies for Multiradio Wireless Mesh Networks: Issues and Solution. IEEE Commun. Mag., 86–93 (November 2007)

4. Cheng, C.-M., Hsiao, P.-H., Kung, H.T., Vlah, D.: Adjacent Channel Interference in Dual-Radio 802.11a Nodes and Its Impact on Multi-hop Networking. In: Proc. of IEEE Globecom (2006)

5. Angelakis, V., Papadakis, S., Siris, V.A., Traganitis, A.: Adjacent Channel Interference in 802. 11a: Modeling and Testbed Validation. IEEE Commun. Mag. 49(3), 160–166 (2011)

6. Ramachandran, K.N., Belding, E.M., Almeroth, K.C., Buddhikot, M.M.: Interference-Aware Channel Assignment in Wulti-Radio Wireless Mesh Networks. In: Proc. of IEEE INFOCOM (2006)

7. Ko, B., Misra, V., Padhye, J., Rubenstein, D.: Distributed Channel Assignment in Multi-Radio 802.11 Mesh Networks. In: Proc. of IEEE WCNC (2007)

8. Subramanian, A.P., Gupta, H., Das, S.R.: Minimum-Interference Channel Assignment in Multi-Radio Wireless Mesh Networks. In: Proc. of IEEE SECON (2007)

9. Kodialam, M., Nandagopal, T.: Characterizing the capacity region in multi-radio multi-channel wireless mesh networks. In: Proc. ACM MOBICOM (2005)

10. Alicherry, M., Bhatia, R., Li, L.: Joint Channel Assignment and Routing for Throughput Optimization in Multi-radio Wireless Mesh Networks. In: Proc. of ACM MOBICOM (2005)

11. Ye, F., Chen, Q., Niu, Z.: End-to-end throughput aware channel assignment in multi radio wireless mesh networks. In: Proc. of IEEE Globecom (2007)

12. Avallone, S., Akyildiz, I.F.: A Channel Assignment Algorithm for Multi-Radio Wireless Mesh Networks. Computer Communications 31(7), 1343–1353 (2008)

13. Giannoulis, A., Salonidis, T., Knightly, E.: Congestion Control and Channel Assignment in Multi-Radio Wireless Mesh Networks. In: Proc. of IEEE SECON (2008)

14. Merlin, S., Vaidya, N., Zorzi, M.: Resource Allocation in Multi-Radio Multi-Channel Multi-Hop Wireless Networks. In: Proc. of IEEE INFOCOM (2008)

15. Rad, A.H.M., Wong, V.W.S.: Joint optimal channel assignment and congestion control for multi-channel wireless mesh networks. In: Proc. of Globecom (2006)

16. Tang, J., Xue, G., Zhang, W.: Interference-Aware Topology Control and QoS Routing in Multi-Channel Wireless Mesh Networks. In: Proc. of ACM MOBIHOC (2005)

17. Dionysiou, T., Siris, V., Stamatakis, G.: Utility-based Channel Assignment and Topology Control in Wireless Mesh Networks. In: Proc. of IEEE Int'l Symposium on a World of Wireless, Mobile and Multimedia Networks, WoWMoM (2010)

18. Raniwala, A., Gopalan, K., Chiuch, T.: Centralized Channel Assignment and Routing Algorithms for Multi-Channel Wireless Mesh Networks. ACM Mobile Computing and Communications Review (MC2R) 8(2), 50–65 (2004)

19. Raniwala, A., Chiuch, T.: Architecture and Algorithms for an IEEE 802.11-Based Multi-Channel Wireless Mesh Network. In: Proc. of IEEE INFOCOM (2005)

20. Jun, J., Peddabachagari, P., Sichitiu, M.: Theoretical maximum throughput of IEEE 802.11 and its applications. In: Proc. of the 2nd IEEE International Symposium on Network Computing and Applications (April 2003)

21. Siris, V.A., Stamatakis, G., Tragos, E.: A Simple End-to-End Throughput Model for 802.11 Multi-Radio Multi-Rate Wireless Mesh Networks. IEEE Communications Letters (2011) (accepted for publication)

22. Garetto, M., Salonidis, T., Knightly, E.: Modeling per-flow throughput and capturing starvation in csma multi-hop wireless networks. In: Proc. of IEEE INFOCOM (2006)

HRAN - A Scalable Routing Protocol for Multihop Wireless Networks Using Bloom Filters

João Trindade[1] and Teresa Vazão[2]

[1] INESC-ID / Department of Computer Science and Engineering,
Instituto Superior Técnico
Av. Prof. Dr. Cavaco Silva, 2744-016 Porto Salvo, Portugal
{jtrindade,tvazao}@tagus.inesc-id.pt
[2] Instituto Superior Técnico, Av. Rovisco Pais, 1049-001 Lisboa, Portugal

Abstract. We propose a novel routing protocol for large scale Mobile Adhoc Networks called HRAN (Heat Route for Ad-hoc Networks). The protocol is able to scale to large composed by many nodes, requires few resources from devices and lowers the global number of control message imposed by the protocol in discovering routes. HRAN maps the paradigm of heat trails in a physical environment to the network topology. In our protocol each node emits a certain quantity of heat and as the node moves a heat trail is formed. After a node leaves a location the heat from surrounding nodes slowly dissipates. This heat information is then used to guide routing queries from the source to the destination. All heat information is represented through the use of bloom filters. We compare our proposed solution with other routing protocols for MANETS and the obtained results show that for large scale networks HRAN reduces the overhead of control messages.

Keywords: Routing Protocol, Large Scale MANETs, Bloom Filter.

1 Introduction

The proliferation of wireless devices in today's world has lead to emergence of Mobile Ad-hoc NETworks also denominated as MANETs. These type of networks are becoming ubiquitous in many human activities, with an increasing number of participants in a wide range of application environments.

MANETs have specific characteristics which are not found in other types of networks, such as the limited lifetime of the node's batteries, the unpredictable signal conditions and node's mobility that lead to frequent topology variation. For these reasons they pose some novel research problems, being routing one of the most challenging as traditional protocols are not able to cope with node mobility. So, as described in various surveys [1] [2] [3], there is a wide variety of routing protocols which were developed to respond to these problems. Some of them, as the Destination-Sequence Distance Vector (DSDV) or the Optimized Link State Routing protocol (OLSR) are a direct evolution of routing protocols that were designed for wired networks, whilst others, as the Zone Routing

X. Masip-Bruin et al. (Eds.): WWIC 2011, LNCS 6649, pp. 434–445, 2011.

Protocol (ZRP) or the Fisheye Routing Protocols (FSR), were designed using new concepts specifically suited for MANET environments.

Nevertheless, as the authors of [4] [5] have shown none of them are able to provide consistent good results in different scenarios. In fact, in [6] and [7] the authors have observed that the efficiency and effectiveness of non-geographical routing protocols does not scale well to MANET composed by hundred of nodes. In most of them, the number of controls messages grows exponentially with the number of nodes, increasing the overhead and decreasing the overall network performance. Geographical routing protocols [8] have the drawback of requiring a positioning sensor, normally a GPS device, for executing their path discovery processes. In many cases the use of such equipment is not adequate as it requires a significant amount of battery resources and increases the monetary value of the nodes. Moreover, route discovery is performed by the use of an additional component, the location-service, which can introduce a significant amount of overhead.

In this work we propose a new routing protocol named Heat Routing for Ad-hoc Networks (HRAN) suited for MANET scenarios. HRAN is scalable to large networks, in which the nodes have limited resources (memory, processing power and bandwidth) and do not requires the use of GPS devices. HRAN relies on the use of bloom filters to store and spread topology information in an efficient way. In the HRAN protocol nodes do not explicitly rebroadcast topology information messages coming from other nodes. Instead, this information is merged by each node with its own topology data and only the result is shared. To reduce the number of messages sent by a node, whenever a route to a destination is requested, HRAN does not flood the network but uses the information present in the node's bloom filters to discover what nodes are potentially useful for the route. This process effectively guides the route query to the destination and avoids unnecessary message transmissions, saving battery power and decreasing the overhead imposed by the protocol over the network.

Previous work of other authors proposed the use of bloom filter in routing protocols [9]. In the Gradient-ascending routing via footprints (GRASP) bloom filters are used to store information of wether a node of a wireless sensor networks belongs to route or not, but it lacks for an efficient mobility support. Other proposal is the Table Attenuation Routing Protocol (TARP) [10], in which bloom filter are use to implement a proactive routing strategy. TARP does not scale to networks with high node density or mobility.

The remainder of this article is structured as follows: Section 2 presents the background and related work, by introducing the concept of bloom filters data structure which will be used by HRAN to represent and exchange topology information. Section 3 describes our new routing protocol and introduces the concept of *Time Aware Bloom* filter. Details of the protocol's three operating phases are also included in this section. Section 4 presents the assessment of our proposal and the comparison against other known routing protocols for MANETs. The simulation setup is described and the results are depicted and analysed. Finally, section 5 draws the conclusions and lists future work.

2   Bloom Filters

2.1   Concept of Bloom Filter

A bloom filter [11] is a probabilistic data structure that is used to test if an element is a member of a set. It is similar to a standard hash table, except that it is more space efficient and does not store the actual value, rather it maps hashed keys related to the object into a bit array.

A bloom filter returns whether *true* or *false* when asked if an object A is a subset of B ($A \subseteq B$). A return of the value *false* is guaranteed to be accurate, but a return of the value *true* has a probability of being a false positive.

In a more detailed description, a bloom filter representing the set $S = \{x_1, c_2, \cdots, x_n\}$, where n is the number of elements, is an array of m bits, initially all set to 0. $H = \{h_1, \cdots, h_k\}$ represents the independent hash functions used by the bloom filter, with each hash function having as output range values $\{1, \cdots, m\}$. Every element $x \in S$ is represented by having the bit $h_i(x) = 1$ for values of i ranging from 1 to k.

To check if an item y is present in set S then all $h_i(y)$ should have the value 1. If this is not the case then it is possible to assure that $y \notin S$. If the contrary happens, $h_i(y) = 1$ for all values of $\{i : 1 < i < k\}$, then either it is a false positive or it is a true positive. A false positive is a situation where the element is not on the set although the bloom filter indicates that it is. A true positive always informs that the element is present in the set.

In order to exemplify an instance of this data structure, Figure 1 presents a bloom filter with $m = 8$ and the set of $k = 3$ hash functions being $H1$, $H2$ and $H3$. In the example we insert two different objects, obj_A and obj_B. In the case of obj_A the result of hashing its identifier is 7 for $H1$, 3 for $H2$ and 2 for $H3$, and thus insertion of obj_A in the bloom filter is achieved by setting the bits 7, 3 and 2. To query if obj_A is present in the bloom filter one just has to check if bits 7, 3, and 2 are all set. For obj_B the result is 5 for $H1$, 0 for $H2$ and 3 for $H3$. To insert obj_B the same operation is performed, but in this case there was a bit collision, as bit 3 was already set by the insertion of obj_A. If we lookup an hypothetical obj_X which has as a result of the group of hashes the values 7, 5 and 4, then the return of the lookup would be true although obj_X was not present in the filter. This is known as a false positive and is caused by the insertion of the previous objects.

3   Heat Routing Protocol for Ad-Hoc Networks

3.1   Time Aware Bloom Filter

The HRAN routing protocol requires the extension of the concept of bloom filter in order to check if a set of bits present in the structure was updated recently. In order to achieve this functionality, we propose a new type of bloom filter, the *Time Aware Bloom* (TAB) filter. This new structure maintains the property which states that false positives may occur but enables the removal of items which have not been updated during a predefined time period.

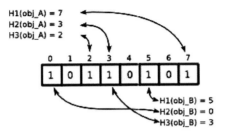

Fig. 1. A Bloom Filter Example

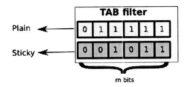

Fig. 2. Time Aware Bloom Filter

The TAB filter is a tuple of two bloom filters, sharing the same size n and the group of k hash functions. These structures are named the *sticky* and *plain* filter and are depicted in Figure 2. The *sticky* filter is used to identify whether a bit was updated in the last δ time interval or not, whilst the *plain* bloom filter contains the bits present in the current plain filter plus the bits set to one in the previous δ time interval.

To add a new element in the TAB filter, the algorithm performs the default bloom filter operation on the *plain* and *sticky* filters. This consists on hashing the inserted element with the k hash functions group in order to get the k corresponding array positions. The bit array positions are then set to 1 on both filters.

To search if an element is in the TAB filter, a query is made only on the *plain* bloom filter. Once again this operation is similar to the default bloom filter lookup function. The element value is hashed by the group of hash functions and the respective bits are checked. If all respective bits are set to value 1 the TAB filter returns a positive value indicating the element is present in the structure.

Finally, at regular δ time intervals, the *plain* filter is erased and its content is then overwritten by the *sticky* bloom filter bit array. After this operation is completed all the *sticky* filter positions are reset to 0 value in order to indicate a new δ time interval.

3.2 HRAN Protocol Description

Conceptually, the HRAN protocol execution is divided into three stages, each one serving a different purpose. This first stage is named heat overlay construction and consists in each node spreading heat information to neighbour nodes. Closer nodes are represented using a stronger heat index than nodes which are farther away. When a node spreads its heat it also spreads the heat it had received from neighbour nodes. This mechanism enables the diffusion of topology information using few control messages. The second stage is named route discovery and is reactive part of the protocol which is activated whenever a node wishes to establish a new route to a destination. The route request message travels the network being guided, where possible by the previously constructed heat overlay. When it does not find any heat information regarding the destination, it acts as a random walk query. Random walks are very easy to implement, but usually lead to non-optimal paths. In order to solve this problem HRAN uses an additional mechanism which shortens unnecessary long routes iteratively. The last stage is designated as route maintenance. This stage serves to the repair broken routes with little overhead, iteratively optimizes active routes in terms of hop numbers, and finally helps to construct heat tunnels useful for guiding future queries which share the same destination.

Overlay Construction. During the overlay construction stage each node spreads its topology information to the neighbour nodes using a pro-active approach. Each node stores the knowledge it has of the network topology through an array of N TAB filters which is designated as E vector. N is a static configuration parameter that represents the level of heat gradients of the heat overlay. Node ids present in E vector index position's closer to 1 are "hotter" than those closer to index N.

In Figure 3a we present an E vector capable of representing three heat gradient levels ($N = 3$), having each tab filter two bloom filter of 8 bits size each. Figure 3b shows the heat overlay of node D on a network where nodes in darker colours layers have node D's identifier in lower index positions than nodes present in brighter layers. Nodes not inside a layer do not have node's D identifier in any layer.

The construction of the heat overlay, mapping the network topology, is created by each node sending HELLO messages at regular time intervals. Each one of these messages contains a vector with $N - 1$ bloom filters because a node does not transmit the bloom filter for colder gradient it knows (index N). The bloom

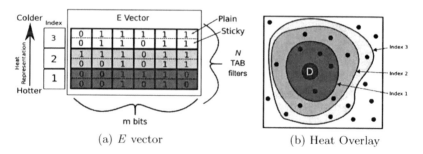

(a) E vector   (b) Heat Overlay

Fig. 3. Overlay construction stage

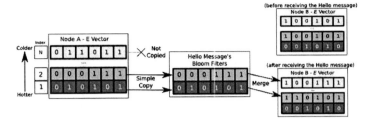

Fig. 4. Hello message exchange between neighbour nodes (for simplicity only plain bloom filters are shown)

filters contained in the HELLO message are a copy of the *plain* filters present at the TAB filters at the sending node's E vector from position 1 to position $N-1$.

When a node receives a HELLO message a bitwise OR operation between the bloom filters present in the messages and its E vector is performed. The iterator in the E vector starts at position 2 while the index that iterates over the array in the message starts at position 1. This operation, presented on Figure 4, is done in order to create heat gradients where information of nodes which are further away is inserted in the colder index positions of the E vector.

Route Discovery. The second stage of the HRAN routing protocol is named route discovery. This stage is responsible for discovering a valid route from the source to the desired destination.

When a source node requests a route to an unknown destination, it initiates a predetermined number of *random walk request* queries (RwREQ) which travels through the network as is shown on Figure 5a. Upon receiving a RwREQ, the node analyses its E vector and checks if it contains the destination node's identification in any one of the *layers*. If this is not the case, the random walk continues to a next neighbour node chosen randomly. If a match is found, the random walk ends and a directed walk is started by sending a *follow heat* (Fo-HEAT) message with the index of the current heat level. FoHEAT messages, as shown on Figure 5b, are only forwarded by nodes that have the destination node identifier in a E vector positions which is hotter than the current heat level passed by the FoHEAT message.

The route discovery mechanism enables the query to rapidly reach the destination with few messages exchanged because only nodes with information of the destination node's heat rebroadcast the query. Nodes do not send twice the same message, as each FoHEAT message contains a unique identifier composed by the route requester id and a sequence number. This way a FoHEAT message is not transmitted if a node has already delivered a message with the same identifier.

Once the FoHEAT query reaches the destination node, the route is given by the list of nodes present in the path log of the message. At this moment the protocols enters in the *go back mode* and the destination sends a *route reply* (RoREP) to the source using the inverted route discovered. This is shown

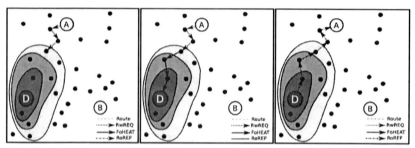

(a) Random Walk Mode (b) Directed Walk Mode   (c) Go Back Mode

Fig. 5. Route Discovery Process

on figure 5c. If the source node, after sending its RwREQ message receives no answer for a predefined amount of time, it falls backs to a reactive source routing protocol (like DSR). This backup procedure is performed in order to ensure the creation of heat tunnels which following queries will be able to use for reaching the same destination. Heat tunnel formation will be explained in the next stage.

Route Maintenance. Route maintenance stage includes three different tasks: heat tunnel creation, route repair and route improvement. The first one aims at creating and maintaining an heat tunnel when a route is being used to transfer data packets. This process helps future route discoveries to quickly find the destination node and supports the route repair stage. Finally, route improvement allows the HRAN protocol to iteratively improve a route as it is being used.

Heat tunnel creation. When a data packet is routed by an intermediate node, a heat tunnel is created or updated with the identifier of the destination. This is accomplished by inserting the destination nodes unique identifier in the respective E vector of the intermediate nodes at position number 0. This operation maintains heat tunnels information on the TAB filters for routes which are actively being used. Inactive routes dissipate with time as their respective heat tunnels information is not updated on the TAB filters.

An example of an heat tunnel formed around the route from node A to node D is shown on Figure 6a, in which nodes in the different shades of grey symbolise the respective amount of heat information regarding the destination. Nodes inside the darker colour layer have the destination identifier in its hotter E vector index position than those nodes on the more light grey layers. Nodes which are not inside a grey layer do not belong to the heat tunnel as they do not have the destination identifier inside their E vectors. Heat tunnels purpose is to help future route requests to quickly find a route to the destination, as is shown on Figure 6b.

Route Repair. When a route failure is detected by the origin endpoint of a communication, the previously created heat tunnel is used to help discover a

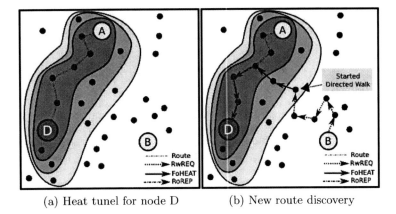

(a) Heat tunel for node D   (b) New route discovery

Fig. 6. Heat tunnel creation

new valid route. To start this process a *route repair* (RoREPAIR) message with the value of $i = 2$ is broadcasted to all the source node's neighbours. If node receives this message and has the destination indentifier in one of its E vector index positions which are lower or equal to i then it rebroadcasts the RoREPAIR message. When the destination receives a RoREPAIR message, it sends a RoREP message to the source using the inverted route discovered. If the source does not receive a RoREP message during a predetermined time period, it performs the same operation, increasing the value of i. This is repeated until i value surpasses the value of E array positions $(i > N - 1)$, at which time the source node considers the route to be irreparable and falls back to the normal route discovery mechanism described earlier in order to find the new route. Through this procedure, route repairs are achieved by incrementally flooding the various levels of the heat tunnel.

Figure 7 shows the route repair procedure on a network, starting at the route fail instant and ending when the new route is discovered.

Route Improvement. Due to the random process of route discovery, in the HRAN protocol it is not guaranteed that discovered routes are the best paths in terms of number of hops. To improve the routes HRAN uses a process which enables the iterative and gradual approximation of the discovered routes to the optimal ones. Also, as nodes move there is the possibility that a potential better route between the source and the destination is created.

HRAN's route improvement process uses the heat tunnel described previously to discover new and faster routes. When a route is being used, HRAN keeps a counter of the number of packets sent by the source node and when a threshold value is reached the source node sends a *route improvement* (RoIMP) message containing the destination ID. Each node which receives this message and has in its E vector the destination, rebroadcasts it. This process happens recursively until the destination node receives the RoIMP message. When this happens a

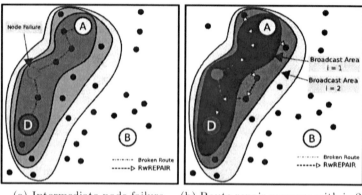

(a) Intermediate node failure   (b) Route repair message with i=2;

Fig. 7. Route Repair process

RoREP message is transmitted through the inverse path. The source node then uses the path reported by RoREP as the new route. By using this mechanism RoIMP messages are only broadcasted inside the heat tunnel. Route improvement can therefore occur using a limited number of transmitted messages and only impacting nodes which are close to the path between the source and the destination. Similarly to FoHEAT messages, RoIMP messages contain an unique identifier in order to prevent messages from being sent twice by the same node.

4   Simulation Results

We used the Qualnet version 5.0 software, due to its ability of simulating MANETs and the relatively large number of routing protocols it includes.

HRAN was implemented in Qualnet in order to be compared with some of the most representative and studied MANET's routing protocols. Several parameters of HRAN protocol were tuned and configured as follows: each bloom filter was configured with a size of $m = 128bits$ and three hashing functions; and the E vector had $N = 3$ heat gradients. HELLO packets were generated each 8s, with a jitter of 800ms to reduce HELLO message collisions.

4.1   Routing Protocol Comparison

To assess the scalability of HRAN protocol we used small, medium and large networks, in which we vary the number of nodes. The coverage area for all maps was $400m^2$ with nodes distributed at random places. The small size network had 50 nodes, the medium network had 100 nodes and the large network had 200 nodes. In all cases, nodes are randomly disposed on a square map and pairs of source/destination were randomly selected, representing 30% of the network nodes.

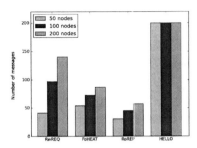

Fig. 8. HRAN messages

CBR/UDP traffic was used in all the simulations, generating data packets of 512 Bytes, at a rate of 2 packets/s. As we want to assess the behaviour of the routing protocols, the MANET must operates in proper conditions without collisions that lead to unwanted packet losses. Thus, a small data generation packet was used.

Figure 8 presents the amount of messages of each type sent by the HRAN protocol when new routes are established. As it is possible to notice the proactive facet, represented by the number of sent HELLO messages, is independent of the network size. The remaining messages types, which are sent only when a new route is requested, seize the heat overlay which was previously spread. This algorithm allows a small number of sent messages even as network size increases.

In the following tests we compared HRAN with three other routing protocols: the reactive protocol AODV, the proactive routing protocol OLSR; and the hybrid protocol ZRP. The overhead was measured as depicted in Eq 1. The results are depicted on Figure 9a.

$$r = \frac{\text{control packets}}{\text{data packets}} \tag{1}$$

As state in the figure, all protocol present a significant overhead, as the amount of data traffic is significantly low (2 packets/s). HRAN outperforms both OLSR and ZRP in all cases and AODV for the large network case. Thus, the reactive nature of this protocol does not seems to be good enough to maintain the overhead results when the network size increases. This results are caused by the small size and reduced number of messages used by HRAN to spread routing information.

Finally, Figure 9b shows the performance of four simulated protocols in terms of the time required to discover new routes to destinations. When analysing this metric we notice that the reactive nature of AODV does not allow it to quickly find new paths. By the contrary, HRAN is able to provide new routes in lower times due to the use of bloom filter to store topology information which effectively guides routing queries to reach the destination.

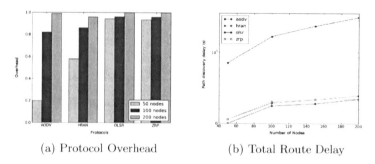

(a) Protocol Overhead   (b) Total Route Delay

Fig. 9. Protocols Comparison

5   Conclusion

This paper proposes a novel hybrid routing protocol specifically designed for large scale MANET that relies on the concept of heat tunnels to discover and maintain active routes. The HRAN protocol spreads topology information across the various nodes by using bloom filters. These special structures are small in size and capable of storing a large number of binary information. As the proposed algorithm requires the removal of values from these structures if they are not updated during a certain time, the *time aware bloom* (TAB) filter structure was developed.

The simulation results demonstrated a case scenario where the HRAN protocol considerably reduced the number of routing messages necessary to find a route, whilst keeping the time to discover new routes acceptable and the number of hops almost optimum. As future work we intend to dynamically adjust HRAN parameters and to improve the random walk performance without introducing significant complexity in the protocol. Also new mechanisms which enable a trade-off between the number transmitted messages inside a heat tunnel and route discovery effectiveness will be studied.

References

1. Jayakumar, G., Gopinath, G.: Ad hoc mobile wireless networks routing protocols - a review. Journal of Computer Science 3, 574–582 (2007)
2. Junhai, L., Danxia, Y., Liu, X., Mingyu, F.: A survey of multicast routing protocols for mobile ad-hoc networks. IEEE Communications Surveys & Tutorials 11, 78–91 (2009)
3. Mauve, M., Widmer, J., Hartenstein, H.: A survey on position-based routing in mobile ad-hoc networks. IEEE Network 15, 30–39 (2001)
4. Wu Chin, K., Judge, J., Williams, A., Kermode, R.: Implementation experience with manet routing protocols. ACM SIGCOMM Computer Communications Review 32, 49–59 (2002)

5. Mohseni, S., Hassan, R., Patel, A., Razali, R.: Comparative review study of reactive and proactive routing protocols in manets. In: 2010 4th IEEE International Conference on Digital Ecosystems and Technologies (DEST), pp. 304–309 (2010)
6. Wang, Y., Dong, L., Liang, T., Yang, X., Zhang, D.: Cluster based location-aided routing protocol for large scale mobile ad hoc networks. IEICE Transactions 92-D, 1103–1124 (2009)
7. Boukerche, A.: Performance evaluation of routing protocols for ad hoc wireless networks. Mob. Netw. Appl. 9, 333–342 (2004)
8. Karp, B., Kung, H.: Gpsr: Greedy perimeter stateless routing for wireless networks. In: Annual International Conference on Mobile Computing and Networking (Mobicom), pp. 243–254. ACM, New York (2000)
9. Broder, A., Mitzenmacher, M.: Network applications of bloom filters: A survey. Internet Mathematics 1, 485–509 (2005)
10. Gilbert, R., Johnson, K., Wu, S., Zhao, B.Y., Zheng, H.: Location independent compact routing for wireless networks. In: Proceedings of the 1st international workshop on Decentralized resource sharing in mobile computing and networking, MobiShare 2006, New York, NY (2006)
11. Bloom, B.H.: Space/time trade-offs in hash coding with allowable errors. Communications of the ACM 13, 422–426 (1970)

Fairness and Satisfaction Model for DTN Applications Using Various Transportation Means

Mohammed Al-Siyabi, Haitham Cruickshank, Zhili Sun, and Godwin Ansa

Centre for Communication Systems Research
University of Surrey
Guildford, UK
{m.alsiyabi,h.cruickshank,z.sun,g.ansa}@surrey.ac.uk

Abstract. Delay Tolerant Network suffers from lack of resources and disconnected contact nature. In DTN, all possible methods are used to transmit data including the physical transportations means. Aircrafts in commercial routes have been proposed to carry data from ground users along their flying routes. Delivery probability is compared when using aircrafts, buses and ferries. Results show that aircrafts provide higher delivery probability which is up to 62% better compared with buses and ferries. Furthermore, when there is lack of resources, it is difficult to satisfy all users' demands for traffic. We propose a Fairness and Satisfaction (FS) model to enhance the users' satisfaction during DTN limited and scarce resources. Various scenarios are tested for the FS model through intense simulations. FS model, when implemented, will improve user's satisfaction up to 18 % and DTN fairness up to 20 % compared with the same scenario lacking the model.

Keywords: Delay Tolerant Network (DTN), Quality of service (QoS), Aircraft and User's Satisfaction.

1 Introduction

Delay tolerant networks work in the environment of limited communication infrastructures where links are disconnected and might not be available for a long time. In addition to using the standard transmission medium in these challenged conditions, transportation means have been used in DTN literature to carry data for DTN applications. Buses, ferries, bicycles, motorbikes and trains have been proposed for DTN[1][2][3][4], sometime by physically transporting the saved data on a storage medium such as USP memory or by wirelessly exchanging data, whenever a transportation vehicle comes in range with the users. We have proposed using aircrafts in commercial routes [5] because they have larger coverage area and fly over remote areas where communication infrastructure is limited. In this paper, we will set a scenario and compare between using buses, ferries and aircrafts. The results show that using aircrafts will provide better delivery probabilities and more user satisfaction. This is mainly because all requesting users are in range with the flying aircraft at most of the time due to the flying high altitude whereas this is not the case with buses and ferries.

X. Masip-Bruin et al. (Eds.): WWIC 2011, LNCS 6649, pp. 446–457, 2011.
© IFIP International Federation for Information Processing 2011

Furthermore, these transportation means are considered as contacts and represent the main resources in DTN. The more number of vehicles will mean more opportunities to send data and therefore more resources. However, these resources are normally scarce and limited in DTN which might degrade its ability to satisfy all users' requests of traffic. The users will compete with each other to get access to the passing contact and this will lead to congestion. Whenever a contact exists, all users will try to get access to it in order to transmit their data but unfortunately not all of them will be able to send theirs due to the contact limited capacity and numbers. However, after another wait, another contact might arrive, where the same competition will be repeated among users and again not all of them will be able to send their data. Therefore, there is a need for a system that should try to improve each and every user chances of getting access to the contact resources especially during severe shortage of resources. The system should be fair to allocate the resources equally among the users and give a chance to as many users as possible to send their data.

Throughout this paper, we will show the improvement in the level of user satisfaction when applying the FS model compared with the same scenario lacking our model. FS model will be applied to aircrafts, buses and ferries which act as intermediate node/gateway to help it decide fairly which user to select. This decision will be used by other vehicles to ensure that they satisfy as many users as possible.

2 Related Work

DTN has increasingly become a hot research topic and the IRTF DTNRG [6] is leading the effort to expand the research of DTN in various topics. In DTN literature, many transportations means are used to carry data for DTN applications. We proposed using an aircraft as a DTN carrier at remote locations [5]. At UMass Amherst [2], they used public buses travelling on scheduled routes to exchange data using Wi-Fi nodes in a project called Diesel Net. Ref [3] proposed using ferries and suggested that the users could schedule their movement to match the ferries movements in order to send their data. We will compare between these three types of transportations in DTN environment in the coming sections.

However, there are limited references that discuss the user satisfaction in DTN. Ref [7] proposed a data delivery method for DTN for various users based on the relative importance of their data requests, which is something like the users class of service CoS classification in DTN. They proposed a carry-and-forward technique to enhance the overall user satisfactions and achieved better users satisfactions compared with the conventional first in first out FIFO method. Our FS model will also consider the class of service CoS of the user, but furthermore, it will consider other metrics such as the history of users previous admissions as we shall see later in the model discussion.

Furthermore, many references in the literature discuss the resources management in DTN but each one is targeting a certain resource. Some of them discuss how to save the buffer resources which is important for some DTN applications like the sensors network. The concept of message ferrying is proposed in [8] where they proposed allocating the buffer resources between users at different connections sessions. In our aircraft application, we assume unlimited buffer space and we consider the aircraft communication bandwidth as the only resource. The bandwidth will increase with the longer time the aircraft stay in line of sight contact with the ground users. Also, more aircrafts will mean more contacts and therefore more resources. Ref [9] also discusses the resource management using adaptive optimal buffer management scheme for various message sizes. It implements a dropping policy to enhance the delivery rate and reduce the delivery delay. Our FS model will decide which users to accept by managing the bandwidth resource of the aircraft.

Many references of DTN resource management are in the form of new routing algorithms while our model is a complementary mechanism applied to the routing algorithms. The Probabilistic Routing Protocol using History of Encounters and Transitivity (PRoPHET) [10] eliminates the production of replications based on history encounters in order to enhance the resource utilizations. Flooding is used in Epidemic routing [11] where the nodes replicate and transmit the bundles to all other nodes which do not have a copy of those bundles and this replication consumes many of the network resources. Spray & Wait routing algorithm [12] sprays a number of copies into the network and waits for at least one of these messages to arrive at destination. The prioritizations concept is implemented in MaxProp [13] and is based on scheduled transmitted and dropped packets where the historical data of past meetings is used to decide the possibility of future meetings. MaxProb routing will be used in our scenario because it the best routing algorithms among the other three to provides better performance.

FS model can be applied to any DTN routing algorithm and we argue that it can provide extra improvements in the performance as we shall see in the coming sections.

3   Fairness and Satisfaction Model Concept

Routing can be considered as a data push operation where each node tries to forward its data bundles to other nodes through various routes, which ensures faster and optimum performance of data delivery from a source to a destination. In the case of DTN, the process will be a store and forward one because the next nodes might not be available for some time. On the other hand, FS model can be considered as a data pull operation where the node decides which one to admit first and which to reject, from a group of interested transmitting nodes.

As shown in Fig.1, which shows pull/push concept, there are 5 users (1 to 5 at area X) who want to send/receive data from/to 5 other users (6-10 at area Y). There are 2 aircrafts (AA and CC) in direct contact with the users while 2 other aircrafts (BB and DD) acting as intermediate nodes. The aircrafts are considered mobile intermediate routers/gateways for the users. FS model is applied at those aircrafts that while receiving the data, they can apply the model to select which to accept among the interested users. This is considered as a pull operation. Now the aircraft wants to forward the data using the routing algorithm to the next contact. This is considered a push operation. For example, aircraft AA applies the pull concept (FS model) from users 1,2,3,4 and 5, while it applies the push concept (Routing) to forward it to intermediate aircrafts BB and DD.

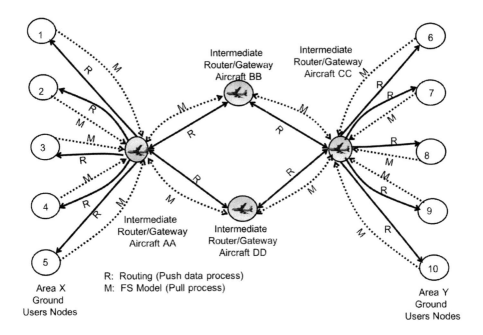

Fig. 1. Push/Pull concept of the FS model

FS model will apply fairness during the selection process and for that we will use Jains fairness index [14] to evaluate the model performance. Jains index will evaluate the fairness of distributed resources for a group of users competing for a common bottleneck channel at a particular time.

3.1 FS Model Design

FS model is working based on collecting feedback administration metrics data from all users of their class of service CoS, Time of their request, number of past acceptances and number of past rejections. FS model will assign a weight value for each metric and decide which user to admit first based on the highest metrics weight. Each contact will use the latest feedback administration data for his decision and these data will be updated after each contact session. The model will allocate the whole bandwidth to users one after another and will not distribute it among users. During scarce resources, if the contact carries a fragment from all users, it might end up - in the worst cases- that none of them is able to process his data because they all haven't received all their fragments. Therefore, FS model is providing fair and better resources allocation using this concept which is more useful at scarce resources only.

3.2 QoS Contact-to-Contact /End-to-End

There are requirements to provide end-to-end QoS and hop-to-hop QoS in traditional networks. However, in DTN the links are not guaranteed and the next hop arrival might not be known and there might be other local hops for the node within its area.

Therefore, providing this concept might be difficult and impractical in DTN environments. Instead, we think the QoS in DTN disconnected environment should be provided per contacts because it is the main resource. Whenever a contact becomes available, it will implement the QoS requirements through collaborations with other contacts by referring to the past data recovered from the nodes. This way, providing the QoS contact-to-contact in DTN is more visible and this can be illustrated in Fig. 1 as users 1 to 5 and aircraft AA or users 6-10 and aircraft CC. Furthermore, end-to-end QoS can be provided based on the performance of the routing algorithms and the availability of contacts and this can be illustrated in Fig. 1 as users 1 to 5 and users 6-10 exchanging data using intermediate aircrafts AA, BB, CC and DD.

We will have two sets of results. The first is contact-to-contact which considers the average results of all contacts applying the model within a group of users' nodes and a particular contact. This set will evaluate the FS model performance results with respect to the satisfied users and fairness. The second set of results will be based on the end-to-end satisfied users and fairness from source to destination. It might consider multiple contacts and the routing algorithms among nodes and contacts.

4   Simulation Results

We will evaluate the performance of using aircrafts compared with using buses and ferries. Furthermore, we will evaluate the performance of FS model.

4.1   Simulation Scenario

The scenario assumes three remote locations, A, B and C where each area has a group of users. These locations have limited communication infrastructure and they use all types of available links including the transportation means of buses, ferries and aircrafts. As shown in Fig. 2, the areas are at the shore of a big lake where buses, aircrafts and ferries operate between the three locations. Whenever any of the vehicles (bus or aircraft or ferry) approaches the area, the ground user will try to send their data to the passing vehicle which in turn will deliver it to the next area and take other data to another area and so on.

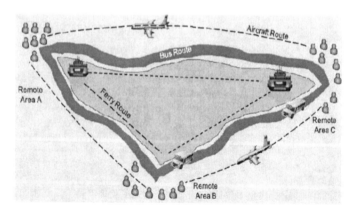

Fig. 2. FS Model Senario

4.2 Simulation Configuration

We have used Opportunistic Networking Environment (ONE) simulator [15] which is a DTN simulator platform for testing the routing and applications protocols. FS model is configured in ONE simulator and the cluster movement model is used for the model scenario as shown in Fig. 3 which illustrates the simulator GUI. The scenario assumed three locations, i.e. A, B and C, which appears in Fig.3 as the group of dotes. The transportation vehicle, which appears in Fig.3 as the circle in route between the clusters locations, is moving between them and collecting data from ground user nodes to send them to other nodes in another area. Every time the vehicle passes by cluster nodes, the decisions of which nodes are selected or rejected will be updated and used by the next vehicle to enable it to take acceptance decision and so on until all vehicles pass throughout the set simulation time.

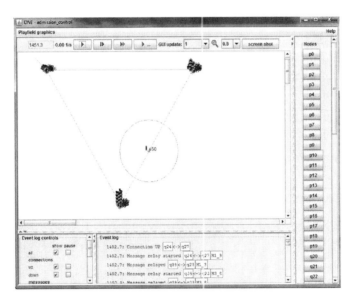

Fig. 3. Scenarios configurations in ONE simulator

Simulation time is in seconds and it is assumed that a full day of 24 hrs is equivalent to 5000 seconds simulation time. 24 hrs is chosen because the transportation means normally have daily schedules of their journeys routes which will be repeated every day. All users and vehicles have equal data rate and ground users create and try to send messages only when the vehicle contact is their LOS range. It is also assumed that all transportation means are in continuous movements in their routes for the whole day and they only stop at the end of the day.

All scenarios are run for 5000 seconds which represent 24 hrs in the scenario time. The scenarios are set for 20 users distributed randomly per location and 2 vehicles for each transportation type. Table 1 shows the setting of the various transportations means. Different vehicle speeds are used where the aircraft is the highest of 900 km/hr and the ferry is the lowest with 60 km/hr. Transportations vehicles are set to stop and wait at each cluster, i.e. the duration time they are in LOS with the ground users. Aircrafts have longer wait time because they fly at high altitude of around 11000 m; therefore, they will have longer contact time and larger coverage range. Each real value will have an equivalent simulator value based on the assumption that 24 hr is equal to 5000 seconds. The performance metric is the delivery probability, user's satisfactions, average processing delay and the fairness. It will be used to evaluate the performance of FS model for various scenarios.

Table 1. Simulator ONE settings

Transportation Mean	Bus	Aircra ft	Ferry
Max Real Speed (Km/hr)	120	900	60 (32.4 knot)
Equivalent Simulation speed (m/s)	33.3	250	16.6
Real Wait Time (min)	5	30	10
Equivalent Simulation Wait Time (s)	17.35	104.1	34.7
Range Km	5	100	5

4.3 Simulation Results

The simulator is run for various simulation times. From 1000 to 5000 seconds and the results are obtained as follows:

4.3.1 Transportation Means Comparison

Fig. 4 shows the obtained delivery probability results for a scenario of 2 vehicles and 20 users per location when FS model is enabled. The delivery probability is the overall delivered messages out of the generated one regardless of the users. It shows that aircrafts have higher delivery probability between 85-95 % compared with buses and ferries whose values range between 20 to 30%. Overall, aircrafts are having up to 62 % improvements over buses and ferries. This is due to that all users are within the aircraft range; therefore, all have better opportunities to send their data. On the other hand, buses and ferries have smaller range because they are at ground level; therefore, not all the users are in their range. Furthermore, the wait time i.e. contact LOS, is larger with the aircrafts because they are at high altitude and therefore can stay longer time over the ground users to enable them to send more data, while the buses and ferries are staying shorter time and they become out of range. This shows the potential of using aircrafts in this special situation and its usefulness at remote locations.

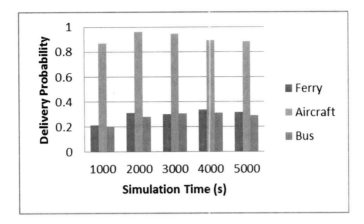

Fig. 4. Delivery probabilty of various transportation means

4.3.2 FS Model Comparison

The previous section compared the results of aircrafts with ferries and buses when FS model is implemented. However, in this section we will compare the results between the three transportation means with and without FS model.

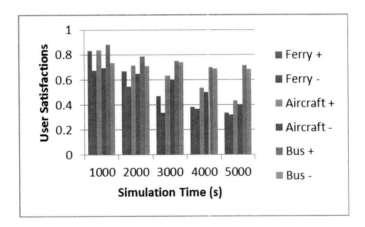

Fig. 5. Contact-to-contact users satisfactions

4.3.2.1. Contact-to-Contact Results. The first set of results is between the ground users and the approaching contacts. The results are obtained for users' satisfaction within contacts. It does not consider the end-to-end routing of data or delivering the data to its final destination. All it considers is the transfer of the user's messages to the passing contact. Users satisfactions is a measure of how many users successfully delivered all their generated messages out of the overall available users. Fig. 5 shows user satisfaction improvements in applying FS model compared with the lack of it for the three transportation means which varies between 2- 18%. Transportation type has no major impact on the model results because the outcome will mainly depend on how long the contact is available for the ground users. As mentioned earlier, messages are generated during contact time only. Therefore, buses have the best user satisfaction because they have the shortest wait time and therefore have less number of generated messages per user, which increases the user's chances of acceptance. Aircrafts have the second best user satisfaction level because they have the highest speed which means more wait time occasions for the ground users.

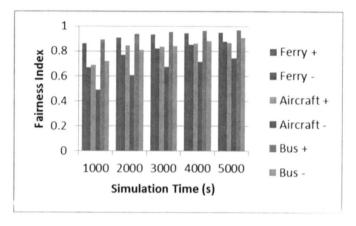

Fig. 6. Contact-to-contact fairness index

Fig. 6 shows Jains fairness index results for allocation of the available resources. The results show improvements in the fairness between 5-20 % compared with the lacking of FS model. Buses and ferries have better fairness results because their users generated fewer messages during the same simulation time compared with aircrafts. However, FS model provides fairness improvements regardless of the transportation means used.

4.3.2.2.   End-to-End Results. The second set of results applies for the end-to-end concept which utilizes the routing to deliver messages to their final destinations. MaxProp [13] DTN routing is used to route the messages for the three transportation means. The obtained results in contact-to-contact section are relatively close to each other between the three transportation means. However, it is not the case with the end-to-end results which indicates a very high priority for using aircrafts compared with buses and ferries.

Fig. 7 shows the user's satisfaction of aircrafts reaching up to 90 % and improvement varies between 5-18 % compared with the lack of FS model. The improvements are higher at the early runs of simulation. On the other hand, buses and ferries have very limited user satisfaction, less than 10 %. These results come to an agreement with the results of the overall delivery probability shown in Fig. 4, but the difference is that Fig. 7 results are per users who delivered all their messages, while Fig. 4 is per overall generated messages regardless of who generated them. Aircrafts have provided higher users satisfactions due to their large coverage which can reach all users, while this is not always the case with buses and ferries. Furthermore, applying FS model has improved this satisfaction by providing better allocations of resources for more users.

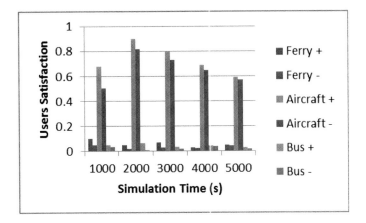

Fig. 7. End-to-end users satisfactions

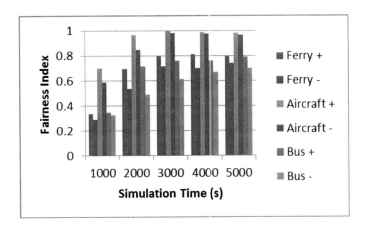

Fig. 8. End-to-end fairness index

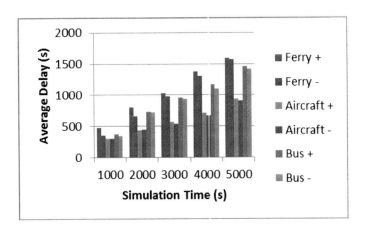

Fig. 9. End-to-end average processing delay

Fig. 8 shows the improvments in end-to-end fairness index for the various transportation means and FS model has improved the fairness for the end-to-end also by 5-18 % compared with the lack of it.

On the other hand, there is a small drawback for the model represented in the slight increase in the processing average delay which is the average time in seconds between message creation and delivery. Applying FS model will sometimes cause the delay to increase between 0 second in the best cases to 100 second in the worst case. Aircrafts have the smallest amount of delay due to their high speed and therefore will mean quicker delivery time and hence less processing time. It is not a very critical increase, and DTN is delay tolerant and hence the extra delay is considered insignificant.

5   Conclusions and Future Work

Various transportation means have been proposed for carrying DTN data due to the scarce and limited resources of its environments. Aircrafts in commercial routes are compared with buses and ferries. The simulation results showed higher delivery probability for using aircrafts due to their large coverage range. Furthermore, FS model is proposed to allocate the resources among users in DTN conditions. The model showed improvements in user's satisfactions and better fairness compared with the same scenario lacking the model. However, FS model will sometimes cause a slight increase in the average processing delay which is not very significant in DTN situation.

As part of our future work, we will implement the aircraft concept together with the FS model in various and more complicated scenarios for a larger number of vehicles and users to analyze its performance.

References

1. Farrell, S., Cahill, V.: Delay-and Disruption- Tolerant Networking, ch. 3, p. 65. Artech House, London (2006)
2. Zhang, X., Kurose, J., Levine, B.N., Towsley, D., Zhang, H.: Study of a bus-based disruption-tolerant network: mobility modeling and impact on routing. In: Proceedings of the 13th annual ACM international conference on Mobile computing and networking, pp. 195–206 (2007)
3. Zhao, W., Ammar, M., Zegura, E.: A message ferrying approach for data delivery in sparse mobile ad hoc networks. In: Proceedings of the 5th ACM international symposium on Mobile ad hoc networking and computing, pp. 187–198 (2004)
4. Jain, S., Fall, K., Patra, R.: Routing in a delay tolerant network. In: Proceedings of the 2004 conference on Applications, technologies, architectures, and protocols for computer communications, pp. 145–158 (2004)
5. Al-Siyabi, M. A., Cruickshank, H., Sun, Z.: Delay/Disruption Tolerant Network Architecture for Aircraft Datalink on Scheduled Routes. Presented at the PSAT10, Rome, Italy, PSA 10 (2010)
6. Home - Delay Tolerant Networking Research Group, http://www.dtnrg.org/wiki (accessed: January 20, 2011)
7. Ishimaru, Y., Sun, W., Yasumoto, K., Ito, M.: DTN-based Delivery of Word-of-Mouth Information with Priority and Deadline. In: The Fifth International Conference on Mobile Computing and Ubiquitous Networking (ICMU 2010), April 26 (2010)

8. Li, Y., Qian, M., Jin, D., Su, L., Zeng, L.: Adaptive Optimal Buffer Management Policies for Realistic DTN. In: GLOBECOM 2009 - 2009 IEEE Global Telecommunications Conference, pp. 1–5 (2009)
9. Chuah, M., Ma, W.: Integrated Buffer and Route Management in a DTN with Message Ferry. In: MILCOM 2006, pp. 1–7 (2006)
10. Huang, T., Lee, C., Chen, L.: PRoPHET+: An Adaptive PRoPHET-Based Routing Protocol for Opportunistic Network. In: 2010 24th IEEE International Conference on Advanced Information Networking and Applications, pp. 112–119 (2010)
11. Vahdat, A., Becker, D.: Epidemic routing for partially connected ad hoc networks. Citeseer (2000)
12. Spyropoulos, T., Psounis, K., Raghavendra, C.S.: Spray and wait: an efficient routing scheme for intermittently connected mobile networks. In: Proceedings of the 2005 ACM SIGCOMM workshop on Delay-tolerant networking, pp. 252–259 (2005)
13. Burgess, J., Gallagher, B., Jensen, D., Levine, B.N.: Maxprop: Routing for vehicle-based disruption-tolerant networks. In: Proc. IEEE Infocom, vol. 6 (2006)
14. Jain, R., Chiu, D.M., Hawe, W.: A Quantitative Measure of Fairness and Discrimination for Resource Allocation in Shared Systems. DEC Research Report TR-301 (1984)
15. Keränen, A., Ott, J., Kärkkäinen, T.: The ONE simulator for DTN protocol evaluation. In: Proceedings of the 2nd International Conference on Simulation Tools and Techniques, pp. 1–10 (2009)

Fuzzy Redundancy Adaptation and Joint Source - Network Coding for VANET Video Streaming*

Alberto J. Gonzalez[2], Kayhan Zrar Ghafoor[1], Ramon Piney[2], Andre Rios[2], Jesus Alcober[2], and Kamalrulnizam Abu Bakar[1]

[1] Universiti Teknologi Malaysia,
Faculty of Computer Science and Information Systems,
81310 Skudai, Johor D.T, Malaysia
kayhan@ieee.org
[2] Technical University of Catalonia/I2cat Foundation,
Department of Telematic Engineering,
08860 Esteve Terradas 7, Castelldefels, Spain
{alberto.jose.gonzalez,ramon.piney,andre.rios,jesus.alcober}@upc.edu

Abstract. Video communication VANETs has many applications, such as emergency video transmission or inter-vehicle entertainment. However, delivering video to high mobile vehicles faces challenges such as packet loss due to intermittent connectivity and channel variations. Thus, designing a reliable approach for video streaming over such harsh scenarios is needed. Hence, we propose a reliable approach based on random practical network coding and source coding. This approach integrates the benefits of network coding with Multiple Description Coding to achieve robust streaming over VANET. Furthermore, we propose a redundancy controller based on fuzzy inference system to adjust the amount of redundant packets based on vehicular traffic density and SNR of the channel. Simulation shows the proposed approach achieves better protection against packet loss, application layer throughput and video quality.

Keywords: VANET, video streaming, network coding, Multiple Description Coding, fuzzy inference system.

1 Introduction

VANETs integrate ad hoc network and WLAN to achieve vehicle to vehicle communications. This inter-vehicle communication fosters the deployment of innovative wireless communication applications based on real time media streaming. These communications have several applications ranging from road safety to entertainment. Furthermore, IEEE 802.11 standard supports video communication over vehicular networks [1]. These networks deal with different traffic scenarios, such as during late night time, rush hour, dense and sparse traffic (e.g. in highways), which cause unstable vehicular network topology. Thus, the

---

* This work was supported by the i2CAT Foundation and the Spanish Government (MICINN) under research grant TIN2010-20136-C03.

X. Masip-Bruin et al. (Eds.): WWIC 2011, LNCS 6649, pp. 458–469, 2011.

communication link will last for a short time due to high mobility of vehicles and dynamic topology. On the other hand, the communication channel between vehicles are prone to packet loss due to high variations (low SNR) together with different forms of fading.

In video communication between vehicles, random and bursty errors may be frequent. One bit error may extend over several packets due to dependency among the frames of a compressed stream. These bursts of errors are accepted [2] as are more severe than random errors. One way of making reliable and robust video communication between vehicles is by using error resilient approaches like Network Coding (NC). In [3] showed that NC can provide robustness and high throughput in wired or wireless networks. The upshot of NC is encoding incoming packets at intermediate nodes. The receiver starts decoding once enough number of coded packets are received. However, a single packet loss can cause a generation of coded packets to be lost. Therefore, NC should be used with a proper error resilient approach for video streaming over VANET-like scenarios. In addition, NC has the potential to increase robustness against packet losses in wireless ad hoc networks [4]. The error resilient capability of NC depends on the number of encoded packets which are produced by intermediate nodes. The usefulness of this redundancy might be varied with vehicular network traffic conditions such as sparse and dense scenarios. In sparse scenarios, number of redundant packets should be increased appropriately to compensate packet losses while in dense scenarios it should be decreased to mitigate bandwidth overload. Thus, we can optimize the redundancy of NC considering vehicular traffic density. Redundancy also can be tuned with error rate of the communication channel. We propose a redundancy controller based on a fuzzy inference system [5], which can effectively adjust the amount of redundant packets to the desired target value.

Multiple Description Coding (MDC) encodes a video file into a number of different independent sub-streams. Thus, MDC can be used to reduce the effects of packet loss [6]. Unlike previous works, which not consider coded packet loss problem of NC, inefficiency of MDC and adjusting the NC redundancy with respect to vehicular traffic conditions and channel error rate variations, we propose fuzzy based NC redundancy control and combined random NC with MDC to achieve reliable video streaming over VANET.

This paper is organized as follows. Section 2 describes related work and details the proposed joint source-network coding. In section 3, we propose NC fuzzy controller based on fuzzy logic. The vehicles communication model is described in section 4. Video transmission end to end delay is investigated in section 5. A simulation setup and performance evaluations are highlighted in section 6. Finally, this paper ends with a conclusion in section 7.

2   Related Work

In recent years, several protocols, approaches and mechanisms are developed for vehicular networks. However, almost all of them deal with short message communication between vehicles. In [7], investigated an architecture for video streaming over VANET whereas no real video data are used in their simulation. In [8], two routing protocols are discussed: Source Based Forwarding (SBF) and Receiver Based Forwarding (RBF). They have used real video data to simulate video streaming over VANET. They also used different traffic conditions for forwarding data between vehicles.

In addition, the challenge of video streaming over VANET can be interpreted by the high channel errors in vehicular traffic conditions. The high packet loss and limited communication range of the vehicles incur frequent link disconnection and uneven network partition. Authors in [9] have combined data mulling technique with three strategies, NC, erasure coding, and repetition coding. Specially, vehicles in the opposite direction are exploited as data mules to relay multimedia data to other vehicles to overcome intermittent connectivity in sparse vehicular scenarios. However, the analysis of the delay for relaying multimedia data is based on mathematical model. Literature on fuzzy inference system exist in variety disciplines of wireless ad hoc networks. Some authors [10] have used entropy based fuzzy logic to construct the new metric-entropy and fuzzy controllers with the help of entropy metric to reduce the number of route reconstruction so as to provide QoS guarantee in the ad hoc networks. T. C Chiang et al. in [11] have introduced fuzzy Petri net agent to be implemented in each node to learn and to adjust itself to fit the dynamic conditions in a multicast ad hoc networks. In our fuzzy based redundancy controller, two metrics has been used to adjust the value of redundant packets.

2.1 Multiple Description Coding Approach

Video coding schemes such as MDC [12] or Scalable Video Coding (SVC) are used to enhance error resiliency. SVC divides the video file into layers referred to as base layer and enhancement layers. The base layer is the most important layer while the enhancement layers are referenced to the base layer. The enhancement layers can not reproduced independently to the base layer. In contrast to SVC, MDC splits (Figure 1) the video signal into multiple sub-streams where each of the sub-streams (descriptors) can be reproduced independently. The receiver can make a reconstruction of the video file when any of the sub-streams is received. The quality of the reconstructed video file is proportional to the number of descriptors received. Thus, the more descriptors are received, the better the perceived video quality. Therefore, MDC is preferable in extreme environments like VANET because it provides increased resilience to packet losses by multiple streams that can be decoded independently. The main parts of MDC system are the splitter and the merger. The splitter is implemented in the source vehicle. The first step of MDC encoder is the pre-processing of the video stream in order to obtain the different N descriptions at the video source, which can be coded and displayed independently. Next, each encoded descriptor is ready to be transmitted.

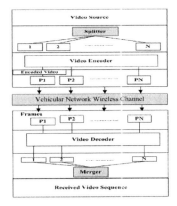

Fig. 1. MDC encoding and decoding system

2.2   Random Linear Network Coding Approach

This work proposes to use Random Linear Network Coding (RLNC). When NC is applied in the video source, the video packets are divided into generations with the same decoding deadline [13]. This approach regards each generation as a vector and applies linear combinations before transmitting the native packets. In more detail, let $N_1, N_2, N_3, , N_K$ K native packets are in a generation. The video source applies linear combination on these K native packets, the output is j coded packets which are referred to as $Y_1, Y_2, Y_3, \cdots, Y_j$, where $Y_j = \sum_{i=1}^{K} e_{i,j} N_{i,j}$ and $j = 1, 2, 3, \cdots, h$. The set of coefficients $e_{j,i} = (e_{j,1}, e_{j,2}, e_{j,3}, \cdots, e_{j,K}) \in GF(2^q)$ denotes the encoding vector which are randomly selected at the source node to encode the native packets.

Intermediate nodes collect the encoded packets of the specific generation, and then re-encode the stored packets. When an intermediate node has received u encoded packets of a given generation, then it will select a new brand of coefficients $\zeta_f = (\zeta_{f,1}, \zeta_{f,2}, \zeta_{f,3}, \cdots, \zeta_{f,u})$ from $GF(2q)$. Thus, the outgoing packets of intermediate nodes are $X_1, X_2, X_3, \cdots, X_k$, where $X_k = \sum_{i=1}^{u} zeta_{f,i} Y_i$. It is worth to observe that the new brand of coefficients with respect to the native packets is $\gamma_k = (\gamma_{k,1}, \gamma_{k,2}, \gamma_{k,3}, \cdots, \gamma_{k,j})$ where $\gamma_{k,f} = \sum_{i=1}^{u} e_{j,i} zeta_{f,i}$,then the intermediate nodes embed it in the header of outgoing re-encoded packets.

When the destination has received K coded packets, it first checks the linear independence of the coefficients in the header of the received coded packets. Next, it builds $K \times K$ matrix using the coded packets. The rows of the formed matrix are represents the coefficients of coded packets. Afterwards, it first computes the inverse of the coefficients matrix and then multiplies it with the received coded packets.

2.3   Proposed Joint Source Coding and Network Coding Approach

The wireless nodes are communicating based on TCP/IP including 802.11 MAC layer. In the protocol stack each protocol layer adds all necessary information to the incoming data. In application layer, the specific header is added whenever the data is passed to the next layer. The source and destination IP addresses and port numbers are added by network and transport layers respectively. These addresses ensure end to end delivery of the packet. In case of link disconnection the network layer drops the packet. On the other hand, MAC and physical layers deals with nearby host communications. Fast channel variation at physical layer will produce packet loss at other layers. Thus, in order to increase robustness of video streaming over VANET, the protocol stack should be modified by embedding coding approaches so that it can tackle packet losses. This can be achieved by joint source coding and NC for video streaming.

The overall block diagram of the proposed joint source-network coding is depicted in Figure 2. In our video streaming environment, a single video source transmits descriptions to a group of receivers over VANET. The MDC is applied for robust transmission over error- prone VANET. The MDC generates several descriptions which are independently decodable. These descriptions are passed down to the next protocol layers for end to end delivery. On the other hand, we implemented the RLNC between network and MAC layer running over an IEEE 802.11 MAC protocol. The reason of this embedding are: 1) processing at lower layers (physical and MAC layers) are faster than upper ones, 2) provide transparent NC operations to upper protocol layers. At the NC shim layer, each description is divided into numbers of generations, this division depends upon the size of generations and MDC descriptions. The outgoing coded packets are recognized by adding generation-ID and description-ID into its header. This information is useful for the receiver to merge generations and descriptions at

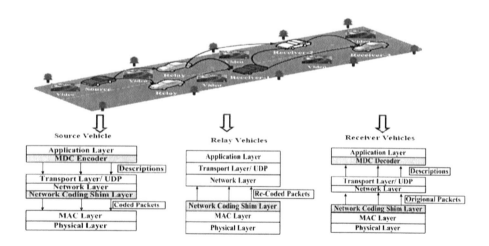

Fig. 2. Proposed joint source-network coding (dark blocks)

the NC and application layers respectively. If receivers collects enough linearly independent coded packets, the decoder part of NC can obtain original data belonging to that generation.

It is well known fact that there is a level of dependency among video frames; loss of one frame may cause other frames to be useless and undecodable. In other words, in certain network conditions a receiver may not decode the original packets which are belonging to the same generation, because it does not receive enough innovative packets based on its maximum flow capacity. In these network conditions, MDC can compensate the effect of coded packet loss by decoding the video, albeit with lower data rate. This is because one description is divided to multiple generations while in NC loss of one generation severely affect the whole video file due to tight correlation between generations to reproduce original video file. Therefore, the reliable approach is proposed to improve the video streaming service by reducing the multiple packet losses over VANET.

3   Proposed Fuzzy Logic Redundancy Control

We know that fuzzy logic simulates the interpretation of uncertain sensory information as sensed by human brain. The appropriate decision making of fuzzy inference system depends on the precise design of membership functions and fuzzy inference rules. However, in VANET the right decision making is difficult due to uncertain movement of vehicles and SNR value of the communication channel. Therefore, fuzzy inference system has been applied to control the amount of redundant packets for improving network load. Concretely, the first step of designing a fuzzy controller is to determine the impact of each input/output parameters and the range of values that each variable can have. The next step is to determine membership functions to the input and output parameters based on the defined range and to design a rule base for the fuzzy inference system. One main characteristic of the fuzzy controller is that it is modifiable. It is easy to tune rules, membership functions, value range or even change the system parameters to enhance its performance. Selection of the most relevant input variables is important. Furthermore, the fuzzy inference system consists of fuzzification , knowledge rule base and defuzzification. A group of rules can be used to represent knowledge base for articulating the control action in linguistic form. The inputs to the fuzzy controller to be designed for adjusting the amount of redundancy are: i) SNR of the communication channel and ii)vehicular traffic density. These two variables make the node's to optimize and adjust the amount of redundancy and then improves the network performance (bandwidth utilization). The overall process involved in calculation of redundant packets is described next.

3.1   Fuzzification of Inputs and Outputs

In order to control the amount of redundant packets,which are produced by using NC operations, the source and intermediate nodes encode m received packets

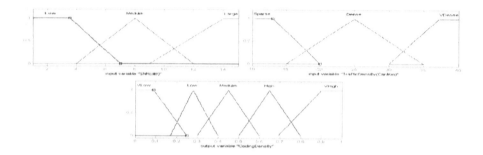

Fig. 3. Membership function for a) SNR ; b) Traffic Density; c) Coding Density

out of all K packets it has received so far [14]. The ratio m/K is refereed to as the coding density (output parameter) and it is used to adjust the degree of redundancy as a function of two input parameters (traffic density and SNR).

The redundancy controller is based on the fuzzy logic. This is because it simplifies the design of stable controller which employed two input variables and also the alterations are easy to perform to the rule inference system in order to enhance the performance of the controller. It is worth to mention the developed controller is implemented in source node and intermediate nodes in a distributed way. We are using traffic density and communication channel SNR in our redundancy controller (see Figure 3 a,b,c). The reason of this selection is that higher traffic density variation in vehicular environment yields high communication channel fluctuation, hence change of SNR. All nodes in a distributed way estimate the channel condition in the form of channel SNR. Furthermore, each node calculates the traffic density based on the proposed method in [15] (see section V). The specific node counts its neighbouring nodes based on the handshaking between them and then adjusts the value of redundancy using fuzzy controller. Moreover, the triangular and trapezoidal functions are chosen as the membership function since they have been extensively used in real-time applications due to their simple formulas and computational efficiency.

3.2   Fuzzy Inference Engine

The fuzzy controller is designed based on 9 rules which are presented in Table 1. Channel SNR is presented on a horizontal axes and traffic density is presented on a vertical axes. In order to demonstrate the designed fuzzy controller, One rule is used to show how the algorithm works and the outputs of each rule are combined for generating the controller decision [5]. Consider a rule "If SNR is Low and Traffic Density is very sparse, the change in coding density is very high" as an example of calculating output of the specified rule. Our fuzzy inference system considers a case where SNR is 2.22 dB and traffic density is 12.9 car/km(this value is increased to 13). The output is 0.891(0.9). This value (0.9) represents the coding density, i.e the intermediate nodes encode 9 packets (in our simulation 10 is total number of packets in each generation) out of all received packets.

Table 1. Rule-based redundancy control

TrafficDensity / SNR	Low	Medium	Large
Sparse	VHigh	High	Medium
Dense	High	Medium	Low
V Dense	Medium	Low	VLow

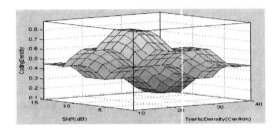

Fig. 4. Correlation between input and output parameters

This high redundancy is because low value of SNR and sparse traffic density. This output is achieved by using Mamdani's fuzzy inference method [5]. Figure 4 depicts the tuning behavior of the redundancy controller.

3.3 Defuzzification

Defuzzification refers to the way a crisp value is extracted from a fuzzy set as a representation value. Our fuzzy controller takes the centroid of area strategy for defuzzification.

4 Delay Constraint of Video Transmission

Consider maximum number of video packets,M, that can be transmitted in a communication session (source to destination) and satisfy maximum allowable delay T. The overall video packet delay (T) consists of three components: 1) the time that it takes for encoding and decoding of generations in NC operations T_{NC}, 2) the time needed to split the video file at the source and merge it at the destination T_{MDC}; and 3) the delay introduced due to video packet transmission from sender to receivers, i.e., the sum of packetization delay, propagation delays over intermediate links and queuing delays in intermediate vehicles T_t. In order to fulfil a video decoding deadline constraint, the worst case scenarios should be considered when calculating maximum allowable video packet delay. Thus, it is necessary to calculate each delay during a communication session.

The delay caused by NC operations is incurred at the encoder and decoder $T_{NC} = T_{Encoding} + T_{Decoding}$. This encoding and decoding delay depends on the number of native packets in each generation. The descriptions are divided to a number generations of the same size, referred to as the native generations

Table 2. Delay Related Parameters

Parameters	Description
n	total number of packets for a given generation
m	encoded packets out of n native packets
f	frame rate (number of frames per second)
$1/(f \times n)$	inter-arrival time between successive native packets
m/n	coding density
z	time needed to inverse coefficient matrix
$T_{Waiting}$	time needed to collect enough coded packets

$(g_1, g_2, g_3, \cdots, g_r)$. The time needed to encode the native packets of each generation is denoted by $T_{Encoding}$ while $T_{Decoding}$ is the time to decode all collected coded packets at the receiver. The decoding delay is shown in (2) under the assumption that the packets are uniformly and periodically received over a frame.

$$T_{Decoding} = T_{Waiting} + T_{Retrieval}. \tag{1}$$

$$T_{Decoding} = (\frac{m}{n} \times \frac{1}{f \times n}) + z \tag{2}$$

For encoding packets at the source and intermediate nodes, it is important to collect enough number of packets belonging to the same generation to produce coded packets. Therefore, the encoding time $T_{Encoding}$ depends on the number of packets of a given generation. Table 2 shows all parameters related to delay.

The main parts of the MDC source coding are the splitter and merger which provide particular processing of the video sequences at the source and destinations respectively. Thus, the time needed for MDC operations is as follow:

$$T_{MDC} = T_{Splitter} + T_{Merger} \tag{3}$$

Therefore, delay parameters should be chosen to satisfy the delay constraint:

$$T \geq T_{MDC} + T_{NC} + T_t \tag{4}$$

5   Performance Evaluation

5.1   Simulation Setup

In this section, we present simulation setup to evaluate the performance of the proposed reliable joint coding approach. The simulation is performed using NS-2 simulator (with default values for MAC and physical layer configuration parameters) integrated with Evalvid [16]. Furthermore, the MDC simulation has been experimented to generate video descriptions [17]. Two different video streaming approaches have been experimented: one was proposed joint coding approach (JSNC) and the other was the NC approach. The SUMO tool [18] has been employed to create the vehicular scenario, and to generate mobility traces of the simulated vehicles. SUMO interposes vehicles in each lanes at a given traffic rate. This mobility model allows us to simulate vehicular scenarios such as speed deceleration/accelerations and different vehicular traffic conditions. The vehicle which is assigned as video source is generated first in one route (each route has its own parameters such as speed, acceleration).

All vehicles in our simulations have a transmission range of 200 meter and 6 Mbps channel capacity. The roadway used is a two-lane road of 5 km length. Vehicles enter the road according to a Poisson distribution and travel at a speed between (10-23) m/second. The simulation is run for 100 seconds, resulting in a total of 125 vehicles generated (Figure 2). In the simulation, the CIF bit stream has been used with resolution 352x288 pixels and 300 frames (Foreman). The CIF Foreman sequence is encoded with a quality 35.68 dB. The encoder includes three types of frames: Intra frames (I-frames) that are independent on other frames, and inter frames that use either P-frames or B-frames temporal prediction from other frames. A number of mutually dependent frames form a group of pictures (GOP). In our experiment, the GOP size is set to 12 frames.

5.2   Simulation Results and Discussions

We consider three different metrics in our evaluation: average Peak Signal to Noise Ratio (PSNR); protection efficiency: average packet loss rate, which represents the robustness of the protocol against packet losses; and application layer throughput: this throughput depends upon packet losses at the lower layers.

Figure 5 a) shows that the overall video quality is higher for proposed approach than that of NC approach. When vehicles are travelling with low speed, the value of PSNR is slight different for both approaches. This is because at low velocity the wireless channel is stable and intermittent connectivity occurs less frequently. As velocity of vehicles increases, the disconnectivity rate between source vehicle and receiver increases frequently as well as the high channel variation leads to coded packet loss. A coded packet loss in one generation causes multiple packet loss of it. As result, the average video quality of the proposed approach is higher than that of the NC approach.

To compare the packet loss rate of the proposed approach with other approach, the video source transmits video packets in a given period of video communication session. The source vehicle transmits the video coded packets from source to receiver by applying NC operations. In the next communication session, we have repeated the video transmission by applying the proposed approach. Subsequently, during off line analysis, we have computed the average packet loss rate through a comparison of receiver and source trace files. We observed that the instantaneous packet loss rate is increasing in both approaches and the overall packet loss rate is lower for proposed approach than that of NC approach as depicted in Figure 5 b). Initially, there is a small difference of instantaneous

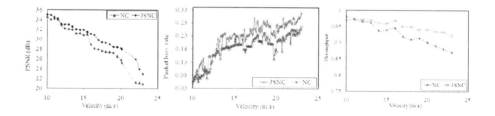

Fig. 5. a) Video quality for different vehicle speeds; b) Instantaneous packet loss rate for different vehicle speeds; c) Application layer throughput for different vehicle speeds

packet loss values for the proposed approach and networks coding approach due to less channel variation (less bit error rate and fading of the channel) as well as less frequent link disruption and hence less number of packet losses. As mobility increases the channel instability (high bit error) and intermittent connectivity increases as well. As a result packet loss increases in both approaches. However, the NC has more coded packet loss than proposed approach at high speed. This is because one coded packet losses has a potential to generate multiple coded packet losses. On the other hand, the MDC increases error resilient of NC by generating multiple descriptions.

We observed similar trends in application layer throughput as we vary the velocity from low to high in Figure 5 c). The NC approach shows significant decrease in throughput due to high speed of vehicles which leads to high coded packet losses, while application layer throughput in our approach does not change as much at high velocity of vehicles. This is because high coded packet losses (due to high speed) at the lower layers reduces effective application layer throughput as well as increases the variation of bandwidth.

6   Conclusions

In this paper, we have proposed joint source coding and NC for reliable video streaming over vehicular networks. In this approach, the NC operations are implemented above MAC layer while MDC operations are embedded in application layer. The MDC descriptions are adapted with NC generations. This two stage of coding increases the robustness of video streaming in vehicular networks. Moreover, the NC redundancy are adjusted using fuzzy inference system controller, the tuning was based on vehicular traffic density and SNR of the communication channel. The mathematical analysis for latency is derived to constrain end to end delay. NS-2 extensive simulations were successfully carried out for significant gains in terms of average video quality, application layer throughput and average packet loss rate. The video streaming with NC has been compared to the proposed joint coding approach and the proposed scheme gives better performance.

References

1. Singh, J.P., Bambos, N., Srinivasan, B., Clawin, D.: Wireless LAN performance under Varied Stress Conditions in Vehicular Traffic Scenarios. In: IEEE International Vehicular Technology Conference, vol. 2, pp. 743–747 (2002)
2. Lee, C.W., Yang, C.S., Su, Y.C.: Adaptive UEP and packet size assignment for scalable video transmission over burst error channels. EURASIP Journal on Applied Signal Processing 2006, 1–9 (2006)
3. Ahlswede, R., Cai, N., Li, S., Yeung, R.: Network information flow. IEEE Transactions on Information Theory, 1204–1215 (2000)
4. Guo, Z., Wang, B., Xie, P., Zeng, W., Cui, J.H.: Efficient Error Recovery with Netowrk Coding in Under Water Sensor Networks. Journal on Ad Hoc Networks 7, 791–802 (2008)
5. Mamdani, E.H.: Application of Fuzzy Logic to Approximate Reasoning Using Linguistic Synthesis, IEEE Trans. on Computers C-26, 1182–1191 (1977)
6. Goyal, V.K.: Multiple description coding: compression meets the network. IEEE Signal Processing Magazine, 74–93 (2001)
7. Gao, M., Ammar, M.H., Zegura, E.W.: V3: a Vehicle-to-Vehicle Live Video Streaming Architecture. In: IEEE International Conference on Pervasive Computing and Communications, Kauai, HI, pp. 404–424 (2005)
8. Xie, F., Hua, K.A., Wang, W., Ho, Y.H.: Performance study of live video streaming over highway vehicular Ad hoc networks. In: International IEEE Vehicular Technology Conference, USA, pp. 2121–2125 (2007)
9. Park, J.S., Lee, U., Oh, S., Gerla, M.: Delay analysis of car-to-car reliable data delivery strategies based on data mulling with network coding. IEICE Transaction on Information and Systems, 2524–2527 (2008)
10. Chen, H., Sun, B., Zeng, Y., He, X.: An Entropy-Based Fuzzy Controllers QoS Routing Algorithm in MANET. In: International Conference on Hybrid Intelligent Systems, pp. 235–239 (2009)
11. Chiang, T.C., Tai, C.F., Hou, T.W.: A knowledge-based Inference Multicast Protocol using Adaptive Fuzzy Petri nets. Journal of Expert Systems with Applications 36, 8115–8123 (2009)
12. Wang, Y., Reibman, A., Lin, S.: Multiple Description Coding for Video Delivery. Proceedings of the IEEE 93(1), 57–70 (2005)
13. Chou, P.A., Wu, Y., Jain, K.: Practical Network Coding. In: Annual Alerton Conference on Communication, Control and Computing, pp. 40–49 (2003)
14. Wang, M., Li, B.: How Practical is Network Coding. In: IEEE International Workshop on Quality of Service, pp. 274–278 (2006)
15. Balon, N., Guo, J.: Increasing Broadcast Reliability in Vehicular Ad Hoc Networks. In: VANET 2006, Los Angeles,California, pp. 104–105 (2006)
16. Evalvid,http://www.tkn.tuberlin.de/research/evalvid/ (accessed March 3, 2011)
17. Multiple Description Coding (MDC), http://140.116.72.80/~smallko/ns2/MDC.htm (accessed March 7,2011)
18. SUMO Mobility Model, http://sumo.sourceforge.net/ (accessed March 5, 2011)

Queue-Management Architecture for Delay Tolerant Networking

Sotirios-Angelos Lenas, Stylianos Dimitriou, Fani Tsapeli, and Vassilis Tsaoussidis

Space Internetworking Center (SPICE),
ECE Department, Democritus University of Thrace, Xanthi, Greece
{slenas,sdimitr,ttsapeli,vtsaousi}@ee.duth.gr

Abstract. During the last years, the interest in Delay/Disruption Tolerant Networks has been significantly increased, mainly because DTN covers a vast spectrum of applications, such as deep-space, satellite, sensor and vehicular networks. Even though the Bundle Protocol seems to be the prevalent candidate architecture for delay-tolerant applications, some practical issues hinder its wide deployment. One of the functionalities that require further research and implementation is DTN queue management. Indeed, queue management in DTN networks is a complex issue: loss of connectivity or extended delays, render occasionally meaningless any pre-scheduled priority for packet forwarding. Our Queue-management approach integrates connectivity status into buffering and forwarding policy, eliminating the possibility of stored data to expire and promoting applications that show potential to run smoothly. Therefore, our approach does not rely solely on marked priorities but rather on active networking conditions. We present our model analytically and compare it with standard solutions. We then develop an evaluation tool by extending ns-2 modules and, based on selective scenarios primarily from Space Communications, we demonstrate the suitability of our model for use in low-connectivity/high-delay environments.

Keywords: DTN, Queue management, Scheduling.

1 Introduction

Queue management in traditional networks is used mainly to regulate traffic fluctuations, as well as to assign priorities to specific traffic classes. It often utilizes dropping mechanisms that signal end-users, implicitly or explicitly, for impeding congestion events. Nevertheless, queue management in Delay/Disruptive Tolerant Networks (DTN) [1] [2], with long delays and disruptions has to address additional issues. While fair resource allocation and traffic classification are still important, queue management needs also to exploit every available contact opportunity and reschedule traffic prioritization and data storage to handle communication disruptions and delays.

We extend further the preliminary architecture proposed in [3] with mathematical analysis, architectural enhancements and systematic evaluation. Our architecture is composed now by three main components: i) an *Admission Control* unit, which determines the criteria that DTN nodes use to accept or reject incoming bundles, ii) a

X. Masip-Bruin et al. (Eds.): WWIC 2011, LNCS 6649, pp. 470–482, 2011.
© IFIP International Federation for Information Processing 2011

Buffer and Storage Management unit, which determines how accepted bundles should be stored, and iii) a *Scheduling* unit, which determines bundle service priorities. Here, we refer to data handled by DTN nodes as bundles, even though the architecture proposed is not confined by the standardized Bundle Protocol [4]. The characteristics of each type of DTN network may vary and the objective each time may be different. Here, we emphasize on space applications: space satisfies both dimensions of DTN, that is, disruptions and long delays. We have primarily two goals: i) to increase the DTN device throughput via efficient link exploitation and ii) to increase application satisfaction.

From an engineer's viewpoint, DTN requires additional supportive functionality primarily for resource management. In DTN, resource management incorporates storage capacity as well, which in turn is associated with long delays for data forwarding and increased complexity for scheduling. For example, unlike typical IP network packets, bundles do not face the danger to be dropped, however they do face the danger to expire. Also, priority-marked packets need not prioritized service in case connectivity disruptions have damaged their scope already.

A traditional FIFO-Droptail queue policy may have been an initial candidate for such system. Apart from its simplicity and the fact that it may perform decently in low-traffic networks, this approach is flawed severely: we cannot assign different priorities to different traffic classes and, on top of that, queuing delays punish uniformly and cumulatively all users, even those that may have a chance to survive a potential short disruption. Alternatively, we could integrate a prioritization algorithm in our scheme, such as Priority Queuing (PQ), Fair Queuing (FQ), Class-based Weighted Fair Queuing [5] (CBWFQ) and Low Latency Queuing (LLQ) [6]. A common, undesirable characteristic, however, is that priorities are typically predetermined and/or static, in the sense that do not incorporate connectivity feedback and hence cannot reflect a scheduling policy to a corresponding forwarding implementation. This non-typical requirement renders them only blind tools for DTN management and hence unsuitable, in their present form, for DTN networks. Additional approaches presented in [7] take account the low expiration time left and the number of times a packet has been forwarded, in order to drop it in cases of congestion. The most notable approach is SHLI (drop shortest life time first) which drops the packet with the lowest expiration time. However, this might have some undesirable side-effects when some packets have been delayed significantly, yet we can still manage to forward them before they expire.

Relevant work on DTN queue management is limited, and usually focuses on specific problems, such as policies or scheduling, providing a narrow approach to the queue management, occasionally isolating joint problems. However, some interesting work exists already. In [8], Amir Krifa et al., focus on queue management policies, and reach similar conclusions; they show that traditional buffer management policies such as *drop-tail* or *drop-front* are sub-optimal for use in DTN networks. Current implementations of the DTN, such as ION [9] and DTN2 [10], at this stage, adopt simple approaches to queue management considering the lack of corresponding standards. For example ION, deploys the bundle protocol approach, via a PQ scheme with three queues of outbound bundles, one queue for each of the defined levels of priority ("class of service") supported by BP. Our approach employs an enhanced classification scheme that integrates both network (i.e., connectivity) dynamics and traffic requirements. Therefore, scheduling is not a product of packet marks and hence, application alone, but rather a joint decision of data priority, application potential to survive disruptions and the network disruptions *per se*.

The rest of the paper is organized as follows. In section 2, we define our queue management model, including only the details necessary for the stochastic analysis, whereas in section 3 we present our stochastic analysis and the corresponding results. In section 4 we apply, validate and compare a part of our model through simulations in ns-2. Finally, in section 5 we conclude and set the framework for future work.

2   Delay Tolerant Queue Management Model

In order to define our queue-management model, hereafter referred as DTQM (Delay-Tolerant Queue Management) we consider the DTN network as a network with low connectivity, high and variable delays and absence of end-to-end path. We define DTQM in a way that allows us to include all the necessary functionality to satisfy a generic set of requirements. Thus, we divide DTQM into three units; i) *Admission Control*, ii) *Buffer and Storage Management*, and iii) *Scheduling*. We discuss all units' functionality, however, due to lack of space we emphasize on the most novel and sophisticated units, namely the *Buffer and Storage Management* and *Scheduling* units.

Admission Control: Admission Control determines how and which data may be accepted from a DTN node and is mainly related to data-custody requests. When custody requests are accepted by a DTN node, that node is obliged to maintain the bundles in its memory, until it is able to forward them, or until they expire.

Buffer and Storage Management: Contrary to traditional networks, where the routing nodes require buffers to implement a store-and-forward strategy, DTN nodes need additional persistent storage to maintain those packets that cannot immediately be forwarded due to limited connectivity. In IP-based routers, the main focus of researchers is to increase channel utilization and decrease delay through scheduling and dropping. This approach inherently assumes that end nodes respond to losses and therefore recover in short time. However, when connectivity is scarce, the requirement for short-time recovery is already violated. Furthermore, DTN networks introduce an additional level of complexity, as a result of combining both volatile and persistent storage. Clearly, the trivial approach to store every incoming bundle in persistent storage and move it to buffer upon request increases the processing delay of all the bundles and fails in cases of applications engaged in low-delay transfers.

In Fig. 1 we depict graphically the Buffer and Storage Management unit. Generally, this model is composed by two units, the Policy unit and the actual Storage unit. The purpose of the Policy unit is to accept all the bundles that enter the node and, depending on the conditions, move them to buffers or storage. Buffer and Storage management is initially differentiated based on whether there is connectivity between the DTN node and the next-hop. During periods of connectivity, packets that enter the node may be immediately routed to the output without being stored first. The total sending rate μ is calculated by the sum of sending rates μ_C and μ_N of the Connectivity and Non-Connectivity buffer, respectively.

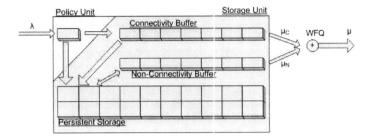

Fig. 1. The Buffer and Storage Management model

In more detail the purpose of each storage unit can be described as follows:

• Connectivity buffer. The Policy unit moves bundles to the Connectivity buffer only when there is connectivity and therefore the corresponding bundles can be forwarded to the next node. After a time-period which is determined by some threshold, when no connectivity exists, bundles that are stored temporarily in the Connectivity buffer move to Persistent storage.

• Persistent storage. The Policy unit moves bundles to Persistent storage in three cases: i) when there is no connectivity, ii) when there is connectivity but no Connectivity buffer space available, and iii) when there is both connectivity and Connectivity buffer space available, however the contact graph, which is known a priori, instructs that time does not suffice to forward bundles to the next hop.

• Non-Connectivity buffer. Bundles are moved from storage to the Non-Connectivity buffer in the following two cases: i) when bundles are of high priority (are either urgent or a scheduled contact is expected) and there is no connectivity and ii) when there is connectivity but other bundles are selected to be forwarded (opportunistic contact). The algorithm that determines which bundles should be forwarded first at a given communication opportunity is described briefly in the Scheduling section.

Our proposed model additionally deals with the problem of increased processing delay. In the event of multiple nodes in a row that are actively connected, transmission is rather straightforward, since packets are transferred from buffer to buffer without the interference of storage. In the event of short connectivity no further delay due to storage retrieval is imposed; bundles have already moved to the Non-Connectivity buffer, and hence bandwidth through short connectivity can be fully exploited.

Scheduling: Scheduling unit reassigns the priorities for each bundle and determines which bundles should be outputted from the DTN node when a communication opportunity occurs. A priority-oriented model should be inevitably considered; this model should incorporate application requirements, data requirements, Time-to-Live (TtL) for bundles etc.

Although we will not delve into more details, our scheduling depends heavily on the arrival timestamp and on TtL. In order to enhance application service, we promote both packets that have recently arrived in the node and packets that are near their expiration. This approach decreases significantly waiting delays and promotes application satisfaction. In Fig. 2 we depict the priority function used, where ToD (Type of Data) is a specific identifier that denotes the packet traffic class and TtL denotes the expiration time.

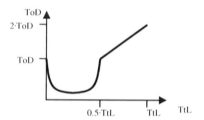

Fig. 2. Scheduling priority function

3   Stochastic Analysis

The purpose of this analysis is to highlight the advantages of our proposed model over traditional scheduling approaches. Our model consists of a primary FIFO queue (Connectivity buffer) and a secondary supportive queue (Non – Connectivity buffer), which serves high-priority bundles. We note that, in the context of Space, the queuing delay involved does not expect to contribute significantly to the total application delay, given the high propagation delay, and furthermore, the potentially very high storage delay involved in typical Space applications. Therefore, a priority queuing (PQ) or a PQ-derived scheduling model for incoming packets does not present conceptually a tempting approach, since it may fail with long-stored packets. Clearly, our approach departs from a FIFO scheme, and therefore, calls for a straightforward comparison with a typical FIFO scheme. However, for completeness, we extend our stochastic analysis also for PQ, which we consider as a theoretical upper bound (only) when connectivity is always present.

It is apparent, from an engineer's perspective, that our model is designed to handle disconnectivity/disruption issues. As such, it is reasonably expected to perform better in environments with limited connectivity, especially against traditional queuing schemes, which do not include a native mechanism to handle intermittent connectivity. Nevertheless, to achieve fairness towards FIFO and PQ, we use a worst-case scenario for DTQM, where connectivity is always available on the system. The results shall indicate to which extent our model is able to perform satisfactorily. In such environments, where connectivity is always available and we do not exploit DTQM's full potential, even a performance comparable to PQ and better than FIFO is acceptable.

We initiate our analysis by modeling network traffic. Packet arrival is modeled as as an exponential process and packet departure as a general distribution process. This is not, however, a globally valid assumption, since different types of traffic can result in different distributions concerning the packet arrival and departure. Nonetheless, as our knowledge on the possible DTN applications is limited, we assume that the environment and the applications under investigation manifest all the necessary characteristics of a M/G/1 system based analysis. The potential existence of self-similar characteristics is not considered here. Furthermore, we assume that all packets have the same size, non-preemptive priority is enforced and flows correspond to different traffic classes.

One might argue, from an analytical perspective, that precision is rather dubious when we attempt to analytically compare different queuing policies with potentially distinct goals. However, there are several occasions when these mechanisms are indeed equivalent and directly comparable. For example, as throughput is decreasing, the behavior of these three systems converges.

We begin our queuing analysis by estimating the average system delay for each flow in a PQ scheme. We consider a single-server PQ system fed by three Poisson streams with arrival rates λ_1, λ_2 and λ_3. Each stream can be considered as a flow of data generated by various applications, in our case Real-time (RT), Telemetry (TM) and Telecommand (TC) applications. The buffers corresponding to different flows are infinite and packets in each buffer are served in the order they arrive. Thus, we use three queues, one per flow, and three priority classes. We limit the overall system utilization by setting $\rho_i<1$ and $\rho_1+\rho_2+\rho_3<1$. This keeps the system from being overloaded and cancels the possibility of flow starvation. Table 1, presents the notation used throughout the present mathematical analysis.

Table 1. Notation

N_i	Average number of packets in each queue
λ_i, λ	Packet arrival rate at class-i queue / Total packet arrival rate
μ_i, μ	Packet service rate at class-i queue / Total packet service rate
ρ_i, ρ	System utilization factor per class-i / System utilization factor
R	Mean residual service time
W_i	Average queuing delay of a class-i packet
T_i	Average system delay of a class-i packet
X^2	Second service moment

That said, we consider the i_{th} data packet arrival at the first queue of the PQ system. Since class-1 packets have the highest priority, the i_{th} packet that has just arrived must wait in queue for a mean residual time R until the end of the current packet transmission, plus the transmission time required for a mean number of packets N_1 currently in the first queue, preceding the i_{th} packet.

$$W_1 = R + \frac{N_1}{\mu} \qquad (1)$$

We calculate the mean residual time, for M/G/1 systems, by the formula ([11]):

$$R = \frac{1}{2}\sum_{i=1}^{n} \lambda_i X_i^2 , \ X_i^2 = \frac{2}{\mu^2} \qquad (2)$$

Now, according to Little's law [12], the average number of packets waiting in the system is equal to the average delay multiplied by the average arrival rate of the system. We apply Little's law to the class-1 queue. As the average queuing delay for class-1 packets is W_1 and the average queue occupancy is N_1 with arrival rate λ_1, we have

$$N_1 = \lambda_1 W_1 \tag{3}$$

$$(1),(2),(3) \Rightarrow W_1 = \frac{R}{1-\rho_1}, \quad \rho_1 = \frac{\lambda_1}{\mu} \tag{4}$$

Similarly, by enforcing non-preemptive priority queuing and according to [11] the average queuing delay for class2 and class-3 packets is accordingly:

$$W_2 = \frac{R}{(1-\rho_1)(1-\rho_1-\rho_2)} \tag{5}$$

$$W_3 = \frac{R}{(1-\rho_1-\rho_2)(1-\rho_1-\rho_2-\rho_3)} \tag{6}$$

Finally, by adding the service time $1/\mu$ of the i_{th} packet in the equations (4), (5) and (6), we can calculate the average system delay for class-k packets:

$$T_k = W_k + \frac{1}{\mu} \tag{7}$$

Next, we estimate the average delay for each flow in a FIFO scheme. In this scheduling scheme, each flow has the same average queuing delay, which depends on the average number of packets in queue N, and the mean residual time, R. According to [11] the average system delay in a FIFO scheme is:

$$T_{FIFO} = W + \frac{1}{\mu} \Rightarrow T_{FIFO} = \frac{1}{\mu(1-\rho)} \tag{8}$$

However, in order to guarantee that the service distribution of the FIFO queue corresponds to an appropriately weighted sum of the service distributions for the different classes in the priority queue scheme, we set:

$$T_{NFIFO} = 3T_{FIFO} - 2R - \frac{2}{\mu} \tag{9}$$

We continue our analysis by estimating the average delay for each flow in a DTQM scheme. We divide the analysis in two parts. Since DTQM uses two outgoing queues (plus the permanent storage – see Fig. 1) one for connectivity and the other for non-connectivity data, we can safely assume that the first one emulates a FIFO queue while the second one approaches the behavior of a PQ scheme. The latter assumption holds since the prioritization function that we apply (see Fig. 2), requires packet sorting. That said, the first queue analysis in terms of average system delay is directly comparable with a FIFO scheme, while the second queue calls for a PQ-based analysis. In order to fairly evaluate our proposed scheme, we omit permanent storage from the mathematical analysis. This allows the three systems to present similar properties and hence be comparable. We consider an average system arrival rate λ equal to the other systems and set arrival rates, without loss of generality, for the two queues $\lambda_a = 0.4\lambda$ and $\lambda_b = 0.6\lambda$. The selection of coefficients 0.4 and 0.6 as the preferred values for our stochastic analysis was based on some initial empirical calculations and will be calibrated further according to emulation results. Finally, the total average system service rate will be μ where $\mu_a=0.4\mu$ and $\mu_b=0.6\mu$ for first and second queues, respectively.

To start off, the average queuing delay for the first queue does not differentiate per flow and can be calculated based on the average number of packets in queue-1 and the mean residual time, using equation (2) and replacing λ_1, λ_2, μ_1 and μ_2 with λ_a, λ_b, μ_a and μ_b respectively.

$$W_{CON} = \frac{N}{\mu_a} + R \qquad (10)$$

By applying Little's law for queue-1 we get:

$$N = \lambda_a W_{CON} \qquad (11)$$

From equations (10) and (11) we get:

$$W_{CON} = \frac{R}{1-\rho_a}, \text{ where } \rho_a = \frac{\lambda_a}{\mu_a} \Rightarrow \rho_a = \frac{0.4\lambda}{\mu_a} \qquad (12)$$

The average system delay for all the flows in queue-1 is:

$$T_{CON} = W_{CON} + \frac{1}{\mu_a} \qquad (13)$$

We now approximate the behavior of the second queue as follows. The queue can split into three sub-queues or subclasses. Each class will be served using a PQ-based scheme. Furthermore, the proportion of packets for each class on the total available capacity of the queue-2 buffer is λ_1/λ for class-1 packets, λ_2/λ for class-2 packets and λ_3/λ for class-3 packets. Therefore, the average queuing delay for class-1 packets is:

$$W_{1NONCON} = \frac{N_1}{\mu_b} + R \qquad (14)$$

By applying Little's law [12], we obtain:

$$N_1 = \frac{\lambda_1}{\lambda} \lambda_b W_{1NONCON} \Rightarrow N_1 = 0.6\lambda_1 W_{1NONCON} \qquad (15)$$

From equations (14) and (15) we get:

$$W_{1NONCON} = \frac{R}{1 - \frac{\lambda_1 \rho_b}{\lambda}}, \text{ where } \rho_b = \frac{\lambda_b}{\mu_b} \Leftrightarrow \rho_b = \frac{0.6\lambda}{\mu_b} \qquad (16)$$

The average queuing delay for the second subclass depends on N_1 packets, which are buffered in the first subclass, plus N_2 packets, which are buffered in the second subclass, plus the residual time R. In our case, unlike the ordinary properties of PQ, our design assumptions do not permit the possibility of higher priority packets to rearrange the queue at any given stage. Therefore, we have:

$$W_{2NONCON} = R + \frac{N_1}{\mu_b} + \frac{N_2}{\mu_b} \Rightarrow W_{2NONCON} = W_{1NONCON} + \frac{N_2}{\mu_b} \qquad (17)$$

$$N_2 = \frac{\lambda_2}{\lambda}\lambda_b W_{2NONCON} \Rightarrow N_2 = 0.6\lambda_2 W_{2NONCON} \qquad (18)$$

From equations (17) and (18) we obtain:

$$W_{2NONCON} = \frac{W_{1NONCON}}{1 - \frac{\lambda_2 \rho_b}{\lambda}} \qquad (19)$$

By the same token, average queuing delay for third subclass is:

$$W_{3NONCON} = \frac{W_{2NONCON}}{1 - \frac{\lambda_3 \rho_b}{\lambda}} \qquad (20)$$

Finally, system's average delay for each subclass is:

$$T_{kNONCON} = W_{kNONCON} + \frac{1}{\mu_b} \qquad (21)$$

Having calculated the average delays for the two queues separately, we will combine these values to acquire the total delay. A statistically acceptable method for doing this is by using weights. Considering the way that we have defined the problem, it is logical to expect that each queue will contribute with a different percentage to the overall system delay. Hence, we will consider that queue-1 and queue-2 will contribute to the total average system delay by 40% and 60%, respectively. Considering the values of λ and μ in each queue, we have.

$$T_{1DTQM} = 0.4T_{CON} + 0.6T_{1NONCON} \, , \, T_{2DTQM} = 0.4T_{CON} + 0.6T_{2NONCON} \, ,$$
$$T_{3DTQM} = 0.4T_{CON} + 0.6T_{3NONCON} \qquad (22)$$

As for the numerical results presented below, the value of system service rate is constant at 10 packets/sec, whereas the values of λ vary in order to obtain the possible range of system utilization, 10% - 90%. The value of service rate, considering packet sizes in the order of KB, provides an acceptable rate of data transmission, especially in space environments and among low energy sensors.

The numerical results of our analysis are presented in Fig. 3. We compare the aforementioned queuing schemes based on the average delay for each queue in each system and the average queue occupancy. The results show that our approach achieves a performance clearly better than FIFO and in some cases better than PQ, especially when the system utilization factor is high.

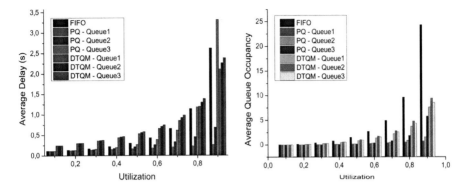

Fig. 3. Numerical results

4 Experimental Evaluation

Evaluating such a queue management policy requires extensive experiments using an actual space network, since DTQM affects both lower-level (battery lifespan) and higher-level (throughput, latency) performance metrics. We implement and evaluate our proposed solution using the ns-2 software simulator [13]. This implementation was not trivial and required significant time considering the fact that ns-2 does not support DTN. In this work, we focus on the full implementation of the second and third component of DTQM, namely the *Buffer and Storage Management* and *Scheduling* parts, leaving the rest of the architecture evaluation as future work.

We apply DTQM to the network topology of Fig. 4. We assume three sending nodes, S_1, S_2, S_3, which are located in space and send traffic generated by various applications (Real-time, Telemetry and Telecommand; all constant bit rate with 0.02 sec, 0.4 sec and 60 sec sending interval respectively) and a receiving node R, which is located on earth. All traffic generated by the sending nodes is routed through the routing node Q in which we deploy DTQM.

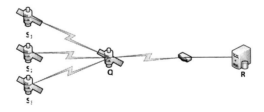

Fig. 4. Simulation topology

Since we assumed that the sending nodes are located in space, the connectivity of the wireless links should be intermittent. In order to emulate a DTN environment where connectivity is not predetermined, thanks to alternative routes and connections, we select a random disconnectivity pattern with uniformly distributed connectivity disruptions spread across the entire duration of the experiment, as the most appropriate for evaluating the proposed architecture. In this context, link S_1-Q is uniformly unavailable in total 1% of the time of the experiment. Similarly link S_2-Q is 5% unavailable, link S_3-Q is 10% unavailable, and finally, link Q-R is 0.5% unavailable. Furthermore, the propagation delay of links S_1-Q, S_2-Q, S_3-Q and Q-R was set respectively to 2sec, 600 sec, 300 sec and 0.6 sec. Finally, we set the total time of the experiments to one hour, and measure the total number of received packets for all three sending nodes, as well as the *Application Satisfaction Index* (ASI) [14] of the network, a metric that highlights the contribution of the queuing delay to the total delay. In order to add reliability to our results and enforce randomness to take effect we repeat the experiment several times. In particular, the performance of DTQM was evaluated in five connectivity scenarios, each one utilizing a different (randomly generated) connectivity schedule. We compare the obtained results with the corresponding results of a FIFO policy. In line with the priority function used (see Fig. 2) we assign ToD for each application as follows: 1 for the RT application, 2 for the TM application and 3 for the TC application.

Furthermore, we set the packet intervals for each application as we would expect in real-life, that is, Real-Time packets are generated with the shortest interval and Telecommand packets are generated with the longest interval; hence the difference in packet numbers.

In Fig. 5 below, we present the results from the comparison of DTQM against Droptail, using *ASI* and *average delay* as our performance metrics. The first observation that we can make is that DTQM outperforms Droptail in any case. In particular, we experience a 60% delay decrease on average and in some cases it can reach up to 90% reduction of the corresponding bundle delay using a typical FIFO scheme. This delay decrease is also reflected on the system ASI, which is increased 20%, on average.

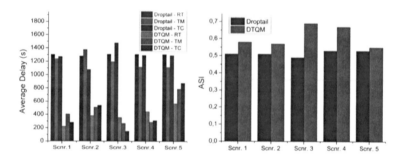

Fig. 5. Experimental results

Tabel 2. Experimental Results

		Best Case			Worst Case		
		RT	TM	TC	RT	TM	TC
Received	FIFO	15680	696	5	15732	645	4
packets	DTQM	15618	754	5	15500	869	7
Average	FIFO	1308	1196	1477	1306	1113	1219
Delay	DTQM	357	267	150	565.9	789.7	877
System	FIFO		0.49			0.53	
ASI	DTQM		0.69			0.55	

Table 2 demonstrates in detail the best and worst case results for DTQM. By viewing Table 2, we notice that the received packets are almost the same in any case (with the exception of the TM packets of the worst case experiment) regardless of queuing policy. Nevertheless, we may experience up to 40% increase in received Telemetry and Telecommand packets when DTQM is deployed, since we assign them with higher ToD. Moreover, the most interesting observation is the undoubtable improvement of the average delay regardless of the application. However, since we transfer the same number of packets in both cases, how can we justify the delay decrease? DTQM uses a sophisticated scheduling algorithm that assigns higher priority to the packets most recently arrived in the node and promotes them in the queue (see Fig. 2). Thus, packets are reordered in the buffer based on the time they entered the routing node. Classic scheduling uses a rigid FIFO approach, which although it seems to promote fairness, in fact it increases the communication time, with the risk of dropping a packet due to TtL expiration.

5 Conclusions

In this paper we proposed a novel architecture for queue management in DTN nodes. Although the available space confines us from presenting a more detailed version and evaluation of our model, we sketched several of its characteristics.

One of the most interesting results was initially introduced by the stochastic analysis, which yielded positive results for the operation of our model that exhibits a behavior far superior to FIFO and comparable to PQ, even in network conditions that are unfavorable for our scheme. We also obtained supportive results from the conducted experiments that alleviate worries from adopting numerous assumptions on the stochastic analysis section. Therefore we can safely claim that DTQM has the potential to achieve smaller queuing delays and higher application satisfaction when connectivity is scarce.

Our next step is to enhance our evaluation towards two directions: i) to present a more detailed analysis, which incorporates total capacity and storage capacity as well, in order to highlight one major property of DTN and ii) to extend the experiments by using the space-oriented testbed [15] that we have developed in our lab.

Acknowledgments. The research leading to these results has received funding from the European Community's Seventh Framework Programme ([FP7/2007-2013_FP7-REGPOT-2010-1, SP4 Capacities, Coordination and Support Actions) under grant agreement n° **264226** (project title: Space Internetworking Center-SPICE).

References

1. Fall, K.: A delay-tolerant network architecture for challenged internets. In: ACM SIGCOMM 2003, Karlsruhe, Germany, August 25-29 (2003)
2. Cerf, V., Burleigh, S., Hooke, A., Torgerson, L., Durst, R., Scott, K., Fall, K., Weiss, H.: Delay Tolerant Networking Architecture. RFC 4838 (April 2007)
3. Dimitriou, S., Tsaoussidis, V.: Effective Buffer and Storage Management in DTN Nodes. E-DTN 2009, St. Petersburg, Russia (October 14, 2009)

4. Scott, K., Burleigh, S.: Bundle protocol specification. RFC 5050 (November 2007)
5. Class-based Weighted Fair Queuing, Cisco IOS Software Releases 12.0 T
6. Low Latency Queuing, Cisco IOS Software Releases 12.0 T
7. Lindgren, A., Phanse, K.S.: Evaluation of queuing policies and forwarding strategies for routing in intermittently connected networks. In: Proc. of IEEE COMSWARE (January 2006)
8. Krifa, A., Barakat, C., Spyropoulos, T.: Optimal buffer management policies for delay tolerant networks. In: IEEE SECON 2008, San Francisco, California, June 16-20 (2008)
9. Jet Propulsion Laboratory: ION: Interplanetary Overlay Network, https://ion.ocp.ohiou.edu
10. The Delay-Tolerant Networking Research Group (DTNRG), http://www.dtnrg.org/
11. Bertsekas, D.P., Gallager, R.: Data Networks. Prentice-Hall, Englewood Cliffs (1991)
12. Little, J.D.C.: A Proof of the Queueing Formula $L = \lambda W$. Operations Research 9 (1961)
13. Network Simulator (1997), http://www.isi.edu/nsnam/ns/
14. Mamatas, L., Tsaoussidis, V.: Differentiating services with Non-Congestive Queuing (NCQ). IEEE Transactions on Computers 58(5), 591–604 (2009)
15. Samaras, C.V., Komnios, I., Diamantopoulos, S., Koutsogiannis, E., Tsaoussidis, V., Papastergiou, G., Peccia, N.: Extending Internet Into Space - ESA DTN Testbed Implementation and Evaluation. In: Mobilight 2011, Athens, Greece, May 18-20 (2009)

Cognitive Radio Access Optimization Using Multi-parameter Match Ability Estimation

Kunqi Guo[1,3], Lixin Sun[1], Xiaoqun Zhao[2], and Shilou Jia[3]

[1] School of Computer Science and Telecommunication Engineering,
Jiangsu University, Jiangsu, China
[2] School of Communication Engineering,
Tongji University, Shanghai, China
[3] Communication Research Center, Harbin Institute of Technology
Harbin, China

Abstract. In this paper, we formulate the optimal channel access of secondary user system in cognitive radio networks as the total reward maximization by Partially Observable Markov Decision Processes (POMDPs). Match Ability is proposed that takes allowable channel transmission rate and bit-error-rate (BER) required by receiving end into account. A heuristic greedy algorithm for channel access is proposed that is based on the local maximum match ability. By combining the utility function of queuing delay with local match ability, we improve the global average delay fairness. It is demonstrated by simulation results that as the average arrival rate increases, the large stable region of low delay can be maintained by adjusting utility function of the average waiting time under the condition that all the control information time overhead is not considered in the centralized global fairness control.

Keywords: Cognitive radio; match ability; utility function; average waiting time.

1 Introduction

A novel solution to radio spectrum underutilization problems is to adopt cognitive spectrum access. It can be realized by first sensing frequency bands that are not used by the primary users and then accessing current idle frequency band. To achieve this goal in an autonomous manner, multiple user cognitive radio networks need to be adaptive to dynamic wireless network characteristics to use radio spectrum most efficiently. In general, the secondary user that is driven by service requirement starts to sense each channel of primary users at any given time, with probable sensing results of channels including (1) a idle (active) channel accurately sensed to be idle (active) and (2) a idle (active)Wrongly sensed to be active (idle). In case (2), the channel usage efficiency can be decreased because the same channel may be simultaneously used by more than two users, or not be utilized by secondary users. In secondary user system, the access decision is determined only according to the result of channel sensing. It can be completed by detecting the signal in frequency bandwidth of primary users at physical layer. A great deal of effort has been made by

X. Masip-Bruin et al. (Eds.): WWIC 2011, LNCS 6649, pp. 483–493, 2011.

considering spectrum detecting method, accessing strategy and traffic tail characteristics estimation in time domain respectively. In [1] and [2], a hierarchical cognitive network is considered for cognitive user transmission opportunities in multiple channel communication system. The queue tail distribution of cognitive users is estimated for the detection of channels of primary users in [3], with closed-form expressions under two primary users.

While there has been much investigation in channel usage in cognitive radio networks including opportunistic access [4, 5, 6, 7], spectrum sharing [8, 9] and stable and efficient access method [10, 11], there is a lack of the efficient effort in spectrum access efficiency of secondary users system that both the efficiency and fairness of the available spectrum utilization are considered. It is a complex multiple variants optimization problem we will face in this paper. Using Partially Observable Markov Decision Processes (POMDPs), we investigate the optimization objective that is formulated as the total reward maximization. The optimization implementation based on POMDP is to obtain the expected total reward by taking a sequence of decision actions. In our objective optimization for channel access, each access decision is made based on the multi-parameter match estimation considering the channel condition, the queuing delay, and the average arrival rate. To address this, we propose a novel channel access scheme using multidimensional parameters *match ability maximization*. In this scheme, for each secondary user, the statistical relationship between context parameters and the quality of service is derived according to queue theory. For wireless packet scheduling, much of efforts is made to achieve efficient wireless packet scheduling in [12], [13] and [14]. Proportionally fair (*PF*) scheduling is investigated in [15], [16] in order to maximize the long-term throughput in terms of user average channel conditions. In cognitive radio network, the interference to primary users may be increased due to the transmission power enhanced by a secondary user using a worse idle channel. In addition, a secondary user will reduce the utilization efficiency of channels being in better condition because its current service queue length is shorter. Thus, the trade-off between channel efficiency and queue length should jointly be considered for optimizing spectrum utilization. It becomes more important for secondary user system in cognitive radio networks using the constrained opportunistic spectrum access for service data transmission. In this paper, we focus on this problem. To our knowledge, as yet, it is not investigated. Considering cognitive access characteristics, we propose a novel metric *Match Ability* for channel access in secondary user system. *Match Ability* is constructed according to the required bit-error-ratio (BER) and the achievable transmission rate while considering the interference caused to its neighboring primary users. For single secondary user, *Match Ability* (*MA*) performs mapping between channel selection and the achieved quality of service (QoS). By this mechanism, secondary user accesses each channel based on *greedy Match Ability maximization* (*GMAM*). However, when more than two secondary users have the requirement of using the same channel, we need to consider the fairness problem of the channel utilization. This motivates us to implement it by combining centralized management control with *GMAM* based local access. To adapt well to the trade-off between queue delay and channel efficiency, we use extended *Match Ability* called *EMA* that is based on the principle of the utility maximization. In this scheme, we combine queue delay with *MA* of each secondary user by the utility function of queue delay. In addition, one of advantages of our methods is that it allows us to use conventional Proportionally fair scheduling (*PF*) as centralized management control by only replacing the single parameters with the integrated parameter *MA*, which can adapt well to the channel efficiency maximization requirement.

2 System Description and Optimization Formulation

In this section, we give the system description for the shared channel usage and analyze the optimization objective by partially observable Markov decision processes (POMDPs).

2.1 System Description

We consider a multiple channels cognitive radio networks with M primary users and N secondary users (cognitive users). In primary user system, each primary user has a channel (frequency band) to exclusively and randomly use. In secondary user system, each secondary user (cognitive user) uses idles channel of primary user to transmit its data queue in dynamic opportunistic way. The same spectrum channel can be shared at the same time between secondary user and primary user. Under this the setting, when we concentrate on idle channel usage, one of key problems we must face is the co-channel interference caused by secondary users to primary users. It mainly is due to two reasons. The first is that secondary users wrongly detect busy channels of primary users as being idle. The second is from how to utilize channels rightly sensed by secondary users as being idle. We focus on the latter one in this paper. Thus, our objective is equivalent to optimizing the utilization of channels shared between primary users and secondary users. The co-channel interference can be avoided when the same channel is used only by a primary user in the prescribed time, however, the spectrum utilization efficiency will be lowered when the space distance between a primary user and a secondary user is long enough to simultaneously use the same frequency band. With the interference protection of primary users, the optimization objective becomes a constrained optimization problem.

Two schemes are considered in our optimization objective implementation. The first one is the distributed spectrum access that the channel access in secondary user system is based on *GMAM*. With the *GMAM* based distributed way, each secondary user can take shorter time from sensing to accessing channel. However, the channel utilization optimization is subject to both the allowable transmission rate and service queue condition that jointly leads to the constrained optimization problem. The total optimization depends on the *optimum match* between the allowable channel transmission ability and the queue condition. This needs a centralized based trade-off control to allocate the same channels that are requested by two or more secondary users. By combining *GMAM* for channel sensing with the queue delay state, we propose the secondary scheme called *GMAMC* that considers trade-off between channel transmission efficiency and queue delay. By maximizing the *utility function* of the average waiting time, *GMAMC* has the global balance ability by controlling *greedy maximization degree* used in *GMAM*, The framework for channel access in secondary user system is shown in Fig. 1.

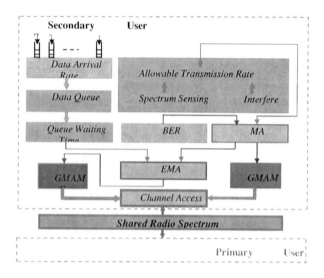

Fig. 1. Framework for Channel Access in Secondary User System

2.2 Optimization Formulation

A POMDP denotes an observation (estimation) and decision process taking a sequence of actions to maximize the reward value under uncertain estimated factors. Let **S**, **A**, and **O**, be a set of states, a set of actions and a set of observations (estimated parameters). If the system is currently in a state $s \in S$, after an action (decision) is taken, the system is driven into a new state s' from s and as a result, a reward value $R(s,a)$ is obtained. Due to uncertain predicted parameters, the end state s' can be modeled as a conditional probability function $T(s,a,s') = p(s'|s,a)$. The optimization objective is to maximize the total reward: $\max \sum_{s \in S, a \in A} R(s,a)$. Let $S_j[k] = 1$ and $S_j[k] = 0$ denote the idle and busy condition of the channel of primary user j in time slot k respectively. Taking channel usage efficiency as the system optimization goal, we represent the system state S by the vector $[S_1, S_2, ..., S_M]$. I_{ij} is the interference caused by secondary user i using channel j to primary user j. We by $I_{threshold}$ denote the maximum interference threshold that primary user can tolerate. For each secondary user, we consider two channel access schemes including the distributed access action and the centralized control. The set of access actions is expressed by A. Let $a_{ij} = 1$ and $a_{ij} = 0$ denote the distributed access and the centralized control scheme respectively for access channel j adopted by secondary user i. Each secondary user can access one channel by one of two ways indicated by $a_{ij} \in A = \{0,1\}$. Let $r_{ij}(a_{ij})$ be the required reliable transmission rate of secondary user i over channel j by accessing mode a_{ij}. By choosing the appropriate access scheme, our objective is to maximize the total system reward in terms of transmission rate

$$\max \sum_{i=1}^{N} \sum_{j=1}^{M} r_{ij}(a_{ij}) \tag{1}$$

$$\text{s.t. 1)} \sum_{i} I_{ij} < I_{threshold} \text{ ; 2) } a_{ij} \in A = \{0,1\}$$

where $\sum_{i} I_{ij} < I_{threshold}$ guarantees that the total interference caused by secondary user to each primary user is under the specified condition. However, the channel utilization efficiency can be reduced because the channel access is determined only according to two states, the busy and idle condition. Dynamic network environment makes it feasible to allocate the same channel at the same time to a secondary user and a primary user due to time-varying user location diversity. We consider secondary user system that time is divided into slots of fixed length T_s and define

$$S_{ij}[k] = \begin{cases} 1, \text{ if } I_{ij}[k] + \sum_{n \neq i} I_{nj}[k] < I_{threshold} \\ 0, \text{ if } I_{ij}[k] + \sum_{n \neq i} I_{nj}[k] \geq I_{threshold} \end{cases} \tag{2}$$

where $i, n \in \{1,2,...,N\}$, $j \in \{1,2,...,M\}$. In (2), $S_{ij}[k]=1$ and $S_{ij}[k]=0$ represent idle and busy condition of channel i in time slot k respectively. It means that a secondary user access a channel of primary user system by considering the interference already suffered by secondary user i and the interference to be caused by secondary user i due to using this channel.

2.3 Multidimensional Parameters

By the effective bandwidth theory [17], [18], we can obtain the probability that the packet delay violates the delay requirements using

$$\Pr\{W_i > D_{max}\} \approx e^{-\theta \delta D_{max}} \tag{3}$$

where D_{max} is the delay requirement and θ is a positive constant referred to as QoS exponent, δ is a constant jointly determined by the arrival process and service process. It means that a large θ implies that a stringent delay requirement can be guaranteed by the system while a small θ implies that a loose delay requirement can be guaranteed by the system. We express by $q_i[k]$ and λ_i the amount of bits of secondary user i waiting for service at time kT_s and the average arrival bit rate respectively. According to Little's principle, we obtain the average waiting time for secondary user i, W_i by $W_i = q_i / \lambda_i$ where $q_i = \lim_{N \to \infty} \sum_{k=0}^{N-1} q_i[k] / N$. By the time low-pass window with length T_w, we obtain the average queue length of secondary user i over the time window, $\overline{q}_i[k]$

$$\overline{q}[k] = (1 - \rho_w)\overline{q}_i[k-1] + \rho_w q_i[k] \tag{4}$$

where $\rho_w = T_s / T_w$. Using this time window, the average waiting time for secondary user i at time kT_s, $W_i[k]$ is estimated by $W_i[k] = \bar{q}_i[k] / \lambda_i$. Let $A_i[k]$ be the amount of arrival bits of secondary user i during time k. We by $R_i[k-1]$ denote the supportable transmission rate of secondary user i for its service during time slot $k-1$, then, its queue length at time kT_s, $q_i[k]$ is

$$q_i[k] = q_i[k-1] + A_i[k-1] - R_i[k-1]T_s \tag{5}$$

Thus, the predicted average waiting time at end of time slot k $W_i[k]$ is the function of the service arrival rate, the average queue length, and the obtainable transmission rate

$$W_i[k] = \frac{(1-\rho_w)\bar{q}_i[k-1] + \rho_w(q_i[k-1] - T_s R_i[k-1] + \lambda_i T_s)}{\lambda_i} \tag{6}$$

Since T_s and ρ_w are known at end of time slot k, $W_i[k]$ is the function in terms of λ_i, $R_i[k-1]$ and $q_i[k-1]$, reflecting the joint effect of multiple parameters on the average waiting time.

3   Channel Access

In this section, we propose two schemes for channel access in secondary user system, *MA-weight channel access* and *Combining queuing delay with MA-weight for channel access*.

3.1   MA-Weight Channel Access (*GMAM*)

During time slot k, secondary user i can decide whether to access channel j based on the maximization of *Match Ability* (*MA*) adopting distributed self-decision. Secondary user i using the channel j can get *Match Ability* MA_i^j

$$MA_i^j[k] = R_i^j[k]S_{ij}[k] \tag{7}$$

where $S_{ij}[k]$ is given by (2) and $R_i^j[k]$ is the achievable transmission rate of secondary user i using channel j that can satisfy the required *bit-error-rate* (BER_i) at receiving end. If QAM modulation is used, we can estimate $R_i^j[k]$ from

$$R_i^j[k] = \log_2\left(1 - \frac{1.5\gamma_i^j[k]}{\ln(5BER_i)}\right) \tag{8}$$

where $\gamma_i^j[k]$ is the *SINR* of the transmission link of the secondary user i using channel j during time slot k [19]. Let $h_{ij}[k]$ and $g_{ij}[k]$ represent the pathloss power gain and the normalized composite of shadowing and fading random variable with unit mean of the transmission link from secondary user i to primary user j respectively. Let where $P_i[k]$ be the transmitting power of secondary user i. If secondary user i complete one transmission during time slot t by $R_i^j[k]$, then we can obtain the power of interference received at primary user $I_{ij}[k]$ by $I_{ij}[k] = P_i[k]h_{ij}[k]g_{ij}[k]$. Due to the location dependence of wireless link, the maximization of the total MA results in the high computation complexity of maximizing the total $MA_i^j[k]$. To reduce complexity, we propose low complexity heuristic distributed algorithm based on *greedy match ability maximization* (*GMAM*) search that is formulated by

$$SU[k] = \arg\max\left\{MA_i^j[k]\right\} \tag{9}$$

where $i = 1,2,...,N$; $j \in D_i[k]$. By (9), each secondary user at end of current time slot k, selects the channel with the *local maximum match ability* out of channels that can be sensed. Two factors, the link supportable transmission rate and the maximum interference power to be tolerated by the primary user are considered in (9). The best short term performance achieved by (9) depends on the available *optimal match* between two factors during current time slot.

3.2 Combining Queue Delay with *MA* for Channel Access (*GMAMC*)

Trade off between resource efficiency and fairness can be realized by maximizing system utility function [20]. Due to the balance ability of maximizing utility, we use the utility function to determine the access priority for secondary users having the requirement of using the same channel. The delay performance is subject to both allowable channel transmission ability and queue condition. Consider both the transmission efficiency and delay fairness, we use the utility function of the average waiting time to control the trade-off between *maximum match ability based transmission efficiency* and *average queuing delay*. The utility function for this purpose is

$$U_i(W_i[k]) = W_i^b[k]; i = 1,2,...,N \tag{10}$$

Let ρ_w be small enough. Since $\Delta U(W_i[k])$ corresponds to the utility addition that should be maximized during current time slot and $R_i[k-1]$ is known before the end of current time slot k, when the arrival process is given, using a first-order approximation of the Taylor's expansion, we can formulate the utility maximization based optimization objective as

$$\max \sum_{i=1}^N \frac{dU_i}{dW_i}\bigg|_{W_i=W_i[k]} \left(\frac{R_i[k]}{\lambda_i}\right) \tag{11}$$

Let $EMA_i^j[k]$ be the extended *Match Ability* at time slot k of secondary user i denoted by $EMA_i^j[k] = W_i^{b-1}[k]MA_i^j[k]$. The total performance optimization is to achieve the optimal trade-off between queue delay and channel transmission efficiency that can be realized by maximizing the total extended *MA*

$$\max\left\{\frac{1}{\lambda_i}\sum_{i=1}^{N}EMA_i^{j}[k]\right\}\qquad\qquad(12)$$

Let $M_i = MA_i^{j}[k]$ $(i = 1,2,...,N)$ and $T_i = W_i^{b-1}[k]/\lambda_i$ be the *match ability* and the factor of service condition of secondary user i in time slot k respectively.

First, we need find *the global optimal trade-off parameter* G_{opt}. It can be realized efficiently by *binary search* (1) Sort M_i $(i = 1,2,...,N)$ in increasing order. (2) Get the lowest T_l and the highest T_h in user service state space $\left\{W_i^{b}[k]/\lambda_i : i = 1,2...N\right\}$. (3) If $T_h - T_l > 0$,   then $T_{center} \leftarrow \lfloor(T_h + T_l)/2\rfloor$ and $T \leftarrow T_{center}$.   (4) If $T - \left(U_h^{'}(W_h)/U_l^{'}(W_l)\right) > 0$, then $T_l \leftarrow T_{center}$; Otherwise $T_h \leftarrow T_{center}$. (5) Let $G_{opt} \leftarrow T_l M_l$.

Second, allocate channel j to the secondary user i which can satisfy $\min\left\{\left|G_{opt} - (W_i^{b-1}[k]M_i[k]/\lambda_i)\right|;i = 1,2,...,N\right\}$. By this method, the channel j is likely allocated to a secondary user that has $W_i^{b}[k]M_i[k]/\lambda_i$ approximating to G_{opt} . The service arrival rate, the queue delay and the allowable transmission rate are jointly considered to determine the current G_{opt} . The complexity of the algorithm is low because of the computing overhead largely depending on in sorting-search for *the global trade-off parameter* G_{opt} [21].

4   Performance Evaluation

In our simulation, each channel used by secondary users is assumed to suffer slow fading. Let the *BER* required by the receiving end of each secondary user be 10^{-6} . It is assumed for *GMAM* that each secondary user can know the interference of its neighboring primary users through its *local spectrum sensing*. An ON-OFF model is used to model the traffic streams of secondary user. The length of time slot is 2 *ms*. The ON period is modeled as Pareto distribution and an exponential distribution is used for OFF duration. The frequency bandwidth of each channel is 20 kHz. Four different rates $\Omega = (1,2,5.5,11)Mbps$ are used for *MA maximization based adaptation* transmission in secondary user system (SUS). First, we consider a square area of size $500\times500m$ in which 10 secondary users and 10 primary users are fixedly and randomly deployed. Let $b = 1,2,3$ respectively for the utility function (10). Figure 2 shows the obvious differences between *GMAM* and *GMAMC* in terms of queuing delay under the average arrival rate $\lambda_i = 60kbps$ of SUS. The best result is achieved by *GMAMC* with $b = 3$. Let *SU* denote the number of secondary users. Figure 3 and 4 show the average delay under different average arrival rates in SUS. Let the exponent of utility function b be 1,2,3,4 and 5 respectively. The effect of the trade-off exponent b on the queuing delay is shown in Figure 5. It can be seen that the maximum lower delay stable region of about 7 ms is achieved by *GMAMC* when $b = 5$ that can allow the average arrival rate of 180 *kbps* in SUS. The better delay performances result from the adaptive trade-off between channel access efficiency and queue delay fairness that can be provided by maximizing the utility function of queue delay.

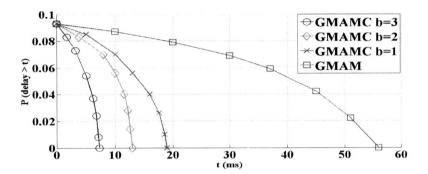

Fig. 2. Delay violation probability difference between *GMAMC* and *GMAM*

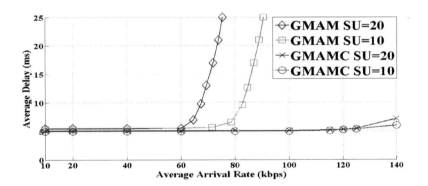

Fig. 3. Delay performance under SU=10 and SU=20

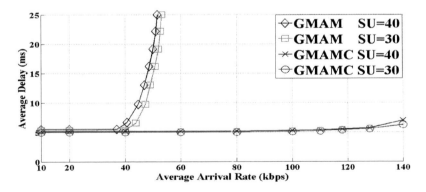

Fig. 4. Delay performance under SU=30 and SU=40

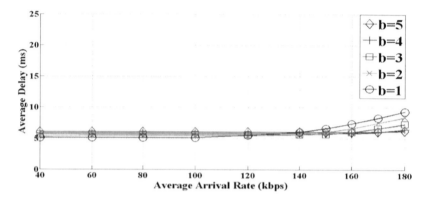

Fig. 5. Delay stable region of *GMAMC* with different trade-off exponent *b*

5 Conclusion

Based on POMDP decision theory, we formulate the optimal channel access of secondary user system in cognitive networks as the total reward maximization. Two schemes for the optimization objective are proposed based on maximizing the short term spectrum efficiency and minimizing the long term delay fairness difference respectively. We demonstrate by simulation results that the large stable region of low the average delay can be maintained by the centralized global fairness control scheme. Combining the schemes proposed in this paper with efficient time window based traffic control is our future research.

References

1. Zhao, Q., Sadler, B.M.: A survey of dynamic spectrum access. IEEE Signal Processing Magazine 55(5), 2294–2309 (2007)
2. Zhao, Q., Tong, L., Swami, A., Chen, Y.: Decentralized cognitive MAC for opportunistic spectrum access in Ad Hoc networks: a POMDP framework. IEEE JSAC 25(3), 589–600 (2007)
3. Laourine, A., Chen, S., Tong, L.: Queuing analysis in multichannel cognitive spectrum access: a large deviation approach. In: IEEE Infocom 2010 preceedings, IEEE Press, London (2010)
4. Chang, N., Liu, M.: Competitive analysis of opportunistic spectrum access strategies. In: Proc. IEEE INFOCOM 2008, IEEE Press, Hong Kong (2008)
5. Chen, Y., Zhao, Q., Swami, A.: Joint design and separation principle for opportunistic spectrum access in the presence of sensing errors. IEEE Trans. Inf. Theory 54(5), 2119–2129 (2007)
6. Huang, S., Liu, X., Ding, Z.: Opportunistic spectrum access in cognitive radio networks. In: Proc. IEEE INFOCOM 2008, IEEE Press, San Francisco (2008)
7. Urgaonkar, R., Neely, M.: Opportunistic scheduling with reliability guarantees in cognitive radio networks. In: Proc. IEEE INFOCOM 2008, IEEE Press, Paris (2008)

8. Wu, Y., Tsang, D.: Distributed power allocation algorithm for spectrum sharing cognitive radio networks with QoS guarantee. In: Proc. IEEE INFOCOM 2009, IEEE Press, San Francisco (2009)

9. Hou, Y., Shi, Y., Sherali, H.: Optimal spectrum sharing for multi-hop software defined radio networks. In: Proc. IEEE INFOCOM 2007, IEEE Press, Madrid (2007)

10. Cao, L., Zheng, H.: Stable and efficient spectrum access in next generation dynamic spectrum networks. In: Proc. IEEE INFOCOM 2008 (April 2008)

11. Geirhofer, S., Tong, L., Sadler, B.M.: Cognitive Medium Access: Constraining Interference Based on Experimental Models. In: IEEE JSAC, pp. 213–223. IEEE Press, Los Alamitos (2008)

12. Lu, S., Bharghavan, V., Srikant, R.: Fair scheduling in wireless packet networks. IEEE/ACM Trans. Networking 7(4), 473–489 (1999)

13. Ng, T.S.E., Stoica, I., Zhang, H.: Packet fair queueing algorithms for wireless networks with location-dependent errors. In: Proc. IEEE INFOCOM 1998, pp. 1103–1111. IEEE Press, San Francisco (2009)

14. Cao, Y., Li, V.O.K.: Scheduling algorithms in broad-band wireless networks. Proc. IEEE 89(1), 76–87 (2001)

15. Viswanath, P., Tse, D.N.C., Laroia, R.L.: Opportunistic beamforming using dumb antennas. IEEE Trans. Inform. Theory, 1277–1294 (2001)

16. Borst, S.: User-level performance of channel-aware scheduling algorithms in wireless data networks. In: Proc., IEEE INFOCOM 2003, pp. 321–331. IEEE Press, San Francisco (2003)

17. Chang, C.-S.: Stability, queue length, and delay of of deterministic and stochastic queueing networks. IEEE Trans. Autom. Control, 913–931 (1994)

18. Courcoubetis, C., Weber, R.: Effective bandwidth for stationary sources. In: Probability in Enginnering and Information Sciences, pp. 285–294. IEEE Press, New York (1995)

19. Qiu, X., Chawla, K.: On the performance of adaptive modulation in cellular systems. IEEE Trans. Commun. 47(6), 884–895 (1999)

20. Song, G., Li, Y.G.: Cross-Layer Optimization for OFDM Wireless. Networks—Part I: Theoretical Framework. IEEE Trans. Wireless Communications 4(2), 2110–2120 (2005)

21. Kruse, R.L., Ryba, A.J.: Data Structures and Program Design in C++. Prentice-Hall, Englewood Cliffs (1999)

Preemptive Performance Monitoring of a Large Network of Wi-Fi Hotspots: An Artificial Immune System[*]

Pheeha Machaka and Antoine Bagula

Intelligent Systems and Advanced Telecommunication Laboratory (ISAT)
Department of Computer Science, Room 317 Computer Science Building, 18 University
Avenue, University of Cape Town, Rondebosch, Cape Town, South Africa, 7701
pheeha.machaka@uct.ac.za,
antoine.bagula@uct.ac.za

Abstract. This paper addresses the problem of network monitoring by proposing an Artificial Immune System (AIS) system to achieve situation recognition and monitoring in a large network of Wi-Fi hotspots as part of a highly scalable preemptive monitoring tool for wireless networks. Using a set of data extracted from a live network of Wi-Fi hotspots managed by an ISP, we integrated an AIS algorithm into a data collection system to detect anomalous performance and aberrant behavior in the ISP's network. The results reveal the efficiency of the AIS system in terms of both anomaly performance and aberrant behavior on several test case scenarios.

Keywords: Performance Monitoring, Non-Self Detectors, Artificial Immune Systems, Anomaly Detection.

1 Introduction

Wireless Fidelity (Wi-Fi) is a wireless networking technology that uses radio waves to provide high-speed wireless internet connections. It is based on the family of IEEE 802.11 standards and builds upon a fast, easy and inexpensive networking approach [1] that uses a client-server model where the access points (AP) also called hotspot, plays the role of server while its client devices range from laptops to cellular mobile devices and Personal Digital Assistants (PDAs). The Wi-Fi APs broadcast signals to Wi-Fi-capable client devices that detect and receive broadcast messages from hotspots within their AP's range, and thus connect to the Internet. These APs are currently installed in different business settings, such as coffee shops, restaurants, hotels and conference rooms to provide wireless Internet access to clients located in these settings.

Performance monitoring is an important task upon which large Wi-Fi network deployment depends. As traditionally implemented, performance monitoring is based on a reactive network approach where the operating system software only warns the network administrators when a problem occurs. This approach leads to both the halting of important network processes and the hampering of critical business processes of the

---

[*] The financial assistance of the National Research Foundation (NRF) and Telkom SA Centre of Excellence (CoE) towards this research is hereby acknowledged.

X. Masip-Bruin et al. (Eds.): WWIC 2011, LNCS 6649, pp. 494–504, 2011.

organization. Pre-emptive network monitoring provides the potential to prevent the occurrence of faults by analyzing the status of the network components to create a fail-safe network status or allow a smooth migration from a faulty to fail-safe network status. The popularity of Wi-Fi technology has led to a large scale deployment of thousands of hotspots networks. These hotspots generate huge amounts of monitoring data which require efficient data handling methods to analyze data, recognize anomalous hidden patterns and implement fault tolerance. While statistical analysis has been deployed in many cases to address this issue, soft computing methods borrowed from the human immune system are emerging as powerful tools used in anomaly detection and security monitoring systems.

1.1 Related Work

There has been work done in the field of AIS, which has mostly focused on intrusion detection, detection of computer viruses and network security [2], [3], [4], and [5]. While [6] addresses anomaly detection for a refrigerator system, the works in [3] and [4] describe AIS mechanisms that differentiate between self and non-self performance with application to a dataset of executable files infected by computer viruses. In [7], a security authentication system inspired by the immune system using the negative selection algorithm is introduced. This system generates a set of anti-passwords (a negative image of the password set) used as a first line of authentication kept separate from the positive authentication system (secured). Using datasets with approximately 2500 most common passwords, the authors generated a set of anti-passwords that defined the non-self of the password authentication system with the objective of providing a proof-of-concept for negative authentication systems using AIS to reduce the effect of brute force attacks on authentication systems by hackers. The tool breakage detection tool developed in [8] aims to detect tooth breakage in different environments. Using this tool, a negative selection technique was successfully implemented to detect the tooth breakage from dynamic variations of the cutting force signal.

Building upon the AIS' success, this paper presents a network monitoring tool that uses the Artificial Immune System (AIS) to achieve pre-emptive monitoring of a large scale live ISP network operating in the city of Cape Town in South Africa. Some of the main goals of this paper consist of providing answers to the following questions:

- What kind of data can be extracted using AIS methods on the network performance?
- How useful is the data that will be extracted?
- How does AIS perform under different network profiles?
- Finally, can we use AIS for network performance monitoring?

The remainder of this paper is organized as follows. Section 2 describes the development of the AIS system while section 3 describes our experimental setting. Section 4 presents the experimental results while our conclusions are presented in section 5.

2 Development of AIS

The Human Immune System (HIS) is a robust, complex network of specialized cells and organs that defend the human body against a sea of harmful microorganisms called antigens. Building upon its capability of differentiating the cells and molecules of the body into self (what belongs) and non-self (what does not belong) [9] and [11], the HIS has led to the development of the Artificial Immune System (AIS) computational paradigm that may solve complex computational problems.

2.1 Human Immune System (HIS)

As depicted by Figure 1, once the body recognizes an invasion by antigens (I-III), the immunological response (IV-VI) consists of neutralizing or destroying the invading antigens through the release and use of B-cells and T-cells (lymphocytes that originate from the bone marrow and play an important role in the immunological response). The B and T-cells will then destroy the invading antigens and remove them from the body.

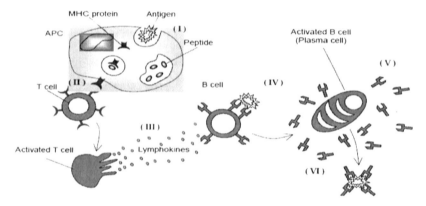

Fig. 1. Pictorial representation of the essence of the acquired immune system mechanism (taken from [10])

2.2 Artificial Immune System (AIS) and Negative Selection

A biologically inspired computational technique, called Artificial Immune System (AIS) has emerged from the HIS metaphor. The HIS features that are of particularly relevant to AIS include matching, diversity and distributed control. These features have been implemented in many AIS mechanisms such as the immune system's Immune Network Theory, Negative Selection mechanism and Clonal Selection Principle to solve real world science and engineering problems. The focus of this paper lies on the negative selection mechanism of the immune system with its application to pattern recognition in Wi-Fi network monitoring.

Negative Selection Mechanism. The HIS mechanism provides tolerance for self cells, and reacts against unknown antigens. The HIS generates antibodies through a pseudo random rearrangement process and undergoes a censoring process in the thymus as described by [9] and [11]. Only those antibodies that do not bind to the self-protein are allowed to leave the thymus to circulate throughout the body to perform immunological functions and protect the body against foreign antigens. This mechanism gave developments to the Negative Selection Algorithm (NSA) described below.

Negative Selection Algorithm. In [3], the negative selection algorithm (NSA) was first proposed as a means of detecting unknown or illegal strings for virus detection in computer systems. This was inspired by a change detection mechanism which is based on the way the human immune system distinguishes self cells from non-self. The algorithm follows the two steps as shown by Figure 2.

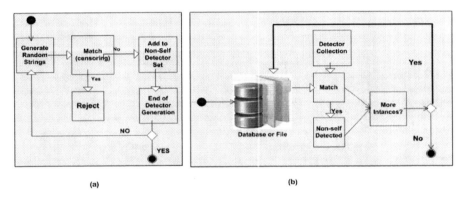

(a)   (b)

Fig. 2. (a) Generation of valid detector set (stage 1); (b) Monitoring the protected strings for changes (stage 2). (Adapted from [3])

1. **Generate a set of detectors.** Each detector is a string representation that does not match any of the protected data (self). This is the censoring stage shown in figure 2(a). The number of detectors generated will vary according to combination of total number of monitored variables and those that are undesired variables. If a non-self detector is found, it is added to the detector set. This process is repeated until the desired number of detectors is reached or no more detectors are found.
2. **Monitor the protected strings.** The AIS continuously monitor for changes in the system, by matching encoded instances from the database/system. If a non-self detector is activated, the correct action will be taken, thus creating an alert and logging this with the monitoring system as show in figure 2(b).

3   The Experimental Model

3.1   The Wi-Fi Network

As depicted by Figure 3, a Wi-Fi network monitoring tool was developed around WRT54GL routers with three components: a storage component, a visualization component and a data collection component. The "Storage component" provides storage for the enormous amount of data that is harnessed during network monitoring. A postgreSQL database was used for this component. The "Visualisation Component" provides visual display of the performance of the network. Google Maps was used as a visual tool as the network monitored covered a large metropolitan city of Cape Town. Google Chart Tools were used to visualize performance statistics and individual router performance. Of most importance was the "Data Collection component" which provided monitoring and data gathering capabilities for the monitoring tool. The data gathering component was implemented using the "Syslog protocol" program installed on each of the 615 Cisco WRT54GL router devices in more than 400 hotspots in the Cape Town network. The program was left to run from 2009-07-03 12h00 to 2009-09-02 04h00 collecting monitoring data at every hour's interval, thus leading to up to 356537 items in the experiment dataset .

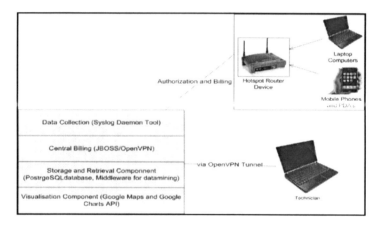

Fig. 3. The Wi-Fi network monitoring tool

3.2 Performance Metrics

We conducted a set of experiments based on three performance metrics which are usually used in performance evaluation of Wi-Fi networks. These include:

Uptime and Downtime. This metric measure the time a device has been up and running. It reveals the availability, stability and reliability of the communication device when used in the network.

Load Average. Measures the "congestion rate" for the device based on the number of users connected to the device.

Radio Noise and Channel. Wi-Fi uses the 2.4 GHz spectrum band which is shared with other devices like cell phones, GPS, RFID tags and Bluetooth devices. Note that the proliferation of devices using the free 2.4 GHz ISM band leads to more congested and noisy Wi-Fi devices.

3.3 Experimental Plan

Our experimental plan consisted of the four stages shown in Figure 4.

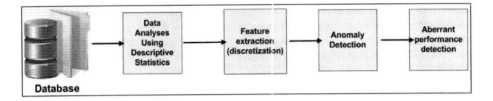

Fig. 4. Experimental Plan

Data analysis. In this stage, descriptive statistics were pulled out of the dataset to reveal the network's performance level in terms of time series characteristics and descriptive summary statistics. This allowed a summary of the observations by considering their central tendency and statistical dispersion.

Feature extraction. At this stage, the readings/observations received were discretized or reduced for further processing.

Anomaly Detection. This stage aimed at discovering those readings/observations associated to unacceptable device performance.

Aberrant behavior. This stage uses the observations obtained from the "Data Analyses stage" to detect aberrant behavior. An observation will fall into the aberrant behavior category when its observed values fall outside the statistical confidence band, an outlier. A total deviation of the observation will depend on a defined Delta (δ) parameter.

3.4 The AIS Implementation

Encoding. Using numeric attributes to encode the three performance metrics, we considered categorical data for our pattern recognition. Therefore, the dataset was discretized for further processing and the following three categories were considered as performance levels achievable by the three performance metrics:

1 $\rightarrow$ LOW LEVELS

2 $\rightarrow$ MODERATE LEVELS

3 $\rightarrow$ HIGH LEVELS

Selection. Each of the three performance metrics was encoded in the following way:

Noise. In the dataset, the noise performance was multiplied by 100 (for calibration purposes) and noise values were categorized using the following encoding:

```
If                  noise < -8500   then encode → 1

Else if  -8500  < noise < -7000   then encode → 2

Else if             noise >-7000  then encode → 3 .
```

Load. The load expressed the UNIX kernel load average multiplied by 100. The load values were categorized using the following encoding:

```
If                      load <70            then 1(LOW)
Else if    70 <    load<100            then 2  (MODERATE)
Else if            load>100            then 3  (HIGH)
```

Uptime or Downtime. The Uptime is the device uptime considered as the current uptime (in minutes) since last reboot. The downtime rate per router is defined by

Downtime rate = $\dfrac{\text{number of reading with uptime=<60 (indicating a device reset)}}{\text{Total number of readings}}$

and the Downtime was categorized using the following encoding:

```
If              downtime-rate>       1%     then 1  (LOW)
Else if 5% <  downtime-rate<       1%     then 2  (MODERATE)
Else if         downtime-rate<       5%     then 3  (HIGH)
```

Similarity Measure or Fitness Function. A fitness function determines if an antigen represented by a string "NLD", where N, L, D express the Noise, Load and Downtime respectively, is fit for further processing. Thus to define the non-self, the following fitness function was used for a three variable antigen "NLD".

```
Fitness Function   (f)  =  (N × L × D)  mod 3
For non-self,       (f)  = 0.
```

Aberrant Performance Detection. To detect aberrant behavior in performance, statistical confidence bands were used. They measured deviations of an observation in a time series. A deviation depended on the Delta (δ) parameter whose sensible values were taken between 2 and 3 [12].

Table 1. Parameter settings for each experiment test case

Test Cases	Noise		Load	Downtime	Confidence Band (δ)
1	high	-7000	100		1.00
	moderate	-8000	70	4%	2.00
	low	-9000	0		3.00
2	high	-7250	100		0.25
	moderate	-8250	75	3%	1.75
	low	-9250	0		2.75
3	high	-7500	100		0.50
	moderate	-8500	80	2%	1.50
	low	-9500	0		2.50
4	high	-7750	100		0.25
	moderate	-8750	85	1%	1.25
	low	-9750	0		2.25

3.5 Test Cases

We conducted experiments using four test case scenarios revealing Wi-Fi operating constraints from loose (e.g. rural setting where QoS is not a issue) to the most stringent(e.g. suburban setting where modern applications demand QoS). In the experiments conducted, four sets of test cases were devised. These test cases are defined by Table 1 in terms of Noise, Load, Downtime rate (overall time the device was down) and the confidence band **δ**.

4   Experimental Results

4.1 Random Detector Generation Stage

We conducted a first set of experiments to find the set of random detectors generated by the first and second stages of the NSA. These detectors fit the non-self description of the NSA problem. As depicted by Table 2, only 18 possible anti-detectors were found by our AIS system.

4.2 Anomaly Detection

Using the parameters described in the test cases of Table 1, we conducted another set of experiments to detect anomalous network performance in terms of percentage of different types of faults (antigens) found by the AIS system and probabilities of finding these faults. As depicted by Table 2, the experimental results revealed that the probabilities of finding non-self detectors (anomalous behavior) increase slightly as the AIS parameters become stricter. This is shown by the increase in detection probability in Table 3 for each test case.

Table 2. Non-self Detectors for the experiment

Antibody Code	Noise	Load	Uptime		Antibody Code	Noise	Load	Uptime
113	low	low	high		311	high	low	low
123	low	moderate	high		312	high	low	moderate
131	low	high	low		313	high	low	high
132	low	high	moderate		321	high	moderate	low
133	low	high	high		322	high	moderate	moderate
213	moderate	low	high		323	high	moderate	high
223	moderate	moderate	high		331	high	high	low
231	moderate	high	low		332	high	high	moderate
232	moderate	high	moderate		333	high	high	high
233	moderate	high	high					

While the first stage of the AIS experiment revealed a set of 18 anti-detectors generated, only 8 antigens were detected as anomalous behavior in the network's performance. This reveals that most of the antigen space was covered by the anti-detectors. The results depicted by Figure 5 were obtained from the following test cases:

Table 3. Detection Rate of Anomaly and Aberrant Faults

Test Case	Anomaly	Aberrant
1	70.53%	29.47%
2	71.64%	28.36%
3	72.45%	27.55%
4	73.41%	26.59%

Test Case 1. It represented the most loose but yet acceptable constraints in terms of network performance. In this test case experiment, above 99% of the faults were of type "311" representing high noise anomalous performance in the network.

Test Case 2. Case 2 revealed similar performance pattern as Case 1 by showing 99% of type "311" faults: high noise anomalous behavior.

Test Case 3. Case 3 revealed a slight shift from the results observed in the test cases 1 and 2. The results revealed more than 99% detectors of type "321" found by the AIS system. This behavior expresses a high level of noise in the network with moderate load performance and low uptime. This kind of shift in anomaly is due to the fact that the load constraints were made stricter, thus picking up moderate load performance.

Test Case 4. The performance constraints for this part of the experiment were stricter for all variables. Test case 1, 2, and 3 followed a similar trend where a 99% detection rate was found for those devices with high levels of noise. In Case 4, more than 99% detection rate was found for type "113" detectors, representing those devices that experience very high levels of downtime.

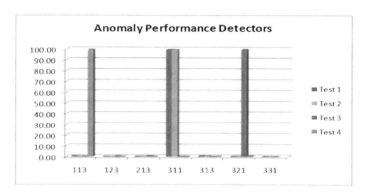

Fig. 5. Bar graph of results showing detection rate for the anomaly detection stage of the AIS experiment

4.3 Aberrant Behavior Detection

We conducted another set of experiments to detect changes in normal performance that are significant enough to be regarded as outlying performance. The parameter that was used to measure deviation from normal performance is the Delta (δ) parameter. This parameter was set to different values for each test case as described in Table 1. Our experimental results revealed that 11 out of 18 detectors were discovered by the AIS system. These results depicted by Figure 6 reveal that:

Test Cases. In all the four cases, a significant percentage of Aberrant Performance detectors of type "113" were successfully detected with a detection rate of ~63.0%. This "113" detector indicates high downtime rate and implies that ~63.0% of the network devices suffered from high variations in the downtime rate. The second most significant aberrant performance detector was of type "313" with a detector rate of 29%. The "313" detector represent devices which have experienced high variations in downtime together with high variations in the level of noise.

The "311" detector type represent devices that are experiencing aberrant behavior in noise levels. Approximately 2.2% of the devices were experienced high noise level variations while they were performing well in terms of load and uptime.

Changes in detection. We conducted another experiment by changing the delta and downtime parameters to evaluate how the change will impact on the detection rate and device type. The results revealed a reduction in the type "113" detectors for each test case, for an average reduction of 0.75%. As the granularity of delta parameter was made coarse, a reduction in detector rate for detector type "313" was discovered and from one test case to the other, the average reduction was 0.25%.

When varying the AIS parameters, for each test case, a different set of results was produced by the AIS system, indicating that different parameter settings lead to the identification of different aberrant behaviors.

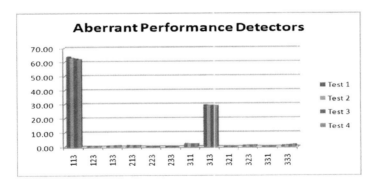

Fig. 6. Aberrant Performance detection stage of the AIs system

4.4 Comparison with Existing Monitoring Tools

MRTG (http://oss.oetiker.ch/mrtg/). It monitors traffic load on network links and uses Simple Network Management Protocol(SNMP) to gather data from device. It uses the SNMP protocol which was found to be more bandwidth intensive in comparison to the Syslog protocol used in our monitoring tool.

RRDTool(http://www.mrtg.org/rrdtool/). It uses Round Robin Database, that stores data and also allows graphing capabilities, but the graphing capabilities are not as scalable and powerful as those presented by our monitoring tool, which includes powerful and intelligent techniques of analyzing and presenting data in a scalable fashion.

5 Conclusion

Building upon a hybrid solution using descriptive statistics and AIS, this paper presents a preemptive Wi-Fi network monitoring system that uses the negative selection algorithm (NSA) to achieve pattern recognition in an ISP network that provides hotspot access to clients in different settings in Cape Town. We present the main steps of our AIS implementation model and show through experimentation that the AIS system can reveal hidden pattern in a large network of Wi-Fi Hotspots in terms of anomalous and aberrant behavior. When deployed in a preemptive monitoring setting, the information resulting from our AIS system can further be used in future situation awareness to predict faulty scenarios in the Wi-Fi network and take preventive measures. This has been reserved for future work.

References

1. Vaughan-Nichols, S.: The challenge of wi-fi roaming. Computer 36, 17–19 (2003)
2. Luther, K., Bye, R., Alpcan, T., Muller, A., Albayrak, S.: A cooperative AIS framework for intrusion detection. In: IEEE International Conference on Communication (2007)
3. Forrest, S., Perelson, A.S., Allen, L., Cherukuri, R.: Self-nonself discrimination in a computer. In: IEEE Computer Society Symposium on Security and Privacy (1994)
4. Forrest, S., Hofmeyr, S.A., Somayaji, A., Longstaff, T.: A sense of self for unix processes. In: IEEE Symposium on Security and Privacy (1996)
5. Dasgupta, D., Gonzalez, F.: An immunity-based technique to characterize intrusions in computer networks. In: IEEE Transactions on Evolutionary Computation (2002)
6. Taylor, D.W., Corne, D.W.: An investigation of the negative selection algorithm for fault detection in refrigeration systems. In: Timmis, J., Bentley, P.J., Hart, E. (eds.) ICARIS 2003. LNCS, vol. 2787, pp. 34–45. Springer, Heidelberg (2003)
7. Dasgupta, D., Saha, S.: A biologically inspired password authentication system. In: Proceedings of the 5th Annual Workshop on Cyber Security and Information Intelligence Research: Cyber Security and Information Intelligence Challenges and Strategies 5 (2009)
8. Dasgupta, S., Forrest, S.: Tool breakage detection in milling operations using a negative-selection algorithm. In: Technical Report Technical Report No CS95- 5, Department of Computer Science, University of New Mexico (1995)
9. Schindler, L.: Understanding the Immune System, p. 40. DIANE Publishing, United States Of America (1991)
10. De Castro, L.N., Von Zuben, F.: Artificial immune systems: Part II–A survey of applications. Technical Report RT DCA 02/00 Universidade Catolica de Santos, Coordenacao de Pos-Graduacao e Pesquisa (COPOP) (2000)
11. Kelly, J.: Understanding the Immune System - How It Works, p. 60. National Institute of Allergy and Infectious Diseases Science Education, United States (2007)
12. Robinson, S.: Simulation: The Practice of Model Development and Use, 1st edn., p. 339. John Wiley & Sons Ltd, Chichester (2004)

Author Index